Kickstart Operating System Design

Master Operating System Design from Core Concepts to Cutting-Edge Applications for Real-Time, Mobile, and Network Systems

Prof. Veerendra Kumar Jain

www.orangeava.com

First Published: February 2025

Published By: Orange Education Pvt Ltd, AVA®

Address: 9, Daryaganj, Delhi, 110002, India

275 New North Road Islington Suite 1314 London,
N1 7AA, United Kingdom

ISBN (PBK): 978-93-48107-60-2

ISBN (E-BOOK): 978-93-48107-36-7

Scan the QR code to explore our entire catalogue

www.orangeava.com

Dedicated To

My Beloved Parents

Shri Manak Chand Jain
Laxmi Devi Jain

And

My Wife Heera Jain

About the Author

Prof. Veerendra Kumar Jain, BE (E), M.Tech (Applied Electronics), FIETE, FIE, and Life Member ISHRAE, is a versatile professional with a distinguished career spanning engineering, academia, and authorship. A retired CPWD engineer, he has authored over 150 technical books on diverse subjects, including computer science, IT, management, engineering, and architecture, with over 130 focused on computer science and IT. His expertise in computing covers a wide range of languages and technologies, from early languages such as COBOL and Fortran IV (which he studied at IIT Kanpur in 1968) to modern tools such as Python, R, and Deno. He also holds a Certificate in PC Awareness from NIIT, New Delhi and received training in Big Data and Hadoop from HCL Noida.

As of 2025, Er. Jain imparts his knowledge in building services at prominent architecture and town planning institutions such as Amity University, Jamia Millia Islamia, Indraprastha University, Sunderdeep Group of Institutions, Vastukala Academy, Accurate Institute (Greater Noida), APG School of Planning and Architecture (Greater Noida), and TMU Moradabad. A renowned MEP consultant engineer and designated ME expert for the AICTE in India, he has contributed to numerous projects across the country.

Beyond his professional pursuits, Er. Jain is a seasoned traveler, having explored over 30 major cities worldwide. His travels have taken him to iconic destinations across Europe, Asia, North America, and the Middle East, including London, Paris, New York, and Dubai.

Acknowledgements

I would like to express my gratitude to a few people for their continued and unwavering support throughout the writing of this book. First and foremost, I would like to thank my wife and grandson for continuously encouraging me to write the book. I could have never completed this book without their support.

I am grateful to the course organizers, such as the All India Council of Technical Education (AICTE), for approving my books on emerging technology. This book will be the fourth. I also extend my sincere thanks for all the behind-the-scenes support provided by Sourabh Dwivedi, CEO of Orange Education Pvt Ltd.

My gratitude also goes to the team of Orange Education Pvt Ltd for being supportive enough to improve my manuscript and for publishing my work in a very short time, providing a lot of facilities and guidance in editing and improving the content.

Preface

This book, *Kickstart Operating System Design*, offers a comprehensive exploration of the fundamental principles and practical implementations of operating systems. It is designed to provide a deep understanding of how operating systems function as the crucial bridge between users and hardware, managing resources and providing essential services.

The book is structured to guide the reader through the key concepts of operating systems, beginning with a foundational introduction. It then delves into core processes, including process management, threading, scheduling, and synchronization, along with the critical issues of deadlock handling. A significant portion is dedicated to memory management, covering both its theoretical underpinnings and practical techniques. The book further explores secondary storage and I/O systems, file systems, and the essential aspects of protection and security.

Recognizing the evolving landscape of computing, *Kickstart Operating System Design* extends its coverage to encompass advanced topics such as distributed operating systems, real-time and embedded systems, multimedia operating systems, and the specialized requirements of mobile, multiprocessor, and network operating systems. This breadth ensures readers gain insight into the diverse challenges and solutions presented by different computing environments.

This book is intended for students and professionals seeking a thorough understanding of operating systems. Whether you are a computer science student, a software developer, or an IT professional, this book will equip you with the knowledge and insights necessary to navigate the complexities of modern operating systems. We believe that by combining clear explanations with practical examples, this book will serve as an invaluable resource in your journey to mastering operating system concepts and techniques.

Get a Free eBook

We hope you are enjoying your recently purchased book! Your feedback is incredibly valuable to us, and to all other readers looking for great books.

If you found this book helpful or enjoyable, we would truly appreciate it, if you could take a moment to leave a short review with a 5 star rating on Amazon. It helps us grow, and lets other readers discover our books.

As a thank you, we would love to send you a free digital copy of this book, and a **30%** discount code on your next cart value on our official websites:

www.orangeava.com

www.orangeava.in (For Indian Subcontinent)

☑ **Here's how:**

Leave a review for the book on Amazon.

Take a screenshot of your review, and send an email to **info@orangeava.com** (it can be just the confirmation screen).

Once, we receive your screenshot, we will send you the digital file, within 24 hours.

Thank you so much for your support – it means a lot to us!

Downloading the code bundles and colored images

Please follow the links or scan the QR codes to download the
Code Bundles and Images of the book:

https://github.com/ava-orange-education/Kickstart-Operating-System-Design

The code bundles and images of the book are also hosted on
https://rebrand.ly/23ea88

In case there's an update to the code, it will be updated on the existing GitHub repository.

Errata

We take immense pride in our work at **Orange Education Pvt Ltd,** and follow best practices to ensure the accuracy of our content to provide an indulging reading experience to our subscribers. Our readers are our mirrors, and we use their inputs to reflect and improve upon human errors, if any, that may have occurred during the publishing processes involved. To let us maintain the quality and help us reach out to any readers who might be having difficulties due to any unforeseen errors, please write to us at :

errata@orangeava.com

Your support, suggestions, and feedback are highly appreciated.

DID YOU KNOW

Did you know that Orange Education Pvt Ltd offers eBook versions of every book published, with PDF and ePub files available? You can upgrade to the eBook version at **www.orangeava.com** and as a print book customer, you are entitled to a discount on the eBook copy. Get in touch with us at: **info@orangeava.com** for more details.

At **www.orangeava.com**, you can also read a collection of free technical articles, sign up for a range of free newsletters, and receive exclusive discounts and offers on Print Books and eBooks.

PIRACY

If you come across any illegal copies of our works in any form on the internet, we would be grateful if you would provide us with the location address or website name. Please contact us at **info@orangeava.com** with a link to the material.

ARE YOU INTERESTED IN AUTHORING WITH US?

If there is a topic that you have expertise in, and you are interested in either writing or contributing to a book, please write to us at **business@orangeava.com**. We are on a journey to help developers and tech professionals to gain insights on the present technological advancements and innovations happening across the globe and build a community that believes Knowledge is best acquired by sharing and learning with others. Please reach out to us to learn what our audience demands and how you can be part of this educational reform. We also welcome ideas from tech experts and help them build learning and development content for their domains.

REVIEWS

Please leave a review. Once you have read and used this book, why not leave a review on the site that you purchased it from? Potential readers can then see and use your unbiased opinion to make purchase decisions. We at Orange Education would love to know what you think about our products, and our authors can learn from your feedback. Thank you!

For more information about Orange Education, please visit **www.orangeava.com**.

Table of Contents

CHAPTER 1
Computer Organization and Hardware Software Interfaces

Introduction

Computer Organization and Hardware-Software Interface is an essential component of contemporary technology that determines how our gadgets work and communicate with us. A fundamental understanding of the organization and design of computers is crucial given the speed at which technology is developing. Computer Organization and Hardware-Software Interface which guarantees smooth operation and communication, takes into account the complex interrelationships between hardware and software components. Investigating the interaction between these two elements to produce the technological marvels we use daily is fascinating. It encompasses the study of how hardware and software work together to form a working computer system. This domain includes computer system design, development, and implementation from both software and hardware standpoints.

Structure

In this chapter, we are going to learn the following topics:

- Overview of Computer Organization
- Working of (Digital Personal) Computers Popular Input and Output Devices
- Introduction to Computer Organization Interface
- Data Transfer Modes
- Using an Interrupt Handler to Pass Control Between a Running Program and OS

Overview of Computer Organization

A computer is a device that processes information. It transforms information (raw data) into a sensible format for direct human use. When we refer to a computer, we really mean a digital electronic computer, which is a personal computer for the majority of uses. The most fascinating thing to humans has been computer technology. We live in a world where computers are ubiquitous and will remain so for centuries to come. There are individuals who hold a science-fiction perspective on computers, believing that they possess sentience and will eventually take over the universe if precautions are not taken.

In fact, the opposite is probably more accurate. Within the limitations imposed by their designers, computers can do whatever they are programmed to do, but not more. They cannot (so far) "*think*" for themselves, but their method of dealing with a problem is similar in many respects to a human's thought processes.

A computer has two main characteristics:

- Follows a predetermined set of instructions and reacts to them in a predictable way.
- Capable of carrying out a program: a recorded set of instructions. Contemporary computers are digital and electronic.

Software refers to the data and instructions, while hardware refers to the actual components, such as circuits, transistors, and wires.

Basic Parts of Computer

The Major Components of The Block Diagram of the Computer System are:

- Input Unit
- Output Unit
- Central Processing Unit (CPU)

Central Processing Unit (CPU) consists of:

- Control Unit (CU)
- Arithmetic and Logic Unit (ALU)
- Memory Unit

The memory unit in turn consists:

- Primary Memory
- Secondary Memory

Input Units

Before using data and information to solve problems, the computer needs the input unit to receive it. Information and data are fed into the computer by the user. We provide information and data through the use of input devices. Different types of input devices make up the input unit, for example, keyboard, mouse, scanner, microphone, and more.

Programs that run on the monitor and provide instructions to the computer's CPU can process those instructions. There must be input devices available for the user to interact with these application programs. To process data entered by the user via input devices, the CPU pauses the application program's instructions and starts processing input signals. The CPU uses the information from input signals to resume processing the instructions from the application program when it receives them.

The following are the main duties of the input unit:

1. Gather user data via input devices
2. Convert electrical signal data into machine language that can be read by computers
3. Tell the CPU to start obtaining data from the input devices
4. Give the CPU access to the converted data via the memory unit so that it can be processed further

Output Device

The output unit of the computer transmits information and processing results to the external environment. The output unit typically reverses the actions of the input unit, translating machine language into electrical signals that the output devices can understand. The most often used output device is the Visual Display Unit (VDU), also known the **monitor**. Other well-liked output devices are speakers, headphones, projectors, and so on.

Central Processing Unit (CPU)

The CPU serves as the system's central nervous system. A computer would be useless without it. This "*brain*" of the computer processes all instructions, or a subset of instructions, that it receives from the user. After receiving instructions and user input, this brain prints out the desired outcome.

The CPU is essential to execute arithmetic and logical operations. It is in charge of managing the functions of other gadgets.

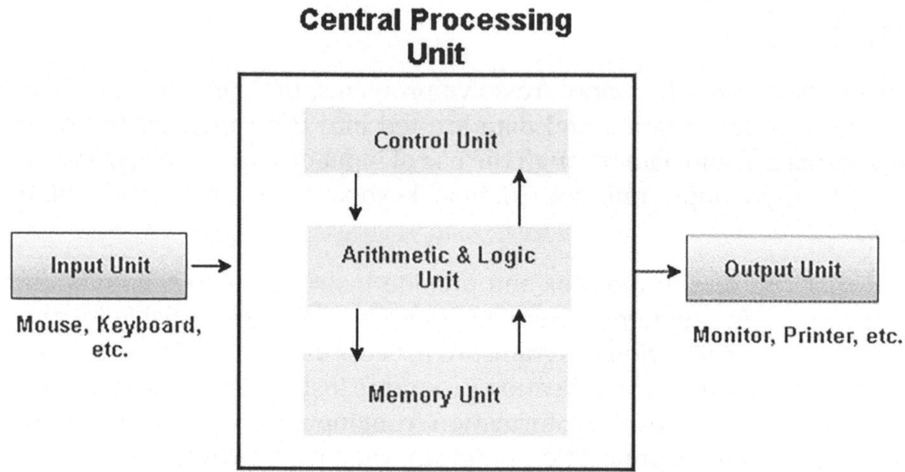

Figure 1.1: *Block Diagram of Computer with Central Processing Unit (CPU)*

Three Major Components of the CPU are Arithmetic Logical Unit (ALU), Control Unit (CU), and Memory Unit (MU):

Arithmetic Logical Unit (ALU)

Arithmetic Logic Unit (ALU) is one of the primary parts of the Central Processing Unit (CPU). It is responsible for managing all of the CPU's calculations, such as arithmetic and logical operations, related operations, and so on. They also operate using comparisons. Additionally, it plays a crucial role in decision-making processes, enabling the CPU to perform the majority of its tasks efficiently.

Control Unit (CU)

When calculations need to be made, the data is passed from the memory unit to the Arithmetic Logic Unit (ALU) by the Control Unit (CU). The computation data is returned to the memory unit by the CU after the computation and the ALU has produced the results. Arithmetic, logical, and bit-shifting operations are carried out by the arithmetic unit.

The control unit (CU) is a crucial component of the central processing unit (CPU). The term "*central nervous system*" refers to the control unit, which is responsible for coordinating and managing the other functional components of the computer.

All CPU operations, such as data flow within the CPU and ALU operations, are managed by the CU. The control unit (CU) performs several crucial tasks for the system, including:

- Directing the input unit where to store data received from users via input devices.

- During program execution, the Govern unit controls the flow of data and instructions from memory to the ALU because the Control Unit (CU) loads instructions from memory one at a time and executes them at the ALU.
- Additionally, CU receives the computation result from the ALU and routes it to the output unit for screen display as well as back to memory. Data transfer from the ALU to the memory and output units is overseen by the Control Unit (CU).

Memory Unit (MU)

This part of the computer is in charge of holding data and information needed by the other operating systems. Before the central processing unit (CPU) processes the data and information from the input unit, it is first stored in the computer's memory unit. You can also refer to a memory unit as a memory unit. In addition, the memory unit performs several crucial roles in the system, including:

- Storing data received from the input unit.
- Information and data are sent to the CPU so that it can be processed further.
- Variables are used to store any information or commands that the CPU generates during intermediate processing.
- Subsequently, the variable records the outcome of the CPU's data processing.
- Delivers the processed data results to the output devices at the end.
- It also keeps information and data for later use.

The Memory Unit is divided into two categories:

- **Primary Memory:** The most rapidly accessible memory unit is the primary memory. Data delivery and reception for processing from these memories happen quite quickly. Also situated close to the main memory are the Control Unit and Arithmetic Logic Unit. The program that is currently running in the CPU, data that the input unit has received, and intermediate and final program results that have been stored and transferred back and forth between memory and the CPU are all commonly kept in this memory. Temporary and volatile memory makes up the main memory. This means that the data is deleted forever if the computer is shut off. Hence, it is unable to store data for very long. To avoid data loss, the computer's secondary memory receives data from the primary memory.
- **Secondary Memory**: Secondary memory stores information for the computer system and has a capacity ranging from gigabytes to terabytes. Applications, documents, audio files, movies, databases, and more can all be kept in secondary memory. Receiving and transmitting data and information is slower than in primary memory. Programs run on the Central Processing Unit (CPU) are executed there. Program execution doesn't start until the CPU asks the

secondary memory to transfer the important data and instructions from the secondary memory into the primary memory.

Working of (Digital Personal) Computers

A computer obtains data or information through some input device. The memory of the device contains this data. Nevertheless, a computer only remembers the data that it has been programmed to store, in contrast to the human brain, which typically remembers all the information entered into it–even though we might not be aware of this. The computer loses any further data. It will compare the two pieces of data if it is programmed to do so and then decide what is best. The computer's output unit receives the result via transmission.

Data is raw Information, especially information in a form that can be used by a computer. It includes text, numbers, sounds, and pictures. A single piece of information is called a Datum.

A computer follows a series of instructions programmed into its memory by the user and operates on data presented to it by the user.

The data input may be in the form of:

Typed or handwritten linguistic data or instructions in the computer's language.

Linguistic Raw data can be:

- Numeric
- Alphabetic
- Alphanumeric

Then this is coded into data acceptable to the computer in its language.

It may be audible, visual, or audio-visual analogic data.

In general, a computer is meant to perform four tasks:

- Receiving input of data, retaining the instructions, data, and other information in its memory and retrieving it when needed.
- Storing data in short-term memory when the power is on and long-term memory when it is off.
- Processing the data in accordance with instructions to transform it into meaningful information.
- Transmitting the data as an output.

The information processing is the core function of any computer system. However, if information is presented in an unexpected way or if the machine is asked to process information in a manner for which it has not been programmed, it will fail to proceed.

Keep in mind that information will only be processed in accordance with the program that was entered into the computer, which is hardly able to think for itself. Since there are many different ways that information can exist, it is necessary for the input and output units to be able to "*translate*" the information into or out of a format that the computer can understand.

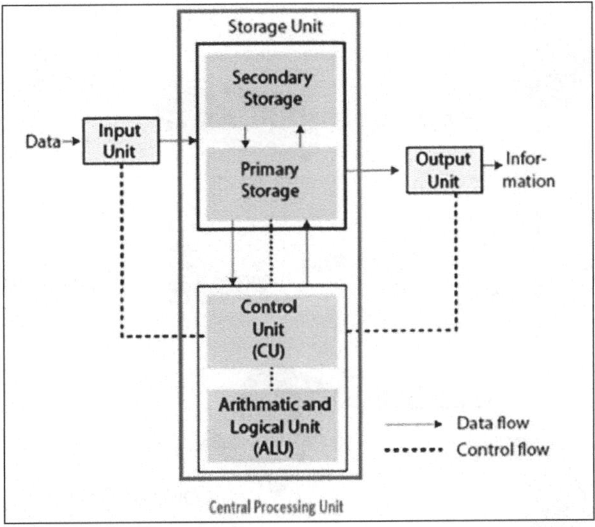

Figure 1.2: *Data Flow in any Personal Computer*

Complete detailed computer organization including some of the input and output units is shown in *Figure* 1.3.

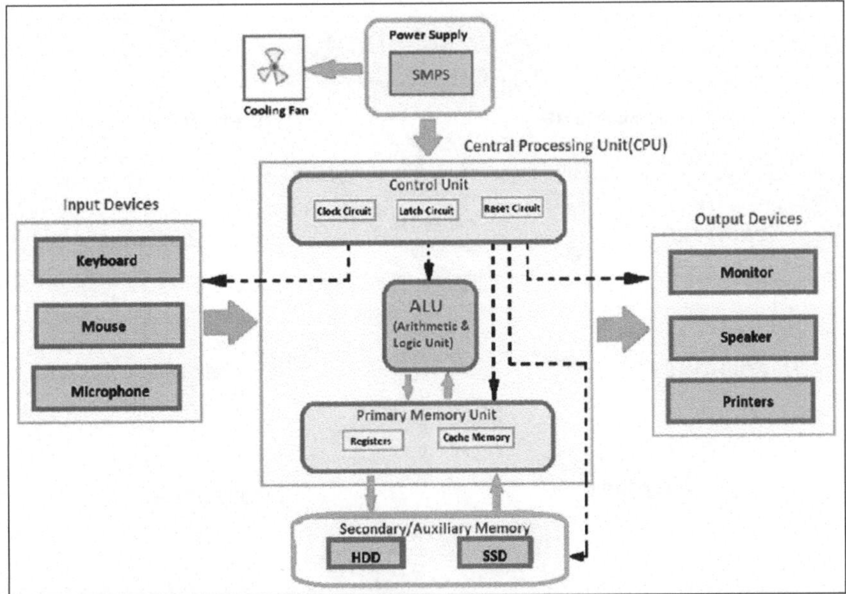

Figure 1.3: *Detailed Computer Organization*

Popular Input and Output Devices

All these components are interconnected and communicate with each other via the bus (Data, Control, and Address Bus). Most of these components in the architecture lie within the motherboard (the backbone of the computer).

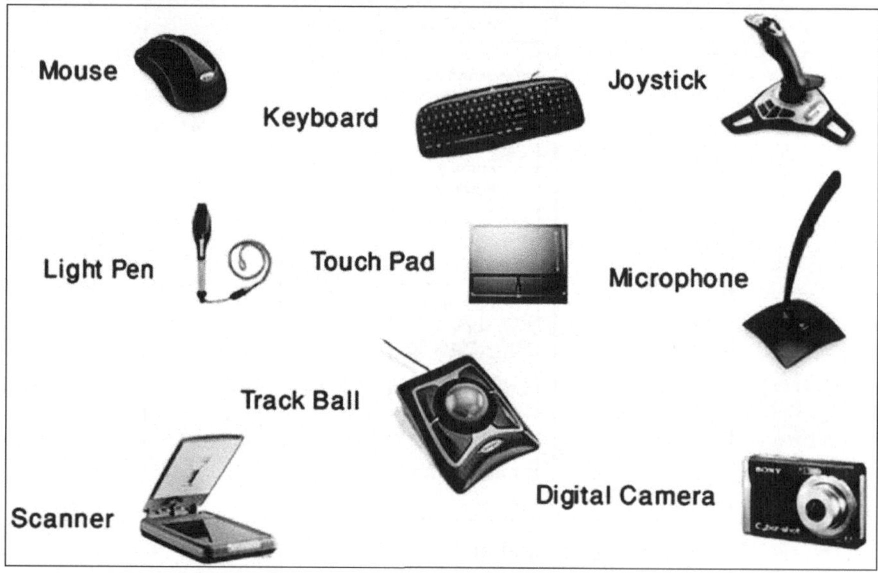

***Figure 1.4**: Some Popular Input Devices*

Following is an illustration of the various output devices:

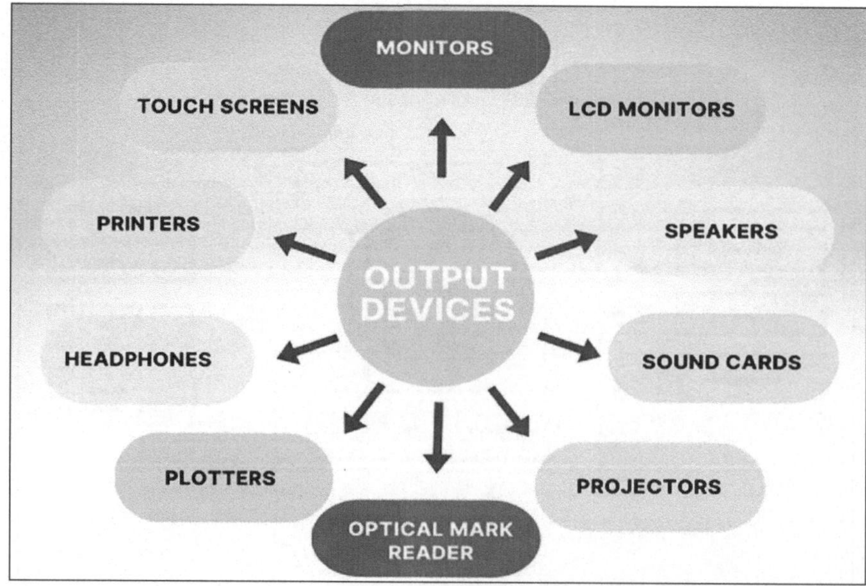

(a)

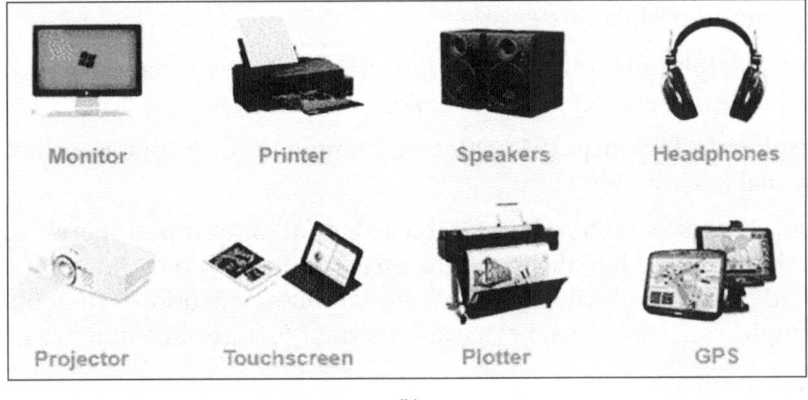

(b)

Figure 1.5: *(a) and (b) Some Popular Output Devices*

Introduction to Computer Organization Interface

Interfaces are tools and concepts that technology developers use as points of interaction between hardware and software components. They help all components within a system to communicate with each other via an input-output system and detailed protocols while also allowing them to function independently.

Interfaces [1]

An interface, which can connect two or more components to the system for communication, is a shared boundary between two distinct computer system components. Interfaces come in two varieties:

- CPU Interface
- I/O Interface

Input/Output Subsystem

An effective way to communicate between the external environment and the central system is through the I/O subsystem of a computer. It manages the computer system's entire input-output process.

Peripheral Devices: Attached to a computer, peripheral devices are input or output devices. These devices, which are regarded as components of the computer system, are made to read data into or out of the memory unit in response to commands from the central processing unit. Another name for these gadgets is peripherals. As an illustration, common peripheral devices include keyboards, displays, and printers.

Three categories of peripherals exist:

- **Input peripherals**: Enable user input from the external environment to the computer, such as keyboard, mouse, and more.
- **Peripherals for output:** Enable the computer to output information to the external environment.
- **Input-output peripherals:** Examples of input-output peripherals are printers, monitors, and other devices that enable output (from the computer to the outside world) as well as input (from the outside world to the computer), for example, touch screens. Let's examine the I/O Interface in more detail.

Input-Output Interface

To interface with the CPU, connected peripherals require dedicated communication links. To regulate or manage the input-output transfers in a computer system, specific hardware components are positioned between the central processing unit and peripheral devices.

These parts establish **communication links** between the processor bus and peripherals, which is why they are referred to as input-output interface units. They give internal systems and input-output devices a way to communicate with each other.

The mode of transferring information between internal storage and external I/O devices is known as I/O interface or input/output interface.

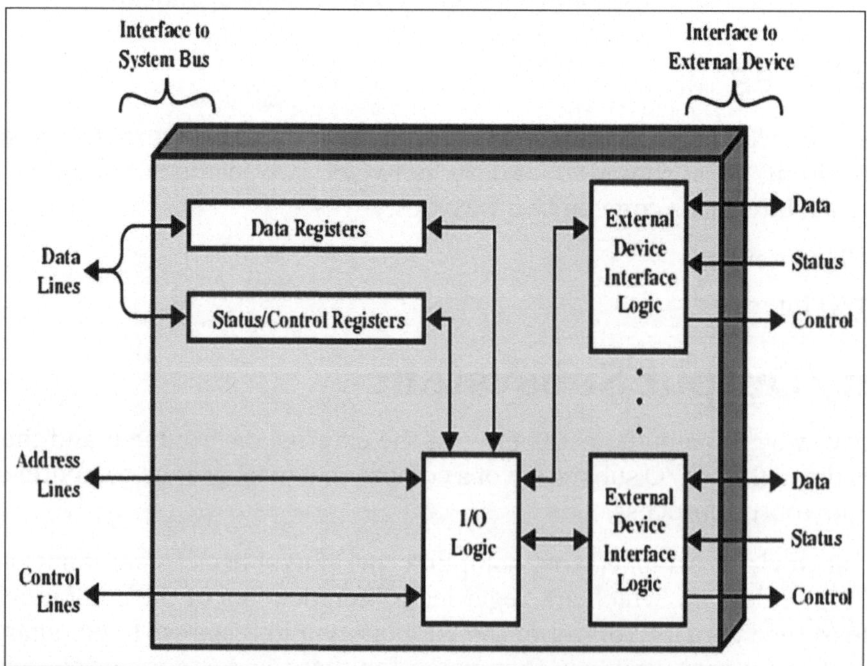

Figure 1.6: *Input/output Interface*

(1)I/O Module Decisions:

1. Protect or reveal device properties to the CPU
2. Support one or more devices
3. Control device functions or delegate them to the CPU

Additionally, O/S decisions – for example, Unix handles every possible thing as a file.

Data Transfer Modes

There are several ways to handle data transfer from the main computer to I/O devices. Three modes of data transfer are generally available between the central unit and I/O devices. These are as follows:

- Programmed I/O
- Interrupt Initiated I/O
- Direct Memory Access

Programmed I/O

Programmed I/O instructions are the result of I/O instructions written in the computer program. Each data item transfer is initiated by the instruction in the program.

Example of Programmed I/O

The I/O device does not have direct memory access when using the programmed I/O method. The CPU must carry out multiple instructions to transfer data from an I/O device to memory. These instructions include an input instruction to move data from the device to the CPU and a store instruction to move data from the CPU to memory. Additional instructions might be required to confirm that the data are accessible from the device and to tally the words transferred. An example of data transfer from an I/O device through an interface into the CPU is shown in *Figure* 1.7.

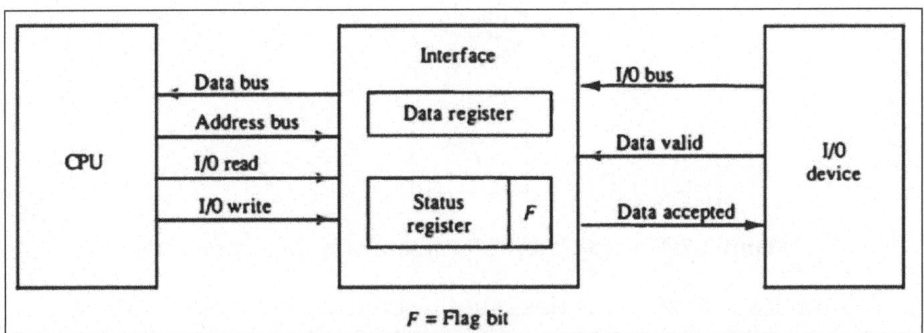

Figure 1.7: *Data Transfer from I/O device to CPU*

The device inserts a data byte into the I/O bus and activates its data valid line as soon as it becomes available. Enabling the data accepted line, the interface takes the byte and stores it in its data register.

The bit in the status register set by the interface is called an F bit, or "*flag*" bit for short. To stop sending data until the interface stops sending data accepted lines, the device can now stop sending data on the data valid line. The computer can run a program to check the status register flag and determine whether an I/O device has written a byte to the data register. To determine the value of the flag bit, the status register must be read into a CPU register. dot.

The CPU reads data from the data register if the flag is equal to 1. Depending on how the interface circuits are built, either the CPU or the interface clears the flag bit to 0.

Upon clearing the flag, the device can proceed to transfer the next data byte as the interface disables the data accepted line.

In *Figure 1.8*, there is a flowchart representing the program that needs to be written for the CPU. A series of bytes that need to be kept in memory are presumed to be being sent by the device.

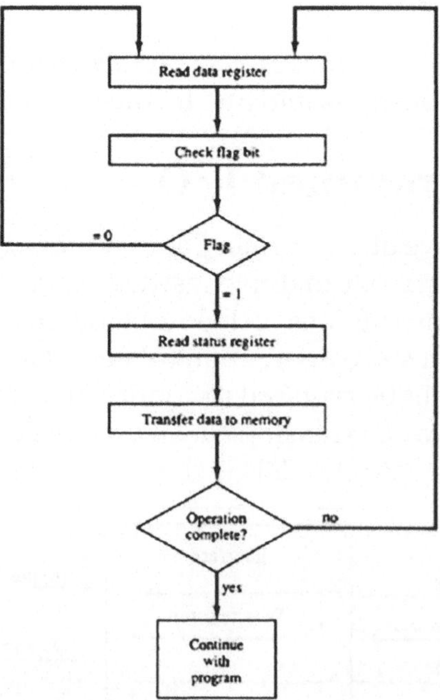

Figure 1.8: *Flowchart for CPU program for Inputting Data*

Small, slow computers or systems designed to continuously monitor a device benefit greatly from the programmed I/O technique. The inefficiency of this type of transfer stems from the differing information transfer rates of the CPU and I/O device. To comprehend why this is inefficient, imagine a typical computer that can perform the two tasks: reading the status register and checking the flag in 1 μS.

Assume for the moment that data is transmitted from the input device at an average rate of 100 bytes per second. This is equivalent to one byte every 10,000 μS. The CPU will perform 10,000 flag checks between each transfer, according to the instructions mentioned here.

Three instructions are needed to transfer each byte:

1. Read the status register
2. Examine whether the flag bit is set, and if it is, branch to step 1; if not, branch to step 3
3. Go through the data register

After being read into a CPU register, each byte is moved to memory following a store instruction. A typical I/O programming task involves moving a word block from an I/O device into a memory buffer.

Data transfer to and from the CPU and peripherals is typically managed by the program. The CPU must constantly keep an eye on the peripherals when transferring data under programmed I/O.

1. CPU sends out I/O operation requests
2. I/O module carries them out
3. I/O module sets status bits
4. CPU checks status bits periodically
5. I/O module does not inform the CPU directly
6. I/O module does not interrupt the CPU.
7. CPU may wait or come back later
8. Under programmed I/O data transfer, each device is assigned a unique identifier
9. Each device is a unique identifier
10. CPU commands contain an identifier (address)

Disadvantage of Programmed I/O:

- The issue with programmed I/O is that it requires a lengthy wait for the relevant I/O module to be ready for data transmission or reception.

- The processor, while waiting, must repeatedly interrogate the status of the I/O module.
- The entire system is severely degraded with respect to Performance

Interrupt Initiated I/O

To transfer data, the CPU in the programmed I/O method remains in the program loop until the I/O unit signals that it is prepared. The processor is kept unduly busy by this procedure, which takes a long time.

By allowing the interface to notify the computer when data is ready to be transferred, the CPU can avoid continuously monitoring the flag. This transfer mode utilizes the interrupt facility. While CPU is executing a program, it does not check the flag.

But when the flag is raised, the computer is alerted of its presence and is briefly forced to break out of its current program. To handle the input or output transfer, the CPU alters its current course of action. Once the transfer is complete, the computer returns to the prior program to carry out its previous task.

To handle the required I/O transfer, the CPU responds to the interrupt signal by first branching to a service routine and then storing the return address from the program counter into a memory stack. Each unit has a different method by which the processor selects the branch address of the service routine.

There are two types of interrupts: vectored interrupt and non-vectored interrupt. The branch address is allocated to a fixed location in memory in a non-vectored interrupt. The source of the interruption provides the computer with the branch information in a vectored interrupt called interrupt vector. The interrupt vector in certain computers is represented by the I/O service routine's first address. On other computers, the interrupt vector is an address that leads to memory where the I/O service routine's start address is kept.

Priority Interrupt

The CPU starts data transfer between an I/O device and itself. However, the CPU cannot initiate the transfer before the device is prepared to communicate with the CPU. An interrupt signal can be used to assess the device's readiness. The return address from the PC is stored in a memory stack by the CPU in response to an interrupt request, and the program then branches to a service routine that handles the necessary transfer.

Additionally, some processors load a fresh PSW for the service routine and push the existing PSW (program status word) onto the stack.

In a typical application, an interrupt request can be initiated by any of the several I/O devices connected to the computer. The primary task of the interrupt system is to identify the source of interrupt. Additionally, multiple sources may make simultaneous service requests. In this scenario, the system has to choose which device to fix first as well.

When two or more requests arrive simultaneously, **a priority interrupt** system sets a priority over the different sources to decide which condition is to be serviced first. In addition, the system can decide under what circumstances the computer can be interrupted while another interrupt is being handled. Requests that could have major repercussions if delayed or interrupted are given higher priority interrupt levels. Keyboards and other slow devices are assigned a low priority, while devices with high-speed transfers such as magnetic disks are assigned high priority.

When two devices interrupt it simultaneously, the computer prioritizes responding to the device with **higher priority.**

Hardware or software can be used to establish the priority hierarchy for concurrent interruptions. In a polling process, software is used to ascertain which source is most important. This method uses a single, common branch address for all interrupts. The interrupt handling program polls each interrupt source sequentially, beginning at the branch address. The order in which interrupts are tested establishes their priority.

First, the highest-priority source is tested, and if its interrupt signal is detected, control branches to a service routine. Subsequently, the source with the lowest priority is examined, and so on. A program that tests the interrupt sources one after the other and branches to one of several potential service routines is thus the initial service routine for all interrupts. The specific service routine that was accessed is associated with the device that has the highest priority among all the devices that caused the computer to interrupt.

If there are a lot of interrupts, polling them could take longer than servicing the I/O device, which is a drawback of the software approach. One way to expedite the process in this scenario is to employ a hardware priority-interrupt unit.

A hardware priority-interrupt unit serves as the general manager in an interrupt system environment. It receives interrupt requests from various sources, chooses the one with the highest priority and then sends an interrupt request to the computer based on this choice.

Every interrupt source can directly access its own service routine through an interrupt vector, which expedites the process. Polling is unnecessary because the hardware priority-interrupt unit is used, as it makes all the decisions.

The hardware priority function can be established by either a serial or a parallel connection of interrupt lines. The serial connection is commonly referred to as the daisy chaining method.

Interrupt-Driven I/O Basic Operation

Details of the Interrupt Driven I/O Basic Operation are as follows:

1. CPU problems with reading commands; I/O module obtains data from peripherals while the CPU performs other tasks
2. I/O module interrupts the CPU; CPU requests data
3. I/O module transfers data

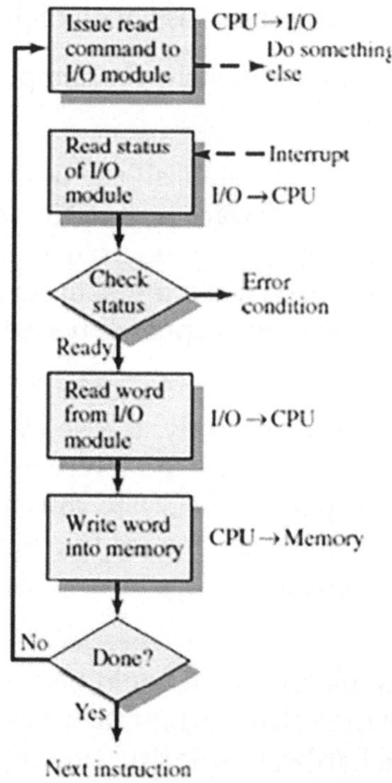

Figure 1.9: *Interrupt Driven I/O*

Interrupt initiated I/O is a solution to this issue. When the interface determines that the peripheral is ready for data transfer, it generates an interrupt. Upon receiving the interrupt signal, the CPU pauses its current task to handle the I/O transfer before proceeding with the previous processing task.

Processor Functioning in Terms of Interrupts

1. Issue read command
2. Take on other tasks
3. Every time an instruction cycle ends, check for interrupts

4. In the event of a disruption:
    a. Store context (registers)
    b. Process interrupt
5. Fetch and store data
6. If there are multiple interrupts:
    a. Each interrupt line has a priority
    b. Higher priority lines can interrupt lower priority lines
    c. If the bus mastering, only the current master can interrupt

Working of CPU in Terms of Interrupts

1. Issue read command
2. Take on other tasks
3. Check for interrupts at the end of each instruction cycle.
4. If interrupted:
    a. Save context (registers)
    b. Process interrupt
5. Fetch data and store
6. In case of Multiple Interrupts:
    a. Each interrupt line has a priority
    b. Higher priority lines can interrupt lower priority lines
    c. If the bus mastering, only current master can interrupt

Direct Memory Access

The transfer speed would be increased if the peripheral device managed the memory buses directly and the CPU was removed from the path. This method is called DMA. In this case, data is transferred between the interface and the memory via the memory bus. The DMA controller facilitates data transfer between the memory unit and peripherals.

Disk drive controllers, graphic cards, network cards, sound cards, and other hardware systems use DMA. Moreover, multicore processors use it for intra-chip data transfer. When a DMA transfer is in progress, the CPU starts it, performs other tasks, and waits for the DMA controller to interrupt it when the transfer is finished.

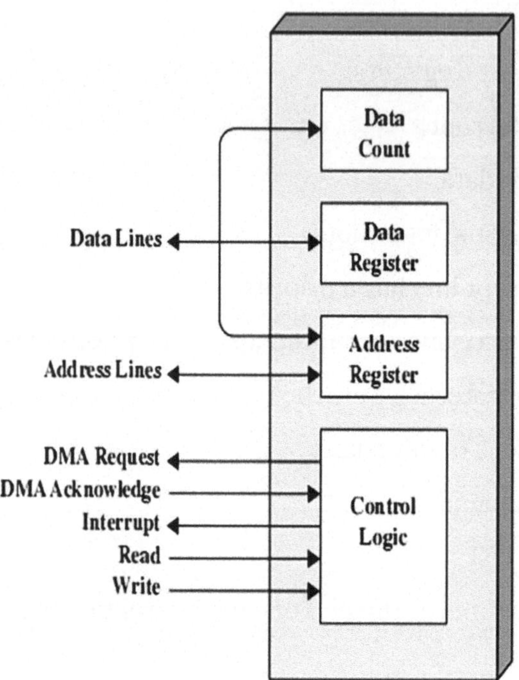

Figure 1.10: *Block diagram of DMA*

DMA Operation:

CPU provides the following instructions to the DMA controller:

1. Read/Write
2. Device address
3. Start address of data memory block
4. Amount of data to be transferred
5. CPU continues with other tasks
6. DMA controller handles transfer
7. The DMA controller sends an interrupt when the transfer is complete

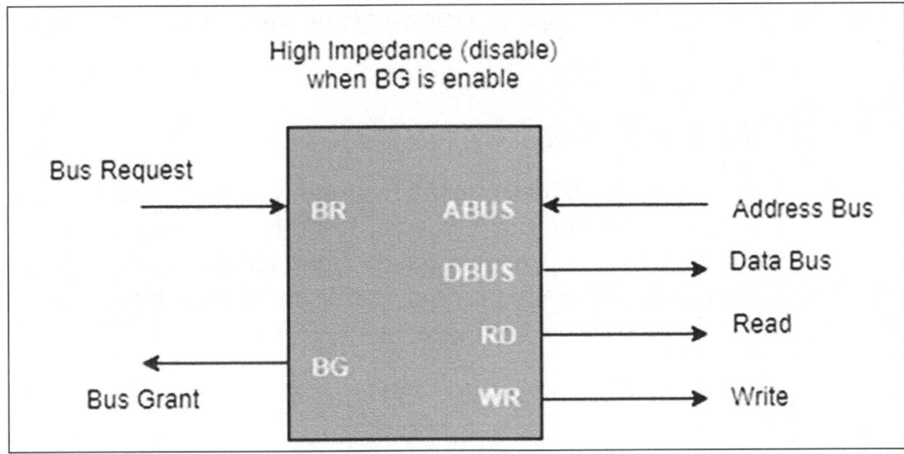

***Figure 1.11**: CPU Bus Signals for DMA Transfer*

Using Interrupt Handler to Pass Control Between a Running Program and an OS

An interrupt is an event that alters the sequence in which the processor executes instructions. An interrupt might be planned (specifically requested by the currently running program) or unplanned (caused by an event that might or might not be related to the currently running program).

Interrupt Handler in OS

Operating systems depend heavily on interrupt handlers to handle time-sensitive events and enable effective multitasking. Let's start by defining an interrupt before talking about interrupt handlers.

In computing, interrupts are used to handle urgent or time-sensitive tasks, react to outside events, or communicate between various parts of a computer system. Program normal execution is momentarily halted and control is passed to an interrupt handler when an interrupt occurs, such as a hardware request or an external event.

Interrupts are used in computing to respond to external events, handle urgent or time-sensitive tasks, and facilitate communication between various parts of a computer system. The normal execution of a program is momentarily halted and control is passed to an interrupt handler when an interrupt occurs, such as an external event or hardware request. This response examines interrupt handlers' purpose, significance, and mechanism in addition to describing the various kinds of interrupt handlers and their unique duties. A specific code routine or function known as an interrupt service routine (ISR) is carried out in reaction to an interrupt event. Upon detecting an interrupt, the CPU transfers control to the corresponding ISR to address the event efficiently.

Interrupt Handlers

The interrupt handlers' responsibilities include responding to interruptions in a timely and efficient manner and carrying out essential tasks related to particular events. Time-sensitive operations such as processing data from hardware devices or reacting to user input are made sure to happen on time, thanks to interrupt handlers.

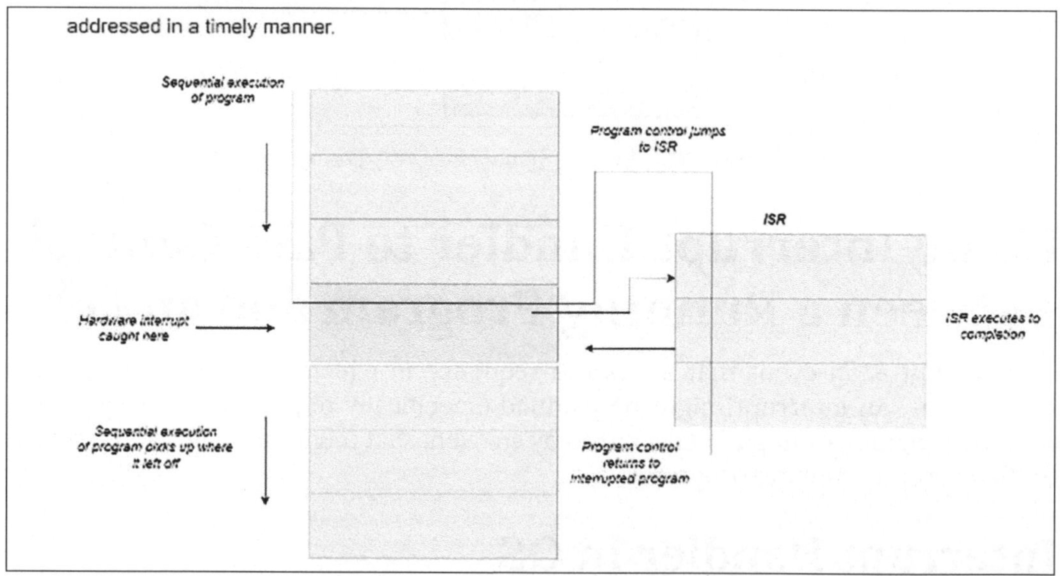

Figure 1.12: *Interrupt Handling Mechanism*

Interrupt handlers aid in preserving system responsiveness and enable the simultaneous processing of several tasks by pausing the running of the current program.

Workflow of Interrupt Handlers

In the event of an interrupt, the CPU first stores the register values and program counter as well as the current state of the interrupted program. Afterward, it recognizes the particular interrupt request (IRQ) linked to the occurrence and responds to the interruption. The interrupt vector table (IVT) is then searched by the processor using the interrupt number or IRQ line to find the appropriate interrupt handler. After that, the code required to handle the interrupt is run at the interrupt handler's memory address. The interrupt handler handles interrupt-specific tasks, such as communicating with hardware or handling data.

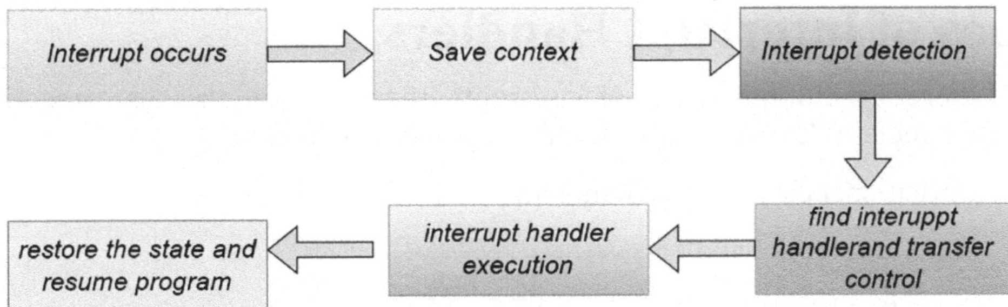

Figure 1.13: *Working of Interrupt Handlers*

Once the interrupt is handled, the saved state is restored, allowing the interrupted program to resume execution from where it left off. This workflow ensures that interrupt events are promptly addressed while preserving the integrity of the interrupted program. By saving and restoring the program state, interrupt handling ensures that the interrupted program can seamlessly resume execution after the interrupt is serviced.

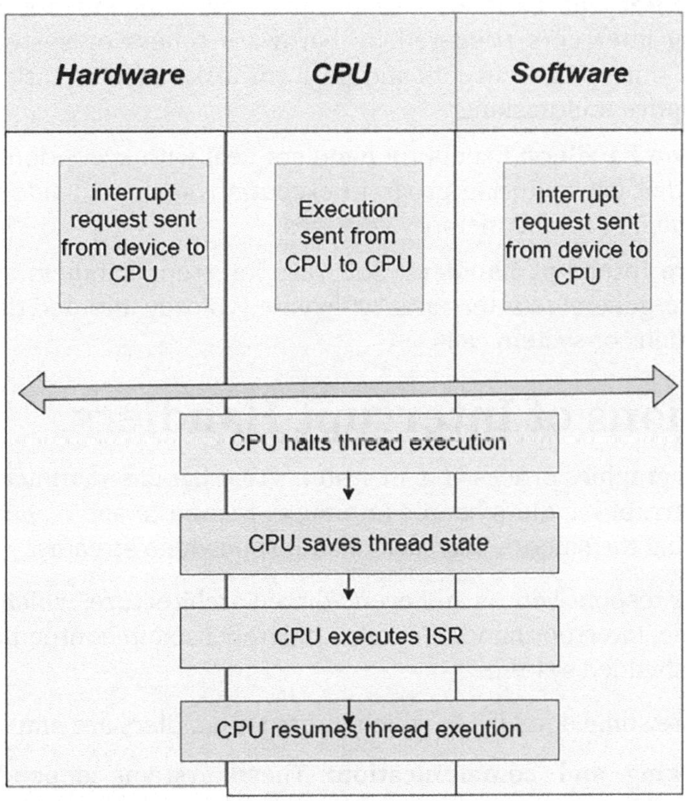

Figure 1.14: *The Process of Interrupt handling*

Types of Interrupt Handlers

Just as there are different types of interrupts, there are also various categories of interrupt handlers. The main types of interrupt handlers include:

1. Device-specific interrupt handlers
2. Timer interrupt handlers
3. Exception handlers
4. Software interrupt handlers

Let's discuss them in detail.

- **Device-specific interrupt handlers**: They handle interrupts generated by devices, such as keyboards, mice, disk drives, and USB devices and interact with the corresponding hardware to perform actions, such as reading or writing data.
- **Timer interrupt handlers**: Timer interrupt handlers are responsible for handling interrupts triggered by hardware timers or system clocks. They manage time-related events and perform tasks such as task scheduling and pre-emptive multitasking.
- **Exception handlers**: Exception handlers deal with exceptional conditions or events that occur during program execution, such as divide-by-zero errors, page faults, or invalid memory accesses.
- **Software interrupt handlers:** Software interrupt handlers are triggered by software-generated interrupts, which are typically initiated through software instructions or system calls.

Applications of Interrupt Handlers

Multimedia and graphics processing: In systems that handle multimedia and graphics processing, interrupt handlers handle interrupts related to audio, video, or graphical events, facilitating the smooth playback of audio and video streams.

Because of their responsiveness and event-driven architecture, which allows them to react in real time, interrupt handlers are extensively used in contemporary operating systems and embedded systems.

The following are some domains in which interrupt handlers are employed:

- **Networking and communication:** These systems depend on interrupt handlers. They support dependable and responsive network communication by facilitating effective protocol handling, data transfer, and network event management.

- **Multimedia and graphics processing**: Interrupt handlers are used to handle audio, video, or graphical event-related interrupts in systems that manage multimedia and graphics processing, enabling the seamless playback of video and audio streams.
- **Power management:** Interrupt handlers are involved in power management mechanisms, such as handling interrupts related to power state changes, sleep/wake events, or power-related events from hardware components. They assist in managing system power modes, transitions between power states, and power-related notifications, optimizing energy consumption and enhancing overall power efficiency.

Conclusion

In this chapter, while learning Computer Organization, we have learnt basic Parts of Computer CPU, ALU including the Input and output Units combinedly known as peripherals. We then learnt various modes of data transfer that included Programmed I/O, Interrupt Driven I/O Basic Operation and Direct Memory Access. We also learned about Priority interrupt and Interrupt handler in OS.

In the next chapter, we will learn about the various aspects of Operating Systems.

Questions

1. With the help of a detailed diagram describe various Basic Parts of the Computer?
2. What are the primary functions of Input Units?
3. What are the primary functions of output Units?
4. What is the primary function of the CPU?
5. Draw a block diagram of a computer with a Central Processing Unit (CPU) and describe their functions in brief.
6. Describe the basic three Major Components of the CPU.
7. What is ALU and what are its components? Describe the function of each of its components.
8. Describe in detail the working of (Digital Personal) Computers.
9. What are the various types of digital devices and Data Flow diagrams of a typical Personal Computer?
10. Define digital Computer Interface?

11. What is included in Input/Output Subsystem and what is meant by Peripherals?
12. What are the different modes of Data Transfer?
13. How is data transfer effected between the central computer to I/O devices? may be handled in variety of modes.
14. Draw a flowchart for the CPU program for inputting data.
15. What is a Programmed I/O method and state the advantages and disadvantages of Programmed I/O?
16. What is Direct Memory Access?
17. Define and describe the working of Interrupt Handlers.
18. How many types of interrupt handlers are there? Describe any one of them.

Reference

[1] Computer Architecture: Input/Output Organisation,https://www.studytonight.com/computer-architecture/input-output-organisation

CHAPTER 2
Introduction to Operating Systems

Introduction

An operating system, a type of specialized software, is installed on every computer, smartphone, and other electronic device. The core component that gives computers and smartphones their usefulness is their operating system(OS). If you work or want to work in the information technology (IT) industry, you should be aware of the various operating system that vary based on the device, manufacturer, and user preference.

Structure

In this chapter, we will learn about the following topics:

- Operating Systems
- Concept of the Kernel in OS and their Types
- Decision on Using the Type of Kernel
- Types of Operating Systems Based on their Method of Operation
- Generations of the Evolution of Operating Systems
- Overview of Main Popular Operating Systems
- Disk Operating Systems, such as MS DOS, Unix Linux and Posix, Windows, Android, and Apple's iOS and iPadOS

Operating Systems

This software interface known as an Operating System (OS) serves as a conduit between the user and the hardware of a device. Users can interact with the device and carry out the required tasks, thanks to this software. Two components that are used by operating systems to control computer programs and applications are as follows:

1. The kernel is the central component that handles data processing on the hardware level and takes care of memory, input-output, and process management.
2. The outermost layer that controls communication between the OS and the user is called the shell. Through the use of shell scripts or user input, the shell can interact with the operating system. A file containing a series of system commands is called a shell script.

Concept of Kernels in OS and Their Types

At the heart of an operating system on a computer is a computer program called the kernel, which typically has total authority over all system operations. Preventing and minimizing conflicts between various processes falls under the purview of the kernel. Interactions between hardware and software are facilitated by this part of the operating system code, which is always present in memory. Complete kernels manage every hardware resource; for example, Device drivers manage resource conflicts (I/O, memory, cryptography) between processes and maximize the use of shared resources. For example Use of file systems, network sockets, and CPU and cache. The kernel loads among the first applications on most systems upon startup, following the bootloader. After converting software requests for input/output (I/O) and memory into instructions, the central processing unit can be used to process data; it manages the remainder of the startup.

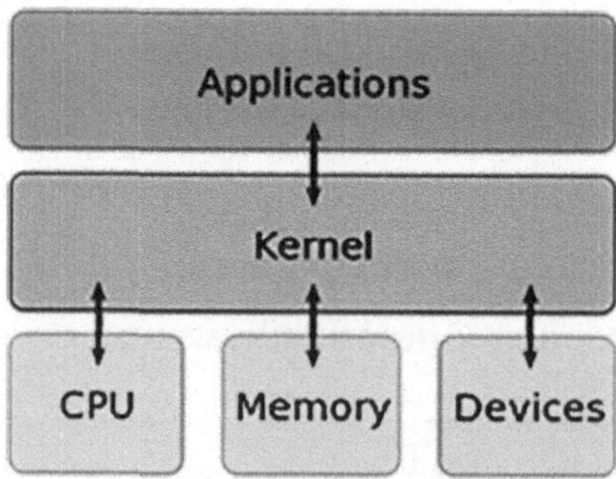

Figure 2.1: *An oversimplification of how a kernel connects application software to the hardware of a computer*

Usually, application software and other less important components of the operating system cannot access the critical code of the kernel as it is located in a separate area of memory. Within this protected kernel space, the kernel carries out its operations, including managing hardware devices such as the hard disk, executing processes, and responding to interrupts. On the other hand, application programs that run on different parts of memory called user space include word processors, video and audio players, and browsers [1].

This section prevents operating system crashes and malfunctioning apps from crashing other apps. It also prevents user and kernel data from interfering with and slowing down the system. Even in systems where application address spaces include the kernel, memory protection ensures unauthorized applications from altering the kernel.

The kernel interface serves as a low-level abstraction layer. When a process requests a service from the kernel, it typically does so through a system call, which is often invoked via a wrapper function.

Types of Kernel Designs/Architecture

There are various kernel architecture designs. Monolithic kernels, optimized primarily for speed, operate entirely within a single address space while the CPU runs in supervisor mode. In contrast, microkernels prioritize resilience and modularity by running most of their services in user space, although not in the same way as user processes. One well-known instance of microkernel design is MINIX 3. The Linux kernel is both monolithic and modular as it allows loadable kernel modules to be added or removed at runtime. As the core component of a computer system, the kernel is responsible for executing programs. It also manages the assignment of active programs to the processor or processors, determining which tasks should run at any given time.

Monolithic Kernels

As they share the same memory space, all OS services in a monolithic kernel operate concurrently with the main kernel thread. This methodology offers rich and potent hardware access. Ken Thompson, a UNIX developer, said that "*implementing a monolithic kernel is easier in [his] opinion.*" Large kernels can be very difficult to maintain; Thompson also noted that "*it is also easier for [a monolithic kernel] to turn into a mess in a hurry as it is modified.*" While monolithic kernels offer performance benefits, they have significant drawbacks. These include dependencies between system components (where a bug in a device driver could crash the entire system) and their large size, which makes maintenance challenging. The operating system's fundamental features and device drivers are all contained in monolithic kernels, which are typically utilized by Unix-like operating systems.

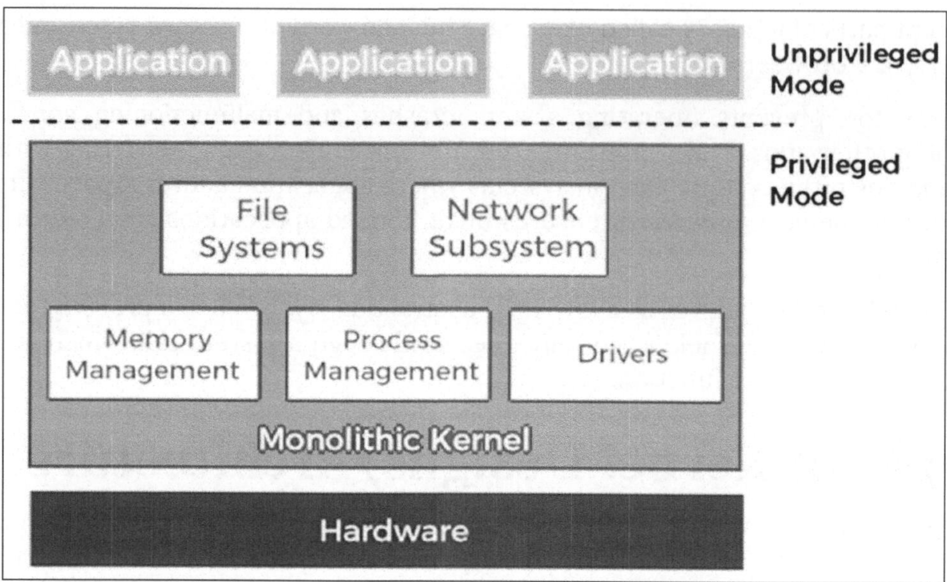

Figure 2.2: *Diagram of a Monolithic Kernel System*

An entire program with all the code required to complete every task pertaining to the kernel is called a monolithic kernel. The kernel contains all components that are needed by most programs but cannot be placed in a library, including file systems, network stacks, schedulers, device drivers, and memory management. A large number of system calls are supplied to enable applications to access all those services. A monolithic kernel can be tuned to run at least as fast as the one that was created especially for the hardware, though it is generally more relevant. At first, it may be loaded with subsystems that are not necessary.

Modern monolithic kernels support loadable kernel modules, which enable modules to be loaded into the kernel at runtime, allowing for easy extension of the kernel's capabilities as needed while helping to minimize the amount of code running in kernel space. Examples of these kernels are the Linux, FreeBSD, AIX, HP-UX, and Solaris kernels, all of which are classified as Unix-like operating systems.

In a monolithic kernel, system calls handle the majority of the work. These are interfaces that typically maintain a tabular structure and provide access to a kernel subsystem, such as disk operations. A verified copy of the request is passed through the system call when calls are essentially made within programs. Therefore, it wouldn't be far to go. Due to its flexibility in dynamic module loading and ease of customization, the monolithic Linux kernel can be made incredibly small. Some versions (like the widely used muLinux) are compact enough to fit alongside numerous utilities and other programs on a single floppy disk while still offering a fully functional operating system. The use of Linux in embedded systems has increased significantly due to its capacity to shrink its kernel.

These kernels are made up of the device drivers and the essential components of the operating system, which can load modules dynamically. They offer rich and robust abstractions of the underlying hardware and a limited range of basic hardware abstractions. To offer additional functionality, they leverage servers, which are applications. Though this method has several shortcomings, it creates a high-level virtual interface over the hardware and uses a series of system calls to implement operating system functions in multiple supervisor mode-running modules, including memory management, concurrency, and process management.

Earlier Examples of Monolithic Operating Systems

Two basic instances of monolithic operating systems are DOS and CP/M. Operating systems that share a single address space with applications are DOS and CP/M. System variables and the application area are the first two addresses in the 16-bit address space in CP/M.

The three operating system components that remain are the BIOS (Basic Input/ Output System), BDOS (Basic Disk Operating System), and CCP (Console Command Processor). The array of interrupt vectors and system variables are at the beginning of DOS's 20-bit address space. Next comes the application area, resident portion of DOS, and lastly, a memory block utilized by the BIOS and video card.

Advantages of Monolithic Architecture

Some benefits of monolithic architecture are:

- Straightforward structure and ease of implementation
- Faster execution because all services are accessed directly

Disadvantages of Monolithic Architecture

- Adding new features or removing outmoded features is extremely challenging in a monolithic architecture.
- As the kernel lacks isolation between different servers, security problems are constant.
- It is challenging to port code written for this operating system (OS).
- Monolithic operating systems are more likely to produce errors and bugs. The rationale is that the kernel and user processes share the same address spaces.
- Adding and removing features from a monolithic operating system is hard. To add or remove any feature, all code must be completely redone and recompiled.

Runtime executable module loading and unloading is possible for modern monolithic operating systems, such as Linux, BSD, SunOS, AIX, and MULTICS as well as modular operating systems. Instead of being at the architecture level, the operating system's modularity occurs at the binary level.

Operating systems that are modular monolithic should not be confused with the inherent architectural modularity of server-client operating systems and their derivatives, which are sometimes referred to as hybrid kernels, that use servers and microkernels. In practice, handling the operating system image at runtime with dynamically loaded modules is far more flexible than rebooting with a different operating system image. The operating systems' capabilities can be easily expanded as needed, thanks to the modules. The cost of dynamically loadable modules is slightly higher than that of integrating the module into the operating system image.

Modular Monolithic Systems

Nevertheless, dynamic module loading can occasionally reduce the amount of code executing in kernel space. This approach is particularly useful for minimizing the operating system's footprint on embedded devices or devices with limited hardware resources. Specifically, it is not necessary to store an unloaded module in randomly allocated memory.

Features of Monolithic System

The following features are offered to users of monolithic operating systems:

- **Simple structure:** This kind of operating system has a simple structure. The kernel contains all the parts required for processing.
- **Functions well for shorter tasks**: Due to its capacity to manage fewer resources, it performs better on shorter tasks.
- **Communication between components**: Every component has direct access to the kernel as well as to each other.
- **Quick operating system**: The code required to create a monolithic kernel is incredibly robust and quick.
- **Challenging:** The inability to use common libraries, such as a feature-rich libc, and the requirement to use a source-level debugger, such as gdb, can make kernel coding difficult at times. It is frequently necessary to restart the computer. For the developers, this is more than just a convenience issue.
- **Code is more likely to be "*buggier*"** when debugging is more difficult and as problems get more severe. Strong side effects can result from bugs in one area of the kernel. Since all functions in the kernel have full access, a bug in one area of the kernel can corrupt the data structure of another, completely unrelated area of the kernel, or of any running program.
- **Kernels frequently grow to be very big** and challenging to manage.
- Although the modules responsible for these functions are isolated from the overall system, the code integration is intricate and challenging to execute accurately.

- The **system can crash due to a bug because all the modules share the same address space.**

The microkernel approach limits the capabilities of the kernel to just those functions necessary for the operation of servers: separate programs that take over the roles of former kernel components, such as GUI servers and device drivers.

Microkernels

The term "*microkernel*" refers to an approach to operating system design wherein the system's functionality is transferred from a traditional "*kernel*" to a collection of "*servers*" that interface with each other via a "*minimal*" kernel, thereby minimizing the amount of space occupied by "*system space*" and optimizing it for "*user space.*" A microkernel built for a particular platform or gadget will only ever have the components necessary for it to function. By defining a basic abstraction over the hardware and using a set of primitives or system calls, the microkernel approach can implement basic operating system functions, such as memory management, multitasking, and inter-process communication. Additional services such as networking, typically supplied by the kernel, are implemented in user-space programs, also known as servers.

Although microkernels are simpler to maintain than monolithic kernels, the sheer volume of context switches and system calls they generate may cause the system to lag compared to plain function calls, which, in kernel space, need to be in a privileged mode: basic memory handling, basic I/O primitives, basic scheduler, or scheduling primitives (IPC). The whole scheduler, memory management, file systems, and network stacks are among the many essential components currently operating in user space. The conventional "*monolithic*" kernel design, in which every system function was contained in a single static program operating in a dedicated "*system*" mode of the CPU, prompted the creation of microkernels. The microkernel handles only the most basic functions, such as managing memory, coordinating message passing amongst processes, and gaining some, but not all, hardware access. A few systems that make use of microkernels are the HURD and QNX. In QNX and Hurd, user sessions can be full snapshots of the system or views as they are called.

Advantages of Using Microkernel Architecture

The microkernel architecture's core benefits are as follows:

- Easy to maintain
- Patches can be tested in a separate instance before being swapped in to take control of a production instance.
- It is possible to test new software quickly even without restarting the kernel.
- If one instance malfunctions, it is feasible to replace frequently with a functional mirror.

To handle requests from one server to another, the majority of microkernels employ a message-passing mechanism. Typically, the message-passing system communicates with the microkernel through ports. For instance, when a request is made for more memory, the microkernel opens a port and sends the request through it. The procedures are the same as the system calls once inside the microkernel. The reasoning behind it was that it would introduce modularity to the system architecture, making it more performative, easier to debug or dynamically modify, and more user-friendly.

Operating systems that include them are GNU Hurd, MINIX, MkLinux, QNX, and Redox OS.

Despite being extremely small on their own, microkernels are frequently larger than monolithic kernels when combined with all auxiliary code they require. The two-tiered architecture of microkernel systems, where most of the operating system does not interact directly with the hardware, is a key point of contention among proponents of monolithic kernels. This structure results in a noticeable loss of system efficiency. The only functions that these kernel types typically offer are process management, inter-process communication (IPC), and memory address space definition. Microkernels are not directly responsible for other tasks, such as managing hardware processes. The drawback of monolithic kernels, according to proponents of microkernels, is that a single kernel error can bring down the entire system. But with a microkernel, you can still stop the system from crashing altogether if a kernel process crashes: restart the service that generated the error.

Additional kernel functions, such as networking, are implemented in user-space programs called servers. Programs can be started and stopped on servers to make changes to the operating system. The networking server, for example, is not started on a machine without networking support. Microkernels are less efficient than monolithic kernels because of the overhead caused by moving data between servers and applications, which involves entering and exiting the kernel.

The microkernel has a few drawbacks. A few of these include:

- A potentially higher running memory footprint
- More software is needed for interfaces
- A possible decrease in performance
- Compared to a single copy in a monolithic kernel, messaging bugs can be more difficult to fix because they must travel a longer distance
- In general, process management can be highly complex
- Microkernels have a great deal of context-specific drawbacks. For instance, when only a few processes are required to run, the difficulties associated with process management are successfully reduced, making them ideal for small, single-purpose (and crucial) systems.

Using multiple operating systems on top of the same unaltered kernel and implementing the remaining portion of the operating system as a standard application program written in a high-level language are made possible by microkernels. It is also feasible to have multiple operating systems open at once and to switch between them dynamically.

Monolithic Kernels versus Microkernels

To reduce the kernel's footprint, extensive editing has to be performed to carefully remove unneeded code. A kernel's footprint refers to the amount of memory it uses. The size and vulnerability of the computer kernel's trusted computing base increase along with the kernel itself, which not only compromises security but also causes issues with memory footprint expansion. Though not all computer architectures support virtual memory, this is somewhat mitigated by advancements in the virtual memory system [2].

With millions of lines of code, a kernel may have subtle dependencies among many of its parts, making it extremely challenging to remove extraneous code carefully without requiring extensive editing. This may lessen the footprint of the kernel. Due to their many disadvantages over microkernels, nearly all operating system researchers felt that monolithic kernels were obsolete by the early 1990s. As a result, a well-known discussion between Linus Torvalds and Andrew Tanenbaum centered on whether Linux was intended to be a monolithic kernel or a microkernel. In the Tanenbaum–Torvalds debate, both sides made valid points. However, it can be challenging to understand non-obvious dependencies between the millions of lines of code that make up a kernel.

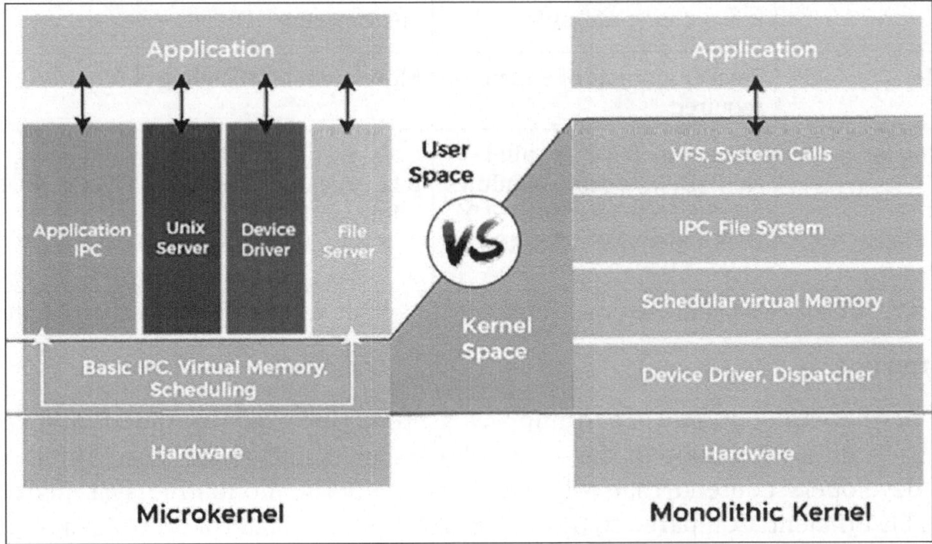

Figure 2.3: *Monolithic Kernels vs. Microkernels*

Table 2.1 compares the several features of Monolithic kernels vs. microkernels Systems.

Features	Monolithic Kernel	Microkernel
Definition	When an operating system's whole system operates inside the kernel, the kernel is said to be monolithic	A microkernel is a kernel that helps to implement an operating system by offering low-level thread management, address space management, and interprocess communication
Address space	The address space used by kernel and user services is shared in a monolithic kernel	Services are kept in separate address spaces in case of microkernel user services and kernel,
Size	The monolithic kernel is larger than the microkernel	The microkernel is smaller in size
Execution	Fast execution	Slow execution
OS services	The kernel contains the OS services in the case of a monolithic kernel system,	Here OS services and kernels are separated in the case of a microkernels-based system
Extendible	The monolithic kernels are complicated to extend	Easily extendible
Security	In case of any service crash, then the whole system crashes	In case of a service crash, it does not affect the working
Customization	Adding new functionalities is very difficult due to which it is not customizable	It is easier to Adding new functionalities to the microkernel is simple and customizable
Code	Smaller amount of coding is required	More amount of coding is required
Example	Linux, FreeBSD, OpenBSD, NetBSD, Microsoft Windows (95, 98, Me), Solaris, HP-UX, DOS, OpenVMS, XTS-400, etc.	QNX, Symbian, L4L.inux, Singularity, K42, Mac OS X, Integrity, PikeOS, HURD, Minix, and Coyotos.

Table 2.1: *Comparison of the several features of Monolithic kernels vs. microkernels Systems*

Performance

Some developers contend that to improve system performance, monolithic kernels must have all of their code in the same address space or kernel space. Additionally, some developers contend that, when written properly, monolithic systems can be incredibly efficient. Compared to the slower IPC system of microkernel designs, which is usually based on message passing, the monolithic model is generally more efficient due to its utilization of shared kernel memory. Microkernels did not perform well in the 1980s or the early 1990s. Studies that evaluated these microkernels' performance empirically, however, did not examine the causes of their inefficiency. The explanations for these data were relegated to "*folklore*," with the supposition that they were caused by a rise in the frequency of context switches, communication between processes, and the transition from "*kernel mode*" to "*user mode*." It was possible to predict in 1995 the reasons for the low performance of microkernels. They were as follows:

- A true inefficiency of the microkernel approach as a whole
- Specific concepts implemented in those microkernels, and
- The specific implementation of those concepts. It was therefore still up for debate whether using the right construction methods–as opposed to earlier attempts–was the way to create an effective microkernel.

Conversely, every time there's an interaction between various protection levels (that is, layers of protection), the hierarchical protection domain architecture that results in the design of a monolithic kernel has a major performance disadvantage. It necessitates message copying by value when a process must manipulate a data structure in both "*user mode*" and "*supervisor mode*".

Hybrid (or Modular) Kernels

The hybrid kernel approach blends the execution safety and modularity of a microkernel with the speed and easier design of a monolithic kernel. Most commercial operating systems, including Microsoft Windows NT 3.2, employ hybrid kernels. 3 points for NT, 5 for NT. 10., NT 4.0, 2000, XP, Vista, 7, 8, and 8.1. Based on code from FreeBSD's monolithic kernel and OSF/1's Mach kernel (OSFMK 7.3),

Apple's macOS runs on a hybrid kernel known as XNU. Except adding extra code to kernel space to improve performance, hybrid kernels are comparable to microkernels. Some developers made modifications by implementing these kernels to accommodate the major benefits of both microkernels and monolithic systems.

These kernel varieties are developments of microkernels with certain monolithic kernel characteristics. Unlike monolithic kernels, these kernels cannot automatically load modules at runtime. To minimize the performance overhead of a traditional microkernel, some services such as the filesystem or network stack, are run in kernel space. However, similar to device drivers, kernel code is still run as servers in user space.

Nowadays, many traditionally monolithic kernels are incorporating module capabilities. Linux is the most popular kernel among these. Parts of the modular kernel can, in essence, be binaries that load into memory on demand or parts that are integrated into the main kernel binary. An operating kernel could become unstable due to a code-tainted module. A driver for a microkernel can be written in a different memory space, tested, and then "*gone*" live. The doorway to potential pollution is opened when a kernel module loads because it adds to the monolithic portion's memory space as needed.

Advantages

The hybrid kernel has several benefits, including:

- Quicker development time for drivers that can function from within modules; testing doesn't require a reboot (as long as the kernel isn't unstable)
- The ability to recompile an entire kernel on demand as opposed to repurposing it for new drivers or subsystems
- Quicker integration of outside technology (relevant to development but not in and of itself)

Modules typically use some module interface to communicate with the kernel. Although specific to a particular operating system, the interface is generalized, so using modules is not always possible. Device drivers frequently require more flexibility than what the module interface provides. In essence, there are two system calls involved, and safety checks that were previously required only once in the monolithic kernel may now need to be performed twice.

Disadvantages of a Hybrid Kernel (or Modular) System

The modular approach has a few drawbacks, including:

- The potential for more bugs because there are more interfaces to go through, which suggests more security holes.
- Some administrators may find maintaining modules confusing when addressing issues such as symbol discrepancies.

Nanokernels

An operating system with a nano kernel architecture only provides the features that are absolutely necessary for the system to run. It does little more than supervise routine computer operations and help systems communicate with one another. More complex tasks are delegated to other operating system components. Microkernels have their roots in the 1980s when they were created to make kernels more straightforward and robust. Nano kernels developed this idea even further by doing even less. They did this to meet the need for safe and efficient systems, especially for embedded and real-time environments.

Nano Kernel Functions

These can vary depending on how the kernel is implemented, but they usually consist of:

- **Low-level hardware management**: Regulates the central processing unit (CPU) and memory of the computer.
- **Changes in context**: Switches attention between various computer processes or tasks.
- **Interprocess communication**: Facilitates the sharing of information across system components.
- **Planning**: Determines which task, albeit occasionally it is delegated to more sophisticated layers, the CPU should work on next.
- **Disruptive management**: Reacts to and controls unforeseen requests or system modifications.

Advantages of a Nano kernel

The advantages of a Nano kernel operating system are as follows:

- **Adjustability:** A modular system that makes it simple to add or remove features as needed is made possible by a nano kernel.
- **Effectiveness and output:** Nano kernels are small, quick, and low power, making them appropriate for systems with constrained resources. safety.
- **Less complexity:** This implies a decreased possibility of mistakes or security problems.

To further reduce the kernel memory requirement compared to a conventional microkernel, a nanokernel assigns almost all functions, including the most fundamental ones such as interrupt controllers and timers, to device drivers.

Exokernels

Exokernel is an operating system kernel developed by the MIT Parallel and Distributed Operating Systems group, and also a class of similar operating systems.

Applications typically access hardware resources through operating systems via high-level abstractions such as (virtual) file systems. Exokernel's concept is to impose as few abstractions as possible on application developers, giving them the freedom to choose as many hardware abstractions as they like. Since exokernel functionality is restricted to resource multiplexing and protection, it is much simpler than conventional microkernels' message-passing implementation and the high-level abstraction implementation of monolithic kernels. This simplicity is why exokernels are small.

The end-to-end principle can be applied to operating systems by using kernels, which spare application programs from having to layer their abstractions on top of other abstractions created with different needs in mind. For instance, the kernel ensures safe disk access by blocking unauthorized reading and writing, but the application or the libraries it uses determines how the disk is abstracted. In the MIT Exokernel project, for instance, the disk is used by the Cheetah web server to store preformatted Internet Protocol packets.

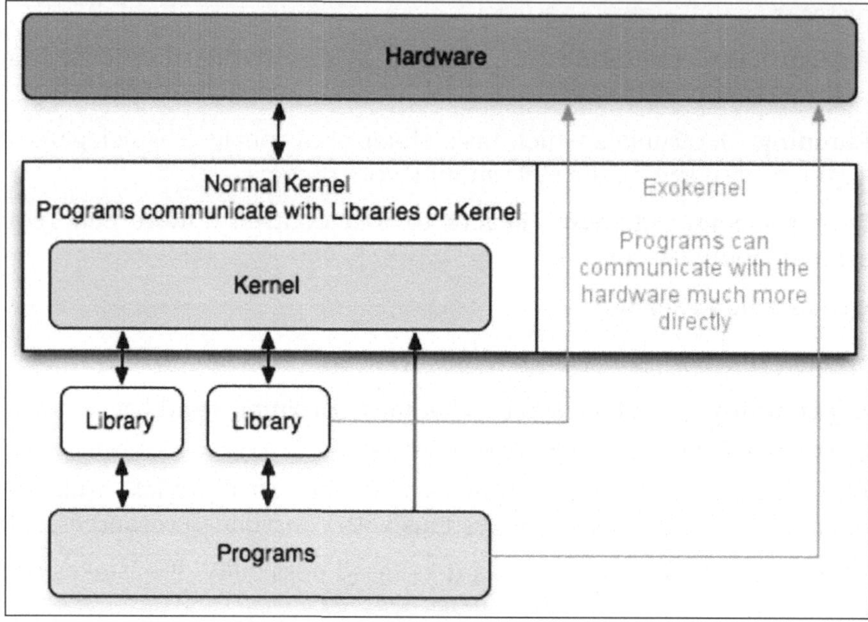

Figure 2.4: *Exokernel System Explored*

A relatively new method of designing operating systems is the use of kernels. Unlike other kernel varieties, they are restricted in their capabilities to safeguard and multiplex the unprocessed hardware; they do not offer any hardware abstractions for the development of applications. Since hardware protection and hardware management are kept apart, application developers can decide how best to utilize the hardware that is available for each unique program. Exokernels are minuscule creatures in and of themselves. They are supported, nevertheless, by library operating systems (also see unikernel), which give application developers access to traditional operating system features.

Exokernels have never taken off because this means that each user must write the remainder of the kernel from scratch. This is a risky, complicated, and intimidating task, especially in a production environment with tight deadlines. The ability to integrate multiple library operating systems, each exporting a distinct API—for instance, one for real-time control and another for high-level UI development—is a key benefit of exokernel-based systems.

Multikernels

When using a multikernel operating system, a multi-core computer is viewed as a network of separate cores, much like a distributed system. Instead of assuming shared memory, it uses message-passing to implement inter-process communications. The term "*multikernel*" was first applied to an operating system, namely Barrelfish. System software is not evolving and diversifying as quickly as computer hardware. For OS designers, a wide range of core counts, caches, interconnect links, IO devices, and accelerators present significant scalability and correctness challenges. Although this hardware bears some similarities to previous parallel systems, it is novel in the realm of general-purpose computing.

In an operating system with multiple kernels, a multi-core computer is viewed as a distributed system consisting of a network of separate cores. The inter-process communications is implemented through message-passing instead of assuming shared memory.

In contrast to traditional high-performance computing applications, multicore systems are becoming more common in a variety of settings, such as data centers and personal computer platforms, with workloads that are typically more OS-intensive and less predictable. Tuning a general-purpose OS design for a particular hardware model is no longer ideal (or useful) since deployed hardware varies greatly and optimizations become obsolete after a few years when new hardware is released. With workloads that are less predictable and frequently more OS-intensive than traditional high-performance computing applications, multicore systems are becoming more and more common in a range of environments, from personal computing platforms to data centers.

A general-purpose OS design cannot be optimized for a specific hardware model any longer, as the deployed hardware varies greatly and the optimizations become outdated when new hardware is released after a few years. These optimizations also involve trade-offs specific to hardware parameters, such as the cache hierarchy, the memory consistency model, and the relative costs of local and remote cache access, making them non-transferable across different hardware types. Often, they do not even apply to updated versions of the same architecture. Hence before developers notice a scalability issue, it typically needs to affect a significant user base. Beyond being a better fit for networked, heterogeneous, and dynamic hardware, the model we propose–dubbed a multikernel (*Figure* 2.4)–enables the application of distributed system principles to address challenges of scale, adaptivity, and diversity in operating systems designed for future hardware.

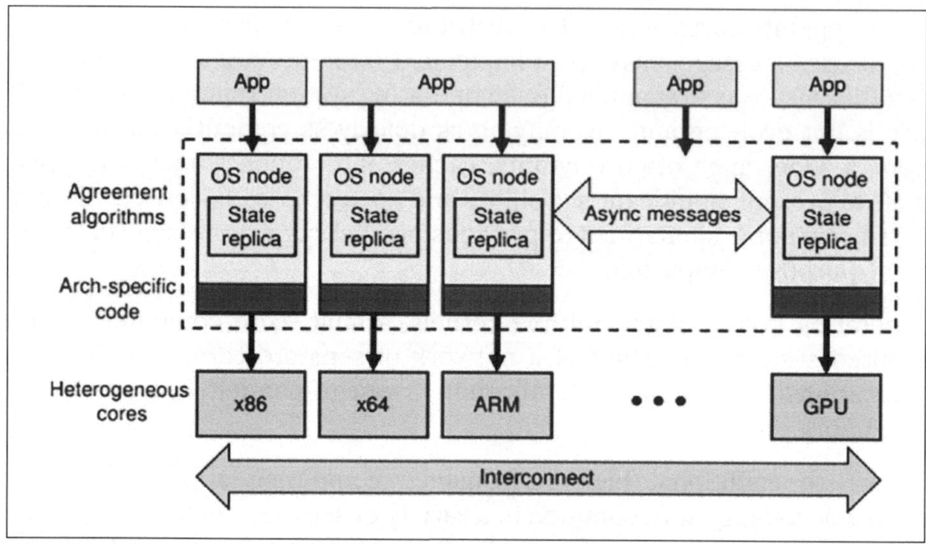

Figure 2.5: *MultiKernel Model*

The ability to pipeline and batch messages encoding remote operations allows a single core to achieve greater throughput and lowers interconnect utilization, as opposed to sequentially manipulating shared data structures, which is constrained by the latency of remote data access. This is true even on current systems with effective cache-coherent shared memory. Building an operating system with message-based rather than shared-data communication offers genuine advantages.

Moreover, the idea naturally supports heterogeneous hardware. Similar to a distributed system, a multicore computer is treated by a multikernel operating system as a network of separate cores. Instead of assuming shared memory, it uses message passing to implement inter-process communications. Barrelfish was the first operating system to be referred to as a multikernel.

Decision on Using the Type of Kernel

In conventional commercial systems, the "*kernel mode*"/"*user mode*" architectural approach to protection–technically known as hierarchical protection domains–causes a monolithic design; in fact, any module that requires protection is ideally integrated into the kernel. The relationship between "*privileged mode*" and monolithic design can be traced back to the fundamental problem of mechanism-policy separation. Although capability-based addressing, the main alternative architectural approach, clearly distinguishes between the two and inevitably leads to a microkernel design, "*privileged mode*" actually blends the protection mechanism and the security policies together.

Microkernels attempt to operate the majority of their services in user space, as opposed to monolithic kernels, which execute all of their code in the same address space (kernel space), to enhance codebase maintainability and modularity. Most kernels are found in the space between these two designs, not precisely in either of these categories. They are referred to as hybrid kernels. Although they exist, less common applications for production systems include more complex designs, such as nanokernels and exokernels; for instance, an exokernel is the Xen hypervisor.

History of Kernel Development

A computer can function without an operating system and, consequently, without a kernel–provided software developers are willing to work without operating system support or hardware abstraction. In such cases, programs can be loaded and run directly on the "*bare metal*" machine. This was how the majority of early computers worked in the 1950s and early 1960s; they were loaded and reset in between running different programs. Eventually, little auxiliary programs were loaded from ROM or kept in memory between runs, such as debuggers and program loaders. As these were created, they served as the model for the initial operating system kernels.

While some embedded systems and video game consoles continue to employ the "*bare metal*" method, most modern computers run modern operating systems and kernels. The RC 4000 Multiprogramming System introduced the notion of a compact core, commonly referred to as the microkernel approach, in 1969, "*upon which operating systems for different purposes could be built in an orderly manner*" for system design.

Basic Functions of an Operating System

An operating system's fundamental features include:

- **Booting:** Controls the starting up of a device.
- **Memory management**: Allows memory to various installed programs on a computer and manages computer applications.
- **Data security**: Shields data from cyberattacks
- **Loading and running programs**: Launches and runs programs
- **Disk and drive management**: Partitions and controls drives in the computers
- **Device control**: Grant or deny access to devices using the operating system
- **User interface (UI):** Let users send and receive data
- **Process management**: Space is allotted by the operating system to support computer functions, such as information sharing and storing

The majority of devices come with pre-installed operating systems. Users can upgrade to a newer version of the operating system or switch to a different one for improved device performance.

Types of Operating Systems

Following are the types of operating systems based on their method of operation. They evolved in different periods in history which is discussed in the earlier sections.

- Serial
- Batch type
- Multi-Programmed Batch System
- Time-Sharing Operating System
- Distributed OS
- Network OS
- Real-time OS
- Mobile OS

History of the Evolution of Operating Systems

The evolution of Operating Systems happened in several stages known as Generations [3].

First Generation (Serial Processing)

The following are the characteristic features of computing devices developed during this generation.

- **Timeline:** The development of electronic computers began in the 1940s and 1950s. They took the place of the previous mechanical trend as the new one.
- **Dimensions and Cost:** The first computers were enormous and expensive.
- **Basic Functions**: They were only capable of basic tasks, despite their size and expense.
- **Absence of an Operating System**: Computers used to operate without an operating system. They completed the tasks one by one.
- **Serial Processing**: The process of moving to the next task after completing the previous one.

Limitations of First Generation

- **Wasted Power:** The CPU, the central processing unit, was often left idle without allowing it to process other tasks. It squandered power, particularly on tasks such as reading data.

- **One Task at a Time**: These systems function similarly to a single-tasking individual as they could only manage one job at a time; everything moved slowly.
- **Extended Wait Times:** They work slowly and one has to wait long time to get the output after assigning a task.

Second Generation (Batch System)

The need for a more optimized strategy became apparent due to the inefficiencies in serial processing, which later on, initiated a system for batch processing. The 1950s and 1960s are referred to as the second generation of operating systems. Similar tasks or jobs are gathered into batches in a batch system, which processes them one after the other without requiring user input. The objective was to reduce setup time and automate job processing.

The Job Control Language (JCL) scripting language was introduced to manage these batches. It enables operators to designate the order in which tasks should be completed. The computer and the batch operating system are not directly connected. A different system separates and assigns related tasks into batches for easier processing and quicker response. For lengthy and time-consuming tasks, the batch operating system is suitable. These systems are used for data entry, bank statement processing, and payroll system management. Each user prepares their tasks offline before sending them to an operator to prevent slowing down a device.

The advantages and disadvantages of using a batch operating system include:

Advantages	**Disadvantages**
The system could better utilize CPU and minimum idle time by processing tasks in batches. Many users can share batch systems. There is little idle time for batch operating systems.	Debugging batch operating systems presents a challenge. Errors cannot be made after the batch has been processed.
The system minimizes setup time and overhead in the processing sequence by clustering related tasks.	There isn't any real-time user interaction, that is, users must wait until the entire batch is processed. Delivering the output takes longer if the batches contain multiple tasks.
It enables the automated completion of tasks, reducing the requirement for manual intervention. Managing heavy workloads becomes feasible.	In case of failure, the backlog is created.
Estimating the amount of time required to complete a task is easy.	It is costly to install and maintain good batch operating systems.

Table 2.2: *Advantages and Disadvantages of Using Batch Operating System*

Third Generation (Multi-Programmed Batch System)

Since the CPUs waits for I/O operations to complete, the systems in the first two generations execute tasks sequentially, one at a time.

The subsequent operating system generations included multiprogramming as a solution to this problem. With multiprogramming, several tasks can run concurrently in the main memory, that is, if a job must wait for an I/O operation, the CPU may move to another one. A CPU with multiple programs can handle more tasks in a given amount of time. More sophisticated memory management was required because several tasks were completed concurrently. Concepts like memory partitioning, paging, and segmentation were developed as a result of these memory demands. Choosing which task to complete first, second, or last is crucial because multiple jobs are completed simultaneously.

The Shortest Job Next (SJN), Round Robin, and First-Come, First-Served algorithms are developed. To help manage files, devices, and other system resources, system utilities were created, and the OS's complexity increased.

Operating systems were accompanied by hardware, such as Integrated Circuit, allowed for smaller, faster, and more reliable computers.

Fourth Generation (Time-Sharing Operating System)

The fourth-generation operating system was more commonly associated with programming languages close to human language and often used for database-related tasks.

Fourth-generation operating systems introduced graphical user interfaces (GUI), which signaled a change in focus toward improving performance and efficiency. The user experience was transformed by these GUIs and improved the intuitiveness of interactions. For example, instead of utilizing text-based commands to navigate through their devices, users can now do so by using icons and menus. This development expedited task execution by streamlining operations.

Another essential component of fourth-generation operating systems was the integration of networking capabilities. These operating system versions made it possible for computers to communicate with one another and share resources easily. Connectivity changed the way people used technology by allowing for effective data exchange and collaborative work environments. Among the features of the fourth generation are:

- Graphical User Interface (GUI), which lets users use windows, menus, and icons to interact with the system: the capacity to execute several programs at once.
- The ability to connect to and use networks, including the Internet, out of the box.
- Identify and set up hardware devices automatically.
- Advanced security features to guard against malware and unwanted access.
- Compatibility with a large variety of hardware components and architectural styles.
- Every task is given a small time slice, or quantum, by the OS.

Advanced Features: These state-of-the-art operating systems improved user experiences significantly with several features. Improved file management was one of these features; it made data stored on the device easier to organize and retrieve. Users could more easily search for specific documents, create folders, and move files between directories.

Fourth-generation operating systems also came equipped with multitasking by default, allowing users to run multiple applications simultaneously without sacrificing system performance. Since users could move between tasks without having to quit one program to open another, this feature increased productivity. Enhanced security was another characteristic that set these cutting edge operating systems apart. The developers incorporated strong security protocols into the OS architecture to guard sensitive data against malicious attacks and unauthorized access.

Future Generations and Emerging Trends

Future generations and emerging trends are further discussed in the upcoming section of this book.

Distributed OS

The foundation of this system is a network of linked, autonomous computers that can communicate with one another over shared communication lines. Every autonomous system has a processor varying in capacity and capability. These operating systems are frequently utilized for peer-to-peer networks, airline reservation controls, and telecommunication networks.

A distributed operating system provides real-time service to numerous users and applications. Next, the processors are assigned different tasks related to processing the data. The potential advantages and disadvantages of distributed operating systems are:

Advantages	Disadvantages
Allows remote working	The system shuts down as a whole if the primary network fails
Facilitates a quicker data exchange between users	Expensive to install
Failure in one site may not cause much disruption to the system.	To maintain them, one must possess a high degree of expertise
Minimizes the load on the host computer	
Improves scalability by allowing the network to accommodate more systems	
Reduces delays in data processing	

Table 2.3: *Advantages and Disadvantages of Distributed Operating Systems*

All features and attributes of Distributed Operating Systems are discussed in detail in *Chapter 10, Distributed OS.*

Network OS

Potential advantages and disadvantages of these systems are:

Advantages	Disadvantages
High stability is provided by Centralized servers	Requires regular updates and maintenance
Security issues are easily handled through the servers	Servers are expensive to buy and maintain
Easily upgradable and integrable new technologies	Users reliance on a central server could be harmful to workflows
Remote access to the servers is possible	No remote access is possible

Table 2.4: *Advantages and Disadvantages of Network OS*

All features and attributes of the Operating Systems are discussed in detail in *Chapter 15, Network Operating System and Ultimate in Operating Systems.*

Real-Time OS

Systems that adhere to stringent time constraints can be supported by real-time operating systems. Typically, they are employed in air traffic control, robotics, medical imaging, and scientific experiments. Processes requiring high precision and sensitivity benefit from the short response time between input, processing, and response. These procedures include running air traffic control, medical, and missile systems, where delays could result in property and human casualties.

There are two types of real-time operating systems: *soft real-time and hard real-time.* Applications with stringent time constraints are installed with hard real-time systems. The system ensures that delicate tasks are finished on schedule. Virtual memory does not exist in hard real-time. Equally strict time requirements do not apply to soft real-time systems. Priority is given to critical tasks over other tasks. The following are possible benefits and drawbacks of real-time operating systems:

- Real-time systems with stringent time constraints must be supported by real-time operating systems.
- Typical applications include air traffic control, robotics, medical imaging, and scientific investigations.
- The short response time between input, processing, and response is beneficial for processes that are extremely sensitive and require high precision.
- Delays in these systems could result in loss of life or property, such as in air traffic control, missile, or medical operations.

Advantages	**Disadvantages**
High stability is provided by centralized servers	Requires regular updates and maintenance
Easier to handle security issues through the servers	Servers are expensive to buy and maintain
Easy to upgrade and integrate new technologies	Workflows may suffer if users become overly dependent on a central server
Remote access to the servers is possible	
More output is provided as they use devices and systems to the maximum	Low capacity to run tasks in a time group
Allows fast shifting from one task to another	Uses heavy system resources
The less focus is put on the queue and more focus, on current tasks	Complex algorithms render themselves not easy to understand
Used in embedded systems	Unsuitable for thread priority due to the system's inability to switch tasks
Real-time systems are free of errors as they are meticulously programmed	
Allows easy allocation of memory	

Table 2.5: *Advantages and Disadvantages of Real-Time OS*

Mobile OS

Smartphones, tablets, and wearables are the only devices that can run mobile operating systems, such as Android, Apple, and Windows Mobile OS. With the addition of features suitable for a portable device, the system combines the functionality of a personal computer. The mobile operating systems launch as soon as a device is powered on to enable access to installed applications. Wireless network connectivity is another feature that mobile operating systems handle.

Potential advantages and disadvantages of mobile operating systems are:

Advantages	**Disadvantages**
Easy for users to learn and operate in most systems	Certain mobile operating systems severely deplete a device's battery, necessitating frequent recharging.
	Some systems are not user-friendly.

Table 2.6: *Advantages and Disadvantages of Mobile Operating Systems*

All features and attributes of Mobile Operating Systems are discussed in detail in *Chapter 13, OS for Mobile Systems.*

Overview of Popular Operating Systems

Following is the list of most common operating systems in use:

- MS DOS
- Unix and Linux, Posix
- Windows
- Android and Apple's iOS and iPadOS

Microsoft Windows has the largest market share (roughly 68%) in the personal computer market as of September 2023. macOS. from Apple Inc. is in the second place (20%), followed by the various Linux versions, including ChromeOS, which come in third place (7%) together. In the mobile sector (including smartphones and tablets), as of September 2023, Android's share is 68.92%, followed by Apple's iOS and iPadOS with 30.42%, and other operating systems with .66%.

MS-DOS

Microsoft created the MS-DOS [4], or Microsoft Disk Operating System that served as a basic operating system. As the main operating system for computers compatible with IBM PCs, it rose to prominence in the 1980s and early 1990s. Users of MS-DOS performed tasks by entering text commands through a command-line interface.

Although graphical user interfaces such as Windows eventually supplanted MS-DOS; it played a critical role in the early days of personal computers by performing necessary tasks for managing files and running software. Nevertheless, its historical significance in the development of operating systems cannot be overlooked. Versions of MS-DOS that exist in different forms are MS-DOS 2.0 (1981), MS-DOS 2.0, MS-DOS 3.0, MS-DOS 4.0, MS-DOS 5.0, MS-DOS 6.0, MS-DOS 6.22, and MS-DOS 7.0 (Windows 95 DOS). With every update, the operating system gained new capabilities and enhancements.

Working of Disk Operating System

MS-DOS works like a command interpreter. Let us understand the workings of the DOS operating system in detail.

Booting: One of the first programs that the computer loads into memory when turned on is Microsoft Windows Operating System. It coordinates with each of the subsequent actions as detailed as follows:

- **Command Line Interface**: Unlike the graphical user interfaces found in contemporary computer systems, MS-DOS lacks one. Rather, we use the keyboard to enter commands through a command line. These commands are like instructions given to the computer to perform a particular task.
- **Command Execution**: Upon entering the command, the user hits the "*Enter*" key. After reading the command, MS-DOS determines what needs to be done, which may involve copying files, erasing folders, or executing programs.
- **Interacting with Hardware**: MS-DOS communicates with the hardware components and issues commands to them.
- **Memory Management**: MS-DOS is also essential to the computer's memory management process.
- **File Management**: Users can create, remove, copy, and move files and folders on the computer's storage with the help of MS-DOS.
- **Task Switching**: MS-DOS is used to move between the various computer programs that are open at the same time, enabling multitasking.
- When shutting down a computer, MS-DOS makes sure that all relevant processes are correctly closed.

Features of MS-DOS

The features of the MS-DOS are as follows:

- **MS-DOS Command Line Interface:** This interface enables users to communicate with the operating system. The user can carry them out by inputting commands into a text-based interface. For instance, one could type

"**DIR**" and hit *Enter* to view the contents of a directory. The commands "**COPY**," "**DEL**," and "**FORMAT**" are also frequently used.

- **File Management**: The FAT file system served as the foundation for MS-DOS's straightforward but efficient file management system. Commands such as "**COPY**" and "**RENAME**" allow users to create, move, copy, and rename files. Additionally, MS-DOS supported subdirectories, enabling users to arrange their files into folders.
- **Memory Management**: MS-DOS's ability to manage memory was constrained. Users could manage conventional memory or memory smaller than 640 KB. The "**MEM**" command allowed users to view their memory's used and free capacities. The users use different memory managers to maximize memory use.
- **Batch Files:** They were scripts that allowed users to run commands sequentially or automate repetitive tasks. Batch files can be created using basic text editors and run in the same manner as other commands. For instance, a batch file can be used to copy files to a remote location and backup important files.
- **Boot Process:** MS-DOS had a straightforward boot process. Both reading the OS files from the disk and running the command interpreter were required. Users are thus able to communicate with the system. Pressing the reset button or turning on the computer started the boot process.

Types of MS-DOS Commands

There are two types of commands in MS-DOS. They are:

- Internal Commands
- External Commands

Internal Commands

The command interpreter, or **COMMAND**, is integrated into and directly performs internal commands. **COMP**). When the system boots up, these commands are loaded into memory with the command interpreter. Since they are pre-invented, they operate more quickly than external commands.

DIR, **CD**, **MD**, **RD**, **COPY**, **DEL**, **TYPE**, and **VER** are examples of internal commands.

Directory, file, and **system** are the three categories of internal commands. To work with directories, use the directory commands (**MD**, **RD**). System management is done with file commands (**COPY**, **DEL**, **REN**, **TYPE**, **XCOPY**, **ATTRIB**). The system is managed using system commands (**CHKDSK**, **FORMAT**, **LABEL**, and **MEM**).

Internal Commands	Use of the Command
`CLS`	Clear the screen
`DIR`	Display a list of files and directories
`CD` or `CHDIR`	Change the current directory
`COPY`	Copy one or more files to another location
`DEL` or `ERASE`	Delete one or more files

Table 2.7: *Internal Commands*

External Commands

External commands are stored on a disc and are executable files that run by themselves. Every time these commands are executed, they are loaded from the disk because they are not part of the command interpreter. As they are kept in memory, they take longer to execute than internal commands.

`FORMAT`, **`CHKDSK`**, and **`EDIT`** are some examples of external commands.

External Commands	Use of the Command
`FORMAT`	Format a disk or drive
`CHKDSK`	Check a disk for errors and fix them
`TREE`	Display the structure of a directory tree
`EDIT`	Starts the MS-DOS editor, a text editor used to create and edit ASCII text files
`XCOPY`	Copy files and directories, with more options
`DISKPART`	Disk partitioning utility

Table 2.8: *External Commands*

Benefits of an MS-DOS Operating System

Especially in the early days of personal computing, MS-DOS offered several advantages during its peak.

- **Simple and Lightweight**: MS-DOS was a lightweight and simple operating system, which made it ideal for the low processing power of early personal computers. Its minimalistic design allowed it to run on machines with relatively low processing power and memory. These are just a few of its noteworthy advantages.
- **Compatibility:** MS-DOS compatibility offered software developers a standardized platform. With a greater degree of consistency across various computer systems, applications created for MS-DOS could operate on a broad spectrum of compatible hardware.

- Users used text commands to communicate with the system via the MS-DOS **command-line interface** (CLI). Experienced users had strong control over the system even though this interface might not seem as user-friendly as more contemporary graphical ones.
- **Can be Booted Straight from Floppy Disks:** MS-DOS was designed to enable users to run the operating system without the need to install it on a hard drive. This was especially helpful when running the system on computers with low storage or for troubleshooting and recovery purposes.
- **Windows OS Foundation**: The Microsoft Windows operating systems were built upon the MS-DOS platform. Microsoft-DOS was still heavily relied upon by Windows versions up to Windows ME (Millennium Edition) for several purposes. OS X was the operating system underneath which Windows 95, 98, and ME functioned as graphical shells. MS-DOS is a 16-bit operating system made to run on computers with little memory.

Drawbacks of an MS-DOS Operating System

Mentioned here are a few drawbacks of the MS-DOS operating systems:

- The maximum memory limit is 640 KB, and this restricts the amount of data and programs that can be saved and used simultaneously.
- Mostly command-line based, it features a limited graphical user interface. For inexperienced users, this makes navigation and use challenging.
- The limited network capabilities of this OS make it unsuitable for use as a network OS, restricting efficient working in a contemporary networked setting.
- It doesn't have user accounts or other security features. Hence viruses and other security risks can exploit it.
- File names can only contain a certain amount of characters. This has a character limit of eight followed by a file extension of three characters. It may result in confusion and difficulty in organizing a large number of files.
- It was designed to function with antiquated technology. Therefore, its compatibility with contemporary hardware, such as USB drives and wireless networks, was restricted.

Starting MS-DOS on Windows

To open MS-DOS in a Windows, follow the steps given here:

On the desktop,

1. Locate and click the Windows Start button. You can also press the Windows key on your keyboard.

2. Next, type **`cmd`** and hit the *Enter* key. By doing this, the MS-DOS command line interface will open.

UNIX

The AT&T Unix, developed in 1969 at the Bell Labs research center by Ken Thompson, Dennis Ritchie, and other individuals, is the ancestor of the Unix family of multitasking, multi-user computer operating systems.

The Open Group authorizes the use of the mark for operating systems that are certified to comply with the Single UNIX Specification (SUS). When AT&T licensed Unix to outside parties in the late 1970s, it was no longer meant for use inside the Bell System. This resulted in a wide range of commercial and academic Unix variants from vendors, such as IBM (AIX), Microsoft (Xenix), Sun Microsystems (SunOS/Solaris), HP/HPE (HP-UX), and University of California, Berkeley (BSD). AT&T sold Novell its rights to the Unix operating system early in the 1990s, and Novell subsequently sold the trademark to The Open Group, an industry association established in 1996. The Open Group permits certified operating systems that adhere to the Single UNIX Specification (SUS) to use the mark.

As the whole operating system is written in C, Unix can run on a variety of platforms. Initially, Unix was not intended to be multitasking or portable. Later on, Unix progressively acquired time-sharing configuration portability, multitasking, and multiuser capabilities. Users started to view Unix as a potential all-purpose operating system for computers of all sizes by the early 1980s.

The Unix environment and the client–server program model were essential elements in the development of the Internet and the reshaping of. Users started perceiving Unix as a potentially all-purpose operating system that could run on PCs of any size by the early 1980s. A key component in the creation of the Internet and the transformation of computing from being cantered on individual computers to networks was the Unix environment and the client-server program model. More machine families have seen the porting of Unix and the C programming language than any other operating system since they were created by AT&T and given to government and academic institutions. Computing is centered in networks rather than on individual computers.

Both Unix and the C programming language were developed by AT&T and distributed to government and academic institutions, leading to both being ported to a wider variety of machine families than any other operating system.

Different versions of Unix are as follows: AIS (IBM), BSD, HP – UX, Solaris, and Iris.

DOS and UNIX commands		
Action	**DOS**	**UNIX**
change directory	`Cd`	`Cd`
change file protection	`attrib`	`Chmod`

compare files	comp	Diff
copy file	copy	Cp
delete directory	Rd	Rmdir
directory list	Dir	Ls
edit a file	Edit	Pico
environment	Set	Printenv
find string in file	Find	Grep
help	Help	Man
make directory	Md	Mkdir
move file	move	Mv
rename file	Ren	Mv
show date and time	date, time	Date
show disk space	chkdsk	Df
show file	Type	Cat
show file by screens type filename	more	More
sort data	Sort	Sort

Table 2.9: *Docs and UNIX Commands (source: Treebeard's Unix Cheat Sheet)*

Following is the aspects mentioned of Docs and UNIX:

Aspect	**DOS**	**Unix**
Operating System Type	Single-user operating system	Multi-user operating system
User Interface	Command-line interface (CLI)	Command-line interface (CLI) and graphical user interface (GUI)
File System	Limited file system support	Hierarchical file system with rich features
Security	Minimal security features	Robust security measures, user permissions, and access controls
Multitasking	Limited multitasking support	Advanced multitasking capabilities
Network Functionality	Basic networking capabilities	Built-in networking capabilities and protocols

Table 2.10: *Aspects of Docs and UNIX*

You don't need Unix skills to use Java, or vice versa, but if you do, then you'll have a good toolbox relevant to any kind of development.

Linux

Linux is an operating system like Windows, iOS, and Mac OS. In fact, Linux powers one of the most widely used platforms worldwide, Android [5]. The components that make up the Linux operating system are as follows:

- **Bootloader** is the program that controls how your computer boots up. This will mostly appear as a splash screen that appears and then disappears when the operating system boots up for most users. The one component of the entire system that is genuinely referred to as "*Linux*" is the kernel.
- **The kernel** that is at the center of the system, controls the memory, peripheral devices, and CPU. The OS's lowest tier is called the kernel.
- **The Init system** is a subsystem responsible for initiating the user space and managing daemons. Systemd, which is also one of the most popular init systems, is also one of the most used. After the bootloader transfers control of the initial boot process, the init system takes over GRAND Unified Bootloader, also known as GRUB. **Daemons** are background services (such as scheduling, audio, and printing, and so on) that you can launch either at boot time or after logging into the desktop.
- The system component that shows graphics on your monitor is called the **graphic server**. It's often called X or the X server. The area that users interact with is the desktop environment.
- One can select from a multitude of **desktop environments**, including KDE, Xfce, Enlightenment, Pantheon, Cinnamon, Mate, and GNOME. ( ) Every desktop environment comes with pre-installed programs (such as web browsers, file managers, configuration tools, and games).

Applications: The complete selection of apps is not available in desktop environments. Just like Windows and macOS, Linux offers thousands upon thousands of high-quality software titles that can be easily found and installed. Most modern Linux distributions include App Store-like tools that centralize and simplify applications.

If free software isn't enough to entice you, how about having an operating system that will function flawlessly for as long as you use it?

Linux is typically far less susceptible to these kinds of assaults. Rebooting the server is only necessary when the kernel has been updated. A Linux server may go for years without needing to be rebooted. This is not unusual. Stability and dependability are essentially guaranteed if you apply the frequently advised updates. Other than your laptop or PC, most devices you can think of operate on a Linux distribution. An open-source operating system based on Unix is called Linux. Developed in 1992, Linux is essentially the name of the kernel. Linus Torvalds is in charge of overseeing the community's development of the Linux kernel.

Apart from the command line interface, Linux has a graphical user interface (GUI) akin to the Windows operating system and applications, thereby making it a complete operating system. Linux Torvalds developed the Linux kernel during the 1990s. Richard Stallman did, however, make a significant contribution to the finished OS under the GNU GPL license. After adding numerous GUI and driver features, and taking inspiration from MINIX, a Unix-like system.

Linus Torvalds created the OS framework that would eventually become LINUX in 1992. On September 17, 1992, the LINUX kernel was made available. A global community of developers contributes free of charge to the advancements in Linux. But, Linus Torvalds, the man who created Linux, has the power to put the development into practice because he has been publishing updates for its kernels.

The standard Linux shell is called BASH (Bourne Again SHell). Numerous command interpreters are supported. Linux is considered to be very secure. Though approximately 60–100 viruses have been identified for Linux to date none of them are actively spreading now.

Originally, Linux was created for Intel's x86 platform. But now, more than twenty CPU types—including ARM—can use the ports.

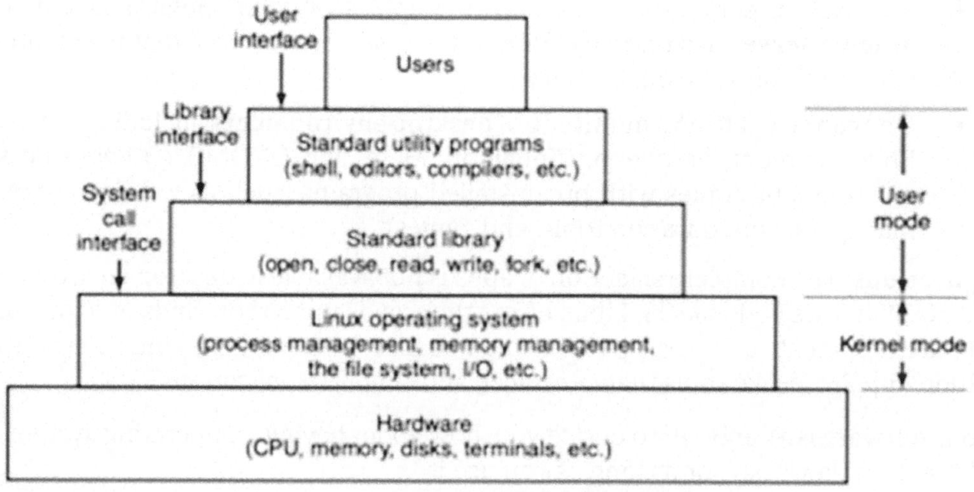

Figure 2.6: *Layers of a Linux system*

Since Linux is free software, all of its derivatives are legally obligated to release their source code under the terms of the GNU General Public License (GPL). Linux was created by programmers for their own use. It emphasizes consistency and simplicity, featuring a small set of fundamental components that can be combined in nearly infinite ways without redundancy.

Its architecture is comparable to that of other UNIX systems without a microkernel. It is written in C and supports both BSD and UNIX System V syntax. Linux supports multiple users and pre-emptive multitasking in addition to the full suite of UNIX tools and standard UNIX networking features. Despite having a simple design at first, Linux is a versatile system that runs on systems with many processors even with less than 16 MB of RAM. Linux distributions consist of a kernel, system libraries, and system utilities, similar to other UNIX systems. Linux offers a command-line interface for accessing the operating system and a graphical user interface (GUI) with a desktop, folder, and file icons.

Android

Android is an operating system that is partly open-source and closely based on Linux. It has gained popularity on smartphones and, to a lesser extent, embedded systems like "*car dashboards, home appliances, medical devices, and smartwatches that require a graphical user interface, or GUI.*" It has consequently emerged as the most popular operating system among consumers. In contrast to Linux, a large portion of Android is object-oriented and written in Java.

Open Source

An open-source license is also used for Linux distribution. The following are the fundamental principles of open source:

- The ability to run the program for any purpose and to examine how the program functions and modify it to suit your needs.
- The ability to freely distribute copies to assist your neighbor.
- The ability to share copies of your altered versions with other people.
- These ideas are essential to comprehending the community that collaborates to develop the Linux platform. The Linux operating system is unquestionably "*by the people, for the people.*" These principles are also a major reason so many people decide on Linux. It's about freedom: freedom of use and freedom of choice.

Popular Linux Distributions

Linux for mobile devices, sometimes referred to as mobile Linux, is the usage of Linux-based operating systems on portable devices, whose primary or only Human Interface Device (HID) is a touchscreen. It mainly comprises smartphones and tablet computers, and also some mobile phones, personal digital assistants (PDAs), and portable media players that come with a separate touchscreen.

Linux Mint, Manjaro, Debian,Ubuntu, Antergos, Solus, Fedora, Elementary OS, Opensuse

The desktop is viewed differently in each distribution. Some choose extremely contemporary UIs (such as Pantheon in Elementary OS and GNOME), while others stick to more conventional desktop environments (openSUSE uses KDE).

Server Distribution

- Red Hat Enterprise Linux
- Ubuntu Server
- CentOS
- SUSE

Enterprise Linux and other server distributions are available for free (such as Ubuntu Server and CentOS) and for a fee (such as Red Hat Enterprise Linux and SUSE Enterprise Linux). Support is another feature of those that come with a cost.

Difference Between Unix and LINUX Operating Systems with Examples

You may have heard of Linux and Unix operating systems before. Unix has its own users, but Linux is more well-known in the modern world. Unix is a proprietary operating system frequently used in internet servers, workstations, and PCs made by Solaris, Intel, HP, and other companies. In contrast, Linux is a popular open-source, free operating system for mainframes, tablet PCs, game development, computer hardware, and software. The original AT&T Unix, the progenitor of the Unix family of multitasking, multiuser computer operating systems, was developed by Ken Thompson, Dennis Ritchie, and other Bell Labs researchers. *Table 2.4* provides the comparison between both the Unix and Linux Operating Systems [6].

Unix	**Linux**
The operating system Unix is proprietary software. Bell Labs created it, as previously mentioned, for internal use, but over time, it was licensed to other tech firms. Although there have been recent developments in GUI on Unix systems, the Unix OS still functions primarily through the Command Line Interface.	Unix is the foundation of the open-source Linux operating system. The Kernel, which was created in 1992, goes by the name Linux. The Linux kernel is developed by the community under Linus Torvalds' direction. To complete its operating system, Linux not only includes a command line interface but also a graphical user interface similar to Windows and applications.

Unix is not a free program. Vendors state that different Unix flavors have different pricing structures.	Linux is available for free download, distribution, and publication in books, magazines, and other media. Although Linux distributions such as Red Hat Linux is paid, they are typically less expensive than Windows.
Compared to Linux, Unix is less flexible. Less hardware of different kinds can be used with it.	Linux is an extremely adaptable operating system that works with most hardware configurations. Almost any device with a processor can run and install Linux OS. Linux is incredibly flexible and adaptable, making it compatible with a broad range of computer hardware, including mainframes, supercomputers, tablets, smartphones, and game consoles.
Only certain CPU machines can run Unix installations, which call for precise and regulated hardware.	No such requirement.
The source code for Unix OS is not accessible because it is not freeware. As such, you cannot alter and market your customized version of Unix.	The source code for Linux OS is freely available due to its open-source nature, that is, you can open, edit, and use it on your computer. Unfortunately, you cannot sell it because it is GNU G licensed.
Unix requires specialized hardware and can only be run on certain CPU processors. Hence its installation is significantly more expensive than that of Linux. Globally, big data servers are primarily where it is utilized.	Wide variety of file systems are supported by Linux, which is also scalable. Since Linux doesn't require specific hardware to operate and the operating system is either free or extremely inexpensive, installing Linux is typically much less expensive than installing Unix.
Very few file systems are supported by Unix in comparison. ZFS, JSON, HFX, GPPS, XFS, GVXFS, and XFS file systems are among those it supports.	Linux supports several file systems, including xfs, ramfs, nfs, vfat, cramfsm, ext3, ext4, ext2, and ext2. ntfs, autofs, devpts, ufs, and numerous others.
There's no portability for the Unix operating system. In comparison, there are fewer Unix operating system versions and distributions.	Linux operating systems come in a relatively larger number of versions or distributions. RedHat, Kali, Slackware, Debian, ArchLinux, Solaris, Ubuntu, CentOS, and Fedora are the Linux distributions that are currently available.

Big MNCs and institutions use the Unix OS primarily on their mainframes, expensive, high-end computer systems, and server systems. AT&T developers are responsible for the development, upkeep, and updates of Unix. They oppose the advancement of open source projects.	Laptops and home computers were the primary target market for Linux OS. However, because of its stability and widespread use, high-end systems, such as like servers, mobile phones, and embedded systems, began using it in offices.

Table 2.11: *Comparison Between the Unix and Linux Operating Systems*

POSIX

Operating System Interface Portable is referred to as POSIX. The set of common OS interfaces that are built on the *nix OS is defined by POSIX. IEEE Standard 1003.1-2017 is the most recent specification. Based on standards, the POSIX is written in C/C++. As you are well aware, threads play an important role in establishing a concurrent process flow. The goal of IEEE, the biggest technical professional association in the world, is to advance technology for the good of humanity. Through its widely cited publications, conferences, technology standards, and professional and instructional initiatives, IEEE and its members uplift the world community.

The IEEE Computer Society has defined a family of standards called the Portable Operating System Interface to ensure operating system interoperability. Application programming interfaces (APIs) for system and user-level software compatibility (portability) with Unix and other operating system variants, as well as command line shells and utility interfaces, are defined by POSIX. The IEEE also owns POSIX as a trademark. Application and system developers are the target audience for POSIX.

The POSIX1 contains four parts:

- **Base Definitions**: This section offers the fundamental definitions for the specifications. It includes details on terms, concepts, syntax, service functions, and command line information.
- **System Interfaces**: This explains the terms and concepts related to interfaces, as well as the functional interfaces that applications can use to access POSIX-conforming systems.
- **Shell and Utilities:** This part describes the commands and utilities that are made available for accessing the POSIX-Conformant systems that include the command language used in those systems.
- **Justification (rationale):** Due to this, certain features are added to or removed from the standard; it also contains historical information about its contents.

The features of the POSIX standard are primarily focused on application development and portability rather than the capabilities themselves. Both application developers and system implementers are intended to use the POSIX standard. While IEEE Std 1003.1-2017 was released in 2017, the first POSIX standard was published in 1988.

The POSIX standard was developed for a variety of reasons, some of which include:

- It was designed to simplify application development and portability, making it suitable for using with both UNIX and non-UNIX systems.
- This standard describes the contract between the operating system and the application; it does not define how the application or the operating system is developed.
- Since this standard is defined at the source code level, applications must have source code that complies with POSIX to run on different systems. This does not imply that this standard provides any object or binary code level of portability.
- Although the POSIX standard is written in C, it is not the only language that application developers can use. Any programming language can be used with the POSIX standard as portability can be achieved without compromising performance.

Because portability can be achieved without compromising performance,

- POSIX is designed to save application developers time and money. Application developers must write code for every system if portability cannot be achieved, which is an expensive and time-consuming procedure.

While Android, FreeBSD, Linux distributions, OpenBSD, and VMware adhere to most POSIX standards but are not POSIX certified, HIX, HP-UX, Solaris, and Mac OS (since 10.5.5 Leopard) are examples of POSIX-Compliant Systems. The Austin Group maintains and updates the POSIX standard regularly. Joining the group is open to anyone who wants to contribute to raising the POSIX standard. Servers, workstations, routers, mobile devices, embedded systems, and so on are all currently using the standard. This explains why developers are becoming more involved in the communities and adding to the POSIX standard.

Microsoft Windows

The Microsoft Windows, developed by Microsoft, is a widely used proprietary computer operating system. A version of Microsoft Windows is preinstalled on the majority of personal computers. Windows's troublesome mobile phone compatibility is one of its drawbacks.

Microsoft created Windows, a graphical operating system that gives users access to the internet and allow them to run applications, play games, watch videos, and view and store files. It was made available for both personal and business use. Microsoft developed and markets a range of proprietary graphical operating systems known as

Microsoft Windows. It is divided into families and subfamilies specific to the computer industry, such as Windows for workstations used by consumers or businesses, Windows Server for servers, and Windows IoT for embedded systems.

Microsoft Corporation created Windows, an operating system (OS) for computers, to usage with personal computers (PCs). The Windows OS quickly took over the PC market, thanks to its introduction of the first graphical user interface (GUI) for IBM-compatible computers. In response to the growing interest in graphical user interfaces (GUIs), Microsoft released the first version of Windows on November 20, 1985, as a graphical operating system shell for MS-DOS. When Microsoft released Windows for the first time in 1985, it was merely a graphical user interface (GUI) added to MS-DOS, their disk operating system at the time. drawn, in part, from ideas that Apple Inc. With Windows, DOS users could now visually navigate a virtual desktop by opening graphical "windows" that displayed electronic folders and file contents with a mouse click, instead of having to type commands and directory paths at a text prompt. Windows was first used for the Macintosh System Software.

More features, such as native Windows File Manager, Program Manager, and Print Manager programs, as well as a more dynamic interface, were added in later versions. Additionally, Microsoft created customized Windows packages for businesses, such as the powerful Windows NT and the networkable Windows for Workgroups. Windows 95, which was released for consumer use in 1995, combined Windows and DOS completely and included built-in Internet functionality, which included the Internet Explorer web browser. According to StatCounter, Windows holds a 70% market share as of March 2023, making it the most widely used desktop operating system globally [7]. However, because of Android's explosive growth in popularity since the early 2010s, Windows is no longer the most widely used operating system when considering both desktop and mobile OSes. Windows 11 Enterprise for businesses, Windows Server 2022 for servers, and Windows 11 for personal computers and tablets are the most recent versions of Windows as of 2024. Certain versions of Windows 10, Windows Server 2016, and later are still supported (and in some cases, paid support is available down to Windows Server 2012 and Windows Embedded POSReady 7).

macOS Operating System (Mac OS)

The operating system (OS) macOS was created by Apple Inc., an American computer company. In 1984, the operating system was released to power the company's Macintosh range of personal computers (PCs). The Macintosh introduced the world to graphical user interface (GUI) systems, and it influenced Microsoft Corporation to create the Windows operating system. The Macintosh's operating system's natural ease of use was a major marketing theme for Apple when it first released the computer.

In contrast to almost all other modern PCs, the Mac OS (originally called System Software, with a version number attached) was based on graphics. Users navigated the Finder, a virtual folder and file system represented by icons, by moving the mouse pointer over text prompts rather than typing commands and directory paths. The GUI model was eventually incorporated into the majority of computer operating systems. Apple and Microsoft reached a deal in the 1980s that let Microsoft incorporate some elements of the Mac interface into the first iterations of Windows. But aside from a brief interval in the 1990s, Mac OS has never been granted a license to run on computers manufactured by companies other than Apple.

Features such as network browsing, Internet file sharing, and multiple user accounts were added in later Mac OS releases. After Steve Jobs left Apple, he founded the competitor NeXT Computers, which Apple acquired in 1996. The company then released Mac OS X in 2001, a significant redesign based on both the NextStep system and Apple's most recent OS release. Operating on a UNIX kernel, which is essentially core software code, OS X provided technological innovations such as pre-emptive multitasking and memory protection, in addition to a more feature-rich Finder, a sophisticated-looking interface called Aqua, and a handy graphical "*Dock*" bar for quickly accessing frequently used apps. Updates for OS X brought new capabilities such as "*Dashboard*" manager for small, convenient apps called widgets and automatic backups.

In 2007, Apple unveiled several mobile Internet-accessible devices, such as the iPad tablet computer and the iPhone smartphone. Apple quickly made a point of highlighting how OS X could interface with these gadgets. Apple released iCloud in 2011, a cloud computing service that allows users to share data between OS X and iOS mobile operating systems and all of their Apple devices. Apple updated OS X, iOS, and later watchOS (the operating system for the Apple Watch smartwatch) with additional features device connectivity. Among these were the options to send and receive text messages and photos between devices as well as make phone calls (to the iPhone). To make the system name more consistent with iOS and watchOS, Apple renamed macOS in 2016.

Android Operating System

The Android operating system is designed primarily for touchscreen devices, such as tablets and smartphones. It is based on additional libre software and a modified version of the Linux kernel. Google is involved in the development of the most widely used version of Android, even though the Open Handset Alliance, a consortium of developers, is principally in charge. The first Android smartphone to go on sale, the HTC Dream, was unveiled in November 2007 and released in September 2008. Android is a Linux-based operating system and software suite intended for use with mobile devices, such as laptops, tablets, smartphones, electronic book readers, set-top boxes, and more. It comes with an operating system based on Linux, middleware, and significant mobile apps. Think of it as the mobile version of an operating system but not limited to smartphone use. These days, it comes in a variety of devices, such as tablets, smartphones, and televisions.

It was developed first by Google and then by the Open Handset Alliance (OHA). Android code is mainly written in Java, though other languages can also be utilized. The goal of the Android project is to create a workable product that improves the mobile experiences of end users. Eighty-four companies, including Google, Samsung, AKM, Synaptics, KDDI, eBay, Intel, Garmin, and Teleca, are part of this alliance. It was established on November 5, 2007, with Google serving as its leader. It is committed to distributing smartphones, providing services, and advancing open standards via the Android Platform. In the fourth quarter of 2023, Android maintained its position as the most popular mobile operating system globally, holding a 70.1% market share. At the same time, Apple's iOS, Android's closest competitor, held a 29.2% market share. The most recent version of Android, version 14, was released on October 4, 2023. The newly released Android 12.1/12L includes improvements made for tablets, desktop screens, foldable phones, and Chromebooks. In 2023, the Samsung Galaxy A14 4G topped the Android phone shipments chart. With its extensive feature set, intuitive UI, and accessibility, Android is undoubtedly the operating system of choice for the most Indian users.

Previously, Kotlin Programming language had been deployed for designing the Android Operating system instead of Java.

Comparison with Apple-owned iOS

The two most popular mobile operating systems currently ruling the world are iOS, owned by Apple, and Android, owned by Google. Here, Android takes the lead in the market for several reasons. Android has become the *de facto* operating system for smartphones, TVs, cars, Internet of Things (IoT) devices, and other electronics. The open-source project is widely used because of its features, which include strong developer support, hardware compatibility, lightweight profile, and extensive app support. Despite its best efforts, Apple's iOS is not even close to matching Android's market share. In these conditions, there is very little competition, which puts us at risk of an Android monopoly. In a situation like this, innovation and competition suffer.

Basically, **Kotlin** is a statically typed, open-source programming language for Android Programming. It runs on Java Virtual Machine (JVM), and also, it can be used to develop Android apps, server-side apps, and much more. It is recommended to start with Kotlin if you want to build an Android application to take advantage of its best features.

Kotlin is an expressive and simple programming language that easily integrates into existing applications and reduces common code errors. According to the yearly Stack Overflow developer survey, Kotlin is rated higher than Java.

Apple iOS

The same company also manufactures tablets and smartphones that run on Apple iOS. This system offers hundreds of applications for users to choose from. The operating system has robust encryption features to prevent unwanted access to users' private data.

The operating system for the iPhone, iPad, and other Apple mobile devices is called Apple iOS. Mac OS, the operating system that powers Apple's lineup of desktop and laptop computers, is the foundation of Apple iOS. The operating system is made to facilitate simple, seamless networking across different Apple devices. When Apple released its first iPhone in 2007, it also introduced iOS (formerly known as iPhone OS).

Apple iOS is the second-most popular mobile operating system. According to Statecounter.com, as of January 2024, Apple iOS held a 30% share of the mobile operating system market, second only to Android which held a 70% market share.

The iPhone is the most popular item sold by Apple. The efficiency of iOS and the iPhone's user-centric design are frequently credited with its success. With almost two billion units sold since launch, the iPhone stands as the most popular product ever made available for the purchase.

Operating System Structure

The way an operating system's various components are arranged and connected is referred to as its operating system structure. There are different ways to approach operating system structure, and each has benefits and drawbacks of its own. Due to the complexity of the structure of an operating system, we need a clear structure to help us tailor it to our specific needs.

Designing an operating system in sections is less complicated to complete than breaking a large problem down into smaller, more manageable subproblems. Each component is a part of the operating system as well. The kernel architecture can be connected to and integrated with various operating system components through using an operating system structure. Several structures are used to implement operating systems. Various structural configurations that use operating systems are as follows:

- Simple Structure
- Monolithic Structure
- Layered Approach Structure
- Micro-kernel Structure

Simple Structure

Simple Structure [8] can only be used for small and constrained systems; it is the most basic operating system structure and is poorly defined. Programs can access I/O routines in this structure because the interfaces and functionality levels are clearly divided. This can lead to unauthorized access to I/O routines.

The MS-DOS operating system uses this structure. Each layer in the MS-DOS operating system has a distinct set of functions.

These layers are:

- Application Program
- System Program
- MS-DOS device drivers
- ROM BIOS device drivers

Layering has an advantage in the MS-DOS operating system as each level can be defined independently and interact with other levels as needed. When a system is constructed in layers, it is simpler to design, update, and maintain. Therefore, Simple Structure can easily construct limited systems with less complexity. The entire operating system crashes when a user program malfunctions. Due to MS-DOS systems' low abstraction level, end users can gain unauthorized access to programs and I/O routines because they are visible to them. The following illustrates layering in a basic structure.

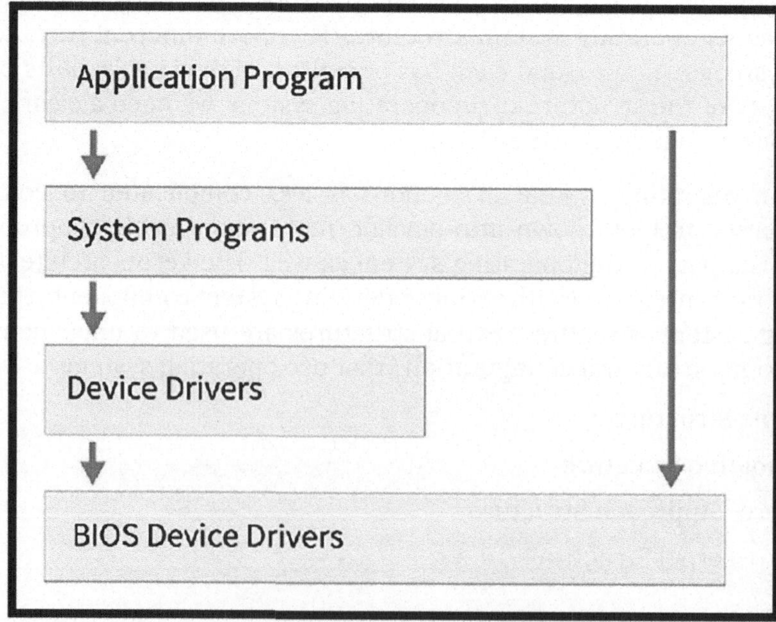

Figure 2.7: *Layering in the Simple Structure of DOS*

Advantages of Simple Structure

- There aren't many interfaces and layers
- Simple to develop; fewer layers separating the hardware and applications which results in good performance
- In environments with limited resources, minimal overhead is appropriate

Disadvantages of a Simple Structure:

- The operating system crashes if a single-user program malfunctions
- Restricted usability since layers are interconnected and communicate with one another.
- **Abstraction** or data hiding is absent
- Layers have access to the operating system's processes, which can change data or crash the operating system

Monolithic Structure In monolithic structure, the operating system is monolithic and the kernel manages all system operations, including memory management, file management, device management, and other operations.

An operating system's (OS) kernel is its central component. All other system components receive their fundamental services from the kernel. It functions as the main interface that the hardware and operating system use to communicate. In systems with a single operating system, the kernel has direct access to all hardware components, such as the keyboard and mouse.

An alternative term for the monolithic operating system is the monolithic kernel. A processor's usability is maximized through multiprogramming through batch processing and time-sharing. Operating System-level, the monolithic kernel manages all hardware elements and performs the functions of a virtual machine. This is an antiquated operating system utilized in banks to carry out insignificant tasks, such as time-sharing and batch processing, allowing numerous users to access the OS at different terminals.

The following is a diagram of the Monolithic Structure:

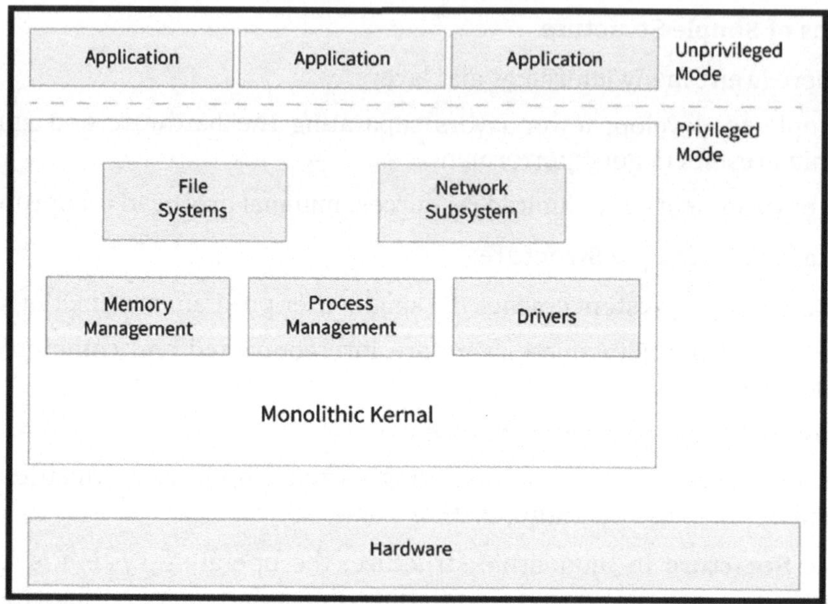

Figure 2.8: *Monolithic Structure*

Advantages of Monolithic Structure:

- It is easy to design and implement since the kernel alone manages all operations and layering is not required.
- Since all of the implementations are done in the same address space, functions such as process scheduling, file management, memory management, and so on are executed more quickly than the functions of typical systems. e Address allocation for new processes is sped up and made faster by using the same address.
- Design and execution are straightforward.

The Disadvantages of a Monolithic Structure are as Follows:

- Since all services in address space are interconnected and have an impact on one another, if one of the monolithic kernel's services fails, the entire system fails.
- Maintenance and extensions are challenging when there is no modularity.
- In addition, adding a new service such as a printer, scanner, and more is not flexible.

Conclusion

In this chapter, we have learned about Operating systems and types of OS and their deployment in various situations. We also learned about the concept of kernels, the types of kernels used in various OS, and how to choose them for one particular application among several OS.

In the next chapter, we shall look into various aspects of the concept of process and system calls.

Questions

1. What is an operating system? Is it a software or hardware?
2. What is the basic purpose of kernel? Illustrate it with the help of sketch.
3. How many types of Kernel Designs/Architecture are there? Briefly mention their name.
4. Explain in brief the various types of kernel mentioning where they are used.
5. Describe the structure of Monolithic Kernel System with the help of a sketch.
6. Enumerate the advantages and disadvantages of using Monolithic Architecture in Monolythic OS.
7. Describe the salient features of Monolithic System.
8. Distinguish between a kernel and microkernel and what feature makes it microkernel? Name the operating systems that utilize microkernels.
9. What are the merits and demerits of using Microkernel Architecture?
10. Distinguish between Monolithic kernels vs. microkernels.
11. What are the features that are utilized in making Hybrid (or modular) kernels?
12. What are the various advantages/disadvantages of Hybrid kernel (or modular) system?
13. How does Nano kernel functions?
14. What was the reason Exokernels have never taken off?
15. On which OS multikernel operating system was tried first?
16. Enumerate the basic functions of an operating system.
17. What are the types of operating systems based on their method of operation?
18. Briefly discuss the various generations of evolution of Operating Systems.
19. Describe the various applications of Real-time OS.
20. What type of OS are used in various gadgets, such as Smartphones, tablets, and wearables?

21. Names the various main popular operating systems an expert programmer needs to know.
22. Write down the benefits of a MS-DOS operating system. Is it a must-use application for all types of computers?
23. What are the limitations of a MS-DOS operating system?
24. Who developed Unix and the C programming language? Is Java necessary for using Unix?
25. Is Linux OS the one of the most popular platforms on the planet? How does it differ from Unix?
26. How did the Linux become most popular OS? Is it used on mobile devices?
27. Discuss the features of Linux kernel. Is Linux is also used for mobile devices?
28. What are the features of the POSIX standard and how it is related with IEEE? What Is IEEE?
29. Why Microsoft Windows is most popular OS and how much was the market share in 2024?
30. Where is the Android Operating System used? What are the other OS that can be used instead?
31. Compare Android OS with Apple-owned iOS.
32. Write a short note on Apple iOS.
33. Discuss the operating system structure explaining its layers. Draw its hierarchical diagram illustrating various layers.
34. Define BIOS and describe its role in computer organization.

References

[1] Kernel (operating system),From Wikipedia, the free encyclopedia,https://en.wikipedia.org/wiki/Kernel_(operating_system)#

[2] Types of Operating Systems (With OS Functions and Examples),https://www.indeed.com/career-advice/career-development/types-of-operating-systems

[3] Evolution of Operating System, Vikram Singh : Assistant Manager - Content,https://www.shiksha.com/online-courses/articles/evolution-of-operating-system/

[4] MS-DOS Operating System, Last Updated: Mar 27, 2024,https://www.naukri.com/code360/library/dos-operating-system

[5] What is Linux? https://www.linux.com/what-is-linux/

[6] What is the difference between Linux and Unix operating systems ? by BMITC CO.,LTD | Tutorials,https://binhminhitc.com/tutorials/what-is-the-difference-between-linux-and-unix-operating-systems/

[7] "Desktop Operating System Market Share Worldwide". StatCounter Global Stats. Archived from the original on January 27, 2020

[8] Operating System Structure, By Tarandeep singhttps://www.scaler.com/topics/operating-system-structure/h,

Chapter 3
Concept of a Process and System Calls

Introduction

In an operating system, a process refers to a piece of running software. Each process must be executed in a specific order. Essentially, a process represents the fundamental task that needs to be completed within a system. To put it another way, we write computer programs as text files, and when these programs are executed, they transform into processes that carry out the tasks outlined in the code. The system call is a function that a user program uses to ask the operating system for a particular service. User programmers can communicate with the operating system to request its services using the interface that is created by a system call.

System calls act as an interface between an operating system and a process. Generally, assembly language instructions are used to create system calls. The handbooks used by programmers who work at the assembly level also address these topics. In user mode, system calls are usually generated when a process needs to access a resource. Next, through a system call, the resource is obtained from the kernel.

Structure

In this chapter, you will be able to learn about following topics:

- Overview of the Concept of a Process
- Unravelling the Components of a Process
- Process States in a UNIX Process
- Process Control Block
- Structure of a Process
- Overview of Process Scheduling
- Inter-process communication (IPC), Shared Memory, and Message Passing
- UNIX signals

- Different Types of System Calls in OS
- Types of System Calls in OS
- Rules for Passing Parameters to the System Call
- Important System Calls Used in OS

Overview of the Concept of Process and System Calls

A process, in the context of computation, is an active program that is currently being executed. It's more than just a computer code; it's an active entity that holds attributes like hardware status, RAM, CPU, and more. A process forms the core of all computation tasks within a system [1].

Defining a Process in an Operating System

In an operating system, a process is simply a piece of running software. Every process has to be carried out in a particular order. An entity that symbolizes the fundamental task that must be completed in a system is known as a process. Stated differently, we write computer programs as text files. These programs become processes that perform all of the tasks listed in the program when we run it. Four parts make up a program when loaded into memory to become a process: stack, heap, text, and data. A process running in the main memory is depicted in simplified form in the following diagram.

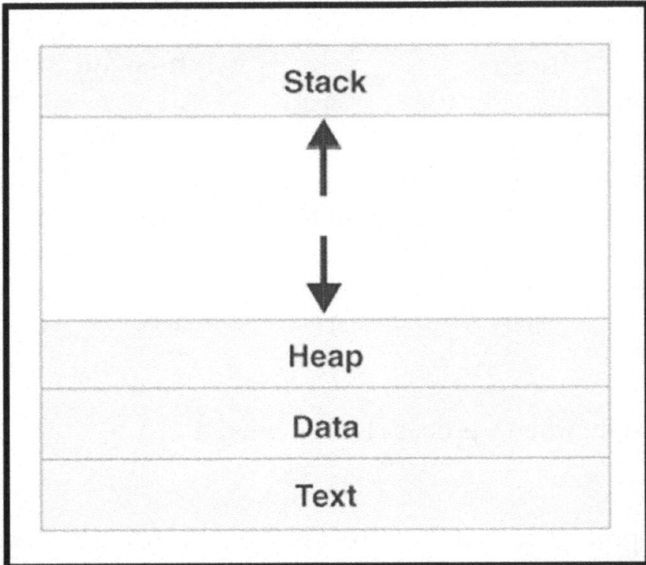

Figure 3.1: *Process Running in the Main Memory*

Unravelling the Components of a Process

A process can be divided into the following four segments:

- **Stack:** The process stack stores temporary data, such as method parameters, return address, and local variables.
- **Heap:** The heap is the memory that is dynamically allocated to a process during its run time.
- **Text:** The text segment includes the contents currently in the processor's registers and the current activity as indicated by the value of the program counter.
- **Data :** This segment includes global and static variables.

Decoding the Process Life Cycle

"A process goes through various states during its execution. Different operating systems may define different stages, and the naming of these states is not standardized. However, in general, a process can be in one of the following five states at any given time."

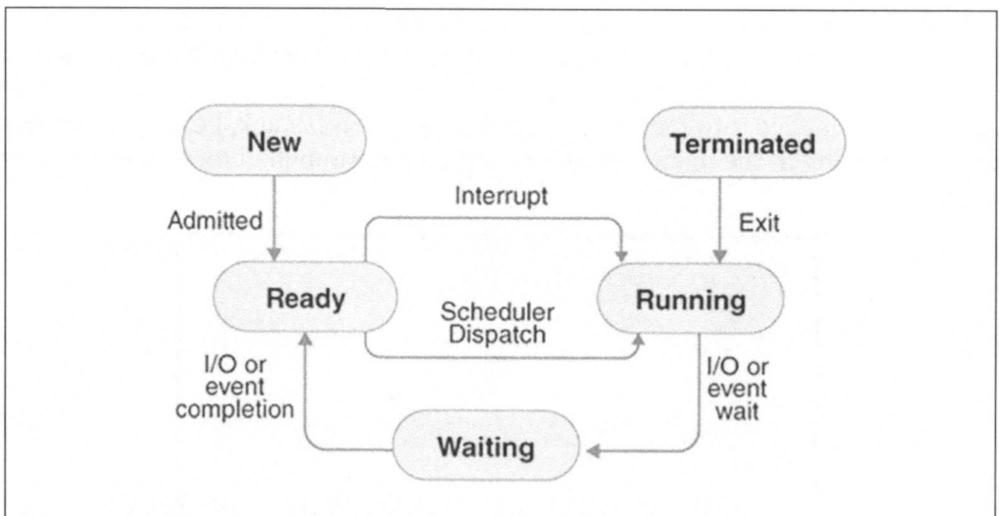

Figure 3.2: *Decoding the Process Life Cycle*

New

This is the initial state when a process is first created.

Ready

In this state, the process is waiting to be assigned a processor. Ready processes are waiting for the operating system to assign them a processor so they can run. The process may enter this state after starting or while running if the scheduler interrupts it to assign the CPU to another process.

Running

When the OS scheduler assigns a processor to a process, the process state is set to running, and the processor executes the process instructions.

Waiting

If a process needs to wait for a resource, such as waiting for user input or for a file to become available, it enters the waiting state.

Terminated or Exit

Once a process has completed its execution or has been terminated by the operating system, it is moved to the terminated state, where it waits for removal from the main memory.

Process States in a UNIX Process

Process is an instance of a program in execution [2]. A set of processes combined together make a complete program. There are two categories of processes in Unix, namely;

- User processes: They are operated in user mode.
- Kernel processes: They are operated in kernel mode.

Understanding the distinction between user and kernel processes is essential for computer science students, especially those preparing for exams such as GATE. Our GATE course offers comprehensive coverage of operating system concepts, including processes and process management in Unix.

The Lifetime of a Process

The lifetime of a process can be divided into a set of states, each with certain characteristics that describe the process. It is essential to understand the following states now:

1. The process is currently executing in user mode.
2. The process is currently executing in kernel mode.
3. The process is not executing but is ready to run as soon as the scheduler chooses it. Many processes may be in this state, and the scheduling algorithm determines which one will be executed next.

4. The process is sleeping. A process puts itself to sleep when it can no longer continue executing, such as when it is waiting for 1/0 to complete.
5. The process is ready to run, but the swapper (process 0) must swap the process into main memory before the kernel can schedule it to execute.
6. The process is sleeping, and the swapper has swapped the process to secondary storage to make room for other processes in the main memory.
7. The process is returning from the kernel to user mode, but the kernel pre-empts it and does a context switch to schedule another process. The distinction between this state and state 3("*ready to run*") will be brought out shortly.
8. The process is newly created and is in a transition state; it exists but is not ready to run, nor is it sleeping. This state is the start state for all processes except process 0.
9. The process executed the exit system call and is in the zombie state. The process no longer exists but leaves a record containing an exit code and some timing statistics for its parent process to collect. The zombie state is the final state of a process.

Since a processor can execute only one process at a time, at most one process may be in states 1 and 2. The two states correspond to the two modes of execution: user and kernel.

"*The states that a Process enters in working from start till the end are known as Process states.*" These are listed as follows:

- **Created:** Process is newly created by system call, and is not ready to run
- **User Running:** The process is running in user mode which means it is a user process
- **Kernel Running**: Indicates process is a kernel process running in kernel mode
- **Zombie**- Process does not exist/is terminated
- **Pre-empted**: When the process runs from kernel to user mode, it is said to be pre-empted
- **Ready to Run in Memory**: It indicated that process has reached a state where it is ready to run in memory and is waiting for kernel to schedule it
- **Ready to Run, Swapped:** Process is ready to run but no empty main memory is present
- **Sleep, Swapped**: Process has been swapped to secondary storage and is at a blocked state
- **Asleep in memory**: Process is in memory (not swapped to secondary storage) but is in blocked state

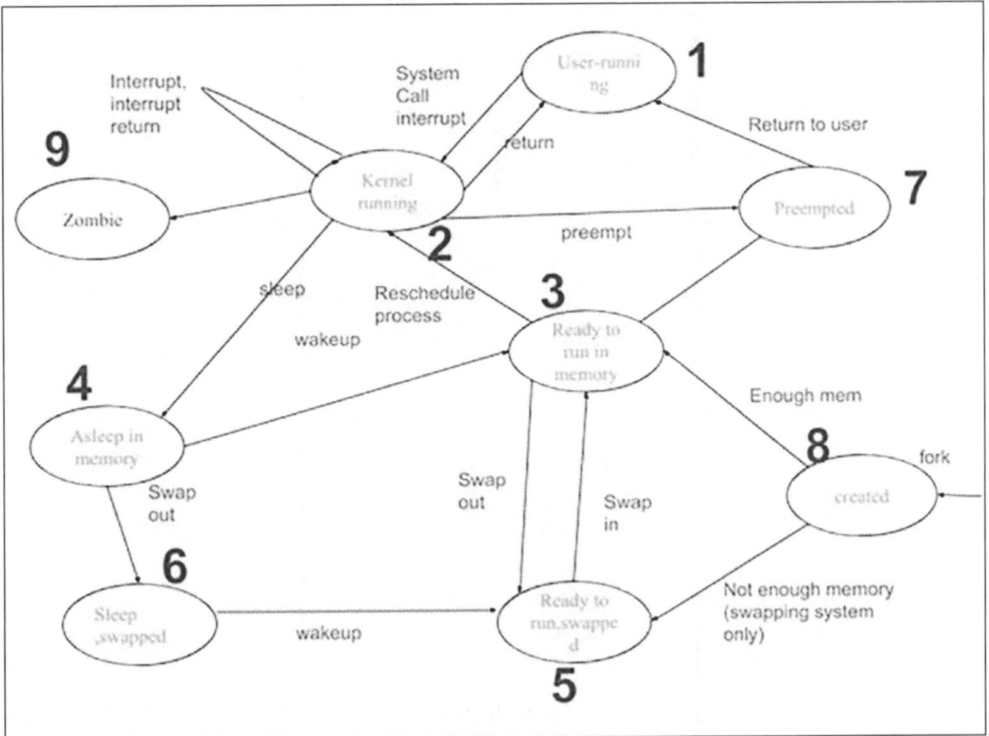

Figure 3.3: *Different Process States. The numbers indicate the steps that are followed*

Process Control Block

An OS data structure called a Process Control Block (PCB) is an essential one that contains information about all the processes running in a computer system. The operating system creates a special PCB in OS for each newly created process instantaneously. This is done to guarantee that the system can effectively manage any resources needed, oversee the process's execution in an efficient manner, and actively monitor its state.

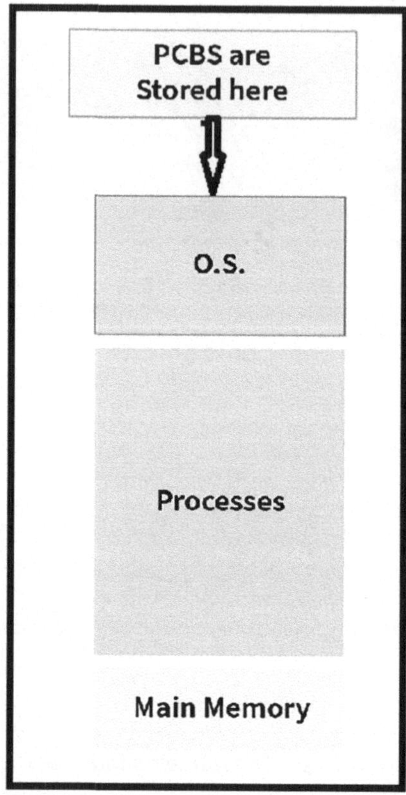

Figure 3.4: *Process Control Block (PCB)*

The PCB in OS functions as a process's "*fingerprint*," giving the OS all the information it needs to administer and regulate the process as efficiently as possible. Operating systems cannot function properly without the PCB because, without it, the OS would not be able to see the processes to control.

Structure of a Process

Process ID, process state, process priority, accounting data, program counter, CPU registers, and other attribute information are all contained in the structure of the process control block.

"*In multitasking operating systems, the PCB stores data needed for correct and efficient process management*" [4]. Though the details of these structures are system-dependent, common elements fall into three main categories:

- Process identification
- Process state
- Process control

1. Status tables exist for each relevant entity, such as describing memory, I/O devices, files, and processes.
2. Memory tables, for example, contain information about allocating main and secondary (virtual) memory for each process, authorization attributes for accessing memory areas shared among different processes, and so on. I/O tables may have entries stating the availability of a device or its assignment to a process, the status of I/O operations, the location of memory buffers used for them, and so on.
3. Process identification data include a unique identifier for the process (almost invariably an integer) and, in a multiuser-multitasking system, data such as the identifier of the parent process, user identifier, user group identifier, and so on. The process ID is particularly relevant since it is often used to cross-reference the preceding tables, for example, showing which process uses which I/O devices, or memory areas.
4. Process state data define the status of a process when it is suspended, allowing the OS to restart it later. This always includes the content of general-purpose CPU registers, the CPU process status word, stack and frame pointers, and so on. During a context switch, the running process is stopped, and another process runs. The kernel must stop the execution of the running process, copy out the values in hardware registers to its PCB, and update the hardware registers with the values from the PCB of the new process.
5. Process control information is used by the OS to manage the process itself. This includes:
    a. **Process Scheduling State:** The state of the process in terms of "*ready*", "*suspended*", and so on, and other scheduling information as well, such as priority value, the amount of time elapsed since the process gained control of the CPU or since it was suspended. Also, in case of a suspended process, event identification data must be recorded for the event the process is waiting for
    b. **Process Structuring Information**: Process's children IDs, or the IDs of other processes related to the current one in some functional way, which may be represented as a queue, a ring, or other data structures
    c. **Interprocess Communication Information:** Flags, signals, and messages associated with the communication among independent processes
    d. **Process Privileges:** Allowed/disallowed access to system resources
    e. **Process State:** *New, ready, running, waiting, dead*
    f. **Process Number (PID)**: Unique identification number for each process (also known as Process ID)

g. **Program Counter** (PC): A pointer to the address of the next instruction to be executed for this process

h. **CPU Registers:** A register set where the process needs to be stored for execution for running state

i. **CPU Scheduling Information:** Information scheduling CPU time

j. **Memory Management Information:** Page table, memory limits, segment table

k. **Accounting Information:** Amount of CPU used for process execution, time limits, execution ID, and more

l. **I/O Status Information** – List of I/O devices allocated to the process

Every process is associated with a process control block, a data structure maintained by the operating system. The PCB is identified by a unique integer process ID (or PID). As given here, the PCB stores all the information needed to keep track of a process.

- **Process State**: This refers to the current state of the process, such as whether it's ready, waiting, running, and so on.
- **Process Privileges**: This is required to allow or deny access to system resources.
- **Process ID:** Each process in the OS has its own unique identifier.
- **Pointer:** This points to the parent process.
- **Program Counter:** The program counter is a pointer that points to the address of the next instruction of the process.
- **CPU Registers:** Various CPU registers must store the processes for execution in the running state.
- **CPU Scheduling Information:** Information such as process priority and other scheduling information is required for the process to be scheduled.
- **Memory Management Information:** This includes information such as the page table, memory limits, segment table, depending on the memory used by the OS.
- **Accounting Information:** This includes information such as CPU usage for process execution, time limits, execution ID, and so on.
- **IO Status Information:** This section includes a list of I/O devices used by the process.

The structure of the PCB depends entirely on the operating system, and different operating systems may include different information.

The PCB is maintained for the duration of a process and is deleted once the process is terminated.

Overview of Process Scheduling

When there are multiple runnable processes, the operating system uses a technique called process scheduling to determine which one should be executed first. A scheduler is a program that makes these choices based on a scheduling algorithm. An effective scheduling algorithm should have the following qualities.

- The response time for users should be minimized.
- The total number of jobs processed per hour should be maximized, which means that a good scheduling system should provide the highest possible throughput.
- The CPU should be utilized to its maximum potential.
- Each process should get an equal share of CPU time.

Inter-process Communication, Shared Memory, and Message Passing)

In this section, we will discuss about inter-process communication, shared memory, and message passing.

Inter-process Communication (IPC)

Inter-process communication (IPC) is the exchange of data and signals between different processes running on the same or different machines. IPC is essential for building concurrent and distributed systems that can perform multiple tasks in parallel and coordinate their actions. There are two main methods of IPC: message passing and shared memory [3].

Message Passing

Message passing is the method of IPC where processes send and receive messages to each other through a communication channel. These messages can be fixed or variable in size and contain data, commands, or signals. The communication channel can be synchronous or asynchronous and uses various protocols and mechanisms, such as pipes, sockets, queues, or remote procedure calls. This method of IPC is suitable for distributed systems, where processes are located on different machines, and for loosely coupled systems, where processes are independent and do not share any resources [3].

Message passing offers several benefits, including the avoidance of race conditions and inconsistent data that can arise from shared memory. As long as they agree on the message format and protocol, it enables processes to communicate across various platforms and networks. Additionally, since processes only need to be aware of the communication channel's interface, it offers a high degree of abstraction and modularity. However, there are also certain drawbacks to message passing. When transmitting lengthy or complex messages, you may face significant overhead associated with message encoding, decoding, and transmission. Furthermore, it can be challenging to set up safe and dependable communication channels for distributed systems that could experience attacks, network outages, or delays. Finally, systems that change over time or have multiple versions may find it difficult to design and maintain the message format and protocol.

Shared Memory

Processes can access a shared memory region mapped to their address space using the shared memory IPC technique. Processes can read and write to this kind of memory directly, without a communication channel, and it can be used to store data, flags, or semaphores. Systems that operate on the same machine or closely coupled systems that frequently need to synchronize their actions or share a large amount of data can benefit from shared memory. Among its many benefits are low-level abstraction and flexibility, ability to transfer data quickly and efficiently, and the fact that it permits processes to use the same data structures and formats. However, it also has some drawbacks, including raising complexity and risk, limiting scalability and portability, and resulting in data inconsistency and race conditions if processes don't coordinate correctly.

Choosing Between Message Passing and Shared Memory for IPC

It can be difficult to decide between shared memory and message passing for IPC because it depends on several variables, including the needs of the system, the environment's capabilities, and the preferences and expertise of the developers. Nonetheless, you can choose more wisely if you follow a few broad principles. If data inconsistency or race conditions need to be avoided, or if communication needs to occur between various machines or platforms, then message passing should be used. The shared memory should be utilized when there is simultaneous communication on the same machine or when high data transfer speeds and efficiency are required. It's crucial to weigh the benefits and drawbacks of each approach, as well as how difficult or easy it will be to implement and maintain. Selecting an ideal approach for your situation can also be accomplished by testing various approaches and evaluating the outcomes. Although IPC is a complicated topic in computer science, you can choose your IPC wisely if you know the advantages and disadvantages of shared memory, message passing, and some general rules of thumb.

UNIX Signals

Signals, to be short, are various notifications sent to a process to notify it of various "*important*" events. By their nature, they interrupt whatever the process is doing at this minute, and force it to handle them immediately. Each signal has an integer number that represents the process (1, 2, and so on), as well as a symbolic name that is usually defined in the file /usr/include/signal.h or one of the files included by it directly or indirectly (HUP, INT, and so on. Use the command '**`kill -l`**' to see a list of signals supported by your system) [4].

A signal handler is a function that is called by the process upon receiving a signal. Each signal may have one. The function is called in "*asynchronous mode,*" which implies that there isn't any code in your program that makes direct calls to this function. Rather, the operating system "*forces*" the process to call the signal handler function by stopping the execution of the process when it receives the signal. The process resumes execution from the location it was in prior to the signal being received, as if this interruption had never happened, when the signal handler function returns.

Sending Signals to Processes

Follow these steps to send signals to the process:

1. **Sending Signals Using the Keyboard:** The most common way of sending signals to processes is using the keyboard. Certain key presses are interpreted by the system as requests to send signals to the process with which we are interacting. They are:

   - *Ctrl-C*: Pressing this key causes the system to send an **`INT`** signal (**`SIGINT`**) to the running process. By default, this signal causes the process to terminate immediately.
   - *Ctrl-Z*: Pressing this key causes the system to send a **`TSTP`** signal (**`SIGTSTP`**) to the running process. By default, this signal causes the process to suspend execution.
   - *Ctrl-*: Pressing this key causes the system to send a **`ABRT`** signal (**`SIGABRT`**) to the running process. By default, this signal causes the process to terminate immediately.

Note *that this redundancy (that is, Ctrl-\ doing the same as Ctrl-C) gives us better flexibility which will be discussed later.*

2. **Sending Signals from the Command Line:** Another way of sending signals to processes is done using various commands, usually internal to the shell:

   `Kill`: The **`kill`** command accepts two parameters: a signal name (or number), and a process ID. Usually, the syntax for using it goes something as follows:

   ```
   kill -<signal> <PID>
   ```

For example, to send the INT signal to process with PID 5342, type:

```
kill -INT 5342
```

It has the same effect as running that process in the shell and pressing *Ctrl-C*. The kill command gets its name because, by default, if no signal name or number is specified, the process will receive a TERM signal, which typically results in its termination.

`Fg`: On most shells, using the '`fg`' command will resume execution of the process (that was suspended with Ctrl-Z), by sending it a CONT signal.

3. **Signal Types - List of Available Signals:** The following signals are supported by Linux. There are several architecture-dependent signal numbers. First, let us see the POSIX-described signals.

Signal		**Value**	**Action**	**Comment**
`SIGINT`		2	A	Interrupt from keyboard
`SIGQUIT`		3	C	Quit from keyboard
`SIGILL`		4	C	Illegal Instruction
`SIGABRT`		6	C	Abort signal from abort (3)
`SIGFPE`		8	C	Floating point exception
`SIGKILL`		9	AEF	Kill signal
`SIGSEGV`		11	C	Invalid memory reference
`SIGPIPE`		13	A	Broken pipe: write to pipe with no readers
`SIGALRM`		14	A	Timer signal from alarm (2)
`SIGTERM`		15	A	Termination signal
`SIGUSR1`		30,10,16	A	User-defined signal 1
`SIGUSR2`		31,12,17	A	User-defined signal 2
`SIGCHLD`		20,17,18	B	Child stopped or terminated
`SIGCONT`		19,18,25		Continue if stopped
`SIGSTOP`		17,19,23	DEF	Stop process
`SIGTSTP`		18,20,24	D	Stop typed at **`tty`**
`SIGTTIN`		21,21,26	D	**`tty`** input for the background process
`SIGTTOU`		22,22,27	D	**`tty`** output for the background process

***Table 3.1:** Signals supported by Linux*

The letters in the "*Action*" column have the following meanings:

A: Default action is to terminate the process

B: Default action is to ignore the signal

C: Default action is to terminate the process and dump core

D: Default action is to stop the process

E : Signal cannot be caught

F : Signal cannot be ignored

4. **Sending Signals Using System Calls**

Using the kill system call is a third way to signal processes. This is the standard protocol for signal transmission between processes. The **'kill'** and **'fg'** commands also use this system call. Here is an example code that causes a process to suspend its own execution by sending itself the **STOP** signal:

```
#include <unistd.h>      /* standard unix functions, like getpid()      */
#include <sys/types.h>   /* various type definitions, like pid_t        */
#include <signal.h>     /* signal name macros, and the kill() prototype */

/* first, find my own process ID */
pid_t my_pid = getpid();

/* now that i got my PID, send myself the STOP signal. */
kill(my_pid, SIGSTOP);
```

An instance in which this code could be helpful is in a signal handler that receives the TSTP signal (recall that it is *Ctrl*-Z) and uses it to perform several actions prior to suspending the process. Later on, we will witness an instance of this.

Catching Signals - Signal Handlers

Catchable and Non-Catchable Signals

The process may be able to intercept most signals, but occasionally it will not be able to and will crash. One such signal is the **KILL** signal, which is -9 on all of the ices. This is why you typically see this signal being used to terminate a process when it becomes "*wild*." The procedure that shuts down the system is the one that uses this signal. First, it gives all processes a **TERM** signal, waits a little, and then uses the **KILL** signal to terminate any remaining processes after giving them a "*grace period*" to end properly.

Similarly, a process that receives a **STOP** signal is unable to continue and must be stopped immediately. This is helpful for debugging programs whose actions are time-dependent. Assume that process A needs to send some data to process B. You would like to verify certain system settings after the message is sent, but before process B receives and processes it. Process A could be run and waited until it sends its crucial message to process B. Alternatively, process B could be suspended by sending a STOP signal. You can check whatever you want to at this point. Process B will then receive and process the message sent by process A. Afterward, you can use the **CONT** signal to resume process B's execution.

The well-known **SEGV** and **BUS** signals are among the numerous other signals that can currently be captured. Programs that have exited with messages such as "*Segmentation Violation - Core Dumped*" or "*Bus Error - Core Dumped*" are likely something you have seen many times. When this happened the first time, your program received a SEGV signal because it was trying to access an invalid memory address. In the second scenario, your program received a BUS signal because it attempted to access a memory address that was not aligned correctly. In either scenario, these signals can be detected and used to perform cleanup tasks, such as ending child processes or possibly deleting temporary files. Although the memory used by your process is probably corrupt in both scenarios, cleanup is usually still achievable because it's likely that only a small portion of the memory was corrupt.

Default Signal Handlers

A set of default signal handlers is set up for your program by the runtime environment if you don't install any custom signal handlers (remember, a signal handler is that function handling a signal). The system call **exit()** is invoked, for instance, by the **TERM** signal's default signal handler. The process dumps its memory image into a file called "*core*" in the current directory of the process and then exits when the default handler for the **ABRT** signal issues the **abort()** system call.

Installing Signal Handlers

Signal handlers can be installed in several methods. For further reading, please refer to the pages in your manual. Here, we'll utilize the simplest format.

The signal() system call is used to specify a signal handler for a particular kind of signal. **Signal()** assigns the given signal to the signal handler function after receiving a signal number and a pointer. For instance, the following code snippet prompts the user to press *Ctrl-C* to cause the program to print the phrase "**Don't do that**."

```
#include <stdio.h>     /* standard I/O functions                         */
#include <unistd.h>    /* standard unix functions, like getpid()         */
#include <sys/types.h> /* various type definitions, like pid_t           */
#include <signal.h>    /* signal name macros, and the signal() prototype */

/* first, here is the signal handler */
void catch_int(int sig_num)
{
    /* re-set the signal handler again to catch_int, for next time */
    signal(SIGINT, catch_int);
    /* and print the message */
```

```
    printf("Don't do that");
    fflush(stdout);
}

.
.
.
/* and somewhere later in the code.... */
.
.

/* set the INT (Ctrl-C) signal handler to 'catch_int' */
signal(SIGINT, catch_int);

/* now, let's get into an infinite loop of doing nothing. */
for ( ;; )
    pause();
```

The complete source code for this program is found in the **catch-ctrl-c.c** file.

Notes: *The process stops running when the **pause()** system call is made, waiting for a signal. It is unquestionably preferable to an endless "**busy wait**" loop. In C/C++, a function's name is a pointer to the function; therefore, you can provide the function's name in place of a pointer when you're asked to supply one. When a signal handler is called on some systems (such as HP-UX), the system immediately sets that signal's handler back to the default handler. Therefore, as soon as we enter the handler function, we reassign the signal handler. If not, the process will terminate (which is the default behavior for INT signals) and this signal will be received again. It never hurts to add this line, so it's a good idea even on systems that don't behave in this manner.*

Pre-defined Signal Handlers

Instead of writing our own signal handler functions, we can write **SIG_IGN** and **SIG_DFL**, two pre-defined functions for our convenience.

SIG_IGN:

Directs the process to disregard the given signal. You can write this to completely ignore *Ctrl*-C, for instance:

```
signal(SIGINT, SIG_IGN);
```

SIG_DFL: Causes the system to set the default signal handler for the given signal (that is, useful for programs that cannot be interrupted in the middle or during critical sections). the same handler the system would have assigned for the signal when the process started running): .

```
signal(SIGTSTP, SIG_DFL);
```

For example, **signal.c**

Pending Signals

From the moment a signal is generated until it is delivered, there is a short interval of time the signal is fulfilled by action. It could cause issues if another signal is generated at this moment. To reset the signal handler, for example, might be your goal, but there's a chance that another signal will arrive first. Signal2 can be used if you do not want your process to be interrupted. Other options include **Sigset**, **Sighold**, **Sigrelse**, **Sigignore**, and **Sigmasuspend.cm**.

Different Types of System Calls in OS

The kernel is the central component of an operating system that controls all of the hardware and services offered by the OS. System calls are interfaces that the OS provides to enable user-level applications to communicate with low-level hardware components and utilize all of the services offered by the kernel. All processes must use these system calls to communicate with the kernel and utilize the services it offers. System calls provide an interface between a process and the operating system. Furthermore, they are the only means of changing from kernel mode to user mode.

A System Call is a way for a user program to interface with the OS. The program requests several services, and the OS responds by invoking a series of System Calls to satisfy the request. The program can be written in assembly language or high-level language, such as C or Pascal. System Calls are predefined functions that the OS may directly invoke if a high-level language is used.

User programs can access OS services through System Call using the Application Program Interface (API). For user-level processes to request help from the OS, it provides a point of contact between processes and the operating system. System Calls are the sole means of gaining restricted access to the kernel. Unless it is interrupted by another System Call, the System Call process operates in user mode. Depending on the priority levels, the System Call is then executed in kernel mode. When the process has finished, the control returns to user mode, allowing user processes to carry on as normal [5].

Example of System Calls in Operating System

The most frequently used system calls on Unix, Unix-like, and other POSIX-compliant operating systems are wait, exec, fork, exit, and kill. Several modern operating systems have hundreds of system calls in them. Linux and OpenBSD, for example, have more than 300 different calls each; NetBSD and FreeBSD have more than 500; and Windows has nearly 2000 system calls, divided between **win32k** and **ntdll**.

A process can be run from scratch and record each system call it makes with the help of tools, such as **truss**, **ftrace**, and **strace**. If the action does not violate the user's permissions, then it can also attach to an existing process and intercept any system calls it makes. Writing program code can copy data from one file into another.

The program's initial requirement is the names of the two files: the input and output files. This kind of program execution requires specific operating system's system calls in an interactive system.

First things first: Type a prompt message on the screen. Next, peruse the characters on the keyboard that denote the two files.

System Call Types in OS

The following figure shows five distinct kinds of System Calls in OS.

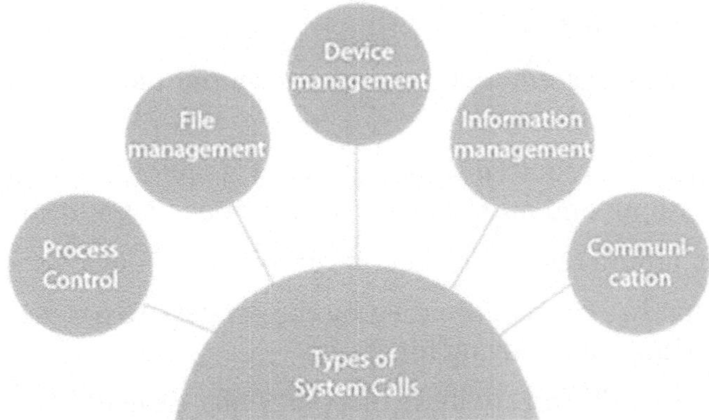

Figure 3.5: *Types of System Calls in OS*

The various features shown in *Figure* 3.5 are explained as follows:

Process Control: Process control heavily relies on System Calls. Applications can use them to start new processes, stop existing ones, and control how they are carried out. The operating system uses System Calls to manage resources and schedule processes when multiple programs run simultaneously.

A key component of process management is the use of system calls. Forking can be used to start new processes, exec to run multiple programs, and exit to end processes. Applications can function without interfering with one another, thanks to these calls.

Example

- **fork()**: Create a new process
- **exec()**: Replace the current process with a new one
- **exit()**: Terminate the current process
- **wait()**: Wait for a child process to terminate

File Management: The file management aspect is linked to a lot of calls. System Calls are responsible for handling an application's requests to open, read, write, and close files. When you save an image in the program or open a text document, for example, the System Calls make it easier to read and write data to and from files. One of the main functions of System Calls is to manage files and directories. Regardless of whether you are opening, reading from, writing to, or ending a file, system calls, such as open, read, write, and close easily manage these programs. These processes underpin everything, including word processing and gaming.

Example

- `open()`: Open a file
- `read()`: Read data from a file
- `write()`: Write data to a file
- `close()`: Close a file

Device Management: A System Call that manages input and output devices provides the following extensive services:

- Devices might be required while a process is operating, such as access to the file system, input and output devices, main memory, and so on.
- As a result, after a task is finished, it can request a device and then release it.
- A device that has been authorized by the process to access data can perform reading, writing, and moving functions.
- To obtain or modify an attribute of a particular device.
- The Call can be used to separate a device from the processor that is executing a command. Read, write, get device attributes, release device, and so on are a few instances of device management.

Example

- `read()`: Read data from a device (for example, keyboard)
- `write()`: Write data to a device (for example, display)
- `ioctl()`: Control device-specific operations

Information Maintenance

Data is moved from the user program to the operating system through System Calls for information maintenance. Due to this, the following services are provided by this kind of call:

- Get the current system time and date and set it
- Gather data about the system and set up the system configuration

- Retrieve details about a file or OS process on the system or any connected devices
- Modify a file or OS process's properties on the computer or any connected devices

Examples of information maintenance include getting system data, set time or date, get time or date, set system data, and so on

Example

- **`getpid()`**: Get the process ID of the current process
- **`getuid()`**: Get the user ID of the current user
- **`time()`**: Get the current time

Communication

In addition, a system call makes the network connection easier for the system. Among the services, they provide are:

- Establish a new connection to send the data. Once the transmission has concluded, cut off the connection.
- Message someone on a specific connection. Obtain correspondence from a particular link.
- Locate a particular remote device and link it to the network. Take a distant computer or gadget off the network.

Example

- **`socket()`**: Create a communication endpoint (socket) for network communication
- **`send()`**: Send data over a network socket
- **`recv()`**: Receive data from a network socket

Working of System Call

The applications run on a section of memory known as user space. A system call connects to the operating system's kernel, which operates in kernel space. Before generating a system call, an application needs to ask the kernel for permission. It accomplishes this by sending an interrupt request, which pauses the running process and gives the kernel control. If approved, the kernel performs the requested action (for example, creating or deleting a file).

The kernel's output is fed into the application as input. The application then carries out the remaining steps after receiving the input. When the operation is finished, the kernel returns the results to the application by transferring data from kernel space to user space in memory.

A simple system call, such as retrieving the current system date and time, may take a few nanoseconds to complete. A more complicated system call, such as one that connects to a network device, could take several seconds to complete.

For each system call, most operating systems start a separate kernel thread to prevent bottlenecks. Multiple system calls can be handled simultaneously because modern operating systems are multi-threaded.

The user program makes a series of system calls to assist in copying the content from one file to another. In an interactive system, the following order of system calls is carried out:

1. Prompt a message on the screen for the user to provide the name of the source and destination files
2. Read the name of the source and destination file character by character from the keyboard
3. Open a source file; open (and if not available Create) the destination file
4. Read from the source file and write to the destination file
5. Close the source and destination files
6. Prompt a message that displays the successful execution of the program
7. Terminate the user program

You can observe how a simple task is performed when seven system calls were executed.

Importance of System Calls

In OSs, System Calls are crucial for various reasons which is illustrated in the following figure:

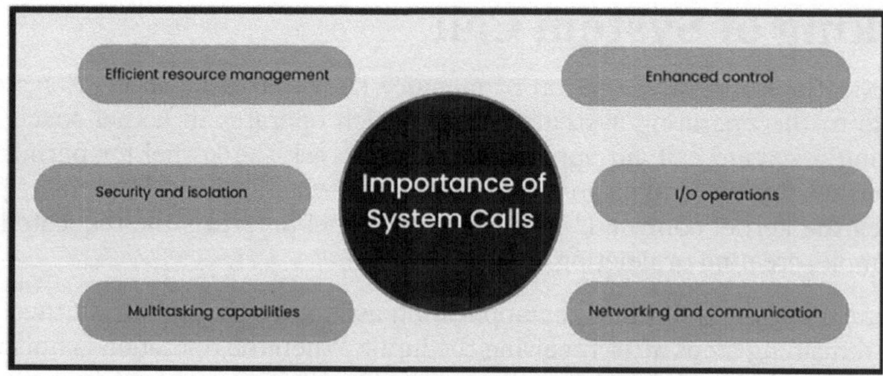

Figure 3.6: *Importance of System Calls*

- **Effective Resource Management**: Calls help allocate and manage memory and allow your computer to operate with methodical resource management. Thus, the programs are guaranteed to function properly and to use no additional resources. This enhances both overall performance and multitasking capabilities.
- **Security and Isolation**: System Calls ensure that one program cannot interfere with or access another program's memory, enhancing the device's general security and stability.
- **Multitasking Abilities**: One of the most important functions of the system call is supporting multitasking strategies. They facilitate easier application switching and increase productivity by allowing multiple programs to run concurrently.
- **Increased Control**: Thanks to system calls, you have a great deal of control over how your device operates. They let you manage files, start and stop processes, and carry out other system-related operations.
- **Input/Output (I/O) Operations**: System Calls enable communication with input and output devices. They ensure that you efficiently utilize your mouse, keyboard, and screen.
- **Networking and Communication**: System Calls facilitate networking and inter-application communication. They make it simple to move data across networks so that you can connect online, send emails, and browse the web.

Examples of System Calls

The following are the most frequently used System Calls on Unix OS and other compatible OS:

- **Open:** This System Call opens or creates files and sets permissions and file access mode.
- **Read and Write**: You can read data from and write data to files using these System Calls.
- **Fork**: The fundamental Unix process creation mechanism, the fork System Call creates the "*child process*," which is a copy of the parent process.
- **Exec:** Following a fork, a new program is loaded into the address space of the running process.
- **Exit:** The exit System Call ends a program and sends its status back to the parent process.

These examples demonstrate how System Calls provide a fundamental interface for apps to communicate with the OS's basic functions, enabling it to perform various operations efficiently [6].

Types of System Calls	Windows	Linux
Process Control	CreateProcess()	fork()
	ExitProcess()	exit()
	WaitForSingleObject()	wait()
File Management	CreateFile()	open()
	ReadFile()	read()
	WriteFile()	write()
	CloseHandle()	close()
Device Management	SetConsoleMode()	ioctl()
	ReadConsole()	read()
	WriteConsole()	write()
Information Maintenance	GetCurrentProcessID()	getpid()
	SetTimer()	alarm()
	Sleep()	sleep()
Communication	CreatePipe()	pipe()
	CreateFileMapping()	shmget()
	MapViewOfFile()	mmap()

Table 3.2: *Example of System Calls in Windows and Unix*

Rules for Passing Parameters to the System Call

The rules for passing parameters to the system call are as follows:

- The floating-point parameters cannot be passed as a parameter to the system call.
- It is possible to pass a finite number of arguments to the system call.
- The memory block is where any additional arguments should be kept if there are any, and the register has the memory block's address.
- Pushing and popping parameters from the stack can only be done by the operating system.

Important System Calls Used in OS

In this section, we will discuss the types of system calls used in OS.

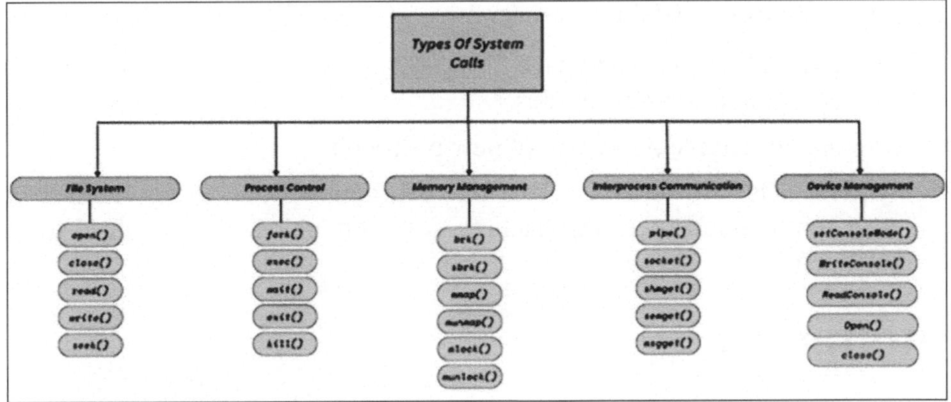

Figure 3.7: *Various Types of System Calls (Courtesy Geeks for Geek)*

1. **`wait()`**: A process may have to wait for another process to terminate to proceed on some systems. The execution of the parent process is halted when it forms a child process, and it continues to run until the child process is completed. A **`wait()`** system call results in the automatic suspension of the parent process. When the child process has finished executing, control moves back to the parent process.

2. **`fork()`**: Processes can duplicate themselves using the OS's fork system call. This mechanism allows the Call parent process to start a child process, which will continue to run while the parent process is stopped.

3. **`exec()`**: This system call is carried out in the context of an active process when an executable file replaces a previous executable file. Although no new process is created, the old process's stack, data, head, data, and so on are replaced by the new process, but the original process identifier remains.

4. **`kill()`**: The operating system signals processes to end using the **`kill()`** system call. Kill system calls are not always used to terminate processes; they can also have other purposes.

5. **`exit()`**: When the program needs to be stopped, the **`exit()`** system call is used. The resources that the process was utilizing were released upon using the exit system call.

Purpose of System Calls in OS

System calls function as an interface between a process and an operating system. Generally speaking, system calls are found as assembly language instructions. The manuals used by the programmers who work at the assembly level also address them.

System calls are usually generated when a user mode process needs to access a resource. Next, a system call is made to the kernel to request the resource.

The following situations call for system calls:

- A system call is required when a file system needs files to be added or removed and to read and write from files.
- Creation and implementation of new protocols.
- System calls are necessary for network connections. This holds true for both sending and receiving packets. A system call is also required to access hardware.

Conclusion

In this chapter, we have learned about processes in OS, the necessity of system calls, and how they are implemented. We have learned in detail about the types of processes and their structure, the scheduling of the processes, and the difference between IPC and shared memory.

In the next chapter, we shall explore the method of making threads for passing and instruction contained by our program and algorithms, and then, working of schedulers.

Questions

1. Define Process in an Operating System.
2. Describe Process and its four content segments.
3. How many stages does a Process go through during its complete execution?
4. How many sets of states can a Process be divided into during its lifetime? Describe them.
5. What is a Process Control Block (PCB), and explain its significance?
6. Describe the contents of a Process Structure.
7. What is Process Control Information, and how does the OS use it to manage processes?
8. What is meant by Process Scheduling and Process Scheduler?
9. Define Inter-Process Communication (IPC) and its function in message passing.
10. What are the several benefits offered by Message Passing?
11. What is meant by the Shared Memory IPC technique, and how is it implemented?
12. In what scenarios should Message Passing and Shared Memory be opted for IPC?

13. How many ways can Signals be passed to Processes?
14. What are Default Signal Handlers, and how are they installed?
15. What is the necessity of a System Call?
16. What are the various types of System Calls in OS? Explain their functions.
17. Describe the working method of a System Call with an example.
18. How long does it take for a System Call to execute? Provide two examples.
19. What is the purpose of System Calls in OS?
20. Illustrate the importance of System Calls.
21. Provide at least five examples of System Calls and describe their purpose.
22. What are the rules for Passing Parameters to a System Call?
23. Describe at least five important System Calls used in OS.

References

[1] Process in Operating System: Understanding Its Components, Life Cycle, and Scheduling,https://testbook.com/gate/process-in-operating-system-notes#:~:text=A%20process%2C%20in%20the%20context,computation

[2] Process states and Transitions in a UNIX Process, Last Updated : 25 Jun, 2024, https://www.geeksforgeeks.org/process-states-and-transitions-in-a-unix-process/

[3] How can you choose between message passing and shared memory for interprocess communication? LinkedIn, https://www.linkedin.com/advice/0/how-can-you-choose-between-message-passing-shared

[4] Introduction To Unix Signals Programming adapted from a tutorial develop by Guy Kerens, https://www.cs.kent.edu/~ruttan/sysprog/lectures/signals.html

[5] System Calls in OS (Operating System), Eliza Taylor, https://www.theknowledgeacademy.com/blog/system-calls-in-os

[6] System Calls in Operating System: Overview, Types & Examples, Blog Author, Abhresh Sugandhi, https://www.knowledgehut.com/blog/web-development/system-calls-in-os

CHAPTER 4
Threads

Introduction

Threads are scheduled for execution based on their priority. Even though threads are executing within the runtime, all threads are assigned processor time slices by the operating system. The details of the scheduling algorithm used to determine the order in which threads are executed vary with each operating system.

Structure

In this chapter, our effort shall be to learn about the following topics:

- Introduction to Processes and Threads
- Process State
- Process Resources
- Threads
- Differences between Process and Thread
- Process Queues
- Major Types of Thread
- Multithreading
- CPU and I/O Bound Processes
- Context Switching
- Scheduler Activations
- Whether Threads or Processes
- Examples of Threaded Programs
- Creating Processes in Linux

Introduction to Processes and Threads

A process is an instance of an operating computer program. A computer program is a set of passive instructions that are kept in the file system and are represented as code. An active process operates by loading and executing the program in memory. A process is an autonomous, self-contained unit of execution that, in the context of computing, symbolizes the execution of a program on a computer system. Program code, ongoing operations, and a special number known as the process ID (PID) are all components of a process.

Every process has its own set of system resources, including variables, file descriptors, and registers, and it operates in its own memory space. Operating systems that support multiple tasks at once are based on processes, which enable them to be managed and carried out simultaneously. The operating system scheduler chooses the sequence and length of each process's execution, allowing users to perceive an illusion of parallelism. Each process runs independently of the others.

To maintain stability and security, processes are usually isolated from one another, though they can communicate with one another through inter-process communication mechanisms. Examples of processes include applications, system utilities, and background services that are currently running on a computer.

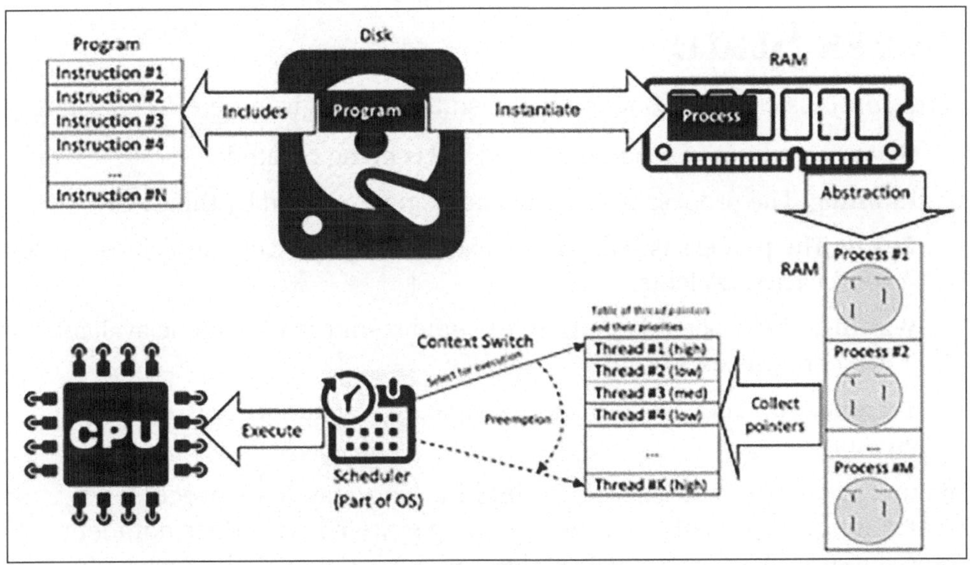

Figure 4.1: *Program vs. Process vs. Thread Scheduling, Preemption, Context Switching*

A computer program is a collection of instructions that are passively stored on a disk in a file, whereas a process is the act of executing instructions once they have been loaded into memory from the disk. A single program can have multiple associated processes. For instance, when multiple instances of the same program are opened, multiple processes are frequently launched. One way to let multiple processes share processors (CPUs) and other system resources is through multitasking.

One process is carried out at a time by each CPU (core). On the other hand, multitasking eliminates the need for each processor to wait for a task to complete to switch between active tasks (preemption). Switches may be made when a task initiates and waits for the completion of input/output operations, when a task voluntarily yields the CPU, in response to hardware interrupts, or when the operating system scheduler determines that a process has used up its fair amount of CPU time. For example, by the Linux kernel's Completely Fair Scheduler.

CPU time-sharing, a technique for dividing up the execution of user processes, threads, and even independent kernel tasks (though the latter is only possible with preemptive kernels like Linux), offers a common way to multitask. Preemption has a significant side effect. In that it gives interactive processes a higher priority than CPU-bound processes. As a result, users can instantly assign computational resources by simply pressing a key or moving their mouse. Moreover, applications with a real-time priority are prioritized over lower-priority processes, such as reproducing music and video. Time-sharing systems execute fast context switches, giving the impression that several processes are running concurrently on the same processor. Concurrency is the apparent simultaneous execution of several processes.

Process State

In short, a process can be in one of several states at any given time. These states are:

- **New:** The process executed by the CPU is being created.
- **Running:** The process is running and being executed by the CPU.
- **Ready:** The process is ready to be executed by the CPU, and all the necessary resources are available.
- **Waiting:** The process is waiting for some resource to become available before it can continue executing.
- **Terminated:** The process has completed execution and is removed from memory.

A computer system that is capable of multitasking may have processes that are in different states. It is possible that the operating system kernel does not identify these different states as such. Nonetheless, they serve as a helpful abstraction for process comprehension.

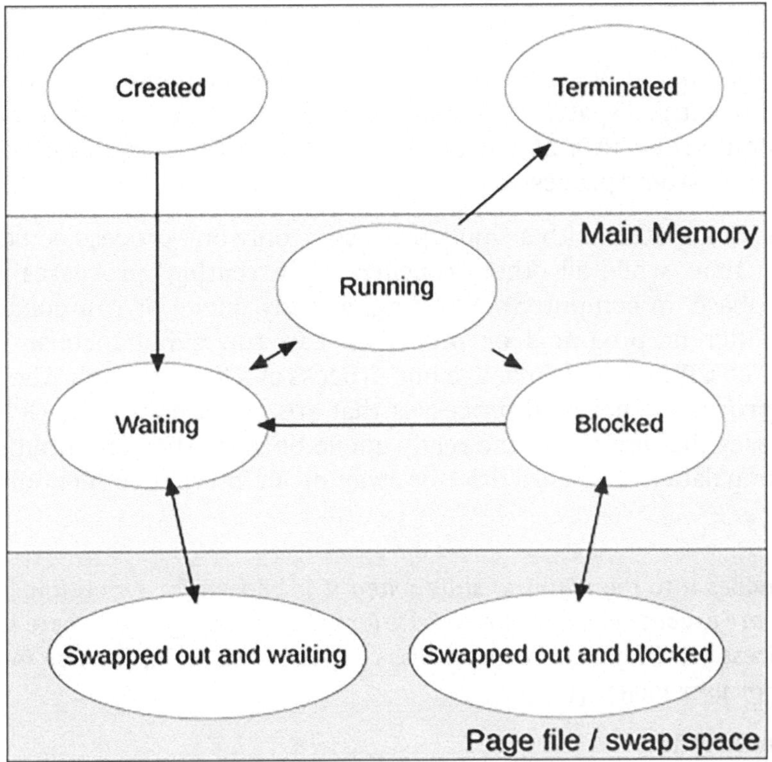

Figure 4.2: Various Process States

"The various process states, displayed in a state diagram, with arrows indicating possible transitions between states - as can be seen, some processes are stored in main memory (yellow), and some are stored in secondary memory (green)." [1]

Primary Process States

The following typical process states are possible on computer systems of all kinds. In most of these states, processes are "*stored*" in the main memory.

1. Created

A process exists in the "*created*" or "*new*" state when it first starts. The process is waiting to be admitted to the "*ready*" state in this state. A long-term, or admission, scheduler will approve or deny admission. This admission will normally be accepted automatically in most desktop computer systems. This admission might, however, take longer for real-time operating systems. Allowing too many processes to enter the "*ready*" state in a real-time system can cause oversaturation and resource contention, making it impossible to fulfill process deadlines.

2. Ready

A "*ready*" or "*waiting*" process has been loaded into main memory and is waiting for a CPU to execute it (the dispatcher, or short-term scheduler, will need to context switch the process onto the CPU). At any given time during the system's execution, there could be several "*ready*" processes.

For instance, in a system with a single processor, only one process could be running at any given time, while all other "*concurrently executing*" processes would be in the waiting phase. In computer scheduling, a ready queue or run queue is utilized. Numerous different programs or processes can run simultaneously on modern computers. The CPU can only manage one process at a time, though. There is a queue for "*ready*" processes that hold processes that are prepared for the CPU. There are other processes that are not in the ready queue because they are awaiting an event, such as loading data from a hard drive or awaiting an internet connection.

3. Running

"*A process moves into the running state when it is chosen for execution. The process's instructions are executed by one of the CPUs (or cores) of the system. There is at most one running process per CPU or core. A process can run in either of the two modes, namely kernel mode or user mode.*" [1]

a. **Kernel Mode**

   a. User mode avoids various catastrophic failures.

   b. There is an isolated virtual address space for each process in user mode.

   c. User mode ensures isolated execution of each process so that it does not affect other processes as such.

   d. No direct access to any hardware device is allowed.

4. Blocked

When an external event or change in state prevents a process from continuing, it enters a blocked state. A process might, for instance, block a call to an I/O device, such as a printer, if the printer is unavailable. Additionally, processes frequently halt when they need user input or access to a crucial area that needs to be carried out atomically. These crucial areas are safeguarded by a synchronization object, such as a mutex or semaphore.

5. Terminated

A process may be terminated, either from the "*running*" state by completing its execution or by explicitly being killed. In either of these cases, the process moves to the "*terminated*" state. The underlying program is no longer executing, but the process remains in the process table as a zombie process until its parent process calls the wait system call to read its exit status, at which point the process is removed from the process table, finally ending the process's lifetime. If the parent fails to call wait, this continues to consume the process table entry (concretely the process identifier or PID) and causes a resource leak. [1]

6. Other Process States

On Unix and Unix-like computer operating systems, a zombie process, also known as a defunct process, is a process that has finished executing (using the exit system call), but it still has an entry in the process table; it is a process in the "*terminated state.*" when operating systems allow virtual memory. Processes are "*stored*" on secondary memory (usually a hard disk) in each of these states.

- **Swapped Out and Ready** This is also known as suspended and ready. The scheduler of a system that supports virtual memory can swap out or move a process from main memory to external storage. It is possible to switch the process back to the waiting state at this point.
- **Switched Out and Blocked** This is also known as blocked and suspended. It is also possible to replace blocked processes. The process is switched out and blocked in this instance; it can be switched back in again under the same conditions as a swapped out and waiting process (though in this scenario, it will transition to the blocked state and might still be waiting for a resource to become available).

Process Resources

A process consists of the following resources:

- **Text** : Machine code of the compiled program
- **Data**: Global, static, constant, and uninitialized variables
- **Heap:** Dynamic memory allocation
- **Stack**: Temporary data such as local variables, function calls, parameters, return address, and so on

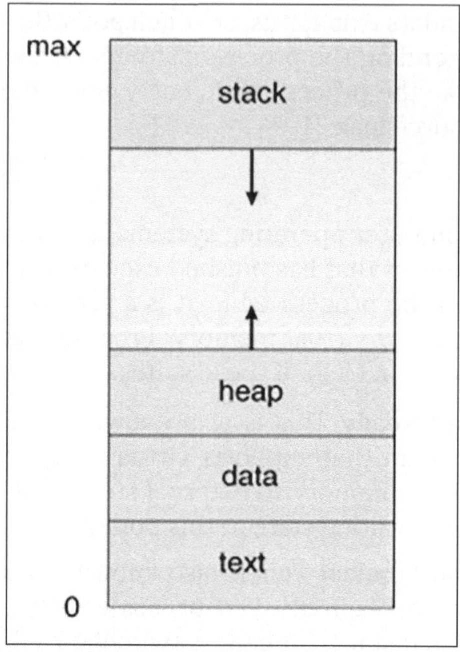

Figure 4.3: *Process Resources*

Threads

"*In computer science, a thread of execution is the smallest sequence of programmed instructions that can be managed independently by a scheduler, which is typically a part of the operating system.*" [2] In many cases, a thread is a component of a process.

Thanks to multithreading capabilities, a process' many threads can run concurrently, (sharing resources such as memory, but separate processes don't share these). To be more precise, all process' executable code, dynamically allocated variable values, and non-thread-local global variable values are shared by all threads at any given time. A process can generate multiple threads. A thread shares the main process' memory and is managed by an operating system in a manner similar to that of a process. A computer program run by one or more threads is referred to as a process in computing.

Operating systems (OS) processes are the basis of nearly all processes, including whole virtual machines. They are composed of program code, allocated system resources, physical and logical access permissions, and data structures to initiate, control, and coordinate execution activity. There are different types of OS processes of which some are lightweight. Multiple threads of execution that carry out instructions concurrently may comprise a process, depending on the operating system.

A computer program is a collection of instructions that are passively stored on a disk in a file; a process is the act of executing instructions once they have been loaded into memory from the disk. A single program can have multiple associated processes. For instance, when multiple instances of the same program are opened, multiple processes are frequently launched.

"In computers, a single process might have multiple functionalities running parallelly where each functionality can be considered as a thread. Each thread has its own set of registers and stack space. There can be multiple threads in a single process having the same or different functionality. Threads in operating systems are also termed lightweight processes."[2]

Need of Threads

A thread is a process's sequential flow of tasks. Within an operating system, threads can belong to the same class or different classes. Applications operate more efficiently when threads are used. Operating system threads enhance the system's overall performance and offer several advantages. Since threads share the same data and code, there is minimal operating cost between them, which is one of the reasons why the operating system needs threads.

In comparison to creating or ending a process, creating and terminating a thread is faster. Threads can switch contexts more quickly than processes can. Every thread possesses a unique set of registers, stack, and program counters. A single process's threads may share the same code, data, or file. Since threads share resources, they are also referred to as lightweight processes. For instance, separate background threads control the audio and video while a movie is being played on a device.

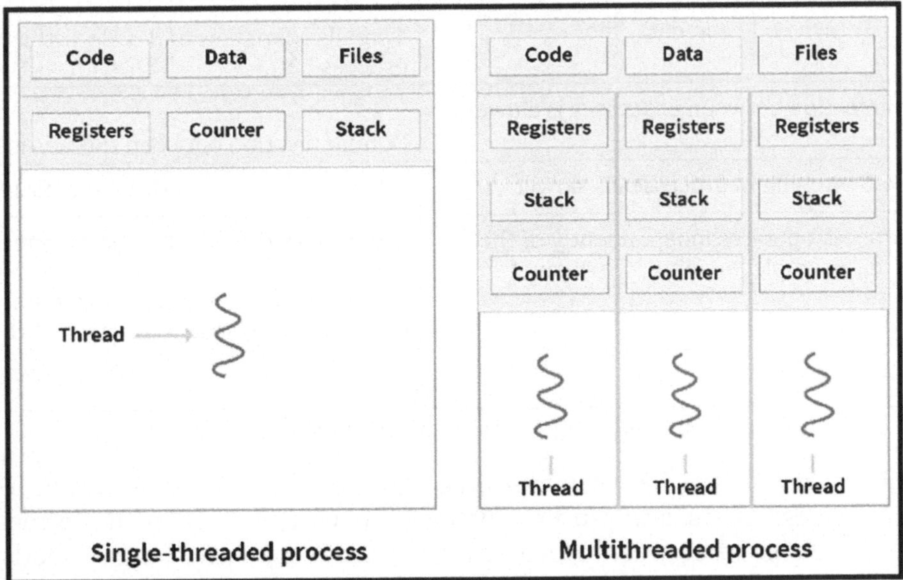

Figure 4.4: *Difference Between a Single-threaded Process and a Multithreaded Process*

A multithreaded process's shared resources and the distinctions between single-and multithreaded processes are depicted in *Figure* 4.4.

Components of Thread

A thread has the following three components:

- Program Counter
- Register Set
- Stack space

Difference between Process and Thread [2]

A process is merely any program that is running, and a thread is a subset of a process. *Table* 4.1 lists the primary distinctions between a thread and a process.

Process	Thread
Processes consume more resources, and hence they are referred to as heavyweight processes	Threads share resources, and hence they are referred to as lightweight processes
Slower process creation and termination times	Faster creation and termination times than processes
Have their own code and data/file.	Threads share files and code within a process
Communication between processes is slower	Communication between threads is faster
Context Switching in processes is slower	Context switching in threads is faster
Each process operates independently of the others, for example, opening two distinct browsers	Conversely, threads depend on one another; they can read, write, and alter data from another thread, for example, using two tabs open in the same browser.

Table 4.1: *Main Differences Between Process and Thread*

The primary distinction between resource sharing in two threads within a single process and resource sharing in two distinct processes is that in the former case, resources are shared between processes, whereas in the latter case, threads share resources.

In contrast to threads, which are dependent on one another within a process, processes are more independent of one another. Inter-thread communication is more user-friendly and efficient than inter-process communication. Threads have lower overhead than processes because they allocate memory and resources separately. Suitable for concurrent execution within the same process, threads are more lightweight.

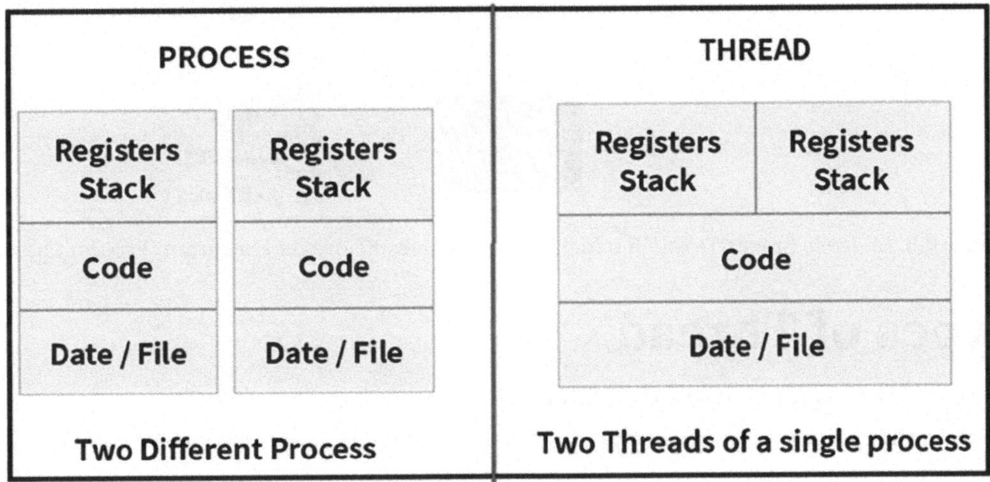

Figure 4.5: *Sharing of Resources in Two Different Processes vs. Two Threads in a Single Process*

The resource sharing between two distinct processes versus two threads within a single process is depicted in the preceding diagram.

Process Queues

There are multiple stages through which a process goes before its execution. A separate queue is maintained for all states.

These process scheduling queues are:

1. **Job Queue**: All the processes stay here in this job queue before their execution. Now, processes are picked up and put in the **READY** queue.
2. **Ready Queue**: The processes waiting to get executed are put in the **READY** queue. They remain here until they are picked up one by one for execution.
3. **Device Queue:** If the process is blocked during execution due to the unavailability of an I/O device, it goes to the Device queue

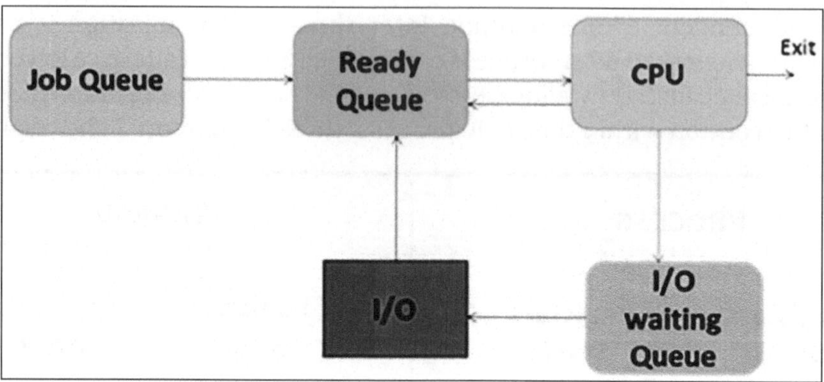

Figure 4.6: *Multiple Stages Through which a Process Goes Before its Execution (Process Queues)*

Types of Thread

There are two major types of threading schemes:

- User Level Threading Schemes
- Kernel Level Threading schemes

User Level Threading Scheme

The kernel is unaware that the user implements and controls user-level threads. User-level libraries are used to implement user-level threads, which are not recognized by the operating system. It can be created and managed more quickly than a kernel-level thread.

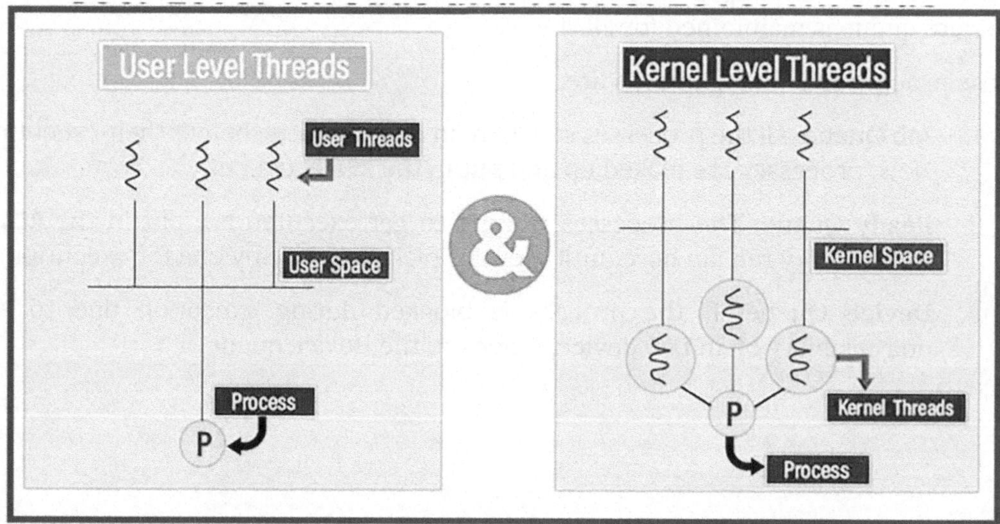

Figure 4.7: *User-level Threads and Kernel-level Threads Gets Active in their Separate Spaces*

In user-level threads, context switching happens faster. The process as a whole is blocked when a blocking operation is carried out by a single user-level thread. For instance, Java threads, POSIX threads, and so on.

- **User-Level Threads Examples [3]**
  - **Java Threads**: Java uses the Java Dot Language to provide its threading model. Class of threads. Java-coded apps can create and control threads without being dependent on the operating system.
  - **POSIX threads**, also known as Pthreads, are a set of guidelines that define how threads behave in operating systems that resemble Unix. C, C++, and other languages can use pthreads. Pthread-based applications can create and control user-level threads.
  - **Windows Thread API**: To create and manage threads, an API is provided by the Windows operating system. Windows provides functions such as `CreateThread` and `ExitThread` for creating and managing threads.
- **Advantages of User-Level Threads**
  - **Enhanced Performance:** User-level threads have less overhead when it comes to creation, management, and context switching. As they are lightweight, jobs are completed more quickly and apps function better overall.
  - **Portability Across Platforms:** User-level thread libraries are frequently more adaptable to various operating systems because they are responsible for managing user-level threads. This portability makes creation and implementation of apps easier on various platforms. Application-specific thread scheduling policies are possible with user-level threads, thanks to customized scheduling. The adaptability of thread management allows developers to customize it to meet the unique needs of their applications, maximizing performance for specific use cases.
  - **Resource Efficiency**: User-level threads can share resources more efficiently and avoid the overhead of kernel-level thread management, making them more resource-efficient than kernel-level threads in certain situations. **Independence from Kernel Support:** Since user-level threads can operate without kernel assistance, applications can utilize threading features even on platforms that lack native threading support. Because there is no need for kernel intervention, thread management operations are very fast.The ease of creation and management of user-level threads is generally higher than that of kernel-level threads, requiring fewer system resources. This effectiveness is useful, especially when creating and managing multiple threads quickly.

- **Deterministic Behavior**: Because user-level threads are managed at the application level, they may exhibit more deterministic behaviour. This predictability is useful in situations where exact timing is essential, such as real-time systems. Without altering the kernel, user-level thread scheduling policies can be tailored or altered for each application. Only the application that is misusing the thread library is impacted by misuse.

- **Disadvantages**
  - **Absence of Kernel Support:** User-level threads exist only in user-level thread libraries and function separately from the kernel. Because of this lack of kernel support, they cannot fully utilize certain features of the operating system, such as direct hardware resource access or thread prioritization.
  - **Problems with Blocking:** Because user-level libraries control user-level threads, a single blocking thread can completely halt a process, as the operating system is unaware of the thread's status. Subpar resource use and responsiveness could result from this restriction.
  - **Restricted Parallelism**: Since the operating system kernel is unaware of user-level threads, they may not fully utilize multicore processors or parallel architectures. As a result, applications meant to take advantage of parallel processing may perform less.
  - **Synchronization Difficulties**: It is difficult to coordinate synchronization between threads at the user level. Kernel support could make mechanisms such as semaphores or mutexes more reliable and effective, which could result in deadlocks or inconsistent data. Problems with
  - **Scalability:** When there are a lot of user-level threads, scalability can become problematic. Ineffective resource management and allocation can be caused by a lack of coordination with the kernel, which can affect the system scalability as a whole.
  - **Interrupt Handling**: User-level threads may find it difficult to handle interrupts effectively. In certain scenarios, responsiveness may be impacted by interrupt-driven events because the kernel is not directly involved in the threading model's integration.
  - **Restricted System Resource Visibility:** For user-level threads to effectively respond to changes in system conditions, they might require additional visibility into system resources. This ignorance may affect thread behavior optimization depending on dynamic resource availability.
  - **Platform Dependency**: Although the implementation of user-level threads is intended to improve portability, it may still rely on a particular platform.

Developers may need to put in extra work to ensure consistent behavior due to variations in operating systems' support for user-level thread libraries. The mapping of user-level threads to physical processors is not direct. A process executing several user-level threads is only allotted one processor, which the threads share. Virtual and physical processor equivalency is distorted by operating system activities, such as multiprogramming, I/O, and page faults. Implementing user-level threads atop kernel threads avoids the problems associated with user-level threads in Mach and Topaz. This means that all issues associated with kernel-level threads are passed down to the thread implementations. When user-level threads are implemented on top of kernel threads, they are preempted, block, resume, and schedule without acknowledging or considering the state of the user-level thread. A lock is being held by a user-level thread.

- **Kernel-level Threading Schemes:**

  The OS implements and controls kernel-level threads. System calls are used to implement kernel level threads, and the operating system is aware of them. Compared to user-level threads, kernel-level threads are more difficult to start and maintain. In a kernel-level thread, context switching is slower. Other threads are unaffected even if a blocking operation is carried out by one kernel-level thread, for example, Window Solaris.

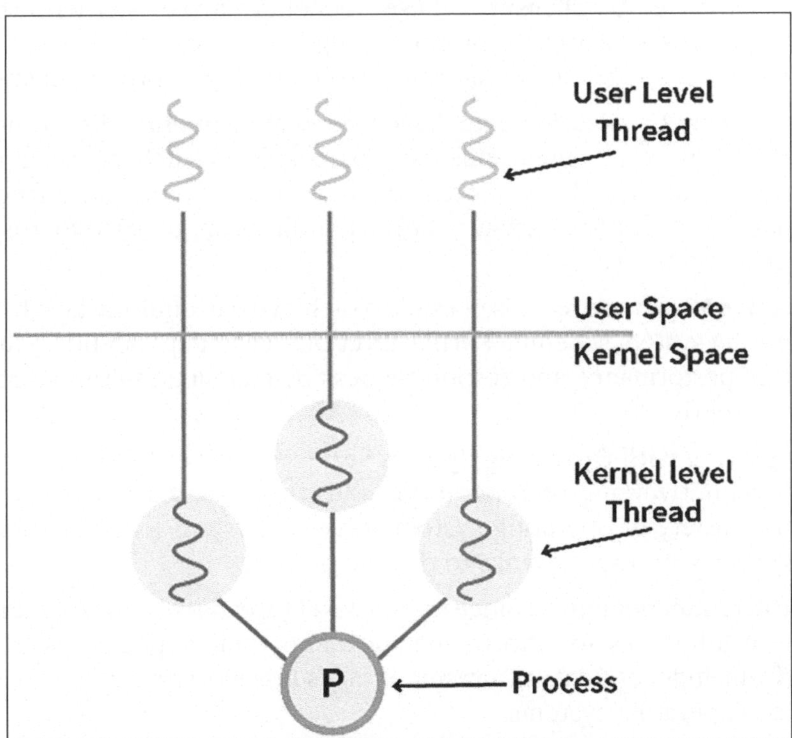

Figure 4.8: *Kernel-level thread*

The preceding diagram shows the functioning of user-level threads in user space and kernel-level threads in kernel space.

Examples of Kernel-Level Threading Scheme [3]

- **Linux Kernel Threads:** The kernel-level task management in Linux is accomplished through kernel-level threads. Typically, Linux kernel threads are represented by kernel structures such as `task_struct`. They are managed directly by the Linux kernel. Threads at the kernel level are made available by Solaris as part of its multithreading architecture.

  In Solaris, the Solaris Thread Library offers an interface for developers to create and manage threads, while the kernel handles thread management.

- **Windows Kernel Threads**: The kernel in the Windows operating system is responsible for overseeing kernel-level threads. Kernel threads are created and scheduled by the Windows kernel to carry out system-level operations. Structures such as `ETHREAD` are used to represent these threads.

Advantages of Kernel-Level Threads

- **Enhanced Parallelism and Scalability**: Kernel-level threads, being directly managed by the operating system, can efficiently utilize multicore processors and enhance parallelism. These benefits make kernel-level threads advantageous in a variety of computing scenarios. This leads to improved scalability in applications requiring a large amount of processing power.
- **Sturdy Synchronization and Resource Management:** The kernel provides direct support to synchronization mechanisms such as semaphores and mutexes, making them more effective and potent. Advanced resource management features ensure optimal utilization of system resources for kernel-level threads.
- **Effective Multitasking**: It is possible to achieve true multitasking by having the operating system schedule Kernel-level threads independently. This improves system performance and responsiveness by enabling multiple threads to run concurrently.
- **Integration with Operating System Services**: Kernel-level threads utilize file systems, networking, I/O operations, and other features to seamlessly integrate with a variety of operating system services. System-level functionalities are efficiently accessible, thanks to this integration.
- **Platform Independence:** Since kernel-level threads rely on common operating system interfaces for thread management, their applications can be more platform-independent. As a result, it takes less work to modify apps to run on various operating systems.
- **Priority-Based Scheduling**: This method provides more precise control over the order in which threads execute because the operating system scheduler

can give Kernel-level threads a priority. Applications with varying task priorities and real-time constraints need to consider this.

- **Support for Blocking Operations**: Kernel-level threads are capable of handling blocking operations, such as waiting for resources or I/O, with ease. The operating system can switch to another thread to make the best use of CPU time when a thread is blocked.
- **Adaptability:** System Conditions can be adapted to dynamically by kernel-level threads. Variations in load or resource availability can be handled dynamically by kernel-level threads. In response to demands that arise in real-time, the operating system can efficiently redistribute resources among threads.
- **Direct Access to Hardware Resources**: System-level software and device drivers, for example, may require low-level operations and interactions with hardware resources, which are made possible by kernel-level threads.

(1) Comparison of Various Prominent Characteristic Features of User-based and Kernel-based Threading.

Table 4.2 compares various prominent characteristic features of user-based and kernel-based threading.

Feature	**User-Level Thread**	**Kernel-Level Threads**
Management	Managed by user-level thread libraries	Managed by the operating system kernel
Context Switching	Lightweight and fast	Involves higher overhead
Parallelism	May not fully exploit multicore CPUs	Efficiently utilizes multicore processors
Synchronization	May lack robust kernel-level support	Strong support for synchronization mechanisms
Resource Management	Limited control over system resources	Direct access to system resources
Portability	More portable across different OSPlatform-dependent	Less portable
Blocking Operations	This may cause blocking of the entire process	Efficient handling of blocking operations
Visibility to OS	Independent of kernel, limited visibility	Directly interacts with the kernel, full visibility
Priority-Based Scheduling	Limited control over scheduling policies	Priority-based scheduling by the kernel
Development Complexity	Simplified, suitable for lightweight apps	Requires a deeper understanding of system concepts

Scalability	May face scalability challenges	Better scalability with proper kernel support
Access to Hardware Resources	Limited access to low-level operations	Direct access to hardware resources

Table 4.2: *Comparison of Various Prominent Characteristic Features of User-based and Kernel-based Threading*

Advantages of Using Threading

- A program runs more efficiently overall when it has threads.
- The program's responsiveness is increased by threads.
- Thread switching occurs more quickly.
- The memory and resources of a process are shared by all threads.
- Threads facilitate faster communication.
- Concurrency within a process is facilitated by threads.
- Increased system throughput.
- Threading improves efficiency by allowing for the simultaneous operation of multiple threads, which maximizes the use of the multiprocessor architecture.

Disadvantages of Using Threading [2]

A multitude of problems can occur when threading.

The semantics of the fork() and exec() system calls are described here, for example, the `fork()` call creates a duplicate child process.

The question of whether the thread that initiated the fork() call should be duplicated along with the entire process comes up during a fork() call. When you use the exec() function, a new program takes the place of the entire process–including all of its threads–that called it.

Thread Cancellation: Thread cancellation is the act of ending a thread before it has finished, and the thread that has been terminated is known as the target thread.

There are two methods for canceling a thread. They are:

Asynchronous cancellation, in which the target thread is terminated instantly by one thread.

Deferred Cancellation is when the target thread determines when to end.

Handling signals: In UNIX systems, a signal is used to inform a process that a specific event has occurred. Signal handling can be divided based on the signal's source:

- **Asynchronous Signal**: A signal that originates outside of the process receiving it. A synchronous signal is produced and delivered simultaneously by a single process.

- **Synchronous Signal:** A signal generated by the process itself due to its execution, often as a result of runtime errors like division by zero or accessing invalid memory.

Multithreading

Creating multiple threads within a single process rather than starting a new one is the idea behind multithreading. Since multithreading is faster in many of the ways that were previously discussed, it is used to achieve parallelism and enhance application performance.

Why is multithreading preferred over creating multiple processes in an operating system?

1. Consumes fewer resources compared to processes
2. Always guarantees better security compared to processes
3. Involves faster context switching than processes
4. Allows independent execution of tasks, unlike processes

Advantages of Multithreading

The list of additional benefits of multithreading is as follows:

A single process's threads share the same resources, including code and data/files [2].

- **Program Responsiveness**: This quality allows a program to continue running even when a section is blocked or needs to complete a time-consuming operation. Consequently, the user will receive more responsiveness.
- **Economy:** Since threads share the resources of a single process, using them is more cost-effective. However, the cost of developing processes is high.

Example of a Multithreaded Program

There are several real-world examples of multi-threading in action. One such example is a web server. A web server typically has multiple threads running concurrently to serve multiple clients simultaneously. A media player is another example of a multithread program.

CPU and I/O Bound Processes

While executing a process needs CPU and I/O devices both. There is a need to have a balanced mix of CPU and I/O bound.

CPU Bound Process

These processes execute at the speed of the computer processor or central processor unit and involve more CPU usage. For example, the processes involving complex calculations are CPU-bound processes.

Note: *These processes involve I/O devices also, but CPU involvement is more.*

I/O Bound Process

These processes are executed at the speed of the I/O subsystem and involve more usage of I/O devices than the CPU. I/O bound process spends a significant amount of time waiting for input or output from a peripheral device; for example, reading/ writing to a disk.

Since these processes can't proceed until the requested data is available, they can often be delayed by other processes that are running on the system. This can cause problems with CPU utilization and lead to overall system instability.

To optimize system performance, it's crucial to identify and allocate resources to I/O-bound processes. This can be done using a variety of schedules, such as the FCFS, SJF, and Round Robin schedulers.

Context Switching

Context switching is the process of temporarily taking control of a computer from its current task and then switching to a different task. This process allows users to perform different tasks on the computer simultaneously. It is one of the most important aspects of operating systems, as it will enable users to access various applications and files easily. Context switching has advantages and disadvantages.

Advantages

- Context switching allows users to quickly switch between tasks, which can be helpful when working on complex tasks.
- Context switching can also be used to keep users updated on various events in the operating system.
- It is so fast that it gives an illusion of execution of multiple processes at the same time.

Disadvantages

- Context switching can be time-consuming and require users to learn new techniques.

- The CPU remains idle and does not do any useful work.

Scheduler Activations

Scheduler activations are a threading technique that offers kernel-level thread functionality with user-level thread performance and flexibility when integrated into an operating system's process scheduler. Using a technique known as "N:M," this mechanism places an M number of kernel entities, or "*virtual processors*," on top of an N number of application threads. This is a trade-off between threading at the user-level ("N:1") and kernel-level ("1:1"). Since both kernel and user-space code modifications are required, 'N:M' threading systems are typically more complex to implement than pure kernel or user threads.

"Scheduler activations were proposed by Anderson, Bershad, Lazowska, and Levy in *Scheduler Activations: Effective Kernel Support for the User-Level Management of Parallelism* in 1991."[4]

Nathan Williams implemented support, but it has since been dropped in favor of 1:1 threading in the NetBSD kernel. Similar threading was implemented by FreeBSD under the name **Kernel Scheduled Entities**, which is likewise being phased out in favor of 1:1 threading. Additionally, scheduler activations were added by Vincent Danjean as a patch for the Linux kernel: Linux Activations, with the user-level implementation taking place in the Marcel thread library. By avoiding their drawbacks, Scheduler Activations aims to combine the advantages of kernel and user-level threads.

A virtual multiprocessor is given to each application. Every application has its own scheduler, which determines which threads on the physical processors the kernel assigns it to execute. Applications can specify how many threads they would like to run, and the kernel will attempt to allocate that number of physical processors to them. When the kernel assigns (removes) physical processors to an application, it does so based on its needs. When such events are required, this is accomplished by having the kernel issue an up-call to the application.

A scheduler activation transfers control from the kernel to the address space thread scheduler in response to a kernel event. The thread scheduler can utilize the activation to execute user-level threads, modify user-level thread data structures, and send kernel requests. The kernel mechanism known as a scheduler activation is what triggers an up-call to the application's thread scheduler when certain events, such as processor allocations and deallocations, must occur.

The interface that the kernel's scheduler activations system uses to alert an application to a scheduling-related event is called an upcall. Utilizing scheduler activations, an application registers a procedure, akin to registering a signal handler, to handle the upcall.

Scheduler Activation Upcalls

Scheduler activation upcalls are a mechanism that allows the kernel to communicate events to user-level threads in an operating system.

Working of Scheduler activation upcalls

Scheduler activation upcalls allow the kernel to send information to user-level threads, such as when a thread returns from the kernel or is preempted.

- Add this processor
- Processor has been pre-empted
- Scheduler activation has been blocked
- Scheduler activation has been unblocked

Application of downcalls

- Add more processors
- This processor is idle

Choosing between Threads or Processes

Use-wise, threads are commonly employed in database systems, web servers, and GUI programming, whereas processes are usually reserved for batch processing and scientific simulations. The decision between threads and processes, however, is dependent on the particular needs of your application; there isn't a universally applicable solution.

It's crucial to consider various aspects when choosing between threads and processes, including the amount of inter-task communication required, the required level of security or data integrity, and the application's performance requirements. Additionally, to ensure that your application functions properly, it's critical to understand and utilize the thread and process management features offered by the Linux operating system, such as the pthreads library.

Differences between Threads and Processes

We have learned about concept of Process in *Chapter 3, Concept of a Process and System Calls.*

A process and a thread are both mechanisms for achieving concurrency in an operating system. However, they have some key differences [5]:

- **Virtual Memory:** The memory space allocated to each process is distinct and separate from the memory spaces of other processes. The memory used by a thread is shared by the process that generated it.

- **Operating System Scheduling**: Threads are scheduled by the operating system to run on multiple CPUs or cores, whereas processes are usually scheduled by the system to run on a single CPU or core.

  Although the kernel schedules both processes and threads for execution, the scheduling algorithm may handle them differently. For instance, the kernel might schedule threads and processes differently.

  Resources are shared by threads and processes, respectively. Processes have their own resources, such as file descriptors and open sockets.

- **Inter-communication**: Processes have their own address space and can't directly communicate with other processes except via inter-process communication (IPC) mechanisms, such as pipes, sockets, and message queues.

  Threads within a process can directly communicate with one another through shared memory and share the same address space.

- **Isolation:** The processes are separate from one another; hence, they are not impacted by the failure of the other. However, since all threads share the same memory, a single thread failure might possibly bring down the entire process. While threads are lightweight execution units that share memory with processes and operate within their context, processes are autonomous entities scheduled by the operating system.

Scheduler Activations are a Threading Technique

Although it always depends on the particular requirements of your application, it can be challenging. A few things to think about when choosing this option are as follows:

- **Memory Space:** Processes are a better option if your application needs distinct memory spaces for various tasks.
- **Shared Data:** Threads are a better option because they share memory space if the tasks need to share data.
- **Synchronization:** Since threads and processes share the same memory, synchronization is typically simpler. Threads might be a better option if your application needs to synchronize data between tasks frequently.
- **Isolation**: Use processes for task isolation, such as ensuring that if one crashes, it won't impact the others.
- **Communication:** Since threads can communicate directly and share the same memory space, they may be more effective if tasks require frequent communication. In contrast, IPC mechanisms such as pipes, sockets, and message queues are usually used by processes for communication.

- **Portability:** The use of threads may be preferred if your application must be portable across various operating systems. This is because threads are commonly implemented using a standard library, such as POSIX threads, which is available on most operating systems.

Not to mention that the performance of your application can be greatly enhanced by selecting the appropriate parallel processing technique. Additionally, both threads and processes can be used in a single application and combined in any way that best fits the application's needs.

Examples of Threaded Programs

Although they have different properties and are best suited for different kinds of tasks, threads and processes are both strong tools for concurrent and parallel execution in a Linux environment. To make the most out of these tools, it is essential to comprehend how the two differ from one another as well as the thread and process management features offered by the Linux operating system.

Threads and processes are both essential ideas that are frequently used synonymously. But to use them effectively in your programming, especially in a Linux environment, there are some significant differences between the two that you should be aware of.

Threads and Processes in Linux

Threads are implemented in Linux as "*lightweight processes*," or "LWP," as a more compact version of processes. They share the same memory space as the parent process and are scheduled by the kernel, which means they can communicate with each other more easily and efficiently. They are therefore ideal for jobs requiring concurrent execution, such as database management, web servers, and GUI programming. [5]

Processes, on the other hand, are independent, self-contained execution environments with their own memory. With its own address space, file descriptors, and other resources, each process is separate from the others and operates independently. Inter-process communication is highly resource-intensive and complex. In scientific simulations and batch processing, for example, processes are usually employed for tasks that don't need to be completed simultaneously.

The task of controlling thread and process execution falls to Linux's scheduler. All threads and processes are assigned a priority value, and an algorithm based on priorities is used to decide which one should be executed next. The scheduler takes this value into account when determining the order in which threads and processes are executed. Higher-priority threads and processes are executed before lower-priority ones.

At the kernel level, the operating system schedules the execution of processes and threads, treating them both as tasks. They use CPU time and memory, and each have a distinct process ID (PID). The primary distinction between threads and processes at the kernel level is in how they share, use, and are scheduled in relation to the system resources.

Furthermore, it is noteworthy that different operating systems may implement threads and processes differently. Threads are implemented as a unique process in Windows, but they are treated as a separate entity from processes in other operating systems, such as Linux. Processes and threads can be created in some operating systems, such as Linux, using the system call **clone()**. The calling task shares all or some of its resources with the new task created by the **clone()** system call. The creation of a new thread or process can be achieved by specifying different flags.

In alternative operating systems, such as Windows, a new process is created using the system call **CreateProcess()**, and a new thread is created using the system call **CreateThread()**.

Under Linux, a new process is created by copying the calling process using the fork() system call, and a new thread is created using the **pthread_create()** system call.

Operating systems can differ in the particular system call that is used to generate processes and threads; however, depending on the flags and parameters that are passed to the system call, it is possible for the same system call to generate both types of objects.

POSIX thread library pthreads

In C, the POSIX thread library, also known as **pthreads**, provides a set of functions for creating and manipulating threads. To create a new thread, you can use the **pthread_create()** function. This function takes three arguments:

```
int id2 = pthread_create(pthread_t* thread_id,pthread_attr_t* attr, void
(*function)(void*),void* param);
```

1. A pointer to a **pthread_t** variable, which will be used to store the thread ID of the newly created thread.
2. A pointer to a **pthread_attr_t** variable, which can be used to set attributes for the new thread (such as the thread's scheduling policy or stack size). This argument is optional and can be set to **NULL** if the default attributes should be used.
3. A pointer to the function that the new thread should execute. This function should have a void *** argument and return void ***.
4. The last parameter is void* which is a parameter to be sent to the thread function from the parent thread or process.

For example, the following code creates a new thread that executes the **myThreadFunction()** function:

```
#include<pthread.h>
void *myThreadFunction(void *arg);

int main() {
    pthread_t myThread;
    pthread_create(&myThread, NULL, myThreadFunction, NULL);
    // ...
    pthread_exit(NULL);
}

void *myThreadFunction(void *arg) {
    // thread code here
    return NULL;
}
```

Figure 4.9: *myThreadFunction() function*

Remember, the thread created with **pthread_create** will operate in parallel with the calling thread.

When the parent thread has finished or terminated, the child thread can continue to run by using the **pthread_exit()** function. The parent thread stops executing along with any other threads still running in the process when it calls **pthread_exit()**. The child thread created using **pthread_create()** operates independently from the parent thread. This is because the operating system's kernel schedules and manages the child thread separately, providing it with its own stack and register values. This independence is particularly useful for running background tasks that need to continue even after the parent thread has completed its execution.

As an illustration, consider a daemon process or a network service that must continue to function even after the parent process ends. Not to mention, the behavior is undefined and may result in resource leaks or other unexpected behavior, if the main thread ends without joining or detaching the child thread.

To wait for the thread to complete its execution, we need to use the **pthread_join()** function which takes two arguments, thread ID and return value pointer.

```
void *thread_result
pthread_join(myThread, &thread_result);;
```

Figure 4.10: *pthread_join() function*

We need to include the **pthread.h** to use the **pthread** functions.

We need to link the **pthread** lib, that is, **lpthread** which is shared **lib(libpthread.so)** to run the threaded programs.

```
g++ pthreadProigram.cpp -lpthread -o pthreadOut
```

The reference programs used here don't check for the return values of thread functions.

But in real code, we need to check the return values of each thread functions, check for any possible errors, and take action.

Creating Process in Linux

A program or application that is running is referred to as a process in Linux. Every process has its own file descriptors, memory space, and distinct process ID (PID).

In Linux, the **fork()** system call can start a new process. A copy of the parent process that is making the call is created by the **fork()** system call. Certain characteristics of its parent process, such as the open file descriptors and environment, are passed down to the child process. The scheduler, which manages processes in the Linux kernel, assigns CPU time to each process. Each process is represented by a data structure called **task_struct**, which contains information about its priorities, resources, and present state.

A process in the Linux kernel is represented by the **task_struct** data structure, which is a kernel data structure. The file **"sched"** in the Linux kernel source code defines the **task_struct** data structure. "**h**". The **task_struct** data structure has the following key fields:

pid_t pid: The process ID of the process

pid_t tgid: The thread group ID of the process

struct task_struct *real_parent: A pointer to the parent process

struct task_struct *parent: A pointer to the real parent process or the thread group leader

struct list_head children: A list of child processes

struct list_head sibling: A list of sibling processes

struct mm_struct *mm: A pointer to the memory management structure for the process

struct task_struct *group_leader: A pointer to the thread group leader

struct files_struct *files: A pointer to the file descriptor table for the process

struct nsproxy *nsproxy: A pointer to the namespace proxy for the process

struct signal_struct *signal: A pointer to the signal handling structure for the process

struct sighand_struct *sighand: A pointer to the signal handlers for the process

struct pid *pids[PIDTYPE_MAX]: An array of pointers to the process ID structures for the process

To decide which process should be executed next, the scheduler employs a scheduling algorithm. A scheduler known as the Completely Fair Scheduler (CFS) is used by the Linux kernel and is intended to distribute CPU time among all processes in an equitable manner. The size of the **task_struct** data structure in the Linux kernel is determined by the system architecture, the kernel version, and the kernel configuration options. **Task_struct** can range in size from a few kilobytes to several hundred kilobytes.

It is significant to remember that the **task_struct** data structure is not exposed to user-space programs through the Application Programming Interface (API); rather, it is a kernel data structure. Therefore, without consulting the kernel source code and the configuration options unique to your system, it is impossible to determine the precise size of **task_struct**.

Furthermore, the features that are enabled in the kernel, such as real-time scheduling, threading on the kernel, CPU and memory hotplug, and other features that might cause the **task_struct** to grow in size, can also affect how big the **task_struct** is.

The first process created when a Linux system boots up is called **init**. It deals with launching and initializing other processes and has the process ID (PID) of 1. All other processes on the system are children of the **init** process, which is also in charge of harvesting the resources of any newly created zombies.

Under Linux, a doubly linked list serves as the task list, which keeps track of all the processes and threads currently operating on the system. A doubly linked list is created by connecting each **task_struct** in the list to the one before and after it uses a set of pointers. As a result, the kernel can quickly iterate through the list and carry out tasks, such as scheduling, context switching, and process management.

The list's head, **init_task**, is an instance of **task_struct** and serves as the list's representation. As the parent task of every other task in the system, **init_task** is created during kernel initialization. The system's **task_struct** structs, which are connected by next and previous pointers, each represent a task.

This doubly linked list is used by the kernel to iterate through all of the tasks and carry out tasks, such as scheduling, context switching, and process management. The task list is used by the kernel to determine which task should be executed next and to track each task's state (such as running, stopped, or zombie). The list is also used to control the resources of each task, including signal handlers, file descriptors, and memory.

To summarize, a doubly linked list is used to represent the task list in Linux. Each task is represented by a **task_struct** struct, which has a set of pointers connecting it to the **task_struct** that comes before and after in the list. This makes it simple for the kernel to navigate the list and carry out tasks, such as scheduling, context switching, and process management.

In addition to initiating other processes such as services and system daemons, the init process is in charge of safely shutting down the system in response to a shutdown signal. In addition to monitoring the system, the init process restarts any services that might have stopped working.

A list of processes that can be executed, known as the run queue, is expanded upon the creation of a new process. Using the scheduling algorithm that is currently in use and the process's priority, the scheduler chooses the next process to run from the run queue.

A single CPU can run multiple processes simultaneously, thanks to the scheduler's multitasking support. Time slicing is used to accomplish this, giving each process a brief window of the CPU to carry out its instructions before preempting it and returning it to the run queue. Later on, the procedure is rescheduled to continue as planned.

Real-time scheduling is another feature of the Linux kernel that enables processes with time constraints to be scheduled with a higher priority than regular processes. This makes it possible to prevent other processes from delaying real-time processes.

To further manage and restrict resources for a group of processes, the kernel also offers a feature known as "*cgroups*." In addition to preventing one process from monopolizing resources and impairing the performance of the other processes, this enables the guarantee of a particular level of resources for a particular set of processes.

The Linux kernel assigns CPU time to processes according to their priority and the scheduling algorithm in use. To manage resources and guarantee a specific level of resources for a specific group of processes, the kernel also provides features, such as time slicing, real-time scheduling, and cgroups. As mentioned earlier, Linux's fork() system call enables the creation of earlier processes. From the **fork()** system call, two returns are obtained: one in the child process and one in the parent.

In the parent process, the child process returns its PID, and in the child process, it returns 0. This enables them to be distinguished and have appropriate responses from the parent and child processes.

fork() call: In Linux, the **fork()** call is used to create new processes and creates a child process that inherits the following:

Identical copies of all parent variables, memory, and CPU registers (apart from one).

Both the parent and the child execute simultaneously after **fork()** returns:

Allocate memory for the child process; copy parent memory and CPU registers to the child's; the execution context of the child process is a copy of the parent's context at the time of the call.

- **Process Death:** In Linux, a process can die for several reasons, including completion of execution, receiving a signal, or crashing. The resources of a dying process are released, and its PID is made available for future use.
- **Death Handling**: A process may wish to pause its own execution until the child process has finished before launching another one. This is accomplished by using the **`wait()`** system call. The **`wait()`** system call stops the calling process from continuing to run until one of its child processes exits, stops, or is restarted by a signal. It also returns the child's PID and exit status. It is possible to ascertain whether a process encountered an error or was successfully finished by looking at its exit status. **`Waitpid()`** is a crucial system call that is connected to handling process death. The difference between this system call and **`wait()`** is that the caller can use the child's PID to indicate which child process to wait for. Furthermore, there's **`waitid()`**, which lets the caller wait for a particular child process and also get additional details about the child's state.

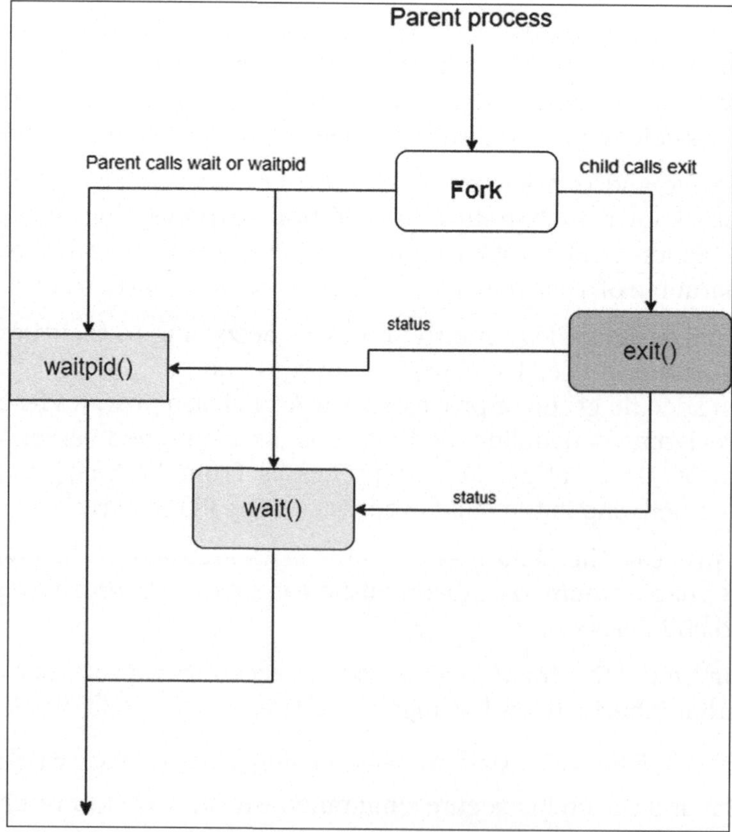

Figure 4.11: *wait() System Call*

Conclusion

We have learned that all computer actions have Processes made of several Threads. We have learned about process' states and resources, process Queues and major types of Thread. We then learned about the differences between process and thread.

We read to understand how is Multithreading made possible by CPU and I/O bound processes. Processes need Context Switching and Scheduler activations. At the end, we learned about Threads and Processes in Linux, Process Creation in Linux, and POSIX thread library pthreads.

In the next chapter, we shall learn about Process scheduling.

Questions

1. What is a process in context of operating system's programming?
2. What is meant by process state and how many process states are there?
3. With the help of a diagram explain how many resources are there in a Process?
4. Explain the concept of threads. Why threads are created and deployed?
5. Explain why threads are needed and intimate whether threads in an operating system can be of the same or different types.
6. Write down the names of three components of a thread.
7. Compare the main differences between Process and Thread.
8. What are Process Queues? Illustrate their type with the help of a diagram.
9. What are the two major types of threading schemes? Describe the user-level scheme in your own words with the help of a sketch.
10. Describe a Kernel-Level Threading schemes with the help of a sketch.
11. State some major advantages of Kernel-Level Threads and major challenges faced.
12. Compare of various prominent Characteristic features of User based and Kernel based threading.
13. What are the advantages of threading and issues faced while making and distributing threads?
14. Why is multithreading adopted and why is it preferred over creating multiple processes in an operating system? Provide at least one example of a multithreaded program.

15. Explain CPU and I/O bound processes individually quoting their examples.
16. What is achieved by Scheduler activations (a threading) technique?
17. Enumerate the differences between Threads and Processes.
18. Describe how the Threads and Processes dealt with in Linux?
19. What is POSIX thread library pthreads and how important is it in?
20. How is a Process created in Linux?

References

[1] Process, https://cio-wiki.org/wiki/Process

[2] Threads in Operating System, By Satyam Vivek, Last updated: 20 Apr 2024, https://www.scaler.com/topics/operating-system/threads-in-operating-system/

[3] User Level Threads and Kernel Level Threads, Narayan Bista,https://www.educba.com/user-level-threads-and-kernel-level-threads/

[4] Anderson, Thomas E.; Bershad, Brian N.; Lazowska, Edward D.; Levy, Henry M. (September 1991). "Scheduler activations: Effective kernel support for the user-level management of parallelism". Proceedings of the thirteenth ACM symposium on Operating systems principles. pp. 95–109. doi:10.1145/121132.121151. ISBN 0897914473.

[5] Thread/Process in Linux, https://www.linkedin.com/pulse/threadprocess-linux-amit-nadiger#:~:text=Thread/Process%20in%20Linux

CHAPTER 5
Scheduling

Introduction

This chapter will explore the need for process scheduling in operating systems and the various types of scheduling along with the algorithms required for efficient management. We will delve into the types of CPU scheduling algorithms, examining their features, advantages, and criteria for effective scheduling.

Time-sharing operating systems and their key characteristics, followed by an overview of multiprocessor scheduling, will also be discussed here. Additionally, we will learn multi-core processors and their programming techniques.

To deepen our understanding, we examine examples of thread scheduling using POSIX threads and learn how to create threads in Linux using the C programming language and the C static library.

Structure

In this chapter, we will study about the aspects of scheduling based on the following points:

- Overview of Scheduling and Scheduler
- The Need for Process Scheduling in OS
- Types of Process Schedulers
- Scheduling Algorithms
- Process Queues
- CPU Scheduling Algorithm
- Types of CPU Scheduling Algorithms with their Characteristic Features and Advantages
- Criteria for Effective CPU Scheduling
- Time-Sharing Operating System and its Key Features
- Multi-processor Scheduling

- Processor Affinity
- Load Balancing
- Multi-Core Processors
- Programming on Multiprocessor Systems
- Thread Scheduling Examples using POSIX Threads
- Creating a Thread in Linux using C Language
- C Static Library

Overview of Scheduling and Scheduler

The OS scheduler determines how to move processes between the ready and run queues. They ensure that processes are executed efficiently, making the best use of CPU resources and maintaining system responsiveness.

Types of Schedulers

There are a few different types of schedulers:

- Batch Operating System
- Time-sharing Operating System
- Multiprogramming Operating System
- Multiprocessing Operating system, and more.

Objectives of Process Scheduling

- Optimize the use of resources present
- Keep the CPU busy and utilize the CPU to the maximum.
- Minimum response time for executing a process means the shortest possible time for process execution

A scheduler is a software that helps schedule the processes in an operating system. It helps to keep all computer resources busy and allows multiple users to share system resources effectively. Let's go through different schedulers in an operating system.

Long-term Schedulers

The created processes exist in the NEW state. The RAM is filled with the programs, so they can run. The processes are therefore added to the READY queue prior to execution. Here's where long-term schedulers (LTS) come in: do they enter the ready queue themselves? It also goes by the name *"job scheduler."* Processes are chosen by these schedulers from secondary memory and added to the ready queue. LTS operates less often. Preserving the level of multiprogramming is LTS's primary goal.

Multiprogramming is the process of using a single processor to run multiple programs. But not all of the processes at once. It implies that if a process is not running for any reason, another process will have an opportunity to run. When multiprogramming is done at its best, the average rate of a process equals the average rate at which it is executed and exits the system.

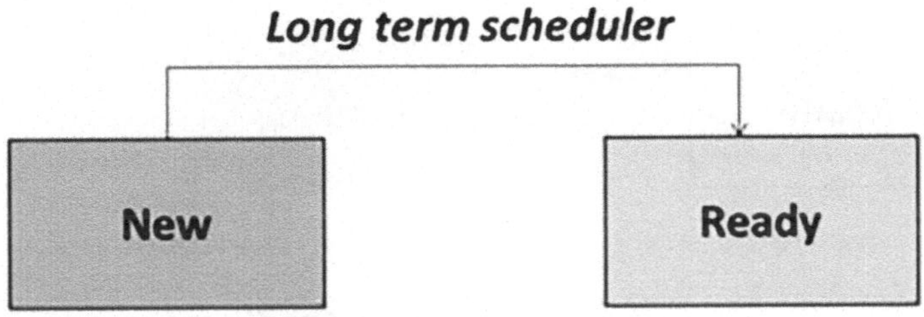

Figure 5.1: *Long-Term Scheduler*

Short-term Schedulers

Another name for it is a CPU scheduler. The processes are ready to be carried out when they are in the ready queue. Thus, one process is chosen from the ready queue by the short-term schedulers, who then move it to the running queue and assign a CPU to it. They are also referred to as the dispatcher since they choose the next process to run. Compared to long-term schedulers, they are faster. The selection of short-term schedulers affects the system's performance. Other processes in the waiting queue will continue to wait in the ready queue if it chooses the processes with the highest burst times. We refer to this state as starvation.

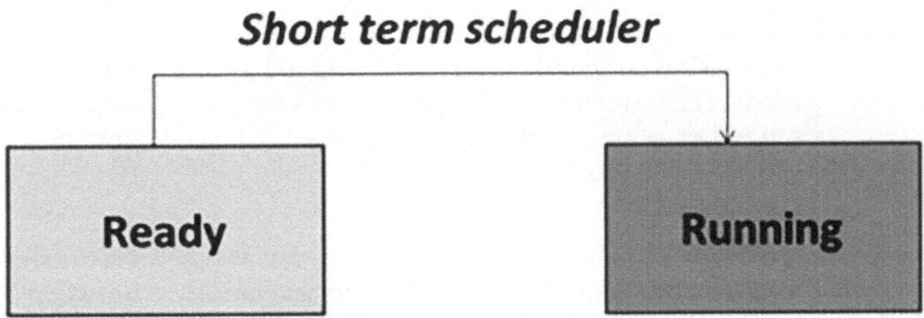

Figure 5.2: *Short-Term scheduler*

Medium-term Schedulers

Sometimes program execution is halted when the process receives a CPU assignment and gets going. An I/O request or a high-priority process could be the cause. Processes that have been suspended in this situation are unable to finish. As a result, the process needs to be ended to free up memory for new ones. The process that was put on hold is returned to the secondary storage. In the given illustration, process 1 was running when it was suspended for some reason. In this case, process 1 is replaced with process 2 in the system. This indicates that there is a swap going on here. We have a medium-term scheduler for swapping.

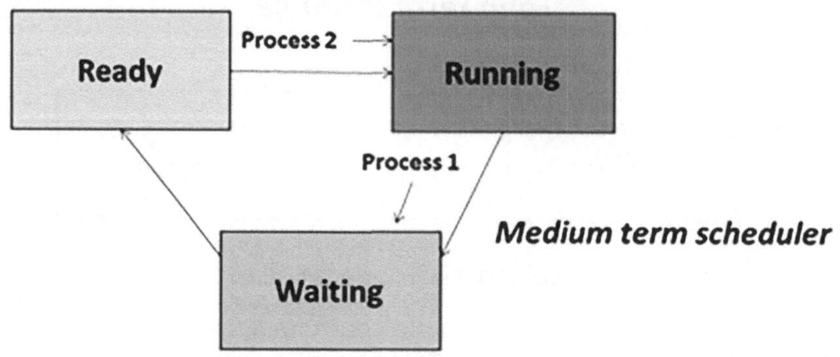

***Figure* 5.3**: *Medium-Term scheduler*

A comparison is shown among long-term, short-term, and medium-term schedulers in *Table* 5.1.

Criteria	**Long-Term Scheduler (LTS)/job scheduler**	**Short-Term Scheduler (STS)/ CPU scheduler**	**Medium-Term Scheduler (MTS)/ swapping scheduler**
Type of process	It chooses a combination of CPU-bound and I/O-bound processes	It chooses the process to be executed	It chooses the process which needs to be swapped in/out
Speed	Have a slower speed than a short-term scheduler as different processes are to be selected	Fastest Speed as one process is selected at one time	It has a medium speed, that is, speed between the other two
Frequency of execution	It executes much less frequently as its job is to load processes in the ready queue only	The short-term scheduler executes more frequently, at least once every 100 milliseconds	Frequency is in between both
Degree of multi-programming	It controls the number of processes in the memory	Ensures less DOM (degree of multiprogramming)	It reduces DOM (degree of multiprogramming)

Working	It selects a process from a pool of processes and loads it into the READY queue	Selects a process in the READY state and put it in the RUNNING state for execution	If some interrupt comes, it swaps the process out and swaps the process back for execution

***Table 5.1**: Comparison of OS Schedulers*

Three Types of Scheduling in OS

Operating systems can have up to three different schedulers: a mid-term or medium-term scheduler, a short-term scheduler, and a long-term scheduler (also called an admission scheduler or high-level scheduler). The names allude to how frequently their respective roles are carried out. An operating system module called the scheduler chooses which jobs and processes will be added to the system next.

Process Scheduler

The operating system component that selects which process to execute at a given time is called the process scheduler. A scheduler that can do this is called a preemptive scheduler; if not, it is referred to as a cooperative scheduler. It can pause an existing process, move it to the back of the running queue, and launch a new one.

Based on the frequency of decision-making, we differentiate between three types of scheduling: medium-term, short-term, and long-term.

Long-term Scheduling

The long-term scheduler, also known as the admission scheduler, determines which jobs or processes are admitted to the ready queue, or main memory. In other words, the long-term scheduler authorizes or delays a program's admission to the set of currently executing processes when an attempt is made to execute it. As a result, this scheduler sets the policies for what processes can run on a system, how much concurrency can be supported at any given time (that is, how many or how few processes can run concurrently), and how to divide up work between CPU- and I/O-intensive tasks. The degree of multiprogramming is managed by the long-term scheduler.

Most processes can generally be categorized as CPU-bound or I/O-bound. A process that dedicates a larger portion of its time to input/output rather than computation is said to be I/O-bound. In contrast, a CPU-bound process spends more time performing computations and generates I/O requests less frequently. A long-term scheduler must carefully choose a balance between CPU- and I/O-bound processes. The ready queue will nearly always be empty, and the short-term scheduler won't have much work to do if every process is I/O-bound. However, if every process is CPU-bound, the system will once more become unbalanced as the I/O waiting queue will nearly never be full and devices will go unused. Processes that are both CPU- and I/O-bound will therefore be present in the system that performs the best. This is used in contemporary operating systems to ensure that real-time processes have adequate CPU time to complete their tasks.

In large-scale systems such as render farms, supercomputers, computer clusters, and batch processing systems, long-term scheduling is also crucial. To avoid processes from blocking because they are waiting on one another, for instance, co-scheduling interacting processes is frequently necessary in concurrent systems. In these situations, in addition to any underlying operating system support for admission scheduling, special-purpose job scheduler software is usually used to support these functions.

Certain operating systems only permit the addition of new tasks when it is certain that all real-time deadlines can still be fulfilled. The admission control mechanism of an operating system is the particular heuristic algorithm that it uses to accept or reject new tasks.

Medium-term Scheduling

Known as swapping out or swapping in (also incorrectly called paging out or paging in), the medium-term scheduler temporarily moves processes from main memory to secondary memory (such as a hard disk drive) or vice versa. To free up main memory for other processes, the medium-term scheduler may choose to swap out a process that hasn't been active in a while: one that has a low priority, one that page faults frequently, or one that uses a lot of memory. The process may then be swapped back in later when more memory becomes available or when it has been unblocked and isn't waiting for a resource.

The medium-term scheduler may act as the long-term scheduler in many modern systems (those that allow mapping virtual address space to secondary storage other than the swap file) by treating binaries as swapped-out processes when they execute. This allows for the on-demand or lazy loading–also known as demand paging–of a binary segment when needed.

Short-term Scheduling

The CPU scheduler, also referred to as the short-term scheduler, determines which of the ready-to-run in-memory processes will be given a CPU to execute when a signal such as an I/O interrupt, clock interrupt, operating system call, or another type of signal occurs. Because scheduling decisions must be made at least after each time slice, which is very short, the short-term scheduler makes scheduling decisions far more frequently than the long-term or mid-term schedulers.

This scheduler can be non-preemptive (also called voluntary or cooperative), in which case it cannot force processes off the CPU, or preemptive (implying that it can forcibly remove processes from a CPU when it decides to allocate that CPU to another process). Preemptive scheduling is based on a programmable interval timer that triggers an interrupt handler to carry out the scheduling function while operating in kernel mode.

Dispatcher

Another part of the CPU-scheduling function is the dispatcher module, which is responsible for assigning the CPU to the process that the short-term scheduler has chosen. A system call or interrupt causes it to take over in kernel mode. A dispatcher's duties include the following:

- The dispatcher loads the initial or previously saved state of the new process after performing context switches, which involve saving the state (also called context) of the thread or process that was previously running and going into user mode.
- Restarting the program by jumping to the appropriate place within the user program, as indicated by its updated status. Given that it is called upon at every process transition, the dispatcher ought to operate as quickly as possible. Repetitive context switches should be avoided since they cause the processor to be essentially idle for a brief period. The dispatch latency is the time it takes for the dispatcher to switch between processes.

Scheduling Algorithms

The operating system executes several programs and procedures to guarantee the computer operates as intended. The demand for CPU and other resources is high because many processes operate simultaneously. The idea of scheduling thus enters the picture. The OS performs scheduling to effectively distribute CPU time to running processes. The various operating system scheduling algorithms can be used to complete the scheduling process. The various methods of scheduling processes to guarantee optimal and effective CPU utilization are defined by scheduling algorithms. The order in which processes should be executed or terminated is decided by the process scheduler using these algorithms. Operating systems have two types of scheduling algorithms: preemptive and non-preemptive.

Process in Programming

A process in computer programming is a program that is running at that particular time. A program should ideally do nothing until and unless the instructions are carried out by a CPU. To put it briefly, a process is a program being carried out. This raises the question of who determines which process to continue running at what time or in what order the programs must be executed. The answer is, of course, process scheduler.

Process Scheduler

In an operating system, process scheduling refers to the process of selecting which process, or when, to execute first, based on a specific strategy or algorithm. The process manager does this by choosing a new process from the queue and removing the current one from the CPU. Most applications are multi-programming, which means that OS scheduling is necessary. They make it possible for several processes to load and share the CPU at once. The manager is responsible for selecting the procedures that needs to be carried out first.

Three Major Process Scheduler Types

The three major process scheduler types are as follows:

- Long-term job scheduler
- Medium-term scheduler
- CPU or short-term scheduler

Another component of process scheduling is the process queues. All the programs and processes in the system are split up into queues as follows:

- **Job queue**: All the programs in the system stay in this queue before they are up for execution.
- **Ready queue**: The programs ready to be executed remain in this queue; just before they are picked up for execution.
- **Device queue**: This queue consists of the processes that have been blocked due to a lack of input/output (I/O) device.

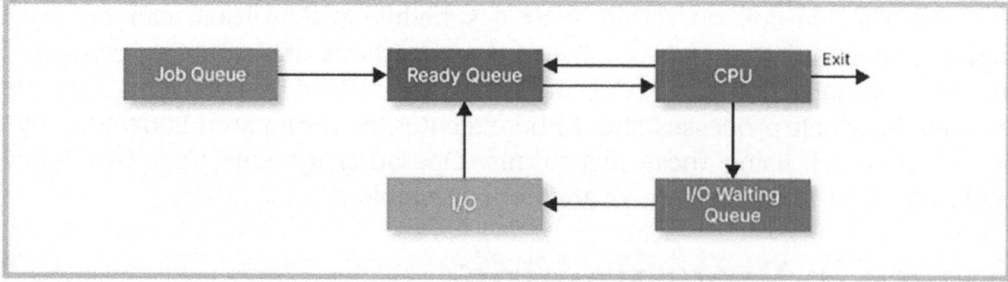

Figure 5.4: *Process Queue in Operating System*

The Need for Process Scheduling in OS

The operating system (OS) has several programs that are waiting to be executed at any given time, as was previously mentioned. For the OS to function properly, these programs must be launched, stopped, and then switched to another program. For the OS to decide which program to run and when to pause and switch, it needs the assistance of a process scheduler.

Through scheduling, the OS can allot CPU time to each process in accordance with a predetermined plan or algorithm. To ensure that the OS makes the best use of CPU time, process scheduling also keeps the CPU busy constantly. As a result, there is less time wasted and a minimum amount of waiting for a program to be executed. Ensuring that the turnaround time for a process's execution is kept to a minimum is necessary. It also lessens or minimizes the programs' response times.

CPU Scheduling Algorithm

Now that we have covered most of the basics, let's discuss what is a scheduling algorithm. A scheduling algorithm in an operating system determines the allocation of CPU time to processes and specifies when each process should receive it. There are two types of scheduling algorithms:

Non-preemptive scheduling algorithms- For these algorithms, once a process starts running, they are not stopped until completion. That is, under non-preemptive algorithms, processes cannot be pre-empted in favor of other high-priority processes before their runtime is over.

Preemptive scheduling algorithms- These algorithms allow for low-priority processes to be preempted in favor of a high-priority process even if they haven't run to completion.

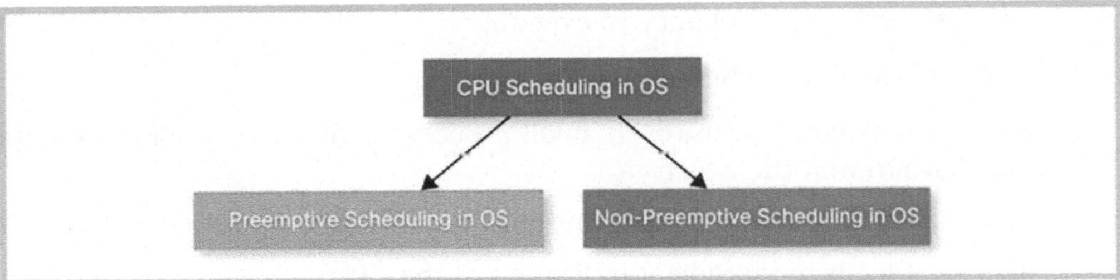

***Figure 5.5**: Two Major Types of Scheduling Algorithms*

The objectives of these process scheduling algorithms are [1]:

- Maximize CPU utilization
- Maximize throughput (that is, number of processes to complete execution per unit time)
- Minimize wait, turnaround, and response time

Different Types of CPU Scheduling Algorithms [1]

There are 10 major types of CPU scheduling algorithms which are discussed in detail ahead.

First Come First Serve (FCFS) Scheduling Algorithm

The FCFS algorithm is the simplest scheduling algorithm in OS. This is because the deciding principle behind it is just as its name suggests: on a first come basis. The job that requests execution first gets the CPU allocated to it, then the second, and so on.

Characteristics of FCFS scheduling algorithm

- The algorithm is easy to understand and implement
- Programs are executed on a first come first serve basis
- It is a non-preemptive scheduling algorithm
- In this case, the ready queue acts as the First In First Out (FIFO) queue, where the job that gets ready for execution first, also gets out first
- This is used in most batch OS

Advantages of FCFS scheduling algorithm

- The fact that it is simple to implement means it can easily be integrated into a pre-existing system
- It is useful, especially when the processes have a large burst time since there is no need for context switching.
- The absence of low or high-priority preferences makes it fairer
- Every process gets its chance to execute

Disadvantages of the FCFS scheduling algorithm

- Since its first come basis, even small processes with a very short execution time, have to wait their turn
- There is a high wait and turnaround time for this scheduling algorithm in OS
- All in all, it leads to inefficient utilization of the CPU

Example of FCFS scheduling algorithm in OS:

Process	Arrival Time	Service Time	Waiting Time	Turnaround Time
A	0	3	3-0-3=0	0+3=3
B	2	6	9-6-2=1	1+6=7
C	4	4	13-4-4=5	5+4=9
D	6	5	18-5-6=7	7+5=12
E	8	2	20-2-8=10	10+2=12
			AVG=4.6	AVG=8.6

Figure 5.6*: FCFS Scheduling Algorithm in OS Example*

Five processes have arrived at the CPU at different times in the preceding table. The first through is the process with the shortest arrival time. Given that the first process has a burst time of three, the CPU will be busy for three units of time. This means that when the second process arrives at T=2, it will have to wait one unit of time. The waiting and turnaround times for each process can be computed in this manner. Additionally, the average waiting time and average turnaround time are provided. This can be compared to alternative algorithms for the same collection of operations.

Keeping track of which process is executed at what stage is made easier by using a queue. Despite being among the most basic algorithms for CPU scheduling, it has a problem with the convoy effect. This happens when several smaller processes are slowed down by a larger process, resulting in a very long average wait time. This is comparable to several vehicles being trapped behind a slow-moving truck on a one-lane road.

Shortest Job First (SJF) Scheduling Algorithm

The Shortest Job First (SJF) is a CPU scheduling algorithm that selects the shortest jobs on priority and executes them. The idea is that jobs with short burst time get done quickly, making CPU available for other, longer jobs/processes. In other words, this is a priority scheduling algorithm based on the shortest burst time.

Characteristics of SJF scheduling algorithm

- This CPU scheduling algorithm has a minimum average wait time since it prioritizes jobs with the shortest burst time
- If there are multiple short jobs, it may lead to starvation
- This is a non-preemptive scheduling algorithm
- Easier to implement the SJF algorithm in Batch OS

Advantages of SJF scheduling algorithm

- Minimizes the average waiting time and turnaround time
- Beneficial in long-term scheduling
- Is better than the FCFS scheduling algorithm
- Useful for batch processes

Disadvantages of the SJF scheduling algorithm

- As mentioned, if short time jobs keep on coming, it may lead to starvation for longer jobs
- Is dependent upon burst time but not always possible to know the burst time beforehand
- Does not work for interactive systems

Example of SJF scheduling algorithm in OS:

Process	Arrival Time	Service Time	Waiting Time	Turnaround Time
A	0	3	3-0-3=0	0+3=3
B	2	6	9-6-2=1	1+6=7
C	4	4	15-4-4=7	7+4=11
D	6	5	20-6-5=9	9+5=14
E	8	2	11-8-2=1	1+2=3
			AVG=3.6	AVG=7.6

Figure 5.7: *SJF Scheduling Algorithm Example*

Here, the first two processes are carried out in the order they arrive, but the fifth process, which has the shortest burst time, immediately moves to the front of the queue. In accordance, the turnaround and waiting times are computed. This is clearly an improvement because there is a noticeable decrease in both average waiting time and average turnaround time compared to FCFS. This algorithm is extremely helpful when there are several incoming processes and their burst times are known ahead of time. It is less when compared with the average waiting time obtained with the first-come, first-served scheduling algorithm.

The Longest Job First (LJF) scheduling algorithm is the OS counterpart of the SJF scheduling algorithm. According to this algorithm, jobs with the longest burst times should be completed first, followed by jobs with shorter burst times.

Characteristic features of LJF Scheduling Algorithm

- Incoming execution requests are sorted based on burst time in descending order
- A non-preemptive CPU scheduling algorithm
- If two jobs have the same burst time, then FCFS is followed
- This priority scheduling in OS is both non-preemptive and preemptive

Advantages of LJF Scheduling Algorithm

The longest job gets done on priority. That is, no other job gets executed until the longest one completes the execution phase.

Disadvantages of LJF Scheduling Algorithm

- It may cause starvation in jobs with a short burst time
- The average waiting and turnaround time is high
- The CPU needs to know the burst time beforehand which is not always possible

P.No.	Arrival Time (AT)	Completion Time (CT)	Burst Time (BT)	Turnaround Time (TAT)	Waiting Time (WT)
P1	1	3	2	2	0
P2	2	21	4	19	15
P3	3	9	6	6	0
P4	4	17	8	13	5

***Figure 5.8**: Example of LJF Scheduling Algorithm*

Following the execution of the first process, the user can choose between the second and third processes. Due to its longer burst time, the third one is chosen. Since the fourth process also has a longer burst time than the second, it is executed next. At last, the second process is given the opportunity to begin. Because shorter processes may have to wait a long time to be executed, this method of CPU scheduling results in extremely high waiting times. This results in the convoy effect mentioned earlier as well.

OS Priority Scheduling Algorithm: The OS prioritizes its CPU scheduling algorithm so that the higher priority jobs are completed first. In other words, the task with the highest priority is completed first, then the task with the second highest priority, and so on.

Characteristics of Priority Scheduling Algorithm

- Jobs are scheduled based on the priority level, in descending order.
- If a job with a higher priority than the one running currently comes on, the CPU preempts the current job in favor of the one with higher priority.
- But for other purposes, it follows a non-preemptive scheduling approach.
- In between two jobs with the same priority, the FCFS process decides which job get executed first.
- The priority of a process can be set depending on multiple factors, such as memory requirements, required CPU time, and so on.

Advantages of Priority Scheduling Algorithm

- This process is simpler than most other scheduling algorithms in OS
- Priorities help in sorting the incoming processes
- Works well for static and dynamic environments

Disadvantages of Priority Scheduling Algorithm

- It may lead to the starvation problem in jobs with low priority
- The average turnaround and waiting time might be higher compared with the other CPU scheduling algorithms

Example of Priority Scheduling Algorithm in OS:

Process	Arrival Time	Service Time	Waiting Time	Turnaround Time
A	0	5	32-10-0=32	22+10=32
B	2	2	6-6-0=0	0+6=6
C	4	4	22-7-1=14	14+7=21
D	6	1	10-4-1=5	5+4=9
E	8	3	15-5-2=8	8+5=13
			AVG=9.8	AVG=16.2

***Figure 5.9**: Priority Scheduling Algorithm Example*

In this case, the incoming processes are given varying priorities. The higher the priority, the lower the number. Since the second process has a higher priority than the first, it will be carried out first. Next comes the turn of the fourth process. We call this scheduling priorities. Although the estimated times might not be the quickest, it helps in giving critical processes precedence over less crucial ones.

Round Robin Scheduling Algorithm in OS: The OS specifies a quantum time or a fixed time frame in this scheduling algorithm. Additionally, each job runs in a cycle for a predetermined amount of time before being preempted to make room for the subsequent job in the ready queue. Before they are finished, jobs that are preempted return to the ready queue to wait for their turn. In operating systems, it is also known as the preemptive FCFS scheduling algorithm.

Example of Round Robin Scheduler

As seen in *Figure* 5.7, the scheduler executes the three incoming processes part by part.

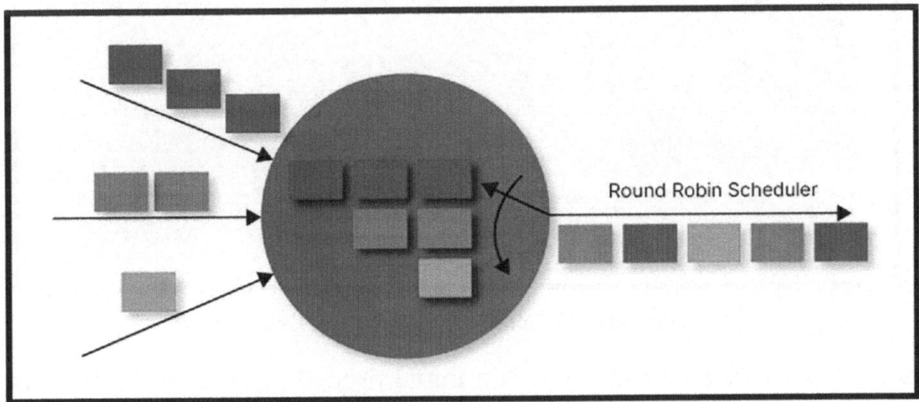

***Figure* 5.10**: *Example of Round Robin Scheduling Algorithm*

Characteristics of Round Robin Scheduling Algorithm

- Once a job begins running, it is executed for a predetermined time and gets preempted after the time quantum is over
- Easy and simple to use or implement
- One of the most commonly used CPU scheduling algorithms in OS
- A preemptive algorithm

Advantages of RR Scheduling Algorithm

- A fair algorithm since all jobs get equal time of CPU
- Does not lead to any starvation problems
- New jobs are added at the end of the ready queue and do not interrupt the ongoing process
- Leads to efficient utilization of the CPU

Disadvantages of RR Scheduling Algorithm

- Every time the job runs the course of quantum time, a context switch happens. This adds to the overhead time, and ultimately the overall execution time

- A low slicing time may lead to low CPU output
- Important tasks aren't given priority
- Difficult to choose the correct time quantum

Example of RR Scheduling Algorithm in OS:

Process	Arrival Time	Service Time	Waiting Time	Turnaround Time
A	0	3	3-3-0=0	0+3=3
B	2	6	17-6-2=9	9+6=15
C	4	4	11-4-4=3	3+4=7
D	6	5	20-6-5=9	9+5=14
E	8	2	19-2-8=9	9+2=11
			AVG=6	AVG=10

Figure 5.11: *RR Scheduling Algorithm Example*

Consider a four-unit quantum time. The initial procedure will start and finish. The second process runs for four units after a one-unit break. Since it has also reached the ready queue, the third one runs next. Four units later, the fourth process starts. This process continues until every step is completed. The minimum average waiting time is higher than for some other algorithms, which is important. Although it takes longer to complete tasks, this method outperforms most other OS scheduling algorithms in multitasking situations.

The preemptive variant of the SJF scheduling algorithm: This is the Shortest Remaining Time First (SRTF) scheduling algorithm. As a result, the job with the shortest burst time remaining must be completed first. Jobs are then preempted based on burst time remaining in ascending order.

Characteristics of the SRTF Scheduling Algorithm

- The incoming processes are sorted based on their CPU-burst time
- It requires the least burst time to be executed first, but if another process arrives that has an even lesser burst time, then the former process will get preempted for the latter
- A process is executed for some specific unit of time and then the scheduler checks if any new processes with even shorter burst times have arrived

Advantages of SRTF Scheduling Algorithm

- More efficient than SJF since it's the preemptive version of SJF
- Efficient scheduling for batch processes.
- Lower average waiting time compared to many other scheduling algorithms in OS

Disadvantages of SRTF Scheduling Algorithm

- Longer processes may starve if short jobs keep getting the first shot
- Can't be implemented in interactive systems
- Frequent context switching, leading to a rise in the overall completion time
- The remaining burst time might not always be apparent before the execution.

An example of the SRTF scheduling algorithm in OS is shown in *Figure* 5.9:

Process	Arrival Time	Service Time	Waiting Time	Turnaround Time
A	0	3	3-0-3=0	0+3=3
B	2	6	15-6-2=7	7+6=13
C	4	4	8-4-4=0	0+4=4
D	6	5	20-5-6=9	9+5=14
E	8	2	10-2-8=0	0+2=2
			AVG=3.6	AVG=7.2

***Figure* 5.12**: *SRTF Scheduling Algorithm Example*

In this case, the first process begins first, and the second process runs for one unit of time after that. The third process, which has a shorter service time, arrives next and preempts the second one. This continues until all processes are executed and the ready queue is empty.

The CPU scheduling algorithm - Longest Remaining Time First (LRTF): This is a rudimentary form of the LJF algorithm. It demands that the jobs with the longest remaining burst time is completed first.

Characteristics of the LRTF Scheduling Algorithm

- The incoming processes are sorted based on their burst time, in descending order
- Schedules the jobs with longer remaining burst time, first

- The CPU scheduler keeps checking for new jobs with long burst times in regular intervals; next, preempts the current job in favor of other longer burst time remaining jobs

Advantages of LRTF Scheduling Algorithm

- More efficient than LJF since it is the preemptive version of the same
- Almost all jobs get done at the same time, approximately
- Prioritizes longer jobs first, leaving shorter ones for later

Disadvantages of LRTF Scheduling Algorithm

- The average waiting and turnaround time are extremely high
- Shorter jobs may be neglected in favor of longer ones, causing starvation
- Burst time should be known beforehand

Example of LRTF scheduling algorithm in OS:

Waiting Time (WT)	Turnaround Time (TAT)	Completion Time (CT)	P.No.	Arrival Time (AT)	Burst Time (BT)
15	17	18	P1	1	2
13	17	19	P2	2	4
11	17	20	P3	3	6
9	17	21	P4	4	8

***Figure* 5.13**: *LRTF Scheduling Algorithm Example*

The first process runs for one unit, after which the second process preempts it. The third process then preempts the second one, which is further preempted by the fourth process. The ones that take the longest are put to death first.

Highest Response Ratio Next (HRRN) Scheduling Algorithm: This scheduling algorithm requires determining the response ratios of each job. Next, it prioritizes the jobs by choosing the one with the highest response ratio to complete. The following formula is used to get the response ratio (RR).

```
Response Ratio = (W+B)/ B
```

where, W is the waiting time, and B is the burst time/ service time.

Characteristics of HRRN Scheduling Algorithm

- The HRRN algorithm selects the job with the highest response ratio and puts it up for execution

- Once this job is executed, all the jobs are again put in the read queue to calculate wait time, and then the response ratio is calculated again, and it goes on
- In case two jobs have the same response ratio, the FCFS method is used to select which is put to execution, first
- This is a non-preemptive algorithm, that is, once a job is put to execution, the next response ratio is not calculated until the job completes the execution process

Advantages of HRRN Scheduling Algorithm

- More efficient than SJF scheduling
- The throughput for this algorithm is high or at least more than many other scheduling algorithms in OS
- While on the one hand, the waiting time for longer jobs is lesser, on the other it encourages the execution of shorter jobs

Disadvantages of HRRN Scheduling Algorithm

- It is not the most implemented algorithm since we cannot always know the burst time for every job beforehand
- Processor overhead may occur

Example of HRRN scheduling algorithm in OS:

Process	Burst Time	Arrival Time
P1	3	1
P2	6	3
P3	8	5
P4	4	7
P5	5	8

***Figure 5.14**: An Example for HRRN Scheduling Algorithm*

In the following figure, Gantt Chart used in the HRRN scheduling algorithm is given:

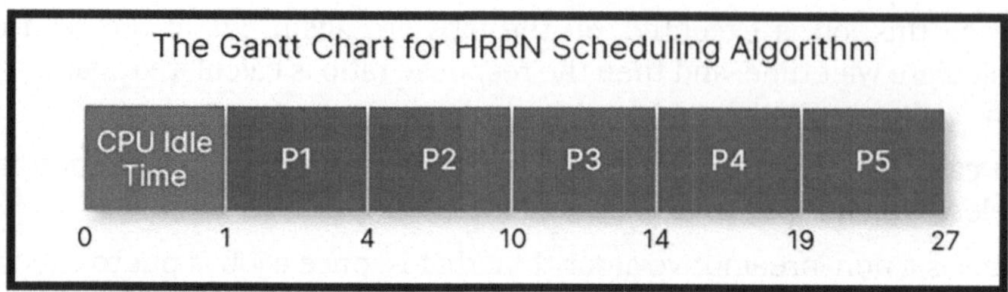

***Figure 5.15**: Gantt Chart used in HRRN Scheduling Algorithm*

At time 0, there is no job in the ready queue, so the CPU remains idle from time 0 to 1. At time 1, P1 comes in and since no other job is available P1 runs to execution without the need to calculate the response ratio. This runs till time 4, at which the only job in the queue is P2, so it runs till completion to time 10. At time 10, all P3, P4, and P5 are available so there is a need to calculate the response ratios, which is done as follows:

```
RR(P3) = [(10-5)+8]/8 = 1.625
RR(P4) = [(10-7)+4]/4 = 1.75
RR(P5) = [(10-8)+5]/5 = 1.40
```

So, at time 10, the response ratio for P4 is the highest which is why this job is executed next. When it runs the completion, the next job to execute is again decided based on the response ratio. And it goes on.

Multiple-level Queue (MLQ) Scheduling Algorithm: The first step in the multiple-level queue scheduling approach is to categorize each process in the ready queue into distinct classes according to how they require scheduling. These result in forming several queues, such as batch and foreground job queues. The OS then handles each of these queues separately, executing various algorithms on them.

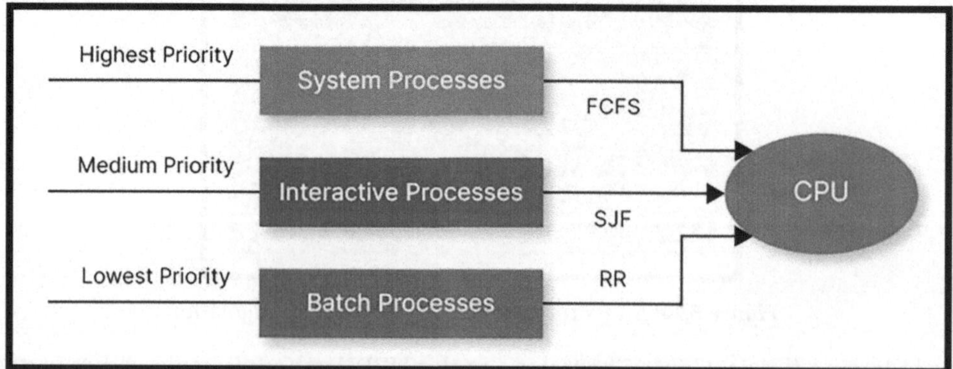

***Figure 5.16**: An Example of MLQ Scheduling Algorithm*

The preceding figure displays how processes are separated based on their priority depending on the type and executed using different algorithms; here, for example, FCFS, SJF, and the Round-Robin (RR) scheduling algorithms.

Characteristics of MLQ Scheduling Algorithm

- Jobs with common characteristics are grouped into individual queues
- Each queue is assigned a scheduling algorithm depending on specific needs
- The queues are then given priority to decide which queue gets CPU time first

Advantages of MLQ Scheduling Algorithm

- Uses a combination of algorithms to provide the best results
- The overhead time is less

Disadvantages of MLQ Scheduling Algorithm

- Once a job is assigned to a queue it cannot be changed, leading to inflexibility and hence inefficiency
- This may lead to a starvation problem if high-priority queue does not allow for low-priority queues to take turns
- Not easy to implement
- Sorting the jobs might become complex

Multilevel Feedback Queue (MLFQ) Scheduling Algorithm: The MLFQ algorithm is similar to the MLQ algorithm, with the primary difference being it preempts depending on feedback. That is, in MLFQ scheduling, there is an allowance for jobs to switch between queues.

Criteria for Effective CPU Scheduling

Let us study the criteria required for effective CPU scheduling:

- **Maximizing CPU Utilization:** Efficient CPU time management involves maximizing the maximum utilization of the central processing unit. This process helps maintain a high level productivity within the system. CPU utilization is crucial in CPU scheduling in operating systems, ensuring the processor is always busy. By keeping the CPU busy, it enhances system performance and efficiency.
- **Maximizing Throughput:** Another important aspect of effective CPU scheduling is maximizing throughput. By focusing on increasing throughput, the system can handle more tasks efficiently, leading to improved overall performance. When considering different scheduling algorithms, selecting one that enhances throughput can significantly benefit system operations. The goal is to complete as many processes as possible within a specific timeframe.
- **Minimizing Waiting Time:** Reducing waiting time ensures that processes are executed promptly once they are ready, contributing to better resource allocation and overall system responsiveness.

Introducing Time-Sharing Operating System

A time-sharing operating system is an advanced framework designed to provide simultaneous services to multiple users. The implementation of this scheme involves slicing up the processor's time into minute, thin pieces and rapidly rotating, feeding each user's program. This gives the impression that each user of a time-sharing system has received a personal computer, even though in real, everyone shares the system. To guarantee efficient use of the processor and other resources, most time-sharing systems were generally designed using multitasking and multiprogramming concepts.

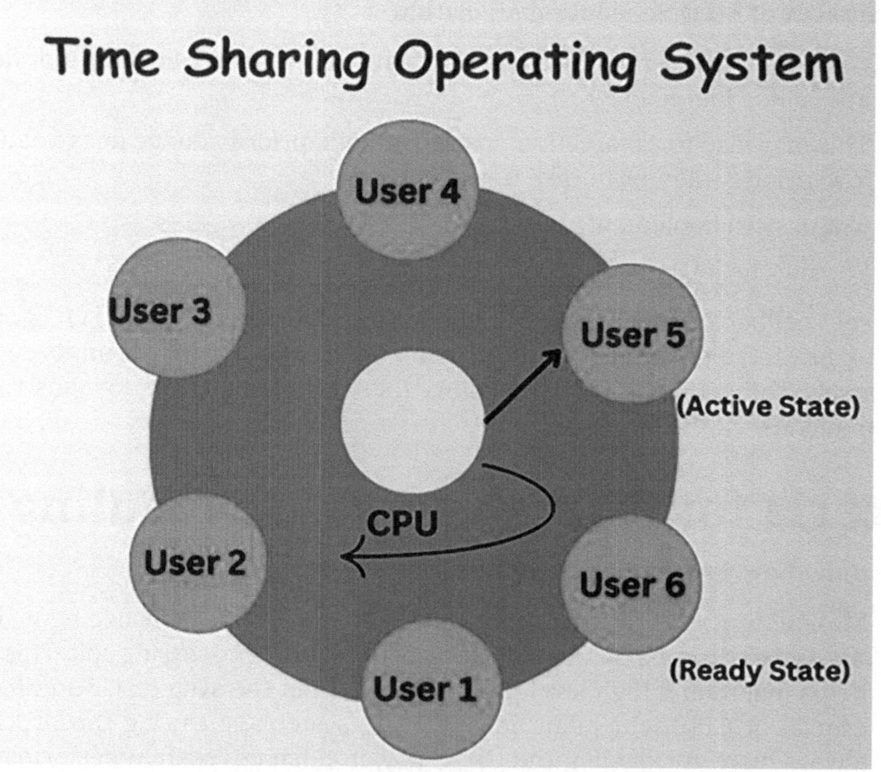

Figure 5.17: *The Concept of Time Sharing*

Key Features of a Time-Sharing Operating System

Many features intended to enhance multi-user environments are included in time-sharing operating systems. Knowing these characteristics makes it easier to understand how these systems operate to give several users an equitable and effective computing environment.

The system has a tight coupling between its parts. Even if a processor fails, the system as a whole continues to function. Several processors (CPUs) share the workload in multi-processor scheduling to enable efficient process execution.

Advantages of the Time-sharing Operating System

The advantages of time-sharing operating systems help to optimize resource utilization and user productivity. Time-sharing operating systems bring many benefits to the table, especially in environments where computing resources need to be maximally utilized across several users. Here are some of the standout advantages:

- **Increased Accessibility**: One of the most significant benefits is the increased accessibility it provides. Multiple users can access the system and its resources simultaneously from different terminals, making it highly suitable for organizations with a large user base.
- **Optimal Resource Utilization**: Time-sharing systems excel in making the most out of the system's processing power and memory. By allocating resources dynamically based on current demands, these systems ensure that no resources are idle.

  By allocating system resources, such as CPU time, memory, and storage among multiple users, time-sharing systems ensure that resources are used efficiently, minimizing wastage.
- **Real-time Interaction**: The interactive nature of time-sharing systems provides users with immediate feedback for their inputs, making these systems ideal for applications that require real-time responses.
- **Enhanced Productivity**: With the ability to perform multiple tasks concurrently and switch between applications seamlessly, users can achieve higher productivity levels.
- **Improved Data Management**: Time-sharing systems often come with sophisticated data management and protection features, ensuring that users' data is securely stored and easily accessible when needed.
- **Cost-Effectiveness**: Time-sharing reduces the need for dedicated hardware for each user, leading to significant cost savings in hardware acquisition and maintenance.
- **User Convenience**: Multiple users can access and work on the system simultaneously from different locations, enhancing convenience and collaboration.
- **Flexibility**: These systems support concurrent running of multiple applications, providing users with the flexibility to work on various tasks without switching devices.
- **Real-Time Processing**: Time-sharing systems offer real-time processing capabilities, allowing immediate interaction and feedback that is essential for applications requiring quick responses.

Disadvantages of the Time-sharing Operating System

Despite their numerous benefits, time-sharing operating systems also come with some challenges:

- **Complexity**: Managing the simultaneous operations of multiple users adds complexity to the system, requiring sophisticated scheduling, memory management, and security measures.
- **Resource Limitations**: High demand from multiple users can strain system resources, leading to potential slowdowns if the system is not adequately provisioned.
- **Security Risks**: With multiple users accessing the system, there's an increased risk of security breaches, making robust security protocols a necessity.
- **Dependency on Network**: For remote access, time-sharing systems rely on network connections, making them susceptible to network-related issues, such as latency and outages.
- **Privacy Concerns**: Sharing a system among multiple users can raise privacy concerns, necessitating stringent data isolation and protection mechanisms.

Overview of Multi-processor Scheduling

A system that shares the same memory, bus, and input/output devices but has multiple processors is called a multi-processor system. Multi-processor scheduling divides the workload among multiple processors (CPUs) to facilitate efficient process execution.

Compared to a single-processor system, the scheduling procedure in a multi-processor system is more complicated. The CPUs could be heterogeneous–different from one another–or homogeneous. A common bus, memory, and other I/O devices are used by all the system's CPUs. There are two methods for scheduling multiple processors: asymmetric and symmetric multiprocessor scheduling [2].

A multi-processor is a system that has more than one processor but shares the same memory, bus, and I/O devices. The bus connects the processor to the RAM, to the I/O devices, and to all the other components of the computer.

Multiple Processors Operating systems are discussed in detail in *Chapter 14, OS for Multy processor Systems*.

The system is a tightly coupled system and works even if a processor goes down. The rest of the system keeps working. In multi-processor scheduling, more than one processor (CPUs) share the load to handle the execution of processes smoothly.

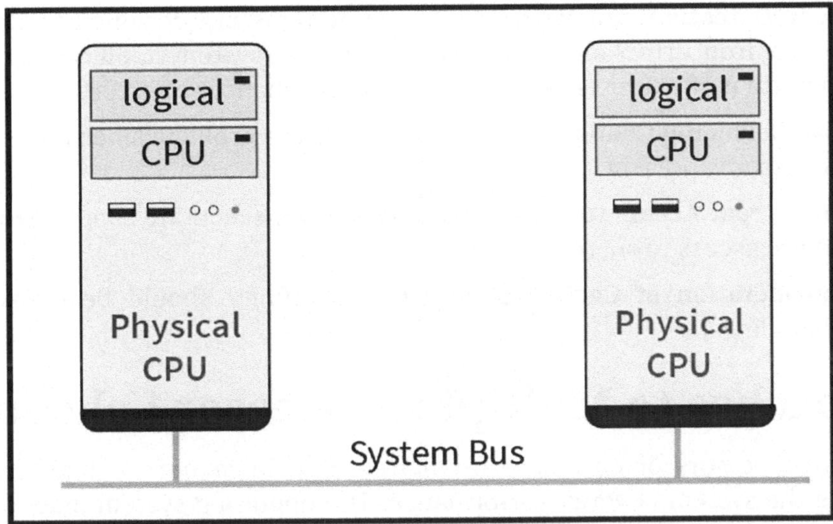

***Figure* 5.18**: *A typical Simultaneous multithreading* (SMT) *Architecture*

The scheduling process of a multi-processor is more complex than that of a single-processor system because of the following reasons:

- **Multiuser Support**: Hallmark of time-sharing systems is their ability to support multiple users simultaneously. This is achieved through efficient scheduling and resource management, allowing users to run programs and perform tasks as if they have the system to themselves.
- **Task Switching**: Time-sharing systems are adept at switching rapidly between tasks. This task switching or context switching allows the CPU to handle multiple processes efficiently, giving each process a slice of the CPU's time.
- **Dynamic Resource Allocation**: These systems dynamically allocate resources as needed. CPU time, memory, and storage are distributed among active users and tasks based on demand, ensuring optimal utilization of system resources.
- **Interactive Processing**: Unlike batch processing systems, time-sharing systems allow for interactive processing. Users can input data during execution and receive immediate output, making these systems ideal for applications that require user interaction.
- **Real-Time Access to Resources**: Time-sharing systems provide real-time access to system resources, enabling users to access databases, applications, and other resources concurrently without significant delays.
- **Security and Isolation**: Time-sharing systems implement robust security measures to protect user data and processes. User authentication, process isolation, and data protection mechanisms are in place to ensure that users' activities remain private and secure.

- **Error Detection and Recovery**: These systems are designed to detect and recover from errors automatically. This ensures system stability and reliability, even in a multi-user environment where the chances of errors are higher.
- **Load Balancing Challenges**: Load balancing is a problem since more than one processor is present.
- **Concurrent Access to Shared Data**: Processes executing simultaneously may require access to shared data.
- **Consideration of Cache Affinity**: Cache affinity should be considered in scheduling.

Approaches to Multiple Processor Scheduling

Numerous processors or cores are frequently used in modern computer systems to increase the system's overall performance. The operating system must be able to effectively schedule processes to execute on various processors, though, to make the best use of these resources.

Multi-processor scheduling involves deciding which processes should be assigned to which processor or core and how long they should be permitted to run. While ensuring that all processes are fairly and appropriately prioritized, the objective is to achieve efficient utilization of the available processors. There are generally two types of approaches adopted:

- **Symmetric Multiprocessing**: The processors self-schedule when using symmetric multi-processor scheduling. Every processor has a scheduler that looks through the ready queue before choosing a process to run. Every processor interacts with one another and uses the same copy of the operating system. The system continues to function even if one of the processors fails.
    - **Symmetrical scheduling with global queues**: The scheduler for each processor looks through this global-ready queue to determine which process to execute if the processes that need to be completed are in a global queue or a common queue.
    - **Symmetrical scheduling using individual queues**: If each processor in the system has a private ready queue, the scheduler for each processor looks through its own queue to choose a process.
- **Asymmetric Multiprocessing**: In asymmetric multi-processor scheduling, there is a master server, and the rest are slave servers. The master server handles all the scheduling processes and I/O processes, and the slave servers handle the users' processes. If the master server goes down, the whole system comes to a halt. However, if one of the slave servers goes down, the rest of the system keeps working.

Processor Affinity

A process prefers the processor it uses to operate. We refer to this as processor affinity.

Let's attempt to comprehend why this occurs. When a process operates on a processor, the processor's cache memory is filled with the data that the process has most recently accessed. The cache memory frequently satisfies the process's subsequent requests for data access.

However, the contents of the first processor's cache memory are invalidated, and the second processor's cache memory needs to be repopulated if this process is moved to another processor for any reason. Process migration from one processor to another is avoided to save money by avoiding the expense of invalidating and repopulating the cache memory.

There are two types of processor affinity:

- **Soft Affinity**: The system has a rule of trying to keep running a process on the same processor but does not guarantee it. This is called soft affinity.
- **Hard Affinity**: The system allows the process to specify the subset of processors on which it may run, that is, each process can run only some of the processors. Systems such as Linux implement soft affinity, but they also provide system calls such as `sched_setaffinity()` to support hard affinity.

Load Balancing

A multi-processor system's processor can have different workloads. Some might be waiting in a long line, while others idle. Load balancing is used as a solution to this issue. The phenomenon of distributing workload in a symmetric multi-processor system so that each processor has an equal workload is known as load balancing. Load balancing is not necessary in systems with symmetric multiprocessing and global queues. In a similar system, a processor looks over the global ready queue and chooses a process as soon as it meets the criteria.

However, in an asymmetric multiprocessor system with private queues, certain processors might be overworked while others remain idle. This can be resolved in two ways:

- **Push Migration**: In push migration, each processor's load is regularly checked by a task. Certain processors might be idle and have lengthy queues. If the workload is not evenly distributed, the burden will be transferred from the overworked processor to an idle or less busy processor.
- **Pull Migration**: In pull migration, a processor that is not in use will take up the load from an overworked processor.

Multi-Core Processors

A processor with multiple cores is a single computing unit with two or more central processing units or cores. The operating system views each core as a distinct physical processor because each core has a register set that preserves its architectural state. An address, an instruction, and so on, can be stored in a processor register. Every core functions as a processor in the system since each has a register set.

Multi-core processors used in symmetric multiprocessing systems enable higher performance at lower energy consumption.

Symmetric Multiprocessor

One operating system which any central processing unit can use, resides in the memory of symmetric multiprocessors. The CPU that made the system call traps the kernel and processes the system call when one is made. The model strives for a dynamic balance between processes and memory. As the name implies, all processors self-schedule and are scheduled using symmetric multiprocessing. Every processor chooses a process to execute after consulting the private or global ready queue.

Remark: The kernel is the main part of the operating system. Through it, the application software and system hardware are connected.

In a symmetric multiprocessor system, conflicts can occur in three different ways:

- **Locking system**: Each processor shares its resources in a multiprocessor system. A locking system is needed to keep these resources safe from the processors. This is done to serialize the processors' resource access.
- **Shared data**: The consistency of the data may be compromised as multiple processors are concurrently accessing the same data. We need to employ a locking system or strategy to prevent this.
- **Cache Coherence**: Should one of the clients modify the memory block, resource data shared among numerous local caches could become invalid. By keeping a uniform perspective of the data, this can be fixed.

Master-Slave Multiprocessor

One CPU functions as a master and the others as slave processors in a master-slave multiprocessor. This implies that all scheduling and I/O operations are managed by the master processor, whereas user processes are managed by the slave processors. Every processor shares the same memory and I/O devices, and they are all connected to the same bus. It schedules processes through asymmetric multiprocessing.

Virtualization and Threading

Operating multiple operating systems on a single computer system is known as virtualization. Hence, a single CPU has multiprocessor capabilities.

Having a host operating system in addition to additional guest operating systems allows for this. Distinct applications function independently of one another on disparate operating systems.

With its CPU, memory, network interface, and storage created on a physical hardware system, a virtual machine is a virtual environment that performs as a virtual computer.

A time-sharing operating system allots 100 milliseconds (ms) to every time slice to provide users with a reasonable response time. Yet, it takes longer than 100 ms, possibly even a second or longer. As a result, users logged into the virtual machine experience slow response times.

The clocks in virtual machines might be off since the virtual operating systems only get a portion of the available CPU cycles. This is because, when using dedicated CPUs, their timers don't take any longer to trigger.

Programming on Multiprocessor Systems

Threads execute sequentially in a time-sliced fashion on a uniprocessor system. In contrast, multiple threads run concurrently on each available processor in a multiprocessor system. Different process threads on different processors can be run to increase overall performance. However, unless it has multiple threads, a single program cannot benefit from multiprocessing.

Because the operating system and the programs it runs handle multiprocessing entirely, most users are unaware of it. Although it's not necessary or advised for everyday use, users can bind their processes to run only on a specific processor. Taking advantage of multiprocessing only requires using multiple threads, even for most programmers. However, while porting or writing code for multiprocessor systems, kernel programmers must contend with several challenges.

- **Identifying processors**: Symmetric multiprocessor (SMP) machines have one or more CPU boards, each of which can accommodate two processors.
- Controlling processor use: This section describes how to control the use of processors on the multiprocessor system.
- **Using Dynamic Processor Deallocation**: Starting with machine type 7044 model 270, the hardware of all systems with more than two processors can detect correctable errors, which are gathered by the firmware. These errors are not fatal and as long as they remain rare occurrences, can be safely ignored. However, when a pattern of failures develops on a specific processor,

it indicates that this component is likely to exhibit an unrecoverable failure soon. This prediction is made by the firmware based-on-failure rates and threshold analysis.

- **Dynamic memory guarding**: AIX systems are designed to be resilient in regard to memory errors. Memory error resilience is the result of both hardware and operating system-level recoveries.
- **Creating locking services**: Some programmers may want to implement their own high-level locking services instead of using the standard locking services (mutexes) provided in the threads library.

Thread Scheduling Examples Using POSIX Threads

Thread operations include scheduling, data management, synchronization (joins, blocking), thread creation, termination, and process interaction. POSIX Threads are often referred to as PThreads. It is a parallel execution model and an execution model that functions independently of a language. For the C programming language, the **`pthread`** library offers a standard interface for thread creation. The **`pthread_create`** function initiates the execution of a new thread.

Scheduling Threads

The threads library offers several tools to manage and regulate the scheduling of threads. Threads can be scheduled. Additionally, it offers tools for managing thread scheduling when performing synchronization tasks such as locking a mutex. There are distinct scheduling parameters for every thread. The thread attributes object can be used to set these parameters prior to the thread creation. During the thread's execution, the parameters may also be dynamically set.

Handling a thread's scheduling can be a challenging task. Because the scheduler manages all threads across the system, a thread's scheduling parameters interact with all other threads within the process as well as with other processes. The following facilities should be utilized first if you wish to manage a thread's scheduling.

The threads library allows the programmer to control the execution scheduling of the threads in the following ways:

- By setting scheduling attributes when creating a thread
- By dynamically changing the scheduling attributes of a created thread
- By defining the effect of a mutex on the thread's scheduling when creating a mutex (known as synchronization scheduling)

- By dynamically changing the scheduling of a thread during synchronization operations (known as synchronization scheduling)

Scheduling Parameters

A thread has the following scheduling parameters:

Parameter	Description
scope	The contention scope of a thread is defined by the thread model used in the thread's library
policy	The scheduling policy of a thread defines how the scheduler treats the thread after it gains control of the CPU
priority	The scheduling priority of a thread defines the relative importance of the work being done by each thread

***Table 5.2**: Scheduling parameters*

It is possible to set the scheduling parameters both before and during the thread's execution. In general, only CPU-intensive threads need to have their scheduling parameters controlled. As a result, the threads library offers default values that are adequate in most situations.

Thread Creation

Thread creation is an essential feature of modern operating systems that allow programs to perform multiple tasks concurrently. The operating system provides thread creation functionality as a system call because it is a low-level feature that is closely tied to the hardware and operating system. While many programming languages provide built-in support for threads, they are typically implemented using the operating system's thread creation functionality.[3]

Higher-level abstractions for creating and managing threads are provided by languages, such as Java and C++. Examples of these abstractions are the Thread class in Java and the std::thread class in C++. Although working with threads is made more convenient and platform-neutral by these abstractions, they still rely on the operating system's inherent thread support.

Programs can leverage platform-specific features and optimizations that may not be accessible through a higher-level threading abstraction by utilizing the operating system's thread creation system call. A program can take advantage of hardware support for threading or optimized scheduling algorithms offered by the operating system by using the thread creation system call.

"Example: Suppose an operating system supports a multi-core processor with hardware-level thread scheduling. In this case, the operating system's thread creation system call

may allow a program to specify that a new thread should be created on a specific core or set of cores using the pthread_attr_setaffinity_np() , CPU_SET()*, to take advantage of the hardware-level thread scheduling.*"[3]

Furthermore, programs written in any language can utilize operating system threads; they are not limited to those with integrated thread support. Using the operating system's thread creation feature, programs written in languages without built-in thread support can now benefit from multi-threading.

A common interface for creating and managing threads in the C or C++ language is offered by the POSIX threads (pthread) library in Linux.

Creating a Thread in Linux Using C Language

The pthread library provides a standard interface for creating threads in C language. The **pthread_create** function creates a new thread and starts its execution. The syntax for **pthread_create** is as follows:

```
int pthread_create(pthread_t *thread, const pthread_attr_t *attr
                   void *(*start_routine)(void *), void *arg);,
```

Figure 5.19: *Using pthread library*

The **pthread_create** function takes four parameters:

- **thread**: A pointer to a **pthread_t** variable that will hold the thread identifier: the same can be obtained from the thread using **pthread_self()**
- **attr**: A pointer to a **pthread_attr_t** structure that contains attributes for the new thread; if NULL is passed, default thread attributes are used and the same can be obtained from thread using **pthread_getattr_np(pthread_self(), &attr)**
- **start_routine**: A pointer to the function that will be executed in the new thread
- **arg**: A pointer to the argument that will be passed to the **start_routine** function

The **pthread_create** function returns zero if the thread is created successfully. Otherwise, it returns an error code indicating the reason for the failure.

Threads made with **pthread_create()** by default take on the calling thread's thread properties. Did you know, by the way, that one thread can give rise to many more? Programs can alter the behavior of newly created threads, though, by utilizing the **pthread_attr_t** structure and companion functions. As an illustration, they can adjust the thread affinity to make use of multi-core processors, the stack size to prevent stack overflow problems, and the thread scheduling policy to maximize thread performance.

```
pthread_attr_t Structure
types .h
```

```
/*
 * attributes for threads, dynamically allocated by library
 */
typedef struct _pthread_attr {
    void    *__pthread_attrp;
} pthread_attr_t;
```

Figure 5.20: *pthread_attr_t Structure*

The **pthread_attr_t** structure is dynamically allocated by the pthreads library (**lpthread** on Linux systems), and its members may vary depending on the underlying architecture and operating system.

Although certain members of **pthread_attr_t** are standardized by the POSIX specification, others are specific to particular implementations of pthreads and may differ. One such example is the **cpuset** member, which some pthreads implementations provide as an extension but is not included in the POSIX standard for thread affinity specification.

```
typedef struct
    int detachstate;              /* Detach state */
    int schedpolicy;              /* Scheduling policy */
    struct sched_param schedparam;  /* Scheduling parameters */
    int inheritsched;             /* Inherit scheduler attribute */
    int scope;                    /* Contention scope */
    size_t guardsize;             /* Stack overflow protection */
    int stackaddr_set;            /* Stack address explicitly set */
    void *stackaddr;              /* Stack address */
    size_t stacksize;             /* Stack size */
    cpu_set_t cpuset;             /* Optional param !! not a part of posix std/spec
} pthread_attr_t;{
```

Figure 5.21: *pthread functions*

The **pthread_attr_t** structure is an important part of the POSIX threads (pthreads) API, as it allows programs to customize the behavior of newly created threads. The **pthread_attr_t** structure contains several thread attributes that can be set using various functions provided by the pthreads API. These attributes include:

- **detachstate**: Specifies whether the thread is created in a joinable or detached state. If it is set to **PTHREAD_CREATE_JOINABLE**, the thread can be joined using

pthread_join(). If it is set to **PTHREAD_CREATE_DETACHED**, the thread will run independently and cannot be joined.

- **schedpolicy**: Specifies the scheduling policy to use for the thread. Possible values are **SCHED_OTHER**, **SCHED_FIFO**, and **SCHED_RR**.
- **schedparam**: Specifies the scheduling parameters for the thread, including the thread's priority and any other relevant parameters for the selected scheduling policy. It is a structure of type struct **sched_param**, which contains a single field **sched_priority**.
- **inheritsched**: Specifies whether the thread should inherit its scheduling attributes from the calling thread (**PTHREAD_INHERIT_SCHED**) or use the default attributes (**PTHREAD_EXPLICIT_SCHED**).
- **scope**: Defines the scope of a thread's scheduling policy. A thread's scheduling scope can either be **PTHREAD_SCOPE_PROCESS**, which means that the thread's scheduling policy and priority are scoped to the entire process, or **PTHREAD_SCOPE_SYSTEM**, which means that the thread's scheduling policy and priority are scoped to the entire system.
- **guardsize**: Specifies the size of the buffer used for stack overflow protection. This field specifies the size of the stack guard area, which is a buffer that protects the thread's stack from overflow.
- **stackaddr_set**: Specifies whether the stack address has been explicitly set (1) or not (0) by the program.
- **stackaddr**: Specifies the address of the stack. Only valid if **stackaddr_set** is 1.
- **stacksize**: Specifies the size of the stack.
- **cpuset**: Optional member is included in the structure and is responsible for setting the CPU affinity of a thread using **pthread_attr_setaffinity_np**.

Note that not all pthreads implementations may support all these attributes; some implementations may provide additional implementation-specific attributes.

Program for Thread Creation

```
#include <stdio.h>
#include <stdlib.h>
#include <pthread.h>
#include <unistd.h>

void *thread_func(void *arg) {
// Thread function code goes here
      int i = 0;
      while(i<5) {
            printf("Hello, I am running in thread\n");
            sleep(1);
```

```
            i++;
        }
return NULL;
}
        int main() {
        pthread_t thread;
        pthread_attr_t attr;
        int ret;

// Initialize attributes to default values
ret = pthread_attr_init(&attr);
if (ret != 0) {
        perror("pthread_attr_init");
        exit(EXIT_FAILURE);
}

// Set stack size attribute
size_t stack_size = 1024 * 1024;
ret=pthread_attr_setstacksize(&attr, stack_size);
if (ret != 0) {
        perror("pthread_attr_setstacksize");
        exit(EXIT_FAILURE);
}


// Create thread with attributes|
ret = pthread_create(&thread, &attr, thread_func, NULL);
if (ret != 0) {
        perror("pthread_create");
        exit(EXIT_FAILURE);
}

int i - 0;
while(i<5) {
        printf("Hello, I am running in main\n");
        sleep(1);
        i++;
}

// Destroy attributes object
ret = pthread_attr_destroy(&attr);
if (ret != 0) {
        perror("pthread_attr_destroy");
        exit(EXIT_FAILURE);
}
```

```
// Wait for thread to finish
ret = pthread_join(thread, NULL);
{
if (ret != 0) {
       perror("pthread_join");
       exit(EXIT_FAILURE);
       }
       return 0;
}

/*
Op =>// amit@DESKTOP-9LTOFUP:~/OmPracticeC++/Threads$ ./a.out
Hello, I am running in main
Hello, I am running in thread
Hello I am running in thread
Hello, I am running in main
Hello I am running in thread
Hello, I am running in main
Hello, I am running in thread
Hello, I am running in main
Hello, I am running in thread
Hello, I am running in main
*/
```

In the preceding example, the stack size attribute is set to 1MB, and the **pthread_attr_t structure** is initialized to default values. Using **pthread_create**, we then create a thread with these properties and look for any potential errors. After the thread is created, we also use **pthread_join** to wait for the thread to finish and destroy the attributes object.

Let us learn more about thread priority, scheduling policy, and stack size default values.

The following program demonstrates getting the default values of stack size, thread priority, and policy.

Defining C Static Library

```
#include <stdio.h>
#include <errno.h>
#include <sched.h>
#include<pthread.h>


void* thread_func(void* arg) {
    pthread_attr_t attr;
    size_t stacksize;
    int priority, policy;

    // Get the attributes of this thread
    pthread_getattr_np(pthread_self(), &attr);
    /*
        suffix "np" stands for "non-portable".
        This indicates that the function is not a part of the portable
        POSIX threads (pthread) standard, but rather it is a non-standard
        extension provided by some implementations of pthreads.
    */
    printf("\n\n");
    // Get the stack size
    pthread_attr_getstacksize(&attr, &stacksize);
    printf("Stack size of %s is : %lu bytes\n",(char*)arg, stacksize);

    // Get the scheduling priority
    struct sched_param param;
    pthread_attr_getschedparam(&attr, &param);
    priority = param.sched_priority;
    printf("Priority of %s is: %d\n", (char*)arg,priority);

    // Get the scheduling policy
    pthread_attr_getschedpolicy(&attr, &policy);
    printf("Scheduling policy of %s is: %d\n", (char*)arg,policy);
        sleep(1);

    // Clean up
    pthread_attr_destroy(&attr);
    return NULL;
}
```

```
int main() {
    pthread_t thread1;

        printf("Policy = SCHED_OTHER => corresponding number    %d \n", SCHED_O
        printf("Policy = SCHED_FIFO  => corresponding number    %d \n", SCHED_F
        printf("Policy = SCHED_RR    => corresponding number    %d \n\n", SCHED_

        printf("RR Min priority = %u\n",sched_get_priority_min(SCHED_RR));
        printf("RR Max priority = %u\n\n",sched_get_priority_max(SCHED_RR));
        printf("FIFO Min priority = %u\n",sched_get_priority_min(SCHED_FIFO));
        printf("FIFO Max priority = %u\n\n",sched_get_priority_max(SCHED_FIFO));
        printf("OTHER Min priority = %u\n",sched_get_priority_min(SCHED_OTHER));
        printf("OTHER Max priority = %u\n",sched_get_priority_max(SCHED_OTHER));

    pthread_create(&thread1, NULL, thread_func, "Thread1");
    pthread_join(thread1, NULL) ;
    return 0;
}
```

```
/*
O/P =>

Policy = SCHED_OTHER => corresponding number    0
Policy = SCHED_FIFO  => corresponding number    1
Policy = SCHED_RR    => corresponding number    2

RR Min priority = 1
RR Max priority = 99

FIFO Min priority = 1
FIFO Max priority = 99

OTHER Min priority = 0
OTHER Max priority = 0

Stack size of Thread1 is : 8388608 bytes
Priority of Thread1 is: 0
Scheduling policy of Thread1 is: 0
*/
```

Figure 5.22: *C Static Library*

If we pass the NULL as second parameter to **`pthread_create()`**, thread will be created with default values.

In the preceding program, the programmer is attempting to create the thread with default values and getting the stack size, thread priority, and scheduling policy of a running thread using:

- `pthread_getattr_np(pthread_self(), &attr)` -> To get the **`pthread_attr_t`** via **`attr`**
- `pthread_attr_getstacksize(&attr, &stacksize)` -> To get the stack size
- `pthread_attr_getschedparam(&attr, &stacksize)` -> To get the sched param and thread priority.
- `pthread_attr_getschedpolicy(&attr, &policy)` -> To Get the sched policy

Note: *We need to clean up the attributes object using* ***`pthread_attr_destroy()`*** *after we are done using it.*

The following are the default values based on the O/P in some systems.

Default stack size = 8388608 bytes, i.e., 8KB

Default Thread priority = 0

Default scheduling policy = 0, i.e., SCHED_OTHER

Changing the Scheduling Policy and Priority

Please note that scheduling policy such as **`SCHED_FIFO`** or **`SCHED_RR`** have stricter requirements compared to **`SCHED_OTHER`**.

It takes particular rights and privileges that are not usually available to regular users to set the scheduling policy to **`SCHED_FIFO`** or **`SCHED_RR`**. The **`pthread_create()`** function will fail with the error code **`EINVAL`** (error code 22 or invalid argument), indicating that the requested scheduling policy is not supported, when you attempt to set the scheduling policy to FIFO or RR using the **`pthread_attr_setschedpolicy()`** function.

You might need to run your program with elevated privileges, such as root, or use capabilities to give your program-specific permissions to use the FIFO or RR scheduling policy. This is because, if applied incorrectly, these policies may deprive other processes of CPU time by giving real-time processes a higher priority than other processes. As an alternative, you can change the kernel configuration to enable the FIFO and RR scheduling policies for non-real-time processes. However, altering the kernel configuration is a difficult and possibly dangerous procedure that calls for in-depth familiarity with Linux system administration.

Note: *Since most Linux systems are not set up by default to permit non-real-time processes to use the* SCHED_RR *and* SCHED_FIFO *scheduling policies, there are situations when you are unable to change the scheduling policy from* SCHED_OTHER *to* SCHED_FIFO *or* SCHED_RR. *These policies usually need the use of special privileges and are only applicable to real-time processes. Thus, you might not be able to use these policies even if you run your program with root privileges.*

To use **`SCHED_RR`** and **`SCHED_FIFO`** policies, we need to modify the kernel configuration (make **menuconfig** -> **General setup** -> **Preemption Model** => **Change its value to Fully Preemptible Kernel (RT)**), or simply use a real-time operating system that supports these policies out of the box.

Meaning of Each Scheduling Policies

Linux supports different scheduling policies for threads and processes. . Every one of these policies possesses unique benefits, constraints, and limitations. The following is a quick rundown of the most popular scheduling policies:

- **SCHED_OTHER**: Linux uses this scheduling policy by default. This policy assigns round-robin CPU time allocations to all processes, treating them equally. With a time slice of 10 milliseconds, the scheduler employs a round-robin scheduling algorithm. Under this policy, CPU time is distributed equally among all processes with a similar priority. Most applications that don't need real-time processing can use this policy.

Advantages: It is fair to all processes, easy to implement, and suitable for non-real-time applications.

Limitations: It does not provide real-time guarantees, and there is no way to prioritize a particular process or thread.

- **SCHED_FIFO**: Applications requiring a deterministic response time in real time use this policy. Processes are scheduled under this policy in order of priority, with the highest priority processes operating first. A process that has the CPU will keep using it until it releases it voluntarily or is interrupted by a higher-priority process. Processes are scheduled using the first-in, first-out (FIFO) scheduling policy. Accordingly, the process that joins the ready queue first will be chosen to run first and will keep running until it chooses to block or give up the CPU. The next process in the queue will be chosen for execution after the first one has finished, and so on.

A process that begins executing under FIFO will not stop until it either blocks or finishes its execution because it is a non-preemptive scheduling policy. This policy works well in real-time applications where quick response times are essential and a higher priority process must complete its execution before a lower priority process can start.

Advantages: It provides a deterministic response time, and processes with higher priority are given precedence over lower-priority processes.

Disadvantages: It can lead to priority inversion, where a high-priority process is blocked by a lower-priority process holding a shared resource.

- **SCHED_RR**: This policy is comparable to FIFO but also provides a time quantum for every process. According to this policy, the highest-priority processes run first in the scheduling hierarchy. Each process, though, is only permitted to operate for a predetermined period of time before being preempted and returned to the scheduling queue. Compared to the SCHED_OTHER policy, this policy's processes are prioritized higher. If a process doesn't require the full quantum of CPU time, it distributes the remaining time to the next process that has the same priority. The process with the highest priority receives CPU time first. Only after all processes with higher priority have been scheduled are those with lower priority scheduled.

Advantages: It provides a deterministic response time and prevents priority inversion.

Limitations: It can lead to priority inversion if a lower-priority process holds a shared resource.

In general, it's critical to select the right scheduling policy according to your application's specifications. The default SCHED_OTHER policy usually suffices for non-real-time applications. Policies such as SCHED_RR or SCHED_FIFO might be more suitable for real-time applications. As previously mentioned, kernel configuration places some limitations on the use of the RR and FIFO. When choosing a policy, it's crucial to consider its restrictions and limitations.

Conclusion

In this chapter, we started learning about the need and types for Process Scheduling in OS along with the requirements of the algorithms involved. We further leaned on types of CPU Scheduling Algorithms with their characteristic features and advantages and Criteria for Effective CPU Scheduling.

We got involved in Time-Sharing Operating Systems and their key features along with Multi-processor Scheduling.

We further learned about Multi-Core Processors and their Programming. Further, it was necessary for us to learn Thread scheduling examples using POSIX threads and creating a Thread in Linux using C Language and C Static Library.

In the next chapter, we shall devote time to learning about how to synchronize the various processes and avoid deadlocks in the flow of operation of operating systems.

Multiple Choice Questions

1. Round Robin scheduling falls under the category of _____________

   a. Non-preemptive scheduling

   b. Preemptive scheduling

   c. All of the mentioned

   d. None of the mentioned

2. With round robin scheduling algorithm in a time-shared system ____________

   a. Using very large time slices converts it into First come First served scheduling algorithm

   b. Using very small time slices converts it into First come First served scheduling algorithm

   c. Using extremely small time slices increases performance

   d. Using very small time slices converts it into Shortest Job First algorithm

3. The portion of the process scheduler in an operating system that dispatches processes is concerned with ____________

   a. assigning ready processes to CPU

   b. assigning ready processes to waiting queue

   c. assigning running processes to blocked queue

   d. All of the mentioned

4. Complex scheduling algorithms ____________

   a. are very appropriate for very large computers

   b. use minimal resources

   c. use many resources

   d. All of the mentioned

5. What is FIFO algorithm?

   a. First executes the job that came in last in the queue

   b. First executes the job that came in first in the queue

   c. First executes the job that needs minimal processor

   d. First executes the job that has maximum processor needs

6. The strategy of making processes that are logically runnable to be temporarily suspended is called ____________.

   a. Non preemptive scheduling

   b. Preemptive scheduling

   c. Shortest job first

7. What is Scheduling?
   a. Allowing a job to use the processor
   b. Making proper use of processor
   c. All of the mentioned
   d. None of the mentioned

8. There are 10 different processes running on a workstation. Idle processes are waiting for an input event in the input queue. Busy processes are scheduled with the Round-Robin time= sharing method. Which of the following quantum times is the best value for small response times if the processes have a short runtime, for example, less than 10ms?
   a. tQ = 15ms
   b. tQ = 40ms
   c. tQ = 45ms
   d. tQ = 50ms

9. Orders are processed in the sequence they arrive if _______ rule sequences the jobs.
   a. earliest due date
   b. slack time remaining
   c. first come, first served
   d. critical ratio

10. Which of the following algorithms tends to minimize the process flow time?
   a. First come First served
   b. Shortest Job First
   c. Earliest Deadline First
   d. Longest Job First

Answers

1. b, 2. a, 3. a, 4. a, 5. b, 6. b, 7. a, 8. a, 9. c, 10. b

Questions

1. What is the need for Process Scheduling in OS?
2. What are the objectives behind process scheduling?
3. Write down the names of various types of Schedulers.
4. With the help of a diagram narrate the working of medium-term schedulers.
5. Distinguish among the three types of schedulers, that is, short, mid, and long-term schedulers.
6. With the help of a sketch, describe the two types of scheduling algorithms and Non-preemptive scheduling algorithm.
7. Enumerate the different types of CPU Scheduling Algorithms.
8. Describe the Round Robin Scheduling Algorithm in OS with its characteristic features and relative advantages and disadvantages.
9. What is Multiple-level Queue (MLQ) Scheduling Algorithm?
10. Describe the Multilevel Feedback Queue (MLFQ) Scheduling Algorithm with its advantages.
11. What are the criteria required for effective CPU scheduling?
12. What is a Time-Sharing Operating System and for what purpose is it utilized?
13. What are some of the key features of a Time-Sharing Operating System?
14. Enumerate some benefits of the Time-sharing Operating System.
15. What are the disadvantages of using Time-sharing Operating System?
16. Justify the statement that the scheduling process of a multi-processor is more complex than that of a single processor system.
17. Discuss the two major approaches, that is, symmetric and asymmetric to Multiple Processor Scheduling.
18. What are two types of Processor Affinity? What are the differences between the two types of Processor Affinity?
19. What is expected by Load balancing?
20. Narrate scheduling parameters of a thread.
21. Describe how a thread is created in Linux using C Language.

References

[1] Scheduling Algorithms In Operating System Explained (With Examples),Shivani Goyal,https://unstop.com/blog/scheduling-algorithms-in-operating-system

[2] Multi-Processor Scheduling | Scaler Topics, Scaler. https://www.scaler.com › topics › operating-system › mu...

[3] Thread creation using POSIX, Amit NadigerAmit Nadiger, https://www.linkedin.com/pulse/thread-creation-using-posix

CHAPTER 6
Process Synchronization and Dead locks

Introduction

The phenomenon known as "*process synchronization*" refers to the coordination of process execution so that no two processes can access the same shared resources and data. This procedure is used to maintain the proper sequence in which cooperative processes are carried out. Different synchronization mechanisms are used to bring the processes into sync. Process synchronization is primarily required in a multi-process system when several processes are operating simultaneously and attempt to access the same shared resource or data at the same time. A process's ability to safely share resources without interfering with one another is known as process synchronization. It is an essential component of operating system design because it guarantees the preservation of resource efficiency and data integrity. A deadlock occurs when two computer programs that are using the same resource are essentially blocking each other's access to it, which causes both programs to stop working. One program could only run at a time on the first computer operating systems. When two computer programs that share a resource effectively block one another from accessing it, it results in a deadlock, which causes both programs to stop working. Only one program could run at a time on the first computer operating systems.

Structure

In this chapter, we will learn about following aspects of process synchronization:

- Process Synchronization in OS- an Overview
- Critical Section Problem
- Hardware Primitives for Synchronization

- Semaphores and their Types
- Implementation of Binary Semaphore (mutex lock)
- Monitors
- Monitor Semantics
- Classical Problems in Synchronization
- Deadlock: Modelling
- Deadlock Characterisation
- Banker's Algorithm
- Starvation

Process Synchronization in OS: An Overview

Process synchronization in OS is the task of coordinating the execution of processes in such a way that no two processes can access the same shared data and resources. It is a critical part of operating system design, as it ensures that processes can safely share resources without interfering with each other.

Process synchronization is beneficial when multiple processes are running simultaneously and more than one process has access to the same data or resources at the same time. Process synchronization is generally used in the multi-process system. When more than two processes have access to the same data or resources concurrently, it can cause data inconsistency, so to remove this, data inconsistency processes should be synchronized with each other. [1]

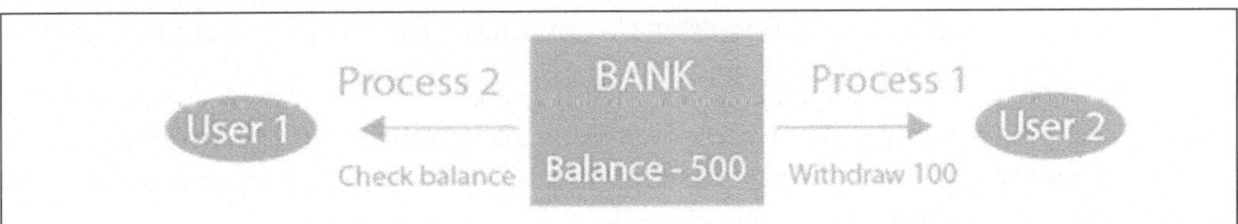

***Figure 6.1**: Example of unsynchronised Bank Transaction*

In *Figure* 6.1, an example of a bank account is shown that has a current balance of 500 and two users who have access to that account. User 1 and User 2 are trying to access the balance. If process 1 is for withdrawal and process 2 is for checking the balance and both will occur at the same time, then user 1 might get the wrong current balance. To avoid this kind of data inconsistency, process synchronization in OS is very helpful.

Working of Process Synchronization in OS with an Example

Let us see an example of different processes trying to access the same data at once [1].

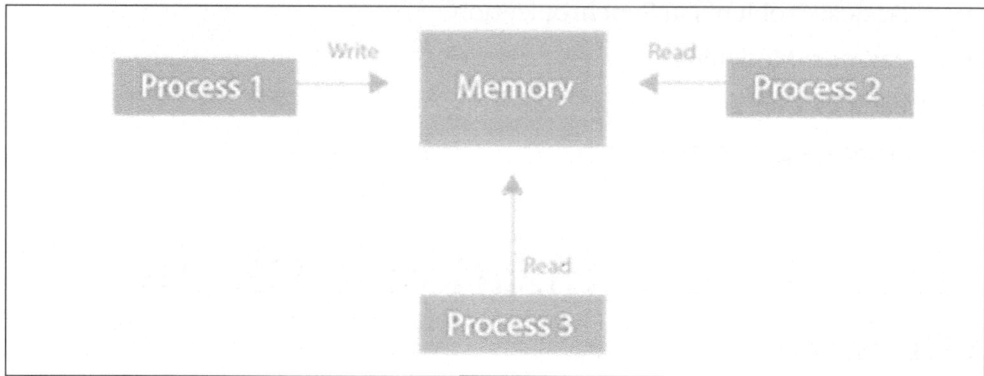

***Figure 6.2**: Example of different processes trying to access the same data*

In the preceding example, there are three processes; Process 1 is trying to write the shared data while Process 2 and Process 3 are trying to read the same data, so there are huge changes in Process 2, and Process 3 might get the wrong data.

Process Synchronization

Problems that emerged during the execution of multiple processes were addressed by introducing of Process Synchronization. It is the task phenomenon wherein processes are coordinated to ensure that no two processes can access the same shared resources and data. It is a process that is necessary to maintain the proper sequence in which cooperative processes are carried out.

There are various synchronization mechanisms to synchronize the processes When multiple processes are executing concurrently and attempting to access the same shared resource or any data at once, process synchronization becomes necessary in a multiprocess system.

Processes are divided into two categories based on synchronization, which are listed as follows:

- **Independent Processes**: Two processes are said to be independent if the execution of one process does not affect the execution of another process.
- **Cooperative Processes**: Two processes are considered cooperative when the performance of one process influences the performance of another. To ensure that the processes are carried out in the correct order, they must synchronize.

Race Condition

At the time when more than one process is either executing the same code or accessing the same memory or any shared variable, there is a possibility that the output or the value of the shared variable is wrong, so for that purpose all the processes are doing the race to say that my output is correct. This condition is commonly known as a race condition. As several processes access and process the manipulations on the same data in a concurrent manner, due to which the outcome depends on the particular order in which the access of data takes place.

This condition mainly occurs inside the critical section. Race condition in the critical section happens when the result of multiple thread execution differs according to the order in which the threads execute. But this condition in critical sections can be avoided if the critical section is treated as an atomic instruction. Proper thread synchronization using locks or atomic variables can also prevent race conditions. [3]

Critical Section Problem

A Critical Section is a code segment that accesses shared variables and has to be executed as an atomic action. It means that in a group of cooperating processes, at a given time, only one process must be executing its critical section. If any other process also wants to execute its critical section, it must wait until the first one finishes. The entry to the critical section is mainly handled by **`wait()`** function, while the exit from the critical section is controlled by the **`signal()`** function. [3]

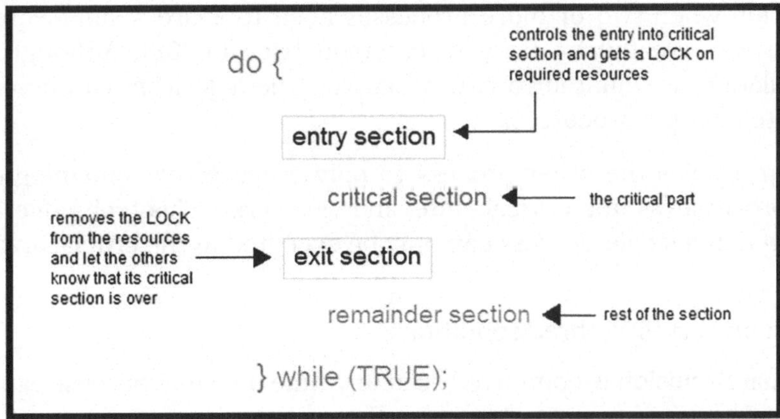

Figure 6.3: *Two subsections of Program for handling Critical Section*

Critical Section Problem has got two subsections as shown in *Figure 6.4*:

- **Entry Section**: In this section, the process mainly requests for its entry in the critical section
- **Exit Section**: This section is followed by the critical section

The Solution to the Critical Section Problem

A solution to the critical section problem must satisfy the following three conditions:

- **Mutual Exclusion**: Out of a group of cooperating processes, only one process can be in its critical section at a given point of time.
- **Progress**: If no process is in its critical section, and if one or more threads want to execute their critical section, then any one of these threads must be allowed to get into its critical section.
- **Bounded Waiting**: After a process requests to get into its critical section, there is a limit to how many other processes can get into their critical section before this process's request is granted. So after the limit is reached, the system must grant the process permission to get into its critical section.

The critical section plays an important role in Process Synchronization so that the problem must be solved.

Some widely used methods to solve the critical section problem are as follows:

Peterson's Solution

This software-based approach is popular for solving important section problems. Peterson, a computer scientist, created the solution, which is why it bears his name. Peterson's algorithm, also known as Peterson's solution, is a concurrent programming technique for mutual exclusion that enables shared memory to be the only means of communication when two or more processes need to share a single-use resource. The formula was created by Gary L. Peterson back in 1981. Although Peterson's initial formulation was limited to two processes, the algorithm can be extended to accommodate multiple processes.

This solution enables the other process to only execute the remaining code when one of the processes is in a critical state, and vice versa. This technique also aids in guaranteeing that a single process can only be executed in the crucial area at a given moment.

This solution preserves all three conditions:

- Mutual Exclusion is comforted as at any time only one process can access the critical section.
- Progress is also comforted, as a process that is outside the critical section is unable to block other processes from entering into the critical section.
- Bounded Waiting is assured as every process gets a fair chance to enter the critical section.

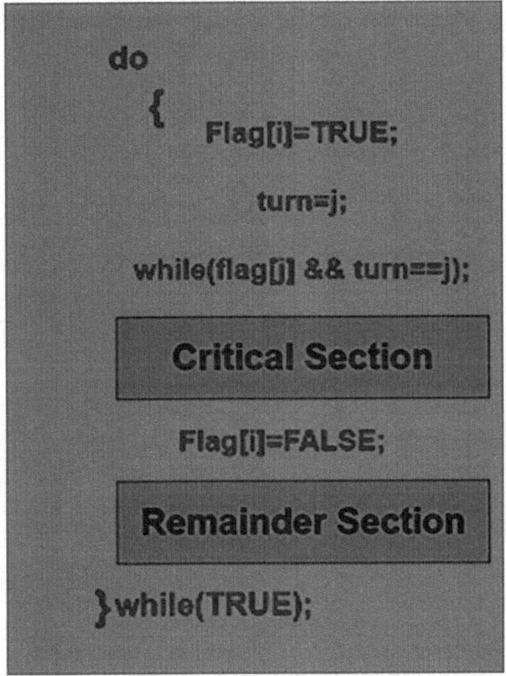

Figure 6.4*: Process Pi in Peterson's solution*

The program snippet of *Figure* 6.5 shows the structure of process Pi in Peterson's solution.

Suppose there are N processes (P1, P2, ..., PN), and at some point in time, every process required to enter the Critical Section.

A **`FLAG[]`** array of size N is maintained here, which is by default false. Whenever a process is required to enter the critical section, it has to set its flag as true.

Example: If Pi wants to enter, it will set **`FLAG[i]=TRUE`**.

Another variable is called **`TURN`** and it is used to indicate the process number that is currently waiting to enter into the critical section.

The process that enters into the critical section while exiting would change the TURN to another number from the list of processes that are ready.

Example: If the turn is 3, then P3 enters the Critical section and while exiting, turn=4, and therefore, P4 breaks out of the wait loop.

Another view of Peterson's solution

A very useful method for solving the critical section problem was provided by computer scientist Peterson. This is a traditional software-based solution. It allows other processes to access the remaining code when one runs concurrently in the critical section and vice versa. The salient feature of this solution is its ability to ensure that a critical section is executed by only one process at a time. Let's go through an example for a better understanding.

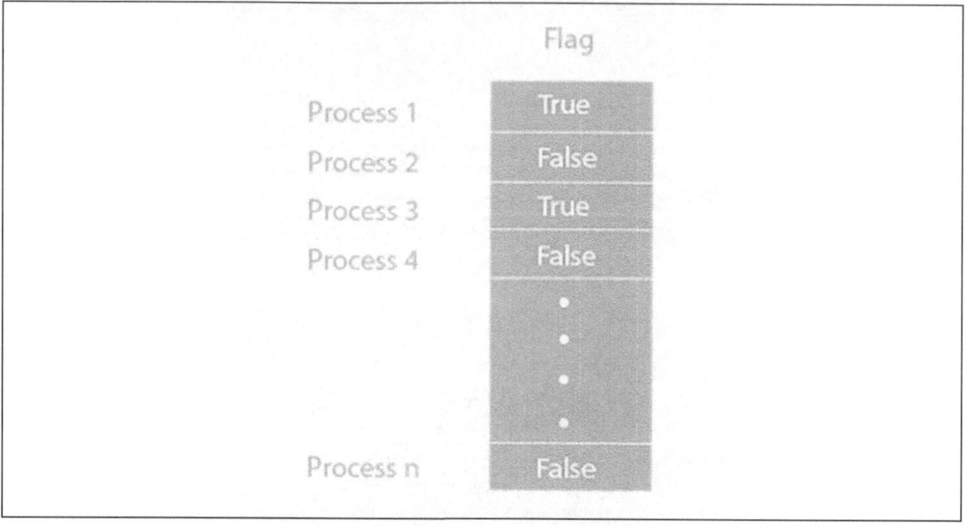

Figure 6.5: *Example of flag array*

```
do{
    // process i will enter in critical section so mark flag of index
    flag[i]=True;
    turn=i;
    while( flag[i]==True && turn==i){
    // the critical section
}
// process i is finished so mark the flag of index i as False
flag[i]=False;
// j is the next process which will enter the critical section
    turn=j;
}
while(True)
```

Figure 6.6: *Program to stop a process by flag Array having critical section*

In the example shown in *Figure* 6.5, there are n processes given (process 1, process 2, process 3, ..., process n). A flag array is also created with a boolean data type and the initial value of all arrays is false. When a process enters a critical section, it marks the flag of that process's index as True. When a process is finished its execution, it marks the flag of that process as False and assigns a turn to the next waiting process.

In this method, a process sends a signal to another process that is waiting on semaphores. Semaphores are variables that are shared between processes. For synchronization among the processes, semaphores utilize the `wait()` and `signal()` functions. We shall read more about semaphores shortly.

Sections and Critical Sections

Let's understand some different sections of a program [1].

- **Entry Section**: Decides the entry of the process
- **Critical Section**: Ensures that only one process accesses and modifies the shared data or resources.
- **Exit Section**: Allows a process that is waiting in the entry section and ensures that finished processes are also removed from the critical section.
- **Remainder Section**: Contains other parts of the code that are not in the Critical or Exit sections.

Rules of Critical Sections

There are three rules that need to be followed to solve critical section problems.

- **Mutual Exclusion**: Ensures that one process is running is the critical section, that is, if one process is accessing the shared data or resources, then no other process enters the critical section at once.
- **Progress**: If there is no process in the critical section and some other processes are waiting to enter into the critical section, then the process that will enter into the critical section is taken by these processes.
- **Bounding Waiting**: There should be some waiting time or bound when a new process requests to enter into the critical section. This bound time is equal to the number of processes that are allowed to access critical sections before it.

Hardware Primitives for Synchronization

Hardware primitives for synchronization are essential components that support efficient and correct communication among concurrently executing threads or processes in a multiprocessor or multi-core system

Synchronization Hardware

"*As the name suggests, we will try to find the solution to the critical section problem using hardware; sometimes, this problem can be solved using hardware. To solve this problem, some operating systems give the feature of locking in this function; when a process enters the critical section, it acquires a lock and the lock is removed when a process exits from the critical section. So, this locking functionality ensures that only one process at a time can enter the critical section because when other processes try to enter into the critical section, it is locked."*

"Many systems provide hardware support for critical section code. The critical section problem could be solved easily in a single-processor environment if we could disallow interrupts to occur while a shared variable or resource is being modified." [3]

By doing this, we could guarantee that the current set of instructions would be permitted to run sequentially without being interrupted. Sadly, in a multiprocessor system, this solution is not workable.

In an environment with multiple processors, disabling interrupts can take some time because the message is sent to each processor.

The system's efficiency declines as a result of this message transmission lag, which delays threads' entry into the crucial section.

Mutex Lock

Since the synchronized hardware method mentioned earlier was difficult, Mutex Locks was introduced. The Mutex Locking Mechanism is used to synchronize access to resources in the critical section. This approach utilizes a lock that is set when a process reaches the crucial part. The lock is released upon a process's departure from the crucial area.

Due to the difficulty of implementing the synchronization hardware solution, Mutex Locks, a stringent software approach, was introduced. With this method, a lock is obtained over the critical resources that are modified and used inside the critical section in the code entry section and released in the code exit section.

Since the resource is locked while a process is completing its crucial part, it cannot be accessed by any other process.

Semaphores

Semaphores are synchronization primitives used to control access to shared resources by multiple threads or processes in a concurrent system.

Introduction to Semaphores

Semaphores are one of the most important tools an operating system has.

"A *semaphore is a communication primitive used in operating systems. It provides blocking, unblocking, and message-passing facilities between processes. A semaphore can be considered an "event queue" for messages waiting to be processed by some other process or thread. A semaphore is a type of mutual exclusion lock that is commonly used in operating systems. It is a primitive synchronization that allows multiple processes to share a resource without conflict."* [4]

"Semaphore ensures process synchronization. Before understanding Semaphore, we need to understand two important terms. Concurrent processes run simultaneously or in parallel and may not depend on other processes. Process synchronization can be defined as the coordination between two processes that have access to common materials, such as common code, resources, and data. Achieving process synchronization is not easy if we have concurrent processes and a common shared code. Here common/shared code means critical section. So here comes the role of the Semaphore to prevent all the processes from accessing the code simultaneously. This is called Mutual exclusion." [4]

Semaphore is an operating system-level memory management technique that can be used to manage the allocation and use of memory resources. In a nutshell, it allows multiple threads or processes to share access to a limited number of resources, such as memory blocks or locks.

A thread first looks up the availability of a shared resource using the Semaphore before attempting to access it. In that case, the thread gets access and is free to continue. In the unavailable event, the thread must wait for the resource to become available. This kind of delay is called a "*semaphore wait*."

Thus, Semaphore offers a means for several processes to use common resources without interfering with one another. You can think of a semaphore as an analog or digital lock that keeps two processes from using the same resource at once.

Need of Using Semaphore

Now that you know what a semaphore is and how it functions, you may be wondering when to use a semaphore in an operating system. The most frequent use of a semaphore is when several threads attempt to access a single resource. This could be a query being made to a database or a file being read or written to.

Semaphore can assist in ensuring that these resources are accessed regularly and systematically, avoiding inconsistent or corrupted data. It can also be used to guard against race conditions, which happen when several threads attempt to use the same resource at the same time.

Advantages of Semaphore

- **Efficient allocation**: Semaphores allow for a more efficient allocation of system resources, which means that memory can be used more effectively
- **Control over multiple processes**: Semaphores give you control over multiple processes, which means you can allocate memory to specific tasks as needed

- **Increased performance**: Semaphore-based memory management can result in increased performance and improved system responsiveness

Disadvantages of Semaphore

- Semaphores are prone to programming errors
- Due to the complexity of semaphore programming, mutual exclusion may not be achieved
- One of the most significant limitations of semaphores is priority inversion; low-priority processes get into a critical section, and high-priority processes keep waiting
- Semaphores can be expensive to implement in terms of memory and CPU usage

Wait and Signaling Operations on Semaphores

There are two operations/functions in the semaphore. They are carried out when an entity enters the critical section (the Wait operation) and leaves the critical section (the Signal operation). The "**P**" and "**V**" functions are used for the wait and signaling operations on the semaphore.

1. **Wait operation**: This semaphore operation, sometimes referred to as a "**P**" feature, sleep, decrement, or down operation, regulates a process's entry into a critical section. A semaphore value will drop by 1 if the process enters the critical section, which is accessible if the mutex/semaphore value is positive.

```
P(Semaphore)
{
While(S==0)
S=S-1;
}
```

2. **Signal Operation:** The signal function is the same as the "**V**" function, also known as the wakeup, increment, or wakeup operation. The semaphore value for the process that allows new processes to enter and access the critical section (shared variables or resources) should be updated when the process exits the critical section. Waiting causes the semaphore value to decrease by one when the process reaches the critical section. For example, if the semaphore's initial value was 1 (S=1), once the process hits the critical section, it will be decreased to 0. If the process exits the critical section after completing its execution, the signal function is called, increasing the semaphore value by 1. Keep in mind that the process only carries out this action once the crucial portion is complete.

```
V(Semaphore)
{
S=S+1;
}
```

Types of Semaphores

Let us learn the types of semaphore [2].

Binary Semaphore

A binary semaphore is a binary (0 or 1) flag that can be enabled or disabled. If a binary semaphore is used as the mutual exclusion mechanism, only the allocated resources will be affected by the mutual exclusion.

Implementation of Binary Semaphore

Binary, as its name implies, means two. There will be two values for this semaphore, that is, O as well as 1. The semaphore value is initially set to 1. Process P1's semaphore value will be 0 when it reaches the crucial part. P2 will not be able to proceed if it reaches the critical section at this point because the value of the semaphore being less than or equivalent to zero. Waiting until the semaphore value is more than 0 would be beneficial. This only occurs when P1 exits the critical region and carries out a signaling action that raises the semaphore's value. Another name for this is mutex lock. This ensures mutual exclusion and prevents either process from accessing the critical section.

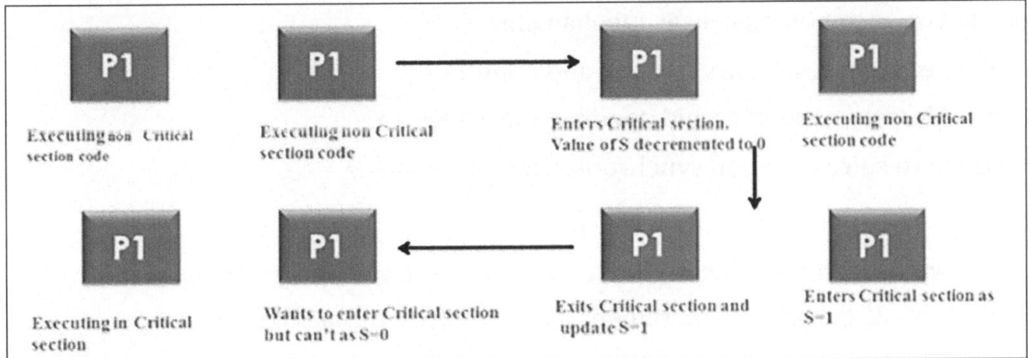

Figure 6.7: Mutex Lock

Counting Semaphore

Semaphores are conceptually integers that are not negative. The number of semaphores is initially set to the total number of available resources, and they are generally used to manage resource access. After that, the value atomically lowers the count when a resource is removed and automatically raises the count when a new resource is added.

Counting Semaphore Implementation

If a resource has three instances, the semaphore's initial value is 3 (that is, S=3). A process calls the wait function and decreases the semaphore value by one whenever it needs to access a crucial area or resource. There is more than zero in the semaphore value. In this instance, the crucial area or resource is accessible to three processes. When the fourth process requires it, it is stopped and placed in a waiting queue. It doesn't wake up until one of the executing processes completes the signaling task. To put it another way, the Semaphore has grown by 1.

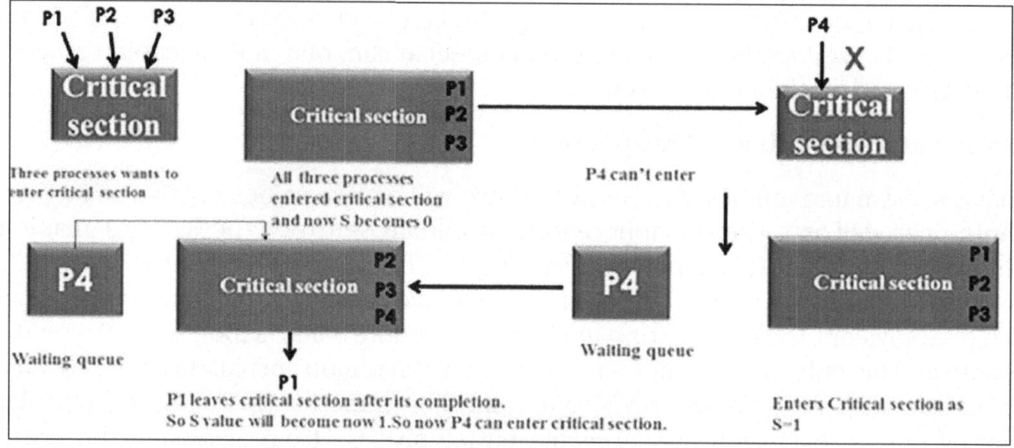

***Figure 6.8**: Three semaphores in critical section*

Look at two common high-level mechanisms:

- **Semaphores**: binary (mutex) and counting
- **Monitors**: mutexes and condition variables

Use them to solve common synchronization problems

Semaphores support two operations [3]:

- **wait**(semaphore): decrement, block until the semaphore is open
- **signal**(semaphore): increment, allow another thread to enter

Blocking in Semaphores

1. Associated with each semaphore is a queue of waiting processes
2. When `wait()` is called by a thread:
    a. If the semaphore is open, the thread continues
    b. If the semaphore is closed, thread blocks on the queue

3. Then **`signal()`** opens the semaphore:
    a. If a thread is waiting on the queue, the thread is unblocked
    b. If no threads are waiting on the queue, the signal is remembered for the next thread

- In other words, **`signal()`** has "**`history`**" (c.f. condition vars later)
- This "**`history`**" is a counter

Semaphores come in two types:

- **Mutex semaphore**
    - Represents single access to a resource
    - Guarantees mutual exclusion to a critical section
- **Counting semaphore**
    - Represents a resource with many units available, or a resource that allows certain kinds of unsynchronized
    - Concurrent access (for example, reading)
        - Multiple threads can pass the semaphore
        - Number of threads determined by the semaphore "count"
- mutex has count = 1, counting has count = N

Readers/Writers Problem

1. An object is shared among several threads
2. Some threads only read the object while others only write
3. We can allow multiple readers
4. But only one writer

We use semaphores to control access to the object to implement this protocol by using three variables:

- **`int readcount`**: number of threads reading object
- **`Semaphore mutex:`** control access to readcount
- **`Semaphore w_or_r`**: exclusive writing or reading

The following is a program

```
// number of readers
int readcount = 0;
// mutual exclusion to readcount
Semaphore mutex = 1;
// exclusive writer or reader
Semaphore w_or_r = 1;

writer {
   wait(w_or_r); // lock out readers
   Write;
   signal(w_or_r); // up for grabs
}
```

```
reader {
   wait(mutex);       // lock readcount
   readcount += 1; // one more reader
   if (readcount == 1)
      wait(w_or_r); // synch w/ writers
   signal(mutex);  // unlock readcount
   Read;
   wait(mutex);       // lock readcount
   readcount -= 1; // one less reader
   if (readcount == 0)
      signal(w_or_r); // up for grabs
   signal(mutex);  // unlock readcount}
}
```

Figure 6.9: Code

Readers/Writers Notes

1. If there is a writer,
   a. First reader blocks on w_or_r
   b. All other readers block on mutex

Once a writer exits, all readers can fall through.

2. Which reader gets to go first?
   - The last reader to exit signals a waiting writer.
   - If no writer, then readers can continue.
   - If readers and writers are waiting on w_or_r, and a
   - writer exits, who goes first?
   - Why doesn't a writer need to use mutex?

Monitors [2]

"A monitor is a programming language construct that controls access to shared data."

- Synchronization code added by compiler, enforced at runtime"

This is an advantage, because of the following:

1. A monitor is a module that encapsulates
   a. Shared data structures
   b. Procedures that operate on the shared data structures
   c. Synchronization between concurrent procedure invocations

2. A monitor protects its data from unstructured access
3. It guarantees that threads accessing its data through
4. Its procedures interact only in legitimate ways

- Monitor Semantics

1. A monitor guarantees mutual exclusion
   a. Only one thread can execute any monitor procedure at any time (the thread is "*in the monitor*")
   b. If a second thread invokes a monitor procedure when a first thread is already executing one, then it blocks, so the monitor has to be in a wait queue.

   If a thread within a monitor blocks, then another one can enter
2. What are the implications in terms of parallelism in monitor?"

Accounting Example is shown in *Figure 6.10*:

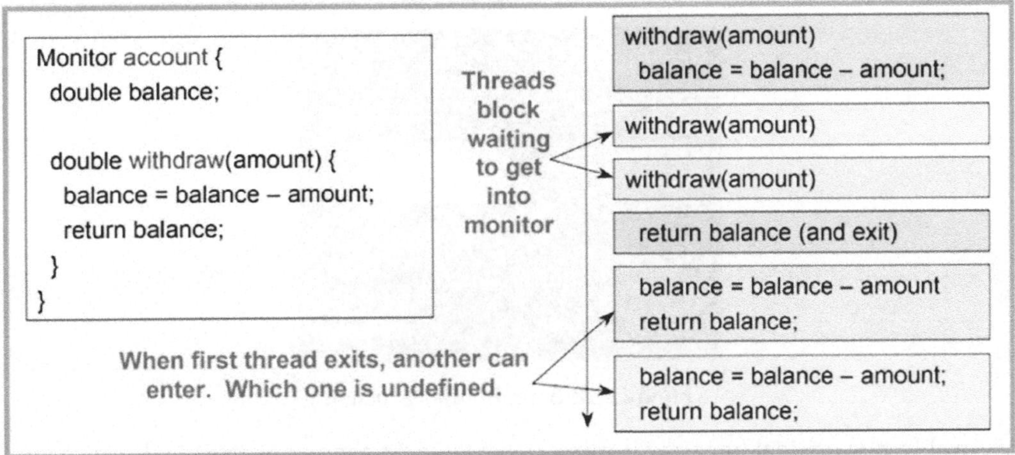

Figure 6.10: *Accounting Example*

Classical problems in Synchronization

But what if a thread wants to wait inside the monitor?

Such as "`mutex(empty)`" by reader in bounded buffer? [5]

Classic synchronization problems include the:

1. **Producer-Consumer Problem** (Bound-Buffer Problem), where producers and consumers share a buffer
2. **Reader-Writer Problem**, where multiple readers can access data simultaneously, but writers must have exclusive access

3. **Sleeping Barber Problem**, where a barber shop has one barber, a barber chair, and a waiting room with several chairs. The challenge arises when the barber must sleep if there are no customers and be woken up as soon as a customer arrives

4. **Dining Philosophers Problem**, where philosophers do nothing but think and eat. The problem is that between each philosopher, there is a fork. A philosopher needs both forks to eat

Synchronization Problems in OS

Bound-Buffer Problem: A classic synchronization problem in computing is the Bound-Buffer problem. It involves handling data in a buffer with a finite amount of space. Imagine a situation in which several processes add data (producers) to the buffer or remove data (consumers) from it. Ensuring that a producer does not add data to an already-full buffer and that a consumer does not attempt to remove data from an empty buffer is crucial.

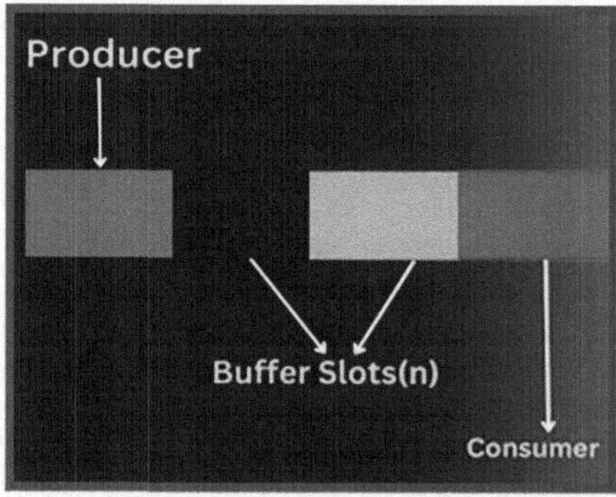

***Figure 6.11**: Bound Buffer Problem*

This problem is critical because it mirrors real-world scenarios in OS where resource allocation needs to be managed efficiently.

Python Code for Bound Buffer Problem

```
import threading
import time
buffer = []
MAX_ITEMS = 10
semaphore = threading.Semaphore()
def producer():
    global buffer
    while True:
        semaphore.acquire()
        if len(buffer) < MAX_ITEMS:
            item = "Data"
```

```
            buffer.append(item)
            print(f"Produced {item}")
        semaphore.release()
        time.sleep(1)

def consumer():
    global buffer
    while True:
        semaphore.acquire()
        if buffer:
            item = buffer.pop(0)
            print(f"Consumed {item}")
        semaphore.release()
        time.sleep(1)

p_thread = threading.Thread(target=producer)
c_thread = threading.Thread(target=consumer)

p_thread.start()
c_thread.start()
```

In this Python example, the buffer is managed via threading and a semaphore. If the buffer isn't empty, the consumer removes an item; otherwise, the producer adds an item. By acting as a lock, the semaphore ensures that only one operation takes place at a time.

The Sleeping Barber Problem: This is an additional intriguing example of synchronization. With one barber, a barber chair, and a waiting area with numerous chairs, it mimics a barbershop. The problem comes when the barber has to go to bed if no one is there and has to wake up as soon as someone does. On the other hand, customers must depart if the waiting area is full. The subtleties of operating system resource allocation and process synchronization are demonstrated by this problem.

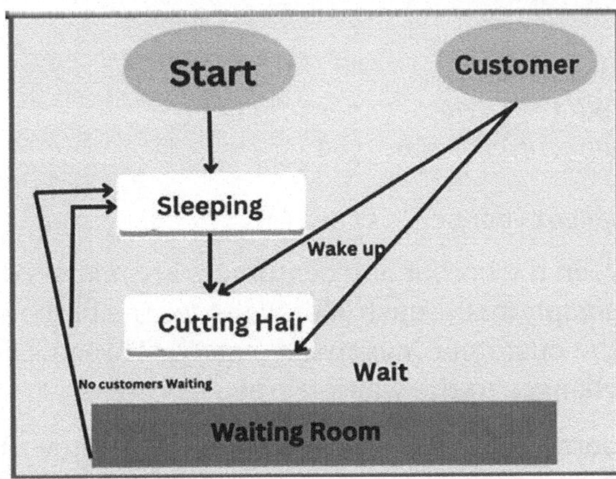

***Figure 6.12**: Example of "Sleeping Barber" Problem*

Python script for Sleeping Barber Problem

```
import threading
import random
import time
waiting_chairs = 5
waiting_room = []
barber_ready = threading.Semaphore(0)
customer_ready = threading.Semaphore(0)
mutex = threading.Lock()

def barber():
    while True:
        customer_ready.acquire()
        mutex.acquire()
        print("Barber is cutting hair")
        waiting_room.pop(0)
        mutex.release()
        barber_ready.release()
        time.sleep(random.uniform(0.5, 2))

def customer():
    mutex.acquire()
    if len(waiting_room) < waiting_chairs:
        waiting_room.append("Customer")
        print(f"Customer sitting in waiting room. Waiting customers:
{len(waiting_room)}")
        customer_ready.release()
        mutex.release()
        barber_ready.acquire()
    else:
        print("Waiting room full, customer leaving")
        mutex.release()

for _ in range(10):
    threading.Thread(target=customer).start()
    time.sleep(random.uniform(0.1, 1))

threading.Thread(target=barber).start()
```

The interactions between the barber and customers are managed in this Python script by mutex locks and semaphores. A customer waits for the barber (**`barber_ready`**), and the barber waits for the customer (**`customer_ready`**). Thread safety is guaranteed by Mutex when making changes to the waiting area.

The Dining Philosophers Problem: This age-old example shows how synchronization problems can arise in an operating system. Five philosophers sit around a circular table and engage in nothing but contemplation and food. A fork exists between each philosopher. Since a philosopher must use both forks to eat, picking up the forks on one's left at once could result in a standoff.

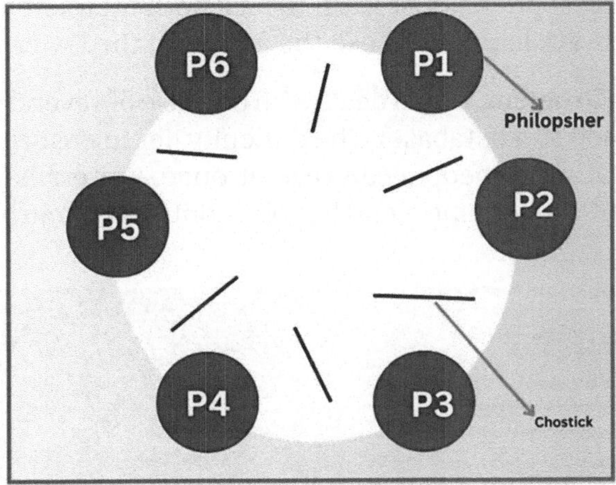

***Figure 6.13**: Example of "Dining Philosopher" Problem*

Python code for the Dining Philosophers Problem

```
import threading
class Philosopher(threading.Thread):
    def __init__(self, index, fork_on_left, fork_on_right):
        threading.Thread.__init__(self)
        self.index = index
        self.fork_on_left = fork_on_left
        self.fork_on_right = fork_on_right
    def run(self):
        while True:
            self.think()
            self.eat()
    def think(self):
        print(f"Philosopher {self.index} is thinking.")

    def eat(self):
        fork1, fork2 = self.fork_on_left, self.fork_on_right
        with fork1:
            with fork2:
                print(f"Philosopher {self.index} is eating.")

forks = [threading.Lock() for _ in range(5)]
philosophers = [Philosopher(i, forks[i%5], forks[(i+1)%5]) for i in
range(5)]

for p in philosophers:
    p.start()
```

The philosophers who dine are modeled by this Python code. Every philosopher is a thread that flips between thought and nourishment. Locks stand in for forks. To avoid a stalemate, philosophers must learn to lock both their left and right forks. They accomplish this by always learning to use the fork with the lower number first.

Readers and Writers Problem, which deals with the case of several processes accessing a shared resource (such as a database). The difficulty lies in ensuring that, even though this is a resource that many people can read at once, writers have exclusive access. This problem is essential to comprehend how OS controls concurrent access to shared resources.

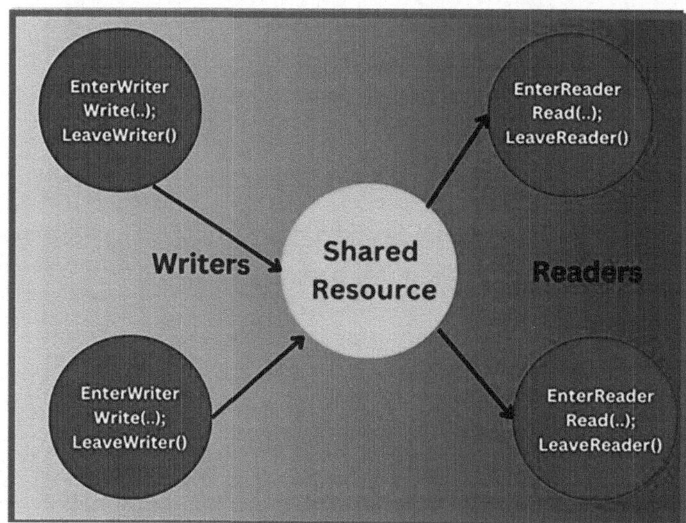

Figure 6.14: *Example of "Readers and Writers" Problem*

Python Code for Readers and Writers Problem

```
import threading
import time
class Database:
    def __init__(self):
        self.readers = 0
        self.resource = threading.Lock()
        self.access_to_readers = threading.Lock()
    def read(self, reader_id):
        with self.access_to_readers:
            self.readers += 1
            if self.readers == 1:
                self.resource.acquire()
        print(f"Reader {reader_id} is reading")
        time.sleep(1)
        with self.access_to_readers:
            self.readers -= 1
```

```
            if self.readers == 0:
                self.resource.release()
    def write(self, writer_id):
        print(f"Writer {writer_id} is waiting to write")
        self.resource.acquire()
        print(f"Writer {writer_id} is writing")
        time.sleep(2)
        self.resource.release()
database = Database()
def reader(id):
    while True:
        database.read(id)
def writer(id):
    while True:
        database.write(id)
for i in range(5):
    threading.Thread(target=reader, args=(i,)).start()
    threading.Thread(target=writer, args=(i,)).start()
```

In this Python example, the Database class uses locks to manage access. The readers counter tracks the number of active readers. If a reader is reading, writers must wait. Writers obtain exclusive access to **resource.acquire()** before writing.

Deadlock

"*All the processes in a system require some resources, such as a central processing unit (CPU), file storage, input/output devices, and so on to execute it. Once the execution is finished, the process releases the resource it was holding. However, when many processes run on a system they also compete for the resources they require for execution. This may cause a deadlock situation.*"[6]

"*A deadlock is a situation in which more than one process is blocked because it is holding a resource and also requires some resource that is acquired by some other process. Therefore, none of the processes gets executed.*"[7]

"*In an operating system, a deadlock occurs when a process or thread enters a waiting state because a requested system resource is held by another waiting process, which in turn is waiting for another resource held by another waiting process.*"[8]

If a process remains indefinitely unable to change its state because resources requested by it are being used by another process, that itself is waiting, then the system is said to be in a deadlock.

Deadlocks are a common problem in multiprocessing systems, parallel computing, and distributed systems because in these contexts, systems often use software or hardware locks to arbitrate shared resources and implement process synchronization.

Deadlocks: Modeling

When multiple processes are halted while each is holding a resource and waiting for another process to obtain another resource, this is known as a deadlock. For instance, in the following diagram, Resource 1 is being held by Process 1, Resource 2 is being acquired by Process 2, and Process 2 is waiting for Resource 1.

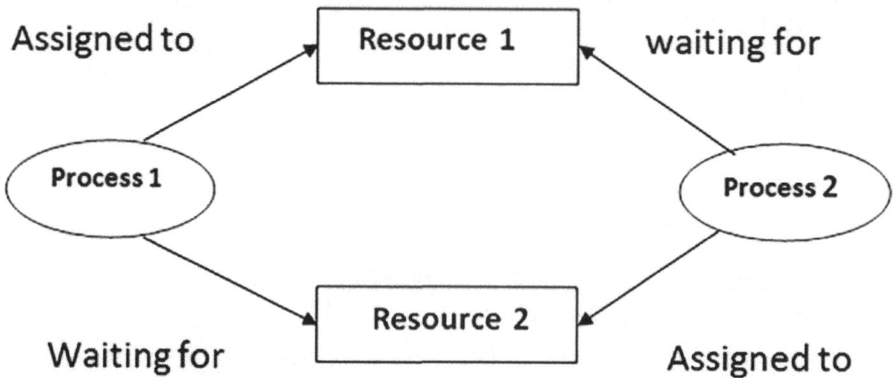

***Figure 6.15**: Deadlock System Model*

System Model

In the context of the deadlock discussion, a system can be conceptualized as a group of finite resources that can be categorized and distributed among numerous processes, each with distinct needs. Resource categories include things such as memory, printers, CPUs, open files, tape drives, CD-ROMs, and more. Every resource in a category is, by definition equal, and any resource in that category can equally fulfil a request from that category. If this isn't true, that is, If resources within a category differ from one another, the category must be further subdivided. For instance, "*printer*" might need to be separated into "*color inkjet printer*" and "*laser printer*." There might be just one resource in some categories. The kernel monitors all of the resources it manages, including which are assigned and which are free, which processes they are assigned to, and a queue of processes awaiting the resource's availability. It is possible to manage application-managed resources (for example, by using mutexes or calls to **`wait()`** and **`signal()`**). G. semaphores that are binary or counting. A set is considered stuck if all its processes are waiting for a resource that is presently allocated to another process within the set.

Operations

Normally, a process asks for a resource before using it and release it when it's done, as the following diagram illustrates.

Request: Should the request not be approved right away, the procedure will have to wait for the necessary resource or resources to become available. For instance, the functions `open()`, `malloc()`, `new()`, and `request()` are used by the system.

Use: The procedure utilizes the resource by reading from a file or printing it to a printer, for example.

Release: The resource is given up by the process so that other processes can use it.

Deadlock Characterization

Before learning this aspect first, let us revise some items which we already learned in previous units.

- **Resources**: A system resource, or simply resource, is any physical or virtual component of limited availability that is accessible to a computer. All connected devices and internal system components are resources. Virtual system resources include files (concretely file handles), network connections (concretely network sockets), and memory areas.[8]
- **Process**: "*A process is the instance of a computer program that is being executed by one or many threads. There are many different process models, some of which are lightweight, but most processes (even entire virtual machines) are rooted in an operating system (OS) process which comprises the program code, assigned system resources, physical and logical access permissions, and data structures to initiate, control, and coordinate execution activity. Depending on the OS, a process may be made up of multiple threads of execution that execute instructions concurrently.*"[8]

  In the multiprogramming operating system, there are several processes which fights for a finite number of resources, and sometimes, the waiting process never gets a chance to change its state because the resources for which it is waiting are held by another waiting process. A set of a process is called a deadlock when they are waiting for the happening of an event that is called by some other event in the same set.

  Here, every process will follow the system model, which means the process requests a resource. If not allocated, then wait; otherwise, the allocated will use the resources and release them after use.
- **Four essential conditions for deadlock to occur:** According to Coffman (1971), a deadlock requires the simultaneous existence of four requirements. If all four of the Coffman requirements are met, there is a deadlock. These requirements, however, do not conflict with one another.

Observation: Edward Grady Coffman Jr. does computer science. He began working at Bell Laboratories in 1979 and remained there for 20 years, retiring in 1979 as a

Distinguished Member of the Technical Staff. The following are the four Coffman conditions that must be met for a deadlock to occur. These requirements, however, do not conflict with one another. They are listed as follows:

- **Mutual Exclusion Requirement**: The resources in question cannot be shared. Justification: Only one process at a time is allowed to claim exclusive control of a resource (thread) if at least one of them is held in a non-shareable mode. The requesting process must wait until the resource has been released if it is one of the processes that request that resource.

  There should be a resource that can only be held by one process at a time. In the following diagram, there is a single instance of Resource 1, and it is held by Process 1 only.

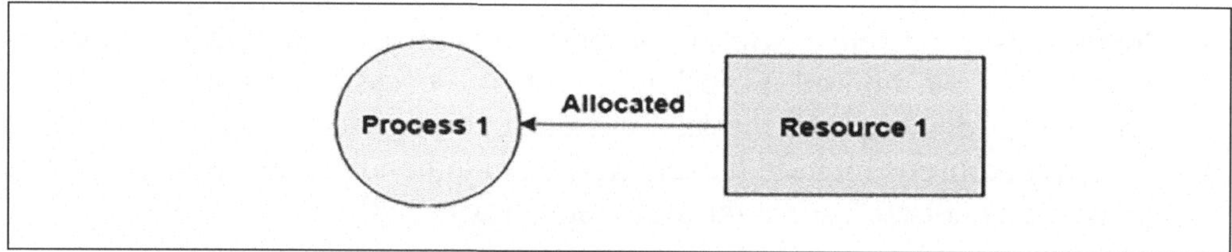

***Figure* 6.16**: *Mutual Exclusion*

- **Hold and Wait Condition:** Requesting process hold already, resources while waiting for requested resources.

  Explanation: There must exist a process that is holding a resource already allocated to it while waiting for additional resources that are currently being held by other processes.

  A process can hold multiple resources and still request more resources from other processes that are holding them. In the following diagram, Process 2 holds Resource 2 and Resource 3 and is requesting Resource 1 which is held by Process 1.

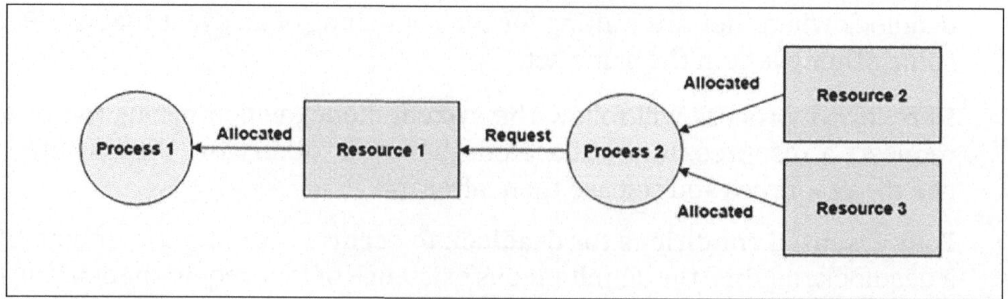

***Figure* 6.17**: *Hold and Wait*

- **No Preemption Condition:** One cannot preempt a process that has already been assigned resources.

Explanation: Resources are either released willingly by the process holding them or they must be used to completion. It is not possible to forcefully remove a resource from a process. A resource can only be released by a process voluntarily. Process 2 is unable to preempt Resource 1 from Process 1 in the following diagram. It won't be made available until Process 1 willingly gives it up following the completion of its execution.

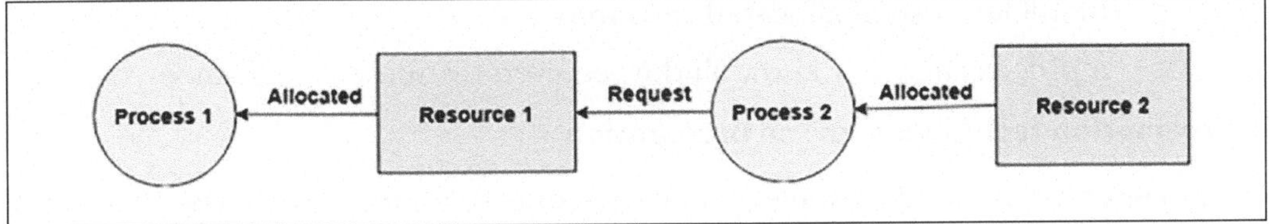

Figure 6.18: *No Preemption*

- **Circular Wait Condition:** Each process in the system's circular list or chain is waiting for a resource that is held by the process after it is in line. One process awaits the resource held by the other, which in turn awaits the resource held by the third, and so on until the final process awaits a resource held by the initial one.

  A circle chain is created by this. As an illustration, Process 1 is assigned Resource 2 and requests Resource 1. In a similar manner, Resource 1 is assigned to Process 2, and it is requesting Resource 2. A circle of waiting is created by this.

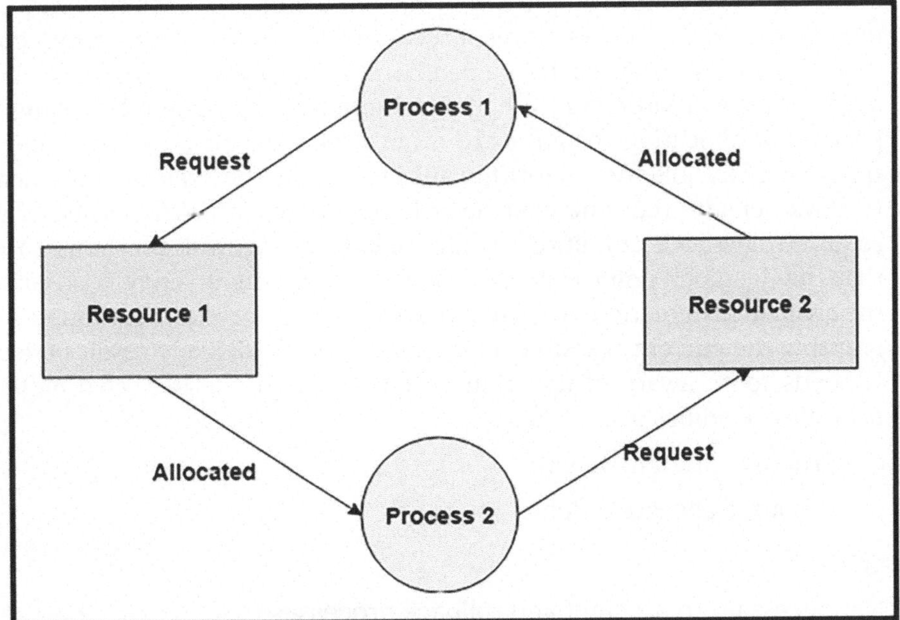

Figure 6.19: *Circular Wait*

Methods for Handling Deadlock

There are mainly four methods for handling deadlock. They are explained as follows:

- **Deadlock Prevention**
    - Long waiting time required
    - Inefficient use of allocated resource
    - A process may not know all the required resources in advance

No preemption techniques for 'no preemption'

If a process that is holding some resource requests another resource that cannot be immediately allocated to it, all resources currently being held are released, and if necessary, requested again together with the additional resource

If a process requests a resource that is currently held by another process, the OS may preempt the second process and require it to release its resources; it works only if both processes do not have the same priority

Circular wait: Ordering all resource types in full and mandating that requests be made by each process in ascending order of enumeration are two ways to guarantee that this condition is never met. If a process receives resources of type R, it is only permitted to request resources of types that come after R in the ordering.

- **Deadlock Avoidance**: The algorithm searches for possible deadlock scenarios ahead of time to prevent them from happening. It accomplishes this by monitoring each process's resource consumption and spotting conflicts that might otherwise result in a deadlock. If the algorithm detects a possible deadlock, it will intervene to end the conflict by, for example, rolling back a process or allocating resources to other processes ahead of schedule. While the Deadlock Avoidance Algorithm aims to reduce the likelihood of a deadlock, it cannot ensure that one won't ever happen. This strategy permits the three required deadlock conditions while making thoughtful decisions to ensure that the deadlock point is never reached. More concurrency is possible than the avoidance detection because it makes a dynamic determination of whether granting the current resource allocation request will likely result in deadlock. It needs to be aware of upcoming requests for processes. Two methods to prevent a deadlock are:
    - Process initiation denial
    - Resource allocation denial

Advantages

- Not necessary to preempt and rollback processes
- Less restrictive than deadlock prevention

Disadvantages

- Future resource requirements must be known in advance
- Processes can be blocked for long periods
- Exists a fixed number of resources for allocation

Banker's Algorithm

The idea of resource allocation graphs serves as the foundation for the Banker's Algorithm. A directed graph with resources represented by edges and processes represented by nodes is called a resource allocation graph. The way resources are currently distributed among processes represents the state of the system. The resource allocation graph would resemble this, for instance, if the system contained three processes, each of which used two resources:

Processes A, B, and C would be the nodes, and the resources they were utilizing would be the edges that connected them.

To determine whether the system is in a safe state or faces the possibility of reaching a deadlock, the Banker's Algorithm examines its current state. The available matrix and the need matrix are the two matrices that the Banker's Algorithm uses to assess whether a system is in a safe state. The quantity of each resource that is presently available is listed in the available matrix. The quantity of each resource needed by each process is listed in the need matrix.

Next, the Banker's Algorithm determines whether a task can be finished without putting too much strain on the system. To achieve this, it adds to the need matrix the quantity of each resource the process uses, deducting it from the available matrix. The process is permitted to continue if the outcome is safe; if not, it is stopped until additional resources are available. The Banker's Algorithm is useful technique for avoiding deadlocks in multiprogramming systems. It is a component of numerous operating systems, such as Linux and Windows. It is also utilized in a wide variety of other systems, including banking and manufacturing systems.

Although it is a strong tool for resource allocation issues, the Banker's Algorithm is not infallible. It can be tricked by both processes that generate more resources than they require and processes that use more than they require. Additionally, it can be tricked by procedures that use resources erratically. It is crucial to keep a close eye on the system to ensure that it is operating safely to stop similar issues.

- **Deadlock Detection:** To eliminate deadlock, an algorithm that monitors circular waiting and terminates one or more processes is used for deadlock detection. The system state is periodically checked to find out if a group of processes is stuck. A process must be stopped and restarted to release all of its resources to break a deadlock.

Neither resource access nor process action is restricted by this technique. When feasible, processes receive the resources they have requested. It makes online handling easier and never delays the start of the process. Preemption losses, by nature, are a drawback.

- **Deadlock Ignorance**: In the method, the system assumes that deadlock never occurs. Since the problem of deadlock situation is not frequent, some systems simply ignore it. Operating systems such as UNIX and Windows follow this approach. However, if a deadlock occurs, we can reboot our system, and the deadlock is resolved automatically.

Note: *The preceding approach is an example of Ostrich Algorithm. It is a strategy of ignoring potential problems on the basis that they are extremely rare.*

Advantages

- ○ Ostrich Algorithm is relatively easy to implement and is effective in most cases
- ○ It helps in avoiding the deadlock situation by ignoring the presence of deadlocks

Disadvantages

- ○ Ostrich Algorithm does not provide any information about the deadlock situation
- ○ It can lead to reduced performance of the system as the system may be blocked for a long time

Deadlock Detection and Recovery

We let the system fall into a deadlock and if it happens, we detect it using a detection algorithm and try to recover.

Some ways of recovery are as follows:

- Aborting all the deadlocked processes
- Abort one process at a time until the system recovers from the deadlock
- Resource Preemption: Resources are taken one by one from a process and assigned to higher priority processes until the deadlock is resolved

When a deadlock occurs, we allow the system to occur, identify it with the help of a detection algorithm, and attempt to resolve it. The following are some strategies for healing.

Deadlock	**Starvation**
A deadlock is a situation in which more than one process is blocked because it is holding a resource and requires some resource that is acquired by some other process	Starvation is a process in which the low-priority processes are postponed indefinitely because the resources are never allocated
Resources are blocked by a set of processes in a circular fashion	Resources are continuously used by high-priority resources
It is prevented by avoiding any necessary condition required for a deadlock or recovery using a recovery algorithm	It can be prevented by aging
In a deadlock, none of the processes get executed	In starvation, higher-priority processes execute while lower-priority processes are postponed
Deadlock is also called circular wait	Starvation is also called lived lock

***Table 6.1**: Difference between Starvation and Deadlocks*

Conclusion

Process synchronization can be achieved by learning about the Critical Section Problem and Hardware primitives for synchronization. We must get involved in Semaphores and their types and learn the process of the Implementation of Binary Semaphore (mutex lock). We need creating Monitors by learning Monitor Semantics. Deadlocks do happen, and we can get alerted by learning Deadlock Modeling and Deadlock Characterization.

In the next chapter, we shall get involved in learning about different types of memories, their types, access time, priority of operation, and their volume.

Questions with Answers

Q1. What are the benefits of process synchronization?

Ans. There are several benefits to process synchronization, including:

- **Data integrity**: Process synchronization helps to ensure that data is not corrupted when multiple processes are accessing it
- **Resource efficiency**: Process synchronization helps to ensure that resources are not wasted when multiple processes are trying to use them at once
- **Increased performance**: Process synchronization helps to improve the performance of applications by reducing the amount of time that processes spend waiting for resources

Q2. What are the challenges of process synchronization?

Ans: There are several challenges to process synchronization, including:

- **Complexity**: Process synchronization can be complex to implement and manage
- **Overhead**: Process synchronization can add overhead to applications, which can reduce their performance
- **Race conditions**: Process synchronization can be difficult to implement correctly, and even a small mistake can lead to race conditions, which can corrupt data or cause other problems

Q3. How do I choose the right synchronization mechanism?

The application's particular requirements will determine which synchronization mechanism is best. To guarantee that only one process can access a resource at a time, for instance, a mutex lock can be employed in situations where two processes need to access the same resource simultaneously. A condition variable can be utilized when two processes must wait for a specific circumstance to occur.

Q4. What are some common mistakes that people make when implementing process synchronization?

Some common mistakes that people make when implementing process synchronization include:

- Not using the right synchronization mechanism for the task at hand
- Not implementing the synchronization mechanism correctly
- Not handling race conditions properly

Q5. What are some tips for implementing process synchronization correctly?

Here are some tips for implementing process synchronization correctly:

- Use the right synchronization mechanism for the task at hand
- Implement the synchronization mechanism correctly.
- Handle race conditions properly

Q6. What do we mean by process synchronization? Why do we need it?

A process that can either influence or be influenced by other processes operating in the system is said to be cooperating. Code and data are exchanged between collaborating processes, and concurrent access to shared data may result in inconsistent data. Process synchronization is a way to ensure that cooperating processes run in unison.

Multiple Choice Questions

1. Race conditions are prevented by requiring that critical regions be protected by locks
   a. True
   b. False

   Explanation: Locks guarantee that only a single thread can access a crucial area at any given time; hence the statement is accurate. By doing this, race conditions–which happen when several threads attempt to access and alter shared data at the same time–are avoided, which can produce unexpected and inaccurate outcomes. Locks are used to protect the critical region so that only one thread at a time can enter it, protecting data integrity and averting race situations.

2. A counting semaphore ____.
   a. Cannot be used to control access to a thread's critical sections
   b. Is essentially an integer variable
   c. Can be modified simultaneously by multiple threads
   d. Is accessed through only one standard operation

   Explanation: Since a counting semaphore regulates which threads may access a shared resource, it can be considered as an integer variable. It keeps track of the resources that are available and decides whether to grant or deny access based on this total. As threads acquire or release resources, they increment or decrement the semaphore's value, which is an integer.

3. Mutex locks and counting semaphores are essentially the same thing.
   a. True
   b. False

   Explanation: Counting semaphores and mutex locks are not exactly the same thing. Both synchronization mechanisms serve distinct purposes in concurrent programming, despite being used in the same context. A shared resource can only be accessed exclusively by one thread at a time with the help of a mutex lock. However, to limit how many threads can access a shared resource at once, a counting semaphore is employed. It keeps track of the number of concurrent thread accesses and permits a predetermined number of them. As such, the claim that counting semaphores and mutex locks are interchangeable is untrue.

4. A race condition ____.

    a. Will result only if the outcome of execution does not depend on the order in which instructions are executed

    b. Results when several threads try to access and modify the same data concurrently

    c. Results when several threads try to access the same data concurrently

    d. None of the above

    Explanation : A race condition occurs when several threads try to access and modify the same data concurrently. In this situation, the outcome of the execution may be unpredictable and inconsistent because the threads may interfere with each other's operations. This can lead to errors and bugs in the program.

5. What is the correct order of operations for protecting a critical section using a binary semaphore?

    a. `Signal()` followed by `wait()`

    b. `Acquire()` followed by `release()`

    c. `Release()` followed by `acquire()`

    d. `Wait()` followed by `signal()`

    Explanation: The correct order of operations for protecting a critical section using a binary semaphore is to first wait for the semaphore (**`wait()`**), which blocks the process if the semaphore value is 0, ensuring mutual exclusion. Then, once the critical section is completed, the process signals the semaphore (**`signal()`**), allowing other processes to enter the critical section. This order ensures that only one process can enter the critical section at a time, preventing race conditions and ensuring synchronization.

6. A mutex lock ______.

    a. Is exactly like a counting semaphore

    b. Is essentially a boolean variable

    c. Can be used to eliminate busy waiting

    d. Is not guaranteed to be atomic

7. The value of a counting semaphore can range only between 0 and 1.

    a. True

    b. False

8. Which one of the following requirements need not be met by a solution to the critical section problem?
   a. Atomicity
   b. Bounded waiting
   c. Progress
   d. Mutual exclusion
9. What is a reusable resource?
   a. One that can be used by one process at a time and is not depleted by that use
   b. One that can be used by more than one process at a time
   c. One that can be shared between various threads
   d. None of the mentioned
10. Which of the following conditions is required for a deadlock to be possible?
    a. Mutual exclusion
    b. A process may hold allocated resources while awaiting assignment of other resources
    c. No resource can be forcibly removed from a process holding it
    d. All of the mentioned
11. A system is in the safe state if _____________
    a. The system can allocate resources to each process in some order and still avoid a deadlock
    b. There exists a safe sequence
    c. All of the mentioned
    d. None of the mentioned
12. The circular wait condition can be prevented by _____________
    a. Defining a linear ordering of resource types
    b. Using thread
    c. Using pipes
    d. All of the mentioned

13. Which one of the following is the deadlock avoidance algorithm?
    a. Banker's algorithm
    b. Round-robin algorithm
    c. Elevator algorithm
    d. Karn's algorithm
14. What is the drawback of a Banker's algorithm?
    a. In advance processes rarely know how much resource they will need
    b. The numbers of processes changes as time progresses
    c. Resource once available can disappear
    d. All of the mentioned
15. For an effective operating system, when to check for deadlock?
    a. Every time a resource request is made
    b. At fixed time intervals
    c. Every time a resource request is made at fixed time intervals
    d. None of the mentioned
16. A problem encountered in multitasking when a process is perpetually denied necessary resources is called _____________
    a. Deadlock
    b. Starvation
    c. Inversion
    d. Aging
17. Which one of the following is a visual (mathematical) way to determine the deadlock occurrence?
    a. Resource allocation graph
    b. Starvation graph
    c. Inversion graph
    d. None of the mentioned
18. To avoid deadlock _____________
    a. There must be a fixed number of resources to allocate
    b. Resource allocation must be done only once
    c. All deadlocked processes must be aborted
    d. An inversion technique can be used

Answers

1. a, 2. b, 3. b, 4. c, 5. d, 6. b, 7. b, 8. a, 9. a, 10. d

11. c, 12. a, 13. a, 14. d, 15. c, 16. b, 17. a, 18. a

Questions

1. Illustrate Process synchronization with an example and a diagram.
2. Illustrate the Working of Process Synchronization in OS works with an example.
3. Why Process Synchronization was introduced in OS, and what are the types?
4. When is a Race Condition encountered?
5. What are three conditions that must be satisfied to get a solution to the critical section problem?
6. Does Peterson's Solution satisfy all three conditions for solving critical section problem?
7. Write down the names of various sections of critical solution.
8. What are the three rules of Critical Sections?
9. Illustrate the two portions of Hardware primitives for synchronization.
10. What is semaphore and how semaphore ensure process synchronization?
11. What is the need of using Semaphore and what are the merits and demerits of using them?
12. Describe how the Wait and signaling operations are effected by programming on semaphores?
13. What is the Implementation of Binary Semaphore?
14. What is mutual exclusion and how is it prevented by mutex lock?
15. With the help of a sketch show how the Counting Semaphore is implemented?
16. What is a Monitor and Monitor Semantics; a software or hardware?
17. Where are monitors run, and what is the effect created?
18. What are the classical problems in synchronization? Write the name of four famous examples of Classical problems in synchronization? Illustrate any one of them.

19. Which famous algorithmic problem teaches the nuances of process synchronization and resource allocation in operating systems?
20. Which is the language normally used for writing synchronization problems in OS?
21. What are the famous four essential conditions (discovered by Coffman) for a deadlock to occur?
22. Write down the names of four essential conditions in which deadlock is ensured. Illustrate any one of them.
23. Which algorithm is an effective way to prevent deadlocks in multiprogramming systems?
24. How is the Deadlock condition detected?
25. Differentiate between Starvation and Deadlocks.

Reference

[1] Understand Process Synchronization with Example?, Naimish Mulani, December 6, 2022,https://www.prepbytes.com/blog/operating-system/process-synchronization-in-os-definition-working-and-example/

[2] Lecture 6: Semaphores and Monitors, CSE 120: Principles of Operating Systems Alex C. Snoeren

[3] Process Synchronization,https://www.studytonight.com/operating-system/process-synchronization

[4] Semaphore in Operating System Shiksha Online,https://www.shiksha.com/online-courses/articles/semaphore-in-operating-system/

[5] Classical Problems of Synchronization in OS, Author Rahul Singh, https://www.naukri.com/code360/library/classical-problems-of-synchronization-in-os

[6] Deadlock in Operating System, Isha Yadav, https://www.scaler.com/topics/operating-system/deadlock-in-os/

[7] Methods for Handling Deadlock in Operating System, By Prerana Jain Last updated : May 07, 2023,https://www.includehelp.com/operating-systems/deadlock-and-method-for-handling-deadlock.aspx

[8] Deadlock (computer science), Wikipedia, the free encyclopedia, https://en.wikipedia.org/wiki/Deadlock_(computer_science)

CHAPTER 7(a)
Computer Memory Part 1

Introduction

Chapter 7 has been divided into two parts covering every aspects of Computer Memory management. In part 1, we shall concentrate on Memory Hierarchy and Features of Memory Hierarchy Design containing primary, secondary memory and RAM and ROM architecture. We shall learn about internal primary memory including, registers, cache memories, RAM and ROM, and types of ROM. We then move on to Main and Virtual Memory, secondary and tertiary memory containing magnetic tape and optical storage, and so on. Also, we shall learn the requirements of Memory Management System at the end of part 1, that is, how exactly memory is managed by swapping and segmentation. In part 2, we shall discuss Demand Paging, Thrashing, and so on and the memory management in two versatile operating systems, Windows and Unix.

Structure

In this chapter, efforts shall be made to learn about following topics:

- Computer Memory Architecture
- Memory Hierarchy
- Characteristic Features of Memory Hierarchy Design
- Primary Memory Arrays
- RAM and ROM Architecture
- Types of ROM: Semiconductor-Based
- Types of Random-Access Memory (RAM)
- Static and Dynamic Random-Access Memory (SRAM and DRAM)
- Modern Memory Hierarchy

- Virtual Memory
- Requirements of Memory Management System
- Cache Memory in Computer Organization
- Segmentation
- Levels of memory
  - Swapping in Operating Systems
  - Segmentation

Overview of Computer Memory

Memory devices such as *registers, cache memory, main memory, flash memory, magnetic disks, magnetic tapes, and so on are all part of our computer systems; each has a unique purpose and performance rate.*

Memory Architecture[1]

"*Memory Architecture describes the methods used to implement data storage in a manner that is a combination of the fastest, most reliable, most durable, and cheapest way to store and collect information.*

The data storage structure consists of individual memory cells arranged in an array of horizontal rows and vertical columns. Each cell is capable of storing 1-bit of binary information. In this structure, there are 2^N *rows also called word lines and* 2^M columns, *also called bit lines.*

Thus, this array's total number of memory cells is 2^N x 2^M. *To access a memory cell, that is, a specific data bit in this array, the corresponding word line and corresponding bit line must be selected according to the address from outside of memory array".*

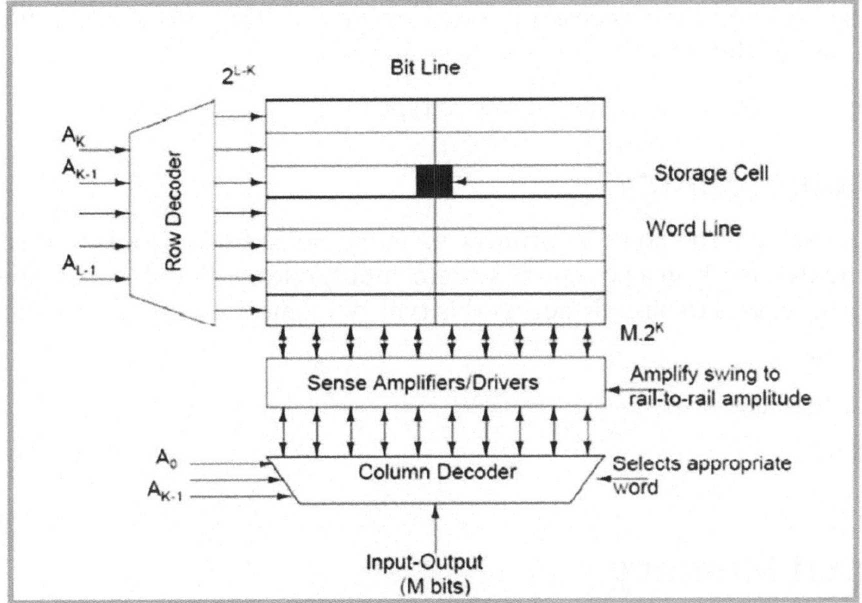

Figure 7a.1: *Basic Memory Organization*

Memory Hierarchy

Memory Hierarchy is the meaningful arrangement and visualization of these various memory devices concerning their performance, access time, and cost per bit, which proves to be helpful while designing a new system to balance its overall performance-to-cost ratio.

When a Computer System is designed, a large number of different devices are used in it, like processors, different memory devices, motherboards, and so on, and these parts are costly, which means we are not free to use them often as we want, meaning we are bound to use each particular part only a specific number of times in the design, to balance the overall cost. [1]

A system's memory devices are arranged in multiple layers, each with varying performance rates and usage, and as a result, their sizes and access times differ significantly from one another.

To optimize a system's performance, the memory hierarchy offers a meaningful arrangement of these different memory types. The memory hierarchy determines how a system's memory is organized to balance performance and overall cost.

The *Figure 7a.1* provides a clear understanding of the memory hierarchy design. You may be wondering why the shape is a pyramid; it represents the size (in bits) and access time of each of these memory layers. The size of the memory layers available inside a system and their access time with respect to the CPU (Central Processing Unit) are the key differences between these layers.

The Memory Hierarchy is divided into two types.

Internal Memory

Internal memory, also known as primary memory, houses data needs to be accessed quickly and frequently in a computer system. Input/output modules allow the system and other processes to directly access this type of memory and that include:

- Registers
- Cache Memories
- RAM
- ROM

External Memory

Large volumes of data are stored in what are known as secondary memories, which are non-volatile memories that continue to store data even during a power outage.

They consist of:

- Magnetic Disks
- Optical Disks
- Magnetic Tapes

Based on speed and intended use, memory can be categorized into five hierarchies. If the processor cannot find what it needs at one level, it advances to the next level. Volatile memory currently resides in the first three hierarchies: registers, cache, and main memory. That is, they lose their data when their power is interrupted. As they are considered as permanent storage, the final two are not volatile.

The final two, which are regarded as permanent storage, are not volatile. Every memory unit has a value of either 0 or 1.

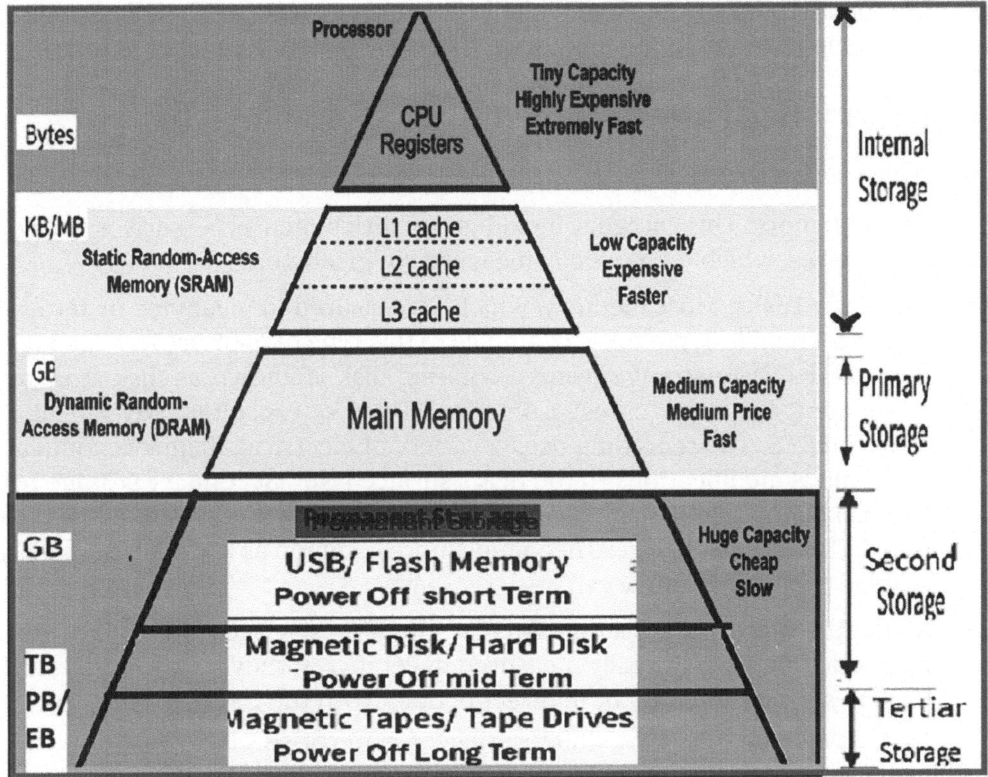

Figure 7a.2*: Memory Hierarchy Pyramid*

Let us understand each of these levels one by one:

- **Registers:** These are extremely small memory devices that can store a variety of types of data, such as general-purpose registers, address registers, and so on. Typically, they can hold bytes of data that are roughly 32-bit to 64-bitin size. Since the registers are directly connected to the CPU, they are the quickest memory that can be found in a system. However, because of this, they are also the most expensive. As a result, they are used in very small quantities and have the quickest access times.
- **Cache Memory**: Also referred to as Static Random Access Memory (SRAM), cache memories are used to store program segments that are frequently accessed by the processor. They are measured in kilobytes or megabytes. Internal memory, which includes registers and cache memories, is the fastest type of memory because it is integrated into the CPU itself. [1]
- **Main Memory (RAM):** The is the most widely used memory, also known as Dynamic Random Access Memory (DRAM). It interacts directly via input and output with the CPU and other memory devices. These are measured in Gigabytes and are less expensive than cache memory.

- The data stored in the three volatile memories mentioned earlier–registers, cache memory, and main memory–will be lost when the power is turned off.

Secondary Storage

Let us explain secondary storage:

- **Flash Memory:** This category includes memories such as pen drives and solid-state drives, which are typically measured in gigabytes.
- **Magnetic Disks:** Most memory, which is measured in gigabytes or terabytes, is slower than flash memory. Examples of this type of memory storage include hard drives. Data storage using a rotating disk is known as disk storage (or drive storage in some cases). Common HDD disk capacities are 500GB, 1TB, 2TB, and 4TB. The recording uses a variety of electrical, magnetic, optical, or mechanical modifications to the disk's surface layer. Secondary storage refers to Flash Memory and Magnetic Disks combined. However, larger sizes such as 6TB, 8TB, and even 16TB are becoming more common as the demand for larger storage capacities increases.
- **Magnetic Tapes Data Storage Media:** The largest-sized and slowest-access magnetic tapes are typically measured in Petabytes; they are primarily used as backup storage and are not in direct contact with the CPU.

  IBM developed the IBM 3592 series of enterprise-class tape drives and matching magnetic tape data storage media formats. The native data transfer rate of this series is up to 400 MB/s, and it can store up to 50 TB of data (uncompressed) on a cartridge. As seen in *Figure 7a.1*, the central processing unit (CPU) is typically positioned at the top of a pyramid-shaped computer architecture.

  Short-term memory serves as a repository for frequently accessed tasks, while long-term memory is used for permanent storage as we descend. As opposed to long-term memory, which can hold many terabytes but operates at a very slow pace (approximately 550 megabytes per second), which is fast (5000–6000 megabytes per second) and has a smaller capacity (a few gigabytes) [1,2]. Let us first examine long-term or storage memories.

Tertiary Storage

The third-level storage system in a computer is called tertiary storage and is where big data is kept for extended periods. Although they are reasonably slow, they are also reasonably priced. Robotic arms are used by tertiary storage devices to deliver removable disks or tapes to reading devices. The old media is ejected from the drive when new media is added. Magnetic tape, optical disks, and optical tapes are a few examples of tertiary storage. Cloud storage, optical jukeboxes, tape libraries, and optical cassettes are also a few example.

Benefits of Memory Hierarchy

Using a memory hierarchy in computer systems has several benefits, including:

- **Faster Access**: Computer systems can offer faster access to frequently accessed data because of the multiple levels of the memory hierarchy. The most often used data is kept in the fastest memory, such as cache memory, which can access data far more quickly than other memory types.
- **Cost-Effective**: Since implementing high-speed memory like cache memory is more expensive than other types of memory like main memory or secondary storage, the computer system can be made more affordable by using a memory hierarchy. The most expensive memory can be used where it is most needed rather than used everywhere by using a memory hierarchy.
- **Effective resource management** is made possible by memory hierarchy, which places frequently accessed information in fast memory and less frequently accessed information in slower memory. This guarantees that high-speed memory is used for data that is rarely accessed, preventing resource waste on the part of the computer system.
- **Boosts Processing Speed:** Computer systems can operate far more quickly, thanks to the use of a memory hierarchy.
- **The system's process**ing speed is increased by the CPU's ability to retrieve data quickly and execute operations more quickly when stored in the fastest memory for frequently used data.
- **Enhanced Capacity**: Memory hierarchy enhances the system's overall capacity by enabling the computer system to store substantial volumes of data in secondary storage and retaining the most frequently accessed data in high-speed memory. As a result, the system can process massive volumes of data without experiencing performance lag.

Overall, the performance and efficiency of computer systems are enhanced by using a memory hierarchy, which makes the system faster, more economical, and more resource-efficient.

Disadvantages of Memory Hierarchy

The memory hierarchy design offers a way to balance costs and maximize system performance overall. It does, however, have certain drawbacks.

- **Complexity**: Because the system must effectively manage several memory layers, it becomes more complex.
- **Access time**: The memory hierarchy design increases system latency even though its goal is to shorten the time it takes to access data. The need to transfer data between layers lengthens the access time.

- **Cost:** The memory hierarchy design raises the system's overall cost even though it seeks to balance it. The system gets more expensive as more layers are added.
- **Restricted capacity**: The system cannot store an infinite amount of data due to the limited capacity of each layer in the memory hierarchy. Occasionally, this restriction may cause problems with performance. Overhead in the management process is added by the need for the system to control the data transfer between the various memory levels.
- **Overhead in the management** process is added by the need for the system to control the data transfer between the various memory levels.

  Memory hierarchy design is still commonly used because it offers an effective means of managing memory and enhancing system performance, despite these drawbacks.

Characteristic Features of Memory Hierarchy Design

This section describes the characteristic features of memory hierarchy design:

- **Performance**: Memory hierarchy was not used when designing computer systems in the past, which caused the speed differences between various memory components and CPU registers to gradually increase and lower system performance. Memory hierarchy designs were introduced to improve this, and as a result, computer systems now perform better.
- **Access Time**: This is the amount of time that passes between when the data becomes available and when read/write requests are made. Going from top to bottom in the memory hierarchy design results in longer access times.
- **Capacity**: The volume of data that the memory can store is indicated by the capacity, which rises from top to bottom.
- **Cost Per Bit**: The registers are the most expensive memory, while secondary and tertiary storage are the cheapest. This is because the cost-per-bit ratio rises from bottom to top. As for the cost, you might assume that since we store petabytes–roughly 1015 bytes–of data on magnetic tapes rather than just a few bytes in registers, the latter should be more expensive than the former. However, the opposite is true; registers are the most expensive of the three when it comes to cost per bit of memory, while magnetic tapes are the cheapest.

  The reason for this cost variation is due to their access times. Specifically, data stored in registers will be accessed at the fastest speed. Cache memory, main memory, flash drives, magnetic disks, and magnetic tapes will follow in order of slower access times.

- **Frequency:** Registers are the memory that the CPU uses the most frequently because they are directly embedded into the CPU, and also, we know that the CPU accesses them even for the smallest tasks, making them the most used memory in any system. Furthermore, magnetic tapes are the least used memory device in a computer system, as they are typically used to store backups, which are regularly accessed but not used normally.

Table 7a.1 describes various characteristic features of various memory systems.

Memory	Type	Access Time (Approx)	Cost per bit
Registers	Internal Memory	1 nano second	Highest among the following
Cache Memory (Static RAM)	Internal Memory	10 nano seconds.	Comparatively Lesser than Registers
Main Memory (Dynamic RAM)	Primary Memory	100 nanoseconds	Comparatively Lesser than Cache Memory
Flash Drives	Secondary Storage	1 microsecond	Comparatively Lesser than Main Memory
Magnetic Disks	Secondary Storage	10 micro seconds	Comparatively Lesser than Flash Drives
External Magnetic Tapes	Tertiary Storage	100 milli-seconds	Comparatively Lesser than Magnetic Disks (Lowest cost of all)

Table 7a.1: *Various characteristic features of memory systems*

Primary Memory Arrays

Memories are also needed in digital systems to store the data that these circuits use and produce. Flip-flop-based registers are a type of memory used to store small amounts of data. Large-capacity memory arrays that are effective at storing data are covered in this section. An overview of the qualities shared by all memory arrays opens this section. The three different types of memory arrays–read-only memory (ROM), static random access memory (SRAM), and dynamic random access memory (DRAM)–are then introduced. Every memory has a unique method for storing information.

This section explains the area and delay trade-offs in brief and demonstrates the use of memory arrays for logic operations in addition to data storage. The HDL for a memory array completes this section.

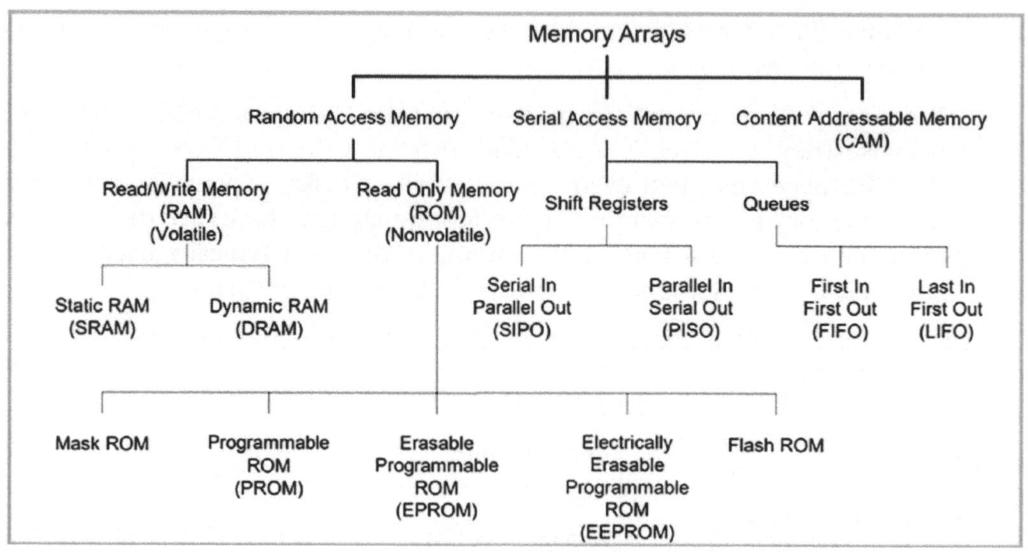

Figure 7a.3: *Concept of Memory Array*

RAM and ROM Architecture

Read-only memory, or ROM, is a form of data storage in computers and other electronic devices that cannot be easily altered or reprogrammed. RAM is referred to as volatile memory and is lost when the power is turned off, whereas ROM is non-volatile, and the contents are retained even after the power is switched off.

Types of ROM: Semiconductor-Based

Classic mask-programmed ROM chips are integrated circuits that physically encode the data to be stored, and thus it is impossible to change their contents after fabrication. Other types of non-volatile solid-state memory permit some degree of modification:

- **A specialized tool known as a PROM** programmer can be used to write to or program programmable read-only memory (PROM), also known as one-time programmable ROM (OTP). This device usually creates or destroys internal links (fuses or anti-fuses) inside the chip by applying high voltages. A PROM can therefore only be programmed once. Erasable programmable read-only memory (EPROM) can be written again using a procedure that requires applying a higher voltage than usual, or it can be erased by exposure to intense UV light (usually for 10 minutes or longer).
- **An EPROM** will eventually wear out from repeated exposure to UV light, but most EPROM chips can withstand more than 1000 cycles of erasing and reprogramming. Packages containing EPROM chips are frequently recognized by the noticeable quartz "window" that lets in UV light. To avoid inadvertent

erasure, the window is usually labeled after programming. Certain EPROM chips are essentially PROM since they have been factory erased before packaging and have no window.

- Contemporary designs exhibit exceptionally high endurance, surpassing 1,000,000 cycles. Modern NAND flash makes efficient use of silicon chip area, resulting in individual ICs with a capacity as high as 32 GB as of 2007. This feature, along with its endurance and physical durability, has allowed NAND flash to replace magnetic in some applications, such as USB flash drives.
- When used to replace older types of ROM, flash memory is sometimes referred to as flash ROM or flash EEPROM; however, this terminology is not appropriate for applications that utilize the fast and frequent modifications that flash memory can perform.

Random-Access Memory (RAM)

RAM is a type of data storage available at any time, from any physical location, and in any order. This is in contrast to other types of storage, such as hard drives, where the time it takes to retrieve data is determined by its physical location. RAM chips can read data faster than ROM because their speed is measured in nanoseconds and their capacity is measured in megabytes.

Types of RAM

The two widely used forms of modern RAM are:

- Static RAM (SRAM) and
- Dynamic RAM (DRAM)

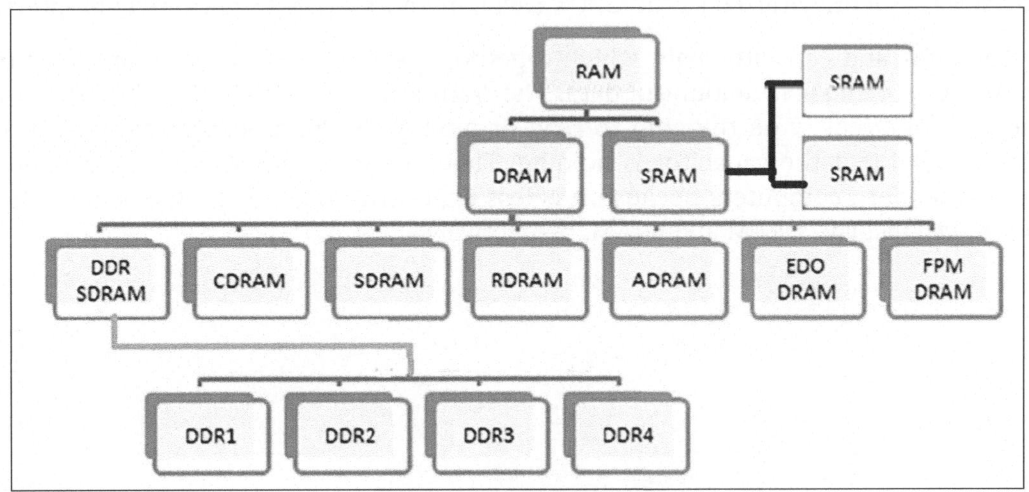

Figure 7a.4: *Types of RAMs*

In general, RAM only refers to DRAM or SRAM, or more precisely, the main memory found in the majority of computers, as solid-state memory devices. While DVD-RAM does not require erasure prior to reuse, it is a bit of a misnomer in the context of optical storage, unlike CDRW or DVD-RW. Though a little slower, a DVDRAM functions very similarly to a hard disk drive.

SRAM	**DRAM**
SRAM has a lower access time, so it is faster compared to DRAM	DRAM has a higher access time, so it is slower than SRAM
SRAM is costlier than DRAM	DRAM costs less compared to SRAM
SRAM requires a constant power supply, that is, this type of memory consumes more power.	DRAM offers reduced power consumption because the information is stored in the capacitor
It is a complex internal circuitry, and it offers less storage capacity compared to the same physical size of a DRAM memory chip	It is the small internal circuitry in the one-bit memory cell of DRAM; the large storage capacity is available
SRAM has a low packaging density	DRAM has a high packaging density

Table 7a.2: *Types of RAM*

Static Random-Access Memory (Static RAM or SRAM)

A six-transistor memory cell's state is used in SRAM to store a small amount of data. (see the right-hand side of *Figure 7a.5*). Although the cost of manufacturing this type of RAM is higher than that of DRAM, it is typically faster and uses less dynamic power. SRAM is frequently utilized as the CPU's cache memory in contemporary computers.

A transistor and capacitor pair, which together make up a DRAM cell, are used by DRAM to store a small amount of data. The transistor functions as a switch to allow the control circuitry on the chip to read or modify the high or low charge (1 or 0, respectively) that the capacitor is holding. This type of memory is most commonly used in modern computers because it is less expensive to produce than static RAM. *Figure 7a.5* displays DRAM and SRAM, respectively.

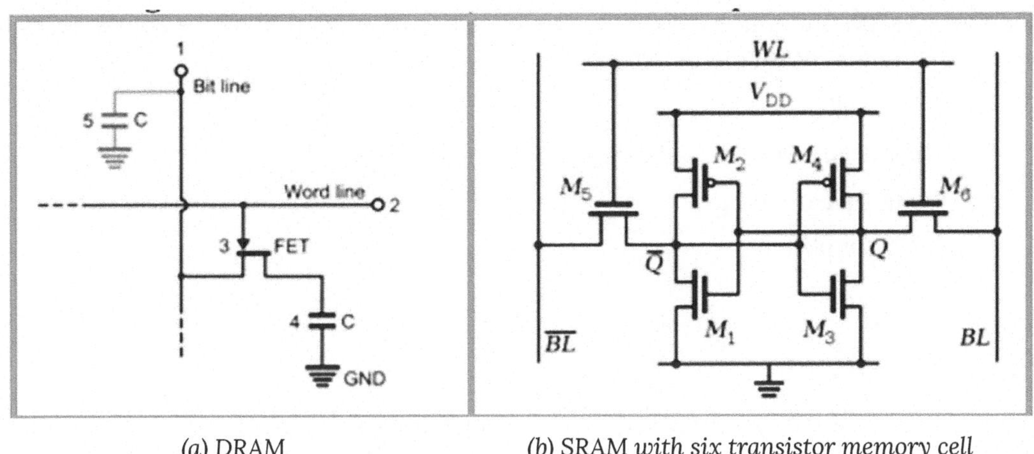

(*a*) DRAM (*b*) SRAM *with six transistor memory cell*

Figure 7a.5: *Circuit of DRAM and SHRAM memory type*

Because the state of both static and dynamic RAM is lost or reset when the system is powered off, they are both regarded as volatile memory. On the other hand, read-only memory (ROM) prevents memory tampering by permanently turning on or off specific transistors that store data. Writeable ROM variations, such as EEPROM and flash memory, combine the advantages of RAM and ROM, allowing data to be updated and maintained without requiring specialized hardware. Solid-state drives, memory cards for cameras and portable devices, and USB flash drives are examples of these durable semiconductor ROM devices. ECC memory, which comes in SRAM and DRAM varieties, has specialized circuitry that uses error correction codes or parity bits to identify and/or fix random faults, also known as memory errors, in the stored data.

Static random-access memory, also known as static RAM or SRAM, is a kind of random-access memory (RAM) in which every bit is stored using latching circuitry, or flip-flops. SRAM is a volatile memory; when the power is turned off, the data is gone. SRAM and DRAM (dynamic random-access memory) are distinguished by the term static. When power is present, SRAM can store data indefinitely, but DRAM needs to refresh data periodically because it deteriorates over time. Although it costs more and takes up more silicon area, it is faster than DRAM. SRAM is typically used for a CPU's cache and internal registers, whereas DRAM is used for a computer's main memory.

"*Fast & low-power* SRAMs *are becoming the main component in many* VLSI *chips. Mainly* SRAMs *are used in cache memories.*"[1]

"SRAMs *are designed to provide a direct interface with the* CPU *at speeds not attainable by* DRAMs *and to replace* DRAMs *in a system that require very low power consumption. In several applications, the embedded* SRAMs *can occupy a larger chip area and contain hundreds of millions of transistors.* SRAMs *need to be not only fast but also reliable; that is, it must be stable and robust for the system to work properly.*

The main SRAM building blocks include various components. All these components or blocks used in the SRAM are listed as follows:

- *SRAM cell*
- *Pre-Charge Circuit*
- *Write Driver Circuit*
- *Sense Amplifier*
- *Row decoder"*

SRAM Cell

The SRAM cell, which stores data, that is, a straightforward latch circuit with two stable operating points, connects two inverters back to back to form the one-bit memory cell. The logic '0' or '1' that corresponds to the data stored in the memory cell depends on the condition of the two inverter latch circuits. Three states are possible for an SRAM cell: writing when the contents are updated, reading when data is requested, and standing by when the circuit is not in use.

When SRAM is operated in read mode, it should have a read-stability, and in write mode, it should have a write-stability.

Typically, an SRAM cell (also called a 6T SRAM cell) consists of six MOSFETs. Each bit in the cell is stored by two cross-coupled inverters made up of four transistors: M1, M2, M3, and M4. In this storage cell, there are two stable states that correspond to 0 and 1. Two additional access transistors control the read and write access to a storage cell. The sixth-generation RAM is the most common type of SRAM.

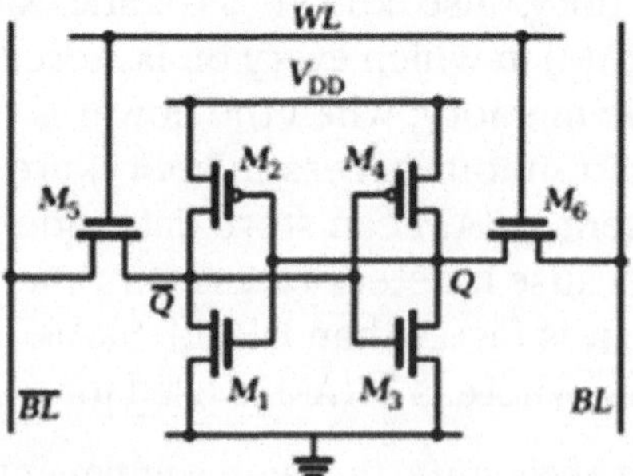

Figure 7a.6: *Transistor SRAM circuit*

SRAM Architecture and Types

Each bit in SRAM is stored using a latching circuit based on flip-flops. The memory cells used by almost all SRAMs are either 4- or 6-transistor designs. As long as the device is powered on, data can be stored in these cell structures for an infinite amount of time. There are two varieties of SRAMs available: Synchronous and Asynchronous.

Synchronous SRAMs: Synchronous SRAMs are devices synchronized with an external signal called a clock. The device will read and write information into the memory only on particular states of the clock. Sync SRAMs is a volatile random-access memory (RAM) that uses flip-flop-based latching circuitry to store each bit. The data bits are retained in memory as long as power is supplied. Unlike Async SRAM, Sync SRAMs has a clocked interface for control, address, and data. Infineon provides the industry's broadest portfolio of Synchronous SRAMs from 2M to 144M.

Asynchronous SRAM: Data on your computer is stored there permanently. Upon installing an application, for instance, your computer either downloads the installation file to your storage or copies the program's files from the installation disc. Documents, images, music, and videos are all stored on your computer using storage as well. You can save a certain number of files on your computer depending on its storage capacity. Large amounts of data can be inexpensively and compactly stored in these. Moreover, since data is not lost during a power outage, these can be utilized for partial or full backup storage. That being said, compared to virtual memory, the access time is somewhat slower.

Design Trade-off Factors of SRAM

To put it briefly, speed is the main benefit. When creating a design, speed, volatility, cost, and many other factors will all need to be traded off.

The speed of an SRAM over a DRAM is one of these factors. Prior to choosing a RAM for our system design, the fastest DRAMs currently available should still be considered. Let us talk about each of these factors that need more than five processor clock cycles to access the first piece of information.

- **Volatility**: SRAM cannot hold the data if the power is removed. The SRAM cells do not need to be refreshed like DRAM. SRAM supports faster read and write times than DRAM.
- **Cost:** If cost is the major factor in a memory design, then DRAMs will be the low-cost option instead of SRAM. If the performance is a critical factor, then using a well-designed SRAM is an effective and cost-performance solution for us.

Modern Memory Hierarchy

A brief hierarchy; memory elements in computer architecture are as follows:

- **The level one** cache represents the second tier within the memory hierarchy.
- **The level two** cache is embedded within the CPU itself and is typically quite compact (ranging from 4KB to 32KB). Despite its small size, it exceeds the

register capacity within the CPU. Being a built-in component of the CPU, this cache cannot be expanded. However, its cost is lower compared to registers.

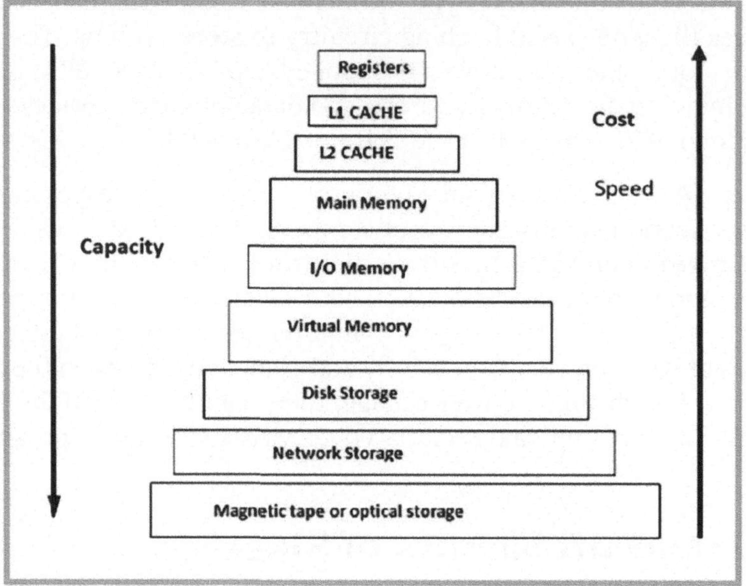

Figure 7a.7: *Modern Hierarchical Levels*

1. **Main Memory:** The main memory system falls right below the level 2 cache memory and is the low-cost and bulk memory available for general purposes. It is relatively fast but bulky, expensive, and volatile.

2. **I/O Memory:** Below the main memory lies the I/O memory, which is used by the peripherals. Such memory access is often slower than the main memory. The video card memory or the flash memory are a few examples of I/O memory.

3. **Virtual Memory:** A virtual memory system is used in most modern computer today. Virtual memory occupies a portion of the disk drive and uses it as main memory. It can transparently copy data between the main memory and the disk as required by the application.

   Disk storage is relatively much cheaper than semiconductor memory; hence, it makes sense to use disk memory as the main memory.

4. **Disk Storage:** Storage is where data is permanently kept on your computer. When you install a program, for example, your computer copies the program's files from the installation disc or downloads the installation file to your storage.

   Your computer also uses storage to save documents, photos, music, and videos. Your storage capacity determines the number of files you can save on your computer.

These can store large quantities of data cheaply and in a small space. Furthermore, these can be used for parament/semi-parament storage as data is not lost when power is removed. However, the access time is slightly slower than virtual memory.

5. **Network Storage:** In the hierarchy, below the disk storage lies the network storage. The programs at this level store data on a remote system connected via a network. Network storage can be used to implement virtual memory, disk storage, and distributed shared memory.

   Network storage can be created by using cheap and unused disk storage spread over a network of computers. Network storage is slower compared to local disk storage.

6. **Magnetic Tape and Optical Storage:** These can both store enormous amounts of data in a tiny amount of space and are cheaper. They are perfect for permanent data storage because they typically use removable media. On the other hand, access times are very lengthy.

   The designer can achieve the best of both worlds and create a comparatively inexpensive system with a high capacity and speed by combining various types of memory into a single system. The computer uses memory as a workspace. The data and programs that the computer uses are stored there. Computer systems always incorporate a variety of memory device types. While some of them might be built-in parts, others might need to be installed separately.

   Memory, sometimes referred to as physical memory or Random Access Memory (RAM), is a part of a PC that stores data while operating. This information can be found on any website you are viewing or in a Word document. Your computer retrieves this data from memory easily and quickly whenever necessary. Your computer's capacity to store and access multiple files simultaneously increases with memory size. For this reason, having enough memory is crucial if you intend to multitask, run resource-intensive applications on your computer, such as AutoCAD® and some games, or have a lot of files.

Virtual Memory

The system's primary memory, or RAM, is expensive and has a limited capacity, as we have already discussed. Secondary memory, on the other hand, comes in larger and cheaper forms, and its capacity can be readily expanded.

A memory management technique called virtual memory gives users the impression of having a very large memory. As was already mentioned, our physical memory is finite. To make storage resources truly accessible on a particular computer, virtual memory enables physical memory to idealize the abstraction of those resources.

This concept offers a unique way to extend apparent primary memory. As a result, we can access secondary memory just like we would main memory. Shifting unused RAM storage to secondary storage is one way to increase this.

Envision your computer's physical memory located in the front portion of your closet. You keep your preferred outfits up front so they are easily accessible. In the aforementioned scenario, visualize yourself as the operating system and the back of your closet as the hard drive. When necessary, you can also access the clothes at the back, though it might take a little longer. You could make a list of the clothing items you have placed where to make searching easier. A page table is a type of mapping mechanism. A portion of the secondary memory of the system that functions and gives the impression that it is a part of the main memory is called virtual memory. A system can run more demanding programs or several programs at once with virtual memory without using up all of the RAM (Random Access Memory). The system can operate specifically as though its total RAM resources were made up of all of the RAM that is physically present as well as all of the RAM that is virtualized.

In essence, virtual memory gives users access to more memory than the system can physically store. With the help of the operating system (OS), installed software, and hardware, it keeps this up to date by transferring data from RAM to the disk. Let us examine how *Figure 7a.6*'s virtual memory functions.

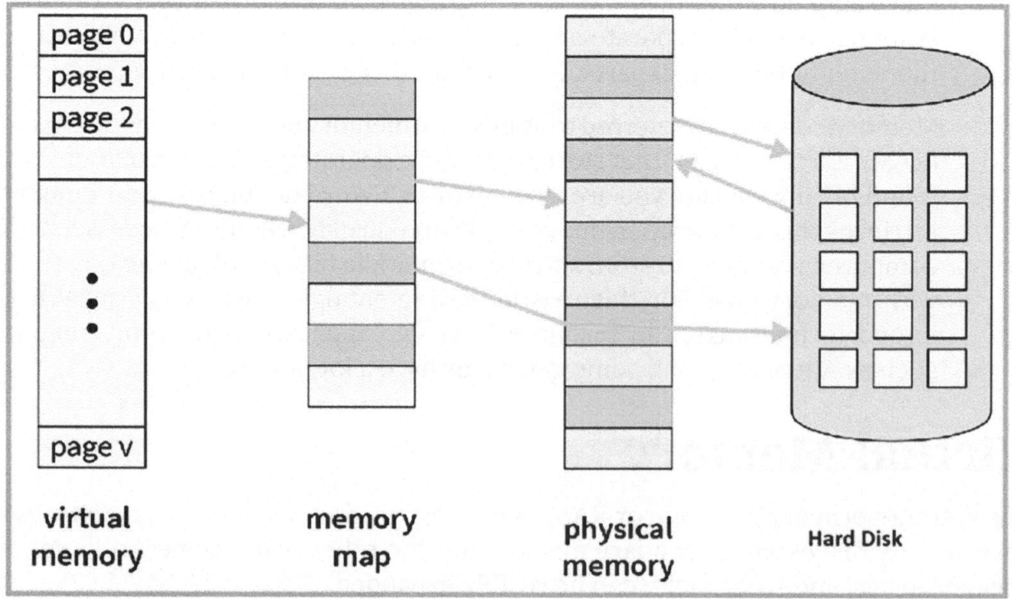

Figure 7a.8: Virtual Memory

A computer's usable memory can be increased beyond what physical RAM can hold using virtual memory. When RAM fills up, the operating system moves rarely used data from RAM to a specific area on the storage device, enabling the system to function properly. A computer system uses both physical and virtual memory for different purposes. Actual hard drives are called physical memory, or RAM.

- **Where is the Virtual Memory?**

  With the aid of the OS, virtual memory takes the form of pages. Massive programs can be stored on these pages, which are atomic units. Software may have a lot of physical address storage available. It is not necessary to load every program because an application only uses a subset of them.

  Envision ourselves engaging in a computer game similar to Grand Theft Auto. The game is installed on a secondary storage device, such as a hard disk when we need to play it. In real, the game's whole file system is not loaded into RAM. Nevertheless, when we launch the game, some of its content is stored in RAM.

- **How Virtual Memory Works?**

  Virtual addresses are mapped to physical addresses via a cooperative effort between the hardware and software. Furthermore, these addresses are translated with assistance from the memory management unit (MMU). In the operating system, we see logical addresses rather than physical addresses. These logical addresses are dynamically translated by the system at load, execute, or compile time. It also depends on how the system is defined or what it is needed for.

  In real-world situations, the resources and processes stored in memory are not constant. The system malfunctions and spreads throughout their physical memory. This is easily accomplished by using a page or segment table and dynamic run-time address translation. Virtual memory, which is a reserved space on the storage device (typically a hard drive or SSD), is used when physical memory runs out. Hardware that offers temporary storage for active data.

Attribute	**Physical Memory**	**Virtual Memory**
Definition	The actual RAM	A memory management technique
Approach	Uses swapping	Uses paging
Accessibility	Access CPU	Cannot access the CPU directly
Size	Limited to the size of the RAM	Limited by the size of the disk
Speed	Faster than virtual memory	Slower compared to physical memory

Table 7a.3: *Differences Between Physical and Virtual Memory*

Benefits of Virtual Memory

For both the user and the operating system, virtual memory offers several advantages. Even if a program's size exceeds the available physical memory, the user can run more than one program at once, thanks to virtual memory. Additionally, it offers protection and isolation for every program since every program has a virtual address space of its own that is inaccessible to other programs. Virtual memory relieves the operating system of the burden of managing memory allocation and management since it does not need to worry about memory fragmentation or physical layout. Moreover, it permits functions such as dynamic loading, memory mapping, and memory sharing.

Drawbacks of Virtual Memory

The efficiency and performance of the computer system are also impacted by a few disadvantages of virtual memory. One of the primary disadvantages is the overhead associated with paging, which entails expensive and time-consuming disk I/O operations. Due to the possibility that some pages are stored in secondary storage and others in physical memory, paging also contributes to latency and inconsistent memory access. The complexity of managing virtual memory, which necessitates the use of extra hardware and software, including the page table, frame table, page fault handler, and page replacement algorithm, is another disadvantage.

How to optimize virtual memory?

There are ways to optimize virtual memory and raise the system's performance and efficiency despite its drawbacks. One method is to change the frame and page sizes, which can impact the size of the page table, the quantity of internal fragmentation, and the quantity of page faults. Alternatively, the hit ratio, the quantity of disk I/O operations, and the frequency of page faults can all be impacted by selecting an appropriate page replacement algorithm. Utilizing prefetching and caching strategies is a third option that helps lower the latency and irregularity of memory access. These strategies involve loading pages ahead of time or storing frequently or recently used pages in a faster memory level, such as the buffer or cache.

Requirements of Memory Management System [3]

Memory management keeps track of the status of each memory location, whether it is allocated or free. It allocates the memory dynamically to the programs at their request and frees it for reuse when it is no longer needed. Memory management is meant to satisfy some requirements that we should keep in mind.

These memory management prerequisites are as follows:

- **Relocation**: Since memory is typically shared by several processes in a multiprogramming system, it is impossible to predict ahead of time which other programs will be running in the main memory during the program execution. The operating system can have a larger pool of processes ready to execute by switching the active processes in and out of the main memory. Because the memory location may still be occupied by another process, it is not always the case that a program that has been swapped out to disk memory will take up residence there when it is swapped back into the main memory. The process might need to be moved to a different region of memory. Swapping, therefore, can trigger moving a program into the main memory.

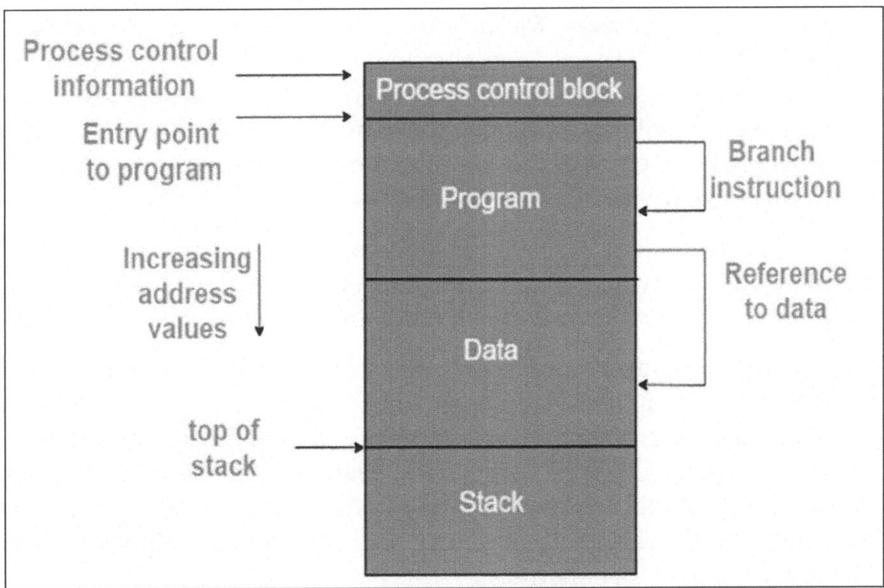

Figure 7a.9: *A process occupying a continuous region of main memory*

A process image is shown in *Figure 7a.9*. A continuous area of the main memory is occupied by the process image. Numerous details, such as the location of process control information, the execution stack, and code entry, must be known by the operating system. Logical addresses are the names given to the memory references found in different instructions throughout a program. Following the program's loading into the main memory, logical addresses are converted into physical addresses by the processor and operating system. The address of the following instruction to be performed is contained in branch instructions. Instructions for data reference include the address of the byte or word of the referenced data.

- **Protection:** Writing to another program's address space is a risk that arises whenever we run multiple programs simultaneously. Therefore, every process must be shielded from uninvited interference when another process tries to write in, whether on purpose or by accident. A trade-off exists between the requirements for protection and relocation, with the fulfillment of the former making the fulfillment of the latter more challenging.

The inability to predict a program's location in main memory makes it impossible to verify the absolute address during compilation to ensure security. Most programming languages permit the dynamic address calculation to occur during execution. Because an operating system cannot control a process that takes up processor resources, the processor itself must meet the memory protection requirement. As a result, memory references can be verified to be valid.

- **Sharing:** It is necessary for a protection mechanism to permit multiple processes to access the same main memory area. There is a benefit to giving every process access to the same copy of the software as opposed to a separate copy. When several processes use the same system file, for instance, it makes sense to load one copy of the file into the main memory and allow the other processes to share it.

  Memory management is responsible for enabling restricted access to shared memory regions while maintaining security. Sharing capabilities that are supported by relocation are enabled through mechanisms.

- **Logical organization:** A series of words or bytes make up the one-dimensional address space that makes up main memory, which is arranged in a linear fashion. Most programs can be divided into modules; some modules have data that can be changed, while others are read-only or execute-only programs. The computer hardware and operating system must support a basic module to provide the necessary protection and sharing when handling a user program. These are some of its benefits.
  - The system resolves all references between modules at run time. Each module is written and compiled separately.
  - Variations exist in the level of protection offered to distinct modules.
  - Module sharing between processes is possible through certain mechanisms.
  - A user can designate the type of sharing they want when sharing is enabled at the module level.
- **Physical organization**: The main memory and secondary memory are the two tiers of a computer's memory structure. The main memory is faster and more expensive than the secondary memory. When the main memory fluctuates, long-term data storage is possible in secondary memory, while the running programs are kept in the main memory. The primary system concern is that understanding the information flow between main memory and secondary memory is not practical for programmers for these two reasons.

The programmer might use a technique called overlaying in the following scenarios:

- When a program's and its data's available main memory might not be enough.
- It permits assigning multiple modules memory to a single memory area.
- For the programmer, it takes a lot of time, which is a drawback.
- The amount and location of memory space that will be available for coding in a multiprogramming environment are unknown to the programmer.

Cache Memory in Computer Organization

Cache Memory is a special and a high-speed memory. It is used to speed up and synchronize with a high-speed CPU. Cache memory is costlier than main memory or disk memory but more economical than CPU registers. Cache memory is an extremely fast memory type that acts as a buffer between RAM and the CPU. It holds frequently requested data and instructions so that they are immediately available to the CPU when needed. Cache memory is used to reduce the average time to access data from the Main memory. The cache is a smaller and faster memory which stores copies of the data from frequently used main memory locations. There are various independent caches in a CPU, which store instructions and data. [4]

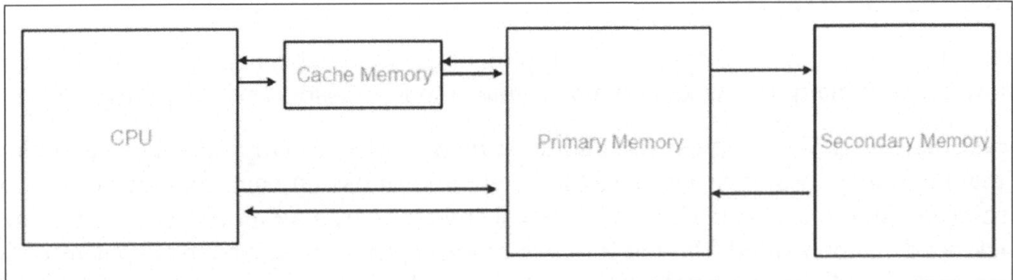

Figure 7a.10: *Cache Memory in Computer Organization*

Levels of Memory [4]

- **Level 1 or Register:** It is a type of memory in which data stored and accepted are immediately stored in the CPU. The most commonly used register is accumulator, program counter, address register, and so on.
- **Level 2 or Cache memory:** It is the fastest memory, which has faster access time where data is temporarily stored for faster access.
- **Level 3 or Main Memory:** It is the memory on which the computer works currently. It is small in size and once power is off, data no longer stays in this memory.

- **Level 4 or Secondary Memory:** It is external memory which is not as fast as the main memory but where data stays permanent.

Cache Performance

When the processor needs to read or write a location in the main memory, it first checks for a corresponding entry in the cache.

- If the processor finds that the memory location is in the cache, a cache hit has occurred, and data is read from the cache.
- If the processor does not find the memory location in the cache, a cache miss has occurred. For a cache miss, the cache allocates a new entry and copies in data from the main memory, then the request is fulfilled from the contents of the cache.

The performance of cache memory is frequently measured in terms of quantity called Hit ratio.

```
Hit ratio = hit / (hit + miss) = no. of hits/total accesses
```

We can improve cache performance using a higher cache block size and higher associativity, reducing miss rate, miss penalty, and the time to hit in the cache.

Cache Mapping [5]

There are three different types of mapping used for cache memory, which are as follows: Direct mapping, Associative mapping, and Set-Associative mapping.

Direct Mapping: The simplest technique, known as direct mapping, maps each block of main memory into only one possible cache line or assign each memory block to a specific line in the cache. If a line is previously taken up by a memory block when a new block needs to be loaded, the old block is trashed. An address space is split into two parts: index field and a tag field. The cache is used to store the tag field, whereas the rest is stored in the main memory. The performance of the direct mapping is directly proportional to the Hit ratio.

```
i = j modulo m
```

where,

`i`=cache line number

`j`= main memory block number

`m`=number of lines in the cache

For purposes of cache access, each main memory address can be viewed as consisting of three fields. The least significant w bits identify a unique word or byte within a block of main memory. In most contemporary machines, the address is at the byte level.

The remaining s bits specify one of the 2s blocks of main memory. The cache logic interprets these s bits as a tag of s-r bits (the most significant portion) and a line field of r bits. This latter field identifies one of the **m=2r** lines of the cache

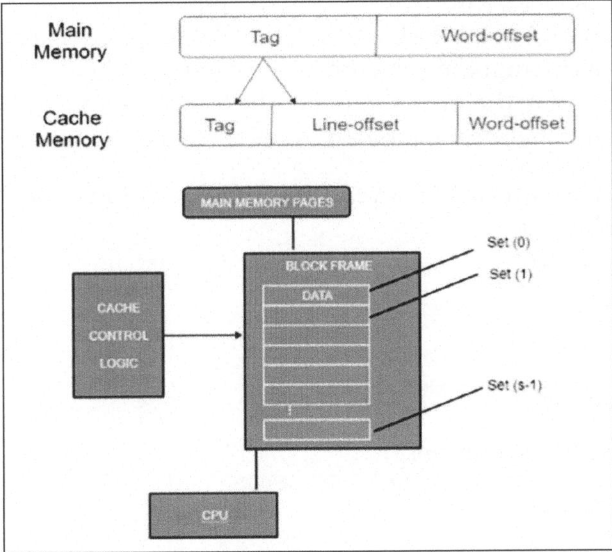

Figure 7a.11: *Direct Mapping*

Associative Mapping: Associative memory is used in this mapping to store addresses and content for the memory word. Any line in the cache can contain any block. In other words, the word **id** bits indicate which word in the block is required, while the tag comprises all other bits. This makes it possible to insert any word anywhere in the cache memory. It is regarded as the most adaptable and quick mapping form.

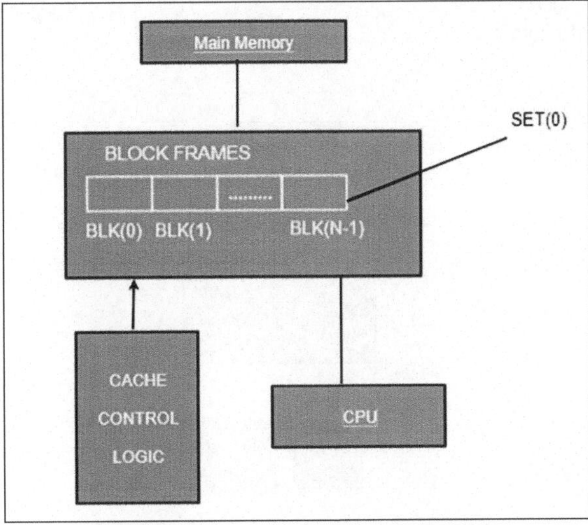

Figure 7a.12: Associative Mapping

Set-associative Mapping: The shortcomings of direct mapping have been eliminated in favor of an improved version of mapping. Set associative solves the issue with potential thrashing in the direct mapping technique. To achieve this, it says, "*We will group a few lines together creating a set*," rather than having a single line in the cache that a block can map to. A memory block can then be mapped to any line within a given set. With set-associative mapping, a word in the cache can have two or more words for the same index address in the main memory. The best aspects of associative and direct cache mapping techniques are combined in set associative cache mapping.

In this case, the cache consists of several sets, each of which consists of a number of lines. The relationships are

```
m = v * k
i= j mod v
```

where

`i`=cache set number

`j`=main memory block number

`v`=number of sets

`m`=number of lines in the cache number of sets

`k`=number of lines in each set

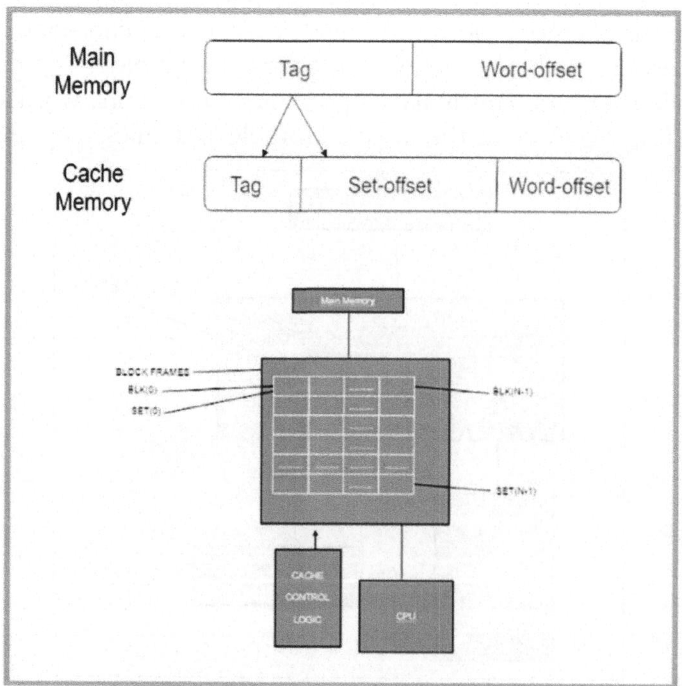

Figure 7a.13: *Set Associative Mapping*

Application of Cache Memory

- Usually, the cache memory can store a reasonable number of blocks at any given time, but this number is small compared to the total number of blocks in the main memory.
- The correspondence between the main memory blocks and those in the cache is specified by a mapping function.

Locality of reference

Since the size of cache memory is lesser than the size of the main memory, checking which part of the main memory should be the priority and loaded in the cache is decided based on the locality of reference.

Types of Locality of Reference

According to the concept of **spatial locality** of reference, an element may be found near the reference point, and if searched the next time, you can observe it even closer than before. The least recently used algorithm will be employed in this case for the **temporal locality of reference**. When a page fault happens within a word, the entire page fault will load as well as the word in main memory. This is because the spatial locality of reference rule states that if a word is referenced, the subsequent word will be referenced in its register. For this reason, the complete page table is loaded, allowing the entire block to be loaded.

C Language Implementation of Memory Mapping

The following code is a C language implementation of memory mapping.

```
#include<stdio.h>
#include<math.h>
#define INT_SIZE sizeof(int)*8
int bin[INT_SIZE];
int power(int b,int e)
{
        int res=1,i=1;
        while(i<=e)
        {
                res=res*b;
                i++;
        }
        return res;
}
```

```
int expo(int a)
{
        int n;
        float x;
        x=log(a)/log(2);
        n=x;
        return n;
}
void binary(int num,int len)
{
        int i,index;
        index=INT_SIZE - 1;
        while(index>=0)
        {
                bin[index]=num&1;
                index--;
                num>>=1;
        }
        printf("\nThe binary representation of %d is: ",num);
        for(i=(31-len)+ 1;i<INT_SIZE;i++)
        {
                printf("%d",bin[i]);
        }
        printf("\n");
}
void Direct(int tot,int lno,int blsize)
{
        int tag,line,word,n,i,j,total,a[100];
        total=tot;
        line=expo(lno);
        word=expo(blsize);
        tag=tot-(line+word);
        printf("\nDirect Mapping:");
        printf("\nTag address: %d",tag);
        printf("\nLine address: %d",line);
        printf("\nWord offset: %d",word);
        printf("\n\nEnter the address of main memory to map to a Direct
mapped cache:\n");
        scanf("%d",&n);
        binary(n,total);
        printf("\nTag of %d: ",n);
        for(i=(31 - total)+ 1;i<(((31- total)+ 1)+(tag));i++)
        {
                printf("%d",bin[i]);
        }
        printf("\nLine of %d: ",n);
        for(i=INT_SIZE-word;i>=INT_SIZE - ((word+line) - 1);i--)
```

```
	{
		printf("%d",bin[i]);
	}
	printf("\nWord of %d: ",n);
	for(i=INT_SIZE;i>=(INT_SIZE-(word- 1));i--)
	{
		printf("%d",bin[i]);
	}
}
void Associative(int total,int blosize)
{
	int tag,word,i,n;
	word=expo(blosize);
	tag=total-word;
	printf("\nAssociative Mapping:");
	printf("\nTag address: %d",tag);
	printf("\nWord offset: %d",word);
	printf("\n\nEnter the address of main memory to map to a
Associative mapped cache:\n");
	scanf("%d",&n);
	binary(n,total);
	printf("\nTag of %d: ",n);
	for(i=(31 - total)+ 1;i<(((31- total)+ 1)+(tag));i++)
	{
		printf("%d",bin[i]);
	}
	printf("\nWord of %d: ",n);
	for(i=INT_SIZE;i>=(INT_SIZE-(word- 1));i--)
	{
		printf("%d",bin[i]);
	}
}
void SetAssociative(int k,int totall,int lineno,int blocksize)
{
	int tag,set,word,i,n,total;
	total=totall;
	word=expo(blocksize);
	set=expo(lineno/k);
	tag=totall-(set+word);
	printf("\nSet Associative Mapping:");
	printf("\nTag address: %d",tag);
	printf("\nSet address: %d",set);
	printf("\nWord offset: %d",word);
	printf("\n\nEnter the address of main memory to map to a Set
Associative mapped cache:\n");
	scanf("%d",&n);
	binary(n,total);
```

```
        printf("\nTag of %d: ",n);
        for(i=(31 - total)+ 1;i<(((31- total)+ 1)+(tag));i++)
        {
              printf("%d",bin[i]);
        }
        printf("\nSet of %d: ",n);
        for(i=INT_SIZE-word;i>=INT_SIZE - ((word+set) - 1);i--)
        {
              printf("%d",bin[i]);
        }
        printf("\nWord of %d: ",n);
        for(i=INT_SIZE;i>=(INT_SIZE-(word- 1));i--)
        {
              printf("%d",bin[i]);
        }
}
void main()
{
        int csize,msize,ws,bs,cs,ms,lines_no,tag,line,word,tot_addr,
choice,k;
        printf("Enter the cache size in KB:\n");
        scanf("%d",&csize);
        cs=csize*power(2,10);
        printf("Cache size in bytes: %d",cs);
        printf("\nEnter the physical memory size in MB:\n");
        scanf("%d",&msize);
        ms=msize*power(2,20);
        tot_addr=expo(ms);
        printf("Physical memory size in bytes: %d",ms);
        printf("\nEnter the word size in B:\n");
        scanf("%d",&ws);
        printf("Enter the block size in B:\n");
        scanf("%d",&bs);
        lines_no=cs/bs;
        printf("\nEnter your choice:\n");
        printf("1. Direct Mapping\t2. Associative Mapping\t3. Set
Associative Mapping\n");
        scanf("%d",&choice);
        switch(choice)
        {
              case 1: Direct(tot_addr,lines_no,bs);
                    break;
              case 2:     Associative(tot_addr,bs);
                    break;
              case 3:     printf("\nEnter the k-way Set Associative\
nie. Enter the number of lines in one set:\n");
```

```
                scanf("%d",&k);
                SetAssociative(k,tot_addr,lines_no,bs);
                break;
          default: printf("\nYou have entered a wrong choice!");
                 break;
      }
}
```

Swapping in Operating Systems

"*Swapping in OS is one of those schemes that fulfill the goal of maximum utilization of CPU and memory management by swapping in and swapping out processes from the main memory. Swap-in removes the process from the hard drive (secondary memory), and swap-out removes the process from RAM (main memory).*

Swapping in OS is done to get access to data present in secondary memory and transfer it to the main memory so that it can be used by the application programs.

Swapping in the operating system is a memory management scheme that temporarily swaps out an idle or blocked process from the main memory to secondary memory, which ensures proper memory utilization and memory availability for those processes that are ready to be executed. Let us suppose there are several processes like P1, P2, P3, and P4 that are ready to be executed inside the ready queue, and processes P1 and P2 are very memory consuming, so when the processes start executing, there may be a scenario where the memory will not be available for the execution of the processes P3 and P4, as there is a limited amount of memory available for process execution."[6]

"*When that memory-consuming process goes into a termination state, it means its execution is over, due to which the memory dedicated to their execution becomes free. Then the swapped-out processes are brought back into the main memory and their execution starts. The area of the secondary memory where swapped-out processes are stored is called swap space. The swapping method forms a temporary queue of swapped processes in the secondary memory. In the case of high-priority processes, the process with low priority is swapped out of the main memory and stored in swap space then the process with high priority is swapped into the main memory to be executed first.*"[6]

Maximum CPU utilization is one of an operating system's primary objectives. This means there should never be a time when a process is not executed, the CPU should be idle, and there should never be any instances of process starvation or blocking. Such operating system goals are achieved by various schemes for memory management and process management.

It may impact on system performance, but by controlling memory, it facilitates the execution of multiple processes. As a result, the memory compaction technique becomes another name for swapping in OS.

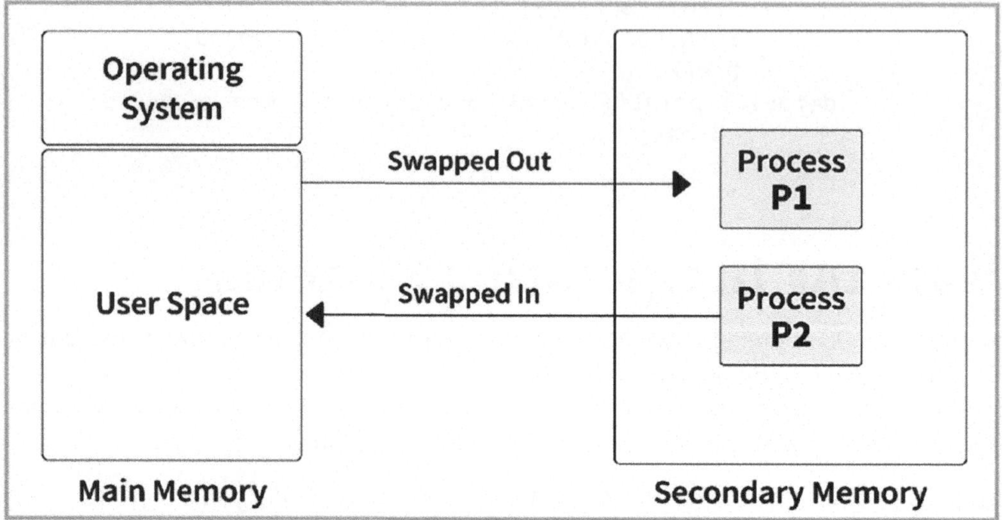

Figure 7a.14: *Swapping Process in Operating System*

There are two important concepts in the process of swapping, which are as follows:

- Swap In
- Swap Out

Swap In: The method of removing a process from secondary memory (hard drive) and restoring it to the main memory (RAM) for execution is known as the swap-in method.

Swap Out: It is a method of bringing out a process from the main memory (RAM) and sending it to the secondary memory (hard drive) so that the processes with higher priority or more memory consumption will be executed, known as the swap-out method.

Note: *Swap-In and Swap-Out method is done by Medium Term Scheduler* (MTS).

Advantages of Swapping in OS

The advantages of the swapping method are listed as follows:

- Swapping in OS helps in achieving the goal of maximum CPU utilization.
- Swapping ensures proper memory availability for every process that needs to be executed.
- Swapping helps avoid the problem of process starvation, meaning a process should not take much time for execution so that the next process should be executed.
- CPU can perform various tasks simultaneously with the help of swapping so that processes do not have to wait much longer before execution.

- Swapping ensures proper RAM (main memory) utilization.
- Swapping creates a dedicated disk partition in the hard drive for swapped processes, which is called swap space.
- Swapping in OS is an economical process.
- Swapping method can be applied to priority-based process scheduling where a high-priority process is swapped in and a low-priority process is swapped out, which improves the performance.

Disadvantages of Swapping in OS

There are some limited disadvantages of the swapping method, which are listed as follows:

- If the system deals with power outaget during bulky swapping activity, then the user may lose all the information that is related to the program.
- If the swapping method uses an algorithm that is not up to the mark, then the number of page faults can be increased, and therefore, decrease the complete performance.
- There may be inefficiency in a case when there is some common resource used by the processes that are participating in the swapping process.

Example: Using the following example, we will better understand the idea of swapping: Let us say we have a user whose process size is 4096 KB. The user in this case is using a standard hard drive with a 4 Mbps transfer rate for swapping. The time it takes to move data from RAM, the main memory, to the hard disk, the secondary memory, will now be calculated.

```
process size of the user is 4096Kb
the transfer rate of data is 4Mbps
Now,
4 Mbps is equal to 4096 kbps
Time taken to transfer the data = process size of user/ transf
Now, coming to the Calculation part:
Time Taken = 4096 / 4096
           = 1 second
           = 1000 milliseconds
```

***Figure 7a.15**: Swapping*

Segmentation

Computer systems can manage their memory by using a technique called segmentation, which splits virtual memory into segments, or variable-sized blocks. A logical entity is represented by each segment, which can be data, code, a stack, or another type of segment. The operating system performs address translation using the segmentation hardware by mapping the segment number to the segment base in the physical memory. Since the segments can differ in size and protection features, this method offers more flexibility in memory management. However, it may also result in increased overhead related to address translation and external fragmentation. Processes are segmented into smaller components called modules. It is not necessary to store the divided segments in a single memory block. There is no internal fragmentation because there is no contiguous memory allocation. The goal of each segment in the user program determines how long the program and memory segments should be. Logical address space, also known as main memory, can be thought of as a collection of segments. [7]

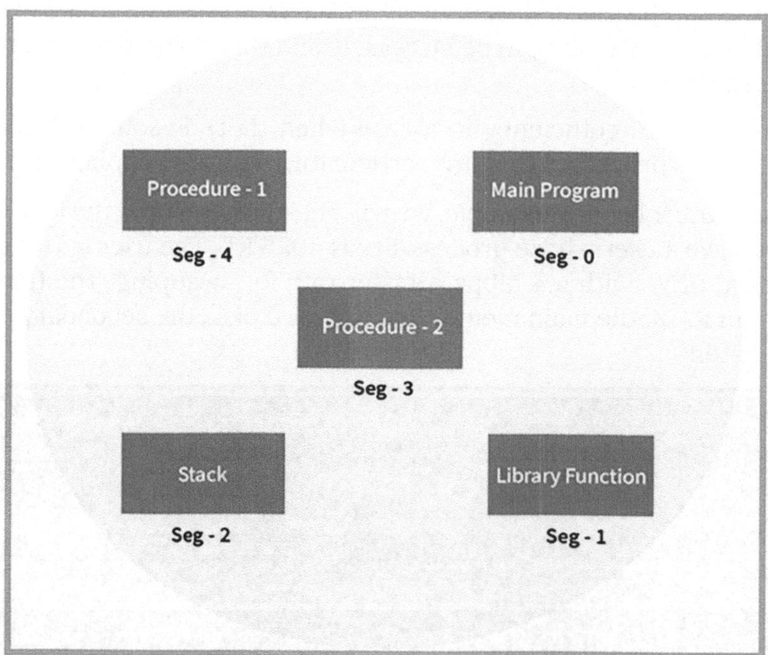

Figure 7a.16: *Segmentation Process in Operating Systems*

Types of Segmentation

There are two categories of segmentation: Virtual memory segmentation and process segmentation.

- **Virtual Memory Segmentation** splits processes into n number of segments.

Not every segment is split at the same moment. Virtual memory segmentation might happen while a program is running or it might not.

- **Simple Segmentation**: In simple segmentation, the processes are also divided into *n* segments, but they are segmented all at once. Simple segmentation happens during a program's runtime. Simple segmentation may disperse the segments into memory in a non-continuous way, allowing one process segment to be at a different location than the other [7].

Need of Segmentation

The issues with the paging technique led to the creation of segmentation. When a function or section of code is divided into pages using the paging technique, it is not considered that the related sections of the code may also be divided. Therefore, to run the process, the CPU needs to load multiple pages into the frames to have all of the relevant code available for execution. To load a process into the main memory, paging requires more pages. To enable the combination of related code into a single block, segmentation–the division of the code into modules–was therefore introduced.

The real view of physical memory is different from the user's view of physical memory, which is a significant disadvantage of other memory management strategies. Segmentation aids in problem solving by breaking up the user's program into manageable chunks based on distinct needs.

Advantages of Segmentation in OS

- **Logical Grouping**: Segmentation enhances the meaning and comprehension of the memory organization by facilitating the logical grouping of related code and data.
- **Protection:** Memory protection and isolation are easier to implement when every segment has a distinct set of protection properties.
- **Sharing**: Segmentation allows multiple processes to share a single segment, which reduces the memory overhead of duplicating the shared data.
- **Flexibility**: By enabling segments of different sizes, segmentation provides more flexible memory management.
- **Relocation:** Segmentation enables dynamic segment movement, which aids in managing the memory requirements of evolving and growing data structures.
- **Performance:** Segmentation enhances performance by lowering internal fragmentation and utilizing memory resources better.
- **Streamlined Memory Management**: Segmentation simplifies memory management by reducing the number of free memory blocks to keep track of and manage.

- **Structured Memory Organization**: Segmentation makes structured memory organization possible, which makes the system easier to maintain and debug.
- **Segmentation:** This can improve address translation performance by lowering the overhead associated with translating virtual addresses to physical addresses.
  - No internal fragmentation is there in segmentation. Segmentation provides better CPU utilization as an entire module is loaded at once.
  - Segmentation is near to the user's view of physical memory and allows users to partition the user programs into modules. These modules are nothing but the independent codes of the current process.
  - The Segment size is specified by the user, but in paging, the hardware decides the page size.
  - Segmentation can be used to separate the security procedures and data.

Disadvantages of Segmentation in OS

- **Overhead:** Because segmentation involves an extra step in mapping the segment number to the segment base, it may result in higher overhead in address translation.
- **External Fragmentation**: Because of the variable-sized segments, segmentation may cause external fragmentation. This can reduce memory utilization and waste memory resources.
- **Complexity**: Segmentation may increase the memory management system's complexity, making it more challenging to set up and keep up.
- **Performance**: Because segmentation increases the overhead associated with address translation and fragmentation, it may lead to a decrease in performance.
- **Restricted Address Space**: Since the segment table needs to be reserved for a certain amount of the address space, segmentation may lead to limited address space.
- **Inefficient Memory Use**: Because segmentation creates internal fragmentation due to the variable-sized segments, it may lead to inefficient use of memory resources.
- **Enhanced Memory Requirements**: Because the segment table must be stored and the segments must be managed, segmentation may result in heightened memory requirements.
- **Compatibility**: Because segmentation hardware and software implementations vary amongst systems, there may be compatibility issues due to segmentation.

- **Security**: Since malicious code may be able to take advantage of the hardware and software used for segmentation to obtain unauthorized access to memory, segmentation may pose security risks.
  - During the swapping of processes, the free memory space is broken into small pieces, which is a major problem in the segmentation technique.
  - Time is required to fetch instructions or segments.
  - The swapping of segments of unequal sizes is not easy.

There is an overhead of maintaining a segment table for each process as well.

A process exits the main memory after it has finished. The unevenly sized process segments are eliminated from the main memory following the completion of the current process. The main memory has holes of varying sizes as a result of the segments' uneven lengths. Because of their tiny size, these gaps in the primary memory may go unfilled.

Characteristics of Segmentation in OS

Some of the characteristics of segmentation are discussed as follows:

- The process of segmentation divides the program into segments or blocks of varying sizes.
- The length and type of modules determine the partition size.
- The idea behind segmentation is that related data should only appear in one segment.

Depending on the segmentation technique selected, portions of the memory may or may not be continuously stored. For every process, the operating system keeps a segment table updated.

Example of Segmentation

Let us take the example of segmentation to understand how it works.

Assume, for the purposes of this discussion, that there are five segments: segments 0 through 4. Initially, the physical memory space is where all process segments are kept before the process is executed. We also have a segment table. The beginning entry address of each segment (denoted by base) is contained in the segment table. Each segment's length (shown by limit) is also included in the segment table.

The base addresses of Segment-0, Segment-1, Segment-2, and so on are as follows: Segment-0's base address is 1400, its length is 1000; Segment-1's base address is 6300, its length is 400; and so on.

The pictorial representation of the preceding segmentation with its segment table is shown in *Figure 7a.16*.

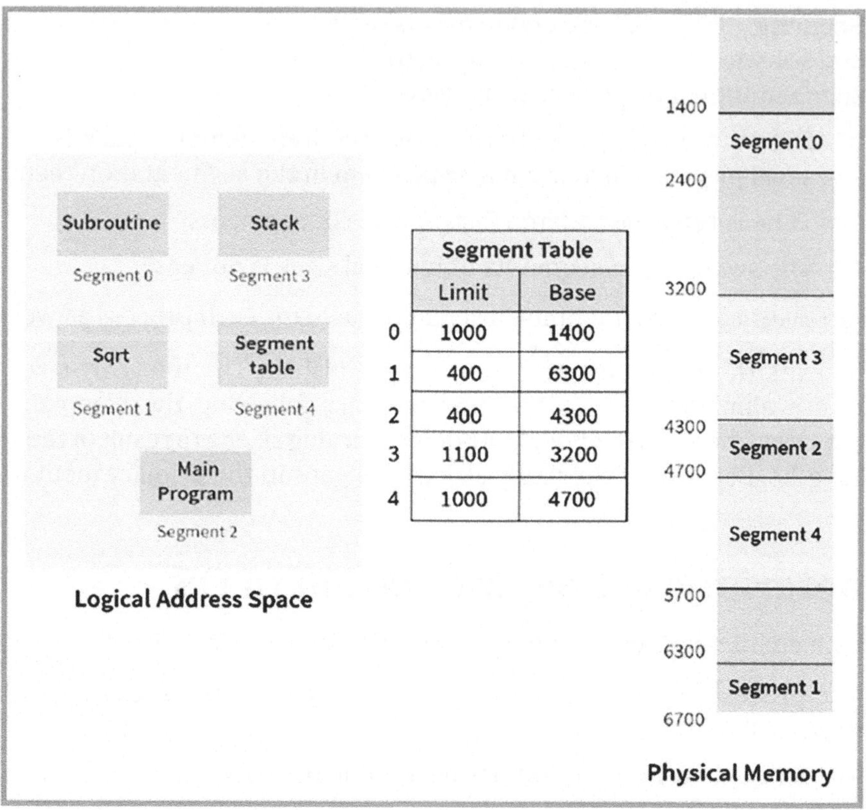

Figure 7a.17: *Example of Segmentation*

Popular Segmentation Architecture

The structure and design of a neural network model used for image or video segmentation tasks is referred to as segmentation architecture. The process of splitting an image into several regions or segments, each of which represents a significant object or area of the image, is known as image segmentation. It is essential to computer vision applications, such as autonomous driving, scene interpretation, and object recognition. In the field of computer vision, a number of well-liked segmentation designs have seen great success. Here are a handful that stand out:

- **Fully Convolutional Network (FCN):** FCN was one of the pioneering architectures for semantic segmentation. It substitutes convolutional layers for the fully connected layers of a conventional convolutional neural network (CNN) to enable dense pixel-wise predictions. FCN combines low-level and high-level features using skip connections for increased segmentation accuracy.
- **Popular U-Net architecture:** This is well-known for its efficiency in biomedical image segmentation applications. It is made up of an expanding path (decoder)

and a contracting path (encoder). While the decoder recovers the spatial information and creates segmentation masks, the encoder records contextual information and decreases the spatial resolution. Skip connections are another method used by U-Net to maintain fine-grained details.

- **DeepLab:** A popular family of segmentation architectures for a range of segmentation applications is called DeepLab. Dilated convolutions, atrous spatial pyramid pooling (ASPP), and a fully connected conditional random field (CRF) are used in the original DeepLab model to refine the segmentation maps. Adding more sophisticated elements, such as feature pyramid networks and encoder-decoder structures, DeepLabv3 and DeepLabv3+ enhance the model even further.
- **Mask R-CNN:** Mask R-CNN integrates instance segmentation and object detection in a single architecture. Including a parallel branch that creates segmentation masks for every object detected, it expands upon the well-liked Faster R-CNN object detection framework. For instance-level segmentation tasks, Mask R-CNN is frequently utilized, where the objective is to segment each object instance accurately within an image.

Problem of Fragmentation

There is one main drawback to segmentation. Processes are loaded into and removed from the main memory during the process-swapping process. According to the segments, switching between processes can occasionally cause the free memory space to fragment. External fragmentation, a significant issue with the segmentation technique, is the term for splitting free space into fragments.

It is important to remember that segmentation does not result in internal fragmentation. Each process is loaded by bringing all of the segments connected to each process into main memory. Each segment is loaded into the main memory by dividing the RAM according to the size of each process segment. Each segment can therefore precisely fit inside the main memory's dynamically generated partitions. Hence, there is no internal fragmentation in segmentation.

Common Segments of a Process

There are segments of text, data, and system data in the running process (or program). Let us learn more about these segments.

- **Text Segment: The program's code is contained in this text segment. A program's** address space segment contains the read-only text segment, also referred to as the instruction segment. Text Segments are initialized using the program's executable file.

- **Data or User Data Segment**: The data segment comprises four data areas: heap area, stack area, non-initialized data, and initialized data.
    - Strings initialized from the program executable file are contained in the initialized section of the data.
    - Global variables are found in the data section that has not been initialized.
    - The area designated for storing the global variables is the heap area, otherwise known as the malloc area. Function calls, function parameters, and local variables are all contained in the stack area. The stack area changes size in response to function calls; it increases when a function is called and decreases when a function returns.
- **System Data Segment**: This section includes information about a segment, such as the process's current directory, user ID (UID), group IDs (GIDs), text, data, stack sizes, and so on. It is important to remember that the system maintains the data segment portion, and the process can only access it through system calls.

Intel x86 Address Translation

A 16-bit segment register is used by the x86 system to determine the actual address from the logical address. Intel Corporation is the developer of the x86 family of microprocessors. Memory segmentation is a feature of Intel-compatible x86 computers' instruction set architecture. Programmers can initially have an address that is no more than 64KB. Segmentation was introduced by Intel to enable programs with addresses larger than 64 KB. However, no memory protection was offered. Any segment can be accessed without any restrictions by any running program. A segment's starting point is all that is needed to identify it; segment length is not necessary. A few years later, the second iteration of segmentation was introduced by the Intel 80286 processor, which included support for memory protection and virtual memory. Only specific segments can be accessed by an operating program while in protected mode. Alternatively, we could state that a program in use is limited to accessing the parts that are part of the active process.

Real mode was the new term for the original x86 Intel model without memory protection. A segment's size in real mode can vary from one byte to 64 KB. The more recent Intel x86 version, now known as protected mode, can accommodate addresses larger than 64 KB.

The x86-64 architecture does not use segmentation in long mode. Instead, they handle programs and their data by utilizing memory paging. Paging (which divides memory into equal-sized pages) is more efficient because it also serves as memory protection, as only specified pages of a process can be accessed by the running program. In later architecture, we shall study Pentium and MIPS systems as well.

Global Descriptor Table (GDT) and Segmentation Using of x86 System

Since the Intel 80286 processor's inception, the Global Descriptor Table has been in use. A binary data structure called the Global Descriptor Table, or GDT, is utilized by Intel x86 processors. The GDT merely provides the CPU with information about the memory segments. It also keeps track of the different parts of the process that is currently running. The size, base address, and access rights (such as the ability to write, read, or execute) of a segment are also preserved by GDT.

A register called the Global Descriptor Table Register, or GDTR, points to the GDT. Segment Selectors loaded into segmentation registers are responsible for accessing the entries in the Global Descriptor Table (more on these later).

Additionally, there is a Local Descriptor Table or LDT. Within the GDT, more than one LDT may be defined. Memory segments private to a particular program are stored in the LDT; global memory segments are found in the GDT.

The basic overview of address conversion is as follows:

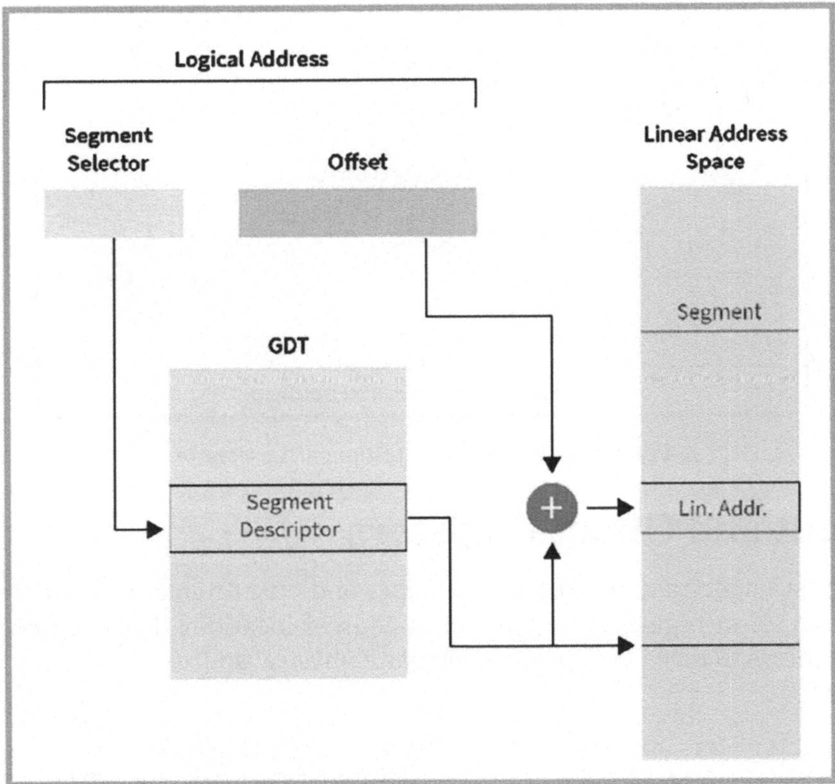

Figure 7a.18: Address Conversion

Segment Descriptor Inside Global Descriptor Table

Selectors for segments are used to identify segment descriptors. The LDT or GDT's segment selector, also known as an index, is used to point to or reference a segment.

Afterwards, the selectors are put into the segment register for later usage. Upon loading a sector or index into the segment register, the processor automatically retrieves the GDT or LDT and stores the segment's properties within the register. Segment base address, segment limit, and segment access rights (such as writing, reading, or executing rights) are all stored in a single memory segment found in the segment descriptor.

Size of Segment Descriptor and its components:

Segment base address in linear address space is defined by the segment description (8 bytes) and base address size (32 bits). Segment Limit size is 20 bits; this indicates a segment's maximum offset. Following is a basic overview of Segment Descriptor.

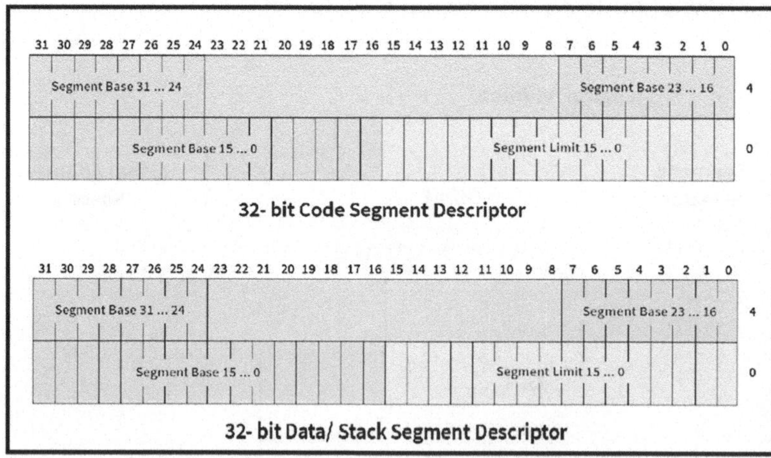

Figure 7a.19: *Overview of Segment Descriptor*

Segment and Offset Registers

We must first understand the segment number and offset number to understand the segment and offset register. The number of address locations that must be added to the base address to reach the specified absolute physical address is typically indicated by an offset.

The segment registers are used to store a segment's starting addresses. The processor combines the segment address in the segment register with the offset value of the location to refer to any memory location within a segment.

We use the segment number (found using the segment register) and offset number (found using the offset register) for the address translation.

Conclusion

In part 1, we have learned on the topic memory hierarchy and features of memory hierarchy design. We have learned that the memory divided as primary, secondary memory and tertiary memory, and also, that the Internal primary memory consist of Registers, Cache Memories, RAM and ROM in the order of their fastness of action in fetching a particular content.

We learned difference between the main and virtual memory, secondary and tertiary memory. In part 2 of this chapter, we shall discuss demand paging, thrashing, and so on, and then memory management in two versatile operating systems, Windows and Unix.

Questions

1. What do you understand by memory hierarchy?
2. Draw a memory hierarchy pyramid duly marked with internal and three types of external storage.
3. What are the advantages of understanding memory hierarchy?
4. Explain what type of memory devices are taken as primary, secondary, and tertiary storage
5. What characteristic features of memory hierarchy design are taken into view while designing a memory system of operating systems?
6. Compare various characteristic features of memory systems.
7. What do you understand by primary memory arrays? Draw a sketch to describe it.
8. What types of ROM: semiconductor-based are used in current usage?
9. What is flash memory, and is it a type of ROM or RAM?
10. With the help of a chart, illustrate various types of ROMs in vogue.
11. With the help of a chart, illustrate various types of RAMs in vogue.
12. Compare the DRAM with SRAM memory with respect to their characteristic properties.
13. What is meant by volatile type memory?

14. Draw a circuit line diagram of SHRAM with a six-transistor memory cell and state whether a four transistor circuits also exist.
15. What are two SRAM architecture types, and describe the working of synchronous SRAMs?
16. Describe the asynchronous types of SRAM, stating where they are used.
17. Describe the design trade-off factors of SRAM in detail.
18. Distinguish among the main memory, I/O memory, and virtual memory. Draw a hierarchy pyramid showing their relative placement to compare their capacity, cost, and access time.
19. Explain the difference between network and disk storage.
20. Describe how the virtual memory is a part of the system's secondary memory and acts as part of main memory.
21. In which form does the virtual memory exist?
22. Explain the differences between physical and virtual memory.
23. Elaborate the benefits and drawbacks of virtual memory.
24. How to optimize virtual memory for improving its performance?
25. Elaborate the various requirements of memory management system.
26. Explain with the diagram showing the functioning of the cache memory in computer organization?
27. Explain how the cache performs its functions.
28. Explain the difference among the three different cash memory mapping schemes, direct mapping, associative mapping, and set-associative mapping.
29. Narrate the swapping in operating systems with the help of a sketch.
30. What are various advantages and disadvantages using swapping operation?
31. What do you understand by segmentation? Mention the types and needs of segmentation.
32. Mention various advantages and disadvantages of segmentation in OS.
33. What are the various salient characteristics of segmentation in OS?
34. Illustrate several popular segmentation architectures that have been adopted.

References

[1] Design And Analysis Of SRAM Array Architectures, B.N. Srinivasa Rao, D. Hemalatha, M. Harish, D.N.V.S. Nooka Raju, A. Swathi 1 DIET College, Visakhapatnam,

[2] Memory Hierarchy Design and Characteristics, Sarveshwar Shukla, https://www.scaler.com/topics/memory-hierarchy/

[3] Requirements for Memory Management,https://eng.libretexts.org/Courses/Delta_College/Operating_System%3A_The_Basics/07%3A_Memory/7.3%3A_Requirements_for_Memory_Management

[4] Cache Memory, https://eng.libretexts.org/Courses/Delta_College / Operating_System%3A_The_Basics/01%3A_The_Basics_-_An_Overview/1.7_Cache_Memory

[5] Memory Mapping of Cache in Computer Organization and Architecture, Anisha, https://github.com/anishaaaaaaa/Memory-Mapping

[6] Swapping in OS, By Mohit Sahay, Last updated: 15 May 2024, https://www.scaler.com/topics/swapping-in-os/

[7] Segmentation in Operating System, Sushant Gaurav, Last updated: 30 Jun 2024, https://www.scaler.com/topics/operating-system/segmentation-in-os/

Chapter 7(b)
Memory Organization Part 2

Introduction

A virtual memory process is made up of numerous pages, and it may not be efficient to swap out all the pages for a specific process at once, because the program might only need a particular page to run the application. The demand paging system, which bears some resemblance to the paging system with swapping, primarily resides in the main memory (usually on the hard disk). Demand paging is the method used to solve this problem by swapping pages only when required.

Memory thrashing is also a problem that arises when the memory is allocated more than the physical memory and is not available in the system. We will therefore learn the methods to avoid such a situation. Also, it shall be our endeavor to learn methods of memory management implementation in Windows and Unix operating system.

Structure

In this chapter, we will learn following topics:

- Paging
- Need of Demand Paging in Operating System
- Common Algorithms used for Demand Paging in OS
- Page Replacement Algorithms
- The Working Set Model
- Thrashing
- Implementation of Windows Operating System
- Implementation of UNIX Operating System
- Linux Operating System
- Memory Management Policies of UNIX System V

- Swapping
- Memory Management Unit (MMU)
- MIPS Architecture
- Pentium Memory Management

Paging

Operating systems use the memory management strategy known as paging to store data in smaller sections of a computer's primary memory called pages. Larger applications than what can fit in memory can be run on the computer by switching the pages between the disk and memory when they are not needed. This mitigates the risk of applications crashing due to memory shortage by facilitating more effective management of memory resources.

Similarities between Paging and Segmentation:

- Both paging and segmentation are memory management techniques used in computer systems.
- Both divide physical memory into smaller units called pages or segments.
- Both aim to improve memory utilization and address the problem of external fragmentation.
- Both allow multiple programs to share the main memory simultaneously.
- Both provide a way for the operating system to manage the allocation and deallocation of memory.
- Both use virtual memory to provide a larger addressing space for programs than the physical memory.
- Both use a page table or segment table to map virtual addresses to physical addresses.
- Both provide protection by allowing the operating system to set permissions for pages or segments, such as read-only or read-write.
- Both have a trade-off between memory fragmentation and overhead due to memory management.

Table 7b.1 explains the differences between paging and segmentation.

Concept	Paging	Segmentation
Definition	Paging is a memory management scheme in which each process is divided into fixed-size pages.	Segmentation is a memory management scheme in which a process is divided into variable-sized segments.
Memory Allocation	Pages are allocated to processes as a whole unit.	Segments can be allocated to processes in a non-contiguous manner.
Memory Management	Paging is managed by hardware through a page table.	Segmentation is managed by software through a segment table.
Memory Utilization	Paging results in less internal fragmentation, but more external fragmentation.	Segmentation results in more internal fragmentation but less external fragmentation.
Page Size	Page size is fixed and determined by the system.	Segment size is variable and determined by the process.
Overhead	Paging has lower overhead due to a simpler memory management scheme.	Segmentation has higher overhead due to a more complex memory management scheme.
Address Translation	Address translation in paging is straightforward as it involves a single table lookup.	Address translation in segmentation is more complex as it involves two table lookups.
Flexibility	Paging is less flexible due to the fixed page size.	Segmentation is more flexible due to the variable segment size.
Performance	Paging has better performance due to the hardware-based management and simpler address translation.	Segmentation has lower performance due to the software-based management and complex address translation.

Table 7b.1: *Differences between paging and segmentation*

Advantages of Paging

- **Effective memory use:** Paging divides memory into smaller pages and allocates them as needed, making better use of the memory resources available.
- **Large virtual memory**: Paging, which temporarily switches pages between the disk and memory, can provide a large virtual memory even in cases where the physical memory is constrained.
- **Optimized system performance**: Paging can enhance system performance by preventing fragmentation and utilizing memory resources.
- **Memory management ease**: The operating system finds it simpler to allocate and deallocate memory as needed when using paging, which offers a straightforward and effective memory management technique.
- **Protection and isolation**: Paging facilitates the assignment of distinct pages to various applications, thereby offering protection and isolation amongst them.
- **Data sharing:** Paging maps the same page to distinct virtual addresses in various processes, allowing multiple processes to share data.

- **Flexibility:** Paging provides the flexibility to resize the memory allocation for a process by adding or removing pages as needed.
- **Dynamic relocation**: Paging enables dynamic relocation of processes, allowing memory to be moved to different physical addresses as needed.
- **Efficient use of disk space:** Paging helps to make efficient use of disk space by temporarily storing inactive pages on disk and swapping them back into memory as needed.

Disadvantages of Paging

- **Page table overhead**: To track pages through paging, a page table must be kept up to date, which can add overhead to the system.
- **Page fault overhead**: A page fault is a processing lag that happens when a page cannot be located in memory and needs to be retrieved from disk.
- **Thrashing:** Thrashing can occur when too many pages are routinely swapped between the disk and memory, decreasing the system's performance.
- **Internal fragmentation**: When paging results in memory that is not a multiple of the page size, part of the available memory within a page is left unused.
- **External fragmentation**: Paging can also cause external fragmentation. . In this scenario, a block of memory may be allocated, but it is dispersed over several non-contiguous pages.
- **Overhead associated with disk I/O**: Paging necessitates disk I/O to swap pages, which adds to the system's overhead.
- **Limitations of page size**: The size of a page can affect the system performance; larger pages may cause less internal fragmentation but more external fragmentation, while smaller pages may cause higher page management overhead.
- **Complex page replacement algorithms**: When a page fault occurs, paging needs to know which page to replace. This requires an algorithm, which can be complicated and affect system performance.
- **Requirements for alignment:** Paging may also impose alignment requirements, such as mandating that data be stored at addresses that are multiples of the page size, which would increase system overhead.

Demand Paging in Operating System

Let us look at demand paging in detail.

Need of Demand Paging

There are many pages in each virtual memory process; in some cases it might not be efficient to swap all the pages for the process at once. Since it is possible that the program will only require a single page to function, think about the following scenario: let us say you have a 500 MB program that only needs 100 MB of page swapping. Here, there is no need to swap all the pages at once.

"There are a lot of pages in one particular process. But to put all the pages of that particular process in the memory will only consume the memory. Now for this problem, the concept of demand paging came into execution. Demand Paging is a method in which a page is only brought into main memory when the CPU requests it.

Let us understand this with the help of an example. Suppose the user did a program to calculate the overall cost of the fencing required for the field. For this, there will be different pages for different codes, such as: [1]"

Page 1: The overall cost of the fence

Page 2: The labour cost

Page 3: The surface area of the field.

The user wants to calculate the overall cost of the fence. Then there is no need for loading all three pages, and this is where the demand paging comes into role. Then only Page 1 will be loaded, not all the pages.

Working of Demand Paging in OS

"When the CPU requests access to any page, the page table is used to find the page in the main memory. If the page is found on the main memory, it is good, and if it is not, then a page fault occurs.

Page fault is when the CPU wants to access the page from the main memory, but it is not present in the main memory. Then, how to overcome this?

For this, swapped-in is usedto swap from the secondary memory. Swapped-in refers to moving a program back to the hard drive from the main memory, or RAM. However, if the page is already in the main memory, it is retrieved from there. The secondary memory is loaded with other pages. There are also valid and invalid bits, which are used to check whether the page is present in the main memory. Valid bits mean that the page is legal and present in the memory, and invalid bits mean the page is not valid or it is not present in the memory."[1]

Common Terms in Demand Paging Operating System

The terms used frequently in demand paging operating systems are as follows:

1. **Page Fault:** A page fault, also called a page miss, occurs when a page reference

is not found in the main memory. The CPU needs to search secondary memory for the absent page. The system's effective access time increases significantly when the number of page faults is high.

2. **Swapping:** Swapping is either deleting every page of the process from memory or labeling the pages so that the page replacement method can remove them. A suspended process indicates that it is not able to continue running. However, we are able to temporarily alter the procedure. The process can be switched by the system over time from secondary memory to primary memory. A process that is busy and has pages coming in and going out of it is referred to as thrashing.

3. **Thrashing**: If there are the same number of page faults as the referred pages, or if the number of page faults is so high that the CPU is only reading pages from the secondary memory, the effective access time will be the amount of time the CPU takes to read a single word from the secondary memory. Thrashing is the term for this. EAT = PF x S + (1 - PF) x (ma) can be used to calculate the effective access time if the page fault rate is PF percent, the service time is S, the memory access time is "ma," and the retrieval time is a page from secondary memory.

Common Algorithms used for Demand Paging in OS

Reducing the amount of page faults is the aim of all algorithms. The following are some popular algorithms for OS demand paging:

- **First In First Out (FIFO)**: This algorithm manages operating system resources, such as memory, CPU time, and input/output operations. The processes that arrive first in the queue are executed first, with the remaining ones having to wait to be done so. To ensure that the processes are added and removed correctly, algorithms are used to manage the queue.
- **Optimal Page Algorithm**: The algorithm that replaces pages with the best results is called the optimal page replacement algorithm. It is used to add new processes to the end of the queue when they arrive. To function, the page from the frame with the lowest future demand is swapped out for another page. Because this algorithm is stack-based, Belady's Anomaly does not occur in this implementation.
- **The Least Recently Used (LRU) algorithm**: It replaces the page that hasn't been used in a while with a new one whenever there is a page fault. Thus, the memory page that has not been used for the longest is replaced. The Least Recently Used (LRU) Algorithm can perform a thorough analysis and produces fewer page faults than any other algorithm.

- **The Page Buffering Algorithm**: It is used to maintain a pool of free frames and initiate a process quickly. The pages that are not used as frequently are substituted by the LFU Algorithm. The page that receives the fewest visits over a specified duration is eliminated. If the frequency of the page doesn't change, the first page gets replaced first.

Advantages of Demand Paging in OS

- Memory can be put to better use
- We can have a lot of virtual memory if we use demand paging.
- By using demand paging, we can run programs that are larger than physical memory
- In demand paging, there is no requirement for compaction
- In demand paging, the sharing of pages is easy
- Partition management is simple in demand paging because of the fixed partition size and the discontinuous loading

Disadvantages of Demand Paging in OS

- Internal fragmentation is a possibility with demand paging.
- It takes longer to access memory (page table lookup).
- Memory requirements
- Guarded page tables
- Inverted page tables

Difference between Swapping Process and On-demand Paging

Table 7b.2 provides the difference between Swapping Process and On-demand Paging.

Attribute	Swapping Process	On-demand Paging
Introduction	A memory management technique to store and acquire data in the RAM	A technics for temporarily removing inactive applications from the computer system's main memory
Purpose	Allows the memory of the process address space to be non-contiguous	Allows multiple programs in the os to run simultaneously
Occurrence	Occurs when only a part of the process gets transferred to the disk	Occurs when the entire process is transferred to the disk

Processes	Paging allows many processes in the main memory to exist and is performed by active processes	Swapping reduces the number of processes in the memory and is performed by inactive processes
Adaptability	More adaptable as relocation of the process is allowed	Less adaptable as the operation goes back and forth
Workloads	Appropriate for heavy workloads	Appropriate for light to medium workloads
Memory Management	Used in non-contiguous memory management	Can be performed without any memory management
Usage	Helps to implement virtual memory	Helps CPU to access processes faster

Table 7b.2: *The difference between Swapping Process and On-demand Paging*

Page Replacement Algorithms

In an operating system that uses paging for memory management, a page replacement algorithm is needed to decide which page needs to be replaced when a new page comes in.

Principle of Page Replacement

The page replacement is done by swapping. The required pages from backup storage to main memory and vice versa. This swapping is done by checking the contents of physical memory. If there is a free frame in the memory, then swap in the required page into the frame which is free.

In case, if there is no frame in physical memory, then first find the frame that is not currently in use. The content of this frame is swapped out from memory to backup storage. Then bring the required page in the frame, which is now free.

As studied in demand paging, only certain pages of a process are loaded initially into the memory. This allows us to get more processes into the memory simultaneously. But what happens when a process requests for more pages and no free memory is available to bring them in? The following steps can be taken to deal with this problem:

1. Put the process in the wait queue, until any other process finishes its execution thereby freeing frames, or
2. Remove some other process completely from the memory to free frames, or
3. Find some pages that are not being used right now, move them to the disk to get free frames.

This technique is called page replacement and is most commonly used.

Page Fault: A page fault happens when a running program accesses a memory page mapped into the virtual address space, but not loaded in physical memory.

Since actual physical memory is much smaller than virtual memory, page faults happen. In case of page fault, the operating system might have to replace one of the existing pages with the newly needed page. Different page replacement algorithms suggest different ways to decide which page to replace. The target for all algorithms is to reduce the number of page faults. [2]

Deployment of Page Replacement Algorithm

Numerous algorithms exist for replacing pages. An algorithm's effectiveness is assessed by calculating the number of page faults it causes when applied to a specific memory reference string. The term "*reference string*" refers to the string of memory references. Artificially created reference strings can also be produced by tracking a system and noting the address of every memory reference. The number of available page frames must also be known to calculate the number of page faults for a specific reference string and page replacement algorithm. Page faults will become less frequent as the number of available frames rises. To illustrate the page replacement algorithm, we will use the following page reference string.

5, 0, 1, 0, 2, 3, 0, 2, 4, 3, 3, 2, 0, 2, 1, 2, 7, 0, 1, 1, 0

for a memory with three frames.

FIFO (First In First Out) Page Replacement

- Simplest page replacement algorithm
- The oldest page in the main memory is the one which will be selected for replacement. Easy to implement, keep a list, replace pages from the tail and add new pages

  1 1 1 1 0 0 0 0 0 0 0 0 0 1 1 1 1 1 1

  Total Page Fault= 11

  Number of Hit= 10

  Rate of page fault = No. of page fault/No. of frames

  11/3= 3.6

Belady's **Anomaly:**

Belady's anomaly is that the page-fault rate may increase as the number of allocated frames increases.

For example, if we consider the following page reference string

0, 1, 2, 3, 0, 1, 4, 0, 1, 2, 3, 4 with number of frame 3, we get a total 9 page faults as shown in the *Figure* (a). But if we increase the number of frame from 3 to 4 we get 10 page faults as shown in *Figure* (b)

Case 1: Frame=3

Total Page Fault= 11

Number of Hit= 10

Rate of page fault = No. of page fault/No. of frames

11/3= 3.6

Advantages

- It is open for full analysis
- Here, we replace the page that is least recently used, thus free from Belady's Anomaly.
- Easy to choose a page which has faulted and hasn't been used for a long time.

Disadvantages

- It requires additional data structure to be implemented.
- Hardware assistance is high.

Optimal Page Replacement

This algorithm states that you should replace that page that will not be used for the longest period of time, that is, future knowledge of reference string is required.

Example: Reference string is 5, 0, 1, 0, 2, 3, 0, 2, 4, 3, 3, 2, 0, 2, 1, 2, 7, 0, 1, 1, 0

Total Page Fault= 12

Number of Hit= 9

Rate of page fault= No. of page fault/No. of frames = 12/3= 4

Advantages

- It is open for full analysis
- Here, we replace the page which is least recently used, thus free from Belady's Anomaly
- Easy to choose page which has faulted and hasn't been used for a long time

Disadvantages

- It requires additional Data Structure to be implemented

- Hardware assistance is high

Optimal Page Replacement

This algorithm states that you replace the page which will not be used for longest period of time, that is, future knowledge of reference string is required.

Example: Reference string is 5, 0, 1, 0, 2, 3, 0, 2, 4, 3, 3, 2, 0, 2, 1, 2, 7, 0, 1, 1, 0

Number of Hit = 12

Rate of page faults= No. of page fault/No. of frames = 9/3= 3

Advantages

- Complexity is less and easy to implement
- Assistance needed is low, that is, data structure used are easy and light

Disadvantages

- Optimal page replacement algorithm is perfect, but not possible in practice, as the operating system cannot know future requests.
- Error handling is tough.

Solved Example: Consider the following page reference string: 1,2,3,4,2,1,5,6,2,1,2,3,7,6 ,3,2,1,2,3,6

Compare the number of page faults for FIFO, LRU, and optimal page replacement. Assume the number of frames is 4.

Sol. FIFO page replacement

Total Page Fault= 14

LRU page replacement

4 4 4 4 6 6 6 6 6 7 7 7 7 1 1 1 1

3 3 3 3 5 5 5 5 5 3 3 3 3 3 3 3 3 3

2 2 2 2 2 2 2 2 2 2 2 2 2 2 2 2 2 2 2

1 1 1 1 1 1 1 1 1 1 1 1 6 6 6 6 6 6 6

H H H H H H H H H H

Total Page Fault= 10

The Working Set Model

Choosing which pages to keep in the main memory (as opposed to paging them out to auxiliary storage) has an important consequence: if a process has too many pages kept in the main memory, then fewer processes can be ready at any given time. The number of active (non-suspended) processes presently running in the system approaches zero when a process has too few pages maintained in main memory, increasing the frequency of page faults in the process. A process is said to be in RAM if and only if it can access all of the pages it is currently using, which is typically determined by looking up the pages it has used most recently.

This is according to the working set model. The model is all-or-nothing, meaning that if a process needs more pages than RAM can accommodate, and there isn't enough space, it will be switched out of memory to make room for other processes.

Heavy-loaded computers frequently have so many processes queued up that, if all of them were permitted to run for a single scheduling time slice, they would refer to more pages than RAM, which would cause the computer to "*thrash*".

When some processes are switched out of memory, even those temporarily removed from memory conclude much faster than they would if the computer tried to run them all at once. Additionally, because it permits other processes to continue operating while one is waiting on the hard drive or another global resource, the processes complete significantly faster than they would if the computer only ran one process at a time. To put it another way, the working set strategy maximizes multiprogramming while minimizing thrashing. Consequently, it maximizes throughput and CPU utilization.

Implementation

Keeping track of the working set is the biggest challenge in putting the working set model into practice. A moving window is the working set window. Every memory reference causes the oldest reference to disappear from one end and a new one to appear at the other. If a page is mentioned in the working set window, it is included in the working set.

The working set is frequently implemented by monitoring the time *t* of the last reference and defining the working set as all pages referenced within a specific amount of time, to avoid the overhead of maintaining a list of the last *k* referenced pages. Although page replacement algorithms can be made only to remove pages that aren't in the working set for a specific process, the working set itself isn't a page replacement algorithm. WSClock, a modified version of the clock algorithm, serves as one illustration.

Variants

The terms "*code working set*" and "*data working set*" refer to two types of working sets. This distinction is crucial when data and code are kept apart at the appropriate level of the memory hierarchy. If either working set is too large to fit there, thrashing will happen. For the process to run smoothly on virtual memory systems, the translation look-aside buffer (TLB) needs to cache the entries of the working set's memory map (which maps virtual memory to physical memory) in addition to the code and data itself. This distinction arises from the fact that address lookup occurs at the page level, while code and data are cached in small blocks (cache lines) rather than entire pages. TLB thrashing results from the virtual address working set possibly not fitting into TLB, even though the code and data working sets fit into the cache if the working sets are divided across multiple pages.

Working set analogs are available for other scarce resources, most notably processes. A set of processes that necessitates frequent communication between different processes has a process working set that needs to be scheduled in order to advance: parallel programs have a process working set that needs to be scheduled for the parallel program to advance (scheduled for execution simultaneously). One interaction per time slice is the fastest the processes can progress if they are not scheduled simultaneously, as would be the case with two processes and one core available for execution.

Additional resources include file handles and network sockets. For instance, copying a file from one location to another is best done using two file handles, one for input and one for output. This results in a "*file handle working set*" of two. Copies can still be made even if only one file handle is available. To do this, get the file handle for the input, read from it (perhaps into a buffer), release it, get the file handle for the output, write to it, release it, get the input file handle again, and so on. In the same way, a server that needs a lot of sockets might have to release and reacquire them frequently if its supply is limited. These resources are usually necessary for the program, so it fails if it cannot obtain enough of them, instead of thrashing around.

Thrashing

The phenomenon of thrashing poses a serious problem for operating systems and can hugely affect system performance. When a computer's virtual memory system is overloaded, it can thrash, resulting in excessive paging and an ongoing, pointless struggle to keep up with the demands of running processes. To maintain the best possible operating system performance, system administrators and developers must comprehend the causes, effects, and mitigation techniques for thrashing. Thrashing is a disruptive phenomenon that has many implications. This exploration explores these implications and the strategies used to address them [3].

Pages are discrete, fixed-size segments of the program that are mapped to the main memory's frames. The fixed size of each program page is the same as the main memory's frame size. Demand paging is used to load a page with the code needed at that moment to implement the idea of virtual memory. Programs kept in the main memory are called processes. A page fault exception is raised when an IO operation (page fault service) is needed to load the requested page from secondary memory into main memory because the requested page for a running process is not in main memory.

Thrashing in Operating System [3]

When virtual memory is used, a phenomenon known as "*thrashing*" happens in operating systems. It happens when the majority of application-level operations are excluded from a computer's virtual memory in favor of fast data exchange with the hard drive. The process is said to be thrashing if the CPU spends more time handling page faults than actually executing pages. The operating system tries to increase the level of multiprogramming in response to the low CPU utilization.

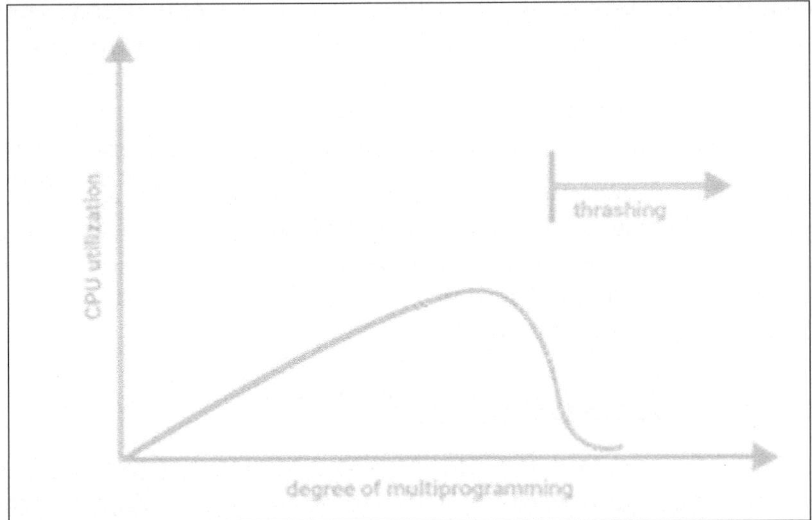

Figure 7b.1: *Graphical representation Concept of Thrashing*

The basic idea is that too many page faults will happen frequently if a process is given insufficient frames.

Consequently, the CPU would be idle, and CPU utilization would sharply decline. Thrashing is a state of an operating system in which there is an extreme decrease in system performance due to excessive paging activity. The operating system has to spend a lot of time switching data between the RAM and the disk when the system is overloaded with requests for more memory than is physically possible. Thrashing is frequently brought on by a high level of multiprogramming or an excessive memory usage by active processes.

Thrashing is the result of the system constantly switching pages when it is trying to meet the demands of too many processes at once, and their combined memory needs are greater than the amount of physical memory that is available.

Next, by putting more processes in memory, the long-term scheduler would attempt to increase CPU utilization and multiprogramming. Regretfully, this would lead to even lower CPU utilization, which would cause a series of larger page faults to occur in succession, increasing the level of multiprogramming and causing thrashing.

Page Replacement Algorithms and Effect of Thrashing

The operating system employs either the local frames replacement algorithm or the global frames replacement algorithm to bring in enough pages in the main memory to handle page faults. Let us examine how thrashing is impacted by these replacement algorithms.

- **Global Page Replacement**: The Global Page Replacement can bring any page and will try to bring more pages if it detects the operating system is thrashing. The operating system begins to thrash more violently as a result of no process can obtain enough frames. In conclusion, the global page replacement technique does not work when the operating system experiences thrashing.
- **Local Page Replacement**: The pages included in that process will be chosen, as opposed to the pages replaced globally. This may lessen the operating system's thrashing. As was previously mentioned, there are several drawbacks to using local page replacement. Therefore, local page replacement is just a substitute for global page replacement.

Causes of Thrashing in OS

The operating system's performance during execution is impacted by thrashing. The performance of the operating system is also lowered by thrashing. A higher level of multiprogramming is achieved when the process scheduling mechanism tries to load multiple processes into memory when CPU usage is low.

There are more processes running in memory in this instance than memory frames available. A higher-priority process will be assigned to a free frame that becomes available when a high-priority process enters memory, provided that no other process is currently using it. If so, the other process will be moved to secondary storage.

Overcoming the Phenomenon of Thrashing in OS

The health of the hard disk and system performance are negatively impacted by OS thrashing. Thus, some safety measures are necessary. Allocating as many frames as each process needs while running will help prevent the operating system from thrashing. The locality model can be used to calculate a process's frame count. A locality is a collection of pages that are frequently used in tandem. The locality model states that a process may overlap its localities as it moves from one to another during execution. To stop page faulting at the current location, we need to provide a process with enough frames. More information on this is provided by the working-set model. The process scheduler can be instructed to halt some of the processes if the system is already thrashing.

The following techniques are provided to help prevent thrashing in OS:

1. **Working Set Model**: This model is predicated on the notion of the locality model mentioned previously. According to the fundamental idea, a process will not stop working until it finds a new locality if we give it enough frames to support it in its current one. Nevertheless, the process will thrash if the allotted frames are less than the current locality's size.

   This model defines the working set as the collection of pages in the most recent 'A' page references, determined by parameter A. All pages that are currently being used would therefore always become a part of the working set. The accuracy of the working set depends on the value of parameter A. If A is too big, working sets might cross over. However, the locality might not be fully covered for smaller values of A.

Let WSSi be the working set size for process I and D be the total demand for frames.

```
D = ∑ WSSi
```

If '`m`' is the number of frames available in memory, there are two options:

When D is greater than **`m`**, that is, thrashing happens when certain processes do not receive enough frames, as the total demand exceeds the available frames. The thrashing would cease if **`D<=m`**. If enough additional frames are available, more processes can be loaded into memory. Stopped (swapped out of memory) processes are necessary if the total of working set sizes is greater than the number of frames available. Thrashing is avoided, and maximum multiprogramming is ensured with this method. It maximizes CPU utilization as a consequence.

2. **Page Fault Frequency**: This idea of Page-Fault Frequency treats thrashing in a more straightforward manner. As thrashing is linked to a high page fault rate, controlling the page fault rate is the idea behind this.

   If the page fault rate is too high, it indicates that the process is receiving too few frames. A low page fault rate, on the other hand, indicates that the process has too many frames.

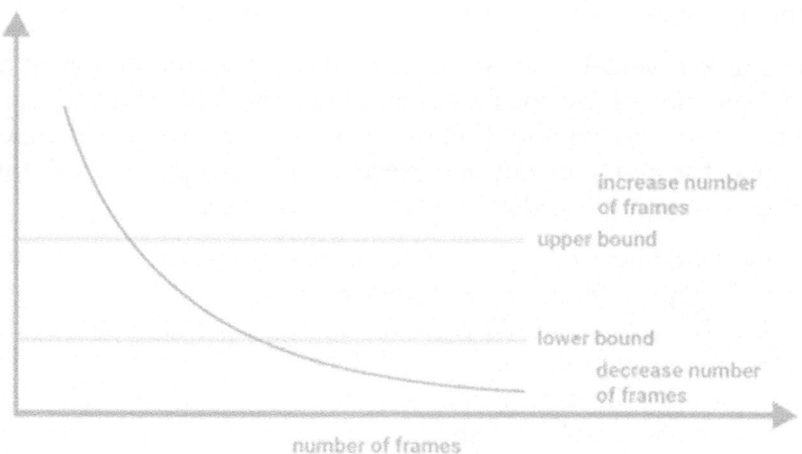

Figure 7b.2: *The Page-Fault Frequency concept*

As illustrated in *Figure 7b.2*, the intended page fault rate can have upper and lower bounds set. Should the rate of page faults drop below the lower bound, frames may be eliminated from the process.

Likewise, extra frames can be assigned to the process if the rate of page faults surpasses the upper limit. Stated differently, only the rectangular area shown in the provided diagram should be allowed to contain the system's graphical state. A process may be suspended and resources reallocated to other processes if it has a high page fault rate and no frames available. It is possible to pick up where the stopped processes left off.

- **Detecting thrashing in an operating system:** Finding signs of thrashing in an operating system, a sudden and significant drop in system performance, a spike in paging-related disk activity, and a reduction in CPU throughput are all indicative of thrashing. Thrashing can be identified early using monitoring tools, such as performance counters or system resource usage metrics.
- **Impact of thrashing on system performance:** Thrashing causes a major reduction in system performance because it uses up valuable CPU cycles and disk I/O bandwidth for excessive paging. This leads to higher latency, slower user application response times, and a general reduction in the system's capacity to carry out operations effectively.

Operating-System Design And Implementation

Here, we talk about issues with operating system design and implementation. While there aren't any perfect answers for these issues, there are strategies that have worked well.

- **Establishing requirements and goals is the first challenge in system design.** At the highest level, the type of system—batch, time-sharing, single-user, multi-user, distributed, real-time, or general purpose—and the hardware selection will impact the system design. The requirements could be considerably more difficult to define after this maximum design level. On the other hand, the requirements can be separated into two fundamental groups:
- **Goals of the system and the user.** Users want certain obvious properties in a system. Convenience, learnability, safety, speed, and dependability are all important features of the system. Naturally, since there is not a consensus on how to accomplish them, these specifications aren't all that helpful when designing the system. Those in charge of system design, creation, maintenance, and operation can define a comparable set of requirements. Easy to design, implement, and maintain, the system should also be flexible, dependable, error-free, and efficient. Once more, these specifications are ambiguous and open to different interpretations.

Mechanisms and Policies

Distinguishing between mechanism and policy is a fundamental principle. Policies determine what will be done, while mechanisms decide how to accomplish tasks. An instance of a mechanism that guarantees CPU protection is the timer construct; however, policy determines how long the timer should be set for a specific user. For flexibility, the division of mechanism and policy is crucial. Policies are probably going to vary over time or between locations. At worst, every policy modification would necessitate a corresponding adjustment to the underlying mechanism.

It would be preferable to have a general mechanism insensitive to policy changes. Then, only a few of the system's parameters would need to be redefined to reflect a change in policy. Take into account, for example, a system that prioritizes some program categories over others. The mechanism can support a policy decision that I/O-intensive programs should take precedence over CPU-intensive programs, or it can be used to support the opposite policy, provided that the mechanism and policy are kept well apart. The allocation of resources depends on policy decisions.

A policy decision must be taken each time it becomes necessary to determine whether or not to allocate a resource. It is always necessary to identify the mechanism when the question is how rather than what.

Implementation

An operating system needs to be implemented after it is created. It is challenging to generalize about operating systems' implementation because they are collections of numerous programs written over a long period by numerous authors. Programming for early operating systems was done in assembly language. Even though assembly language is still used to write some operating systems, most modern operating systems are now written in higher-level languages like C or even higher-level languages like C++. It is true that an operating system can be written in multiple languages. Assembly language could be the lowest level of the kernel. Shell scripts, and interpreted scripting languages like PERL or Python, or C or C++ may be used for system programs and higher-level routines. Programs written in these languages are likely included in a particular Linux distribution.

Implementation of Windows Operating System

Windows Operating System was introduced into the market in the year 1985, and as a robust and comprehensive kind of software, has almost 90% market share over and above other operating system [4].

"*The Microsoft Operating System as a family of Microsoft Windows was created as a graphical layer over that of old MS-DOS with its root from MS-DOS Command line and this it retains till date with DOS Box command prompt that is cmd.exe.* "[5].

With its prominent and overwhelming presence in business and industrial buildings, in addition to its obvious presence in personal computers. However, the overwhelming interest in open source operating systems is thought to refute this claim once more.

The original Windows NT core was the first to appear in the OS/2 operating system, the foundation for all subsequent iterations. Windows OS, DEC Alpha, PowerPC architectures, Windows OS, and MIPS are all compatible with 32- and 64-bit AMD and Intel systems, as well as low- and mid-range servers. The Windows operating system can also use databases and web servers. Microsoft has demonstrated in recent years that it has what it takes to run any enterprise application on Windows, both in terms of interoperability and financial stability. This has been demonstrated through both marketing and financial efforts.

Merits of Windows OS

- **Technical/Maintenance support:** Support is made available either online or offline because of its general acceptability by so many users.
- **Compatibility:** Windows accommodates almost every application, game works, and different types of drivers.
- **Enormous quantity of functions:** Getting used to Windows, one would realize that there are many functions one can do almost anything quite easily with when called up.

Demerits of Windows OS

- **Viruses**: Need to purchase an antivirus program that needs to be activated frequently, and this can be done in auto or manual mode, although free antivirus exists with limitations.

- **Slow:** Windows operating system, particularly Vista and Windows 7 needs a lot of system resources, such as registers, cache, main memory, processor, disk space, and this makes the system run slower.
- **Price:** The cost of purchasing the Windows operating system is high, and very few users can afford it and this necessitates cracking and makes pirated software versions available.

Implementation of UNIX Operating System [6]

As one of the few operating systems from the recent ICT era that is still widely available and in use today, UNIX is primarily meant for use by huge enterprise computing systems. Despite its unassuming appearance, its interface design and mode of operation make it somewhat hidden. It so happens to be one of the widely used operating systems on servers and other PCs that make up the vast majority of the Internet.

Even though UNIX may never be used on a local PC, it is used indirectly every time someone logs on to the internet. There are many different UNIX operating system versions available for UNIX PCs, one of which is "UNIXy," which most users have installed on desktop computers. Very few users run UNIX on their personal systems.

With its various versions, Linux emerges as the most widely used and well-liked platform for personal computers. There are numerous variations and features available in the basic UNIX interface. A UNIX OS is stable, reliable, and resource-efficient, but it can be challenging to set up and operate without extensive knowledge. UNIX OS uses the "UNIX file system". However, most file systems used by UNIX OS are impartially similar but different uniquely from other operating systems file systems, such as DOS or Windows. The trademark UNIX® is been owned by the Open Group; only PCs fully compliant with and certified to the Single UNIX specification qualify as "UNIXR", others are referred to or known as "Unix system-like" or "Unix-like."

Between the latter and early part of 1970s and 1980s respectively, UNIXs way in academic circles led to large-scale acceptance of UNIX by commercial businesses, the most prominent of which is Sun Microsystems. Nowadays, operating systems like UNIX and examples like Linux and BSD products are frequently encountered in addition to certified UNIX computer systems. UNIX has its pros and cons, and besides being a free system, it is run on most machines.

Merits of UNIX

UNIX provides more control by the user. Some OS such as Windows and Mac, are based on icons and mouse, making them more user-friendly; users can also activate what the operating system allows. On UNIX, the user has no limitations, as anything can be done as much as the operating system offers it. What it means is that user can work freely without the fear of thinking that the system can be messed up even when the user does not know what he/she is doing. UNIX offer both freedom and danger because the operating system can be changed and made more compatible with what one wants to do. If one knows what it takes to work perfectly well with UNIX, the operating system can be so powerful that it can be customized, and because it has been in use for a long time, most bugs have been cleared, and this fact makes it highly reliable.[6]

Demerits of UNIX

An expert must be present in the system for UNIX to be used successfully. If one is not an expert in UNIX, even simple installations of new products and updates could be challenging. Because utilizing the UNIX command line to interact with a system is challenging—especially for a beginner—only experienced users use UNIX. The UNIX operating system is highly configurable, with multiple dialects and languages available in various versions. For instance, the operating system code had to be changed at one point because the Berkley UNIX group did not feel comfortable with how UNIX categorizes users. As a result, a seasoned UNIX user in one domain might encounter significant learning curve difficulties in a different domain.

Linux Operating System

Linux is the GNU's response to both Windows and the Mac. It is true that Linux is a free operating system; downloading, editing, and sharing are all free of charge. Regarding operating systems, Linux is comparatively new. It was revised for modern use in 1991 after being written.

You can think of Linux and Windows as an entity whose roofs and floors are either replaceable or not. But with Linux, the floor and roof can be moved in any direction as an entity, whereas Windows' floor and roof are so rigid that they cannot be moved. You are limited to what Microsoft has created. In the 1991 design of Linus Torvalds, Linux was the leader of a new wave of open-source Unixes that emerged in 1990 and include Darvin, FreeBSD, NetBSD, and OpenBSD. These are all illustrations of the design direction that was decided upon by the group as a whole.

Although Linux code is completely different from the original UNIX source tree code, it still adheres to UNIX standards to function as a UNIX. Because developers in the open-source Linux community want to control a significant portion of end-user desktops, Linux is expected to have a larger user base than traditional Unix users, who are afraid of losing market share in the server and workstation space. Since UNIX and Linux are proprietary systems, Linux applications must exhibit a higher level of ruggedness than their counterparts running proprietary UNIX systems. This increased concern for ease of installation and troubleshooting software distribution stemmed from the aspiration to reach end users.

Merits of Linux OS

- **Price**: Linux is F-R-E-E in price. It doesn't cost anything to download, install, use, or modify.
- **Variety:** Linux is merely a kernel and not a full OS. Given that it is a kernel, additional software add-ins are needed. There are numerous distributions, or distros, of this type.
- **Virus:** Although it is less vulnerable than a Mac due to its open-source nature, this does not guarantee that it is immune to virus attacks.

Demerits of Linux OS

- **Complicated:** Although some Linux distributions are relatively simple to use, using them requires a good deal of computer knowledge.
- **Compatibility:** While Linux shares a small portion of the market with Mac, it lacks the same number of apps and games as Windows.
- **Vendors:** There aren't many Linux vendors offering Linux computers; if one requires one, they may have to buy a Windows computer, format the hard drive, and then install Linux on it.

Memory Management Policies of UNIX System V [7]

Traditionally, UNIX systems moved entire processes–aside from shared text–between the swap device and main memory. However, individual process components were never moved. Swapping is the term for such a memory management strategy. On the PDP 11, where the maximum process size was 64K bytes, it made sense to implement such a policy. The amount of physical memory available on a system serves as the process size limit for this policy. Demand paging was first implemented in a big way by the BSD system (release 4.0), which transfers memory pages rather than processes to and from a secondary device.

More recently, UNIX System V's Memory Management Policies have also supported demand paging. A process does not always need to run in main memory; in fact, the kernel loads pages when it needs them, as long as it refers to them. The benefit of a demand paging policy is that it allows for more flexibility in how a process's virtual address space is mapped into the physical memory of a machine. This typically enables multiple processes to run concurrently in main memory and allows process sizes to be up to ¾ larger than the available physical memory. A swapping policy's benefit is that it requires less system overhead and is simpler to implement.

Swapping

There are three parts to the description of the swapping algorithm: managing space on the swap device, swapping processes out of the main memory, and swapping processes into the main memory.

Allocation of Swap Space [7]

The swap device is a block device in a configurable section of a disk. When as the kernel allocates space for files one block at a time, it allocates space on the swap device in groups of contiguous blocks. Space allocated for files is used statically; since it will exist for a long time, the allocation scheme is flexible to reduce the amount of fragmentation and, hence, unallocatable space in the file system. However, the allocation of space on the swap device is transitory, depending on the pattern of process scheduling. A process that resides on the swap device will eventually migrate back to the main memory, freeing the space it had occupied on the swap device. Since speed is critical and the system can do I/O faster in one multiblock operation than in several single block operations, the kernel allocates contiguous space on the swap device without regard for fragmentation. Because the allocation scheme for the swap device differs from the scheme for file systems, the data structures that catalog free space differ too. The kernel maintains free space for file systems in a linked list of free blocks, accessible from the file system superblock, but it maintains the free space for the swap device in an in-core table, called a map. Maps, used for other resources besides the swap device (some device drivers, for example), allow a first-fit allocation of contiguous "*blocks*" of a resource.

A map is an array in which each entry is the address of an allocatable resource and the number of resource units that are available there. The address and units are interpreted by the kernel based on the type of map. A map initially has a single entry that lists the address and the resources. For example, the address is treated as a block offset from the start of the swap area, and each unit of the swap map is treated by the kernel as a collection of disk blocks. The first swap map, shown in *Figure 7b.3*, has 1,000,000 blocks and begins at address 1.

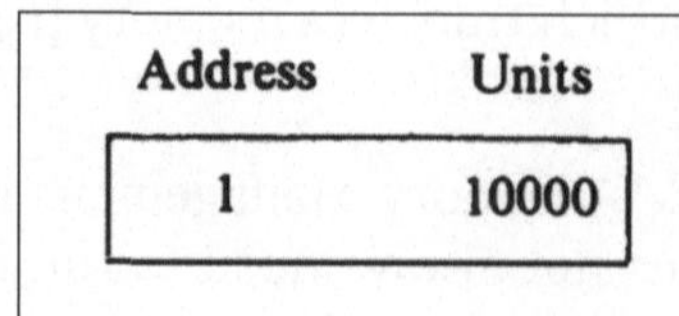

Figure 7b.3: *Initial Swap Map*

The malloc algorithm is shown in *Figure 7b.4* for space allocation from maps.

```
algorithm malloc        /* algorithm to allocate map space */
input:  (1) map address         /* indicates which map to use */
        (2) requested number of units
output: address, if successful
        0, otherwise
{
        for (every map entry)
        {
                if (current map entry can fit requested units)
                {
                        if (requested units == number of units in entry)
                                delete entry from map;
                        else
                                adjust start address of entry;
                        return (original address of entry);
                }
        }
        return(0);
}
```

Figure 7b.4: *Algorithm for allocating space for maps*

The request is fulfilled by the kernel when it finds the first entry on the map with sufficient space. Should the request utilize every resource in the map entry, the kernel eliminates the entry from the array and reduces the size of the map (that is, one fewer entry). If not, the entry's address and unit fields are modified based on the resource allocation. The swap map configuration sequence is displayed in *Figure 7b.5* following the allocation of 1 00 units, 50 units, and 1 00 units once more. The swap map is modified by the kernel so that it now displays 9750 free units beginning at address 25 1 and that the first 250 units have been allocated. The kernel uses the address to determine the resources' correct location in the map before freeing them. Three scenarios could happen.

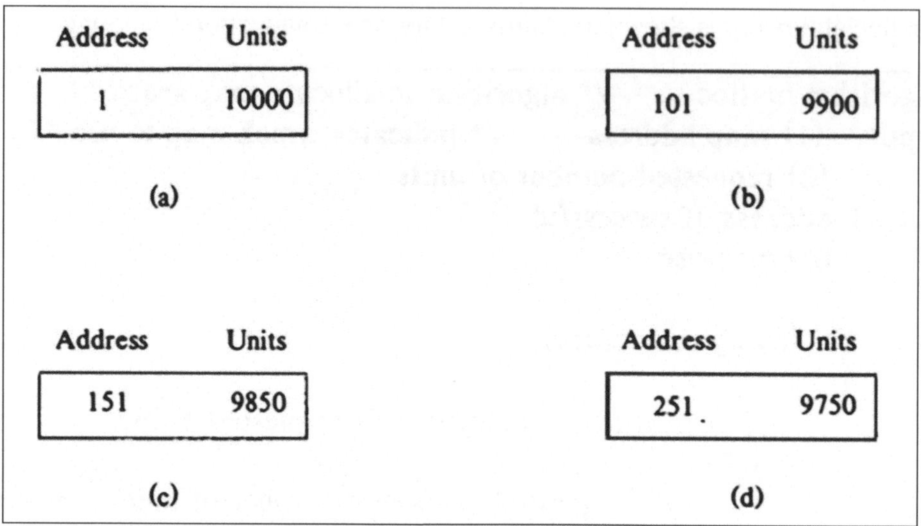

Figure 7b.5: *Allocating Swap Space*

- The resources that were released entirely cover a gap in the map since they are adjacent to entries whose addresses would both come before and after them on the map. Here, the newly released resources and the two already-existing entries are combined by the kernel into a single map entry.
- The resources that have been released fill in a gap on the map. The kernel modifies the address and unit fields of the appropriate entry to take into account the resources that have just been freed if the address of the released resources is contiguous with either the entry that would come right before them or the entry that would come right after them, but not both. The map still has the same amount of entries.
- The released resources do not connect to any other resources on the map; instead, they only partially fill a gap. The map's entry is created by the kernel, which then places it in the appropriate location.

Going back to the earlier example, the swap map has a new entry for the resources that were freed if the kernel releases 50 units of the swap resource beginning at address 101. This is because the returned resources are not adjacent to already existing entries in the map. The first entry of the swap map is altered if the kernel then releases 1,000 units of the swap resource, beginning at address 1. This is because the freed resources are adjacent to those in the first entry. The order of swap map configurations that correspond to these occurrences is shown in *Figure 7b.6*.

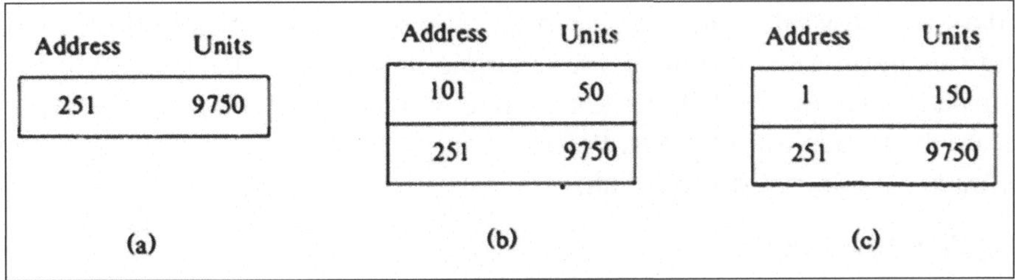

(a)

Address	Units
251	9750

(b)

Address	Units
101	50
251	9750

(c)

Address	Units
1	150
251	9750

Figure 7b.6: *Freeing Swap Space*

Assume that 200 units of swap space are now requested by the kernel. Finally, let us say the kernel releases 350 units of figure swap space beginning at address 15 1. This is because the first entry in the swap map only has 1 50 units, so the kernel fulfills the request from the second entry (see *Figure 7b.7*). The 350 units were allotted separately, but the kernel was unable to release them all at once. This is not the same for swap space, because requests for swap space are separate from one another.

(a)

Address	Units
1	150
251	9750

(b)

Address	Units
1	150
451	9550

Figure 7b.7: *Allocating Swap Space from the Second Entry in the Map*

Conventional UNIX system implementations use a single swap device, but the most recent System V implementations allow multiple swap devices. The kernel recognizes that the freed resources fit neatly into the hole between the first and second entries in the swap map and creates one entry for the former two (and the freed "*resources*").

If the swap device has enough contiguous memory, the kernel selects it using a round-robin algorithm. Swap devices are dynamically added and removed by administrators. The kernel does not swap data to a swap device when it is being removed; instead, it empties as data is swapped out of it until it is free to be removed.

Allocating Swap Space from the Second Entry in the Map

With no intermediate buffer cache, the kernel swaps as much data as possible per I/O operation directly between the user address space and the swap device. The kernel program must repeatedly move one memory page at a time if the hardware transfer multiple pages in a single operation. The disk controller's capabilities and the memory management system's implementation, among other things, determine the precise data transfer rate and how it works. The data to be swapped out is probably discontinuous in physical memory, for example, if memory is arranged in pages. For the disk driver to set up the 110, the kernel needs to compile the page addresses of the data that needs to be swapped out. Before swapping out additional data, the swapper waits for each I/O operation to finish.

Swapping Processes Out

The kernel swaps a process out if it needs space in memory, which may result from any of the following:

1. The **fork** system call must allocate space for a child process
2. The **brk** system call increases the size of a process
3. A process becomes larger by the natural growth of its stack
4. The kernel wants to free space in memory for processes previously swapped out and should now swap in.

The case of fork stands out because it is the only case where the in-core memory previously occupied by the process is not relinquished. When the kernel decides that a process is eligible for swapping from main memory, it decrements the reference count of each region in the process and swap the region out if its reference count drops to 0. The kernel allocates space on a swap device and locks the process in memory (for cases 1-3), preventing the swapper from swapping it out while the current swap operation is in progress. The kernel saves the swap address of the region in the region table entry.

For instance, if memory is organized in pages, the data to be swapped out is likely to be discontinuous in physical memory. The kernel must gather the page addresses of data to be swapped out, and the disk driver may use the collection of page addresses to set up the 110. The swapper waits for each I/O operation to complete before swapping out other data.

The kernel doesn't need to write the entire virtual address space of a process to a swap device. Instead, it copies the physical memory assigned to a process to the allocated space <**tn**> Unassigned virtual addresses are ignored by the swap device. The kernel can reassign the process to the appropriate virtual addresses when it swaps the process back into memory because it is aware of the virtual address map of the process. By reading the data into physical memory locations that were previously configured to comply with the virtual address locations, the kernel removes an extra copy from a data buffer to physical memory.

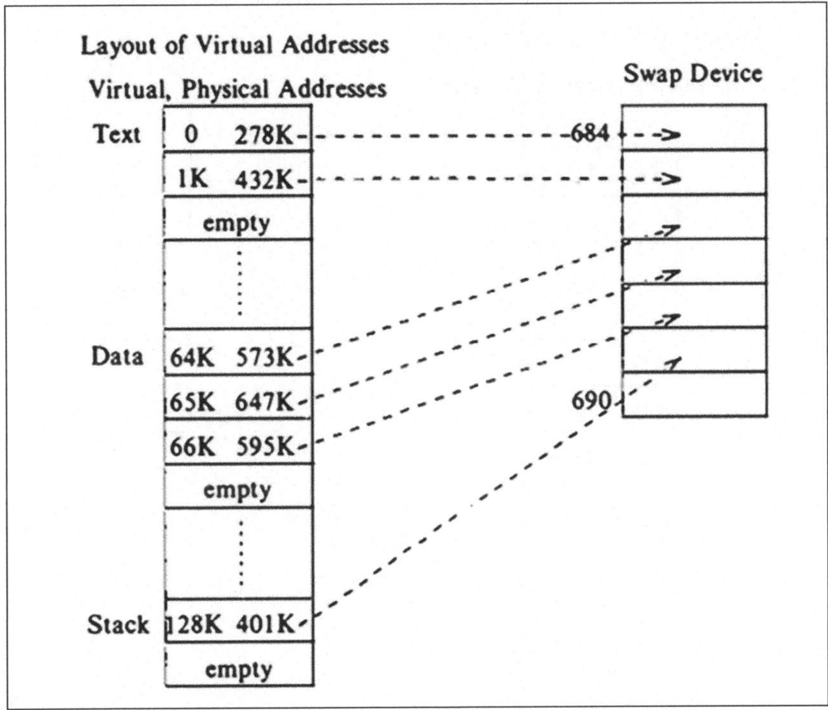

Figure 7b.8: *Mapping Process Space onto the Swap Device*

A process's in-core image can be mapped onto a swap device as shown in *Figure 7b.8*. The process is divided into three regions: text, data, and stack. The data region begins at a virtual address of 64K, while the text region ends at a virtual address of 2K, leaving 62K bytes in the virtual address space between them. Instead of allocating swap space for the empty 62K bytes between the text and data regions or the empty 61K bytes between the data and stack regions, the kernel fills the swap space continuously when it swaps out the process. This involves swapping the pages for virtual addresses 0, 1 K, 64K, 65K, 66K, and 128K. The kernel recognizes the process when it switches it back in. By looking at the process memory map, it determines that there is a 62K-byte hole and allocates physical memory appropriately. This case is illustrated in *Figure 7b.8*.

A comparison of *Figures 7b.7* and *7b.8* shows that the physical addresses occupied by the process before and after the swap are not the same; however, the process does not notice a change at user-level, because the contents of its virtual space are the same.

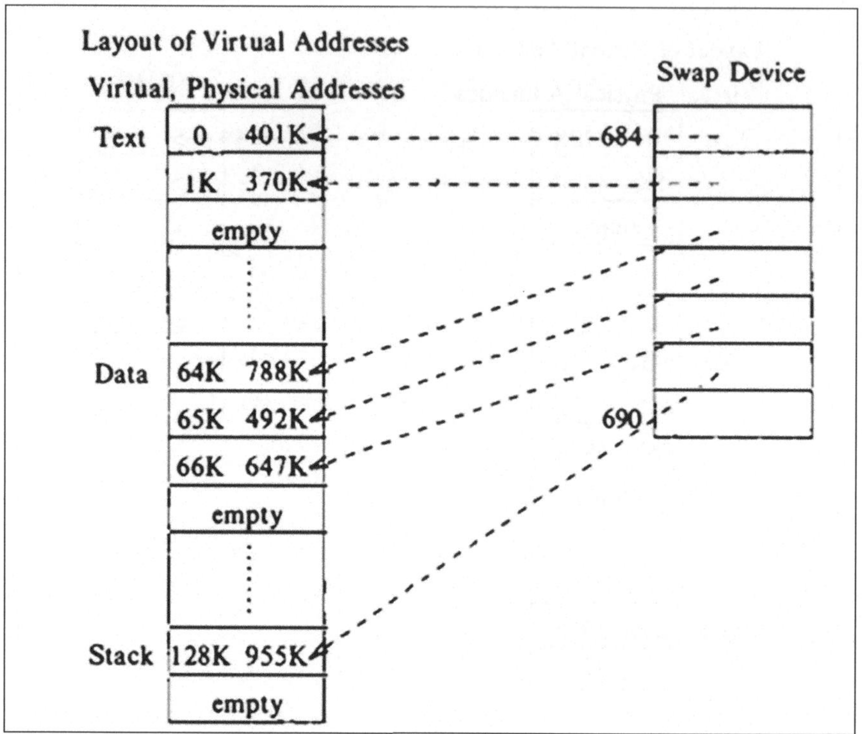

Figure 7b.9: *Swapping a Process into Memory*

If a sensitive operation is running, the kernel may temporarily lock a region into memory. However, in theory, any memory space occupied by a process, including its u area and kernel stack, is eligible to be swapped out. But in practice, if the u area holds the process's address translation tables, kernel implementations do not swap it out. If a process is unable to swap itself out and needs to ask another process to do so, it is also determined by the implementation.

Memory Management Unit (MMU)

A computer hardware device known as a memory management unit (MMU), also known as a paged memory management unit (PMMU), analyzes every memory reference on the memory bus and converts these requests—also referred to as virtual memory addresses—into physical addresses in main memory. Program addresses in contemporary systems typically access the 32- or 64-bit theoretical maximum memory of the computer architecture. The addresses from each program are mapped by the MMU into distinct physical memory regions, which are typically substantially smaller than the theoretical maximum. Programs rarely use large amounts of memory at one time, which makes this possible.

Most contemporary operating systems (OS) collaborate with an MMU to enable virtual memory (VM) functionality. When a program references a location on a page not in physical memory, the MMU will trigger an operating system interrupt. The MMU tracks memory use in fixed-size blocks known as pages. After choosing a less-used block of memory, the OS will read the page from backing storage into that block, set up the MMU to map the block to the originally requested page so the program can use it, and write the block to backing storage—such as a hard drive—if it has changed since it was read in. We call this demand paging.

Most modern MMUs also carry out extra memory-related functions. Memory protection keeps malicious code from reading data from another program or misbehaving programs from exhausting memory by preventing them from attempting to access memory they haven't been asked for. Additionally, they frequently oversee a processor cache, which minimizes the need to communicate with the slower main memory by storing recently accessed data in very fast memory. They are also in charge of bus arbitration in certain implementations, which manage memory bus access among the various computer components that need access.

The range of addresses that the processor uses, known as the virtual address space, is normally divided into pages by modern MMUs. Each page has a size that is a power of two and is typically a few kilobytes, though they can be much larger. Programs use the machine's natural address size, which is usually 32 or 64 bits in modern systems, to refer to memory. The address's lowermost bits—the offset within a page—remain unaltered. Virtual page numbers are represented by the upper address bits.

Most MMUs use an in-memory table of items called a page table, containing one-page table entry (PTE) per virtual page, to map virtual page numbers to physical page numbers in main memory. Multi-level page tables are often used to reduce the size of the page table. An associative cache of PTEs called a translation lookaside buffer (TLB) is used to avoid the necessity of accessing the main memory every time a virtual address is mapped.

Other MMUs may have a private array of memory, registers, or static RAM that holds a set of mapping information.

The virtual page number can be used as an index into the page table or other mapping information directly, or it can be further divided into two or more levels of indexing, with bits at one level serving as an index into a table of lower-level tables into which bits at the next level down serve as an index.

The entire physical address is obtained by combining the page offset and the physical page number. Information about whether the page has been written to (the dirty bit), when it was last used (the accessed bit, for a least recently used (LRU) page replacement algorithm), what types of processes (user mode or supervisor mode) may read and write it, and whether it should be cached are all possible additions to a page table entry or other per-page information.

Access to a specific virtual page may occasionally be blocked by a page table entry or other per-page data, possibly because no physical random-access memory (RAM) has been assigned to that virtual page. Here, the MMU alerts the CPU to a page fault. The operating system (OS) then takes care of the matter, possibly by attempting to locate a free frame of RAM and configuring the page map to map it to the virtual address that has been requested. When no RAM remains free, selecting an already-existing page—referred to as a victim—might be required using a replacement algorithm and saving it to disk (a procedure known as paging). There may be a PTE scarcity with some MMUs; in that scenario, the OS must free up one for the new mapping.

In addition, the MMU may produce invalid page faults or illegal access error conditions in response to unauthorized or non-existent memory accesses, respectively. These errors can cause segmentation faults or bus error conditions, which the operating system must handle.

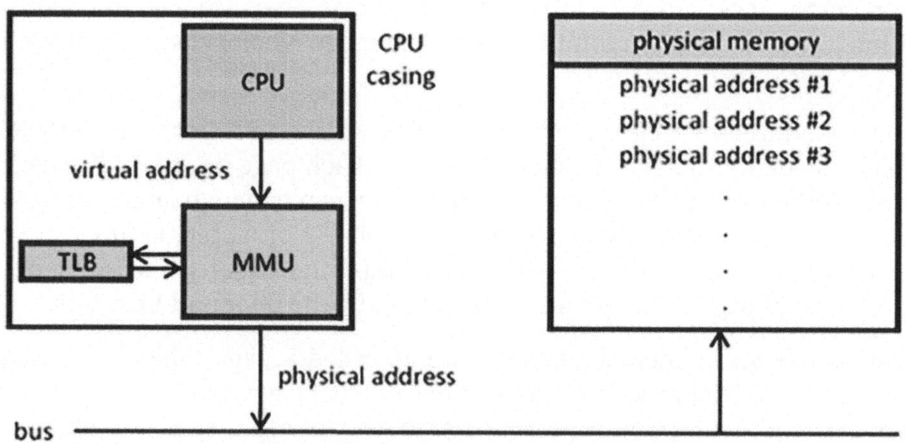

Figure 7b.10: *Schematic of the operation of an MMU*

MIPS Architecture

In the early 1980s, Stanford University conducted VLSI research that resulted in the development of the MIPS processor. The development of MIPS began with a graduate student brainstorming session taught by Professor John Hennessy, who is currently the president of the university. The development of the processor, which became one of the first RISC processors, was aided by the readings and brainstorming sessions. Berkeley and IBM were also developing processors at roughly the same time.

Because the Stanford research group had a strong background in compilers, they could develop a processor whose architecture would represent a departure from the long-standing hardware industry design philosophy of raising hardware to the software level and lowering the compiler to the hardware level.

As a result, the MIPS processor used a more condensed and straightforward instruction set. The chip design contained instructions that each completed in a single clock cycle. To process instructions more quickly, the processor employed a method known as pipelining.

A bit pattern of this size is called a word, and MIPS used 32 registers, each 32 bits wide.

Instruction Set

The MIPS instruction set consists of 111 instructions, each represented in 32 bits. The following is an example of an MIPS instruction:

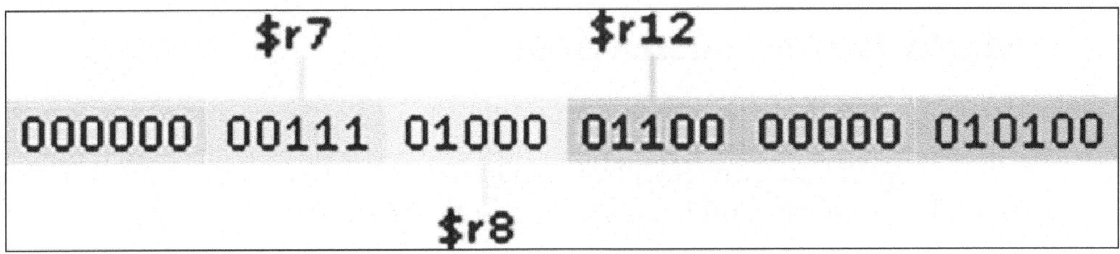

Figure 7b.11: *MIPS instruction set*

Reduced instruction set computing, or RISC, is a technique used in the architecture of MIPS microprocessors. To put it another way, it is a method of arranging the computer processor so that speed and simplicity are the main priorities. To create a commercial version of the prototype chip, members of the Stanford research team founded the MIPS corporation in 1984. The R2000 microprocessor, which debuted in 1985, was their first product. The R2010 floating-point coprocessor was released in 1987. Several of the early workstations were able to use both chips successfully. With the same instruction set as the R2000, the R3000 was the next generation of MIPS processors, designed with low-cost embedded systems in mind.

The preceding figure is a representation of an MIPS addition instruction in binary (right) and assembly (left). The processor is instructed by the instruction to add the values in registers 7 and 8 and store the result in register 12. Use the dollar signs to denote a register operation. A MIPS instruction's six fields are depicted in the colored binary representation on the right. The binary numbers in the first and last fields help the processor determine what kind of instruction it is. In this instance, the CPU recognizes that the instruction is an addition based on the 20 in the last field and the zero in the first field. The blue and yellow fields indicate the operands, while the fourth (purple) field displays the desired result location. The shift amount, which is not utilized in addition operations, is represented by the orange field.

The instruction set consists of a variety of basic instructions, including:

- 21 arithmetic instructions (+, -, *, /, %)
- 8 logic instructions (&, |, ~)
- 8-bit manipulation instructions
- 12 comparison instructions (>, <, =, >=, <=, ¬)
- 25 branch/jump instructions
- 15 load instructions
- 10 store instructions
- 8 move instructions
- 4 miscellaneous instructions

Basic MIPS Implementation

For all instructions, the first two steps are common:

1. Set the program counter (PC) to the memory location that contains the code and fetch the instruction from that memory location.
2. Read one or two registers, using the fields of the instruction.

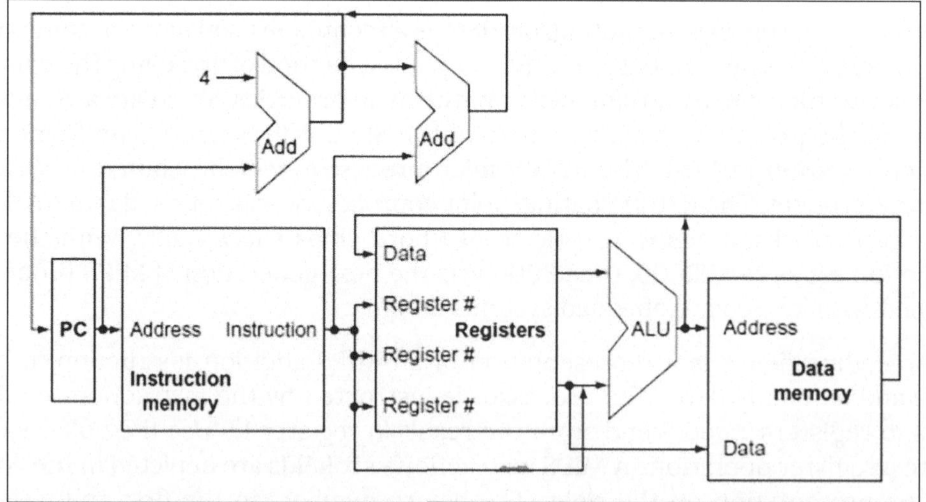

Figure 7b.12: *An abstract view of the implementation of the MIPS subset showing the major functional units and the major connections between them*

3. After these two steps, the actions required to complete the instruction depend on the instruction class.

Three commonly used instruction classes are:

- Memory Reference
- Arithmetic Logical
- Branches

For each of the three instruction classes, the actions are exactly the same, independent of the exact opcode.

Across instructions, there are some similarities.

- For example, all instruction classes, except jump, use the arithmetic-l(ALU) after reading the registers.
- The memory-reference instructions use the ALU for an address calculation, thearithmetic-logical instructions for the operation execution and branches for comparison.
- After using the ALU, the actions required to complete various instruction classes differ.
- A memory-reference instruction will need to access the memory to read data for a load or write data for a store. An arithmetic-logical or load instruction must write the data from the ALU or memory back into a register.
- Lastly, for a branch instruction, we may need to change the next instruction address based on the comparison; otherwise, the PC should be incremented by 4 to get the address of the next instruction.
- *Figure 7b.12* shows the high-level view of an MIPS implementation, focusing on the various functional units and their interconnection.
- The program counter provides the address of the next instruction to be fetched.
- After the instruction is fetched, the register operands are fetched.
- Once the register operands have been fetched, they can be operated on to compute a memory address (for a load or store), to compute an arithmetic result (for an integer arithmetic-logical instruction), or to compare (for a branch).
- If the instruction is arithmetic-logical, the result from the ALU must be written to a register.
- If the operation is a load or store, the ALU result is used as an address to either store a value from the registers or load a value from memory into the registers.

This processor and its system-on-a-chip implementations are still popular and used in millions of devices (for example, printers) even today. Since then, several improved variants of the original instruction set have been introduced:

- MIPS-I: The first 32-bit instruction set, still widely used.
- MIPS-II: An enhanced instruction set that includes numerous new instructions. The R4000 series uses the 64-bit MIPS-III instruction set.
- MIPS-IV: This is an enhanced version of MIPS III.

The TLB can have one to 64 entries supported by the MIPS architecture. Prior to synthesis, the CPU configuration allows for the customization of the TLB entry count. There are two TLB entries. Depending on the least significant bit of the virtual address not included in the page mask, each TLB entry maps a virtual page number (VPN2) to one of two-page frame numbers (PFN0 or PFN1). The page mask bits and this bit are not kept in the VPN2. Every TLB entry possesses a unique page size, ranging from 1 KB to 256 MB in multiples of four.

A TLB entry contains three PFNs: a dirty, a valid, and a caching attribute. A VPN2 has an OS-assigned ID that, when the global status bit is set to zero, takes part in the virtual address TLB entry match, as well as a global status bit. The physical address is stored in a PFN without the page mask bits. When the mapped virtual address is not matched by any entries in the TLB, a TLB refill exception is raised. When there is a match but the entry is flagged invalid, a TLB invalid exception is raised. When the dirty status of the matching entry is not set and a store instruction references a mapped address, a TLB modified exception is raised. A double fault TLB exception is a TLB exception that arises during processing and is forwarded to a different exception handler.

MIPS32 and MIPS32r2 support 32 bits of virtual address space and up to 36 bits of physical address space. MIPS64 supports up to 64 bits of virtual address space and up to 59 bits of physical address space.

Pentium Memory Management

Since the introduction of the 32-bit architecture, microprocessors have evolved sophisticated memory management schemes that build on the lessons learned with medium- and large-scale systems. In many cases, the microprocessor versions are superior to their larger-system antecedents. Because the schemes were developed by the microprocessor hardware vendor and may be employed with a variety of operating systems, they tend to be quite a general purpose. A representative example is the scheme used on the Pentium II. The Pentium II memory management hardware is essentially the same as that used in the Intel 80386 and 80486 processors, with some refinements.

Address Spaces The Pentium II includes hardware for both segmentation and paging. Both mechanisms can be disabled, allowing the user to choose from four distinct views of memory:

- **Unsegmented, unpaged memory:** In this case, the virtual address is the same as the physical address. This is useful, for example, in low-complexity, hyper-performance controller applications.
- **Unsegmented, paged memory:** Here memory is viewed as a paged linear address space. The memory protection and management are done via paging. This is favored by some operating systems (for example, Berkeley UNIX).
- **Segmented, unpaged memory:** Here memory is viewed as a collection of logical address spaces. The advantage of this view over a paged approach is that it affords protection down to the level of a single byte, if necessary. Furthermore, unlike paging, it guarantees that the translation table needed (the segment table) is on-chip when the segment is in memory. Hence, segmented, unpaged memory results in predictable access times.
- **Segmented paged memory**: Segmentation is used to define logical memory partitions subject to access control, and paging is used to manage the memory allocation within the partitions. Operating systems such as UNIX System V favor this view.

An Intel microprocessor line that was compatible with the x86 architecture is known as Pentium. First available on March 22, 1993, was the Pentium I. Before Intel's Core processor line debuted in 2006, Pentium served as the company's flagship processor line for over ten years. Following the naming convention of previous generations (286, i386, i486), the original Pentium-branded CPUs were supposed to be dubbed 586 or i586. Intel's first P5-based processor came after the company's earlier series of microprocessors, which included the 8086, 80186, 80286, 80386, and 80486.

Several major changes make the Pentium significantly faster than the 486. The primary change is that two integer pipelines can be used to execute two instructions simultaneously. Many instructions have improved timings, especially floating-point instructions. A new branch prediction feature allows the processor to predict the destination of a branch instruction to eliminate branch delays. Most of the other changes help alleviate the inevitable bottlenecks that occur when executing more instructions at a faster rate. Here is a brief list of the changes:

- 64-bit bus
- 8K code cache and 8K data cache (vs. 8K combined cache on 486)
- Fewer clock cycles for some instructions (especially floating point)
- Branch prediction logic
- Dual integer pipelines
- Higher clock speeds"

The "*superscalar pipelined architecture*" of the Pentium is what is known about it. Superscalar refers to a CPU that can carry out two or more instructions in a single cycle. More specifically, the Pentium can process the output of two instructions in a single clock cycle. A CPU that performs each step of an instruction in separate steps is said to have a pipelined architecture. Following the completion of a stage, one instruction moves to the next stage, and another instruction starts executing in the first stage. Five stages make up the pipelines of the Pentium and 80486.

There are two pipelines on the Pentium: the U pipe and the V pipe. Because of inconsistencies in register usage or address generation, certain instructions may at some point in the pipeline prevent other instructions from progressing.

Bigger Cache

The Pentium cache is now 8K for data versus code and 8K for data. 8K aggregated on the 486. Note: A 16K combined cache is now present in some more recent 486 CPUs. Having the data and code caches kept apart has benefits. The code cache is used for instruction fetches, and the data cache is used for reading and writing data. Because of this division, there are fewer internal bus conflicts that might result in delays. But more significantly, this makes it possible for the code cache to hold extra details about every byte stored there. The Pentium keeps track of the pairing information for each instruction. Later chapters contain more details on this.

Pentium II Segmentation

Each virtual address (referred to as a logical address in the documentation) is made up of a 32-bit offset and a 16-bit segment reference when segmentation is employed. The protection mechanism takes up two bits of the segment reference, leaving 14 bits available for identifying a specific segment. Therefore, the user's virtual memory is GBytes when using unsegmented memory. A user's perception of the total virtual memory space with segmented memory is measured in terabytes (TBytes). For a maximum of 4 GBytes, the physical address space uses a 32-bit address. It is possible for virtual memory to exceed 64 TBytes in size. This is so that the processor can interpret a virtual address differently depending on the process running at the time. There are two sections to virtual address space. In the virtual address space (8K), half is global and shared by all processes, and the other half is local and unique to each process.

Two types of protection are linked to each segment: access attribute and privilege level. The four privilege levels are as follows: level 0 is the most protected, and level 3 is the least protected. A data segment's "classification" is the privilege level linked to it, whereas a program segment's "clearance" is the privilege level linked to it. "An executing program can only access data segments if the data segment's privilege level is equal to or less privileged than the clearance level of the data segment."

How these privilege levels are used is determined by the design and implementation of the operating system, not by the hardware. Preference level 0 was supposed to be used for the tiny percentage of the OS dedicated to memory management, security, and access control, while level 1 would be used for the most OS. Two levels remain for application. Applications typically live at level 3 in many systems, with level 2 being idle. Suitable candidates for level 2 are specialized application subsystems that need to be secured since they use their own security measures. Database management systems, office automation systems, and software engineering environments are a few instances.

The privilege mechanism restricts the use of specific instructions in addition to controlling access to data segments. Certain instructions can only be performed at level 0, such as those pertaining to memory management registers. Only a specific OS-designated level, usually level 1, can be reached when executing I/O instructions. The read/write or read-only permissions for a data segment are indicated by its access attribute. The read/execute or read-only access for program segments is specified by the access attribute.

The process of translating a virtual address into a linear address is known as the address translation mechanism for segmentation, please refer (*Figure* 7*b*.13).

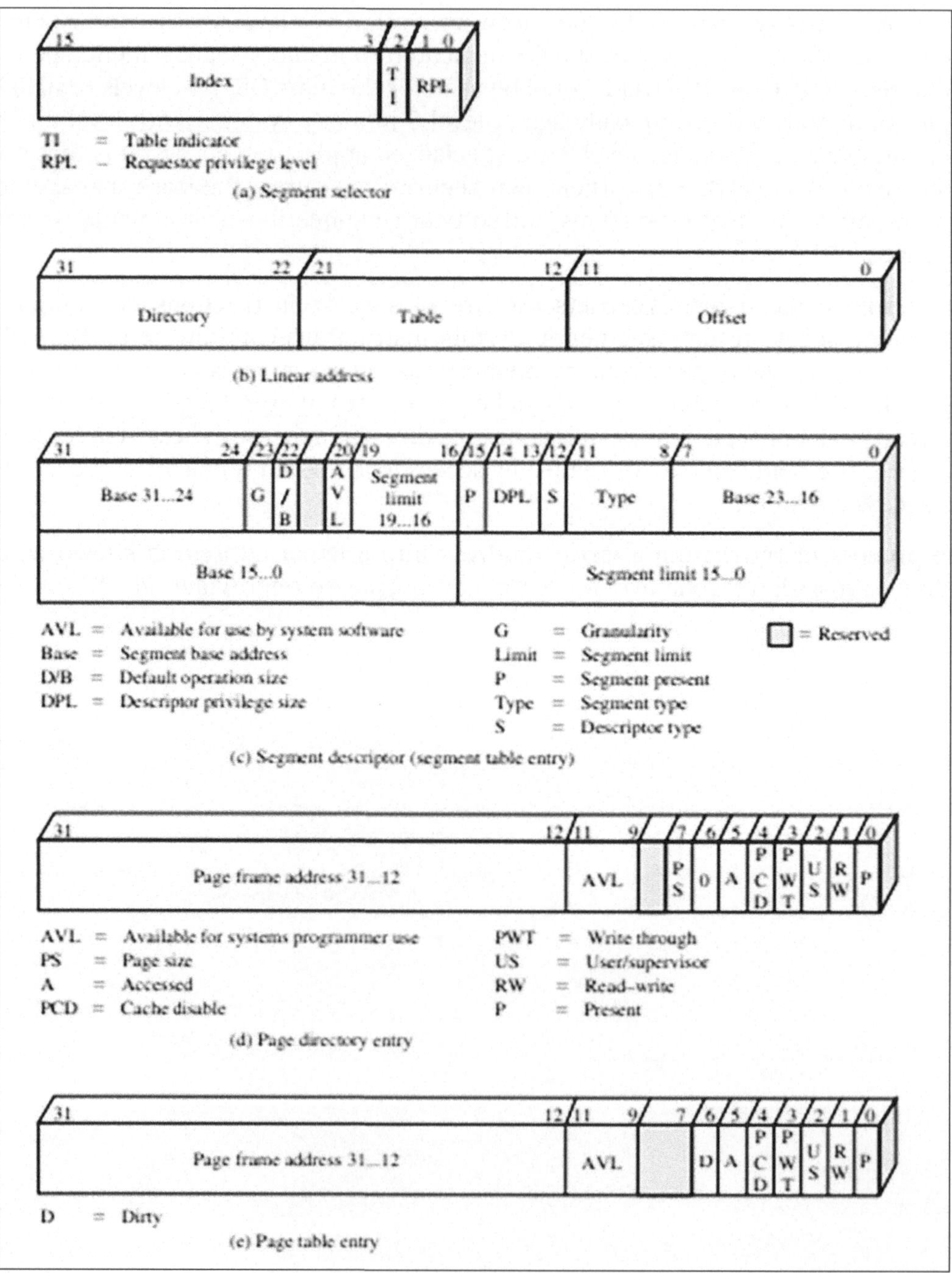

Figure 7b.13: *Segmentation in Pentium*

A virtual address consists of the 32-bit offset and a 16-bit segment selector (*Figure 7b.13*).

The segment selector consists of the following fields:

- **Table Indicator (TI)**: Indicates whether the global segment table or the local segment table should be used for translation.
- **Segment Number:** The number of the segment; this serves as an index in the segment table.
- **Requested Privilege Level (RPL)**: The privilege level requested for this access.

Each entry in a segment table consists of 64 bits, as shown in *Figure 7b.13*. The fields are defined in *Table 7b.3*.

Segment Descriptor (Segment Table Entry)

Base
Defines the starting address of the segment within the 4-GByte linear address space.

D/B bit
In a code segment, this is the D bit and indicates whether operands and addressing modes are 16 or 32 bits.

Descriptor Privilege Level (DPL)
Specifies the privilege level of the segment referred to by this segment descriptor.

Granularity bit (G)
Indicates whether the Limit field is to be interpreted in units by one byte or 4 KBytes.

Limit
Defines the size of the segment. The processor interprets the limit field in one of two ways, depending on the granularity bit: in units of one byte, up to a segment size limit of 1 MByte, or in units of 4 KBytes, up to a segment size limit of 4 GBytes.

S bit
Determines whether a given segment is a system segment or a code or data segment.

Segment Present bit (P)
Used for nonpaged systems. It indicates whether the segment is present in main memory. For paged systems, this bit is always set to 1.

Type
Distinguishes between various kinds of segments and indicates the access attributes.

Page Directory Entry and Page Table Entry

Accessed bit (A)
This bit is set to 1 by the processor in both levels of page tables when a read or write operation to the corresponding page occurs.

Dirty bit (D)
This bit is set to 1 by the processor when a write operation to the corresponding page occurs.

Page Frame Address
Provides the physical address of the page in memory if the present bit is set. Since page frames are aligned on 4K boundaries, the bottom 12 bits are 0, and only the top 20 bits are included in the entry. In a page directory, the address is that of a page table.

Page Cache Disable bit (PCD)
Indicates whether data from page may be cached.

Page Size bit (PS)
Indicates whether page size is 4 KByte or 4 MByte.

Page Write Through bit (PWT)
Indicates whether write-through or write-back caching policy will be used for data in the corresponding page.

Present bit (P)
Indicates whether the page table or page is in main memory.

Read/Write bit (RW)
For user-level pages, indicates whether the page is read-only access or read/write access for user-level programs.

User/Supervisor bit (US)
Indicates whether the page is available only to the operating system (supervisor level) or is available to both operating system and applications (user level).

Table 7b.3: *Pentium II Memory Management Parameters*

Paging in Pentium

It is possible to disable segmentation, which is an optional feature. Program addresses are virtual addresses and are transformed into linear addresses, as previously mentioned, when segmentation is in effect. Programs use linear addresses when they do not use segmentation. Changing that linear address into a real 32-bit address is the next step in either scenario. In reality, the Pentium II paging mechanism is a two-level table lookup operation, which is necessary to comprehend the structure of the linear address. Up to 1024 entries can be found in the page directory at the first level. As a result, 1024 page groups, each 4 MBytes in length and having its own page table, are created from the 4-GByte linear memory space. There can be up to 1024 entries in each page table, each representing a single 4-KByte page.

Memory management can use a single-page directory for every process, a single-page directory for every process, or a mix of the two. Main memory is always home to the page directory for the active task. Virtual memory may contain page tables.

Table 7b.2 defines the fields, and *Figure 7b.13* displays the formats of entries in page tables and directories. Keep in mind that page-level or page group-level access control mechanisms are available.

A translation lookaside buffer is another feature used by the Pentium II. Entries from 32-page tables can fit in the buffer. Buffer clearing occurs each time the page directory is modified.

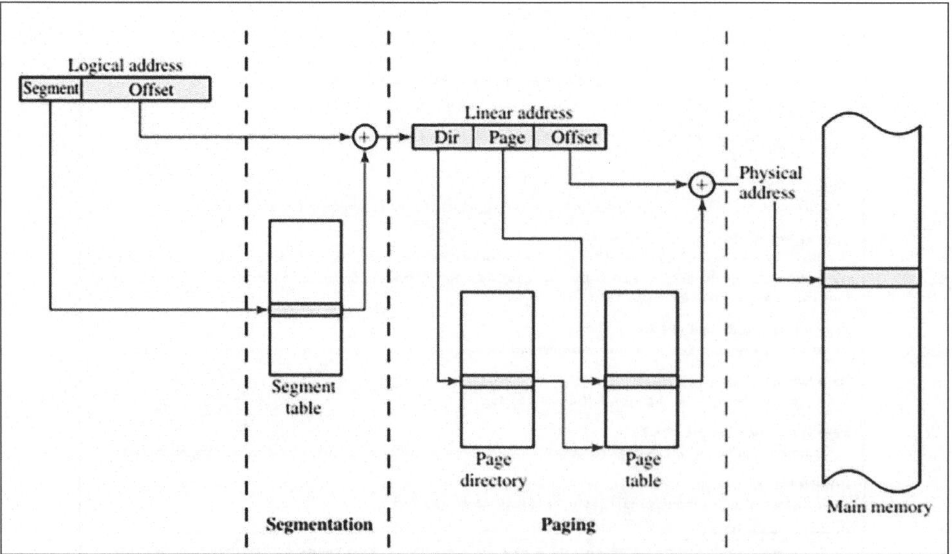

Figure 7b.14: *Pentium Memory Address Translation Mechanisms*

Figure 7b.14 illustrates the combination of segmentation and paging mechanisms. For clarity, the translation lookaside buffer and memory cache mechanisms are not shown.

Finally, the Pentium II includes a new extension not found on the 80386 or 80486, the provision for two-page sizes. If the PSE (page size extension) bit in the control register 4 is set to 1, then the paging unit permits the OS programmer to define a page as either 4 KByte or 4 MByte in size.

When 4-MByte pages are used, there is only one level of table lookup for pages. When the hardware accesses the page directory, the page directory entry (*Figure 7b.7*) has the PS bit set to 1. In this case, bits 9 through 21 are ignored, and bits 22 through 31 define the base address for a 4-MByte page in memory. Thus, there is a single-page table.

Using 4-MByte pages reduces the memory-management storage requirements for large main memories. With 4-KByte pages, a full 4-GByte main memory requires about 4 MBytes of memory just for the page tables. With 4-MByte pages, a single table, 4 KBytes in length, is sufficient for page memory management.

Conclusion

In this chapter, we continued learning memory management further to part I; thereby, paging demand and thrashing. Also learned about the implementation of the memory management of two vulnerable operating systems: Windows and UNIX Operating System. In the next chapter, we shall learn about secondary storage and interfacing Input/Output (I/O) devices.

Questions

1. What is paging in memory organization? Enumerate the differences between segmentation and paging.
2. What are the advantages and disadvantages of paging?
3. How does demand paging in OS work?
4. Write a brief note on page fault and thrashing.
5. For what purpose is the LRU algorithm used?
6. What is the principle of the page replacement technique?
7. How is working set model implemented?
8. What is thrashing in an operating system?
9. What are the causes of thrashing in the OS method of overcoming the phenomenon of thrashing?
10. How can thrashing in an operating system be detected?

11. What goals are to be adopted in operating-system design and implementation?
12. Write an exploratory essay on the implementation of the Windows Operating System.
13. What merits of Windows OS made it extraordinary in its adoption worldwide?
14. Explain the workings of a Memory Management Unit (MMU) with the help of a diagram.
15. What special arrangement were made for working with 32-bit memory management, Pentium memory management, and including hardware for both segmentation and paging?
16. How paging is done in the Pentium microprocessor?

References

[1] Demand Paging in OS (Operating System), Rinki Deka, Naukri.com, https://www.naukri.com › code360, https://www.google.com/search?q=Demand+Paging+in+OS%2C+Rinki+Deka&oq=Demand+Paging+in+OS%2C+Rinki+Deka&gs_lcrp

[2] Page-Replacement-Algorithms - Operating System: https://www.studocu.com › document › page-replacemen...

[3] Thrashing in OS, Prepbytes, Ankit Kochar, https://www.prepbytes.com/blog/operating-system/thrashing-in-os/

[4] Merits and Demerits of The Operating Systems: Windows, Unix, Linux, Mac, Android, And Ios

[5] The Design Of The Unix Operating System,Maurice J. Bach

[6] Computer Organization And Architecture Designing For Performance Eighth Edition William Stallings

[7] This article is based on material taken from Memory+management+unit at the Free On-line Dictionary of Computing prior to 1 November 2008 and incorporated under the "relicensing" terms of the GFDL, version 1.3 or later

Chapter 8
Secondary Storage and Interfacing I/O Devices

Introduction

Data that is not accessed as frequently as data in primary storage is stored in secondary storage, also known as auxiliary storage. It is a non-volatile memory medium that holds onto data until it is either overwritten or erased. Secondary storage may be housed in the cloud, on an external device, or on-site. Secondary storage allows businesses to store data in a few megabytes to petabytes due to the variety of media types that are available. Since these storage devices are typically external, the input and output channels aid in connecting them to the computer. It has a bigger storage capacity than primary storage and is non-volatile. It is made up of external and internal memory. For example, backup storage, such as floppy disks, USB drives, and so on.

Structure

In this chapter, we shall concentrate over following topics:

- Secondary Storage and Input/Output Devices
- Computer System Architecture
- Device Controller
- Communication with I/O Devices
- Direct Memory Access (DMA)
- Polling vs. Interrupts
- Device Driver
- Common Challenges and Issues with Device Drivers

- Free Space Management in the Operating System
- Disk Management in the Operating System
- Disk Management Types
- Disk Scheduling Algorithms
- Redundant Array of Independent Disks (RAID)

Secondary Storage and Input/Output Devices

In this section of the book, we first introduce the idea of an input/output (I/O) device and demonstrate how the operating system may communicate with it before getting into the main body of work. I/O is obviously very important to computer systems; consider an application that does not have any input (it would always produce the same result); now consider an application that does not have any output. It is obvious that both input and output are necessary for computer systems to be interesting.

Computer System Architecture

To begin our discussion, let us look at a "*classical*" diagram of a typical system (*Figure 8.1*).

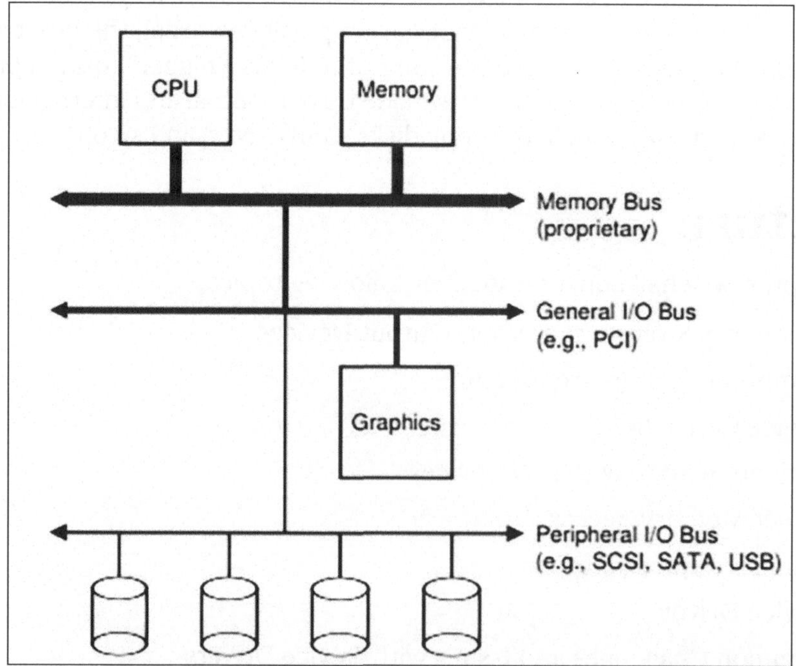

Figure 8.1: *Prototypical Computer System Architecture*

The figure depicts a single CPU connected by some type of memory bus or interconnect to the system's main memory. In many modern systems, secondary storage devices are connected to the computer through interfaces like PCI (Peripheral Component Interconnect) or its many advanced derivatives, such as PCIe (PCI Express).

Lastly, even lower down is one or more of what we refer to as a peripheral bus, such as SCSI, SATA, or USB. These link sluggish devices–such as disks, mouse, and keyboards–to the computer. You might wonder why, in a nutshell, physics and cost require such a hierarchical structure. A high-performance memory bus has limited space for plugging in devices and other accessories because a bus's length increases with its speed.

Furthermore, building a bus for optimal performance comes at a high cost. As a result, system designers have embraced this hierarchical architecture, placing parts closer to the CPU that require high performance, like the graphics card. Distance is a measure of lower performance components. There are many advantages to mounting disks and other slow devices on a peripheral bus, not the least of which is the capacity to mount many devices there. Naturally, to increase performance, modern systems are using faster point-to-point interconnects and specialized chipsets more and more.

An approximation of the Z270 Chipset schematic is shown in *Figure* 8.2. The CPU and memory system are connected most closely along the top, but it also has a high-performance connection to the graphics card, which connects to the display, allowing gaming and other graphically demanding apps.

The CPU is connected to an I/O chip through a variety of interconnects, while the other devices are connected to this chip through Intel's exclusive DMI (Direct Media Interface). The ATA (the AT Attachment), SATA (for Serial ATA), and now eSATA (for external SATA) represent an evolution of storage interfaces over the past decades, with each step forward increasing performance to keep pace with modern storage devices. On the right, one or more hard drives connect to the system via the eSATA interface. Several USB (Universal Serial Bus) connections are found below the I/O chip. In this illustration, these connections allow a keyboard and mouse to be connected to the computer. USB is used for low-performance devices like these on many modern systems. Lastly, PCIe (Peripheral Component Interconnect Express) allows for the connection of additional, higher-performance devices to the system on the left. A network interface is shown as being connected to the system in this diagram; higher-performance storage devices, such as NVMe persistent storage devices, are frequently connected here.

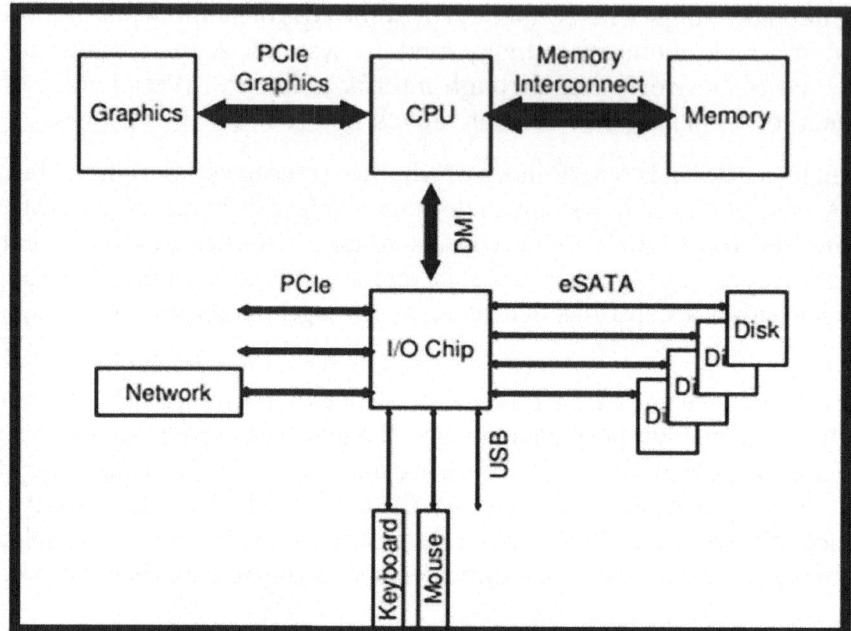

Figure 8.2: *Modern System Architecture*

A Canonical Device

Let us now examine a canonical device, which is not real, and use it to inform our understanding of some of the equipment needed to enable effective device interaction. *Figure* 8.3 shows that a device consists of two crucial parts. The hardware interface it uses to communicate with the rest of the system is the first. Similar to software, hardware needs to have an interface that the system software can use to control how it operates. Because of this, every device has a designated interface and protocol for normal communication.

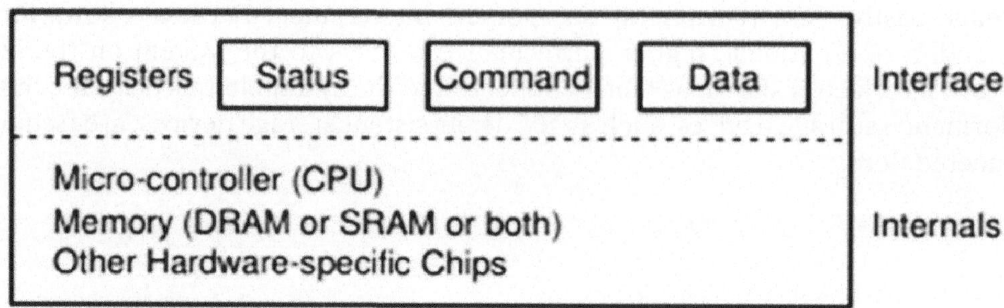

Figure 8.3: *Structural composition of any Digital Computer device*

An apparatus's internal structure makes up its second component. The device's implementation of the abstraction it presents to the system is handled by this implementation-specific component. Simpler devices rely on one or a few hardware chips to carry out their functions, whereas more sophisticated devices use a basic CPU, some general-purpose memory, and additional device-specific chips to complete their tasks. For instance, hundreds of thousands of lines of firmware could make up a modern RAID controller (that is, software inside a hardware device) to carry out its operation.

Device Controller

The management of multiple input/output devices (I/O), such as keyboards, mice, touch pads, disk drives, display adapters, USB devices, bit-mapped screens, LEDs, analog-to-digital converters, on/off switches, network connections, audio input/output, printers, and so on.) is one of an operating system's significant tasks [1].

An input/output system must receive an input/output request from an application, send it to the physical device, and then receive and relay back to the application the response from the device. Two types of I/O devices exist: block devices and non-block devices.

A block device is one that the driver interacts with by transmitting complete data blocks, for instance, USB cameras, disk-on-key, and hard drives.

Character devices: When a driver communicates with a character device, it sends and receives single characters (bytes, octets). As an illustration, consider sound cards, serial ports, and parallel ports.

Device drivers are software modules that can be plugged into an OS to handle a particular device. The operating system takes help from device drivers to handle all I/O devices.

Between a device and a device driver, the device controller functions as an interface. I/O devices (for example, printers, mice, keyboards, and so on, usually comprise two parts: an electronic component known as the device controller and a mechanical component.

Every device that interacts with an operating system has a device driver and a device controller. A device controller can manage several devices. Its primary function as an interface is to convert a serial bit stream to a block of bytes and carry out error correction as needed.

A plug and socket are used to connect any device to the computer, and the socket is linked to a device controller. Here is a model that shows how the CPU, memory, controllers, and I/O devices are connected. The CPU and device controllers communicate with each other via a common bus.

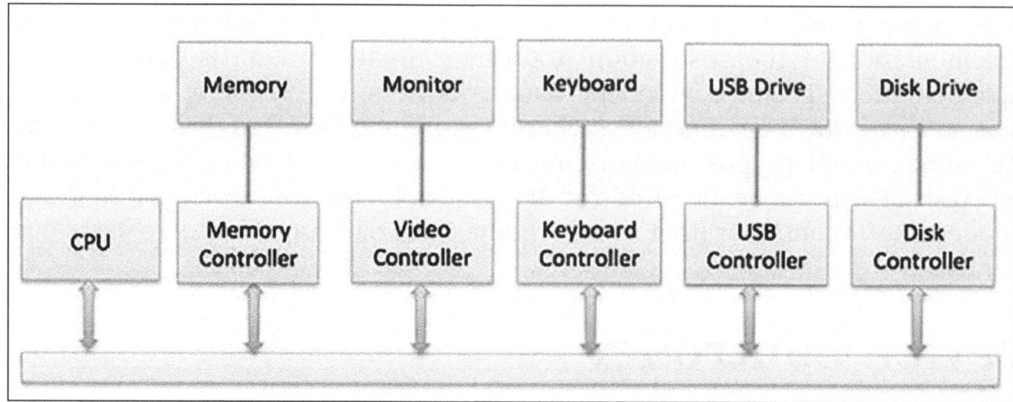

Figure 8.4: *Device Controller*

- Synchronous vs. asynchronous INPUT/OUTPUT
- Synchronous I/O – In this scheme CPU execution waits while I/O proceeds
- Asynchronous I/O – I/O proceeds concurrently with CPU execution

Explore our latest online courses and learn new skills at your own pace. Enroll and become a certified expert to boost your career.

Communication with I/O Devices

The CPU must have a way to pass information to and from an I/O device. There are three approaches available to communicate with the CPU and device.

- Memory-mapped INPUT/OUTPUT
- Direct memory access (DMA)
- Special instruction INPUT/OUTPUT

This uses CPU instructions that are specifically made for controlling I/O devices. These instructions typically allow data to be sent to an I/O device or read from an I/O device.

Memory-mapped INPUT/OUTPUT

When using memory-mapped INPUT/OUTPUT, the same address space is shared by memory and I/O devices. The device is connected directly to certain main memory locations so that the I/O device can transfer blocks of data to/from memory without going through the CPU.

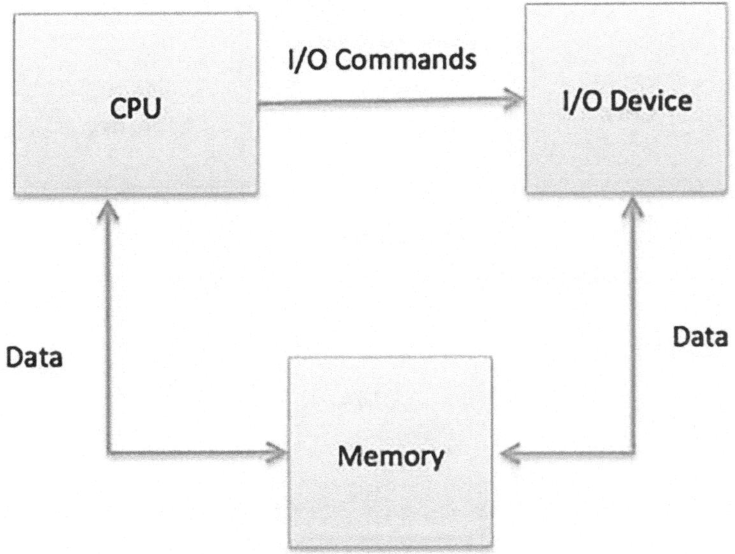

Figure 8.5: *Memory mapped IO*

To send data to the CPU using memory-mapped I/O, the operating system (OS) allocates a buffer in memory and instructs an I/O device to use it. I/O devices work in tandem with CPUs asynchronously, interrupting the latter once completed. This approach has the benefit of allowing any instruction that has memory access to control an I/O device. For most high-speed I/O devices, such as disks and communication interfaces, memory-mapped I/O is utilized.

Direct Memory Access (DMA)

To transfer each byte, slow devices–such as keyboards–cause an interrupt to the main CPU. The operating system would have to spend most of its time handling interrupts if a quick device, like a disk, generated one for every byte. Therefore, most computers use direct memory access (DMA) hardware to minimize this overhead. The CPU gives I/O modules permission to read from or write to memory directly through Direct Memory Access (DMA).

The DMA module manages data transfer between the I/O device and main memory. Only at the start and finish of the transfer does the CPU get involved; it is not interrupted until the entire block has been transferred.

The DMA controller (DMAC), a specialized piece of hardware required for DMA, controls data transfers and arbitrates access to the system bus. The controllers have settings, which include I/O and memory types, interrupts, and CPU cycle states, as well as source and destination pointers, which tell them where to read and write data, and counters, which count the number of bytes transferred.

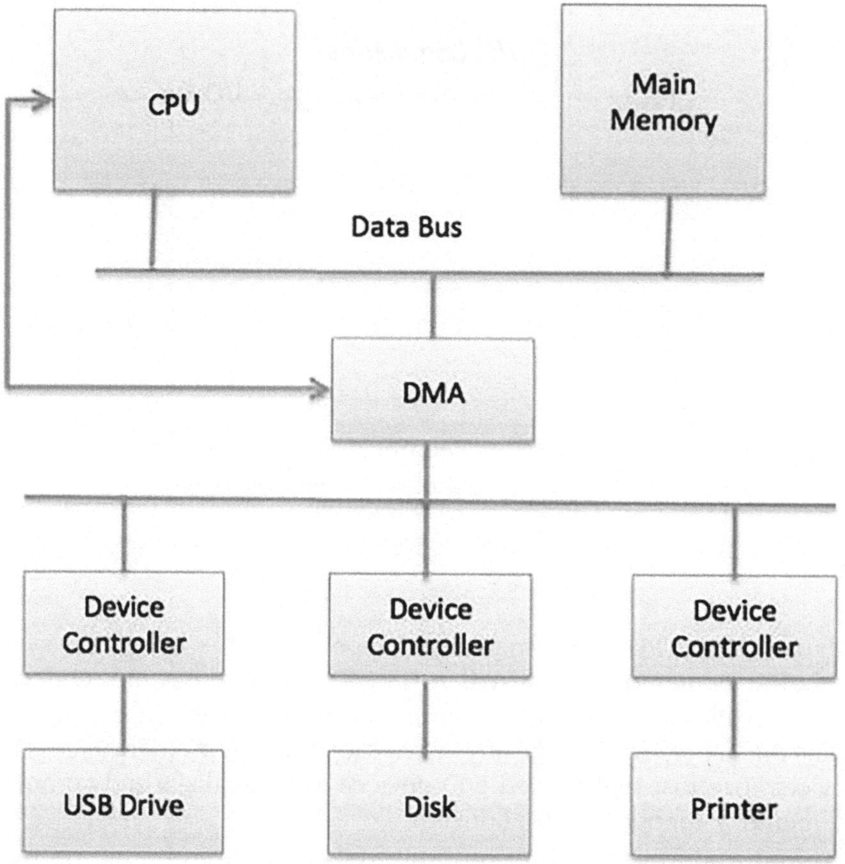

Figure 8.6: *DMA controller*

The operating system uses the DMA hardware as follows:

Step	Description
1	Device driver is instructed to transfer disk data to a buffer address X.
2	Device driver then instructs disk controller to transfer data to buffer.
3	Disk controller starts the DMA transfer.
4	Disk controller sends each byte to DMA controller.
5	DMA controller transfers bytes to the buffer, increases the memory addresses, and decreases the counter C until C becomes zero.
6	When C becomes zero, DMA interrupts CPU to signal transfer completion.

Table 8.1*: Steps to use the DMA Hardware*

Polling versus Interrupts INPUT/OUTPUT

A computer must have a way of detecting the arrival of any type of input. There are two ways that this can happen: polling and interrupts. Both of these techniques allow the processor to deal with events that can happen at any time and that are not related to the process it is currently running.

Polling INPUT/OUTPUT

The simplest method for an I/O device to communicate with the processor is through polling. Polling is periodically determining whether the device is ready for the next I/O operation. The processor needs to retrieve the data from the I/O device, which merely stores it in a status register.

In most cases, devices do not need to be attended to, and when they do, they must wait until the polling program asks it again. A significant portion of the processor's time is wasted on pointless polls with this inefficient method.

Compare this approach to a teacher asking each student in the class, one by one, if they need help all the time. Of course, it would be more effective if students told the teacher whenever they needed help.

Interrupts INPUT/OUTPUT

The interrupt-driven method is a different approach to handling I/O. An interrupt is a message sent by a device that needs to be attended to by the microprocessor. When a CPU receives an interrupt, a device controller sends an interrupt signal to the bus, saves its state, and uses the interrupt vector–addresses of OS routines to handle different events–to invoke the relevant interrupt handler. Following the resolution of the interrupting device, the CPU resumes its initial task as if it had not been interrupted. The following layers are commonly used to organize I/O software:

- **User Level Libraries**: These libraries offer a basic interface for the user program to perform input and output. For instance, the programming languages C and C++ come with the library studio. Device drivers can communicate with the device controller and device-independent I/O modules by using Kernel Level Modules.
- **Hardware:** This layer consists of the actual hardware and the hardware controller that communicates with the device drivers to bring the hardware to life. One of the main ideas behind the design of I/O software is that it should be device-independent, meaning that programs should be able to access any I/O device without specifying it beforehand.

  For instance, a program designed to read files as input ought to be able to read files from various media types, such as CD-ROMs, hard drives, and floppy disks, without requiring modifications to the program for each device.

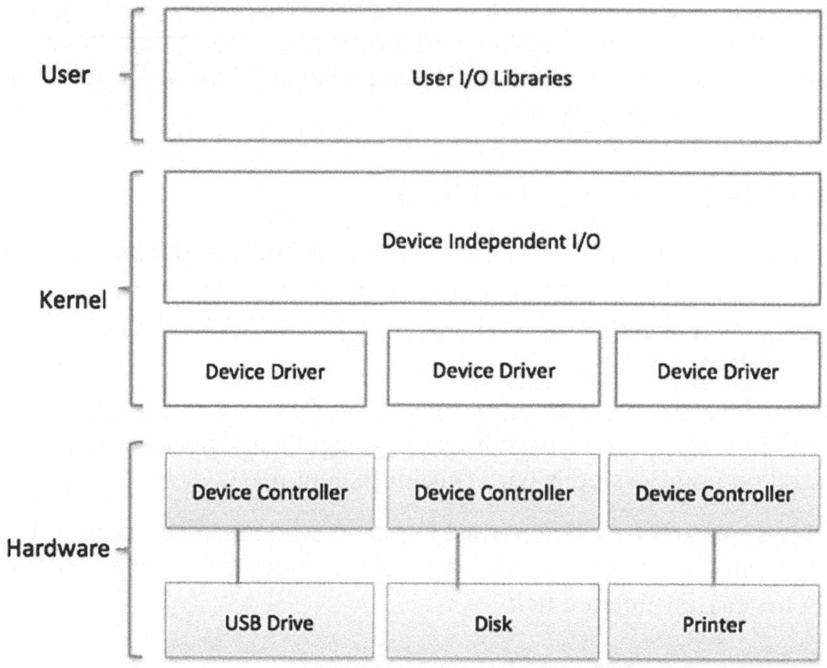

Figure 8.7: *I/O software*

Device Driver

Device drivers are the unsung heroes of the computing world. The operating system of your computer can communicate with hardware, such as printers, keyboards, and graphics cards, thanks to these specialist software applications. They are a crucial aspect of daily computing, because without them, your computer would not be able to connect with these vital components. We will go into the topic of device drivers, explaining what they are, how they function, and why they are crucial. Whether you are a tech geek or just interested, we will translate the technical jargon into understandable language so you can grasp these essential software elements. By the conclusion, you will understand the importance of device drivers for contemporary computing and how they keep your computer operating properly. [2]

Device drivers are specialist software programs that act as a bridge between a computer's operating system and hardware. They enable the operating system to communicate with various hardware devices, such as network adapters, graphics cards, and printers, without necessitating the operating system to be knowledgeable about their internal mechanisms.

Device drivers are critical components of computers because they enable hardware and software to work together flawlessly. They make it easier for different components to communicate with each other and to manage data flows and hardware resources. If device drivers were missing, a computer would not use its hardware, leading to compatibility issues, subpar performance, and the inability to use certain features. Device drivers are essentially necessary for modern computer systems to operate correctly and smoothly.

Function of Device Drivers in a Computer System

Device drivers serve as a vital bridge between software and hardware. Their main job is to facilitate communication between the operating system and other hardware components, such as printers, graphics cards, and hard drives.

Because different devices behave differently, the operating system would not be able to interact with or manage the hardware without device drivers. The driver converts the operating system's generic orders into precise instructions that the hardware can comprehend. This eliminates the need for software programs to understand the complex workings of the hardware to utilize its capabilities. Device drivers essentially ensure that a computer's components can function together seamlessly, offering a flawless user experience.[2]

Types of Device Drivers

Device drivers come in different types, each designed to control specific operations within a computer system. These drivers ensure that various hardware components are properly managed and that they work in tandem with the operating system. You can better understand how your computer works and manages the different pieces of hardware that are attached to it by learning about the many types of device drivers. Developers may distinguish the following types of device drivers:

Kernel-mode Drivers

Device drivers operating at a low level within the operating system of the computer are referred to as Kernel-mode drivers. With direct access to the hardware and essential features of the computer, they can perform vital tasks required for its proper operation.

Kernel device drivers are pieces of generic hardware loaded into the OS (operating system) as part of it. They consist of processors, motherboards, and BIOS. Whenever necessary, they are called upon and loaded into the random-access memory (RAM). The machine may stutter when multiple of them are working simultaneously. For every

OS, there is therefore a minimal requirement. Layers separate kernel device drivers. Higher-level drivers, which support drive functionality, receive data from applications, filter it, and then transfer it to a lower-level driver, such as file system drivers. Kernel device drivers are implemented as separate, modular parts with a predetermined set of necessary features.

Examples of Kernel-mode Drivers:

- **Graphics Drivers:** These control the graphics card and manage how images and videos are displayed on your screen.
- **Network Drivers:** These manage network adapters, allowing your computer to connect to the internet and other networks.
- **Disk Drivers:** These handle data transfers between the computer's storage devices, such as hard drives and SSDs.

Advantages of Kernel-mode Drivers:

- **High Performance**: Because they have direct access to hardware, kernel-mode drivers can perform tasks quickly and efficiently.
- **Greater Control:** They offer more control over hardware operations, which is essential for tasks that require precise timing or resource management.
- **Essential for Core Functions**: They are crucial for the basic operations of the computer, such as managing memory, processes, and hardware devices.

Disadvantages of Kernel-mode Drivers:

- **Security Risks:** Since kernel-mode drivers have deep access to the system, any bugs or vulnerabilities can potentially be exploited to harm the computer or compromise security.
- **System Stability**: Errors in kernel-mode drivers can lead to system crashes or the infamous "*blue screen of death,*" as they operate at such a fundamental level.
- **Complex Development**: Writing kernel-mode drivers requires a deep understanding of the operating system and hardware, making them more challenging to develop and maintain.

User-mode Drivers

User-mode drivers are device drivers that operate under tighter restrictions than kernel-mode drivers. Because they run in the user space of the operating system, they lack direct access to the hardware or main system resources. This limitation enhances the system's stability and security.

These device drivers are deployed by users to possibly activate while in a session. System users might bring in their own external devices—such as plug-and-play devices–to utilize. For these devices to work, drivers are also necessary. User-mode device drivers in Windows systems act as a bridge between kernel-mode drivers or other operating systems and Win32 applications. To ease the burden on computer resources, users have the option to write these drivers to the disk.

Examples of User-mode Drivers include:

- **Printer drivers**: They control how the operating system and printer communicate by sending print jobs, among other things.
- **USB Device Drivers**: These programs control USB-connected devices, such as cameras and external storage.
- **Sound playback:** Sound playback and recording are made possible by the sound card drivers, which regulate the audio hardware.

Benefits of User-mode Drivers:

- **Enhanced Security**: User-mode drivers are less likely to result in serious mistakes or security lapses because they do not have direct access to the system's essential components.
- **System Stability**: Because user-mode drivers operate in a distinct, isolated environment, errors in them are less likely to cause the system to crash as a whole.
- **Easier Development**: Because user-mode drivers do not require deep access to the internal workings of the system, their development can be less complicated and risky than that of kernel-mode drivers.

The following are some **drawbacks of user-mode drivers**:

- **Lower Performance**: User-mode drivers may not work as well as kernel-mode drivers when processing large amounts of data quickly because they are operating in a restricted environment.
- **Limited Control**: They do not have as much control over the system's hardware and resources, which can be a problem for some applications that need careful hardware management.
- **Dependency on Kernel Services**: To complete some low-level operations, user-mode drivers frequently rely on kernel-mode drivers, which can add complexity and overhead.

Virtual Device Drivers

Virtual device drivers are specialized drivers that create a virtual environment so that multiple operating systems or applications can share hardware resources as if they were separate. They are crucial to virtualization technology because they transform physical components into their "*virtual*" equivalents, increasing hardware efficiency.

Virtual machines, or VMs, require virtual device drivers to function. They function in environments with and without virtualization. These drivers simulate the host device's hardware in virtualized environments. They regulate or oversee the host device's resource hardware to guarantee that the guest and host devices function as intended.

For instance, for a guest operating system to access hardware while running on a host, function calls to virtual device drivers are made. Furthermore, they simulate events such as interrupts at the processor level and forward them to the virtual machine.

- **Virtual Network Adapters:** They, for instance, enable numerous virtual machines (VMs) on a single physical host to connect to the internet or communicate with one another as though they each had a separate physical network card.
- **Virtual Disk Drives:** These let each virtual machine (VM) function as though it had its own dedicated storage device by imitating a physical hard drive. Virtual sound cards give virtual machines audio capabilities so they can process sound just like they would if they were physical sound cards.

Virtual device drivers have the following **benefits:**

- **Resource Optimization**: By sharing hardware resources across several VMs, virtual device drivers enable the effective use of those resources and eliminate the need for dedicated hardware for each VM.
- **Flexibility and Scalability**: They facilitate easier system scaling up or down by adding or removing virtual devices as needed without changing the physical hardware.
- **Isolation and Security**: By limiting direct access to physical hardware and guarding against potential threats, virtual devices add an extra layer of isolation between VMs.

Virtual device drivers have the following **drawbacks:**

- **Performance overhead**: Using virtual devices can be slower than using physical devices directly because virtual devices depend on the hardware and software of the host system to operate.
- **Complexity**: Compared to working with physical hardware, managing and configuring virtual devices can be more difficult, requiring specific skills and equipment.
- **Limited Functionality:** Virtual devices may not always support every feature of their physical counterparts, which could make them less useful for some uses.

Character Drivers

Hardware can be accessed in an unstructured manner through character device drivers. They move data between devices without utilizing a particular device address. They facilitate the sequential data reading and writing of one byte at a time. Character drivers are paired with block devices to get around the buffer cache and provide raw input/output (I/O) operations directly to the user's program address space. They can handle I/O more freely because they do not handle I/O through the buffer cache. Memory mapping, device polling, and I/O control commands are some of the extra interfaces they offer. Modems and bus controllers are two examples.

Device drivers in the form of block drivers provide organized access to the hardware. They carry out I/O using file system block-sized buffers from a buffer cache that the kernel supplies. A buffer cache is a memory pool that the kernel created to hold frequently accessed blocks via block devices. Fewer I/O queries require an I/O operation from the device, thanks to the buffer cache.

Furthermore, block device drivers show data durability and offer accessible block-oriented I/O. They receive a file system request and send the requested block to the disk via I/O operations. USB memory keys and disk drives are two examples.

Device Drivers for Digital Cameras

A program known as a digital camera driver enables communication between the camera and other devices, including computers. The operating system will not recognize this device without the drivers. Since Linux systems lag, most digital cameras are only compatible with Windows OS. Photo transfers from the camera to the computer are made possible by digital camera drivers.

They make it possible for digital cameras to print pictures directly from a PictBridge-capable computer printer to a computer without using a computer. Users can choose one video or photo at a time to be displayed on television by using drivers in the video output port.

- **Mobile devices running Android operating systems** require drivers to connect to computers. Most phones' firmware includes drivers, which enables computers to load them up to support hardware even in cases where the OS is not specified. However, for drivers to be installed and enable data transfer, users occasionally might need to install OEM PC software first.

  Drivers enable the integration of peripheral devices running operating systems like Android Things and Android, such as game controllers and keyboards. Hardware access and control are made possible by the drivers. They also make it possible for smart devices to run customized apps.

- **Device drivers for better video performance** Graphic cards are essential parts of a computer system in charge of providing better video performance for graphically demanding tasks, such as games and computers. For graphic cards to operate at their best, graphic drivers are necessary because they enable the cards to communicate with the computer's operating system.

Updates for graphic drivers and other Windows 11 (or older) drivers can improve performance, resolve issues, and occasionally even bring new features to users. One way to decrease lag is by increasing frames per second through game driver updates.

- **Original equipment manufacturer (OEM) drivers:** Device drivers fall into two categories: (1) OEM-*specific* and (2) *generic*. Device drivers included with the original equipment manufacturer's operating software are referred to as generic drivers. Generic drivers can be used with various brands of a specific type of device. For example, Linux comes with several generic drivers that can be used without requiring the installation of any additional software.

  OEMs are free to design their own proprietary device drivers, which must be installed independently of the operating system. Hardware, like keyboards, can communicate with the host operating system, thanks to OEM drivers. For example, OEM drivers allow features like Google Assistant and Alexa's lighting control system integration with OEM hardware.

  Open-source drivers are made available under a free and open-source license. If the display is a component of the graphics hardware, for example, its output is managed by open-source graphic drivers. Collaboration on software projects is facilitated by the open-source drivers' source code being accessible to all. Because anyone can examine them to look for any malicious code, they are more reliable. More privacy is provided by open-source drivers. People can redistribute a copy of the software with the tracking disabled if they track users.

Essential building blocks of personal and enterprise computing are used in the following ways:

- **On a computer, the most basic driver is the Basic Input Output System (BIOS)**. The fact that it is housed in a read-only memory (ROM) chip guarantees that BIOS will continue to function even if the hard drive is formatted. It is responsible for starting a computer and giving it instructions while it does so. Additionally, it carries out the necessary power-on self-tests (POST) at startup. The BIOS also supplies drivers for basic hardware, such as keyboards and monitors, to interface with the operating system and perform as intended.
- **Motherboard drivers** are small programs that can be used with Linux and Windows. They are part of the operating system and allow basic computer functions. These drivers are programs that enable the USB devices and I/O ports on the keyboard and mouse to function. There are motherboard drivers that support both audio and video.

  Motherboard drivers are unique to the chipset model—for example, B460 for computers made by Intel. Users might need to install extra drivers for the motherboard to function to its full potential and for connected components to function properly.

Open-source drivers ensure that even after the company stops distributing them, a copy endures because more people continue to make improvements to them.

- **Device drivers for accessing storage systems:** Users can store and retrieve data from computer storage systems as needed. They consist of both internal and external gadgets, such as hard drives, network-attached storage, and USB flash drives. Storage systems can communicate with computers thanks to drivers. This guarantees the computer's ability to query its internal and external storage systems, access them, and permit data transfer. Without drivers, it becomes difficult to connect storage devices to the computer because the operating system cannot detect them. Hard drives and CD-ROMs are typically detected by the operating system and do not need drivers to be manually installed. When drivers are not found automatically, users must install them from the manufacturer's website.
- **Device drivers for input and output devices**: These drivers work with the operating system of the computer to guarantee that the hardware performs as intended. Keyboards and mice are examples of input devices, and monitors and other display devices are examples of output devices. Plug-and-play devices include monitors, keyboards, and mice. Plug-and-play device drivers are typically generic and installed automatically by the computer's operating system. They do not usually need to be manually installed. Users might have to download and manually install the drivers from the installation disc if an external device is not plug-and-play. As a result, the OS will be able to identify these devices. .

How do Device Drivers Work?

Device drivers are essential to the proper communication between the operating system and hardware on your computer. A device driver is a specialized software application that runs as part of the operating system and communicates with a device connected to a computer. Here is a basic explanation of how they function. It is merely a piece of OS code that gives you access to the precise commands you need to run the related device.

The operating system (OS) oversees and regulates the connected devices by giving the software applications the functionality they need to control various aspects of the devices. OS accomplishes this by fusing software and hardware technologies. The OS communicates with the I/O hardware by using device driver software.

Every device has its device driver software. Device drivers are essentially low-level programs that give computers the ability to communicate with a wide variety of hardware devices.

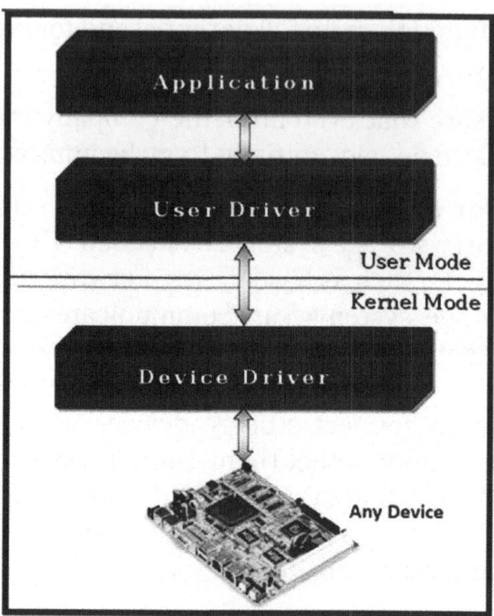

Figure 8.8: *Device Driver*

- **The operating system and hardware communicate through device drivers**: Device drivers serve as a bridge between the operating system and hardware components. An application or the operating system instructs the device driver to carry out a task, such as printing a document or displaying an image. After that, the driver converts this command into a format that the hardware can comprehend. If you send a print command, for instance, the printer driver translates it into a set of instructions that the printer can follow, printing your document.
- **A device driver's ability to provide an abstraction layer** is one of its primary roles in converting high-level commands into low-level hardware instructions. In other words, the driver converts high-level commands from applications or the operating system into low-level hardware instructions. This abstraction speeds up the development process by removing the need for software developers to comprehend the nuances of each hardware device's operation. Rather than assuming responsibility for the details, they can depend on the driver, enabling a more efficient and uniform communication between the hardware and software.

The Lifecycle of a Device Driver

The device drawer has to go through the following activities throughout its entire life:

- **Installation:** The initial stage of a device driver's lifecycle, installation is followed by initialization, usage, and termination. The driver is loaded onto the system and set up to function with the particular hardware during this phase.

- **Setting up required system**: Settings and transferring driver files to the proper locations are common steps in this process.
- **Initialization:** After installation, the driver goes through a **setup phase** in which it gets ready to control the hardware. To do this, you may need to configure device settings, set up communication protocols, and ensure that the hardware is operational.
- **Use:** The driver controls data exchange between the hardware and the operating system while it is in operation. It manages requests, executes instructions, and guarantees a proper hardware operation. The development of the driver is crucial in this situation since it dictates how well and quickly the hardware completes its tasks.
- **Termination:** The driver experiences termination when the system shuts down or the device is no longer in use. This stage entails clearing out temporary settings and data, stopping hardware connections, and optimizing available resources.

The Importance of Device Drivers

Device drivers are essential to the proper functioning of your computer's hardware and software.

- **Ensuring Hardware Compatibility and Performance**: Device drivers ensure that your operating system is compatible with a range of hardware components, such as printers, graphics cards, and USB devices. This is why they are crucial. They allow these components to function as effectively and accurately as possible. Without the appropriate drivers, hardware may not function at all or may not function as intended.
- **Effectively Managing Hardware Resources**: Device drivers help to regulate how hardware resources are used. They manage and distribute resources such as memory and processing power to ensure that each device gets the resources it needs without causing conflicts or performance issues. Effective management of the system is essential to its stability and overall performance.
- **Error Handling and System Stability**: Maintaining system stability and handling errors depend on device drivers. They are designed to deal with hardware issues and provide solutions or workarounds to prevent crashes and other issues. A well-designed driver contributes to system stability even during hardware issues.
- **Improving User Experience with Seamless Device Integration**: Well-written device drivers ensure that hardware devices easily interface with the operating system and applications, enhancing the user experience. They facilitate simple and trouble-free tasks, such as printing documents, playing audio, and

connecting to the internet by making it simple for the user to interact with their devices.

Common Challenges and Issues with Device Drivers

Device drivers can present their own set of difficulties, but they are essential for communication between hardware and software.

- **Driver conflicts and compatibility issues**: Occasionally, different drivers may not work correctly with the operating system or may interact with one another. These are some common issues you might run into. This could lead to device failure entirely or to hardware issues. Compatibility issues can arise, especially during operating system updates or new hardware installations, leading to conflicts that make normal operation difficult.
- **Security Vulnerabilities in Device Drivers**: Malicious software or hackers may exploit security holes in device drivers. Because drivers have extensive access to system resources, any flaws in their code could pose a serious threat to system security. Knowing about these vulnerabilities is essential to protecting your system from possible attacks.
- **Drivers that are corrupted or outdated and cause system instability:** Drivers may become outdated as new versions are released to fix bugs or add features. Using out-of-date or corrupt drivers may lead to hardware malfunctions, crashes, and system instability. This could be because the drivers do not work perfectly with the newest software or they still have issues that need to be fixed.
- **The Value of Regular Driver Updates:** Maintaining the stability and performance of your system depends on keeping your drivers up to date. Regular updates fix bugs and security holes and ensure that drivers work with the newest operating systems and hardware modifications. This maintains the security and effectiveness of your system.

The Future of Device Drivers

Device drivers are a field that is rapidly changing due to new developments in software development and technological advancements. This is a preview of what lies ahead for device drivers:

- **AI and Machine Learning Integration:** Artificial intelligence (AI) and machine learning (ML) are expected to have a significant influence on device driver development. Advanced error detection and correction made possible by these technologies can improve driver performance and flexibility. For instance, AI algorithms can analyze driver behavior and predict issues before they happen, leading to more dependable and efficient hardware interactions. Additionally, machine learning can assist in driver optimization for specific hardware configurations, enhancing system performance generally and reducing the requirement for manual upgrades.

- **Open-Source Drivers and Community Contributions:** Open-source drivers are becoming more significant in the driver development landscape. Through open-sourcing driver code, programmers and enthusiasts around the world can collaborate to improve and update drivers quickly. Community contributions help with bug fixes, new feature introductions, and hardware compatibility assurances. This collaborative approach accelerates driver development, fosters innovation, and permits greater customization and openness.
- **Impact of New Hardware Technologies on Driver Development:** New hardware innovations present opportunities as well as obstacles for driver development. Modern network connections, fast graphics cards, and high-speed storage units all need drivers to make the most of these innovations. To guarantee performance and compatibility, driver developers must stay up-to-datewith these developments. For instance, drivers that can manage low latency and high-resolution graphics are needed as virtual reality and augmented reality technologies gain traction. Developing drivers that support the newest technologies and provide the best user experience requires keeping up with hardware developments.

Free Space Management in the Operating System (OS)

You are aware of the space limitations of the hard drive in our system. The hard disk's memory or space should therefore be used appropriately.

The files on the hard drive are allotted memory by the operating system. There is void or free space on the hard drive left over after memory has been allocated to the files. Furthermore, multiple files are concurrently saved and removed from the memory. Thus, making a file disappear from memory also frees up space. The operating system controls the hard drive's available space.

Operating systems refer to this as free space management. The operating system tracks the amount of free disk space by keeping a free space list. Every available disk block that is not assigned to a file or directory is included in the free space list. The operating system looks through the free space list to find the necessary disk space before allocating it to the file to save it on the disk. An allocated file's space is added to the list of free space when it is deleted.

Commonly Used Free Space Management Techniques

There are five commonly used free space management strategies:

- **Linked Allocation:** This stores files in disk blocks using a linked list structure. Every block has the address of the block after it.
- **Contiguous Allocation**: This method stores files in a single, contiguous block of disk space. Files are kept using the **Indexed Allocation technique**, which involves storing files in a linked list of disk blocks where each file's directory entry also includes an index block. The addresses of a linked list's initial few blocks are contained in the index block.
- **File Allocation Table (FAT):** Tables are used in this method to monitor how disk space is allocated. Every entry states if a block is free or allocated, and if allocated, it also specifies which block it belongs to.
- **Volume Shadow Copy**: This operating system feature takes a snapshot of a volume at a given moment in time.

Methods of Free Space Management in OS

There are four methods of doing free space management in operating systems. These are as follows:

- Bit Vector
- Linked List
- Grouping
- Counting

First, let us discuss the Bit Vector method.

Bit Vector

The first method that we will discuss is the bit vector method. Also known as the bit map, this is the most frequently used method to implement the free space list. In this method, each block in the hard disk is represented by a bit (either 0 or 1). If a block has a bit 0, then it means that the block is allocated to a file, and if a block has a bit 1, then it means that the block is not allocated to any file, that is, the block is free.

For example, consider a disk having 16 blocks where block numbers 2, 3, 4, 5, 8, 9, 10, 11, 12, and 13 are free, and the rest of the blocks, that is, block numbers 0, 1, 6, 7, 14, and 15, are allocated to some files. The bit vector for this disk will look as follows:

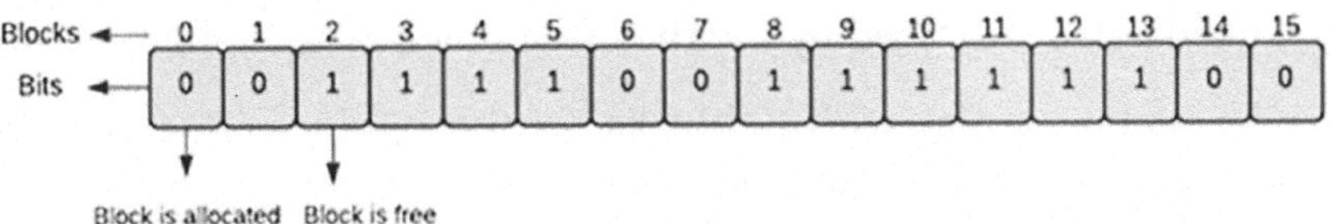

Figure 8.9: *Bit vector*

We can find the free block number from the bit vector using the following method:

```
Block number = (Number of bits per word)* (number of 0-value words) +
(offset of first bit)
```

We will now find the first free block number in the preceding example.

The first group of 8 bits (00111100) constitutes a non-zero word since all bits are not 0. After finding the non-zero word, we will look for the first 1 bit. This is the third character of the non-zero word. Hence, offset = 3.

Therefore, the first free block number = 8 * 0 + 3 = 3.

Advantages

The advantages of the bit vector method are:

- Simple to understand
- Efficient
- Occupies less memory

Disadvantages

The disadvantages of the bit vector method are:

- For finding a free block, the operating system may need to search the entire bit vector.
- Special hardware support is needed to detect the first 1 in a word that is not 0 using this method. Keeping the bit vector in the main memory is possible for smaller disks but not for larger ones. For example, a 1.3 GB disk with 512-byte blocks would need a bit vector of over 332 KB to track its free blocks. Giving away 332 KB just to maintain its free block space is not so efficient in the long run.

Linked List

A linked list is another technique that operating systems use for managing free space. With this method, a linked list is created by connecting all of the free blocks on the disk. There is a memory location where the address of the first free block is kept. The address of the following free block is contained in a pointer found in each free block. The end of the linked list is indicated by the final free block, which points to null.

For illustration, let us take a disk with 16 blocks. Of these, blocks 3, 4, 5, 6, 9, 10, 11, 12, 13, and 14 are free, and the remaining blocks, that is, blocks 1, 2, 7, 8, 15, and 16, are assigned to certain files. If we keep a linked list, a pointer to Block 4 will be found in Block 3, and a pointer to Block 5 will be found in Block 4.

In the same way, Block 5 will connect to Block 6, Block 6 to Block 9, Block 9 to Block 10, Block 10 to Point 11, Block 11 to Point 12, Block 12 to Point 13, and Block 13 to Pin 14. The 14th block will point to null. The first block's free address, that is, the Block 3, will be kept in some location within the memory. This is also represented in the following figure:

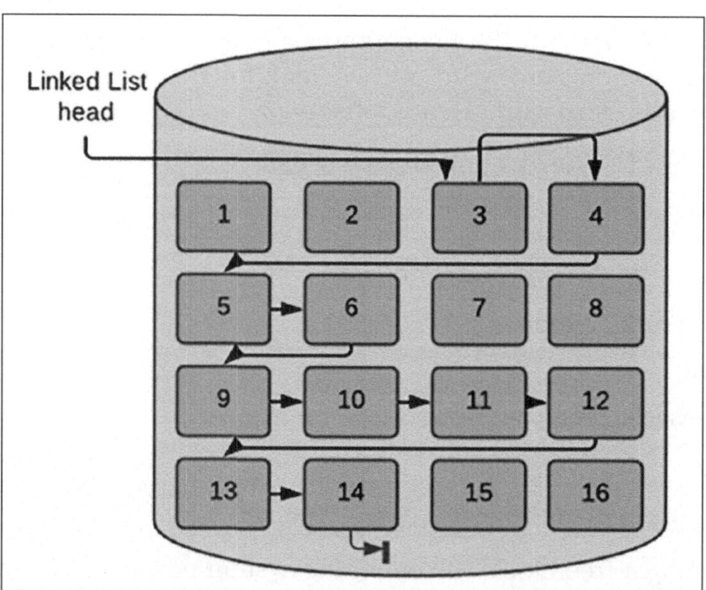

Figure 8.10: *Linked List Methods of Free Space Management in OS*

Advantages

The linked list allocation prevents external fragmentation, which is one of the linked list method's **benefits**.

- This eliminates the waste of memory blocks as opposed to contiguous allocation.
- Additionally, expanding our file is a fairly easy process. All we need to do is attach a fresh block of files to our linked list. This way, the file can grow as long as memory blocks are available.
- Linked list allocation relieves some of the directory's overhead because it only needs to store the file's beginning and ending pointers.

Disadvantages

The linked list approach has a few **drawbacks.**

- First, it is inefficient because it requires reading each block to traverse the list, adding to the I/O time.
- Maintaining the pointer has an overhead.
- In linked list allocation, random or direct memory access is not supported.
- To access a particular file block, we have to look through the entire linked list to find the right block.

Grouping

Grouping is the third method of free space management in operating systems. This method is the modification of the linked list method. In this method, the first free block stores the addresses of the n free blocks. The first *n*-1 of these blocks is free. The last block in these n free blocks contains the addresses of the next *n* free blocks, and so on.

For example, consider a disk having 16 blocks where block numbers 3, 4, 5, 6, 9, 10, 11, 12, 13, and 14 are free, and the rest of the blocks, that is, block numbers 1, 2, 7, 8, 15 and 16 are allocated to some files.

If we apply the Grouping method considering n to be 3, Block 3 will store the addresses of Block 4, Block 5, and Block 6. Similarly, Block 6 will store the addresses of Block 9, Block 10, and Block 11. Block 11 will store the addresses of Block 12, Block 13, and Block 14. This is also represented in the following figure:

Block 3 -> 4, 5, 6
Block 6 -> 9, 10, 11
Block 11 -> 12, 13, 14

Figure 8.11: *Applying Grouping Method*

The drawbacks of the linked list approach are addressed by this one. It is possible to locate the addresses of many free blocks rapidly by simply accessing the first or nth free block. The linked list method required paging through the entire list, which is not necessary here.

Benefits: The grouping method has the following benefits:

- A large number of free blocks' addresses can be quickly located.

- One advantage of this approach is that it can be used to quickly find the addresses of a group of blank disk blocks.
- It is a tweak to the free list methodology. Thus, going through the entire list is not necessary.

Cons

The grouping method has the following drawbacks:

- One block's worth of space is wasted storing addresses. The addresses of the next n free blocks are stored in the nth block. Since it is impossible for us to keep track of all n free disk addresses, we only store the address of the first free block.
- Maintaining the block index comes with a cost. The fourth technique for managing free space in operating systems is counting. This technique also modifies the linked list approach.
- This technique utilizes the possibility that multiple adjacent blocks may be allocated or released at once. This approach keeps a linked list, but it also keeps track of the number of free contiguous blocks that come after the first block, in addition to the pointer to the next free block. Consequently, every free block on the disk will have two contents: a pointer to the following free block. how many free, consecutive blocks come after it.

For illustration, let us take a disk with 16 blocks. Of these, blocks 3, 4, 5, 6, 9, 10, 11, 12, 13, and 14 are free, and the remaining blocks, that is, blocks 1, 2, 7, 8, 15, and 16, are assigned to certain files. Using the counting method, Block 3 will store the count 4 and point to Block 4 because Blocks 3, 4, 5, and 6 are all adjacent. Block 9 will also point to Block 10 and maintain the count of six because Blocks 9, 10, 11, 12, 13, and 14 are adjacent. This is also represented in the following figure:

Block 3 -> 4
Block 9 -> 6

Figure 8.12: *Grouping*

Since the entire list does not need to be traversed, this method also addresses the drawbacks of the linked list method.

Benefits:

- The counting method offers several benefits, including the quick allocation of numerous consecutive free blocks.
- The free block can be accessed at random.
- The list as a whole is shorter.

The following are the **drawbacks** of the counting method:

- More disk space is needed for each free block to maintain the count, to perform traversal, insertion, and deletion tasks quickly.
- We must keep the entries in the B-tree. The area is shrunk altogether.

Advantages of free space management techniques in operating systems

- **Efficient use of storage space**: Space management techniques help in optimizing the use of storage space on the hard disk as well as secondary storage devices.
- **Easy to implement**: Some techniques in space management are easy to implement, like linked allocation. It requires less overhead in terms of processing and memory resources.
- **Reduce Fragmentation**: Free space management techniques such as contiguous allocation help in reducing disk fragmentation, which results in faster access to files.

Disadvantages of free space management techniques in operating systems

- **Complex**: Some space management techniques are complex to implement and manage.
- **Performance overhead**: Free space management techniques can contribute to adding some performance overhead because some techniques require frequent updates to the free space list.
- **Vulnerability to corruption:** If the free space list is not properly maintained, there is a chance of corruption.

Disk Management in Operating System

The process of setting up and maintaining physical storage devices in a computer system, such as hard disk drives and solid-state drives (SSDs), is known as disk management in an operating system.

It involves generating, modifying, formatting, partitioning, and controlling disk volumes to effectively store and retrieve data. The operating system controls the read and write processes related to these files and drives, as well as keeping track of them. Among other things, you can create, delete, and format disc partitions with the help of the operating system's helpful built-in feature called disk management.

- **Windows Operating System:** The Windows operating system uses a graphical interface to carry out disk management tasks, such as controlling the hard drives and storage. To make various portions of our disks easier to access, we can create, format, resize, and assign letters to or rename them.
- **Disk Management commands in Windows operating systems**: The "`diskmgmt.msc`" command is used to start the disk management tool in Windows

operating systems. Disk partition management, disk formatting, drive letter assignment, and other disk-related operations are all possible with this tool. Windows' disk management is divided into two primary sections: the lower section provides details about the selected disk or partition, and the upper section shows a graphical representation of the system's disks and partitions. By comparison, the Linux operating system lacks Windows' graphical tool. It features a command-line utility known as "*fdisk*." which enables comparable operations, such as the creation, removal, and management of disk partitions.

Disk Management Types

Basic disk management and **dynamic disk management** are the two varieties. The conventional disk partitioning method is known as basic disk management, whereas dynamic disk management enables more sophisticated features, such as fault tolerance and disk spanning.

The Operating System's Disk Management Procedures

The operating system's disk management procedures include:

- Disk Format (or low-level format or physical format)
- Booting from disk
- Bad block recovery

We will learn these aspects in detail:

- **Disk Format:** Setting up a storage device, such as a USB flash drive, solid-state drive, or hard drive, for the first-time use is called disk formatting. To facilitate data storage and retrieval, it entails partitioning the disk into sectors and tracks, creating a file system, and creating the relevant data structures. Depending on the needs and operating system, a disk format can be FAT (File Allocation Table), NTFS (New Technology File System), exFAT (Extended File Allocation Table), and more. Formatting removes all data from the disk, so before doing this operation, make a backup of any crucial files.
- **Booting from disk (bootstrap loader):** The boot block, sometimes referred to as the bootstrap loader, is a little bit of code that is kept at the very start of a storage device (such as an SSD or hard drive). When the computer is turned on or restarted, its main job is to start the operating system's boot process. Typically, the boot block holds instructions on how to load the kernel of the operating system into memory and begin its execution. To help with the boot process, the boot block may occasionally also include error-checking codes or details about the disk's partition layout.

- **Bad block recovery**: Damaged or faulty physical portions of a disk or storage device that are unable to store data consistently are known as bad blocks. These blocks could be the product of physical harm, manufacturing flaws, or aging.
  To avoid storing data in those areas and to prevent data corruption, operating systems and disk management software keep track of bad blocks.
  During formatting or routine disk maintenance, bad blocks can be identified and marked by mechanisms found in many modern file systems and disk management tools. When a bad block is found, it is usually labeled as unusable, the data inside is moved to an available spare area, or the block is just avoided in subsequent data storage operations.

What does disk management do?

An operating system's disk management feature gives users the ability to monitor and regulate storage devices such as solid-state drives (SSDs) and hard disk drives (HDDs) in computers. Among the main functions of disk management are:

1. **Partitioning**: Several partitions can be made on a single disk by users using disk management. Additionally, we can resize the disk partitions to suit our needs without losing any data.
2. **Formatting**: Partitions with particular file systems, such as FAT32, NTFS, and so on, can be formatted using options provided by disk management.
3. **Disk Cleanup**: Tools for managing disk space can also be used to help clean up the disk by eliminating junk and superfluous files.
4. **Disk Encryption:** This is a feature that certain disk management tools offer to protect the data kept on disks.

Disk Scheduling Algorithms

Operating system services request data from a disk drive in a certain order, which is determined by disk scheduling algorithms. The idea is to reduce the total seek time–that is, the amount of time it takes the disk's read/write head to travel between various disk platter tracks. The following are a few popular disk scheduling algorithms:

- **FCFS (First-Come, First-Served):** Handle requests in the order that they come in. Basic but may cause requests farther down the disk to become starved. The request that takes the least amount of time to seek from the current head position is handled by **SSTF (Shortest Seek Time First)** cuts down on seek time, but for distant requests, it might cause starvation.
- **SCAN: As** the head travels back and forth across the disk, it responds to requests in that direction. Suitable for systems that are overloaded but slow for requests that are made far from the current position.

- **Circular SCAN, or C-SCAN** for short, is similar to SCAN except it uses the disk as a circular track, responding to all requests in one direction before turning around.

Spooling and Buffering

Spooling and buffering are techniques used to improve data transfer efficiency between devices with different speeds.

- **Spooling:** Spooling is a process that allows the computer to work on other tasks while creating a temporary storage area to hold data that needs to be processed by a slower device, such as a printer. This is how it operates:
  - A print job is submitted by a user. A disk file receives the spooled data.
  - A print job queue is managed by the spooler software.
  - One job at a time, the printer pulls data from the queue and prints it.

  System performance is enhanced by spooling, which enables the computer to send data to the printer much faster than the printer can print it.
- **Buffering:** Buffering transfers data between devices by using a temporary memory space. It facilitates the balancing of disparities in data transfer speeds among devices. A summary of buffering is as follows: Data is transferred from a source device, such as a disk, to a memory buffer. The buffer holds on to the data until a complete block is prepared. From the buffer to the intended device (such as a network), the data block is moved. Buffering increases data exchange efficiency by lowering the number of necessary data transfers.

Advantages of Disk Management in OS

- **Storage Organization:** Users can effectively arrange their hard drives and storage devices, thanks to disk management. It offers tools for formatting drives, making partitions, and carrying out related read and write operations. Even the disks' sizes can be changed to suit our needs.
- **Enhanced Efficiency**: By releasing space and reducing system lag, disk management in an operating system helps to enhance a computer system's performance. This makes it possible to access files more quickly, improving system performance.
- **Enhanced Security**: By securely storing files, OS disk management improves data security. Users can add an extra layer of security to protect sensitive data and prevent data loss or theft by encrypting their disks or specific partitions using disk encryption features that some disk management tools offer.
- **Improved Backup:** Data can be stored in files that are arranged logically with

the aid of disk management. This offers an improved backup system that guards against data loss from power outages and other sources.

- **Disk Monitoring**: Diagnostic and monitoring features are also provided by disk management. Disk health data, such as performance, temperature, and other characteristics, can be obtained.

Disadvantages of Disk Management in OS

- **Increased complexity**: Beginners with little technical knowledge may find disk management challenging. The more disk partitions there are, the more complicated it becomes.
- **Risk of data loss:** Data loss may occur if the disk management tools are not used properly. When resizing or partitioning a disk, for instance, the user might unintentionally erase its contents.
- **Time-consuming operations**: When working with big volumes of data, disk defragmentation and partition resizing are two examples of disk management procedures that can take a while.

Redundant Array of Independent Disks (RAID)

Disk transfer rates are increasing, but not nearly as quickly as CPU performance.

We can use multiple disks to increase performance by striping files across them (that is, placing portions of each file on a different disk). We can also use parallel I/O to improve access time.

Striping reduces reliability; 100 disks have 1/100th the MTBF (mean time between failures) of one disk. Therefore, we need something to help with availability and reliability in addition to striping.

A RAID is a Redundant Array of Inexpensive Disks.

- Disks are small (physically) and inexpensive, making it simple to put many disks (10s to 100s) in one box for increased availability and storage.
- Data and some redundant information are striped across the disks in some way.
- The method of striping is crucial to both performance and reliability.

Some RAID tradeoffs

- Granularity – fine-grained: stripe each file over all disks
- High throughput for the file

- Limits transfer to one file at a time – coarse-grained: stripe each file over only a few disks
- Limits throughput for one file
- Allows concurrent access to multiple files
- Redundancy – uniformly distribute redundancy information on disks
- Avoids load-balancing problems – concentrate redundancy information on a small number of disks
- Partition the disks into data disks and redundancy disks

The RAID consists of seven levels, zero through six. These levels designate different design architectures that share three common characteristics: RAID is a set of physical disk drives viewed by the operating system as a single logical drive. Data are distributed across the physical drives of an array in a scheme known as striping, described subsequently. Redundant disk capacity stores parity information, guaranteeing data recoverability during a disk failure.

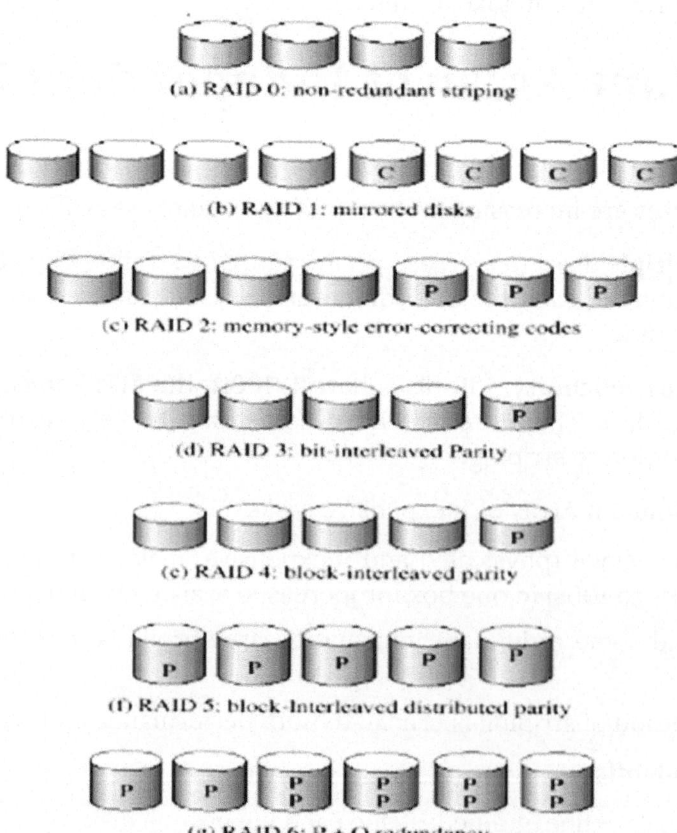

Figure 8.13: *Pictorial Depiction of various versions of RAID storage Technology*

Several physical disk drives are combined into a single logical unit using the RAID storage technology, which can be used to increase performance, data redundancy, or both. There exist multiple RAID levels, each with unique attributes and applications. Whichever version you use, the NFS will operate differently. There are currently three versions of NFS available for use, each has distinct operating standards.

- RAID-0 (striping)
- RAID-1 (mirroring)
- RAID levels 2, 3, and 4 employ parity disks or error-correcting code
- RAID-5 (block-level striping with distributed parity)
- RAID-6 (block-level striping with two parity bits)

RAID-0 (Striping)

RAID 0, often referred to as "*striping*," is a basic RAID configuration. In RAID 0, data is divided into blocks and distributed across multiple hard drives or SSDs, which allows for improved read and write performance as multiple drives can be accessed simultaneously. However, RAID 0 lacks data redundancy or fault tolerance. The following are the key characteristics of RAID 0:

Data Striping: Data is split into blocks or stripes, with each block written to a different drive in the RAID 0 array.

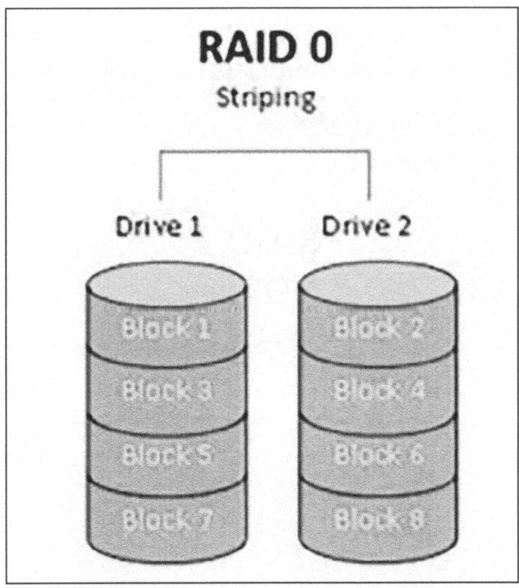

***Figure 8.14**: RAID 0 Array and Data Striping*

- **No Redundancy**: RAID 0 does not provide fault tolerance or data redundancy. The RAID 0 configuration loses all of its data if one of the array's drives fails.
- **Performance Improvement**: Since multiple drives can be used to read and write data simultaneously, RAID 0 can greatly improve read and write performance.

Because of this, it can be used for apps like gaming and video editing that require fast data access.

- **Drive Requirements**: RAID 0 can have more drives than the minimum of two. Performance improvement is more likely when there are more drives in the array. **Capacity Utilization**: Lacking redundancy or mirroring, RAID 0 utilizes of every drive's capacity within the array.
- **Use Cases**: When performance is essential but data redundancy is not a concern, RAID 0 is frequently employed. Workstations used for video editing, gaming systems **Use cases**, and other programs that value speed are examples.
- **Risk:** The main disadvantage of RAID 0 is that it is not fault-tolerant. All data is lost if any drive in the array fails. As such, it is not recommended for use in conjunction with other RAID levels such as RAID 1 (mirroring) or RAID 10 (striped mirrors) for additional redundancy when storing critical data. In conclusion, RAID 0 is a RAID level that does not offer fault tolerance or data redundancy, but it does improve performance through data striping. While it works well in scenarios where speed is crucial, it should not be used to store vital data without additional redundancy or backup systems in place.

RAID-1 (Mirroring)

RAID 1 (Mirroring) is a RAID configuration that prioritizes data redundancy and fault tolerance. In RAID 1, data is duplicated or mirrored across two or more drives in the array. This means that every piece of data is simultaneously written to at least two drives, creating identical copies. Key characteristics of RAID 1 include:

Data Mirroring: Data is duplicated across multiple drives, ensuring that each drive contains an identical copy of the data.

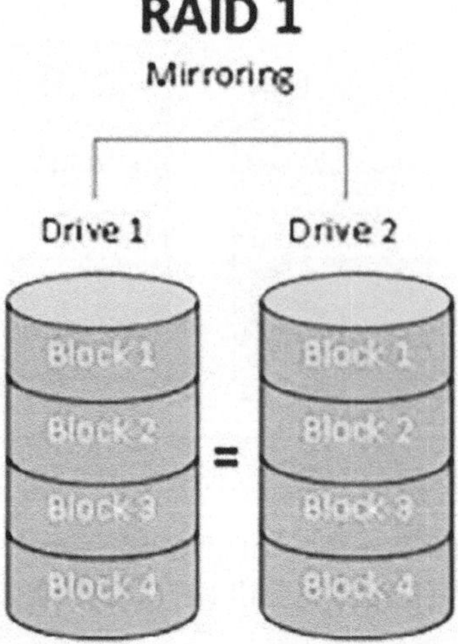

Figure 8.15: *RAID 1 (Mirroring) configuration*

High levels of fault tolerance and redundancy are offered by RAID 1. The data is still accessible from the other drive(s) in the array if one fails. As a result, there is less chance of data loss from hardware malfunctions.

- **Performance:** RAID 1 can result in moderate improvements in read performance, but it cannot match the performance improvement of RAID 0. It is possible to read data simultaneously from several drives. However, compared to using a single drive, write performance might not significantly improve.
- **Minimum Drives:** RAID 1 can have more drives, but it needs at least two. An exact duplicate of the data is kept on each drive in the array.
- **Capacity Utilization:** Because every piece of data is mirrored, RAID 1 only uses half of the total drive capacity for data storage. For instance, you have 1 TB of usable storage in a two-drive RAID 1 array with 1 TB drives because the other 1 TB is used for mirroring.
- **Use Cases:** When fault tolerance and data integrity are crucial, RAID 1 is the best option. It is frequently used for storing crucial documents or files where data loss is unacceptable, as well as in server environments and database systems.
- **Risk:** RAID 1's high degree of data redundancy and fault tolerance is its main benefit. Compared to RAID 0, it has less storage capacity, and the requirement for multiple drives raises the hardware cost.

To sum up, RAID 1 mirrors data across several drives to provide data redundancy and fault tolerance. Although it does not offer as much performance improvement as other RAID configurations like RAID 0, it is appropriate for situations where data integrity and reliability are crucial.

RAID levels 2, 3, and 4 use ECC (error correcting code) or parity disks

For example, each byte on the parity disk is a parity function of the corresponding bytes on all the other disks.

- A read accesses all the data disks
- A write accesses all the data disks plus the parity disk
- On disk failure, read the remaining disks plus the parity disk to compute the missing data

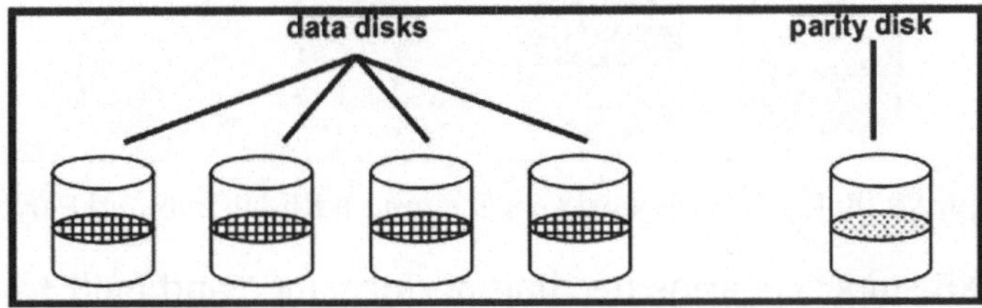

Figure 8.16: *RAID levels 2, 3, and 4 use ECC (error correcting code) or parity disks*

Refresher: What is parity?

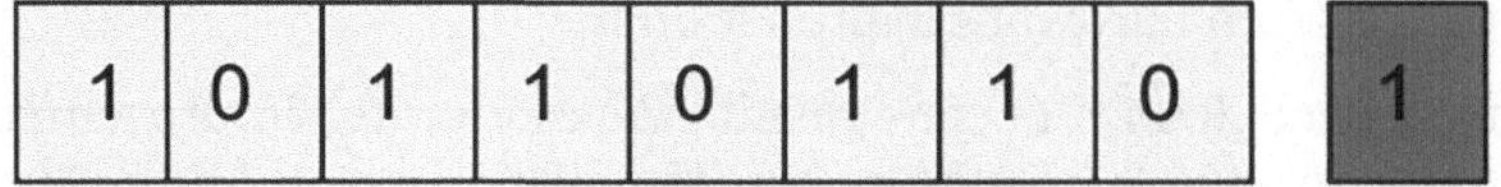

Figure 8.17: *Parity*

- To each byte, add a bit set so that the total number of 1's is even
- Any single missing bit can be reconstructed

RAID-5 (Block-Level Striping with Distributed Parity)

RAID 5 is a configuration that combines data striping with distributed parity for both performance enhancement and data redundancy.

RAID 5 requires a minimum of three drives and combines data striping, similar to RAID 0, with distributed parity. During a single drive failure, data can be reconstructed using the parity information distributed across the remaining drives, with no downtime. While read speed is fast, write speed can be slower due to parity calculations. This RAID level is well suited for file and application servers with a limited number of data drives.

Unlike RAID 0, which offers no redundancy, RAID 5 provides fault tolerance through parity. It does come with a trade-off in terms of storage space. Using three drives, RAID 5 loses approximately 33 percent of its storage capacity to parity information. However, configurations with four drives are more popular as they reduce the lost storage space to approximately 25 percent. RAID 5 can be implemented with up to 16 drives, allowing scalability while maintaining data redundancy.

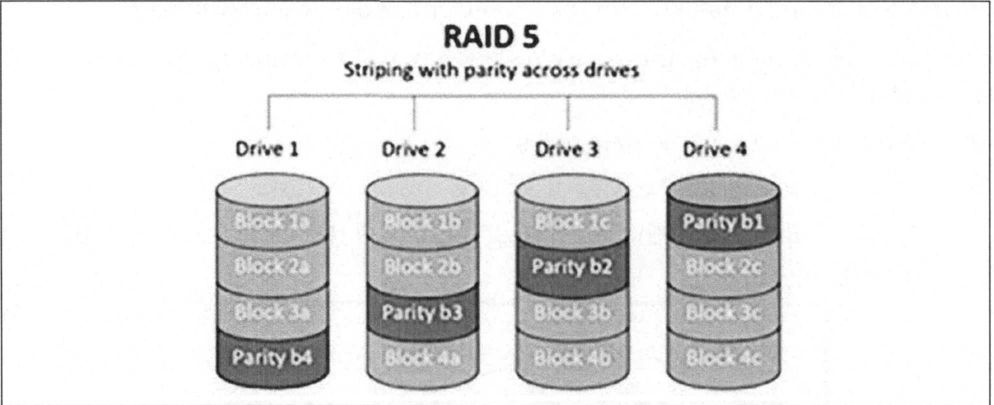

Figure 8.18: RAID-5 (*Block-Level Striping with Distributed Parity*)

Use Cases: RAID 5 suits scenarios needing performance and fault tolerance, such as file servers, NAS devices, and small to medium-sized businesses.

In summary, RAID 5 combines data striping with distributed parity for improved performance and fault tolerance. It is suitable for scenarios requiring both speed and data redundancy but carries some risk during drive rebuilds.

RAID-6 (Block-Level Striping with two Parity Bits)

RAID 6 is a RAID configuration that builds upon the principles of RAID 5 but offers higher fault tolerance by using dual-distributed parity. In RAID 6, like RAID 5, data is divided into blocks and striped across multiple drives. However, it differs in using two separate parity blocks to protect against two drive failures simultaneously, whereas RAID 5 can only tolerate one drive failure.

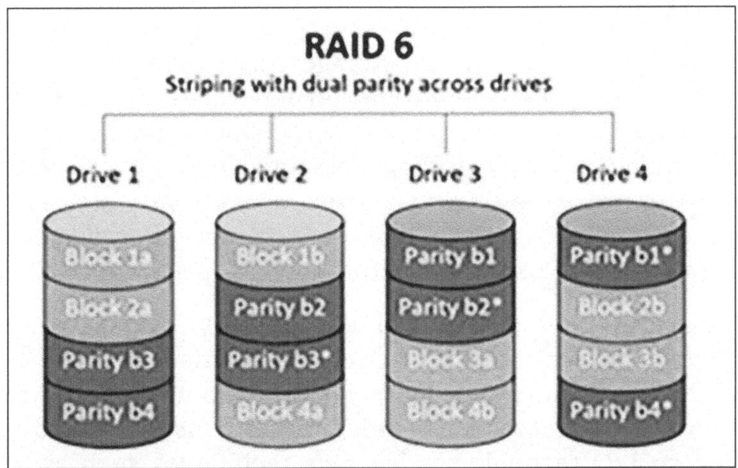

Figure 8.19: *RAID-5 (Block-Level Striping with two Parity Bits)*

- **Dual Distributed Parity:** RAID 6 uses two separate parity blocks, each distributed across all the drives in the array. This redundancy allows it to withstand the failure of two drives concurrently without data loss.
- **Redundancy and Fault Tolerance:** RAID 6 provides a high level of fault tolerance. If two drives fail within the array, data can still be reconstructed using the dual parity information, minimizing the risk of data loss.
- **Performance Improvement**: Similar to RAID 5, RAID 6 offers performance improvement for both read and write operations because data can be read from and written to multiple drives simultaneously.
- **Minimum Drives:** RAID 6 typically requires a minimum of four drives due to the dual parity setup. However, larger arrays with more drives can be created for greater storage capacity and performance.
- **Capacity Utilization**: RAID 6 efficiently utilizes drive capacity, with two drives dedicated to storing parity information. This means more drive space is used for redundancy compared to RAID 5.

- **Use Cases:** RAID 6 is suitable for environments where data integrity and fault tolerance are critical. It is commonly used in scenarios, such as file servers, database servers, and storage systems where both read and write operations are important.

In summary, RAID 6 is a RAID level that provides a high degree of fault tolerance by using dual-distributed parity. It offers a good balance between data protection and performance, making it suitable for various applications where data integrity is essential.

Conclusion

This chapter explains that secondary storage serves as a critical component in computer systems, providing the persistent and non-volatile memory needed to store large amounts of data. Unlike primary memory, secondary storage retains information even when the system powers off, making it essential for long-term data preservation and large-scale data processing. Various forms of secondary storage, such as hard drives, solid-state drives, optical disks, and cloud storage, offer diverse capabilities to cater to specific user needs, balancing factors such as speed, capacity, and cost.

Interfacing I/O devices is equally pivotal, as it bridges the gap between users and computers or between computers themselves. The interface design ensures efficient, secure, and synchronized data exchange, facilitating smooth operation and interaction with peripheral devices, such as keyboards, printers, monitors, and more complex machinery. Modern I/O technologies leverage techniques such as direct memory access (DMA) and buses such as PCI, USB, and Thunderbolt to enhance performance and reliability. In the next chapter we will explain the file system.

Questions

1. What is the function of device drivers in a computer system?
2. How many types of device drivers are there?
3. At what level within the operating, the kernel mode device drivers work?
4. Write down the advantages and disadvantages of the kernel mode device driver.
5. What is secondary storage?
6. What are the basic functions of the device controller concerning to input-output units?
7. What is DMA and what is its function? How does the operating system use the DMA hardware?

8. What is the function of the device driver? Is it software or hardware?
9. What is the role of device drivers between software and hardware?
10. State different types of device drivers.
11. How do device drivers work?
12. Provide some examples of user-mode drivers.
13. Write down the advantages and disadvantages of the user mode device driver.
14. Illustrate the working of kernel-mode drivers with some practical examples.
15. Describe the working of kernel-mode drivers, giving some practical examples.
16. How is a virtual environment created with the help of virtual device drivers?
17. State the merits and drawbacks of virtual disk drives.
18. Describe the communication of the operating system and hardware through device drivers with the help of a diagram.
19. Describe the various stages through which a device driver must go..
20. Which is the most basic driver used in a computer system?
21. How does the basic input-output system (BIOS) work?
22. Write an essay on common challenges and issues faced by device drivers.
23. Describe how the device drivers may be deployed in near future.
24. What are commonly used free space management techniques?
25. What are the four main methods of doing free space management in operating systems? Describe any one of them in detail.
26. Write a short note on disk management in the operating system.
27. What are two basic types of disk management?
28. Name the four disk scheduling algorithms and describe FCFS (First-Come, First-Served)?
29. What techniques are used to improve data transfer efficiency between devices with different speeds?
30. Enumerate the advantages of disk management in OS.
31. Present and discuss some trade-off features of RAID systems.
32. Discuss the main features as to how they progressed in increasing data read and writing speed in seven levels of the RAID?

References

[1] Operating System - I/O Hardware, https://www.tutorialspoint.com/operating_ system/os_io_hardware.htm

[2] Understanding Device Drivers: The Backbone of Modern Computing,https://drishinfo.com/understanding-device-drivers-the-backbone-of-modern-computing/

[3] Free Space Management in Operating System (OS), Naukri.com, https://www.naukri.com › ... › Disk Management

[4] Disk Management in Operating System, Prashant Singh, https://www.naukri.com/code360/library/disk-management-in-operating-system

[5] What is RAID structure and different levels of RAID configuration?_Anshuman,

Chapter 9
File System

Introduction

Files are used for all input and output (I/O) of information in the operating system to standardize access to both software and hardware. Input occurs when the contents of a file are modified or written to. Output occurs when the contents of one file are read or transferred to another file. A file is a named collection of related information recorded on secondary storage, such as magnetic disks, magnetic tapes, and optical disks. In general, a file is a sequence of bits, bytes, lines, or records whose meaning is defined by the file creator and user.

Structure

In this chapter, we are going to learn about following topics related with file systems in different operating systems:

- Files
- File Types
- File Access Mechanisms
- Internal structure of Files in the UNIX System
- File System Layout
- Inode
- Hierarchical Arrangement of Directories and File System
- Categories of File Types in a Unix system
- File Types in a Unix system
- Pathname
- File System Calls
- File I/O Functions available UNIX System

- File Descriptors
- File Sharing
- v-node
- The UNIX File Abstraction
- File Persistence
- File System Navigation
- Additional File Attributes
- Understanding and Modifying File Permissions
- Network File System (NFS)
- Virtual File System (VFS) Module
- Distributed File System (DFS)
- Mount in Unix-like Operating Systems

Computer Files

On secondary storage devices such as magnetic disks, magnetic tapes, and optical disks, a file is a named collection of related data. A file is generally defined as a series of bits, bytes, lines, or records that the user and creator of the file have chosen to represent. A file structure ought to follow a necessary format that the operating system can comprehend. Depending on its type, a file has a specific defined structure.

- A text file consists of a series of characters arranged in lines
- A source file is a series of steps and operations
- An object file is a series of machine-understandable bytes arranged into blocks

Operating systems include the code necessary to support the various file structures they define. MS-DOS and Unix support the bare minimum of file structures. Discover the newest courses we offer online and pick up new abilities at your own speed. To advance your career, enroll and earn your certification as an expert.

File Types

File type refers to the ability of the operating system to distinguish different types of files such as text files, source files, binary files, and so on. Many operating systems support many types of files. Operating systems such as MS-DOS and UNIX have the following types of files:

- **Ordinary files**
  - These files contain user information
  - These contain text, databases, or executable programs
  - The user can apply various operations on such files, such as add, modify, delete, or even remove the entire file
- **Directory files**
  - These files contain list of file names and other information related to these files
  - Special files
  - These are also known as device files
  - These files represent physical devices, such as disks, terminals, printers, networks, tape drives, and so on
  - These files are of two types:
    - **Character special files:** Data is handled character by character as in case of terminals or printers
    - **Block special files:** Data is handled in blocks as in the case of disks and tapes

File Access Mechanisms

File access mechanism refers to how the records of a file can be accessed. There are several ways to access files:

- **Sequential access:** A sequential access means the records are accessed in some sequence, that is, the information in the file is processed in order, one record after the other. This access method is the most primitive one. Example: Compilers usually access files in this fashion.
- **Direct/Random access:** Random access file organization provides accessing the records directly. Each record has its own address on the file, helping to access it for reading or writing directly. The records need not be in any sequence within the file, and they need not be in adjacent locations on the storage medium.
- **Indexed sequential access:** This mechanism is built on the base of sequential access. An index is created for each file that contains pointers to various blocks. Index is searched sequentially, and its pointer is used to access the file directly.

Space Allocation in Files

Files are allocated disk spaces by the operating system. Operating systems deploy the following three main ways to allocate disk space to files.

- **Contiguous Allocation**
  - Each file occupies a contiguous address space on disk
  - The assigned disk address is in linear order
  - Easy to implement
  - External fragmentation is a major issue with this type of allocation technique
- **Linked Allocation**
  - Each file carries a list of links to disk blocks
  - Directory contains link / pointer to the first block of a file
  - No external fragmentation
  - Effectively used in the sequential access file
  - Inefficient in case of direct access file
- **Indexed Allocation**
  - Provides solutions to problems of contiguous and linked allocation
  - An index block is created having all pointers to files
  - Each file has its own index block, which stores the addresses of disk space occupied by the file
  - Directory contains the addresses of index blocks of files

Internal Structure of Files in the UNIX System [1]

The internal representation of a file is given by an inode, which contains a description of the disk layout of the file data and other information, such as the file owner, access permissions, and access times. The term inode is a contraction of the term **index node** and is commonly used in literature on the UNIX system. Every file has one inode, but it may have several names, all of which map into the inode. Each name is called a link. When a process refers to a file by name, the kernel parses the file name one component at a time, checks that the process has permission to search the directories in the path, and eventually retrieves the inode for the file.

The kernel contains two other data structures, the file table and the user file. descriptor table. The file table is a global kernel structure, but the user file descriptor table is allocated per process. When a process opens or creates a file, the kernel allocates an entry from each table, corresponding to the file's inode. Entries in the three structures–the user file descriptor table, file table, and inode table–maintain the state of the file and the user's access to it. The file table keeps track of the byte offset in the file where the user's next read or write will start and the access rights allowed to the opening process. The user file descriptor table identifies all open files for a process.

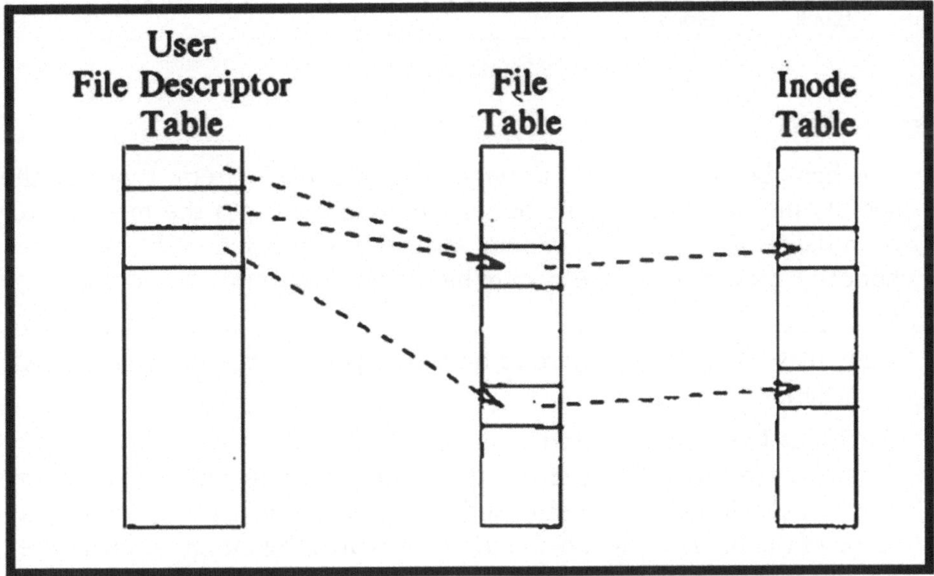

Figure 9.1: *File Descriptors, File Table, and Inode Table*

Figure 9.1 shows the tables and their relationship to each other. The kernel returns a file descriptor for the open and create system calls, which is an index into the user file descriptor table. When executing read and write system calls, the kernel uses the file descriptor to access the user file descriptor table, follows pointers to the file table and inode table entries, and, from the inode, finds the data in the file.

File System Layout

A file system consists of a sequence of logical blocks, each containing 512 (=2^9), 1024, 2048, or any convenient multiple of 512 bytes, depending on the system implementation. The size of a logical block is homogeneous within a file system but may vary between different file systems in a system configuration. Using large logical blocks increases the effective data transfer rate between disk and memory because the kernel can transfer more data per disk operation and therefore make fewer time-consuming operations. For example, reading 1 K bytes from a disk in one read operation is faster than reading 512 bytes twice. However, if a logical block is too large, effective storage capacity may drop. For simplicity, this book will use the term "*block*" to mean a logical block, and it will assume that a logical block contains IK bytes of data unless explicitly stated otherwise.

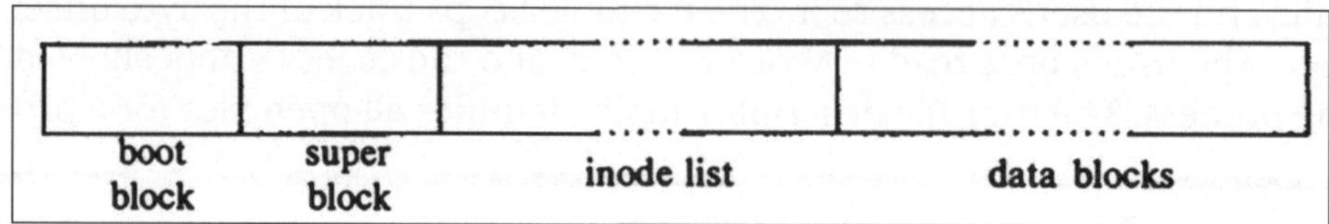

***Figure* 9.2:** *File System Layout*

A file system has the following structure (*Figure* 9.2):

- The **boot block** occupies the beginning of a file system, typically the first sector, and may contain the bootstrap code read into the machine to boot, or initialize, the operating system. Although only one boot block is needed to boot the system, every file system has a (possibly empty) boot block.
- **The super block** describes the state of a file system–how large it is, how many files it can store, where to find free space on the file system, and other information.
- The **inode list** is a list of inodes that follows the super block in the file system. Administrators specify the size of the inode list when configuring a file system. The kernel references inodes by index into the inode list. One inode is the root inode of the file system: it is the inode by which the directory structure of the file system is accessible after execution of the mount system call.
- **The data blocks** start at the end of the inode list and contain file data and administrative data. An allocated data block can belong to one and only one file in the file system.

INODES

Every file on a UNIX system has a unique inode. The inode contains the information necessary for a process to access a file, such as file ownership, access rights, file size, and location of the file's data in the file system.

Inodes exist in a static form on disk, and the kernel reads them into an in-core inode to manipulate them. Disk inodes consist of the following fields:

- **File owner identifier:** Ownership is divided between an individual owner and a "*group*" owner and defines the set of users who have access rights to a file. The superuser has access rights to all files in the system.
- **File type:** Files may be of type regular, directory, character or block special, or FIFO (pipes).
- **File access permissions:** The system protects files according to three classes:

the owner and the group owner of the file, and other users; each class has access rights to read, write, and execute the file, which can be set individually. Because directories cannot be executed, execution permission for a directory gives the right to search the directory for a file name.

- **File access times:** This gives the time the file was last modified, when it was last accessed, and when the inode was last modified.
- **Number of links to the file:** This represents the number of names the file has in the directory hierarchy. We will discuss file links in detail.

  Table of contents for the disk addresses of data in a file. Although users treat the data in a file as a logical stream of bytes, the kernel saves the data in discontiguous disk blocks. The inode identifies the disk blocks that contain the file's data.
- **File size.** Data in a file is addressable by the number of bytes from the beginning of the file, starting from byte offset 0, and the file size is 1 greater than the highest byte offset of data in the file. For example, if a user creates a file and writes only 1 byte of data at byte offset 1000 in the file, the size of the file is 1001 byte.

Processes access files by a well-defined set of system calls and specifies a file by a character string that is the path name. Each path name uniquely specifies a file, and the kernel c<>converts the path name to the file's inode. The inode does not specify the path name(s) that access the file.

owner vkj
group os
type regular file
perms rwxr-xr-x
accessed Oct 23 1:45 P.M.
modified Oct 22 '2024 10:30 A.M
inode Oct 23 '20241:30 P.M.
size 6030 bytes
disk addresses

Figure 9.3: *Sample Disk inode*

Figure 9.3 shows the disk inode of a sample file. This inode is that of a regular file owned by "*vkj*," which contains 6030 bytes. The system permits "*mjb*" to read, write, or execute the file; members of the group "os" and all other users can only read or execute the file, not write it. The last time anyone read the file was on October 23,

2024, at 1:45 pm, and the last time anyone wrote the file was on October 22, 2024, at 10:30 am. The inode was last changed on October 23, 2024, at 1 :30 pm, although the data in the file was not written at that time. The kernel encodes the preceding information in the inode. Note the distinction between writing the contents of an inode to disk and writing the contents of a file to disk. The contents of a file change only when writing it. The contents of an inode change when changing the contents of a file or while changing its owner, permission, or link settings. Changing the contents of a file automatically implies a change to the inode, but changing the inode does not imply that the contents of the file change.

The in-copy of the inode contains the following fields in addition to the fields of the disk inode:

- The status of the in-core inode, indicating whether the inode is locked;
  - a process is waiting for the inode to become unlocked,
  - the in-core representation of the inode differs from the disk copy as a result of a change to the data in the inode, the in-core representation of the file differs from the disk copy as a result of a change to the file data, the file is a mount point
- The logical device number of the file system that contains the file.
- The inode number. Since inodes are stored in a linear array on disk, the kernel identifies the number of a disk inode by its position in the array. The disk inode does not need this field.
- Pointers to other in-core inodes. The kernel links inodes on hash queues and on a free list in the same way it links buffers on buffer hash queues and the buffer free list. A hash queue is identified according to the inode's log device number and inode number. The kernel can contain at most one in-core copy of a disk inode, but inodes can be simultaneously on a hash queue and the free list.
- A reference count, indicating the number of instances of the file that are active (such as when opened).

Hierarchical Arrangement of Directories and File System [2]

The UNIX file system is a Inode hierarchical arrangement of directories and files. Everything starts in the directory called root, whose name is the single character /. A directory is a file that contains directory entries. Logically, we can think of each directory entry as containing a filename along with a structure of information describing the attributes of the file. The attributes of a file are such things as the type of file (regular file, directory), the size of the file, the owner of the file, permissions for the file (whether other users may access this file), and when the file was last modified. The stat and fstat functions return a structure of information containing all the attributes of a file.

We make a distinction between the logical view of a directory entry and the way it is actually stored on disk. Most implementations of UNIX file systems do not store attributes in the directory entries themselves because of the difficulty of keeping them in sync when a file has multiple hard links.

Introduction to the Unix File System

The Unix file system is a methodology for logically organizing and storing large quantities of data to make the system easy to manage. A file can be informally defined as a collection of (typically related) data, which can be logically viewed as a stream of bytes (that is, characters). A file is the smallest unit of storage in the Unix file system.

A file system consists of files, relationships to other files, as well as the attributes of each file. File attributes are information relating to the file but do not include the data contained within a file. File attributes for a generic operating system might include (but are not limited to):

- a file type (that is, what kind of data is in the file)
- a file name (which may or may not include an extension)
- a physical file size
- a file owner
- file protection/privacy capability
- file time stamp (time and date created/modified)

Additionally, file systems provide tools that allow the manipulation of files, provide a logical organization and provide services that map the logical organization of files to physical devices.

From the beginner's perspective, the Unix file system is essentially composed of files and directories. Directories are special files that may contain other files.

The Unix file system has a **hierarchical (or tree-like**) structure with its highest-level directory called root (denoted by /, pronounced slash). Immediately below the root level directory are several subdirectories, most of which contain system files. Following this are system files, application files, and/or user data files. Similar to the concept of the process parent-child relationship, all files on a Unix system are related to one another. That is, files also have a parent-child existence. Thus, all files (except one) share a common parental link, the top-most file (that is /) being the exception.

Figure 9.4 shows a "*typical*" Unix file system. As you can see, the top-most directory is / (slash), with the directories directly beneath being system directories. Note that as

Unix implementations and vendors vary, so will this file system hierarchy. However, the organization of most file systems is similar.

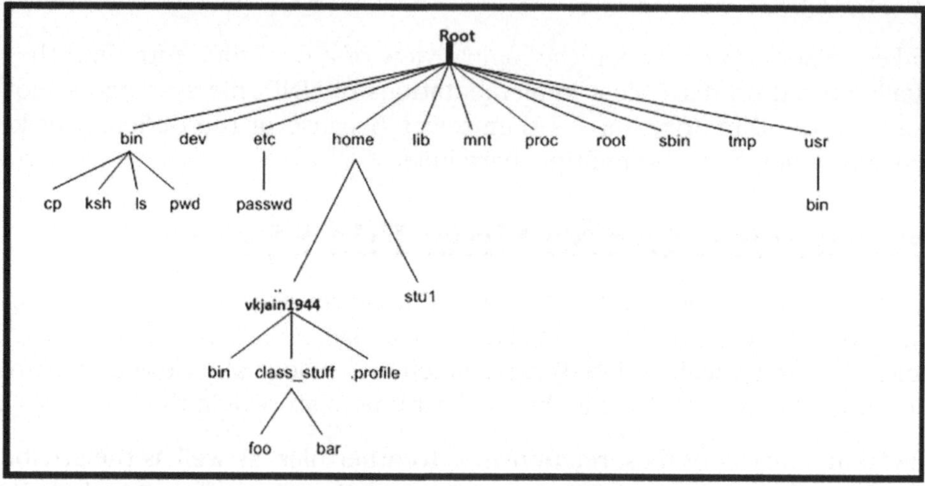

Figure 9.4: *Typical Unix file system hierarchical (or tree-like) diagram*

While this diagram is not all-inclusive, the following system files (that is, directories) are present in most Unix filesystems:

- **`bin`**: short for binaries, this is the directory where many commonly used executable commands reside
- **`dev`**: contains device-specific files
- **`etc`**: contains system configuration files
- **`home`**: contains user directories and files
- **`lib`**: contains all library files
- **`mnt`**: contains device files related to mounted devices
- **`proc`**: contains files related to system processes
- **`root`**: the root users' home directory (note this is different than /)
- **`sbin`**: system binary files reside here. If there is no sbin directory on your system, these files are most likely stored elsewhere
- **`tmp`**: storage for temporary files which are periodically removed from the filesystem
- **`usr`**: also contains executable commands

Categories of File Types in a Unix System

From a user perspective in a Unix system, everything is treated as a file, even devices such as printers and disk drives.

How can this be, you ask? Since all data is essentially a stream of bytes, each device can be viewed logically as a file.

All files in the Unix file system can be loosely categorized into three types, specifically:

- Ordinary files
- Directory files
- Device files

While the latter two may not intuitively seem like files, they are considered "special" files.

The **first type** of file in the preceding list is an ordinary file, that is, a file with no "special-ness". Ordinary files are comprised of streams of data (bytes) stored on some physical device. Examples of ordinary files include simple text files, application data files, files containing high-level source code, executable text files, and binary image files.

Note that unlike some other OS implementations, files do not have to be binary images to be executable.

The **second type** of file in the preceding list is a special file called a directory (it is not a folder). Directory files act as a container for other files of any category. Thus we can have a directory file contained within a directory file (this is commonly referred to as a subdirectory). Directory files do not contain data in the user's sense of data; they merely contain references to the files contained within them.

It is perhaps noteworthy at this point to mention that any "*file*" that has files directly below (contained within) it in the hierarchy must be a directory, and any "file" that does not have files under it in the hierarchy can be an ordinary file, or a directory, albeit empty.

The **third** category of file mentioned in the preceding list is a device file. This is another special file that describes a physical device, such as a printer or a portable drive. This file contains no data whatsoever; it merely maps any data coming its way to the physical device it describes.

Device file types typically include: character device files, block device files, Unix domain sockets, named pipes, and symbolic links. However, not all these file types may be present across various Unix implementations.

Filename

The names in a directory are called filenames. The only two characters that cannot appear in a filename are the slash character (/) and the null character. The slash separates the filenames that form a pathname (described next) and the null character terminates a pathname. Two filenames are automatically created whenever a new directory is created: . (called dot) and .. (called dot-dot); dot refers to the current directory, and dot-dot refers to the parent directory. In the root directory, dot-dot is the same as dot.

The Research UNIX System and some older UNIX System V file systems restricted a filename to 14 characters. BSD versions extended this limit to 255 characters. Today, almost all commercial UNIX file systems support at least 255-character filenames. Nevertheless, it is good practice to restrict the characters in a filename to a subset of the normal printing characters. (If we use some of the shell's special characters in the filename, we have to use the shell's quoting mechanism to reference the filename, and this can get complicated.). Indeed, for portability, POSIX.1 recommends restricting filenames to consist of the following characters: letters (a-z, A-Z), numbers (0-9), period (.), dash (-), and underscore (_).

Example

Listing the names of all the files in a directory is not difficult. *Figure* 1.3 shows a bare-bones implementation of the ls(1) command.

```
#include "apue.h"
#include <dirent.h>
int
main(int argc, char *argv[])
{
DIR *dp;
struct dirent *dirp;
if (argc != 2)
err_quit("usage: ls directory_name");
if ((dp = opendir(argv[1])) == NULL)
err_sys("can't open %s", argv[1]);
while ((dirp = readdir(dp)) != NULL)
printf("%s\n", dirp->d_name);
closedir(dp);
exit(0);
}
```

Note: *The* ***apue.h*** *header file is a cross-platform header file that defines constants and function prototypes for the code in advanced programming in the UNIX environment.*

Pathname

A sequence of one or more filenames, separated by slashes and optionally starting with a slash, forms a pathname. A pathname that begins with a slash is called an absolute pathname; otherwise, it is called a relative pathname. Relative pathnames refer to files relative to the current directory. The name for the root of the file system (/) is a special-case absolute pathname that has no filename component.

They start with the root directory, represented by a forward slash (/), and then provide the full path to the file or directory. For example, "**`/home/user/Documents`**" is an absolute path to the "**`Documents`**" directory in the home directory of the user "**`user`**".

Types of Pathname[3]

Navigating through files and directories is a common task while working in a Linux system. To access a file or directory, you need to specify its path.

Linux supports two types of paths: absolute path relative path

An absolute path is a complete path to a file or directory from the root directory. The root directory is the top-level directory of the file system and is represented by a forward slash (/). Absolute paths always start with the root directory and provide the full path to the file or directory.

For example, the absolute path to the home directory of a user named "**`waqas`**" would be "**`/home/waqas`**."

On the other hand, a relative path is a path to a file or directory relative to the current directory. It specifies the location of the file or directory about the current directory. Relative paths do not start with the root directory and are usually shorter than absolute paths.

For example, if you are currently in the home directory of "**`waqas`**" and want to access a file named "**`example.txt`**" in a subdirectory called “documents,” the relative path would be "**`documents/example.txt`**."

The main difference between absolute and relative paths is how they are interpreted. Absolute paths always point to the same location regardless of the current directory, whereas relative paths may point to different locations depending on the current directory.

Absolute paths are useful when you refer to a file or directory from anywhere in the system. For example, if you want to create a symbolic link to a file located in a different directory, you would use an absolute path to specify the file location.

Relative paths are more convenient when working within a specific directory or subdirectory. They allow you to specify the location of a file or directory relative to your current location, saving you time and typing.

In conclusion, both absolute and relative paths have advantages and are useful in different situations. Understanding the difference between the two can help you navigate through the file system more efficiently and work more effectively in a Linux environment.

Advantages of the absolute path

- **Unambiguous:** Absolute paths are unambiguous and provide the exact location of a file or directory in the file system. This means that regardless of the current directory you are in, an absolute path will always point to the same location. This can be useful when working with scripts, as you can be sure that the correct file or directory is being accessed.
- **Easy to Use**: Absolute paths are easy to use once you understand the syntax. They start with the root directory, represented by a forward slash (/), and then provide the full path to the file or directory. For example, "/home/user/Documents" is an absolute path to the "Documents" directory in the home directory of the user "user".
- **Useful for Remote Access**: Absolute paths are useful when accessing files or directories remotely. For example, if you are accessing a file or directory on a remote server, you can use an absolute path to ensure that you are access the correct file or directory.
- **Useful for Symbolic Links:** Symbolic links are files that act as shortcuts to other files or directories. Absolute paths are useful when creating symbolic links because they ensure link points to the correct location, regardless of the current directory. For example, if you want to create a symbolic link to a file in a different directory, you would use an absolute path to specify the file location.
- **Useful for System Administration**: System administrators often need to work with files and directories located in different parts of the file system. Absolute paths are useful for system administration tasks because they allow administrators to access files and directories from anywhere in the file system. For example, an administrator might need to access log files in the /var/log directory. An absolute path would allow them to access these files from any directory in the system.

Advantages of relative path [3]

- **Shorter and Simpler**: Relative paths are shorter and simpler than absolute paths. They are specified relative to the current working directory, meaning they do not need to include the entire path to a file or directory. This can be useful when working with long and complex file paths by saving time and reducing typing errors.
- **Easier to Move Around**: Relative paths are relative to the current working directory, meaning they can be easily moved around within the file system without breaking the path. For example, if you are working in the directory /home/user/documents and want to access a file in the directory /home/user/pictures, you can use the relative path ../pictures/file.jpg to access the file, even if you move to a different directory.

- **Useful in Scripts:** Relative paths are useful in scripts because they can be used to reference files and directories relative to the script's location. This can be useful when creating portable scripts that can be run from different locations without modifying the file paths.
- **Useful in Web Development**: Relative paths are commonly used in web development to reference files, such as images, scripts, and stylesheets. Using relative paths makes it easier to move a website from one server to another, as the file paths will remain valid as long as the directory structure is maintained.
- **Useful in Collaborative Work:** When working collaboratively on a project, relative paths can be useful as they allow team members to reference files and directories relative to their own working directory. This can help avoid confusion and ensure that everyone is referencing the same files.

Working Directory

Every process has a working directory, sometimes called the current working directory. This is the directory from which all relative pathnames are interpreted. A process can change its working directory with the `chdir` function.

For example, the relative pathname doc/memo/joe refers to the file or directory joe, in the directory memo, in the directory doc, which must be a directory within the working directory. From looking just at this pathname, we know that both doc and memo must be directories, but we cannot tell whether joe is a file or a directory. The pathname /usr/lib/lint is an absolute pathname that refers to the file or directory lint in the directory lib, in the directory usr, which is in the root directory.

Home Directory

When we log in, the working directory is set to our home directory. Our home directory is obtained from our entry in the password file.

File system calls for the file

We have read about system calls in early in *Chapter 1, Computer Organization and Hardware Software Interfaces* of this book. This section starts with system calls for accessing existing files, such as open, read, write, /seek, and close, then presents system calls to create new files, namely, `create` and `mknod`, and then examines the system calls that manipulate the inode or that maneuver through the file system: `chdir`, `chroot`, `chown`, `chmod`, `stat`, and `fstat`.

File system calls

System calls serve several important functions, which include:

- **User-Kernel Boundary.** System calls serve as the authorized gateway for user programs when requesting services from the kernel. They ensure that user programs cannot arbitrarily access kernel functions or critical system resources.

- **Resource Management**. User programs can request and manage vital resources, such as CPU time, memory, and file storage, via system calls. The OS oversees the process and guarantees that it is completed in an organized manner.
- **Streamlined Development**. System calls abstract the complexities of hardware. This allows developers to perform operations such as reading and writing to a file or managing network data without writing hardware-specific code.
- **Security and Access Control**. System calls implement checks to ensure that requests made by user programs are valid and that the programs have the necessary permissions to perform the requested operations.
- **Inter-Process Communication (IPC).** System calls provide the mechanisms for processes to communicate with each other. They offer features such as pipes, message queues, and shared memory to facilitate this inter-process communication.
- **Network Operations**. System calls provide the framework for network communications between programs. Developers can devote their attention to building their application's logic instead of focusing on low-level network 9.5.2

Workings of System Calls

This high-level overview explains how system calls work:

- **System Call Request**. The application requests a system call by invoking its corresponding function. For instance, the program might use the read() function to read data from a file.
- **Context Switch to Kernel Space**. A software interrupt or special instruction triggers a context switch and transition from user mode to kernel mode.
- **System Call Identified**. The system uses an index to identify the system call and address the corresponding kernel function.
- **Kernel Function Executed**. The kernel function corresponding to the system call is executed. For example, reading data from a file.

The following figure explains how the system calls work.

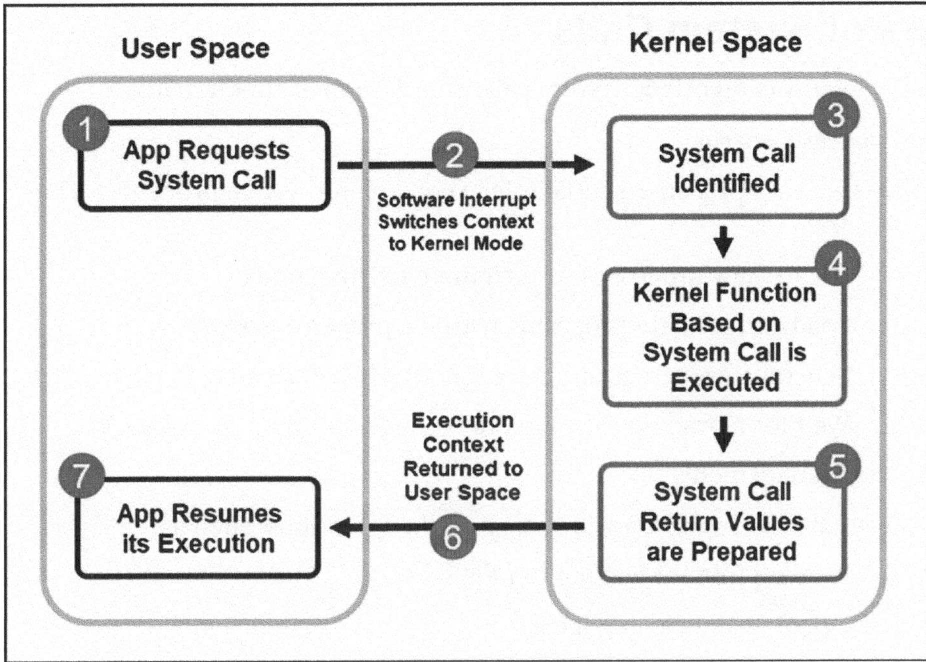

***Figure* 9.5**: *Working of system calls in Unix*

- **System Prepares Return Values**. After the kernel function completes its operation, any return values or results are prepared for the user application.
- **Context Switch to User Space**. The execution context is switched back from kernel mode to user mode.
- **Resume Application**. The application resumes its execution from where it left off, now with the results or effects of the system call.

Note: The exact number of steps and the functionality of system calls can vary depending on the operating system.

File Operations via System Calls

- **Device Management**. System calls enable processes to request device access, perform read or write operations on these devices, and release them afterward.
- **Resource Management**. System calls help allocate and deallocate resources, such as memory, CPU time, and I/O devices.
- **Maintenance**. System calls are used to obtain or configure system information, such as the date and time or process status.
- **Communication**. System calls allow processes to communicate with each other and synchronize their actions.
- **Error Handling**. When a system call cannot be completed, it returns an error code that the calling program can process.

Types of System Calls

The following list categorizes system calls based on their functionalities:

1. **Process Control**

   System calls play an essential role in controlling system processes. They enable you to:

   a. Create new processes or terminate existing ones

   b. Load and execute programs within a process's space

   c. Schedule processes and set execution attributes, such as priority

   d. Wait for a process to complete or signal upon its completion

2. **File Management**

   System calls support a wide array of file operations, such as:

   a. Reading from or writing to files

   b. Opening and closing files

   c. Deleting or modifying file attributes

   d. Moving or renaming files

3. **Device Management**

   System calls can be used to facilitate device management by:

   a. Requesting device access and releasing it after use

   b. Setting device attributes or parameters

   c. Reading from or writing to devices

   d. Mapping logical device names to physical devices

4. **Information Maintenance**

   This type of system call enables processes to:

   a. Retrieve or modify various system attributes

   b. Set the system date and time

   c. Query system performance metrics

5. **Communication**

   The communication call type facilitates:

   a. Sending or receiving messages between processes

   b. Synchronizing actions between user processes

c. Establishing shared memory regions for inter-process communication

d. Networking via sockets

6. **Security and Access Control**

System calls contribute to security and access control by:

a. Determining which processes or users get access to specific resources and who can read, write, and execute resources.

b. Facilitating user authentication procedures.

Examples of System Calls

The following table lists common Unix and Windows system calls and their descriptions.

Unix System Calls	Description	Windows API Calls	Description
Process Control			
`fork()`	Create a new process	`CreateProcess()`	Create a new process
`exit()`	Terminate the current process	`ExitProcess()`	Terminate the current process
`wait()`	Make a process wait until its child processes terminate	`WaitForSingleObject()`	Wait for a process or thread to terminate
`exec()`	Execute a new program in a process	`CreateProcess() or`	Execute a new program in a new process
		`ShellExecute()`	
`getpid()`	Get the unique process ID	`GetCurrentProcessId()`	Get the unique process ID
File Management			
`open()`	Open a file (or device)	`CreateFile()`	Open or create a file or device
`close()`	Close an open file (or device)	`CloseHandle()`	Close an open object handle
`read()`	Read from a file (or device)	`ReadFile()`	Read data from a file or input device

write()	Write to a file (or device)	WriteFile()	Write data to a file or output device
lseek()	Change the read/write location in a file	SetFilePointer()	Set the position of the file pointer
unlink()	Delete a file	DeleteFile()	Delete an existing file
rename()	Rename a file	MoveFile()	Move or rename a file
Directory Management			
mkdir()	Create a new directory	CreateDirectory()	Create a new directory
rmdir()	Remove a directory	RemoveDirectory()	Remove an existing directory
chdir()	Change the current directory	SetCurrentDirectory()	Change the current directory
stat()	Get file status	GetFileAttributesEx()	Get extended file attributes
fstat()	Get status of an open file	GetFileInformation ByHandle()	Get file information using a file handle
link()	Create a link to a file	CreateHardLink()	Create a hard link to an existing file
symlink()	Get the status of an open file	CreateSymbolicLink()	Create a symbolic link
Device Management			
brk() or sbrk()	Increase/decrease the program's data space	VirtualAlloc() or VirtualFree()	Reserve, commit, or free a region of memory
mmap()	Map files or devices into memory	MapViewOfFile()	Map a file into the application's address space
Information Maintenance			
time()	Get the current time	GetSystemTime()	Get the current system time
alarm()	Get the status of an open file	SetWaitableTimer()	Set a timer object
getuid()	Set an alarm clock for the delivery of a signal	GetUserName() or LookupAccountName()	Get the username or ID

`getgid()`	Get the group ID	`GetTokenInformation()`	Get the group information of a security token
Communication Calls			
`socket()`	Create a new socket	`socket()`	Create a new socket
`bind()`	Bind a socket to a network address	`bind()`	Bind a socket to a network address
`listen()`	Bind a socket to a network address	`listen()`	Listen for connections on a socket
`accept()`	Accept a new connection on a socket	`accept()`	Accept a new connection on a socket
`connect()`	Initiate a connection on a socket	`connect()`	Initiate a connection on a socket
`send()` or `recv()`	Send and receive data on a socket	`send()` or `recv()`	Send and receive data on a socket
Security and Access Control			
`chmod()` or `umask()`	Change the permissions/ mode of a file	`SetFileAttributes()` or `SetSecurityInfo()`	Change the file attributes or security info
`chown()`	Change the owner and group of a file	`SetSecurityInfo()`	Set the security information

Table 9.1: *Common Unix and Windows system calls and their descriptions*

Note: *System call behavior, parameters, and return values might differ depending on the OS and version. Consult the OS's manual or documentation for detailed information.*

Relationship between the System Calls and the Algorithms

Figure 9.6 shows the relationship between the system calls and the algorithms described previously. It classifies the system calls into several categories, although some system calls appear in more than one category:

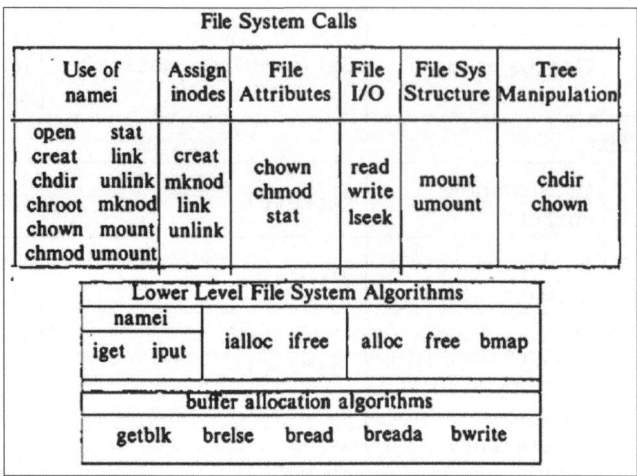

Figure 9.6: *Relationship between the system calls and the algorithms*

- System calls that return file descriptors for use in other system calls
- System calls that use the namei algorithm to parse a path name
- System calls that assign and free inodes, using algorithms ial/oc and ifree
- System calls that set or change the attributes of a file
- System calls that do 1/0 to and from a process, using algorithms al/oc, Jree, and the buffer allocation algorithms
- System calls that change the structure of the file system
- System calls that allow a process to change its view of the file system tree

1. OPEN

The **open** system call is the first step a process must take to access the data in a file. The syntax for the open system call is

```
fd = open (pathname, flags, modes) ;
```

where **pathname_** is a file name, **flags** indicate the type of open (such as for reading or writing), and **modes** give the file permissions if the file is being created. The open system call returns an integer' called the user file descriptor. Other file operations, such as reading, writing, seeking, duplicating the file descriptor, setting file I/O parameters, determining file status, and closing the file, use the file descriptor that the open system call returns.

The kernel searches the file system for the file name parameter using the algorithm namei (see *Figure* 9.7). It checks permissions for opening the file after it finds the in-core inode and allocates an entry in the file table for the open file. The file table entry contains a pointer to the inode of the open file and a field that indicates the byte offset in the file where the kernel expects the next read or write to begin. The kernel initializes the offset to 0 during the open call, meaning that the initial read or write starts at the beginning of a file by default. Alternatively, a process can open a file in write-append mode, in which case the kernel initializes the offset to the size of the file. The kernel allocates an entry in a private table in the process area, called the user file descriptor table, and notes the index of this entry. The index is the file descriptor that is returned to the user. The entry in the user file table points to the entry in the global file table.

```
algorithm open
inputs:  file name
         type of open
         file permissions (for creation type of open)
output:  file descriptor
{
        convert file name to inode (algorithm namei);
        if (file does not exist or not permitted access)
                return(error);
        allocate file table entry for inode, initialize count, offset;
        allocate user file descriptor entry, set pointer to file table entry;
        if (type of open specifies truncate file)
                free all file blocks (algorithm free);
        unlock(inode);                  /* locked above in namei */
        return(user file descriptor);
}
```

Figure 9.7: *Algorithm for Opening a File*

Suppose a process executes the following code, opening the file "`/etc/passwd`" twice, once read-only and once write-only, and the file "*local*" once, for reading and writing.

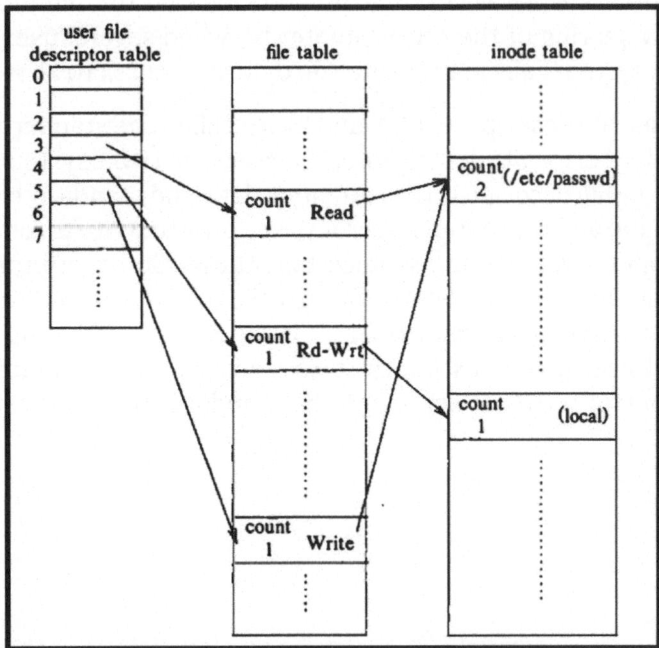

Figure 9.8: *Data Structures after Open*

```
fd 1 = open ("/etc/passwd", O_RDONLY) ;
fd2 = open ("local", 0 RDWR) ;
fd3 = open ("/etc/pass d", O_WRONLY) ;
```

Figure 9.8 shows the relationship between the *inode table, file table,* and *user file* descriptor data structures. Each open returns a file descriptor to the process, and the corresponding entry in the user file descriptor table points to a unique entry in the kernel file table even though one file ("/etc/passwd") is opened twice. The file table entries of all instances of an open file point to one entry in the in-core inode table. The process can read or write the file "**/etc/passwd**" but only through tile descriptors 3 and 5 in the figure. The kernel notes the capability to read or write the file in the file table entry allocated during the open call. Suppose a second process executes the following code.

```
fd 1 = open ("/etc/passwd", O_RDONLY) ;
fd2 = open ("private", 0 _ RDONL Y) ;
```

Figure 9.9 shows the relationship between the appropriate data structures while both processes (and no others) have the files open. Again, each open call results in an allocation of a unique entry in the user file descriptor table and the kernel file table, but the kernel contains at most one entry per file in the in-core inode table. The user file descriptor table entry could conceivably contain the file offset **fqr** the position of the next I/O operation and point directly to the in-core inode entry for the file, eliminating the need for a separate kernel file table. The preceding examples show a one-to-one relationship between user file descriptor entries and kernel file table entries. Thompson notes, however, that he implemented the file table as a separate structure to allow sharing of the offset pointer between several user file descriptors. The dup and fork system calls manipulate the data structures to allow such sharing.

The first three user file descriptors (0, 1, and 2) are called the standard input, standard output, and standard error file descriptors. Processes on UNIX systems conventionally use the standard input descriptor to read input data, the standard output descriptor to write output data, and the standard error descriptor to write error data (messages). Nothing in the operating system assumes that these file descriptors are special. A group of users could adopt the convention that file descriptors 4, 6, and 11 are special file descriptors, but counting from 0 Gn C is much more natural. Adoption of the convention by all user programs makes it easy for them to communicate via pipes. Normally, the control terminal serves as the standard input, standard output, and standard error.

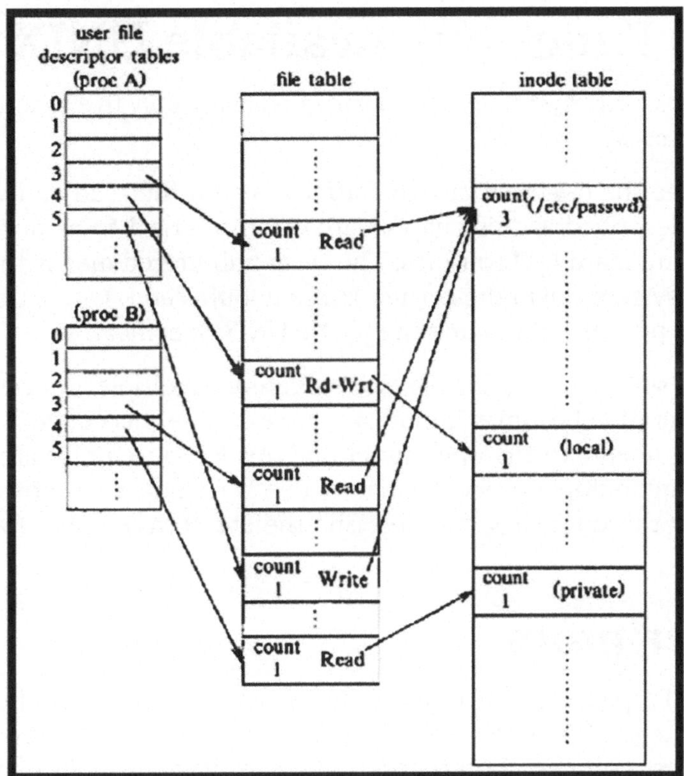

***Figure 9.9:** Data Structures after Two Processes Open Files*

Due to shortage, we shall discuss only a few processes and readers are advised to go through Chapter 5 of the book *The Design Of The Unix® Operating System* by Maurice J. Bach.

2. READ

The syntax of the **read** system call is

```
number = read (fd, buffer, count)
```

where **fd** is the file descriptor returned by open, **buffer** is the address of a data structure in the user process that will contain the read data 01, 1 successful completion of the call, **count,** the number of bytes the user wants to read, and number, the number of bytes actually read.

3. WRITE

The syntax for the **write** system call is

```
number "" write(fd, buffer, count);
```

where the meaning of the variables **fd**, **buffer**, **count**, and **number** are the same as they are for the read system call.

File I/O Functions Available UNIX System

Most file I/O on a UNIX system can be performed using only five functions: *open*, *read*, *write*, *lseek*, and *close*.

We then examine the effect of various buffer sizes on the read and write functions. The functions described in this chapter are often referred to as unbuffered I/O, in contrast to the standard I/O routines. The term unbuffered means that each read or write invokes a system call in the kernel. These unbuffered I/O functions are not part of ISO C but are part of POSIX.1 and the Single UNIX Specification.

Whenever we describe the sharing of resources among multiple processes, the concept of an atomic operation becomes important. We examine this concept concerning file I/O and the arguments to the open function. This leads to a discussion of how files are shared among multiple processes and which kernel data structures are involved. After describing these features, we describe the **dup**, **fcntl**, **sync**, **fsync**, and **ioctl** functions.

File Descriptors

To the kernel, all open files are referred to by file descriptors. A file descriptor is a non-negative integer. When we open an existing file or create a new file, the kernel returns a file descriptor to the process. When we want to read or write a file, we identify the file with the file descriptor that was returned by open or create as an argument to either read or write.

By convention, UNIX system shells associate file descriptor 0 with the standard input of a process, file descriptor 1 with the standard output, and file descriptor 2 with the standard error. This convention is used by the shells and many applications; it is not a feature of the UNIX kernel. Nevertheless, many applications would break if these associations were not followed.

Although their values are standardized by POSIX.1, the magic numbers 0, 1, and 2 should be replaced in POSIX-compliant applications with the symbolic constants **STDIN_FILENO**, **STDOUT_FILENO**, and **STDERR_FILENO** to improve readability.

These constants are defined in the **<unistd.h>** header.

File descriptors range from 0 through **OPEN_MAX-1**, (Recall *Figure* 2.11). Early historical implementations of the UNIX System had an upper limit of 19, allowing a maximum of 20 open files per process, but many systems subsequently increased this limit to 63.

With FreeBSD 8.0, Linux 3.2.0, Mac OS X 9.6.8, and Solaris 10, the limit is essentially infinite, bounded by the amount of memory on the system, the size of an integer, and any hard and soft limits configured by the system administrator.

File Sharing

The UNIX System supports the sharing of open files among different processes. Before describing the dup function, we need to describe this sharing. To do this, we will examine the data structures used by the kernel for all I/O.

The following description is conceptual; it may or may not match a particular implementation. The kernel uses three data structures to represent an open file, and the relationships among them determine the effect one process has on another about file sharing.

- Every process has an entry in the process table. Within each process table entry is a table of open file descriptors, which we can think of as a vector, with one entry per descriptor. Associated with each file descriptor are:
    - The file descriptor flags (close-on-exec; refer to *Figure* 3.7 and Section 3.14)
    - A pointer to a file table entry
- The kernel maintains a file table for all open files. Each file table entry contains:
    - The file status flags for the file, such as read, write, append, sync, and nonblocking; more on these in Section 3.14
    - The current file offset
    - A pointer to the v-node table entry for the file
- Each open file (or device) has a v-node structure that contains information about the type of file and pointers to functions that operate on the file. For most files, the v-node also contains the i-node for the file. This information is read from disk when the file is opened so that all the pertinent information about the file is readily available. For example, the i-node contains the owner of the file, the size of the file, pointers to where the actual data blocks for the file are located on disk, and so on.

Linux has no v-node. Instead, a generic i-node structure is used. Although the implementations differ, the v-node is conceptually the same as a generic i-node. Both point to an i-node structure specific to the file system.

Figure 9.10 shows a pictorial arrangement of these three tables for a single process that has two different files open: one file is open on standard input (file descriptor 0), and the other is open on standard output (file descriptor 1).

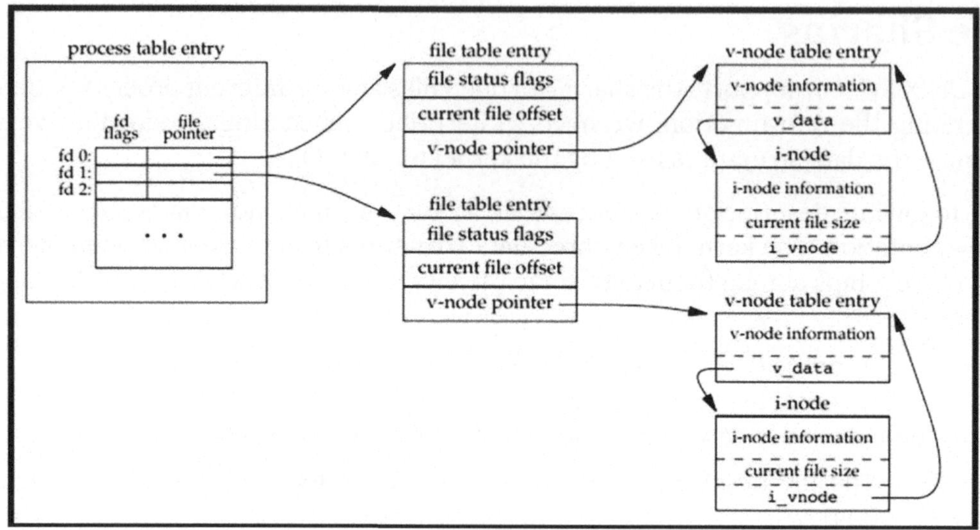

Figure 9.10: *Kernel data structures for open files*

The arrangement of these three tables has existed since the early versions of the UNIX System [Thompson 1978]. This arrangement is critical to the way files are shared among processes. We will return to this figure in later chapters when we describe additional ways that files are shared.

v-node

The v-node was invented to provide support for multiple file system types on a single computer system. The v-node propagated through various vendor implementations as support for Sun's Network File System (NFS) was added. The first release from Berkeley to provide v-nodes was the 4.3BSD Reno release when NFS was added.

Instead of splitting the data structures into a v-node and an i-node, Linux uses a file system–independent i-node and a file system–dependent i-node. If two independent processes have the same file open, we could have the arrangement shown in *Figure 9.11*.

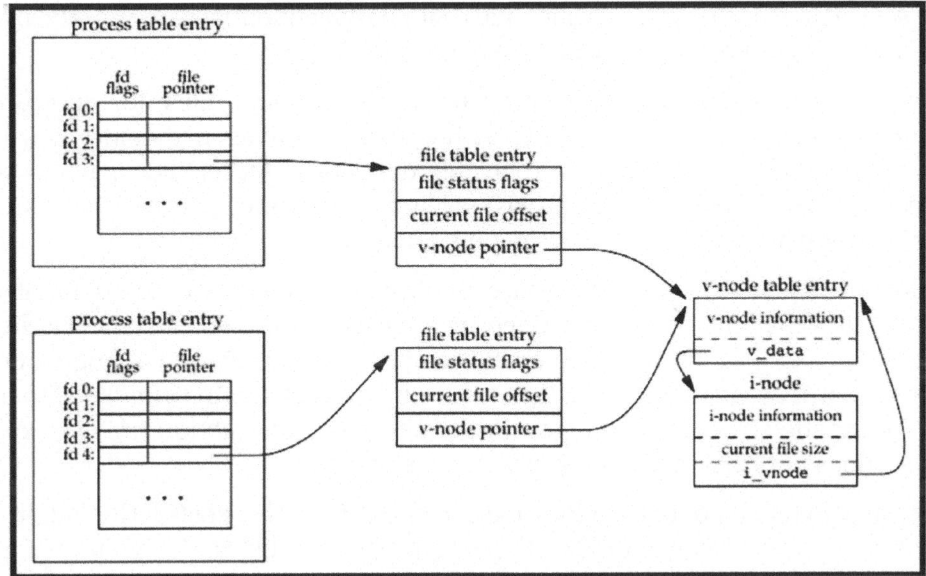

***Figure 9.11**: Linux's file system–independent i-node and a file system–dependent i-node*

We assume here that the first process has the file open on descriptor 3 and the second process has that same file open on descriptor 4. Each process that opens the file gets its own file table entry, but only a single v-node table entry is required for a given file. One reason each process gets its own file table entry is so that each process has its own current offset for the file.

The UNIX File Abstraction

When multiple processes exist on a single machine, they rely on virtual memory to create the illusion that they have sole access to the CPU; the context switch mechanism prevents one process from accessing another process's register values, stack, heap, and so on. However, processes ultimately do not have sole access to the entire machine. There are many resources, such as a network interface, storage devices, user input devices, and so on, that must be shared with other processes on the same machine. As such, processes act as a unit of ownership for instances of access to these resources.

The UNIX file abstraction, widely used in modern OS design, provides a uniform interface to these various shared resources. This abstraction relies on two features: a file is a sequence of bytes and everything is a file. It is important to emphasize that this definition is different from the common usage of the term "file," which is typically associated with persistent data storage. The key differences between this common usage and the UNIX file abstraction are as follows:

Arbitrary or bidirectional access to a file is not necessarily possible. In some cases, once a byte has been read from the file, that byte no longer exists in the file; there is no way to seek a previous position in such files. Similarly, sequential access of the bytes in order may be required, with no way to skip ahead.

Files may not have names or persistent storage. Some files for interprocess communication, commonly referred to as IPC, exist solely as in-memory constructs at run time, identified only by an integer file descriptor. Other files (such as /dev/random on UNIX and Linux systems) exist solely as an abstract interface to a hardware component or generate data at run-time on demand.

Files do not necessarily have structure or typing. Readers are like a family with persistent files that can be distinguished by a file extension. For instance, a file with the .pdf extension has a different internal structure than one with a .png extension; programs that read or write these files must ensure that the bytes adhere to a pre-defined semantic structure. However, in the UNIX file abstraction, this pre-defined structure does not exist; a file is just a sequence of bytes.

By removing so much contextual information about files, this abstraction might seem to lose much of its meaning or utility. On the contrary, this abstraction greatly simplifies the work of dealing with a variety of resources; there are certain operations (creating, deleting, opening, closing, reading, writing) common to the lifecycle of all files. The UNIX file abstraction provides a single, consistent interface for these operations, thus eliminating much of the complexity of supporting many such resources.

When a process completes (or crashes), any data stored in the main memory is lost. But data stored on a hard disk drive (HDD) or solid state drive (SSD) is "persistent;" that is, it survives after the process completes, even if the computer shuts down.

Hard disk drives are complicated. Data is stored in blocks, laid out in sectors, which make up tracks, arranged in concentric circles on platters.

Solid-state drives are simpler in one sense because blocks are numbered sequentially, but they raise a different complication: each block can be written a limited number of times before it becomes unreliable.

As a programmer, you do not want to deal with these complications. What you want is an appropriate abstraction of persistent storage hardware. The most common abstraction is called a "*file system.*"

Abstractly:

A "*file system*" is a mapping from each file's name to its contents. If you think of the names as keys and the contents as values, a file system is a kind of key-value database (see https://en.wikipedia.org/wiki/Key-value_database).[4]

A "file" is a sequence of bytes.

File names are usually strings and are usually "hierarchical"; that is, the string specifies a path from a top-level directory (or folder), through a series of subdirectories, to a specific file.

The primary difference between the abstraction and the underlying mechanism is that files are byte-based and persistent storage is block-based. The operating system translates byte-based file operations in the C library into block-based operations on storage devices. Typical block sizes are 1–8 KiB.

For example, the following code opens a file and reads the first byte:

```
FILE *fp = fopen("/home/downey/file.txt", "r");
  char c = fgetc(fp);
  fclose(fp);
```

When this code runs:

1. **fopen** uses the filename to find the top-level directory, called /, the subdirectory home, and the sub-subdirectory downey.
2. It finds the file named file.txt and "*opens*" it for reading, which means it creates a data structure that represents the file being read. Among other things, this data structure keeps track of how much of the file has been read, called the "*file position.*"
3. In DOS, this data structure is called a File Control Block, but we want to avoid that term because, in UNIX, it means something else. In UNIX, there is no good name for it. It is an entry in the open file table, so we will call it an **OpenFileTableEntry**.

When we call **fgetc**, the operating system checks whether the next character of the file is already in memory. If so, it reads the next character, advances the file position, and returns the result.

If the next character is not in memory, the operating system issues an I/O request to get the next block. Disk drives are slow, so a process waiting for a block from disk is usually interrupted so that another process can run until the data arrives.

When the I/O operation is complete, the new block of data is stored in memory, and the process resumes. It reads the first character and stores it as a local variable.

When the process closes the file, the operating system completes or cancels any pending operations, removes data stored in memory, and frees the **OpenFileTableEntry**.

The process for writing a file is similar, but there are some additional steps. Here is an example that opens a file for writing and changes the first character.

```
FILE *fp = fopen("/home/downey/file.txt", "w");
  fputc('b', fp);
  fclose(fp);
```

When this code runs:

1. Again, **fopen** uses the filename to find the file. If it does not already exist, it creates a new file and adds an entry in the parent directory, **/home/downey**.

2. The operating system creates an **OpenFileTableEntry** that indicates that the file is open for writing and sets the file position to 0.
3. **fputc** attempts to write (or re-write) the first byte of the file. If the file already exists, the operating system has to load the first block into memory. Otherwise, it allocates a new block in memory and requests a new block on disk.
4. After the block in memory is modified, it might not be copied back to the disk right away. In general, data written to a file is "buffered," which means it is stored in memory and only written to disk when there is at least one block to write.
5. When the file is closed, any buffered data is written to disk, and the **OpenFileTableEntry** is freed.

To summarize, the C library provides the abstraction of a file system that maps from file names to streams of bytes. This abstraction is built on top of storage devices that are actually organized in blocks.

The file abstraction is really a "stream of bytes" abstraction, which is useful for many things, not just file systems.

One example is the UNIX pipe, a simple form of inter-process communication. Processes can be set up so that output from one process is taken as input into another process. For the first process, the pipe behaves like a file open for writing, so it can use C library functions, such as **fputs** and **fprintf**. For the second process, the pipe behaves like a file open for reading, so it uses **fgets** and **fscanf**.

Network communication also uses the stream of bytes abstraction. A UNIX socket is a data structure that represents a communication channel between processes on different computers (usually). Again, processes can read data from and write data to a socket using "*file*" handling functions.

Reusing the file abstraction makes life easier for programmers, since they only have to learn one API (application program interface). It also makes programs more versatile since a program intended to work with files can also work with data coming from pipes and other sources.

The **/home/mthomas** directory has one (note that there may be many) child, which is **/home/mthomas/bin** in absolute form and bin in relative form. You might be wondering, "*How do we use this?*" One uses this to move around the file system. The **cd** command, which enables a user to switch directories, is used for file system navigation. Entering **$ cd [Enter]** will take the user to their "**home**" or login directory (as indicated by the **$HOME** variable 4) in the most basic use of this command. If a user wants to switch to a different directory, they type **$ cd file_spec [Enter]**. If **file_spec** is a valid directory, this directory location will now be their current working directory. Keep in mind that the file specification may always be either absolute or relative. If we want to switch directories to the **/home/mthomas/bin** directory, we can type **$ cd /home/mthomas/bin** [Enter] - absolute, will work from anywhere, or **$ cd** .. We type as before, and the system returns the following: **$ pwd** [Enter] **/home/mthomas/class_stuff**. [Insert] i, go up one directory, relative. e. Proceed to the bin directory or **$ cd** . by moving down to the parent **$ cd bin** [Enter] relative. Sometimes, novice users ask which file specification method is better or which they should use. /bin [Enter] relative, both steps in one file spec. The simple yet ambiguous answer is "*It depends*". In other words, it is contingent upon one's objective and existing position in the file system hierarchy. This depends on several factors, including the file specification's length, the ease with which special characters can be typed, one's familiarity with the current position within the file system hierarchy, and other factors. After some investigation, look at the file system in your Unix implementation and observe how it varies from the preceding diagram. (1) Since each component is a file, I prefer to call this a file specification, even though some might call it a path name or path specifier. System administrators frequently use fully qualified path names, or FQPN, because they are used to working with DNS. You can find more information by searching for fully qualified path names using your preferred search engine. (2) As an alternative, a user can navigate to their "**home**" directory by using the command cd ~ (tilde), where the ~ character indicates the user's "home" directory. CD and CD ~ are interchangeable in a fundamental sense. However, much more complex behavior can be achieved with the ~ character as it is presented here.

File Persistence

The maximum time that modified data may stay at each level before being archived to the next level of the storage hierarchy is specified by a set of per-file time constraints (one for each level of the storage hierarchy), which maintain the continuity of the persistence spectrum. The sooner data is archived to the next level of the storage hierarchy, the less likely it is to be lost because each level of the hierarchy offers increasing guarantees for persistence.

On the other hand, the likelihood of data surviving drops if it intends to stay at the higher levels. Every storage level has modified data tracked by a daemon process, which archives the data to the subsequent lower level after a predetermined amount of time. Until space becomes scarce, data archived to the next level stays at the current level. Conceptually, the level of persistence of the file should rise in proportion to the cost of recreating the data. One way to avoid the need for data regeneration later is to move files to stable storage after a certain amount of time, even though they may be relatively easy to regenerate (for example, an executable compiled from sources) and may never need to hit stable storage. When a file is very active, it means that... E. being created regularly, like an object code file (. o), although the temporal delay stops the intermediate file versions from being sent down the hierarchy, the data will eventually be archived after the active period has ended.

Extra File Properties

The **ls** command is used to view the files that are currently in our working directory. With this command, the user can easily list their files. Using this command with the **-l** (that is, ell) option results in the output shown below from root (/).

permission modes	# links	owner	group	size (bytes)	date (modified)	file name
drwxr-xr-x	2	root	root	4096	Mar 21 2002	bin
drwxr-xr-x	17	root	root	77824	Aug 11 14:40	dev
drwxr-xr-x	69	root	root	8192	Sep 25 18:15	etc
drwxr-xr-x	66	root	root	4096	Sep 25 18:15	home
dr-xr-xr-x	46	root	root	0	Aug 11 10:39	proc
drwxr-x---	12	root	root	4096	Aug 7 2002	root
drwxr-xr-x	2	root	root	8192	Mar 21 2002	sbin
drwxrwxrwx	6	root	root	4096	Sep 29 04:02	tmp
drwxr-xr-x	16	root	root	4096	Mar 21 2002	usr
-rw-r--r--	1	root	root	802068	Sep 6 2001	vmlinuz

Figure 9.12: *ls Command*

As we can see from the preceding output, each file contains seven attribute fields. The attribute fields are as follows, from right to left: modification date: the date the file was last edited, that is, the file name, which is the name attached to the file (note that any type of file can be included). E. E. "*Time-stamp*.". If no changes have been made to the file in the past year (six months for Linux users), the year of the last modification is evident. size: the bytes of the file (that is, E. E. characters). Two groups: the group's owner; the number of links linked to the file; the number of additional links linked to the file; and permission modes: the permissions granted to the file for the owner, the group, and all other individuals. Note that this listing is only an example and might not be an accurate or complete representation of the root (/) directory. The number of characters in the file, not its actual size on disk, is referred to here because files are written to disk in blocks of 1024 bytes. If the file is a directory, keep in mind that this is the size of the structure needed to control the directory hierarchy.

Understanding and Modifying File Permissions

As displayed in the following diagram, each file has a permission field with ten characters, as you can see if you closely inspect the previous permission field.

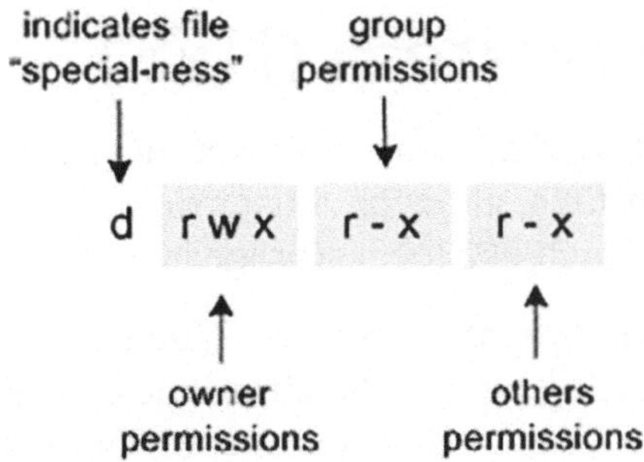

Figure 9.13: *File Permissions*

A file's "*type*" is indicated by the first (leftmost) character. Another way to put this is to ask if the file has any unique characteristics. If the file is a standard one (that is, no special characteristics), it will be preceded by a dash. This is where the letter "d" will appear if it is a directory file. Or it will have the letter l (ell) in this first position if it is a link to another file. Examples of a directory and a regular file are shown in the ls -l output above. There are other unique qualities that are not worth talking about here. Three groups of three characters each comprise the next nine characters: three for the file owner's permissions, three for the group's permissions, and three for the permissions of every other user. The user's permissions on that specific file are indicated by the three characters, which stand for read (r), write (w), and execute (x). In the above diagram, the file owner has all permissions (shown by rwx), a user in this group has read and execute permissions (shown by r-x), and all other users have read and execute permissions. You will notice that a dash will appear in place of the appropriate letter if a user lacks the necessary authorization.

Overview of the Command

- **`cat`:** display entire file(s) in the terminal window (also see more command later)
- **`cd`:** change the current directory (see bash-built-ins note)
- **`cp`**: copy file(s)
- **`chmod`:** change file(s) protection modes
- **`lpr`:** send file(s) to the line printer
- **`mkdir`:** create (make) a new directory
- **`more`**: nicely view the contents of file(s)
- **`mv`:** move (and/or rename) file(s)
- **`pwd`**: print absolute pathname of current working directory
- **`rm`:** remove file(s)
- **`rmdir`:** remove an empty directory
- **`umask`:** set file mode

Network File System (NFS)

Network File System (NFS) is a distributed file system protocol originally developed by Sun Microsystems (Sun) in 1984, allowing a user on a client computer to access files over a computer network much like local storage is accessed.

NFS is often used with Unix operating systems (such as Solaris, AIX, HP-UX), Apple's macOS, and Unix-like operating systems (such as Linux and FreeBSD). It is also available to operating systems, such as Acorn RISC OS, AmigaOS, the classic Mac OS, OpenVMS, MS-DOS, Microsoft Windows, OS/2, ArcaOS, Novell NetWare, and IBM i.

The NFS is a distributed file system that allows users to access files over a computer network as if they were local files. It is a client-server architecture, where the server exports directories to clients, and the clients can mount the exported directories.

NFS uses a remote procedure call (RPC) protocol to communicate between the client and server. This makes it relatively easy to implement and deploy.

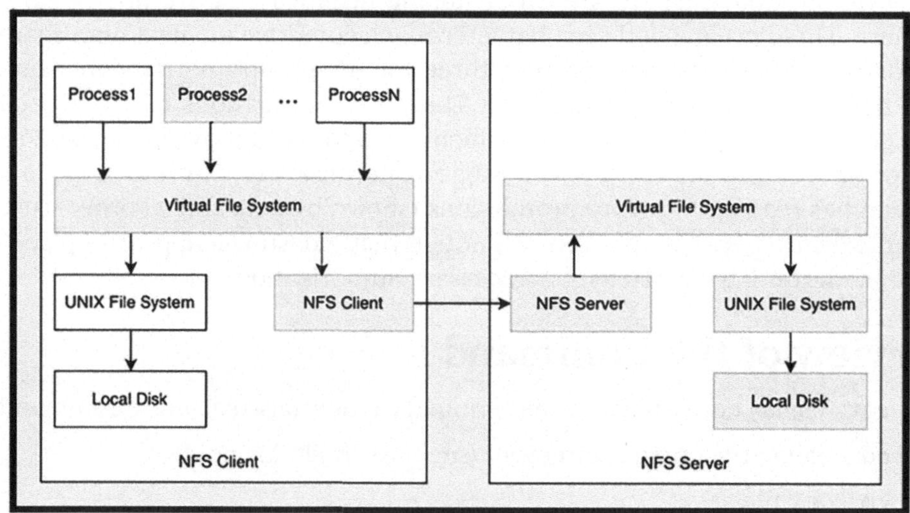

Figure 9.14: *NFS Architecture*

- **NFS Client System**

  The NFS client system is integrated with the kernel (OS). It performs RPCs to the NFS server system for DFS operations, such as reading and writing files, creating and deleting files, and moving and renaming files.

- **NFS Server System**

  The NFS server system plays the role of both flat file service and directory service. It allows the mounting of files and directories.

Mounting a file or directory means that the client makes the file or directory appear as if it is part of the client's local file system. For example, if a client mounts the directory `/usr/edison/inventions` into the directory `/usr/tesla/my_competitors`, then the client can access the file `/usr/tesla/my_competitors/foo` as if it were the file `/usr/edison/inventions/foo`.

Mounting files and directories does not clone (copy) the files. It simply creates a symbolic link to the files on the server. This means that the client can access the files without downloading them to the client machine.

Server Optimizations

Server caching is one of the big reasons NFS is so fast with reads. Server caching stores some of the recently-accessed blocks (of files and directories) in memory. This means that when a client requests a block that is already in the cache, the server can return the block immediately without having to read it from disk. This can significantly improve the performance of read operations.

Most programs tend to have a locality of access. This means that blocks accessed recently will likely be accessed soon in the future. Server caching takes advantage of this locality of access by keeping recently accessed blocks in memory.

There are two main flavors of writes in NFS:

- **Delayed write:** With delayed write, the server writes the data to memory and then flushes it to disk every 30 seconds (or via the Unix sync operation). This is faster than write-through, but it is not as consistent. If the server crashes before the data is flushed to disk, the data may be lost.
- **Write-through:** With write-through, the server writes the data to disk immediately before acknowledging the client's request. This is more consistent than delayed writing, but it may be slower.

The choice of which write flavor to use depends on the application. Applications that require consistency, such as financial applications, should use write-through. Applications that require speed, such as streaming media applications, may be able to use delayed write.

Other Server Optimizations in NFS

Asynchronous INPUT/OUTPUT: NFS servers can use asynchronous I/O to improve performance. Asynchronous I/O allows the server to continue processing other requests while waiting for I/O operations to complete.

Multiple threads: NFS servers can use multiple threads to improve performance. This allows the server to handle multiple client requests simultaneously.

Load balancing: NFS servers can be load-balanced to distribute the load across multiple servers. This can improve performance and reliability.

Using server optimizations such as caching, asynchronous INPUT/OUTPUT, multiple threads, and load balancing, NFS servers can provide high performance and reliability for a variety of applications.

Client Caching

Client caching is similar to server caching in that it stores some of the recently-accessed blocks (of files and directories) in memory. However, there are a few key differences:

- Client caching is performed by the NFS client, while server caching is performed by the NFS server.
- Client caching is used to improve the performance of read operations, while server caching is used to improve the performance of both read and write operations.
- Client caching can lead to inconsistencies, while server caching is always consistent.

Each block in the client cache is tagged with the following information:

- `Tc`: The time when the cache entry was last validated.
- `Tm`: The time when the block was last modified at the server.

A cache entry at time `T` is valid if (`T-Tc` < `t`) where t is the freshness interval. It is a compromise between consistency and efficiency. Sun Solaris sets t adaptively between 3-30 seconds for files and 30-60 seconds for directories.

When a block is written, the client performs a delayed write to the server. This means the client writes the data to the cache and then sends a write request to the server. The server does not acknowledge the write request until it has flushed the data to disk. This approach is faster than write-through, but it is not as consistent. If the client crashes before the data is flushed to the server, the data may be lost.

Client caching can significantly improve the performance of read operations, especially for applications that access the same files frequently. However, it is important to be aware of the potential for inconsistencies. Applications that require consistency should not rely on client caching.

Here is an example of how client caching can lead to inconsistencies:

- A client opens a file and reads a block into the cache
- The client modifies the block and writes it back to the cache
- The client crashes before it can flush the changes to the server

- Another client opens the same file and reads the block from the cache
- The second client sees the old version of the block, even though the first client modified the block

To avoid this inconsistency, applications should use write-through semantics or flush the cache before closing a file.

An NFS is a protocol that lets users on client computers access files on a network, making it a distributed file system. A Network File System, or NFS, is necessary for helping your business share files over a network. You can access remote data and files from any remote computer or device that links to the network you will use. All people within a network will have access to the same files, making file-sharing efforts easier.

The NFS protocol has been evolving since Sun Microsystems first introduced it in 1984. It continues to change today, as it is an open standard solution where anyone can implement the protocol on all operating systems and adjust it as necessary.

The General Concept

An NFS uses a basic system where a "`mount`" command will prompt the server to link with many clients. The clients will get access to the same files on the server through the proper platform. The design can use security protocols to dictate who will access certain files, producing a simplified and safe approach to work.

An NFS can also use a file-locking system that allows many clients to share the same files. The NFS can manage multiple applications or compute threads for operation.

- The NFS uses several hosts that will access the same files. It does not require one application for its operation, providing a simple design for handling the content one will read.
- The Transmission Control Protocol, or TCP, works in this NFS format. The TCP links between an application and an IP. It keeps tabs on data segments and only needs to receive the lost frames in the TCP set when something must be sent for a second time.
- The server will also accept TCP port 2049 commands. This port is one of the more commonly used ports on the market. It does not have to interact with daemons like the **`rpcbind`** and **`lockd`** options.

What Services Are Necessary?

You will require a few services to make an NFS file system work:

- **`nfs:`** The nfs service will start the server and the RPC processes necessary for accepting shared systems.
- **`Nfslock:`** The **`nfslock`** service starts the RPC processes and allows NFC clients to lock files.

- `Portmap`: You can take port reservations from local services with this one; `portmap` will respond to messages stating that certain ports are available for file access.

NFS File Share

You can use NFS for these scenarios:

- You have a local network with all Unix-based machines (including Linux-based environments) on the network
- Large file sizes are required

What Makes An NFS Useful?

You've got many positives surrounding an NFS to explore:

- Everyone in your network can access the same files when they become clients on the same NFS
- The mounting process for the file system remains transparent, giving clients an idea of how they can handle the content you manage
- The NFS may be more secure, as you will not have as many removable drives and disks on hand
- Multiple computers can share the same applications; they do not have to use excess disk space, and store things as often..

Are There Any Concerns?

There are a few drawbacks to the NFS to notice:

- A firewall is necessary for running an NFS to keep unwanted parties from entering. Any NFS that does not use this protection will be at risk of harm.
- It may be tough for multiple parties to access a file simultaneously, especially if the file is more massive in size.
- Some protocols allow for up to 1 MB of data to move in each read or write request. While today's protocols can handle immense amounts of requests, the 1 MB standard may be too weak.

Today there are only two versions of the NFS protocol left in use: Version 3, published in 1995, and version 4 in 2000. NFS 3 is still by far the most common version of the protocol and is the only one supported by Windows clients.

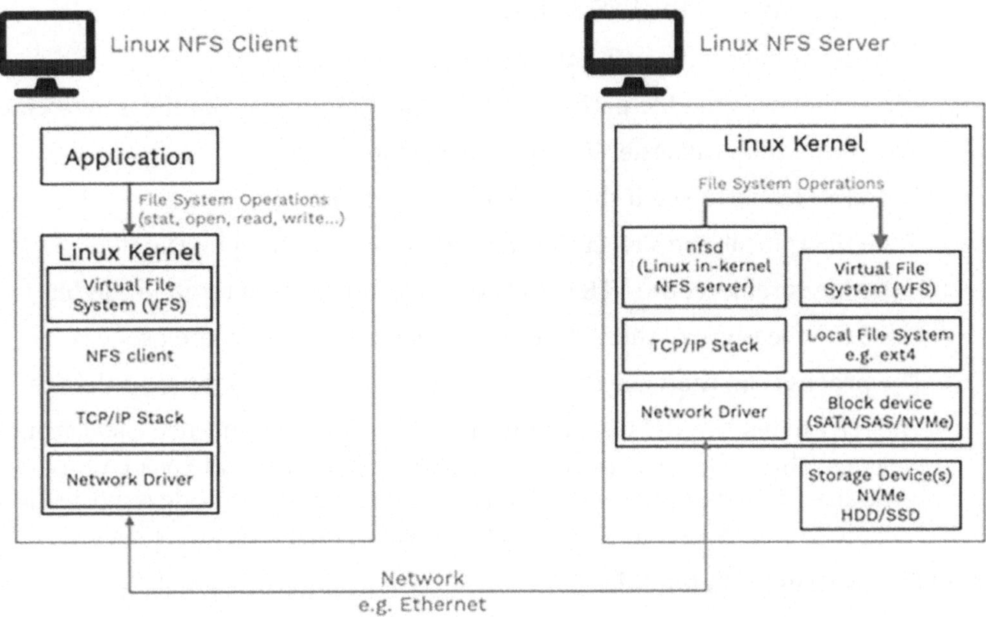

***Figure 9.15:** Illustration of a Linux NFS client communicating with a Linux NFS server (nfsd, in-kernel NFS server) and the components of the Linux kernel involved*

Virtual File System (VFS) Module

The VFS is a layer of abstraction between the kernel and the file system. It allows processes to access files via file descriptors such as local Unix files. This makes local and remote files indistinguishable from processes, which gives transparency.

The VFS keeps a data structure for each mounted file system. This data structure contains information about the file system, such as its type and location.

The VFS also keeps a data structure called a v-node for all open files. The v-node is a cache of information about the file, such as its size, permissions, and location. If the file is local, then the v-node points to the local disk i-node. If the file is remote, then the v-node contains the address of the remote NFS server.

For a given file access, the VFS decides whether to route the request to the local file system or the NFS client system. This decision is made based on the file handle. The file handle is a unique identifier for a file. It is generated by the NFS server and is returned to the client when the client opens the file. The VFS uses the file handle to identify the file system on which the file is located and to determine which file system operations to perform.

The VFS is a critical component of the Unix operating system. It allows processes to access files in a transparently and efficiently.

Here is an example of how the VFS works:

- A process opens a file using the **open()** system call
- The kernel uses the file path to find the file system that the file is located on
- The kernel then calls the VFS to open the file
- The VFS checks to see if the file is local or remote
- If the file is local, the VFS calls the local file system to open the file
- If the file is remote, the VFS calls the NFS client system to open the file
- Once the file is open, the VFS returns a file descriptor to the process
- The process can then use the file descriptor to read and write to the file
- The VFS hides the details of how the file is located and accessed from the process. This makes the process code more portable and easier to maintain. (v-node → file descriptor → inode). This means that the v-node is at the highest level, followed by the file descriptor, and then the inode.

Virtual File System (VFS) Module

While both Network File System (NFS) and **Server Message Block** (SMB) can be used across operating systems, the SMB protocol is the native Windows file-sharing default. Windows functionality is built around SMB. You need external tools such as Samba to use SMB on Linux computers to access remote Windows server files.

In contrast, the NFS protocol was designed specifically for Unix systems. It is a native file-sharing protocol–and the default file-transfer protocol–in most Linux distributions.

There are three types of NFS mounts: predefined, explicit, and automatic. Exporting and mounting directories must be understood to administer NFS. The /etc/exports file indicates all directories that a server exports to its clients.

SMB has been built so you can share a wide range of network resources, including file and print services, storage devices, and virtual machine storage.

This is in contrast to NFS, which only has built-in support for sharing files and directories.

Client-client communications

SMB allows clients to communicate and share files with each other by using the server as a mediator.

NFS only allows client-server operations.

When to use NFS versus SMB

Typically, NFS and SMB are used to create and manage local area networks (LANs) with homogenous operating system environments. In these environments, shared storage needs to be accessed like local files. NFS and SMB are also used in legacy networked environments over distance and hybrid cloud environments via gateways.

SMB file share

If you want to set up network-attached storage (NAS) in a LAN, SMB is the easiest choice to share and access files over the network. This remains true whether you run Windows, Mac, or Linux operating systems.

Other use cases of SMB

The following examples are other common use cases:

- Windows-based local area networks for organizations where several client machines require shared storage
- Enterprise environments with larger storage arrays that prioritize efficiency and scalability
- Advanced sharing operations that require native support

Distributed File System (DFS)

A distributed file system (DFS) is a file system that is spread across multiple servers or locations. It allows clients to access files as if they were stored locally, even though they may be physically located on different servers. DFSs are used to improve scalability, performance, and fault tolerance.

Some popular DFS systems include:

- **Network File System (NFS):** NFS is a popular DFS widely used in Unix and Linux environments. It uses a client-server architecture, where the server exports directories to clients, and the clients can mount the exported directories.
- **Hadoop Distributed File System (HDFS):** HDFS is a DFS designed for large-scale data processing. It uses a master-slave architecture, where the master node manages the metadata for the files, and the slave nodes store the data.
- **GlusterFS**: GlusterFS is a distributed file system built on top of TCP/IP. It uses a distributed hash table (DHT) to distribute the data across multiple servers.
- **Ceph**: Ceph is a unified distributed storage system that provides object storage, block storage, and file system storage. It uses a RADOS (Reliable Autonomic Distributed Object Store) architecture to distribute the data across multiple servers.

Desirable Properties of a DFS

The desirable properties of a DFS include:

- **Transparency:** The DFS should be transparent to the client, meaning that the client should be able to access files in the DFS as if they were local files.
- **Support for concurrent clients**: The DFS should be able to support multiple client processes accessing the same file concurrently.
- **Replication:** The DFS should store multiple copies of the file on different servers to improve fault tolerance and performance.
- **Scalability:** The DFS should be able to scale to support several clients and files.
- **Security:** The DFS should provide security features to protect files from unauthorized access.
- **Performance:** The DFS should provide good performance for both read and write operations.

Copy Update Semantics

This refers to the idea that when a file is replicated within a Distributed File System, the contents of the file, as visible to clients, should not appear any different than when the file has only one replica.

In other words, whether a file is replicated or not, clients accessing the file should see consistent and coherent data. This consistency ensures that the behavior of the file system is predictable for users, regardless of the number of replicas.

At Most Once Operation vs. At Least Once Operation:

- **At most once operation**: An at most once operation is an operation that is guaranteed to be executed at most once, even if there are failures in the system. At-most-once operations are useful for applications where idempotency is important, such as financial applications.
- **At least once operation**: An at least once operation is an operation that is guaranteed to be executed at least once, even if there are failures in the system. At-least-once operations are useful for applications where durability is important, such as logging applications.

  The choice between "*At Most Once*" and "*At Least Once*" semantics depends on the nature of the operation and the desired behavior.

- **At Most Once**: Suitable for operations where repetition could lead to undesirable consequences, such as data duplication.
- **At Least Once:** Appropriate for idempotent operations where repetition does not introduce issues.

Security in DFS

Authentication is the process of verifying that a given user is who they claim to be. This is typically done by requiring the user to provide a username and password or by using another form of authentication, such as biometric authentication.

Authorization is the process of verifying that a user is allowed to access a particular resource.

Access control lists (ACLs) specify who has access to a particular resource and what type of access they have. ACLs are typically associated with individual resources, such as files and directories.

Capability lists specify what resources a particular user has access to and what type of access they have. Capability lists are typically associated with individual users. Capabilities are indivisible units of authority. Each capability grants the holder permission to perform a specific operation on a specific resource.

Mount in Unix-like Operating Systems

A file system organizes and stores files on a storage device, such as a hard disk or a partition. Common file systems in Unix-like systems include ext4, XFS, and NFS.

In Unix-like operating systems, the term "**moun**t" refers to the process of associating a file system with a particular directory in the system's directory tree. This allows the files and directories within that file system to be accessed by users and applications as if they were part of the overall directory structure.

A mount point is an existing directory in the file system hierarchy where the contents of a separate file system are attached. When a file system is mounted at a specific mount point, the files and directories in that file system become accessible through that directory.

Once a file system is mounted, you can navigate to the specified mount point and access the files and directories within that file system as if they were part of the local file system. This flexibility allows Unix-like operating systems to manage various storage devices and network resources seamlessly.

For example, if a client mounts the directory **`/dev/sda1`** into the directory **`/mnt/external/sda1`** (maybe using **`sudo mount -t ntfs /mnt/external/sda1`**), then the client can access the files inside sda1 directory, that is, **`/mnt/external/sda1/foo.txt`**.

Conclusion

In this chapter, we have learned about file systems and their types in different operation systems along with their file access mechanisms. This included a hierarchical arrangement of directories and file system with an internal structure of files in the UNIX system. We learned about file system calls and file I/O functions available UNIX System. After this, we learned about file descriptors, file sharing, and additional file attributes. Apart from what we discussed, we learned on Network File System (NFS), Virtual File System (VFS) Module, and Distributed File System (DFS). Finally, we discussed mount in Unix-like operating systems.

In the next chapter, we shall go for distributed operating systems enables multiple independent computers to work together as a unified system.

Questions

1. What is a known computer file? State the number of types of files.
2. How do we find a particular file by file access mechanisms? How many types of file access mechanism are there?
3. Describe what indexed sequential access is and how it is managed?
4. How are the disk spaces for files allocated by the operating system?
5. How is the internal representation of a file made by an inode (Index Node)?
6. What are the two basic data structures contained by the kernel? Define the file table and the user file.
7. With the help of a diagram, explain file descriptors, file tables, and inode tables.
8. A file system that consists of a sequence of logical blocks is called ....
9. Draw a diagram of the logical block of file system layout and state the function of each component.
10. What is inode, and which fields are narrated in disk inodes?
11. Draw a Typical Unix file system hierarchical (or tree-like) diagram.
12. Describe the three main file types in a Unix system.
13. How can files be loosely divided into three categories in a Unix system?
14. Distinguish between absolute and relative path names and state their advantages.
15. What is the file system calls, and why are they needed?
16. Describe different types of system calls.
17. Describe five main Unix system calls used in process control.
18. What are the seven attribute fields listed for each file?

19. What are the desirable properties of a DFS?
20. Describe when to use NFS vs. SMB.
21. What is the purpose of having mount in Unix-like operating systems?
22. What do we mean by file permissions and how they are given and modified?

References

[1] The Design Of The Unix® Operating System Maurice J. Bach, published by Pearson Education, Inc., publishing as Prentice Hall Pearson Education Inc., ISBN-978-81-203-Q516-8

[2] Advanced Programming in the UNIX ® Environment, Third Edition W. Richard Stevens Stephen A. Rago,, https://xesoa.com/wp-content/uploads/2014/04/APUE-3rd.pdf

[3] System Calls in Operating System Explained, https://phoenixnap.com/kb/system-call

[4] Hard disk drive, From Wikipedia, the free encyclopedia, https://en.wikipedia.org/wiki/Hard_disk_drive /topics/hard-disk-drive-vs-solid-state-drive

CHAPTER 10
Distributed OS

Introduction

We have already discussed single-node, monolithic operating systems. But in contrast, distributed operating systems work over several nodes simultaneously.

Although it consists of multiple nodes, it appears to users and applications as a single node. A distributed operating system is system software over a collection of independent software, networked, communicating, and physically separate computational nodes. They handle jobs that are serviced by multiple CPUs.

Structure

In this chapter, we will learn the following topics:

- Distributed Operating Systems
- Real-life Example of Distributed Operating System
- Types of Distributed Operating Systems
- Five Challenges in Building Distributed Systems
- Advantages of Distributed Operating System
- Disadvantages of Distributed Operating System
- Architecture of Distributed Systems
  - Software Architecture
  - System Architecture
- Key Components of a Distributed System
- Examples of a Distributed System
- Three Guarantees of Distributed System: CAP Theorem

Distributed Operating Systems

Distributed operating systems allow several separate computers to function as a cohesive system. In addition to offering a unified, cohesive user interface, they enhance performance and dependability by managing resources and operations across networked machines. A distributed operating system runs concurrently on multiple computers. Clients can access the operating system on a personal computer, mainframe, or server. In addition to their many benefits, distributed operating systems have several drawbacks. One crucial kind of operating system is a distributed one. An operating system is essentially a program that serves as an interface between the user and the system hardware.. It also manages all of the communication between the hardware and software.[1]

A distributed operating system is one in which multiple computer systems are connected through a single communication channel. Additionally, these systems have separate processors and memory. In addition, these processors communicate over high-speed buses or telephone lines. These individual systems connected by a single channel are considered a single entity. We can also call them loosely coupled systems. Each component or system of the network is a node. In *Figure 10.1*, we have different computers (at different locations) attached to each other through the network and can communicate. [2]

Distributed computing is defined as a system consisting of software components spread over different computers but running as a single entity. A distributed system can be an arrangement of different configurations, such as mainframes, computers, workstations, and minicomputers. This article gives in-depth insights into the workings of distributed systems, the types of system architectures, and essential components with real-world examples.

A distributed operating system (DOS) enables the connection of two or more systems to support real-time applications. Systems can be connected to one another to share resources, thanks to a type of DOS called a Network Operating System (NOS). In contrast to a network operating system (NOS), a distributed operating system (DOS) enables systems to be connected to one another to share resources, whereas a NOS enables systems to be connected to serve real-time applications. The Network Operating System (NOS) type known as a Distributed Operating System (DOS) enables sharing resources between two or more systems.

Distributed computing is a system of software components spread over different computers but running as a single entity. A distributed system can be an arrangement of different configurations, such as mainframes, computers, workstations, and minicomputers.[3]

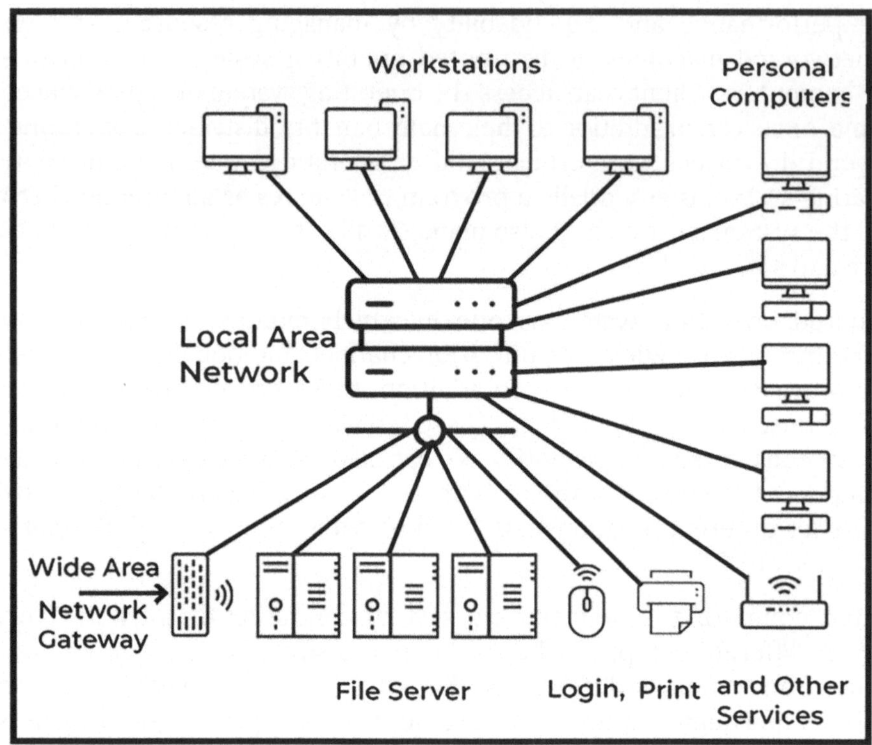

Figure 10.1: *Distributed System*

Sharing resources such as hardware, software, and data is one of the principles of cloud computing. With different levels of openness to the software and concurrency, it is easier to process data simultaneously through multiple processors. The more fault-tolerant an application is, the quicker it can recover from a system failure.

Organizations have turned to distributed computing systems to handle the data generation explosion and increased application performance needs. These distributed systems help businesses scale as data volume grows. This is especially true because adding hardware to a distributed system is simpler than upgrading and replacing an entire centralized system made up of powerful servers.

Distributed systems consist of many nodes that work together toward a single goal. These systems function in two general ways, and both have the potential to make a huge difference in an organization.

The first type is a cohesive system where the customer has each machine, and the results are routed from one source.

The second type allows each node to have an end user with their own needs, and the distributed system facilitates sharing resources or communication.

Examples of distributed operating systems:

- Micros
- DYNIX
- Mach
- Ubuntu
- Linux
- Locus
- OSF/1 operating system
- OSF/1AIX IBM RS/6000 computer operating system. Solaris is the operating system for workstations with multiple processors. Mach/OS is an operating system compatible with UNIX that supports multitasking and multithreading.

Real-life Example of Distributed Operating System

- **Web search:** We have different web pages, multimedia content, and scanned documents that we need to search. The purpose of web search is to index the content of the web. So to help us, we use different search engines, such as Google, Yahoo, Bing, and so on. These search engines use distributed architecture.
- **Banking system:** Suppose a bank with headquarters in New Delhi has branch offices in cities, such as Ludhiana, Noida, Faridabad, and Chandigarh. You can operate your bank by going to any of these branches. How is this possible? It is because whatever changes you make at one branch office are reflected at all branches. This is because of the distributed system.
- **Massively multiplayer online games:** Nowadays, you can play online games where you can play games with a person sitting in another country in a real-time environment.

Types of Distributed Operating System

There are mainly three types of distributed systems:

- Client/Server Systems
- Peer-to-Peer Systems
- Middleware

Client-Server System

In this system, clients request resources from servers. The server, in turn, makes this resource available to clients. A client connects to only one of the servers at a time. A single server can handle multiple clients simultaneously. Clients and servers connect through a computer network within the system. Client-server systems are also called "*tightly coupled operating systems.*" This system is primarily intended for multiprocessors and homogeneous multi-computers. A client-server system acts as a central server, authorizing all requests issued by client systems.

Peer-to-Peer System

Nodes play an important role in this system. All work is evenly distributed among the nodes. Nodes here refers to the computer, electronic devices, or workstation. Additionally, these nodes can share data or resources depending on your requirements. Again, you need a network to connect.

The peer-to-peer system is known as the "*loose pairing system.*" This concept is used in computer networking applications because they contain many processors that do not share memory or clocks. Each processor has its local memory, interacting with each other through various communication methods, such as telephone lines or high-speed buses.

Middleware

Message-oriented middleware is another name for this kind of software. It facilitates the connection and real-time operation of two or more systems. In this type, messages are used to communicate between systems.

Five Challenges in Building Distributed Systems

Building and operating distributed systems is hard.

However, if you embrace these challenges and factor them into your design, you can reap the true benefits of distributed systems. Let us look at these challenges one by one.

Communication [4]

A distributed system is distributed on the network. There is multiple nodes, and in most cases, they are separated geographically. No distributed system can function without communication between its various nodes. Even the seemingly simple task of browsing a website in your web browser requires significant communication between different processes.

When we visit a URL, our browser contacts the DNS to resolve the server address of the URL. Once it gets hold of the address, it sends an HTTP request to the server over the network. The server processes the request and sends back a response.

System designers should ask a few important questions regarding the communication aspects:

- How are request and response messages represented over the wire?
- What happens in the case of a network outage?
- How do we guarantee security from snooping?

We can handle many communication challenges by falling back on abstractions, such as TCP and HTTPS.

However, abstractions can leak. For example, TCP attempts to provide a complete abstraction of the underlying unreliable network. But TCP cannot do much if the network cable is cut or overloaded. When this happens, the challenge falls back on the system designer.

Coordination [4]

Imagine there are two generals with their respective armies. They need to coordinate with each other to attack a city at the same time. Only if they attack at the same time can they capture the city. For that, they need to agree on the time of the attack. Since the armies are geographically separated, the generals can communicate only by sending a messenger. Unfortunately, the messengers have to go through enemy territory and may captured.

How can the two generals agree about the time of the attack?

One could propose a time to the other by sending a messenger and waiting for the response. But what if there was no response? Could the messenger have been captured? Could the messenger be injured and take longer than expected? Should the general send another messenger?

The problem is not trivial.

Figure 10.2: *Generals Approaching the Castle*

No matter how many messengers are sent, neither general can be sure that the other army will attack the city at the correct time. Sending more messengers can increase the chances of successful coordination, but the chances can never reach 100%.

In distributed systems, this problem is known as the two-general problem. Generals are like nodes in a distributed system. To make the system work, the nodes should coordinate with each other. However, a node can fail at any time due to a fault.

While starting, every developer feels they will build a fault-free system. Of course, it was a naive pursuit that was bound to fail. You cannot build a system completely free from faults. The larger the distributed systems, the higher the probability of faults. A fault-tolerant system can continue to operate despite the presence of one or more faults. The trick is to make the nodes in the system coordinate with each other in the presence of failures.

Scalability[4]

Scalability often commands the greatest attention from system designers when building distributed systems. At a basic level, scalability is a measure of a system's performance with increasing load.

But how do we measure the **performance** and load of a distributed system?

For performance, we can use two excellent parameters: throughput and response time. Throughput denotes the number of operations processed per second. Response time is the total time elapsed between a client request and response.

Measurement of system load is more specific to the system use case. For example, system load can be measured as the number of concurrent users, communication links, or the ratio of writes to reads. Performance and load are inherently tied to each other. As the load increases, it will eventually reach the system's capacity. The capacity may depend on the physical limitations of the system, such as:

- The memory size or the clock cycle of the node
- Bandwidth and latency of the network links

When the load reaches capacity, the system's performance either plateaus or worsens.

If the load on the system continues to grow beyond the capacity, it will eventually hit a point where most operations fail or time out. Throughput goes down and response times rocket upwards. At this point, the system is no longer scalable. See the following graph that shows this situation.

Point where most operations fail or time out

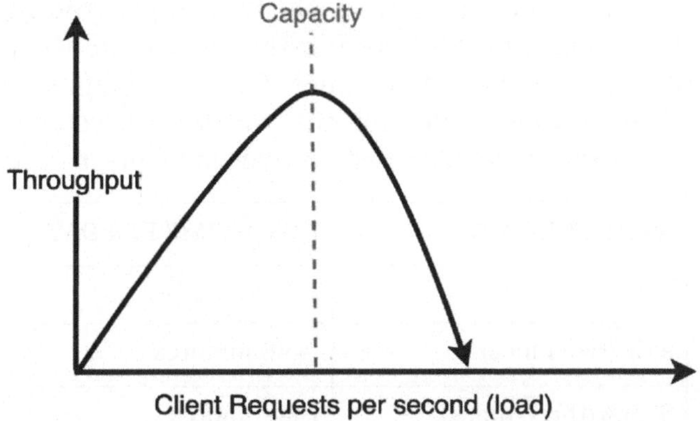

Figure 10.3: *Performance Evaluation*

How Do We Make the System Scalable?

If the load exceeding capacity is the cause of performance degradation, we can make a system scalable by increasing the capacity. A quick and easy way to increase capacity is by buying more expensive hardware with better performance metrics. This approach is known as scaling up.

Though it sounds good on paper, this approach will hit a brick wall sooner or later. The more sustainable approach is scaling out by adding more machines to the system.

Resiliency [4]

Failures are pretty common in a distributed system due to several reasons:

- Firstly, scaling out increases the probability of failure. Since every component in the system has an inherent probability of failing, the addition of more pieces compounds the overall chances of failure.

- Second, more components mean a higher number of operations, which increases the absolute number of failures in the system.
- Lastly, failures are not independent. Failure of one component increases the probability of failures in other components.

When a system is operating at scale, any failure that can happen will eventually happen. An ideal distributed system must embrace failures and behave in a resilient manner. A system is considered resilient when it continues to do its job even when failures occur.

We can use several techniques such as redundancy and self-healing mechanisms, to increase a system's resiliency. However, this is not a zero-sum game. No distributed system can be 100% resilient. At some point, failures dent the system's availability. Availability is an important metric; It is amount of time the application can serve requests divided by the duration of the period measured.

Organizations often market their system's availability in percentage terms using the concept of nines. Three nines (99.9%) are mostly considered acceptable for a large number of systems. Anything above four nines (99.99%) is highly available. An even higher number of nines may be needed for mission-critical systems. Here is a handy chart that demonstrates the availability percentages in terms of actual downtime.

AVAILABILITY %	DOWNTIME PER DAY
90% (one nine)	2.40 hours
99% (two nines)	14.40 minutes
99.9% (three nines)	1.44 minutes
99.99% (four nines)	8.64 seconds
99.999% (five nines)	864 milliseconds

***Table 10.1**: Availability percentages vs. actual downtime*

Operations [4]

Among the other challenges, operating a distributed system is probably the most difficult. Also, the most significant innovations are happening in this area. Like any other software system, distributed systems also need to go through the software development lifecycle of development, testing, deployment, and operations.

However, gone are the days when developing a piece of software and its operations were done by two separate teams or departments. The complexity of distributed systems has given rise to DevOps. Now, the same team that designs and develops a system is expected to operate it in a production environment. This creates several difficulties for the development team that they ignored earlier.

- New deployments need to be rolled out continuously in a safe manner
- Systems need to be observable
- Alerts need to be fired when service-level objectives are at risk of being breached

There is a positive side to this change as well. There is no better way for developers to find out where a system is falling short than by providing on-call support.

Advantages of Distributed Operating System

Following are the advantages of using the distributed operating system:

- **Data Sharing:** Distributed systems allow one component to share data with other components in the system easily. This is possible because, in a distributed system, nodes are connected for collaboration.
- **Ability of extension:** Scalability means changing a particular system's size and scope. The distributed system offers unparalleled scalability as we can easily add more nodes to a particular network.
- **Error management:** A distributed system does not depend on a single node. Thus, even in the event of a malfunction of one node, the other nodes continue to function normally. So the system is intact.
- **Reliability:** For a system to be reliable, it must handle errors efficiently. Since distributed systems easily handle system problems, they are quite reliable.
- **Improved scalability**: Distributed computing clusters are a great way to scale your business. They use a 'scale-out architecture,' which makes adding new hardware easier as load increases.
- **Enhanced performance**: This model uses 'parallelism' for the divide-and-conquer approach. In other words, all computers in the cluster simultaneously handle a subset of the overall task. Therefore, as the load increases, businesses can add more computers and optimize overall performance.
- **Cost-effectiveness:** The cost efficiency of a distributed system depends on its latency, response time, bandwidth, and throughput. Distributed systems work toward a common goal of delivering high performance by minimizing latency and enhancing response time and throughput. They achieve this goal using low-cost commodity hardware to ensure zero data loss, making initial deployments and cluster expansions easy.
- **Effective:** Distributed systems are efficient because they involve many computers, saving users time. In addition, they can provide superior performance compared to centralized systems.

- **Less delay:** In today's world, time is a major constraint for salespeople and users. The distributed system provides low latency. Let' us take the example of a user who uses the Internet and loads a web page. The system ensures that the button closest to the user performs the loading task to save time.
- **Other benefits:** The following are the advantages of utilizing a distributed operating system:

The real-time applications and resource sharing are made possible by connecting two or more systems.

The distributed system can be scaled to accommodate business demands, increasing its adaptability and effectiveness.

Control and monitoring of the system are made easier by the possibility of central management. Big data's ascent and the demand for real-time applications have led to a growing popularity for distributed systems.

Disadvantages of Distributed Operating System

The following are the drawbacks of utilizing a distributed operating system:

- **Security issues:** Security issues often arise in many software and hardware devices. The same is true for distributed systems. Such security risks occur because there are many nodes and connections in an open system environment, which makes it challenging to provide adequate security.
- **High setup cost:** Installation and initial configuration costs are high due to the wide variety of hardware and software devices. Other maintenance costs associated with the system add up to the total cost, making it even more expensive.
- **Lost data:** There may be cases where the data sent from one node to another may be lost halfway through its journey from the source node to the destination node. This leads to losing some important messages, which is detrimental to the business.
- **Difficult to manage:** The hardware and software of a distributed system are quite complex. The maintenance and operation of hardware components for enterprises is very complex. In addition, the complexity of software forces companies to pay special attention to software components.
- **Overload problem:** Overload problems can arise in the system if all nodes in the distributed system try to send data at a certain time.
- **Other disadvantages**: A distributed operating system can also be more challenging to administer and manage, which is one of its drawbacks.

The increased number of systems and points of failure increases the likelihood of system failure. A distributed system can be expensive to set up and maintain.

Note: *Despite these drawbacks, a distributed system typically has more benefits than drawbacks.*

As big data and real-time applications become more prevalent, distributed systems are growing in popularity and will remain crucial to computing in the future. In conclusion, if used appropriately, a distributed operating system such as Linux can save time and money. Some requirements include secure IP addresses and restricted accessibility from specific client devices.

Architecture of Distributed Systems

Cloud-based software, the backbone of distributed systems, is a complicated network of servers that anyone with an internet connection can access. In a distributed system, components and connectors arrange themselves to ease communication. Components are modules with well-defined interfaces that can be replaced or reused. Similarly, connectors are communication links between modules that mediate coordination or cooperation among components.

A distributed system is broadly divided into two essential concepts: **software** architecture (further divided into layered architecture, object-based architecture, data-centered architecture, and event-based architecture) and **system architecture** (further divided into client-server architecture and peer-to-peer architecture).

Let us understand each of these architecture systems in detail:

Software Architecture

Software architecture is the logical organization of software components and their interaction with other structures. It is at a lower level than system architecture and focuses entirely on components; for example, the web front end of an e commerce system is a component.

The four main architectural styles of distributed systems in software components entail:

Layered Architecture

Layered architecture provides a modular approach to software. Separating each component makes it more efficient. For example, the Open Systems Interconnection (OSI) model uses a layered architecture for better results. It does this by contacting layers in sequence, which allows it to reach its goal. In some instances, the implementation of layered architecture is in cross-layer coordination. Under cross-layer, the interactions can skip any adjacent layer until it fulfills the request and provides better performance results.

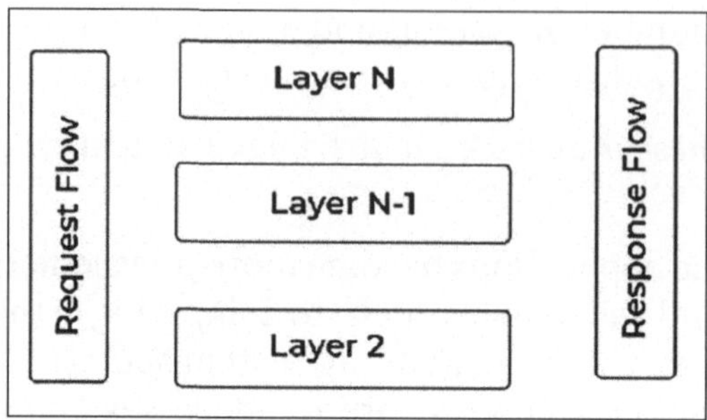

Figure 10.4: *Layered Architecture*

Layered architecture is a type of software that separates components into units. A request goes from the top down, and the response goes from the bottom up. The advantage of layered architecture is that it keeps things orderly and modifies each layer independently without affecting the rest of the system.

Object-Based Architecture

Object-based architecture centers around an arrangement of loosely coupled objects with no specific architecture, such as layers. Unlike layered architecture, object-based architecture does not have to follow any steps in a sequence. Each component is an object, and all the objects can interact through an interface (or connector). Under object-based architecture, such interactions between components can happen through a direct method call.

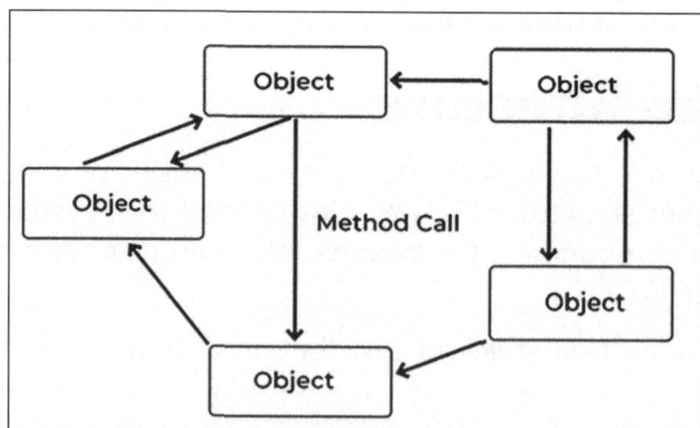

Figure 10.5: *Object-based Architecture*

At its core, communication between objects happens through method invocations, often called remote procedure calls (RPC). Popular RPC systems include Java RMI, Web Services, and REST API Calls. The primary design consideration of these architectures is that they are less structured. Here, component equals object, and connector equals RPC or RMI.

Data-Centered Architecture

Data-centered architecture works on a central data repository, either active or passive. Like most producer-consumer scenarios, the producer (business) produces items to the common data store, and the consumer (individual) can request data from it. Sometimes, this central repository can be just a simple database.

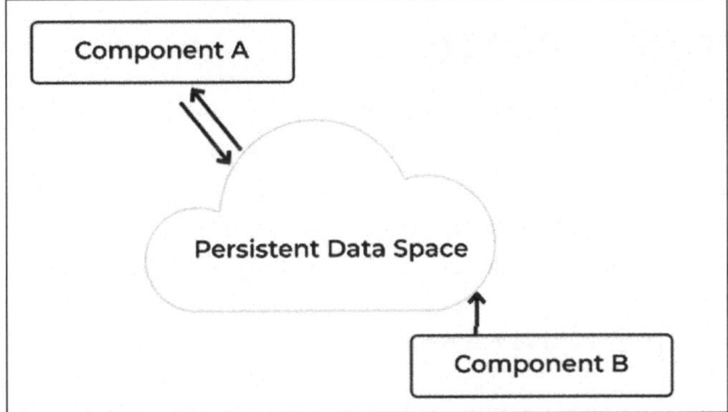

Figure 10.6: *Data-centered Architecture*

All communication between objects happens through a data storage system in a data-centered system. It supports its stores' components with a persistent storage space such as an SQL database, and the system stores all the nodes in this data storage.

Event-Based Architecture

In event-based architecture, the entire communication is through events. When an event occurs, the system gets the notification. This means that anyone who receives this event will also be notified and have access to information. Sometimes, these events are data, and, at other times, they are URLs to resources. Also, the receiver can process the information they receive and act accordingly.

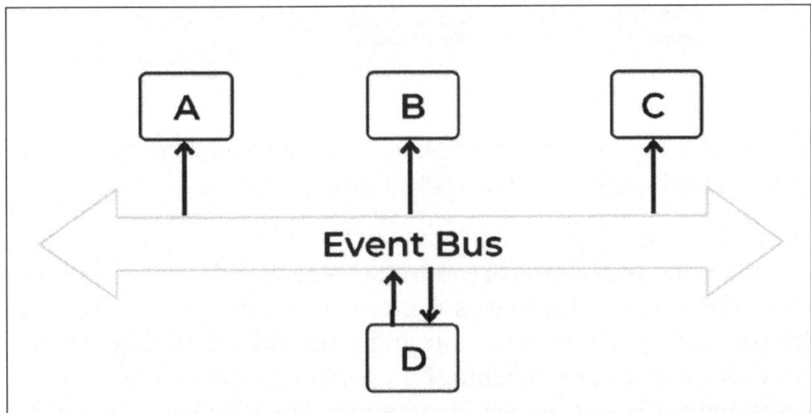

Figure 10.7: *Event-Based Architecture*

One significant advantage of event-based architecture is that the components are loosely coupled. Eventually, it is easy to add, remove, and modify them. To better understand this, think of publisher-subscriber systems, enterprise services buses, or akka.io. One advantage of event-based architecture is allowing heterogeneous components to communicate with the bus, regardless of their communication protocols.

System Architecture

System-level architecture focuses on the entire system and the placement of components of a distributed system across multiple machines. The client-server architecture and peer-to-peer architecture are the two major system-level architectures that hold significance today. An example would be an e-commerce system that contains a service layer, a database, and a web front.

Client-Server Architecture

As the name suggests, client-server architecture consists of a client and a server. The server is where all the work processes are, while the client is where the user interacts with the service and other resources (remote server). The client can then request from the server, and the server will respond accordingly. Typically, only one server handles the remote side; however, using multiple servers ensures total safety.

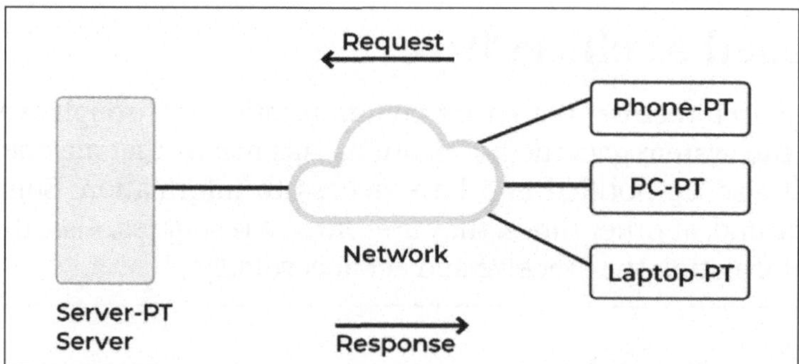

Figure 10.8: *Client-server Architecture*

PT in Server commonly refers to Permission Table, a crucial component in managing user access and permissions within a system or application.

Client-server architecture has one standard design feature: centralized security. Data such as usernames and passwords are stored in a secure database for any server user to access this information. This makes it more stable and secure than peer-to-peer. This stability comes from client-server architecture, where the security database can allow resource usage in a more meaningful way. The system is much more stable and secure, even though it is not as fast as a server. The disadvantages of a distributed system are its single point of failure and not being as scalable as a server.

Peer-to-Peer (P2P) Architecture

A peer-to-peer network, also called a P2P network, works on the concept of no central control in a distributed system. A node can either act as a client or server at any given time once it joins the network. A node that requests something is called a client, and one that provides something is called a server. In general, each node is called a peer.

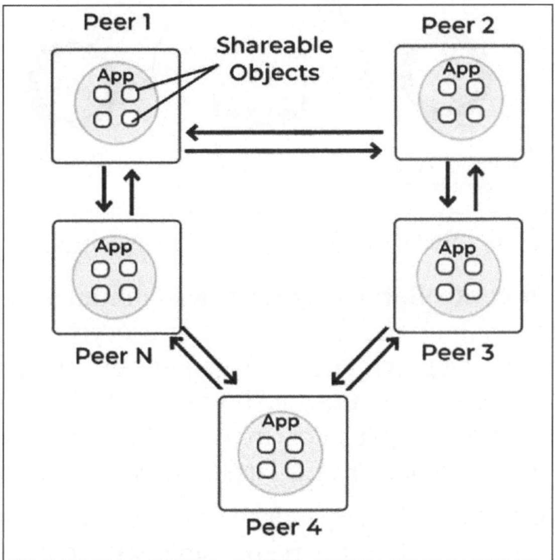

Figure 10.9: *Peer-to-Peer Architecture*

If a new node wishes to provide services, it can do so in two ways. One way is to register with a centralized lookup server, which will then direct the node to the service provider. The other way is for the node to broadcast its service request to every other node in the network, and whichever node responds will provide the requested service.

P2P networks of today have three separate sections:

- **Structured P2P:** The nodes in structured P2P follow a predefined distributed data structure
- **Unstructured P2P:** The nodes in unstructured P2P randomly select their neighbors
- **Hybrid P2P**: In a hybrid P2P, some nodes have unique functions appointed to them in an orderly manner

Key Components of a Distributed System

The three basic components of a distributed system include the primary system controller, system data store, and database. In a non-clustered environment, optional components consist of user interfaces and secondary controllers.

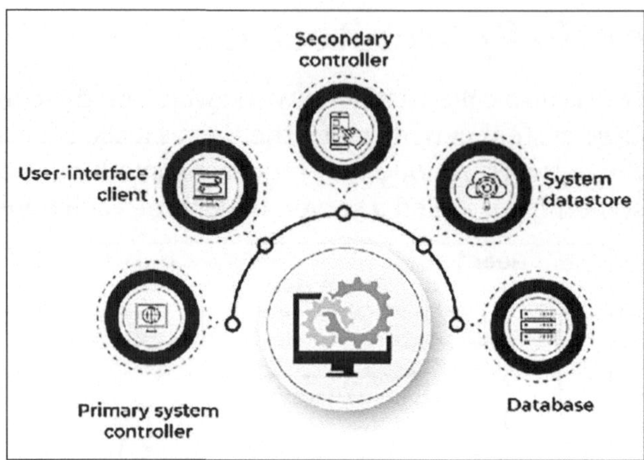

Figure 10.10: *Main Components of a Distributed System*

- **Primary system controller:** The primary system controller is the only controller in a distributed system and keeps track of everything. It is also responsible for controlling the dispatch and management of server requests throughout the system. The executive and mailbox services are installed automatically on the primary system controller. In a non-clustered environment, optional components consist of a user interface and secondary controllers.
- **Secondary controller:** The secondary controller is a process controller or a communications controller. It is responsible for regulating the flow of server processing requests and managing the system's translation load. It also governs communication between the system and VANs or trading partners.
- **User-interface client:** The user interface client is an additional element in the system that provides users with important system information. This is not part of the clustered environment and does not operate on the same machines as the controller. It provides functions that are necessary to monitor and control the system.
- **System datastore:** Each system has only one data store for all shared data. The data store is usually on the disk vault, whether clustered or not. For non-clustered systems, this can be on one machine or distributed across several devices, but all these computers must have access to this data store.
- **Database:** In a distributed system, a relational database stores all data. Once the data store locates the data, it shares it with multiple users. Relational databases can be found in all data systems and allow multiple users to use the same information simultaneously.

Examples of a Distributed System

When processing power is scarce, or when a system encounters unpredictable changes, distributed systems are ideal and help balance the workload. Hence, distributed systems have boundless use cases, varying from electronic banking systems to multiplayer online games. Let us check out more explicit instances of distributed systems:

- **Networks:** The 1970s saw the invention of Ethernet and LAN (local area networks), which enabled computers to connect in the same area. Peer-to-peer networks developed, and e-mail and the internet continue to be the biggest examples of distributed systems.
- **Telecommunication networks:** Telephone and cellular networks are other examples of peer-to-peer networks. Telephone networks started as an early example of distributed communication, and cellular networks are also a form of distributed communication systems. With the implementation of Voice over Internet (VoIP) communication systems, they grow more complex as distributed communication networks.
- **Real-time systems:** Real-time systems are not limited to specific industries. These systems can be used and seen throughout the world in the airline, ride-sharing, logistics, financial trading, massively multiplayer online games (MMOGs), and e-commerce industries. The focus in such systems is on the correspondence and processing of information with the need to convey data promptly to plenty of users who have an expressed interest in such data.
- **Parallel processors:** Parallel computing splits specific tasks among multiple processors. This, in turn, creates pieces to put together and form an extensive computational task. Previously, parallel computing only focused on running software on multiple threads or processors accessing the same data and memory. As operating systems became more prevalent, they too fell into the category of parallel processing.
- **Distributed database systems:** A distributed database is spread across numerous servers or regions. Data can be replicated across several platforms. A distributed database system can be either homogeneous or heterogeneous in nature. A homogeneous distributed database uses the same database management system and data model across all systems.

  Adding new nodes and locations makes it easier to control and scale performance. On the other hand, multiple data models and database management systems are possible with heterogeneous distributed databases. Gateways translate data across nodes and are typically created due to the merger of two or more applications or systems.
- **Distributed artificial intelligence:** Distributed artificial intelligence is one of the many approaches of artificial intelligence that is used for learning and entails complex learning algorithms, large-scale systems, and decision-making. It requires a large set of computational data points located in various locations.

A few real-world examples of distributed systems include:

- Video-rendering systems
- Scientific computing
- Airline and hotel reservation
- Cryptocurrency processors such as Bitcoin
- P2P file-sharing such as BitTorrent
- Multiplayer video games
- E-learning applications
- Distributed supply chains such as Amazon

Three Guarantees of Distributed System: CAP Theorem

A distributed operating system can also be more challenging to administer and manage, which is one of its drawbacks. The increased number of systems and points of failure increases the likelihood of system failure.

A distributed system can be expensive to set up and maintain.

Note: *Despite these drawbacks, a distributed system typically has more benefits than drawbacks. As big data and real-time applications become more prevalent, distributed systems are growing in popularity and will remain crucial to computing in the future.*

In conclusion, if used appropriately, a distributed operating system such as Linux can save time and money. Some requirements include secure IP addresses and restricted accessibility from specific client devices.

In general, the ability of a database to handle transactions concurrently while maintaining data integrity is referred to as eventual consistency. In short, inconsistency is the assurance that a READ will return the outcome of the most recent successful WRITE. Although this seems straightforward, it is very challenging to provide such a guarantee in a globally distributed database topology, which consists of several clusters with numerous nodes each. "ACID guarantees" are typically offered by relational databases that support "*strong consistency*."

The acronym ACID is intended to encompass the fundamental components of a highly consistent database. ACID compliance is a complicated and frequently disputed topic.

Its components are as follows:

- **Atomicity**: If a transaction fails at any point, the entire operation rolls back
- **Consistency:** The database remains structurally sound with every transaction

- **Isolation:** Each transaction is independent of any other transaction
- **Durability:** All transaction results are permanently preserved. Actually, confirming vendor consistency claims is the focus of one well-liked analytical framework, the Jepsen tests. Because of this, databases that adhere to ACID standards are typically slow, costly to operate and maintain, and challenging to scale. Notably, certain RDBMS systems allow for the relaxation of ACID guarantees. This drawback is shared by all SQL databases, though they differ in how much they adhere to ACID. Implementing distributed, resilient SQL database deployments is extremely costly and challenging.

Conclusion

In this chapter, we have paid attention to real-life examples of distributed operating systems and their key components of a distributed system. We learned about types of DOS and challenges we face in building distributed systems. We understood the advantages/disadvantages of distributed operating systems. Then we learned about the architecture of distributed systems: Software Architecture and System Architecture, giving examples of a distributed system. At last, we learned about CAP Theorem Definition distributed system.

In the next chapter, we are going to explore on real-time operating systems and embedded operating systems.

Questions

1. What is a distributed system?
2. Explain the concept of distributed systems.
3. What are the key challenges in building distributed systems?
4. What is the CAP theorem? Explain its implications.
5. What is consistency in distributed systems?
6. Explain the difference between strong consistency, eventual consistency, and eventual strong consistency.
7. What is the difference between horizontal and vertical scaling?
8. Explain ACID properties and how they apply to distributed systems.
9. What is the difference between a distributed transaction and a local transaction?
10. What are some common concurrency control mechanisms in distributed systems?

11. Explain the concept of distributed consensus. What are some algorithms used for achieving consensus?
12. What is the role of leader election in distributed systems?
13. What is a distributed lock and why is it necessary?
14. What is sharding, and how does it help in distributed databases?
15. What is the difference between synchronous and asynchronous communication in distributed systems?
16. What are message queues, and how are they used in distributed systems?
17. Explain the concept of eventual message delivery.
18. What is the difference between a distributed system and a decentralized system?

Multiple Choice Questions

1. In a distributed system, each processor has its own ____________
    a. local memory
    b. clock
    c. both local memory and clock
    d. none of the mentioned
2. If one site fails in the distributed system then ____________
    a. the remaining sites can continue operating
    b. all the sites will stop working
    c. directly connected sites will stop working
    d. none of the mentioned
3. Network operating system runs on ____________
    a. server
    b. every system in the network
    c. both the server and every system in the network
    d. none of the mentioned
4. Which technique is based on compile-time program transformation for accessing remote data in a distributed-memory parallel system?
    a. cache coherence scheme
    b. computation migration

   c. remote procedure call
   d. message passing
5. The logical extension of computation migration is ____________
   a. process migration
   b. system migration
   c. thread migration
   d. data migration
6. Processes on the remote systems are identified by ____________
   a. host ID
   b. hostname and identifier
   c. identifier
   d. process ID
7. Which routing technique is used in a distributed system?
   a. fixed routing
   b. virtual routing
   c. dynamic routing
   d. all of the mentioned
8. In distributed systems, link and site failure is detected by ____________
   a. polling
   b. handshaking
   c. token passing
   d. none of the mentioned
9. The capability of a system to adapt to the increased service load is called ____________
   a. scalability
   b. tolerance
   c. capacity
   d. none of the mentioned
10. Internet provides ________ for remote login.
   a. telnet
   b. http
   c. ftp
   d. rpc

Answers

1. c
2. a
3. a
4. b
5. a
6. b
7. d
8. b
9. a
10. a

References

[1] Distributed Operating System, Definition, Types and ...by toppr.com, https://www.toppr.com › guides › computer-fundamentals

[2] Distributed Operating System, Shiksha Online,https://www.shiksha.com/online-courses/articles/distributed-operating-system/, Updated on Mar 20, 2024

[3] What Are Distributed Systems? Architecture Types, Key Components, and Examples, Remya Mohanan, https://www.spiceworks.com/tech/cloud/articles/what-is-distributed-computing/

[4] 5 Challenges in Building Distributed Systems, Saurabh Dashora, https://dzone.com/articles/5-challenges-in-building-distributed-systems

Chapter 11
Real-Time Operating Systems and Embedded Operating Systems

Introduction

In this chapter, we will have an overview of real-time operating system (RTOS) i/c their types, basic functions, working with them, and their architecture. RTOs operating systems are either employed on huge physical systems or in tiny Embedded systems. These are QNX Embedded Operating System, INTEGRITY OS, or VxWorks and we will move on to development of embedded applications with Qt and Felgo.

Structure

In this chapter, the following topics will be covered:

- Overview of Real-Time Operating System (RTOS)
- Working with Real-Time Operating System
- Basic Functionalities of an RTOS
- RTOS Architectures
- Embedded Operating Systems
- Tools and Ecosystem of Embedded Linux Development
- QNX-Embedded Operating System
- Introduction to INTEGRITY OS
- Embedded Operating System – VxWorks

- Embedded Operating System Comparison Table
- Development of Embedded Applications with Qt and Felgo
- Real-Time System Examples
- The Changing World of Embedded and Real-Time Operating Systems [4]
- Factors for Choosing a Commercial RTOS

Overview of Real-Time Operating System (RTOS)

When we hear the word operating system, what comes first to our mind is the operating system used in laptops and computers. Generally, we use different operating systems, such as Windows XP, Linux, Ubuntu, Windows 7, 8.8.1, and 10. The operating systems used in the smartphones are KitKat, Jellybean, Marshmallow, and Nougat. In a digital electronic device, there is some sort of operating system that is developed by the microcontroller program. Although various operating system types can be developed by microcontrollers, here we have focused on the real-time operating system.

Development of Embedded Applications with Qt and FelgoRTOS is an operating system; it is the brain of the real-time system and responds to inputs immediately. In the RTOS, the task will be completed by the specified time and it responds in a predictable way to unpredictable events. The structure of the RTOS is shown as follows:

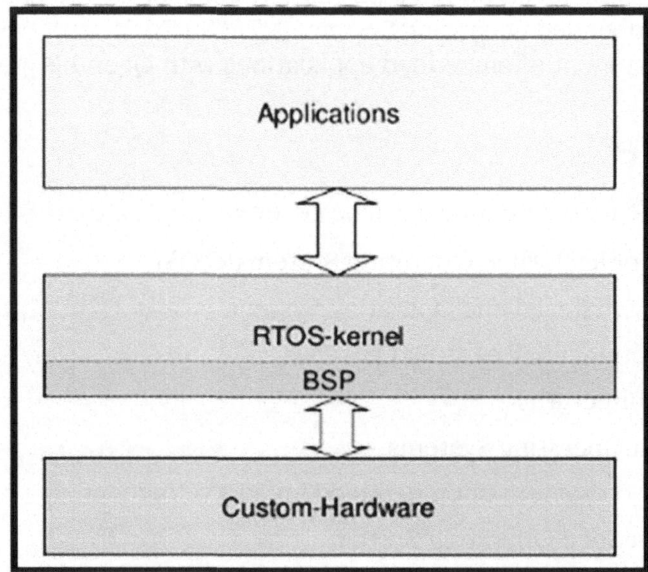

Figure 11.1: *Structure of RTOS*

There are three different types of RTOS, they are:

- Soft real-time operating system
- Hard real-time operating system
- Firm real-time operating system

Soft Real-Time Operating System

The soft real-time operating system has certain deadlines that may be missed, and they will take the action at a time t=0+. The soft real-time operating system is a type of OS and is not constrained to extreme rules. The critical time of this operating system is delayed to some extent. The digital camera, mobile phones and online data, and so on are a few examples of this operating system..

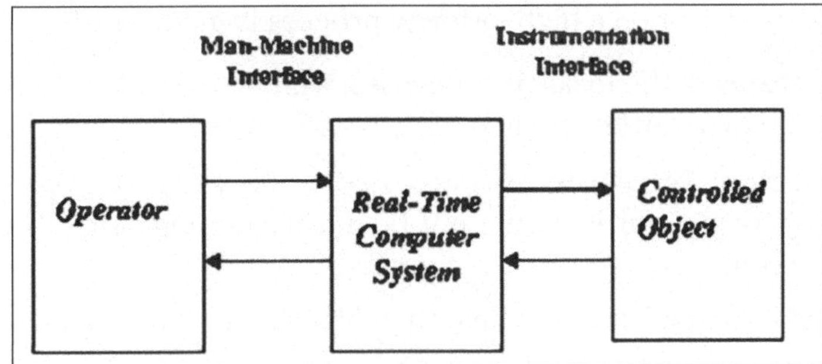

Figure 11.2: *Soft Real-Time Operating System*

Hard Real-Time Operating System

This is also a type of OS, and it is predicted by a deadline. The predicted deadlines will react at a time t = 0. Some examples of this operating system are airbag control in cars, anti-lock brake, engine control system, and so on.

Firm Real-Time Operating System

In the firm real-time, an operating system has certain time constraints; they are not strict and may cause undesired effects. A visual inspection in industrial automation is an example of this operating system.

Working with Real-Time Operating Systems

There are different types of basic functionalities of an RTOS. They are:

- Priority-based scheduler

- System clock interrupt routine
- Deterministic behavior
- Synchronization and messaging
- RTOS service

Priority-Based Scheduler

In the priority-based scheduler, most RTOS is between 32 and 256 possible priorities for the individual tasks or processes. This scheduler will run the process with the highest priority. If the task runs on the CPU, the next highest priority task runs and continues the process.

In the system, the highest priority process will have the CPU. If the original task is preempted by the new one, then a high-priority process is made ready.

There are **three states** of the tasks or processes, which are ready to run, and the other one is blocked. The description of each state is as follows:

- **Ready to Run:** The ready to run is said to be when the process has all the resources to run, but it should not be in the running state. Then it is called a ready-to-run.
- **Running:** If the task is executing, then it is said to have a running state.
- **Blocked:** In this state, if it does not have the enough resources to run, then it is sent to the blocked state.

Three techniques are modified to schedule the task. They are:

- **Cooperating Scheduling:** In this type of scheduling, the task will run until the execution is completed
- **Round-Robin Scheduling:** In this scheduling, each process is assigned a fixed time slot, and the process needs to complete its execution, or else the task loses its flow and data generation.
- **Preemptive Scheduling:** The preemptive scheduling involves priority time-dependent time allocation. In general, 256 priority levels are used, and each task has a unique priority level. There are some systems that support the higher-priority level, and multiple tasks that have some priorities.

System Clock Interrupt Routine

To perform the time-sensitive operation, the RTOS will provide some sort of system clock. If there is a 1ms system clock, then you have to complete the task in 50 ms. Usually, there is an API that follows you to say, "*In 50ms wake me up*". Hence the task would be in a sleeping position until the RTOS will wake you up. We have two notices that the woken-up will not ensure it runs exactly at that time, it depends on the priority, and if the higher priority is running currently, it would be delayed.

Deterministic Behavior

The RTOS goes to great lengths to ensure that whether you have taken 100 tasks or 10 tasks; it does not make any difference in the distance to switch context and determines the next highest priority task. In the prime area, deterministic RTOS does the interrupt handling. When the interrupt line is signalled them, the RTOS immediately takes the action of the correct interrupt service routine, and interrupt is handled without any delay.

We must note that the project developers will write the hardware specific ISR's. Before, the RTOS gave the ISR's for the serial ports and system clocks; it may be a networking hardware, but if there is anything specialized, such as pacemaker signals, actuators, and so on, are not be a part of the RTOS.

This is all about gross generalizations, and there is a large variety of implementations in the RTOS. Some of the RTOS are operated differently, and the preceding description is capable for the large portion of existing RTOS.

Synchronization and Messaging

The synchronization and messaging provide the communication between the task of one system to another system, and the messaging services are as follows. To synchronize the internal activities the event flag is used and to send the text messages we can use in the mailbox, pipes, and message queues. In the common data areas, the semaphores are used.

RTOS Service

The most important part of the operating system is the kernel. To monitor the hardware, the task should be relieved, and the kernel manages and allocates the resources. If the task cannot obtain the CPU's attention for every time, then there are some other services provided by the kernel. The following are:

- Time services
- Interrupt handling services
- Device management services
- Memory management services
- Input-output services

Benefits of RTOS

- When all devices and resources are idle, the RTOS maximizes system consumption and increases output
- Due to the RTOS's error-free nature, errors cannot occur while a task is run
- In this system, memory allocation is the easiest to handle; there is very little shifting time in this kind of system
- Transport and other embedded systems use the Real-Time Operating System (RTOS) due to its small program size

Basic Functions of RTOS

RTOS is a specialized operating system made for highly reliable and precisely timed applications. Unlike general-purpose OSs, which execute several tasks at once, RTOSes are single-tasked.

Task scheduling is one of a Real-Time Operating System's (RTOS) primary features. It arranges tasks to guarantee that they are carried out in a predictable and deterministic way.

- **Runtime operations** include the ability to create, delete, suspend, and modify the priority of tasks.
- **Handling interrupts**: An interrupt is a signal that alerts the processor to a situation that needs to be addressed right away.
- **The interrupt handler system:** RTOS manages these signals. To handle the interrupt, RTOS can pause the running task.
- **Memory management:** Memory blocks are allocated or released by the RTOS as needed.
- **Security:** RTOS maintains process separation to prevent interruptions between tasks. It facilitates the ability to communicate and synchronize between different tasks as well as device driver management.

Characteristics of an RTOS [2]

- **Determinism**: Repeating an input will result in the same output.
- **High performance:** RTO systems operate quickly and nimbly, frequently finishing tasks in a fraction of the time required by a traditional operating system.
- **Safety and security**: RTOs are commonly used in critical systems, such as flight controllers or robotics, where failures could have disastrous effects. They need more dependable safety features and higher security standards to protect people nearby.

- **Schedules:** The tasks based on priorities are prioritized, meaning that tasks with higher priorities are carried out first, and tasks with lower priorities are carried out later. This implies that an RTOS will always carry out the task that is most crucial.
- **Minimal Footprint**: RTOSes are significantly smaller than their bulky general OS counterparts. Windows 10, for instance, uses about 20 GB when post-install updates are enabled. Conversely, VxWorks® has a file size in the low single-digit megabytes, about 20,000 times less.

RTOS Architectures

Aside from the minute details, two prevailing design philosophies affect RTOS design: monolithic kernel versus microkernel. These systems are differentiated by their structure; monolithic kernel systems run in a single space, while microkernel systems compartmentalize different components of the architecture.

- **Microkernel Systems:** In microkernel architecture, components are stored in separate "*rooms*," which are independent of one another but share a similar space. A room can be renovated without impacting those around it. However, to get from one to another, you must step out through the doorway and head down the hall, which takes time. Any action has to return to the kernel before it can move to the component it references, meaning some operations take much longer than necessary.
- **Monolithic Systems:** In a monolithic system, there are no "*walls*" between the rooms; you can step from one to another much more quickly. Rather than implementing a small kernel, monolithic kernels provide services of their own as well as regulate those of other areas. With exceptions, operations are executed in the kernel space, removing the recurrent need to return to the kernel and improving speed and performance.

Embedded Operating Systems

An embedded system is a device with a computer designed for a specific purpose. To achieve that, the device needs an operating system that can respond fast and is prepared to keep working in any event. That is why we cannot rely on a general-use OS but an embedded operating system.

An embedded operating system is an OS designed and optimized to:

- Improve the efficiency of managing the hardware resources
- Reduce response times specifically for the task the device was created for
- Some examples of embedded systems are industrial robots, smart devices, IoT machines, drones, medical systems, video game consoles, and many others.

- The related hardware has to be miniature as they are to be embedded.

Operating Systems for General-Use versus Embedded Systems[3]

As mentioned before, the embedded operating system differs from other operating systems in many cases, as detailed in the following table.

Features	**Embedded Operating Systems**	**General-use Operating Systems**
Primary Goal	Run a single application	Run many applications
App Distribution	Typically, a single image containing the system and the application is distributed	The applications and the operating system are distributed separately
Architecture	Designed for a specific purpose	Designed for general use to solve all kinds of tasks
Processing	MCUs and CPUs	

***Table 11.1**: Operating Systems for General Use vs Embedded Systems*

The Difference Between OS and RTOS

Another thing you have to take into account is how fast your application has to react to an event. If you require that the system reserves resources to execute our task in real-time, or, in other words, at the moment an event occurs, it will be a good idea to choose a **real-time operating system (RTOS)**.

An RTOS is an operating system that manages resources in such a way that it processes data at the time it is inputted into the system, lowering the processing time.

One use case for RTOS is in self-driven vehicles. In these vehicles, we have real-time inputs that we must process fast to avoid a car crash and ensure the safety of the passengers.

Types of Embedded Operating Systems [3]

There are three types of Linux-based RTOS: *Hard RTOS, Firm RTOS, and Soft RTOS.*

- **Hard RTOS:** If any task misses a deadline, even if only once, it generates a total system failure. Delivering results in real-time is a hard requirement for the system.
- **Firm RTOS**: If tasks infrequently miss the deadline, it may degrade the system quality. In case the system frequently fails to deliver in time, it cannot operate correctly.

- **Soft RTOS:** The system can still operate correctly if a deadline is missed. If a task takes too long, then the quality of the service is degraded.

Choosing a real-time system will depend on how fast your system must react. For example, a Hard RTOS is used for medical systems, and soft RTOS is used in video streaming such as Chromecast.

Now that you know basic concepts about embedded operating systems, let us see the different choices you have at the moment to start an embedded system project.

Mastering Embedded Linux Programming[3]

Embedded Linux refers to the use of Linux in robots, routers, prototyping boards, or any electronic device that possesses a microcontroller (MCU). Embedded Linux differs from Linux mainly in size, because a great part of the system is not required for your embedded device.

With Embedded Linux, you have a variety of options. You can build the system image yourself using Yocto Project or Buildroot. You can also use a prebuilt image such as OpenWrt if you are working with routers or Ångström if you have a prototyping board such as BeagleBoard or Raspberry Pi. Also, you can use a more known distribution, such as Debian, Ubuntu, or even Android (please note that Android is not a Linux distribution but uses Linux as its kernel). Additionally, depending on what board you choose to use, you may have a Linux image already being distributed by the manufacturer.

If we need an operating system with enough flexibility and customization options, then we can choose the Linux version that fits our requirements better.

Security, Performance, and Features of Embedded Linux Development

You can achieve great performance with Embedded Linux. However, due to a variety of options, it will depend on what distribution you choose or how you desire to build it. Because of that, Linux will be a great place to learn how to tweak things around and get a customized experience.

In terms of security, Linux is a very secure OS. But still, if you choose to build it, you will have to configure it yourself in most cases, especially if you are planning to implement networking capabilities into your application.

Some features that embedded Linux distributions share are:

- Free license and open-source software
- Support around 150 processors

- True multitasking
- Real-time kernel
- Support for many file systems
- Protected mode so programs or users cannot access unauthorized areas.
- Networking with TCP/IP and other protocols.
- Multi-user capability

Tools and Ecosystem of Embedded Linux Development [3]

You can find a large set of toolkits, software development kits (SDKs), and libraries for Linux. As your embedded programming language, C and C++ are used the most in embedded systems. C++ brings a lot of advantages at the time of developing an embedded application. One of them is the number of libraries that C++ has in its arsenal. Among them is Qt, which counts with great growth in the embedded system world.

Linux has a plethora of documentation and resources online for free. You can consult on forums, blogs, wikis, IRC, email lists, YouTube channels, and user groups. Also, there are big communities that can help you. If your project needs professional support, you can use the paid support service offered by the system developer, or you can choose from many companies that specialize in embedded Linux support.

Embedded Linux is used in a vast number of fields. It is safe to say that it is a general-purpose embedded OS; routers, Chromecast, and GPS are some of the devices where you can find Linux or Android. As you can see, due to the flexibility of the system, Linux can be used in any application.

Overview of Embedded Linux Development[3]

The usability and learning curve will depend on which option you choose for your operating system. If the system is not provided by the manufacturer or if you need to customize the system for your application, you will need to learn how to build a Linux operating system. You will also need to learn how to create the image of the system and how to configure and use the cross-compile toolkit for the programming tools you choose. If you are just starting in the embedded world, it is advised to choose a prebuilt distribution and start learning from there.

You can also find free versions of the system online. Thus, it is a perfect choice if you are a beginner or prototyping a device.

Regarding the licensing, Linux is free software licensed under the GPL.

Advantages of the Embedded Linux System

- Free license
- Inexpensive
- Plenty of documentation
- Offers free and paid support
- Highly customizable

Disadvantages of the Embedded Linux System

- Difficult to use
- The security must be implemented
- If you choose to build your own Linux, the performance will depend on how you configure your system

QNX-Embedded Operating System [1]

QNX is designed with critical mission situations in mind. You can create an embedded system that ensures your application completes its tasks within the time frame that is required by your project. The system is mostly utilized in the industrial, automotive, and medical fields.

QNX has a proprietary license with the option to acquire an academic license. You need to get in contact with the company to discuss your use cases and project to get a price offer.

Building Embedded Systems with QNX

Originally developed by Quantum Software Systems in the early 1980s, it is owned by Blackberry now. QNX is an embedded RTOS destined to develop critical mission systems and is a UNIX-like microkernel-based operating system.

Security, Performance, and Features of the QNX Embedded OS

QNX is a real-time embedded operating system that focuses on performance and reliability. Its features are designed to keep the embedded device running its task without flaws and on time.

Characteristics of QNX-Embedded Operating System

Some of the most relevant QNX characteristics are:

- Microkernel architecture

- Support for multicore
- Hardware optimized composition manager supporting HTML5, Kanzi, OpenGL ES, Qt 5, Storyboard, Video, and other third party HMI technologies
- Supports multi-touch input and video capture
- Secure boot
- Encrypted file system
- Self-verifying file system
- Heap, stack, and memory protection
- ASLR
- Rootless execution
- POSIX PSE52 certified
- WiFi 802.11 a/b/g/n
- Full IPv6 and IPv4 stack support
- USB 3.x, Host, Device and OTG support
- Bluetooth v4.2 Classic and Low Energy
- Support for the latest ARMv8 and x86-64 processors
- Continued 32-bit support for ARMv7 and x86

Tools and Ecosystem of the QNX Operating System

For QNX you can choose between C++, HTML5, Qt, Python, or Java as your programming language to develop your application. Also, you can port your Linux applications to QNX.

You can choose the QNX SDP and the QNX Momentics Tool Suite with Eclipse or Qt Creator as your development tool.

The QNX website offers full documentation about the operating system and the SDK. Also, you have forums and technical support programs to ask for assistance. For using the Qt framework on QNX you can find some resources on the Qt or Felgo website.

Real-life Examples of QNX System

QNX is being used in the following fields:

- Automotive
- Heavy Machinery

- Industrial Control
- Medical Devices
- Rail
- Robotics

One use example of QNX is in the Jaguar Land Rover.

Benefits of the QNX Embedded System

It is a real-time operating system that supports numerous architectures; Linux applications can be ported to QNX; it is compatible with Qt5 and Felgo.

Demerits of QNX Embedded System

The QNX Embedded System's drawbacks are that it is highly costly and has a private license.

Introduction to INTEGRITY OS [3]

INTEGRITY OS comes with an extended group of partners. Many companies use this operating system for their embedded application development. On the downside, existing reviews about the development environment state that it is hard to use compared to other tools. Still, if you are planning to develop a great scale project in your company, INTEGRITY may very well fit your needs.

The INTEGRITY OS has a private license, and the MULTI development environment costs $6000 per developer.

Integrity is a POSIX-certified RTOS developed by Green Hills. One of the most relevant aspects of this system is that it is a hard real-time operating system.

Security, Performance, and Features of the INTEGRITY OS

INTEGRITY is an RTOS for embedded devices applied in many areas such as satellites, rail trains, or industrial robots. Because of its features, its use is very extended, which makes it a very tested and stable OS.

INTEGRITY comes with:

- Wi-Fi support: WPA2, Bluetooth, 3G
- Pv4/IPv6 host and routing networking stacks
- FFS, FAT, NFS, and journaling file systems
- 2D, 3D, and OpenGL graphics

- Security and Safety certification for medical devices, railway control systems, industrial control systems, automotive, and others
- Support many architectures such as x86, Power Architecture, ARM, MIPS, OMAP, and others
- Hard real-time
- Advanced multicore support

Tools and Ecosystem of the INTEGRITY Operating System

INTEGRITY offers its very own development kit: MULTI. It supports C, C++, Embedded C++, and ADA as programming languages. Nintendo used MULTI as the development environment for the Wii U game console. There are reports from some game developers that MULTI is hard to use and time-consuming during the linking and debugging process compared to other tools.

Qt is also supported by INTEGRITY and uses MULTI's toolchain to cross-compile applications for the INTEGRITY OS.

Green Hills offers support to its customers. You can also find supporting documentation on Qt's and Felgo's website.

If you want to know how to develop your application for INTEGRITY, feel free to schedule a consulting session with one of Felgo's embedded development experts.

Real-life Examples of INTEGRITY OS

Embedded operating system - Integrity example 3

The INTEGRITY operating system is used in aerospace, automotive, military, industrial, medical, and consumer fields. Some examples of the devices that used the OS are:

- Boeing 787 Dreamliner
- F-22 Raptor Jet
- Toyota Prius
- Ford Lincoln Aviator
- Bombardier Train Control Management System
- Stryker Endoscopy Arthroscopy Resection System

INTEGRITY Operating System

INTEGRITY is a leading real-time operating system (RTOS) widely utilized across various industries. Many companies rely on INTEGRITY for developing their embedded applications due to its robust performance and extensive partner ecosystem.

The INTEGRITY operating system has the following:

Benefits

- It is a hard, real-time operating system
- It tests on a wide range of devices
- It supports a large variety of CPU and MCU architectures

Disadvantages

- It is relatively expensive
- Finding the right source for the documentation can be time-consuming
- Reports indicate that the MULTI IDE is slower and more difficult to use than its competitors

Embedded Operating System - VxWorks

VxWorks is the last operating system currently (As of 2024). It is an RTOS developed by Wind River Systems. VxWorks is a proprietary system designed for several industries like aerospace and defense, medical devices, industrial equipment, robotics, energy, transportation, network infrastructure, automotive, and consumer electronics.

- **Overview of VxWorks Embedded OS**

  The system has a simulator and continuous integration tools that will make your life easier developing for this platform. Also, it is very widely used and has a lot of resources and documentation.

  The license is private, and you must register as a customer to know the pricing. They offer a 30-day evaluation period.

- **Security, Performance, and Features of the VxWorks OS**

  Although VxWorks comes with many security features, last year ARMIS exposed 11 critical vulnerabilities of the system, including remote code execution, denial of service, information leaks, and logical flaws. ARMIS publishes a video on YouTube showing how to exploit these vulnerabilities to get unauthorized access to a network where a VxWorks device is connected.

Characteristics Features of Adopting VxWorks

VxWorks have the following characteristics:

- Support for single and multicore

- Separation between the kernel and memory-protected user-space environments
- POSIX Conformant
- Support for ARM, IA-32, Intel 64, MIPS, PowerPC, SH-4, StrongARM, xScale architectures
- Support C++ 11, 17 and 20, Python and Rust programming languages
- Support dos-FS and HRFS file systems
- General-purpose and real-time IPv4/IPv6 network stack
- Time-sensitive networking (TSN)
- EEE 1394
- Socket Controller Area Network (SocketCAN)
- USB (host, target, and OTG)
- Support for multimedia: OpenCV, OpenGL ES 1 and ES2, JPEG and PNG image libraries, PCM audio and mouse, touch, screen, and keyboard support
- Secure boot, ELF loader, and storage
- Kernel hardening
- Security events
- Built-in access controls
- Advanced user management
- Cryptography
- Arm TrustZone with OP-TEE support
- TPM 2.0 support
- Network security protocols
- GE Digital® Achilles Level II certified for compliance with IEC 62443 part 4-2
- Safety certifications for DO-178C, IEC 61508, IEC 62304, and ISO 26262

Tools and Ecosystem of the VxWorks Operating System

For VxWorks application development, there are two tools by Wind River Systems:

- The first one is Wind River Workbench, an Eclipse-based IDE.
- The second one is Wind River Simics, a simulator that will let you virtualize your hardware and make the development process easier. It also comes with continuous integration tools.

VxWorks development tools let you use the C++ 11 and C++ 14 standard, as well as cross-platform libraries, such as Boost, OpenCV, and Qt5 to create applications.

VxWorks has almost as many documentation resources as Linux. On their website, you can find many resources about how to program applications for the OS and how to apply continuous integration to your development process. You can find blogs, webinars, whitepapers, and even an academy. VxWorks also offers a great support service.

Real-life Examples of the VxWorks Embedded OS

VxWorks is used in a long list of embedded devices. One example is Honda's robot Asimo or NASA's Curiosity Rovers. These are some more fields where the embedded system has been used so far:

- **Spacecraft:** Curiosity Rover, the Mars Reconnaissance Orbiter, the Deep Impact space probe, the SpaceX Dragon, and so on.
- **Aircraft:** Airbus A400M Airlifter, Boeing 787
- Space Telescopes
- **Automotive:** European Volkswagen RNS 510 navigation systems, Bosch Motorsports race car telemetry system
- Industrial Robots
- Test and Measurement
- Transportation
- Controllers
- Storage Systems
- Imaging
- Medical

Advantages of VxWorks include:

- a simulator
- support for cross-platform libraries
- support for numerous 32- and 64-bit architectures
- testing on a wide range of devices and online documentation

Disadvantages of the VxWorks include:

- limited programming language support
- a minor security flaw

Embedded Operating System Comparison Table

So, let us see our four embedded operating systems side by side. In *Table* 11.2, the embedded operating systems will be compared based on the following eight categories: *programming tools available, documentation and support, supported hardware, and licensing & pricing.*

Features	**Embedded Linux**	**QNX**	**INTEGRITY**	**WxWorks**
Programming Languages Supported	You can use any programming language	C++, C, HTML5, Java, Python	C++, C, Ada	C++
Qt & Felgo Support	Yes	Yes	Yes	Yes
CPU/MCU arch supported	A wide range of MCU and CPU architectures are supported. To view the list of supported processors, use this link: bit. ly/397Tikz.	IA-32, MIPS, PowerPC, SH-4, ARM, StrongARM, XScale	ARM, XScale, Blackfin, ColdFire, MIPS, PowerPC, x86	
Usability	Hard to use depending on your choice	Easy to use	Hard to use	Easy to use
Documentation	A great number of resources online	Can find Documentation on the OS website, paid training. Also, tutorials can be found on YouTube and online resources	Offers documentation with the purchase of the license	A lot of documentation and on VxWorks website and courses in their Academy

License	Free	Private	Private	Private
Support	Forums, communities, mailing list, amount others; paid support available	Forums and paid support	Paid support	Paid support
Pricing	Free	Depends on the project	$6000 per developer	Depends on the project

Table 11.2: *Comparison of Four Major os for Embedded Systems*

Development of Embedded Applications with Qt and Felgo

Fortunately, all the previous operating systems also support Qt as a feature-rich development framework. This means you also have the option to use Felgo. But before getting into it in more detail, let us take a look at how to use Qt.

Each of the embedded operating systems offers its own development tool to create embedded applications, especially Linux, which offers a plethora of languages, tools, IDEs, and so on. But one of the advantages that you can exploit as a developer is the support and portability that you get when using Qt.

Qt is a C++ cross-platform library that covers everything from the user interface to networking and multimedia. One of the biggest benefits of using Qt is that the library supports all the systems previously mentioned in this article.

With Qt, you can develop your application once and deploy it in any system, including Android. So imagine you are working with Linux and suddenly you need to migrate your application to VxWorks. With Qt, you only need to configure the VxWorks compiler in the Qt Creator (Qt's IDE) and run your application in the new system without virtually changing anything in your code. That portability means a reduction of costs and time in the event of migration, removing the necessity to retrain your development team, and making the change transparent for every part involved in the project.

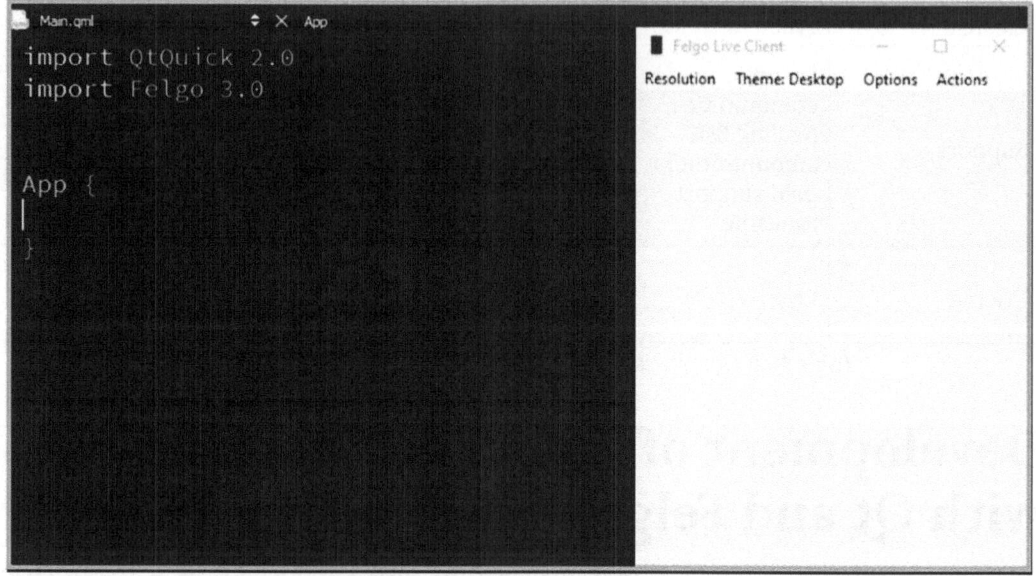

***Figure 11.3:** QT and Felgo Main QML*

And this is the point where Felgo makes its entry. Felgo extends Qt and makes the development even easier. But how? Felgo comes with a lot of components that offer great features for your embedded applications. These are only some examples:

- **Adaptive UI, Navigation Components, and Controls**: Felgo allows you to create state-of-the-art user experiences and brings best practices from the mobile development world to other supported platforms, such as embedded, desktop, or web. You get all the tools you need for creating user interfaces that look and feel nice while also supporting all kinds of different screen sizes and densities.
- **Maps, GPS and Sensors**: You can use these components to create an application that tracks the position of the embedded device. For example, in a vehicle or to show maps to the user, you can access the native sensor of your hardware and start getting location data really easily.
- **Connectivity and Networking**: With Felgo, you do not have to implement the communication between your client and server parts from scratch. With the `HttpRequest` API, you can connect to RESTful services quickly. You can also dynamically fetch assets or code at runtime with downloadable resource. This allows you to keep the initial app size minimal and load content as required.

Apart from the SDK components, Felgo also provides tools that will ease your development process.

- The first one that will save you a lot of time is QML Hot Reload. This feature will let you see changes in your code in real time.

- The second one is the Cloud Builds CI/CD. Felgo offers a continuous integration and continuous deployment service to test and deploy your software for any platform, such as embedded systems, Android, iOS, desktop or web. By using Qt and Felgo services, you can simplify the development process and put yourself in a more advantageous position.

If you would like to jump-start your embedded app development, feel free to contact Felgo's team of experts. From comprehensive, remote or on-site training, webinars to professional consultation and app development services, Felgo provides all the resources you need to develop your next embedded application.

Real-Time System Examples

Over two billion devices worldwide are powered by VxWorks, one of the many products that uses RTOSes. Real-time operating systems are used by embedded systems in a variety of devices, such as car engines, Mars rovers, helicopter guidance systems, and deep-space telescopes.

A&D	**Telecom**	**Transportation**	**Medical**	**Manufacturing**
Flight display controller	5G modem	Functional safety systems	Magnetic resonance imaging	Factory robotics systems
Engine turbine	Satellite modem	Emergency braking systems	Surgery equipment	Safety systems
Drones	Base station	Engine warning systems	Ventilators	Oil and gas vibration monitors

Table 11.3: *Example of uses of Real-Time System Operating Systems*

The Changing World of Embedded and Real-Time Operating Systems [4]

To guarantee that the device can react to sensory inputs within the time constraints set by the embedded software, real-time embedded systems are those that include a real-time operating system. Their prerequisites are one of the primary distinctions between embedded and real-time operating systems. If an EOS needs to fit into a hardware environment with limited resources and optimize for efficiency, an RTOS needs to adhere to tight time constraints and guarantee that tasks are completed by the deadline.

- **New Methodologies**: Operating systems that power embedded systems are subject to expectations that trickle down from above. Real-time operating systems need to use contemporary development techniques and stay up to date with emerging technologies. This entails maintaining compatibility with the frameworks, languages, and development techniques used by the newest generation of embedded system programmers without sacrificing any aspect of performance, security, safety, or dependability.

- **Maintaining Legacy Systems:** Cutting-edge developments in performance, connectivity, and design cycles are beginning to render even brand-new goods outdated. The issue of how to manage legacy systems is brought up by this. The cost of recoding embedded applications is prohibitive. Conversely, system developers would rather leverage pre-existing code wherever feasible, particularly in cases where software certification has already been funded and applications can now be consolidated, thanks to advancements in multi-core-based hardware platforms. The final shipped product can be made smaller, lighter, and less expensive, thanks to the ability of a single chip to hold anywhere between two and sixty-four CPUs. Additionally, virtualization is quickening embedded system development. It is now possible to run multiple embedded systems in virtualized form on a single piece of hardware by using a hypervisor. For manufacturers looking to get the most out of their investment in current intellectual property while facilitating the migration of legacy applications to new platforms, this is essential.

Factors for Choosing a Commercial RTOS

Real-time systems were first introduced nearly seven decades ago. British information technology consultant James Martin was well-known. RTOS has changed a lot in the last few years. Each RTOS has an exclusive feature of its own. Developers are not taking full advantage of this field's growth, though, because most RTOS is expensive and requires licensing. Between RTOS, peripheral support and stack availability also differ significantly. The few available free/open source real-time operating systems have limited support for proprietary protocols. The luxury of time to customize RTOS to project requirements is not afforded to developers. They are therefore resistant to altering their present working circumstances. In recent years, there has been a lot of activity in the real-time operating system research domain. Numerous RTOSs with a wide range of concepts, tenets, and paradigms have been developed in the field. More hands-on practice with these RTOSs is preferred, though.

- **Commercial RTOS Advantages Compared to Open Source:** Open-source or community-based operating systems are an alternative to proprietary RTOS options available to developers. They lack certain important features, even though they offer some advantages of a real-time operating system. Developers are investing a lot of money in hardware because larger deployments frequently use boards that cost hundreds of thousands or even millions of dollars. Implementing an open-source system can present challenges that quickly cause budgets and deadlines to balloon. Additionally, the lack of organized support for open source systems can lead to incomplete documentation or unfixed bugs. A well-organized and experienced engineering team that can offer clarifications or troubleshoot problems is a benefit of a commercial system.

- **Common Business Challenges Affecting Commercial RTOS**
  - **Implementation**: Keeping platform costs down
  - **reducing time-to-market** and development risks for deploying real-time systems
  - **allocating engineering resources efficiently** between sustaining existing products and developing new ones
  - **managing increasing complexity** across multiple technologies, product lines, development organizations, and geographies
  - **capitalizing on the massive growth opportunity** of the Internet of Things

Conclusion

In this chapter, we have gone through working with real-time operating system, their basic functionalities and RTOS architectures. We have further learned about embedded operating systems. Moreover, we learned in history how the tools and ecosystem of embedded Linux development were adopted. The four major types of RTOS used in history are QNX Embedded Operating System, INTEGRITY OS, VxWorks, and Qt and Felgo.

We have also seen embedded operating system comparison table and development of embedded applications with Qt and Felgo. We further studied the examples of real-time. Finally, we studied system the futuristic possible deployment of embedded real life-time operating systems and factors for choosing a commercial RTOS.

In the next chapter, we are going to learn about characteristic features of multimedia operating systems.

Questions

Real-Time Operating Systems

1. What are some common features of an RTOS?
2. What is an RTOS, and how does it differ from a traditional OS?
3. What are some examples of applications that use an RTOS?
4. How is task scheduling different in an RTOS?
5. What are some advantages of using an RTOS?

6. What are some challenges associated with using an RTOS?
7. What is the best RTOS for Arm?
8. How can I learn about RTOSes in the field of embedded systems?
9. How does a real-time operating system (RTOS) work?
10. What are the functions of the kernel?
11. How are tasks prioritized in an RTOS?
12. Where are RTOSes used?
13. What RTOS works with ROS or ROS2?

Embedded Systems

1. What is a real-time embedded system?
2. What are microcontrollers?
3. What are the differences between a microcontroller and a microprocessor?
4. State the differences between a mutex and a semaphore.
5. Differentiate between operating systems for general use vs. embedded systems.
6. Enumerate various advantages and disadvantages of the embedded Linux system.
7. Describe the characteristics/features of QNX embedded operating system.
8. Quote some real-life examples of QNX system.
9. Quote some real-life examples of INTEGRITY OS.
10. Describe the main characteristics features of adopting VxWorks.
11. What is Qt and Felgo? Are they mutually dependent?
12. Describe the major area of applications for real-time operating systems.
13. Discuss which are the various factors for choosing a commercial RTOS?
14. Which is the common business challenges affecting commercial RTOS implementation?
15. What RTOS works with Raspberry Pi?
16. What is embedded Linux?
17. What version of Linux is best for embedded systems?

References

[1] What is Real-Time Operating System (RTOS) and How It works? https://www.elprocus.com/real-time-operating-system-rtos-and-how-it-works/

[2] What Is a Real-Time Operating System (RTOS)?,https://www.windriver.com/solutions/learning/rtos

[3] Top 4 Embedded Operating Systems with Examples (2024 Update),Jan 1, 2024, https://blog.felgo.com/embedded/embedded-operating-systems

[4] What Is a Real-Time Operating System (RTOS)?,https://www.windriver.com/solutions/learning/rtos

Chapter 12
Multimedia Operating Systems

Introduction

In this chapter, we will learn about real-time and multimedia systems and their characteristics. Since they involve deadlines, we will look into it in detail.

Moving on, we will learn how the resource and processes are managed. Next, we will present real-time scheduling system models. Disk file systems in multimedia OS systems are managed in a slightly different manner using disk scheduling using disk scheduling algorithms.

Structure

In this chapter, we will learn the following topics:

- Overview of Multimedia Operating Systems
- Characteristic Features of Multimedia Operating Systems
- Real time and Multimedia
- Deadlines
- Resource Management in Multimedia Systems
- Process Management
- Real-time Scheduling System Models
- File System in Multimedia OS Systems
- Disk Scheduling
- Disk Scheduling Algorithms

Overview of Multimedia Operating Systems

Operating systems may handle multimedia data among other types of data. Multimedia data has become increasingly prevalent in computer systems in recent years. Conventional files and continuous media in the form of audio or video files are examples of multimedia data. Unlike conventional data, continuous media data has time constraints that must be met to deliver files, such as audio, video, or picture frames. The term "*multimedia*" describes a broad range of frequently used applications in modern times.

This term refers to a wide range of audio and video files, including movies, short video clips, MP3 audio files, flash/animation files containing news stories or movie trailers, and movies. Multimedia additionally comprises live webcasting, that is, broadcasting of different events or sports via the World Wide Web.

A multimedia application can consist of both audio and video, though not always necessary. Similar to other types of data, multimedia files are kept at the file system-specific rate, but there is no need for any specific timing when accessing a standard file. A video is typically composed of a fast-paced series of images called frames. The smoother the video appears to the user, the faster the frames display. For the video to look smoother to the human eye, a frame rate of 24–30 frames per second is usually required.

When data is delivered from the local file system, it is called '*local playback*.' Multimedia files can also be stored on a remote server and delivered to a client across a network using called streaming.

There are two types of streaming techniques:

- Progressive download
- Real-time streaming

Progressive download and real-time streaming are the two methods for downloading media files, including audio and video. Progressive download is used to download and store the media file on the user's local file system. Real-time streaming, on the other hand, enables the media file to be streamed to the client without being downloaded or stored by the client. For media files, like long videos and Internet radio or TV broadcasts, that are too big to store on the client system, real-time streaming is the recommended option. For those who wish to save space on their devices, real-time streaming is a better option because the media file is not stored on the client system. The requirements of traditional applications are not the same as those of multimedia systems. The following qualities are possible for multimedia systems:

- Multimedia files can be relatively large. For example, a 100-minute MPEG-1 video file uses roughly 1.125 GB of storage, and 100 minutes of high-definition television needs approximately 15 GB of storage.
- Continuous media might need very high data rates. Think of a digital video wherein a frame of color is displayed at a resolution of 800 x 600.
- Multimedia applications are pretty sensitive to time delays at some point in playback.

Characteristic Features of Multimedia Operating Systems

- The operating system provides a comfortable environment for the execution of programs, and it ensures effective utilization of the computer hardware. Speed and efficiency are not the main characteristics of real-time systems.
- The OS offers various services related to the essential resources of a computer: CPU, main memory, storage, and all input and output devices.
- In multimedia applications, a lot of data manipulation (for example, A/D, D/A and format conversion) is required and this involves a lot of data transfer, which consumes many resources.
- The integration of discrete and continuous multimedia data demands additional services from many operating system components.
- The major aspect in this context is the real-time processing of continuous media data.
    - Processing guarantees for time-sensitive tasks is necessary for real-time systems to behave in a deterministic and predictable manner.
    - A real-time system is distinguished by the following features:
- Predictably fast response to time-critical events and accurate timing information:
- An elevated level of schedule to fulfill the deadlines. The critical task is taken care of first for stability under temporary overload.
- A real-time process is a process that delivers the results of the processing in a given time-span.
- The main characteristic of real-time systems is the correctness, that is, errorless computation of the computation.
- The moment of result presentation (for example, G. The timing of the video data presentation should be appropriate—neither too fast nor too slow). It is also necessary to consider the timing and logical dependencies between various related tasks that are processed concurrently.

Real Time and Multimedia

The real-time requirements of traditional real-time scheduling techniques usually have a high demand for security and fault tolerance. (Most of them involve system control.)

Real-time requirements of multimedia systems are:

- The fault-tolerance requirements of multimedia systems are usually less strict than those of real-time systems with a direct physical impact.
- For many multimedia system applications, missing a deadline is not a severe failure, although it should be avoided, for example, when playing a video sequence. Scheduling considerations for periodic tasks are much simpler because, in general, all time-critical operations are periodic.
- Continuous media typically has a negotiable bandwidth requirement and is scalable.

Issues concerned with multimedia operating systems

The following issues are tackled in multimedia operating systems:

- Process management: A brief presentation of traditional real-time scheduling algorithms
- File systems: Outlines disk access algorithms, data placement, and structuring
- Interprocess communication (IPC) and synchronization
- Memory management
- Database management
- Device management
- Process management must consider the timing requirement imposed by the handling of multimedia data.

Concerns in process management (Scheduling):

	Traditional OS	**MM OS**
Timing requirement	No	Yes
Fairness	Yes	Yes

Table 12.1: *Comparison of MMos with traditional OS*

- To adhere to timing constraints, single components are considered f as resources reserved beforehand. This resource reservation must include all resources on a data path.

- The communication and synchronization between single processes must meet the restrictions of real-time requirements and timing relations among different media
- Memory management must provide access to data with a guaranteed timing delay and efficient data manipulation functions. (for example, minimize physical data copy operations)
- Database management should rely on file management services.

Deadlines

A deadline represents the latest acceptable time for the presentation of a processing result. Deadlines are set in two manners:

- **Soft deadline** is a deadline that cannot be exactly determined and which, failing does not yield an unsatisfactory outcome. As long as its miss could be accepted,
  - not too many deadlines are missed and/or
  - the deadlines are not missed by much.
- **Hard deadline** is a deadline that should never be broken since doing so results in a system failure. The physical properties of real-time processes dictate it.

Resource Management [1]

Despite data compression and the use of new technologies, multimedia systems with integrated audio and video processing are at the limit of their capabilities. The demand sharply rises.

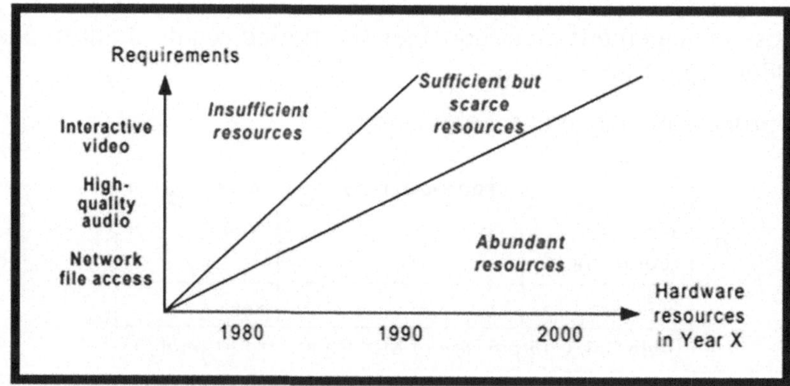

Figure 12.1: *Evolution of changing multimedia requirement over time*

- There is no reason to anticipate resource capacity redundancy anytime soon
- Timing guarantees for processing continuous media in a multimedia system must be followed throughout the data path
- The actual prerequisites are contingent upon
  - the kind of media and
  - the kind of supported applications
- Careful allocation is necessary due to the scarcity of resources
- The resource is managed after it has been allocated
- The resource management ensures the new "*connection*" is established during the connection establishment phase; It does not violate performance guarantees already provided to existing connections
- When it comes to operating systems, resource management includes file system, device, memory, and CPU management (including process management)
- While each resource has a different management, all resources have the same reservation made for them.

Resources

A resource is a system entity required by tasks for manipulating data.

- A resource is a system entity required by tasks for manipulating data.
- Resources can be either passive or active, for example, current resources.
- It offers a service; it processes protocols via a network adapter or CPU. Both active and passive resources exist.

Active resource: The current resource is, for example, for processing protocols, the CPU or a network adapter; it offers a service.

Inactive asset: For example, file systems, main memory, or communication capacity. It indicates a system capability that is necessary for resources to be active.

- A resource may be shared by multiple processes or utilized only by one process at a time.
- Passive ones can typically be shared, but active ones are frequently exclusive.
- Every resource has a time-span capacity. (for example, CPU processing time, memory storage capacity, and other factors.)
- For real-time scheduling, only the temporal division of resource capacity among real-time processes is of interest. prerequisites [2].

The transmission and processing requirements of local and distributed multimedia applications can be specified according to the following characteristics, which are known as the QoS parameters:

- **Throughput:** Determined by the data rate of the connection to satisfy the application requirements and the size of the data units
- **Local and end-to-end delay**
    - **Local delay**: The maximum period for the completion of a certain task being performed by the resource
    - **End-to-end delay:** The total delay for a data unit to be transmitted from the source to its destination
- **Delay jitter:** The maximum allowed variance in the arrival of data at the destination

Error detection and correction systems are examples of reliability. Errors can be reported, fixed, or ignored. While individual applications may have their own requirements specified as constants, generally there are boundaries within which the application will still receive an acceptable service. Forward error correction mechanisms are more appropriate for time-critical data because re-transmitting the correct data implies a delay that will probably violate the timing requirements. This is why the resource manager and the client application negotiate resource allocation. A QoS specification will be provided by the client when requesting a resource. Upon reviewing its own resource utilization, the resource manager will determine if the reservation request can be fulfilled. Requests are queued if they cannot be fulfilled right away. Though this may sound strange, it is crucial to remember that in a real-time setting, smooth playback of a continuous data stream is more significant than starting the stream's playback right away. If playback starts right away but experiences jitter delays, it might be more acceptable for the user to wait a while before it can begin uninterrupted. Upon receiving a resource request, the resource manager will conduct a scheduling test to ascertain whether the resource has enough capacity to handle the request. The resource manager will next allocate the necessary capacity (resource reservation) after performing a QoS calculation to ascertain the best possible guarantee for the request. Finally, inbound connections' messages are scheduled based on the specified QoS guarantees via resource scheduling. There are various scheduling algorithms that can be defined for various resources. Based on the scheduler's algorithm, the schedulability test, QoS computation, and resource reservation are performed.

Components and Phases

The relationship between clients and their respective resource managers may serve as the basis for resource management and allocation.

- The client selects the resource and requests a resource allocation by specifying its QoS specification.

- After assessing its own resource usage, the resource manager determines whether or not to fulfill the reservation request.
- After acceptance, performance can be assured. Phases of resource management and reservation:
    - Scheduling
    - The resource manager verifies the specified QoS parameters (for example, G. dependability and throughput).
    - Quantity of Service (QoS) computation: The resource manager determines the optimal performance. For example, the resource can ensure that the new request is processed without delay.
    - Resource reservation: Scheduling of resources, assigns the necessary capacity to every request to fulfill the QoS guarantees.
- Incoming messages (that is, LDUs) from connections are scheduled according to the given QoS guarantees.

Allocation Scheme

Here, both optimistic and pessimistic approaches can be used to reserve resources.

- The former prevents resource conflicts by planning ahead for the worst-case scenario (It is highly traditional.)
- Only an average workload is used to reserve resources in the optimistic approach.

Attributes	Pessimistic approach	Optimistic approach
Account for	Worst case	Average case
QoS	Guaranteed	Best effort
Utilization	Low	High
Remarks		May need a monitor to detect overload situation and act

Table 12.2: *Comparison between optimistic and pessimistic approaches to reserve resources*

Continuous Media Resource Model [2]

The chain of resources that data travels through on its end-to-end path is frequently modeled using the continuous media resource model to manage resources while ensuring a quality of service in a distributed environment.

This is predicated on the Linear Bounded Arrival Processes (LBAP) model. Logical Data Units (LDUs) make up the data stream in this model. One data unit in a series of time-dependent units is called an LDU. LDUs are referred to as messages in the context of LBAP (see below). As a result of sampling the original analog signal to retrieve continuous data, the data stream is highly periodic and requires that the samples be played at regular intervals. Because each sample's compressed data may require a different amount of bandwidth (if it is variable length coded), the compressed data that makes up each sample could be extremely irregular. There is a set maximum message size, though. Messages that arrive ahead of schedule make up a burst of messages in the LBAP model. Three parameters define the message arrival process at a resource (LBAP):

M stands for maximum message size in bytes;

R for maximum message rate in seconds;

B for maximum burstiness in messages.

For example, two workstations are connected via a LAN. One workstation has a CD player attached. The other computer with speakers connected, receives single-channel audio data from the CD player via the network. 44,100 samples of the audio signal are taken per second, and each sample has a 16-bit code. Thus, the rate of data is. $R_{byte} = 44100Hz \times (16bits/8bits/byte) = 88200bytes/second$

The CD prepares data for transmission as messages by assembling samples into frames. The CD-format standard decrees that 75 frames are assembled per second of audio (R). Therefore, the maximum message size is

M = (88200bytes/second / 75messages/second) = 1176bytes/message

For transmission over the LAN, up to 12000bytes are assembled into a packet. The maximum number of messages per packet is

B = (12000bytes/1176bytes/messages) >= 10 messages

This represents a *burst*, where data is being carried over the network in bulk. We assume that there is only one route between the client and server, so it is not possible for packets to arrive out of sequence. The LAN may also be capable of carrying 10 Mbits of data per second (roughly equivalent to 1.2Mbytes/s, or less than 1000 audio frames per second). However, a single second of audio can be carried by only 75 frames. We need to limit the number of frames that are transmitted so that we do not overload the client and the network. We can state that during a time interval t, the maximum number of messages received by the client must not exceed

M' = B + (R x t) messages

For example, assuming that *t* is 1 second:

M' = 10 *messages* + (75 *messages* x 1 *second*) = 85 messages

This allows for short-time violations of the rate constraint. The maximum average data rate of the LBAP is $R' = M \times R$ bytes per second

For example, $R' = 1176\,bytes/message \times 75\,messages/s = 88200$ bytes per second

We must specify a buffer size to hold messages on the client temporarily because only a certain number of messages can arrive earlier than needed. Data will be lost if the buffer size is too small, but memory will be underutilized if the buffer size is too large. The buffer size is defined to be $S = M \times (B + 1)$ bytes

For example:

$S = 1176$ bytes/message $\times (10 + 1)$ messages $= 12936$ bytes

Through these computations, we can approximate the following: the guaranteed logical delay (the maximum amount of time that separates a message's earliest arrival time from its latest completion time), the logical arrival time of messages (the earliest time a message can arrive ahead of schedule when all messages arrive at their rate), and the number of work-ahead messages (the number of messages that arrive ahead of schedule and which can be processed immediately if the resource is idle). If the logical arrival time of a message has passed, it is considered critical.

- Maximum burstiness (message), maximum message rate (message/second), and maximum message size (byte/message) are the three parameters that determine the resource where the message arrival process known as LBAP takes place.

Example: Single channel audio data are transferred from a CD player attached to a workstation over the network to another computer

- As CD audio is handled, the bit rate is constant.
- The audio signal: sampled at 44.1 kHz, each sample is coded with 16 bits.
- Samples are grouped into 75 frames of equal size (corresponds to messages) in a second and transmitted in CD-format standard.
- Assume up to 12000 bytes are assembled into 1 packet and transmitted over the LAN.

Then, we have

data rate	= 44100x16/8	= 88200	bytes/s
R	= 75 messages/second		
M	= 88200/75	= 1176	bytes/message
B	= 10 messages	≤ 12000/1176	

That B=10 means we receive 1 packet at a time and each of them carries 10 messages, which implies we receive no more than 10 messages at a time.

Figure 12.2: *Transfer of audio data from CD Player to another computer*

Burst: During a time interval of length t, the maximum number of messages arriving at a resource must not exceed M = B + R×t (message). Maximum buffer size. Messages arriving ahead of schedule must be queued in a buffer. When traffic congestion occurs and data is moved from disk in bulk transfer mode, bursts are produced after messages are put together to form bigger packets.

- The buffer size is S = M ×(B +1) (bytes).

Logical backlog: The number of messages that are "ahead of schedule" when that message m arrives is known as the logical backlog.

- Let a_i be the actual arrival time of message m_i for $0 \le i \le n$. Then b(i) is defined by

$$\begin{cases} b(m_0) = 0 \\ b(m_i) = \max(0, b(m_{i-1}) - (a_i - a_{i-1})R + 1) \end{cases}$$

Unit: message

- **Example:**

The time increases by t upon the arrival of message M5. Since it is expected to consume tR messages during this time, *b*(M5)=*b*(M4)-tR+1 should be the number of messages currently in the buffer. The newest member is the last one.

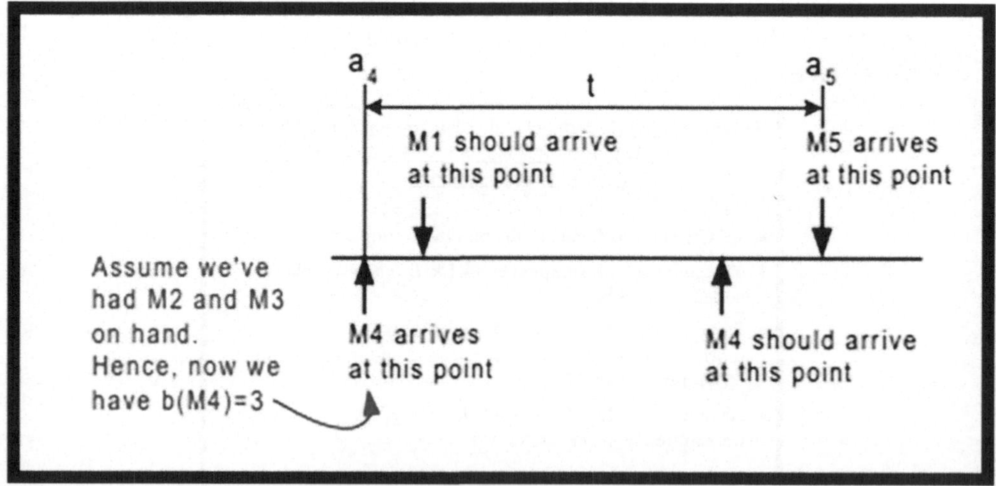

Figure 12.3: *Arrival of message*

$$l(m_i) = a_i + \frac{b(m_i)}{R}$$

or

$$\begin{cases} l(m_0) = a_0 \\ l(m_i) = \max\left(a_i, l(m_{i-1}) + \frac{1}{R}\right) \end{cases}$$

Logical arrival time

- The logical arrival time defines the earliest time a message m_i can arrive at a resource when all messages arrive according to their rate.

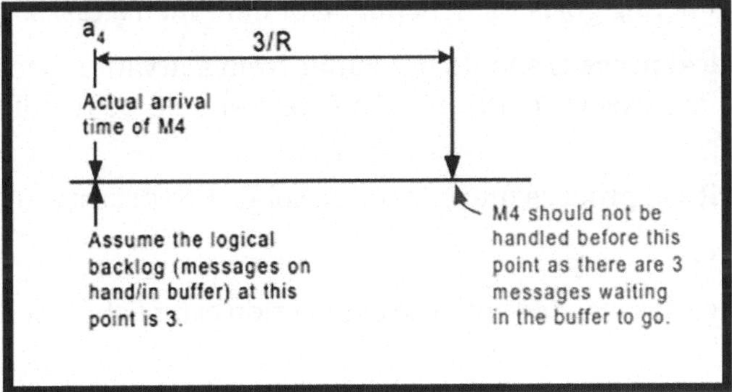

Figure 12.4: *Logical arrival time*

Guaranteed logical delay

- A message's guaranteed logical delay (GLT) is the longest period that can pass between a message's logical arrival time and its most recent valid completion time (deadline).
- **Workahead messages**: Workahead messages are those that can be processed instantly when they arrive "ahead of schedule" and the resource is idle.
- When a message is handled "ahead of schedule," the backlog grows logically rather than physically.

Process Management

All management work is handled by the process manager. The process manager maps single processes onto resources according to a specified scheduling policy such that all processes meet their requirements. One of the following four states can apply to a process that the process manager is in charge of.

The process manager is the scheduler. The scheduler transfers a process into the ready-to-run state by assigning it a position in the respective queue of the dispatcher.

The dispatcher is the essential part of the operating system kernel. The next process to run is chosen according to a priority policy. If two or more processes are equally important, then the one with the longest ready time is selected.

Real-Time Processing Requirements

The real-time process manager determines a schedule for the resource CPU that allows it to make reservations and give processing guarantees. Each of them can meet its deadlines.

In a multimedia system, continuous and discrete media data are processed concurrently. There are two conflicting goals for scheduling of multimedia tasks.

- **An uncritical process** should not suffer from starvation because time-critical processes are executed. (for example, text should be handled while handling video.)
- **A time-critical process** must never be subject to priority inversion.

One should reduce:

- The overhead associated with the connection establishment and schedulability test; and
- The expenses related to scheduling each message because they happen regularly; the latter is more serious.

Traditional Real-time Scheduling

The goal of traditional scheduling on time-sharing computers is optimal throughput, optimal resource utilization, and fair queuing. The main goal of real-time tasks is to provide a schedule that allows all, respectively, as many time-critical processes as possible, to be processed in time, according to their deadline.

Two basic algorithms for solving real-time scheduling problems:

- Earliest deadline first algorithm and
- Rate monotonic scheduling

Real-time Scheduling: System Model

A task is a scheduled entity of the system. In a hard real-time system, a task is characterized by its timing constraints and its resource requirements.

We will discuss only periodic tasks without precedence constraints, that is, the processing of two tasks are mutually independent.

- The time constraints of the periodic task T are characterized by the following parameters (s,e,d,p)

  s : Starting point

  e : Processing time of T

  d : Deadline of T

  p : Period of T

r : Rate of T (r=1/p) whereby $0 \leq e \leq d \leq p$

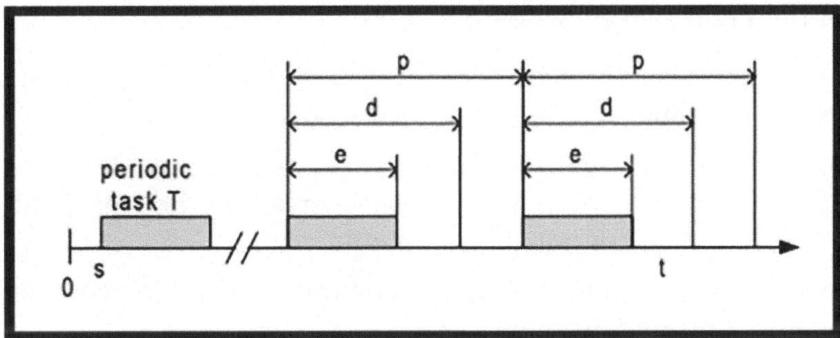

***Figure* 12.5:** *Characterization of periodic tasks*

It is assumed that the ready time of period k (i) is the deadline of period (k-1) for continuous media tasks. e. d=p), a phenomenon referred to as deadline-avoiding congestion. Unless otherwise indicated, all CPU-processed tasks are regarded as preemptive. The scheduling algorithm in a real-time system has to figure out a schedule for a limited, exclusive resource used by several processes at once so that none of them misses a deadline. A scheduling algorithm guarantees that a task will be completed before its deadline if it does so.

Performance Metrics:

- **Guarantee ratio:** The total number of guaranteed tasks versus the number of tasks that could be processed.
- **Processor utilization:** The amount of processing time used by guaranteed tasks versus the total amount of processing time = $U = \sum_{i=1}^{n} \frac{e_i}{p_i}$
- Note that for each task i, the processor utilization is e_i / p_i. Many tasks are running in parallel, so we have,

$$U = \sum_{i=1}^{n} \frac{e_i}{p_i}.$$

Earliest deadline first (EDF) algorithm

The highest priority is assigned to the task with the earliest deadline. EDF is an optimal, dynamic algorithm. At every new ready state, the scheduler selects the task with the earliest deadline among the tasks that are ready and not fully processed.

At any arrival of a new task, EDF must be computed immediately, leading to a new order, and the new task is scheduled according to its deadline. The running task is preempted.

Cons: It is impossible to guarantee that any task will be processed; its overhead is high.

Extension of the Time-Driven Scheduler (TDS)

In the event of an overload, the scheduler terminates jobs that are no longer able to be completed by the deadline.

- The scheduler eliminates tasks that are not as crucial to the system if there is still an overload situation. An additional version of the EDF divides each task into mandatory and optional components.
- Even if a task is not finished at this point, it is ended in accordance with the mandatory portion's deadline.
- Assignments are planned in accordance with the due dates for the required components. If the resource capacity is not fully utilized, the optional parts are processed.
- The optional portions are canceled in the event of an overload.
- Scalable video is favored in this implementation.

Rate Monotonic Algorithm

For preemptive, periodic tasks, this static, priority-driven algorithm is ideal. The fact that it can produce the same schedule as any static algorithm makes it optimal. To use the rate monotonic algorithm, there are five prerequisites that must be met:

- All tasks that have deadlines must have periodic requests.
- Each task must be completed before the next request occurs.
- Every task is carried out independently.
- Run-time for each request of a task is constant.
- Any non-periodic task in the system has no required deadline.

At the start of processing, a static algorithm schedules a process. Priorities are determined at the outset of each task and followed throughout. No additional planning time is needed. Tasks are given static priorities based on request rates once the connection is established.

How to assign a priority

Higher request rates will result in higher priorities for tasks. The job with the shortest turnaround time is given top priority. The period between the request and the task's completion is known as the response time. When multiple processes with a higher priority task to be processed simultaneously, this time limit is reached. The critical instant occurs at the precise moment when this occurs (the fewer, the better).

Rate Monotonic Algorithm

The period between the critical instant and task completion is known as the critical time zone (the shorter, the better).

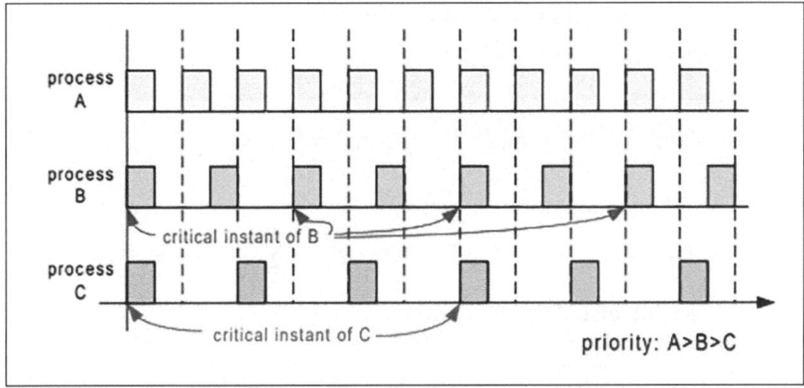

***Figure* 12.6:** *Rate Monotonic Algorithm*

EDF and Rate Monotonic: Context switches

A scheduler using the rate monotonic algorithm will likely experience more context switches than one using the EDF algorithm if multiple streams are processed concurrently in the system.

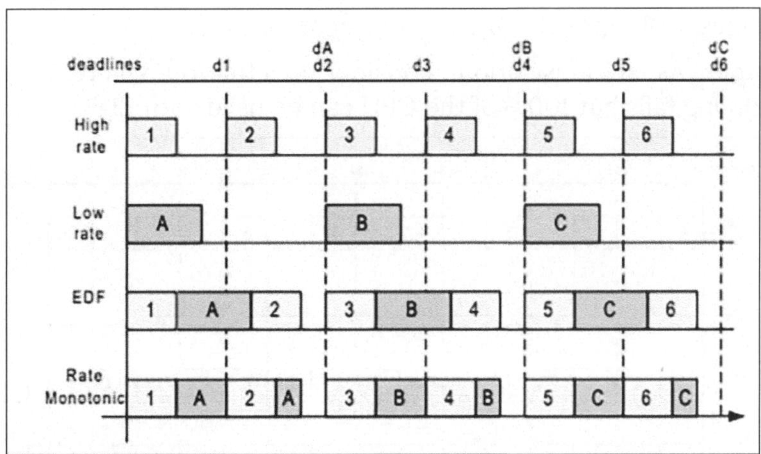

***Figure* 12.7:** *Rate monotonic vs. EDF: context switches in preemptive systems*

EDF and Rate Monotonic: Processor Utilization

Rate Monotonic Algorithm

The quantity, duration, and intervals of the scheduled tasks determine how much processor that has an upper bound is used. The critical instant determines the upper bound of the processor utilization. If m is independent, periodic tasks have a fixed priority and are set up in this way, they will always meet their deadline.

- A set of m independent, periodic tasks with fixed priority will always meet its deadline if
$$U(m) = m\left(2^{1/m} - 1\right) \geq \frac{e_1}{p_1} + \cdots + \frac{e_m}{p_m}$$
Note: $U(m) = m\left(2^{1/m} - 1\right) \geq \ln 2 = 0.6931$

- When a new job is coming, to save effort, just check if $U_k = U_{k-1} + \frac{e_k}{p_k} \leq \ln 2$, where $U_k = \sum_{i=1}^{k} \frac{e_i}{p_i}$. If yes, go ahead, else deny it.

The fact that most of the time the average task execution time is significantly less than the worst-case execution time contributes to the issue of underutilizing the processor. Even in cases where the bottleneck utilization is significantly higher than 80%, the rate monotonic algorithm guarantees the fulfillment of all deadlines. A higher processor utilization cannot be attained by any other static algorithm, hence, it is ideal.

- **EDF**: Since all tasks are dynamically scheduled in accordance with their deadlines, EDF U(m) of 100% can be accomplished.
- **Example**: As an illustration, consider a situation where rate monotonic scheduling fails but 100% of the CPU can be used with EDF.

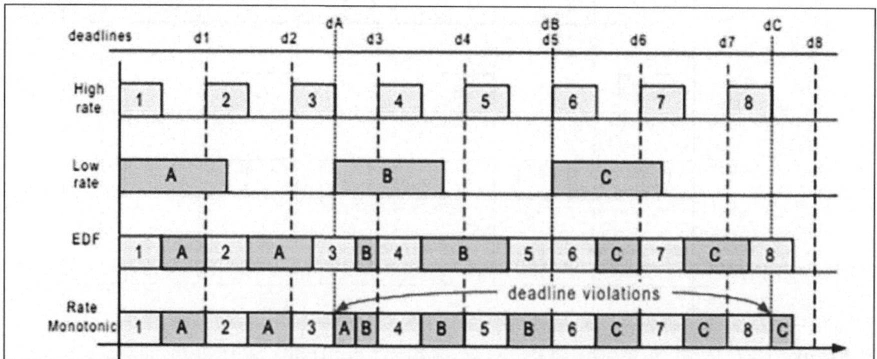

Figure 12.8: *Rate monotonic vs. EDF: processor utilization*

Extensions to rate monotonic scheduling separates a task into two parts: required and voluntary. Processing the required portion yields a result that the user can accept. Only the outcome is refined by the optional portion. The rate monotonic algorithm determines the scheduling of the mandatory portion. Alongside other policies, the optional portion is scheduled. If a system has aperiodic tasks, what can we do? If the aperiodic request is an aperiodic continuous stream, we try to convert it to a periodic stream. A sporadic server is used to answer aperiodic requests if the stream is not continuous.

Advantages: It takes full advantage of the periodicity of the data, making it especially well-suited for processing media data continuously. Since the algorithm is static, there is no scheduling overhead.

Disadvantages: Data streams that do not have a consistent processing time for each message can cause issues. The easiest way to deal with this is to schedule these tasks based on their maximum data rate, but doing so will use less processor power.

Other Algorithms for In-time Scheduling

Least Laxity First (LLF)

- The task with the shortest remaining laxity is the first to be scheduled
- The difference between the actual time t and the deadline, less the amount of processing time left, is known as the laxity.

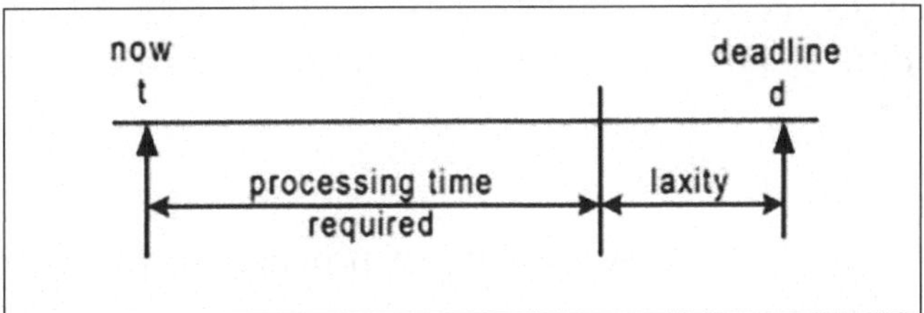

***Figure* 12.9:** *Laxity Time*

For exclusive resources, LLF is a dynamic, optimal algorithm.

Challenges with laxity-dependency:

- It is impossible to predict processing times precisely in advance, making it difficult to determine laxity.
- Over time, the laxity of waiting processes varies dynamically. We always consider the worst-case scenario.

LLF's drawbacks include the potential for multiple context switches. Every time a task is scheduled, its laxity needs to be reevaluated.

Shortest Job First (SJF): The task whose remaining computation time is the shortest is selected for execution. If every task has the same deadline, then in an overload scenario, it is guaranteed that the greatest number of tasks will meet their deadlines. The rate monotonic algorithm in various variations is used in the majority of multimedia systems with preemptive tasks.

Preemptive vs. Non-preemptive task scheduling

- When a task is non-preemptive, it is processed continuously until it is completed or more resources are needed.
- When tasks are handled as non-preemptive, the scheduler is usually unaware of the arrival times, processing times, and deadlines until the task is completed.
- An algorithm is considered optimal when it maximizes the number of tasks completed.
- In this situation, resource management and processing guarantees are not feasible.
- Tasks for periodic processes are typically treated as preemptive to ensure their processing and obtain a workable schedule for periodic task sets.

Reasons

- Increased preemption capability lessens the consequences of priority inversion.
- Unfortunately, certain non-preemptive task sets may not permit the identification of an ideal schedule, but preemptive scheduling offers this opportunity.

Scheduling of Preemptive Tasks

Let us understand more about scheduling of preemptive tasks from the following figure:

- A task set of m periodic tasks with processing times e_i and request periods p_i for all $i \in \{1,2 \cdots m\}$ is schedulable:
- With fixed priority assignment if $\Sigma \frac{e_i}{p_i} \leq \ln 2$
- For deadline-driven scheduling if $\Sigma \frac{e_i}{p_i} \leq 1$
- The preemptiveness of tasks is a prerequisite to check their schedulability.

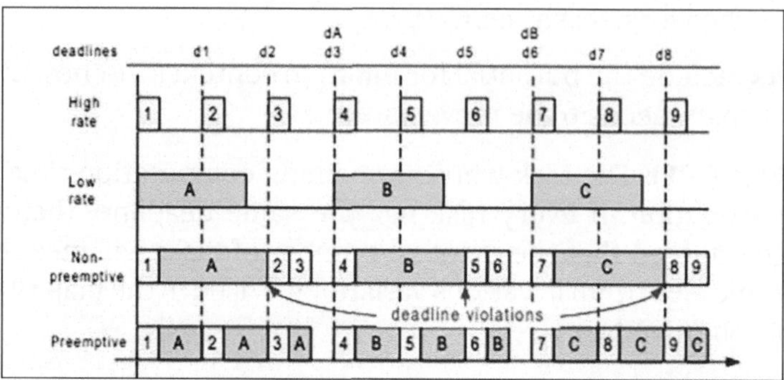

Figure 12.10: *Preemptive vs. Non-preemptive scheduling*

- **Non-preemptive task scheduling**: If a set of m periodic streams has processing times e_i, deadlines d_i, and request periods p_j for all **i** $\in$**{1,2m}**, then they can be scheduled using the non-preemptive fixed priority scheme.

$$d_m \geq e_m + \max_{1 \leq i \leq m} e_i$$

$$d_i \geq e_i + \max_{1 \leq j \leq m} e_j + \sum_{j=i+1}^{m} e_j F(d_i - e_j, p_j)$$

$$\text{where } F(x, y) = ceil\left(\frac{x}{y}\right) + 1$$

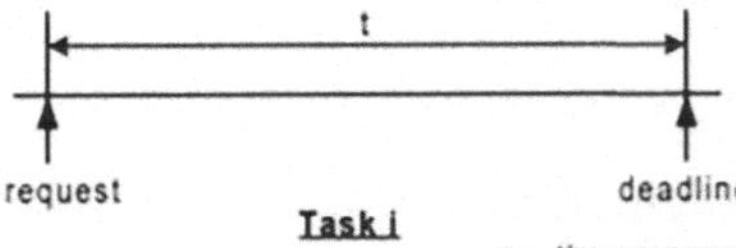

t

request

deadline

Task i

$$t \geq e_i + \sum_{k \in \Omega} e_k + e_m$$

e_i: the processing time of task i
Ω: all tasks of higher priority than task i
e_m: longest task among all

- The time between the logical arrival time and the deadline of a task t_i has to be larger or equal to the sum of its processing time *ei* and the processing time of any higher-priority task that requires execution during that time interval, plus the longest processing time of all lower- and higher-priority tasks $\max_{1 \leq j \leq m} e_j$ that may be serviced at the arrival of task t_i

Schedulability test for the following tasks:

- Given *m* periodic tasks with periods p_i and the same processing time E per message, let $d_i = p_i + E$ be the deadline for task t_i. Then, the streams are schedulable:
    - With the non-preemptive rate monotonic scheme with $\Sigma \frac{E}{p_i} \leq \ln 2$
    - With deadline-based scheduling, the same holds with $\Sigma \frac{E}{p_i} \leq 1$
- Non-preemptive tasks are less favorable because the number of schedulable task sets is smaller compared to preemptive tasks.
- It must be more conservative as it has to be played safe, so the number of schedulable task sets is smaller.

File Systems in Multimedia Systems

A file is a sequence of information held as a unit for storage and use in a computer system. Files are stored in secondary storage. In **traditional file systems**, the information types stored in files are sources, objects, libraries and executables of programs, numeric data, text, payroll records, and so on.

In **multimedia systems**, the stored information also covers digitized video and audio with their related real time `'read'` and `'write'` commands.

The file system provides access and control functions for the storage and retrieval of files.

Two issues are addressed here: the organization of the file system and disk scheduling.

Traditional File Systems

Main goals of traditional files systems are:

- To provide a comfortable interface for file access to the user
- To make efficient use of storage media

File Structure

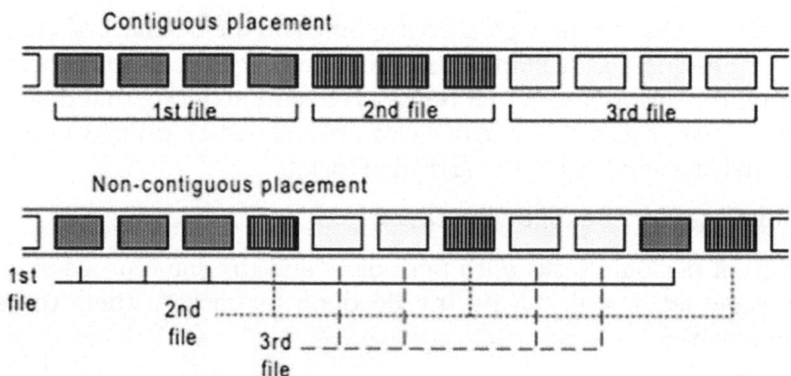

***Figure* 12.11:** *Contiguous and Non-contiguous Storage*

Sequential storage:

- Each file is organized as a simple sequence of bytes of records
- Files are stored consecutively on the secondary storage media
- A file descriptor is usually placed at the beginning of the file

Principal benefits:

- It is effective for both direct and sequential access
- Minimizes disk access time for writing and reading
- Caching can help to further improve performance

Cons:

- You cannot expand a file without copying it in its entirety to a bigger location
- Several creation and deletion operations result in the splitting and fragmentation of second storage

Non-sequential storage

- The data items are stored in a non-contiguous order.

  Two approaches:

  - To use linked blocks
  - Physical blocks containing consecutive logical locations are linked using pointers
- The file descriptor must contain the number of blocks occupied by the file, the pointer to the first and the last blocks.

Disadvantage: The cost for random access is high as all prior data must be read.

Example: In MS-DOS, a File Allocation Table (FAT) is associated with each disk.

To store block information in mapping tables:

- Each file is associated with a table where information, such as owner, file size, creation time, last access time, and so on, are stored

In UNIX, a small table called an i-node is associated with each file.

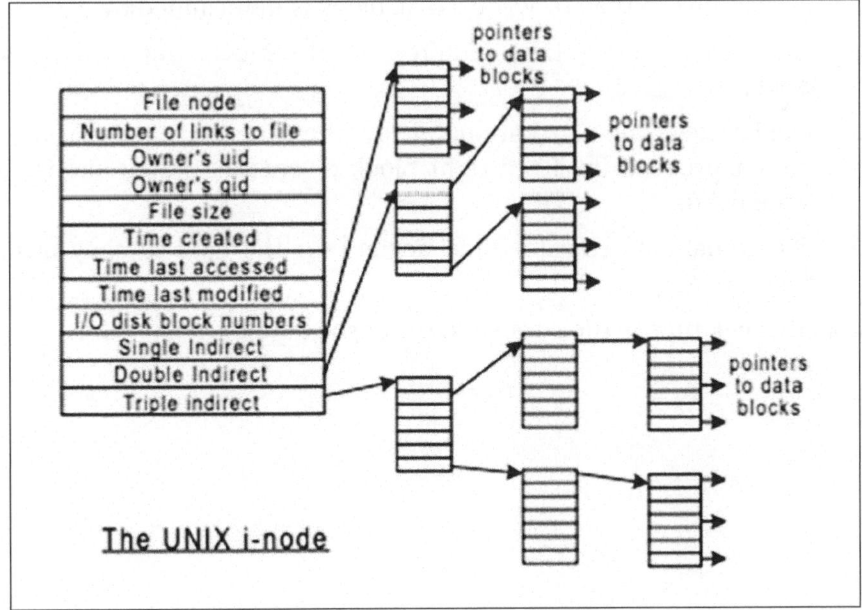

Figure 12.12: The Unix i-node

Directory structure

- Files are usually organized in directories (especially, tree-structured directories).
- In multimedia systems, it is important to organize the files in a way that allows easy, fast, and contiguous data access.

Disk management

- Disk access is a slow and costly transaction.
- Typical methods for lowering disk access in conventional systems include:
  - **Employ block caches**: Data is stored in memory for the expectation that it will be accessed again during read or write operations in the future.
  - **Reduce the motion of the disk arm by considering rotational positioning.**
- Blocks that are likely to be accessed in sequence are placed together on one cylinder.
- The mapping tables on the disk should be placed in the middle of the disk to minimize the average seek time.
- Use the same cylinder for the storage of mapping tables and referred blocks.

Disk scheduling

- For random access storage devices, every file operation may require movements of the read/write head (seek operation).
- The actual time to read or write a disk block is determined by:
  - The seek time (the time required for the movement of the read/write head).
  - The latency time or rotational delay (the time during which the transfer cannot proceed until the right block or sector rotates under the read/write head).
  - The actual data transfer time needed for the data to copy from disk to main memory.
- Usually, seek time is the largest factor of the actual transfer time.

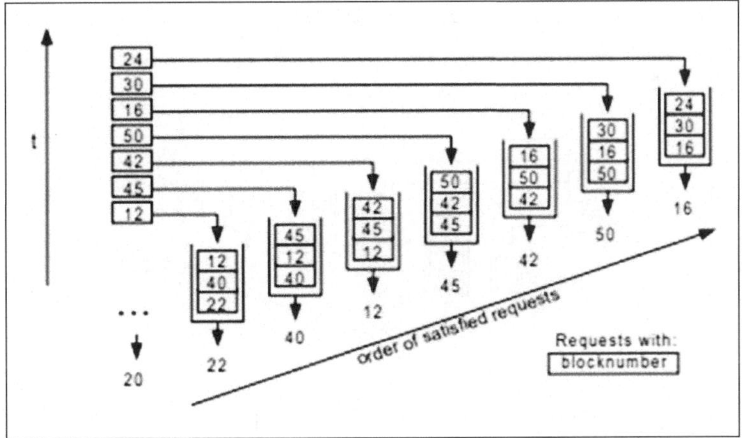

Figure 12.13: *FCFS Disk Scheduling*

Requests are accepted one at a time by the disk driver, which then fulfills them in incoming order.

Benefits: Simple to program, inherently equitable

Drawbacks: Head movement is not optimal

Shortest-Seek-Time First (SSTF)

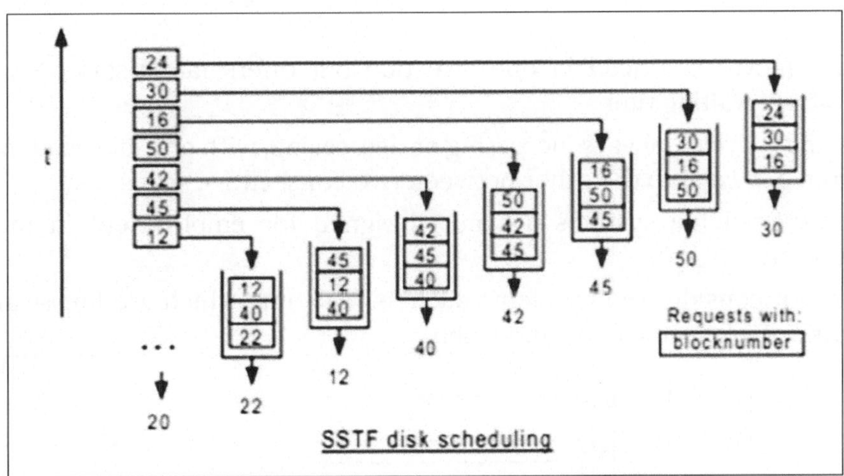

Figure 12.14: *SSTF Disk Scheduling*

- At every point in time, when a data transfer is requested, SSTF selects among all requests the one with the minimum seek time from the current head position
- Minimize the seek time, and it is optimal in this sense
- May cause starvation of some requests
- It favors middle tracks

SCAN

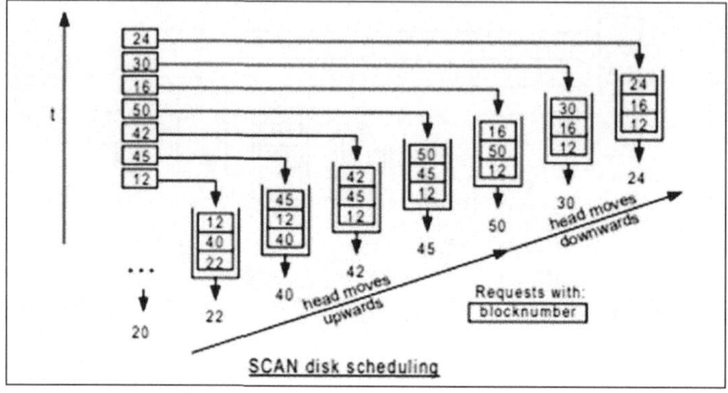

Figure 12.15: SCAN *disk scheduling*

Like SSTF:

- Takes the direction of the current disk movement into account
- Serves all requests in one direction until it does not have any requests in this direction anymore
- Provides a very good average seek time
- Improved service for edge tracks as c.w. SSTF

C-SCAN

- Also moves the head in one direction but offers fairer service with more uniform waiting times
- Scans in cycles, always increasing or decreasing, with one idle head movement from one edge to the other between two consecutive scans.
- Traditional file systems are not designed for employment in multimedia systems
- Do not consider requirements such as real-time which are important to the retrieval of stored audio and video.

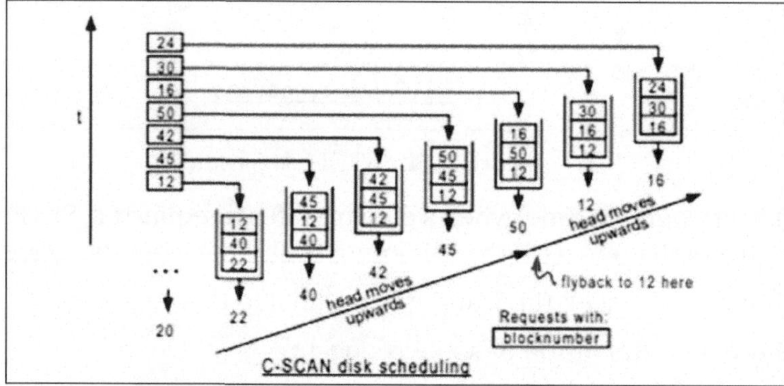

Figure 12.16: C-SCAN *disk scheduling*

Multimedia file systems

- Continuous media data are different from discrete data in:

Real-time characteristics:

- Data presented (read) before a well-defined deadline with small jitter only.

File size:

- Huge video size and audio size
- Must organize the data on disk in a way that efficiently uses the limited storage

Multiple data streams

- Must support different media at one time
- Must consider tight relations between different streams arriving from different sources

Storage Devices

- Tapes are inadequate for multimedia systems because they cannot provide independent accessible streams, and random access is slow and expensive.
- Disks can be characterized in two different ways:
  - How information is stored on them: rewriteable, write-once or read-only
  - The method of recording: magnetic or optical

	Seek time	**Rotation speed**
Optical	~200ms	CLV
Magnetic	~10ms	CAV

Table 12.3: *Comparing the features of two disk Systems*

Note: *CLV, or constant linear velocity, is a standard for rotating storage media that refers to the rated speed of an optical disk drive or the writing speed of recordable disks.*

Whereas Constant Angular Velocity (CAV) is a technique for accessing data from rotating disks by keeping the disk spinning at a fixed rate, measured in Revolutions per Minute (RPM).

- Different algorithms for magnetic and optical disks are necessary.
- File systems on CD-ROMs are defined in ISO 9660. File Structure and placement on disk
- Main goal of the file organization in conventional file systems:
  - To make efficient use of the storage capacity (that is, to reduce internal and external fragmentation)
  - To allow arbitrary deletion and extension of files

Main goal of the file organization in multimedia file systems:

- To provide a constant and timely retrieval of data.
- Internal fragmentation occurs when blocks of data are not entirely filled.
- External fragmentation occurs when files are stored in a contiguous way in where the gap cannot be filled after deleting a file.
- Two basic approaches to support continuous media in file systems:
    - Use special disk scheduling algorithms and sufficient buffer to avoid jitter.
    - Optimize the organization of audio and video files on disk for their use in multimedia systems.

Approach 1 : Providing enough buffer

Advantages:

- It is flexible. (Do not need to store files in a contiguous way.)
- External fragmentation can be avoided.
- The same data can be used by several streams (via reference).

Disadvantages:

- There are long initial delays at the retrieval of continuous media.
- Large buffers must be provided.
- Transfer rate is restricted.

Approach 2: Utilizing a designated disk layout

Goal: Reduce the expense of obtaining and storing streams; this approach is supported by the characteristics of continuous media data.

Advantages:

- Constant media streams are mostly of the write-once-read-many variety.
- It is likely that streams will be played back simultaneously if they are recorded simultaneously.
- Continuous media data should be stored on disk in big data blocks that are sequential.

Disadvantages:

- External fragmentation and overhead in copying when inserting and deleting.
- The constrained block allocation of the continuous media is the solution.

- The continuity requirement is met if,

$$T_{play}(s) \geq \frac{M(in\ sectors) + G(in\ sectors)}{r_{dt}(in\ sectors / s)}$$

where $T_{play}(s) =$ the duration of its playback

M = the size of the blocks

G = the size of the gaps

- In this case, we assume that the disk rotation rate (sectors/s) and the data transfer rate (dt r) are equal.
- This ensures that the necessary data can be retrieved prior to playback.
- Occasionally, readahead and buffering of a predetermined number of blocks must be added to meet continuity requirements.

Disk Scheduling Algorithms

- Main goals of traditional disk scheduling algorithms:
  - To reduce the cost of seek operations
  - To achieve a high throughput
  - To provide fair disk access for every process
- Systems without any optimized disk layout for the storage of continuous media depend far more on reliable and efficiency disk scheduling algorithms than others.
- The overall goal of disk scheduling in multimedia systems is to meet the deadlines of all time-critical tasks.
- The scheduling algorithm must find a balance between time constraints and efficiency.

Earliest deadline first (EDF)

- The block of the stream with the nearest deadline would be read first.
- It results in poor throughput and excessive seek time.

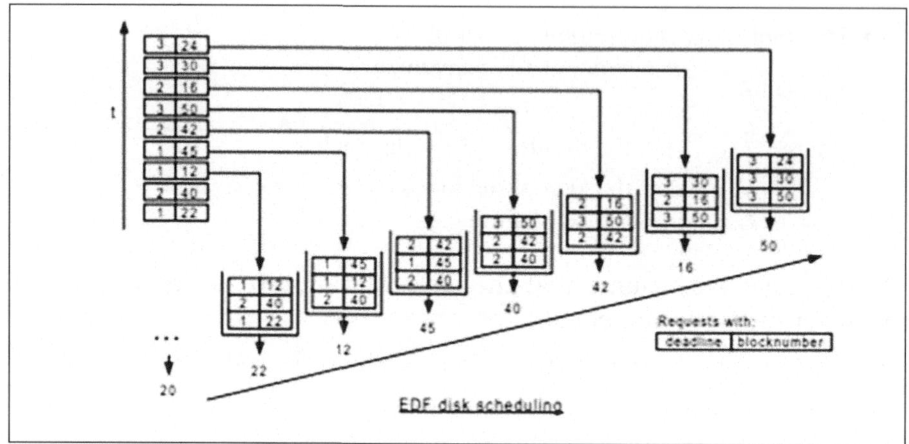

Figure 12.17: *The EDF Disk Scheduling*

SCAN-Earliest Deadline First (SCAN-EDF)

- The request with the earliest deadline is always served first.
- Among requests with the same deadline, the specific one that is first according to the scan direction is served first.

Group Sweeping Scheduling (GSS)

- Requests are served in cycles in a round-robin manner.
- Streams are grouped in such a way that all of them comprise similar deadlines.
- Groups are served in fixed order.
- Individual streams within a group are served according to SCAN.
- GSS is a trade-off between the optimization of buffer size and arm movements.

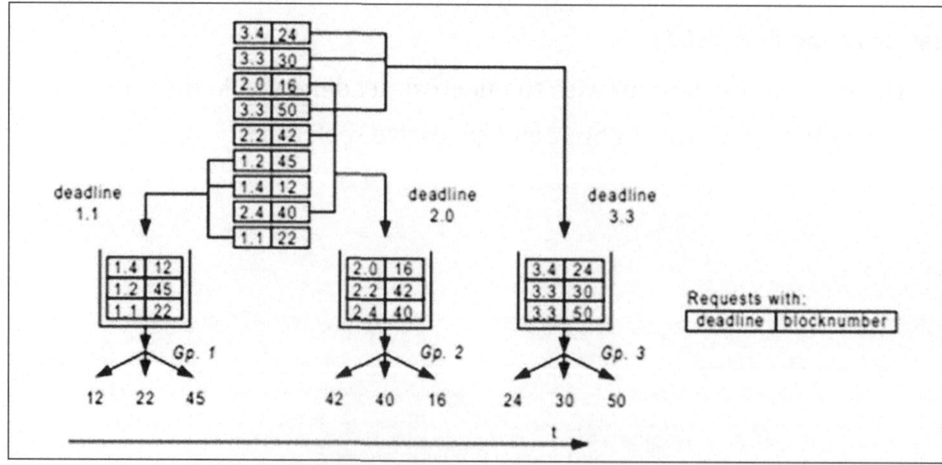

Figure 12.18: *The Group Sweeping Scheduling (GSS)*

Mixed Strategy

This mixed strategy is based on both the balanced strategy and the shortest seek. To meet process requirements with a constrained buffer space, the objective is to maximize transfer efficiency by minimizing seek time and latency. .

- Shortest seek, the method that determines which data block is closest is served first.
- The balanced strategy chooses the process which has the least amount of buffered data for service because this process is likely to run out of data.
- Two criteria must be fulfilled:
  - The number of buffers for all processes should be balanced.
  - The overall required bandwidth should be sufficient for the number of active processes' status of buffers: balanced buffers and SSTF buffers.

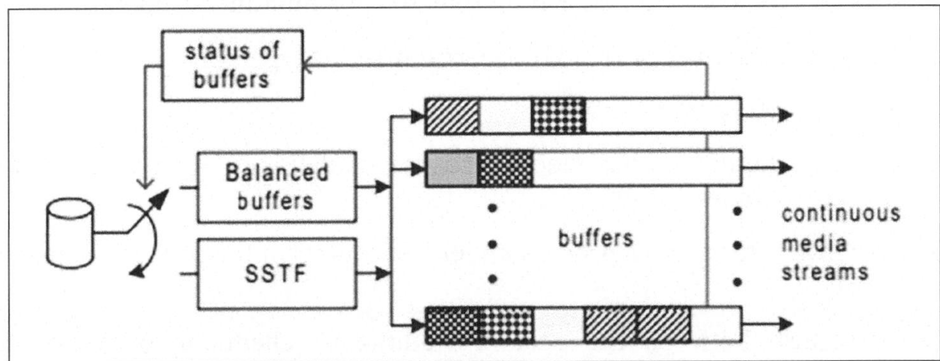

***Figure 12.19:** Mixed disk scheduling strategy*

- The urgency is the sum of the reciprocals of the current 'fullness' (amount of buffered data).
- If the urgency is large, the balance strategy will be used; if it is small, it is safe to apply the shortest seek algorithm.

Conclusion

In this chapter, we have studied the characteristic features of real-time multimedia operating systems and deadlocks normally encountered and how to overcome them in real life.

Then we discussed resource and process management in multimedia systems. as well as real-time scheduling system models and their file system. Ultimately, we learned about disk scheduling and scheduling algorithms.

In the next chapter, we will discuss mobile device operating systems.

Questions

1. What is multimedia?
2. Which types of content are included in multimedia?
3. What are the two types of streaming techniques?
4. What is called a streaming technique?
5. Multimedia files can be relatively large. True or False?
6. What are the main characteristics of multimedia operating systems?
7. What are the real-time requirements of multimedia systems?
8. What are deadlines and types of deadlines?
9. What are the characteristics requirements of a multimedia operating system?
10. What actions are performed by the resource manager?
11. What are QoS parameters?
12. Describe the continuous media resource model along with Linear Bounded Arrival Processes (LBAP).
13. How many states can a process under the control of the process manager can be in?
14. Distinguish between the goal of traditional scheduling on time-sharing computers and the main goal of real-time scheduling.
15. What are two basic algorithms for solving real-time scheduling problems?
16. Describe the Earliest Deadline First (EDF) algorithm and its disadvantages.
17. What is the extension of EDF (Time-Driven Scheduler (TDS))?
18. What is the Rate Monotonic Algorithm, and how the priority is determined?
19. What is the Least Laxity First (LLF) approaches for in-time scheduling, and its disadvantages?
20. Distinguish between preemptive versus non-preemptive task scheduling.
21. Distinguish between traditional file systems and multimedia file systems.
22. Enumerate the advantages and disadvantages of the sequential storage and non-sequential storage.

23. Distinguish between CLV and CAV, stating for which type of disk storage systems they are related.
24. What are the main goals of the file organization in multimedia file systems?

References

[1] Multimedia operating systems, http://www.eie.polyu.edu.hk/~enyhchan/mt-os.pdf

[2] Lecture 10 - Multimedia Operating Systems, https://staff.um.edu.mt/csta1/courses/lectures/csa3020/mm10.html

Chapter 13
OS for Mobile Devices

Introduction

In this chapter, we will discuss the definition of a mobile device and move on to the introduction to android operating system and its features, comparing it with Apple-owned iOS (its world rival). Then we will try to understand the categories of android applications which necessitate learning Android Studio. To understand android, we must learn its architecture with main components; it is necessary to go for Android Studio Integrated Development Environment for easily developing and creating a project. In the end, we will learn mobile Linux.

In this chapter, you shall achieve insight into following Android OS:

- The basics of Android OS, including its system architecture, connectivity, power, interaction, and camera
- How Android OS works, including its default user interface (UI), home screen, and status bar
- How Android OS implements the principle of least privilege to keep apps secure
- How Android OS's modular and customizable architecture allows developers and device manufacturers to tailor the user experience
- The history of Android OS and various versions

Structure

In this chapter, we will cover the following topics:

- Mobile Devices
- Android Operating System: Introduction
- Comparison with Apple-owned iOS
- Categories of Android Applications
- Dealing with Android Studio
- Features of Android

- Android Architecture with Several Main Components
- Android Studio Integrated Development Environment
- Developer Workflow Basics
- Creating a Project
- Mobile Linux

Mobile Devices

A mobile device is a type of portable computing device that satisfies one of the following criteria:

- It is small enough to be carried by one person
- It is made to function without a physical connection (for example, sending and receiving data wirelessly)
- Have local, non-removable data storage; and
- Run continuously on a self-contained power source for extended period.
- Additionally, having voice communication features, onboard sensors that enable the device to record (for example, record, take a picture, or pinpoint a location) data, as well as integrated tools for coordinating local data with distant locations.

E-readers, tablets, and smartphones are a few examples of mobile devices. In practical terms, a mobile device is a tiny, portable gadget with a touch-sensitive display, a QWERTY keyboard, and the ability to make and receive phone calls. It should be noted that a device is classified as portable storage rather than mobile if it can only store data and cannot process, transmit, or receive data.

Android Operating System: Introduction

Android is a mobile operating system primarily meant to run on touchscreen devices, such as smartphones and tablets. It is built on a modified version of the Linux kernel along with additional libre software. Although the Open Handset Alliance, a group of developers, is primarily responsible for the development of Android's most popular version, Google is also involved. November 2007 saw its unveiling, and September 2008 saw the release of the HTC Dream, the first Android smartphone for sale. Android is an operating system and software package based on Linux and is designed for use with mobile devices, including tablets, laptops, smartphones, electronic book readers, set-top boxes, and more. Along with middleware and important mobile apps, it includes an operating system based on Linux. Consider it an operating system for mobile devices. It is not, however, exclusive to smartphones. Today, it is found in a wide range of gadgets, including televisions, tablets, and smartphones.

Google initially developed it, followed by the Open Handset Alliance (OHA). While other languages can be used, Java is primarily used to write Android code. The objective of the Android project is to develop a viable product that enhances end users' mobile experiences. It is an alliance of eighty-four companies, including Google, Samsung, AKM, Synaptics, KDDI, Garmin, Teleca, eBay, Intel, and more. On 5 November 2007, it was founded under Google's leadership. It is dedicated to using the Android Platform to distribute smartphones, offer services, and promote open standards.

With a 70.1% market share, Android continued to be the most widely used mobile operating system worldwide in the fourth quarter of 2023. Android's closest rival, Apple's iOS, held a 29.2 percent market share during the same period. 4 October, 2023, saw the release of Android 14, the most recent version. Improvements designed for tablets, desktop screens, foldable phones, and Chromebooks are included in the recently released Android 12.1/12L. The Samsung Galaxy A14 4G led the shipment of Android phones in 2023. As a result of its accessibility, rich feature set, and user-friendly interface, Android is clearly the preferred operating system for the vast majority of Indian consumers.

Comparison with Apple-owned iOS

The two most widely used mobile operating systems currently dominating the globe are Google-owned Android and Apple-owned iOS. Here, Android has become the market leader for a variety of reasons. For cell phones, Internet of Things (IoT) gadgets, automobiles, TVs, and other electronics, Android has emerged as the de facto operating system. Due to its extensive app support, lightweight profile, hardware compatibility, robust developer support, and other features, the open-source project is implemented practically everywhere. Although it is making a strong effort, Apple's iOS is not even close to matching Android's market share. We are in danger of an Android monopoly in the market under such circumstances, as there is hardly any competition; competition and innovation suffer in such a setting.

Android Versions

Android, Inc. began developing the Android operating system in 2003. Later on, in 2005, Google acquired it. On 5 November 2007, the Android OS beta was made available while the software development kit (SDK) was released on November 12, 2007. Android creators had a practice of naming the various versions akin to confectionary name, but after version 10, they stopped this practises.

Table 13.1 provides the history and details of various versions.

Year	Version	Name	Details
September 23, 2008	Android 1.0	Alpha (API 1)	Google Maps, browser, calendar, camera and scroll down the notification bar, Gmail integration, Contacts, and Google Synchronization, Wireless supports - Wi-Fi and Bluetooth
February 9, 2009	Android 1.1:	Beta (API 2)	Feature of display details and reviews for locations, clicking on the business
April 30, 2009	Android 1.5	Cupcake (API 3)	On-screen keyboard and search function; Uploading videos and images
September 15, 2009	Android 1.6	Donut (API 4)	Handling Wi-Fi, Bluetooth, and GPS
December 3, 2009	Android 2.0	Eclair (API 5)	Updated UI
....			
August, 2018	Android 9	Pie (API 28)	Most widely used OS, compatibility for AI, and hybrid gesture/button navigation system
September, 2023	Android 10		Totally reimagined interface for Android gestures, with this version, Android dropped the naming tradition of each major release along with an item of confectionery
September, 2020	Android 11		Android 11 also made it more difficult for apps to request the ability to detect your location in the background
October-21	Android 12	Snowcane	Biggest reimagining of Android's interface since 2014's
August 15, 2022	Android 13	Tiramisu	A whole new interface design for both tablets and foldable phones, with a renewed focus on creating an exceptional large-screen experience
October 23	Android 14	Upside Down Cake	More customizable lock screen and AI generation of wallpapers
Fall of 2024	Android 15	Vanilla Ice Cream	Satellite connectivity for phone calls and text

Table 13.1: *History of various versions*

Features of Android

After discovering what Android is, let us examine its features. The following are some of Android's key characteristics:

- It is open source.
- The Android Platform is customizable by anybody.
- The consumer has a wide selection of mobile applications to select from.
- It has several interesting features, such as live RSS (Really Simple Syndication) feeds, the opening screen, and weather information.
- It supports a web browser, SQLite storage, GSM, CDMA, Bluetooth, Wi-Fi, and other connectivity options in addition to messaging services (MMS and SMS).), media, phone configuration, etc.

Categories for Android Apps

The market is filled with a wide variety of Android applications. The top categories include:

- Travel and Local
- Social Media
- Video
- Entertainment Tools
- Communication
- Productivity
- Personalization
- Music and Audio

Android Architecture with Multiple Primary Components [1]

An Android platform's architecture is made up of several software components that are intended to work with a wide range of Android-capable devices. Based on a layered architecture of software stacks, this mobile operating system consists of an application framework, a runtime environment, a Linux kernel, supporting libraries, and a collection of applications. Building a system this complex requires careful structural attention to ensure that no component of Android architect conflicts with any other component.

The architecture of Android keeps each of its many components' separate functionalities intact while safeguarding them against crashing altogether. The following succinctly describes some advantages of Android's layered architecture: It guarantees that various issues will be divided into smaller components and addressed at different stages. By employing a layered architecture, Android software developers can steer clear of low-level issues every time they create new code.

Rather than focusing on the minutiae, they can concentrate on providing business value associated with the layer they are working on. It is unnecessary for developers working on apps to worry about how the application framework is actually implemented. These duties will be assigned to the system developers in charge of putting the application framework into practice. Android is structured in layers, so updates with bug fixes or enhancements can be applied to each layer separately. Maintaining the independence of changes within layers is essential to prevent their effects from overlapping. Developers working on different operating system versions can collaborate without interfering with one another. This is especially crucial for updating and releasing new operating system versions.

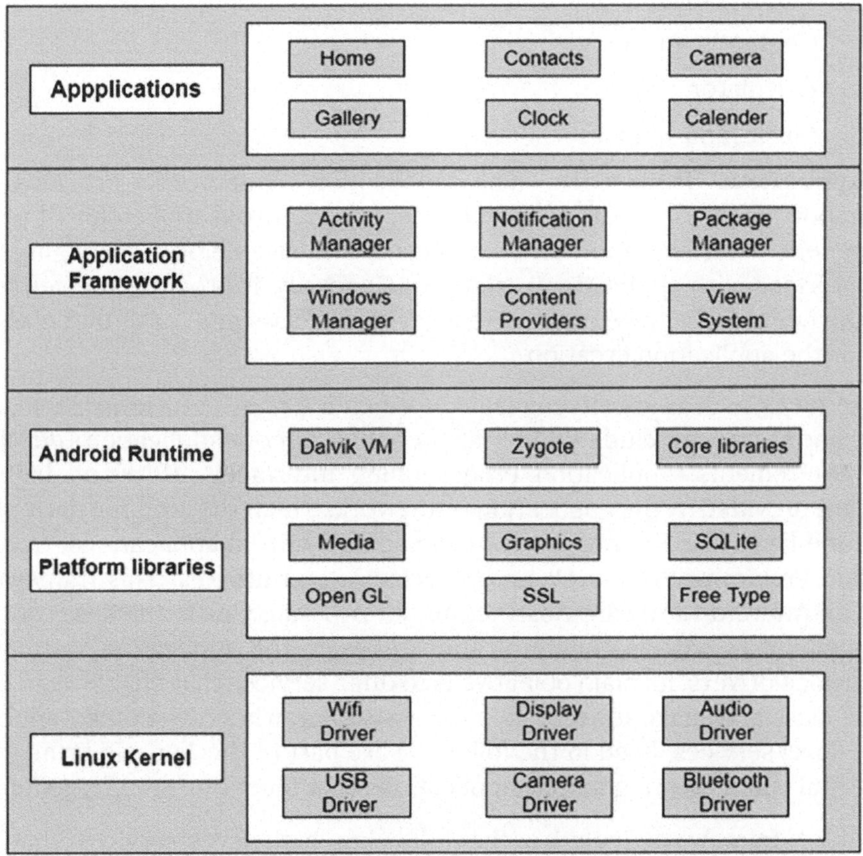

Figure 13.1: *Pictorial representation of android architecture with several main components and their sub-components*

- **Applications**: Applications occupy the topmost layer within the Android architecture's layers. Pre-installed apps on the device include the gallery, contacts, music, app store, cameras, and more, as well as those that can be downloaded from the Google Play Store; these include professional, gaming, and social applications. The classes and services offered by the application framework are used by applications as they execute within the Android runtime environment. Most Android users' interactions with this layer are for standard tasks, such as using the Web browser, placing phone calls, accessing galleries, and so on. A selection of the standard apps that are pre-installed on all devices are as follows:
  - SMS client app
  - Dialer
  - Clock
  - App store
  - Web browser
  - Contact manager
  - Calculator
  - Music, and so on.
- **Application framework:** The application framework provides several important classes that are used to create an Android application. It provides a generic abstraction for hardware access and also helps in managing the user interface with application resources. Generally, it provides the services with the help of which we can create a particular class and make that class helpful for the application creation.

Various services such as activity manager, notification manager, view system, package manager, and so on are included, which are beneficial for our application's development by the requirements. Application Programming Interfaces (APIs) and higher-level services are provided by the application framework, which sits atop the native libraries and runtime layer. For the purpose of developing Android applications, the Android Application Framework offers classes, interfaces, and utilities. This framework also includes an Android Hardware Abstraction Layer (HAL), which enables resource and UI management as well as communication between the application and hardware-specific device drivers. Its main objective is to offer services that enable us to establish a specific class and make it accessible for assistance when developing applications. The high-level services listed in the following are part of the Android framework and can be useful when creating mobile applications that meet our requirements.

The Android framework includes the following high-level services that can be beneficial for developing mobile applications according to our prerequisites:

The following services are deployed for application services:

- **Activity Manager:** Plays a crucial role in bringing all aspects of the applications lifecycle and activity stack under control.
- **Content Providers**: These providers enable applications to publish data online and share it with other applications.
- **Resource Manager**: Assists in accessing non-code embedded resources, such as strings, color settings, and layouts for user interfaces.
- **Notifications Manager:** Allows applications to show alerts and notifications to users via the user interface of the application.
- **View System**: It serves as a base class for widgets and handles events.
- **Android Runtime:** Android Runtime environment is one of the most important aspects of Android. It contains components such as core libraries and the Dalvik virtual machine (DVM). Mainly, it provides the base for the application framework and powers our application with the help of the core libraries.

Dalvik Virtual Machine (DVM) is a register-based virtual machine, similar to Java Virtual Machine (JVM), that is specifically tailored and optimized for Android to guarantee that a device can run multiple instances efficiently. For low-level memory management and threading, it is dependent on the Linux kernel. With the help of the core libraries, we can create Android apps in either Kotlin or standard Java. Android application developers can create Android apps using the Java programming language, thanks to the core libraries provided by the Android runtime.

Like JVM, DVM is a register-based virtual machine that is specially designed and optimized for Android to ensure that a device can run multiple instances efficiently. It depends on the layer of the Linux kernel for threading and low-level memory management. The core libraries enable us to implement Android applications using the standard JAVA or Kotlin programming languages.

The Android runtime provides core libraries which let Android application developers develop Android applications in the Java programming language.

- **Platform libraries:** The Platform libraries include various C/C++ core libraries and Java-based libraries, such as media, graphics, surface manager, OpenGL, and so on to provide a support for Android development.

  The Linux kernel is topped with several native libraries. The library gives the device a set of instructions so that it can appropriately handle various kinds of data. Native libraries, most of which are open-source, are necessary for Android development. It is an assortment of Java-based and C/C++ core libraries that facilitate Android development, including Graphics, Libc, SSL

(Secure Socket Layer), SQLite, Media, Webkit, OpenGL (Open Graphic Library), Surface Manager, and others. The following provides information about some of the most important Android development libraries.

- A media library used for playing, recording, and editing audio and video formats.
- A surface manager library that provides display management functionality.
- Surface manager responsible for managing access to the display subsystem.
- SGL and OpenGL are both cross-language, cross-platform application program interfaces (API) are used for 2D and 3D computer graphics.
- SQLite provides database support, and FreeType provides font support.
- Web-Kit, an open-source web browser engine that provides all the functionality to display web content and to simplify page loading.
- SSL (Secure Sockets Layer), a security technology that establish an encrypted link between a web server and a web browser.

- **Linux Kernel:** Linux Kernel is the heart of the Android architecture. It manages all the available drivers, such as display drivers, camera drivers, Bluetooth drivers, audio drivers, memory drivers, and so on, which are required during the runtime. The Linux Kernel will provide an abstraction layer between the device hardware and the other components of Android architecture. It is responsible for management of memory, power, devices, and so on.

The features of the Linux kernel are:

- **Security**: The Linux kernel handles the security between the application and the system.
- **Memory Management**: It efficiently handles memory management, thereby providing the freedom to develop our apps.
- **Process Management**: It manages the process well and allocates resources to processes whenever they need them.
- **Network Stack:** It effectively handles the network communication.
- **Driver Model**: It ensures that the application works properly on the device and hardware manufacturers are responsible for building their drivers into the Linux build.

Overview Android Studio Integrated Development Environment (IDE) [2]

Android Studio is the official Integrated Development Environment (IDE) for Android app development. Based on the powerful code editor and developer tools from IntelliJ

IDEA , Android Studio offers even more features that enhance your productivity when building Android apps, such as:

- A flexible Gradle-based build system
- A fast and feature-rich emulator
- A unified environment where you can develop for all Android devices
- Live Edit to update composable in emulators and physical devices in real-time
- Code templates and GitHub integration to help you build common app features and import sample code

Extensive Testing Tools and Frameworks

The functionality, performance, and usability of Android apps are tested using Android testing tools and frameworks. It is essential to conduct thorough mobile app testing to guarantee a consistent app experience across multiple devices. Several factors need to be considered by developers and testers when selecting an automated testing platform. It should integrate with necessary tools, be easy to use, support widely used testing frameworks, enable tests to run on actual devices rather than emulators, be reasonably priced, and scale effectively as the test suite grows. Productivity can also be greatly increased by integrating continuous integration and continuous delivery (CI/CD) workflows seamlessly. Android testing frameworks and tools are useful in this regard. The following tools and frameworks are used to test Android apps' functionality, performance, and usability. In this article, you will learn about six of the most popular Android testing tools available.

- Lint tools to catch performance, usability, version compatibility, and other problems
- C++ and NDK support
- Built-in support for Google Cloud Platform, making it easy to integrate Google Cloud Messaging and App Engine

This section provides an introduction to basic Android Studio features.

Project Modules

In Android Studio, a project includes all components that make up your app's workspace, including assets, test code, build configurations, and source code. A group of source files and build parameters known as a module enables you to separate your project into distinct functional units. One module may depend on another module, and your project may consist of one or more modules. Each module can be built, tested, and debugged on its own. When building code libraries for your own project or when you want to develop distinct sets of resources and code for various device types–such as phones and wearables–while maintaining the scope of all the files within the same project and sharing some code, additional modules come in handy. Each project in Android Studio contains one or more modules with source code files and resource files. The types of modules include:

- Android app modules
- Library modules
- Google App Engine modules

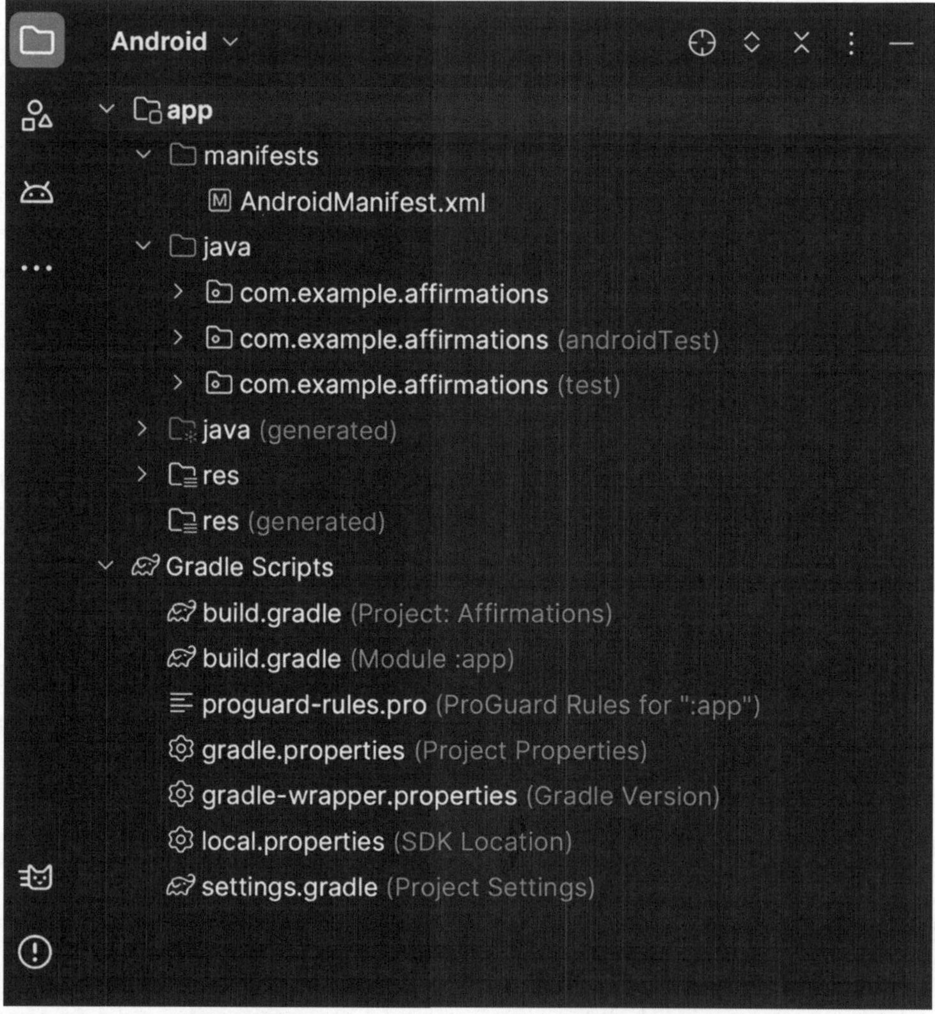

Figure 13.2: *Project files in Android project view*

By default, Android Studio displays your project files in the Android project view, as shown in *Figure* 13.2. This view is organized by modules to provide quick access to your project's key source files. All the build files are visible at the top level, under Gradle Scripts.

Each app module contains the following folders:

- **manifests**: Contains the AndroidManifest.xml file.
- **java:** Contains the Kotlin and Java source code files, including JUnit test code.
- **res:** Contains all non-code resources such as UI strings and bitmap images.

The Android project structure on disk differs from this flattened representation. To see the actual file structure of the project, select Project instead of Android from the Project menu.

Gradle Build System

The Android Gradle plugin adds more Android-specific functionality to the build system, which is based on Gradle and used in Android Studio. This build system operates without requiring the command line, functioning as an integrated tool from the Android Studio menu. The following can be accomplished by utilizing the build system's features:

- **Expand, customize, and set up the build process:** Make several APKs for your application with distinct functionalities by utilizing identical projects and modules. Utilize code and resources from different source sets. You can accomplish all these without changing the essential source files for your app by utilizing Gradle's flexibility.

`Build.gradle` is the name of the build files used by Android Studio. **`Build.gradle`** if you are using Groovy, or kts if you're using Kotlin (strongly advised). These are just text files with components from the Android Gradle plugin configured for the build using the Kotlin or Groovy syntax. For every project, there is a single top-level build file and distinct module-level build files for every module. Android Studio automatically creates the required build files when you import an existing project.

Note: *We may make use of the* **`build.gradle`**. *In the documentation, they are referred to as* **`build.gradle`** *files or kts files, but they are conceptually equivalent. Take* **`build.gradle`**, *for instance. You can think of the Groovy DSL as the* **`build.gradle`** *file (and vice versa) if you use it to configure your build*

- **Build variants:** Using a single project, the build system enables you to produce multiple iterations of the same application. This is helpful if your app has both a paid and a free version or if you wish to distribute different APKs on Google Play for various device setups.
- **Support for multiple APKs:** This feature enables you to quickly create multiple APKs according to screen density or ABI. For instance, you can make different APKs of the same app for hdpi and mdpi screen densities, but treat them as one variant and allow them to share ProGuard settings, javac, dx, and test APKs.

- **Resource shrinking**: When you use Android Studio's resource shrinking feature, any unnecessary resources from your packaged app and library dependencies are automatically removed. For instance, resource shrinking can get rid of the different drawable assets for the `SignInButton` buttons if your app uses Google Play services to access Google Drive functionality and you are not using Google Sign-In at the moment.

Note: *Resource shrinking works in conjunction with code shrinking tools, such as ProGuard.*

- **Manage dependencies:** In the module-level build script, dependencies are listed by name for your project. Gradle locates dependencies and adds them to your build. Declaring module, remote, and local binary dependencies in your `build.gradle` configuration is possible.
- **KTS file**: By default, Android Studio sets up projects to use the Maven Central Repository. This configuration is part of the project's top-level build file.
- **Debugging and profiling tools:** Android Studio is equipped with debugging and performance analysis tools to help you debug and optimize your code.
- **Inline debugging**: By verifying references, expressions, and variable values inline, inline debugging improves code walkthroughs in the debugger view.

Inline debug information includes:

- Inline variable values
- Objects that reference a selected object
- Method return values
- Lambda and operator expressions
- Tooltip values

To enable inline debugging, in the Debug window, click Settings and select Show Variable Values in Editor.

- **Performance profilers:** With the performance profilers offered by Android Studio, you can effortlessly monitor the memory and CPU usage of your application, identify deallocated objects, pinpoint memory leaks, enhance graphics performance, and examine network requests. To use performance profilers, choose View > Tool Windows > Profiler to launch the Android Profiler while your app is running on a device or emulator. Heap dump:

You can start the Java heap dump and garbage collection simultaneously in Android Studio. A file in the Android-specific HPROF binary format contains the heap snapshot. This is helpful for memory usage profiling. You can use the HPROF viewer, which displays classes, instances of each class, and a reference tree, to monitor memory usage and spot memory leaks.

- **Memory Profiler**: Use Memory Profiler to monitor memory usage and see where objects are allocated during particular actions. These allocations help you optimize your application's performance and memory usage by changing the method calls linked to those actions.
- **Data file access:** For in-depth app analysis, the Android SDK tools, such as Systrace and Logcat, produce performance and debugging data. Open the Captures tool window to see the generated data files that are available. To view the data, double-click a file in the list of generated files. To convert any HPROF file to the standard, simply right-click on it. Examine the format of your RAM usage file.
- **Code inspections** Android Studio performs configured lint checks and other IDE inspections automatically during program compilation to make it simple for you to find and fix issues with the structural quality of your code. The lint tool examines the source files of your Android project to look for possible bugs and optimize them for accuracy, security, speed, usability, accessibility, and internationalization.

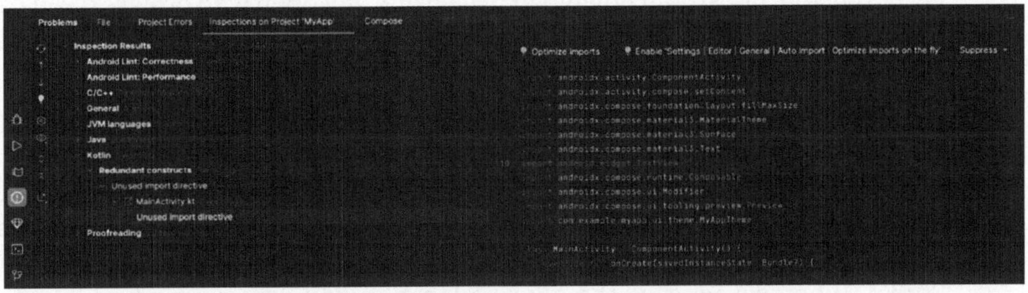

Figure 13.3: *Android Studio's lint inspection results*

Android Studio streamlines your coding workflow by performing IntelliJ code inspections and validating annotations in addition to lint checks.

Annotations in Android Studio

Android Studio offers annotations for variables, parameters, and return values to help you find errors such as null pointer exceptions and conflicts in resource types. The Android SDK Manager bundles the Jetpack Annotations library in the Android Support Repository for use with Android Studio. Code inspection is used by Android Studio to ensure that the configured annotations are accurate.

Log messages: After building and launching your app with Android Studio, you can see device log messages and adb output in the Logcat window. You can use Firebase and other tools that require authentication by logging into your Android Studio developer account. You give those tools permission to access and manage your data across all

Google services by logging in. You can sign in to your developer account or switch developer accounts after opening a project in Android Studio by doing the following:

- Click the profile icon located at the end of the toolbar.
- Choose one of the following actions from the window that pops up:
  - Click **`Sign In`** to enable Android Studio to access the services that are listed if you have not already.
  - Click **`Add Account`** to sign in with a different Google account if you're already logged in.

Alternatively, to sign in to a different account, click **`Sign Out`** and follow the previous instructions once more.

Installing Android Studio

Two steps are required:

1. Go to the Android Studio download page using any open web browser. You can download Android Studio from this website for Android developers. This page automatically finds out what operating system you have.
2. Follow these steps: Click Android Studio Download. Opening the Android Studio License Agreement is the Terms and Conditions page. Go over the license agreement. If you accept the terms and conditions, check the box that says, "**`I have read and agree with the above terms and conditions`**," at the bottom of the page. To begin the download, click Download Android Studio. When asked, save the file to a location you can quickly find, like the Downloads folder. Await the download's completion.

Downloading Android Studio

During downloading procedure, you will be asked to confirm through following screen:

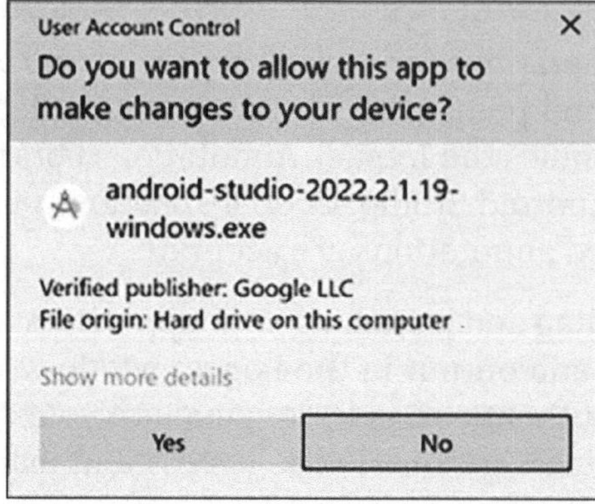

Figure 13.4: *User's confirmation Screen*

After confirmation, user is to go for setting procedure:

Figure 13.5: *Guide screen Before setup*

To install Android Studio on Windows

- Navigate to the folder in which you saved and downloaded the installation file. After downloading, double-click the file. In case a User Account Control prompt appears requesting permission for the installation to modify your computer, select "**`Yes`**" to validate the installation.
- Click **`Next`** to start the installation.
- Accept the default installation settings for all steps.
- **`Click Finish`** when the installation is done to launch Android Studio.

Figure 13.6: *Intimation regarding final stage of Installation*

During Android Studio launch, select your preferred theme: light or dark. Select your preferred theme; screenshots in this course use the light theme.

A mobile UI (mobile user interface) is the graphical and usually touch-sensitive display on a mobile device, such as a smartphone or tablet, that allows the user to interact with the device's apps, features, content, and functions.

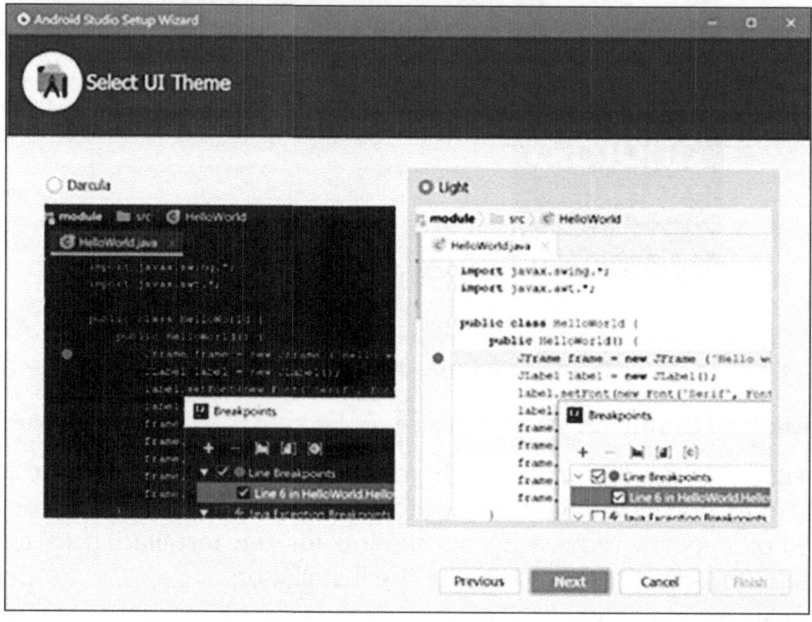

Figure 13.7: *Selecting User Interface theme*

The setup wizard downloads and installs extra files and tools required for developing Android apps during the installation process. Your internet speed may determine how long this takes. You might see a Windows Command Processor `User Account Control` dialog during this time. To accept the dialog, click `Yes`.

Figure 13.8: *Asking confirmation for installing command Processor*

You may also receive a Windows Security Alert about **`adb.exe`**. Click **`Allow Access`**, if needed, to continue the installation.

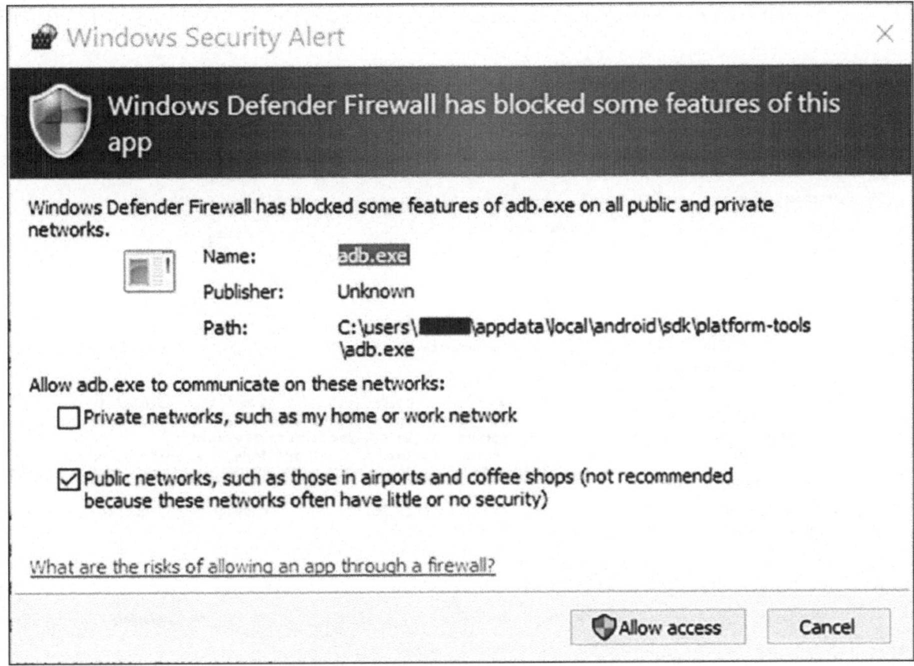

Figure 13.9: *Selecting Access permission*

When the download and installation are completed, click **`Finish`**.

The **`Welcome to Android Studio`** window displays, and you are ready to start creating apps!

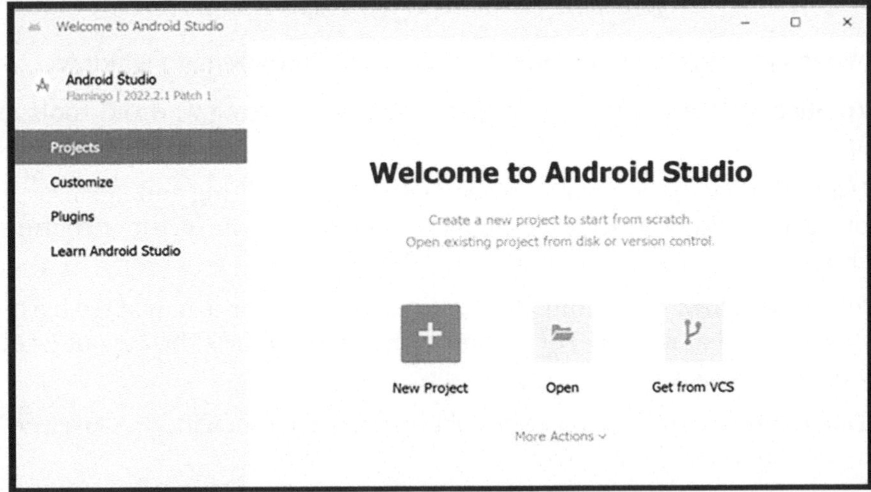

Figure 13.10: *Welcome to Android Studio window*

Get to know the Android Studio UI [4]

The Android Studio main window consists of several logical areas as shown in *Figure 13.4.*

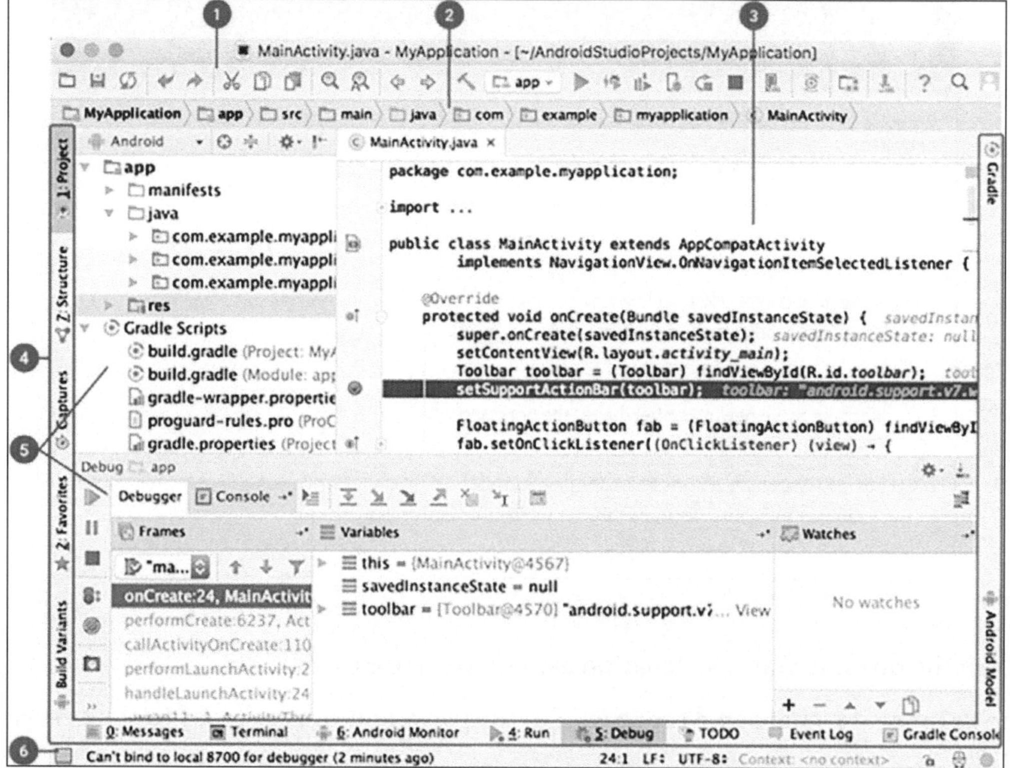

***Figure 13.11:** The Android Studio main window*

The following are the main components of Android Studio's main window:

- **Toolbar**: Perform a variety of tasks, such as starting Android tools and your app.
- **Using the navigation bar**, you can open files for editing and move around your project. It offers a more condensed representation of the structure that is shown in the Project window.
- **Editor window:** Write and alter programs. The editor may alter based on the type of file that is open. For instance, the editor shows the Layout Editor when viewing a layout file.
- **Tool window bar:** To expand or collapse specific tool windows, use the buttons located outside the IDE window.

- **Tool windows:** Provides access to particular functions, such as version control, search, and project management. Expanding and collapsing them are possible.
- **Status bar**: This shows the current state of the IDE and your project, along with any alerts or messages. Tool windows and toolbars can be moved or hidden to reorganize the main window to free up more screen real estate. Keyboard shortcuts are another way to access most IDE features. One of the following can be used to search through your source code, databases, actions, UI elements, and more: double-press the Shift key. Click the magnifying glass, on the top right corner of the Android Studio window. If, for instance, you are trying to find an IDE action that you have forgotten how to trigger, this can be very helpful.

Tool Windows

As you work, Android Studio recognizes your context and automatically opens the appropriate tool windows, saving you the trouble of switching between preset perspectives. The most often used tool windows are, by default, pinned to the application window's tool window bar. Use the following to navigate the tool window:

Click the tool's name in the tool window bar to expand or collapse the tool window. Moreover, tool windows can be attached, detached, pinned, and repinned.

Click `Window` > `Restore Default Layout` to bring the current tool window back to its default layout. Click `Window` > Store Current Layout as Default to change the default layout.

Click the window icon on the Android Studio window's lower left corner to reveal or conceal the full tool window bar. Hover your cursor over the window icon and choose the desired tool window from the menu to find it.

Keyboard shortcuts are another way to open tool windows. The most popular tool windows' shortcuts are listed in the following table.

Tool window	**Windows and Linux**
Project	*Alt+1*
Version Control	*Alt+9*
Run	*Shift+F10*
Debug	*Shift+F9*
Logcat	*Alt+6*
Return to Editor	Esc
Hide All Tool Windows	*Control+Shift+F12*

Table 13.2: *Keyboard shortcuts for tool windows*

Click **`View`** > **`Enter Distraction Free Mode`** to hide the editor tabs, tool windows, and toolbars altogether. Click **`View`** > **`Exit Distraction Free Mode`** to get out of Distraction Free Mode. Use Speed Search to search and filter within most Android Studio tool windows. . Choose the tool window and enter your search term to utilize Speed Search.

Code Completion

Android Studio has three types of code completion, which you can access using keyboard shortcuts.

Type	**Description**	**Windows and Linux**
Basic Completion	Provides fundamental recommendations for variables, types, procedures, expressions, and so forth. You see more results, including private members and non-imported static members, if you call basic completion twice in a row.	*Control+Space*
Smart Completion	Shows options that are appropriate given the context. The anticipated type and data flows are recognized by smart completion. You see more results, including chains, if you call Smart Completion twice in a row.	*Control+Shift+Space*
Statement Completion	Puts in the missing parentheses, brackets, braces, formatting, and other elements to finish the current statement for you.	*Control+Shift+Enter*

Table 13.3: *Keyboard shortcuts for code completion*

To perform quickfixes and show intention actions, press *Alt+Enter*.

Find Sample Code

The Code Sample Browser in Android Studio helps you find high-quality, Google-provided Android code samples based on the currently highlighted symbol in your project.

Navigation

Here are some pointers to get you started with Android Studio.

- To navigate between your recently accessed files, use the Recent Files action.
- To open the Recent Files action, press *Control+E*. The most recent file that was accessed by default is selected. You can also use the left column to access any tool window by using this action.
- To quickly navigate to any part of your current file and view its structure,

use the File Structure action. Press Control+F12 to bring up the File Structure action.

In your project, you can find and navigate to a particular class by using the **Navigate to Class** action. Several advanced expressions are supported by Navigate to Class, such as camel humps, which allow you to search for an element by its capitalized name; paths, line navigate to, which allows you to navigate to a specific line within the file; middle name matching, which allows you to search for a portion of the class name; and many more. It displays the outcomes from the project classes if you call it twice in a row.

- Use the Navigate to File action to navigate to a file or folder: Press *Control+Shift*+N to open the Navigate to File action.
- Press *Control*+N to open the Navigate to Class action. Put a "/" at the end of your expression to search for folders rather than files.
- Press *Control+Shift+Alt*+N to open the Navigate to Symbol action. This action allows you to navigate to a method or field by name. *Alt*+F7 will bring up every line of code that references the class, method, field, parameter, or statement that is currently in the cursor position.

Style and Formatting

Android Studio automatically applies formatting and styles according to the code style settings as you edit. Programming language-specific code style settings allow you to specify formatting conventions for spaces, tabs, indents, wrapping and braces, and blank lines. You can call the Reformat Code action explicitly, even though the IDE applies to format automatically as you work. To customize your code style settings, click **File** > **Settings** > **Editor** > **Code Style** (Android Studio > Preferences >). Hold down **Control+Alt+L** . to initiate the action. Press **Control+Alt+I** to automatically indent all lines (*Figures* 13.12 and 13.13).

```
public void onCreate(Bundle savedInstanceState) {
    super.onCreate(savedInstanceState);
        setContentView(R.layout.activity_main);
  mActionBar = getSupportActionBar();
        mActionBar.setDisplayHomeAsUpEnabled(true);
```

***Figure* 13.12:** *Code before formatting*

```
public void onCreate(Bundle savedInstanceState) {
    super.onCreate(savedInstanceState);
    setContentView(R.layout.activity_main);
    mActionBar = getSupportActionBar();
    mActionBar.setDisplayHomeAsUpEnabl...(true);
                          Formatted 7 lines
                          Show reformat dialog: ⌥⇧⌘L

    // Get reference to the drawer layout and set event listener
```

***Figure* 13.13:** *Code after formatting*

Accessibility Features

The accessibility features in Android Studio, such as keyboard navigation, are covered in this document. Since release 2021.1 of IntelliJ IDEA is the foundation for Android Studio Bumblebee, updates to accessibility features have also been made for all subsequent versions of Android Studio. Complete instructions for enabling screen readers and modifying the IDE for improved accessibility can be found in the IntelliJ documentation.

Use the keyboard: To access all of Android Studio's controls, use keyboard shortcuts.

Note: *Only when utilizing your screen reader's object navigation feature are some Android Studio elements keyboard-accessible.*

This section includes useful keyboard shortcuts for navigating around Android Studio. For a complete guide to the default Android Studio keyboard shortcuts, read Keyboard shortcuts.

Activate the Main Menu

To open the main menu and other top-level menus, use these shortcuts:

1. To open the main menu, press F10.

   To open a top-level menu on a Windows machine, press Alt+[mnemonic]. For example, to open the File menu, press *Alt+F*.

2. Navigate between files and tool windows

   To navigate between files and tool windows, use these shortcuts:

3. To move to a tool window, press *Alt+[number]* (on macOS, *Command+[number]*). For example, to move to the Project structure tool window, press *Alt+0* (on macOS, *Command+0*).

4. To move between files and tool windows, press *Control+Tab* (on macOS, *Command+Tab*). To move through all entries, keep pressing *Control+Tab*.

5. Use the navigation bar

   The navigation bar lets you move between files in a project using the following shortcuts:

   a. To activate the navigation bar, press *Alt+Home* (on macOS, *Option+Fn+Left*).

   b. To switch between items in the navigation hierarchy, press the left arrow or the right arrow.

   To open a popup window displaying the contents of the current item, press the spacebar.

Disable Code Folding

By default, the Android Studio editor folds part of the text into expandable regions. For example, the list of imports at the beginning of a Java source file is folded into a single line containing the text "*import* ...".

Navigating a screen reader can be challenging when code folding is present.

To change the code folding options, go to **File** > **Settings** > **Editor** > **General** > **Code Folding**. Turn off the auto-insertion features.

By default, Android Studio inserts parentheses, quotes, and closing curly braces. It may not be helpful to use automatic insertion when using a screen reader. Disable automatic code completion popup. By default, Android Studio automatically shows the code completion popup when specific keystrokes are typed, and if it finds only one match, it automatically inserts that match.

To change the automatic insertion options, navigate to **File** > **Settings** > **Editor** > **General** > **Smart Keys**. Screen readers may become confused by this behavior.

Access errors, warnings, and code inspections with your keyboard to view and navigate through them. To change the auto popup and auto-insertion options for code completion, go to **File** > **Settings** > **Editor** > **General** > **Code Completion**.

Examine all of the project's files for errors. The Messages window displays all warnings and errors that arise when you select **Build** > **Make Project**.

Use these shortcuts to review errors in the Messages window: *Alt*+0 opens the Messages window; the up and down arrows move you through all messages. As an alternative, you can view and navigate through every error using the text editor.

- Review errors and code inspections in a single file using the editor, press *Control*+Alt+Up/Down. To review errors in a single file, use the following shortcuts: F2 or *Shift*+F2 (F2 or *Shift*+F2 on macOS) to move to the next or previous error. Press Control+F1 to bring up a tooltip with the error message.
- To view all code inspections, not just errors, select **File** > **Settings** > **Editor** > General. Deselecting "N*ext error*" only applies to issues of the highest priority.
- Use tab indentation: By default, Android Studio indents text using the space character. Tab indentation may be preferred by screen reader users due to its more concise verbalization. Go to **File** > **Settings** > **Editor** > **Code Style** > **Java** > **Tabs** and Indents to switch to tab indentation. Make use of the tab character.

Fundamentals of the Developer Workflow [5]

Developing an Android app follows a conceptually similar process to developing apps for other platforms. But you need a few specialized tools to create an Android app that is well-designed and quickly built.

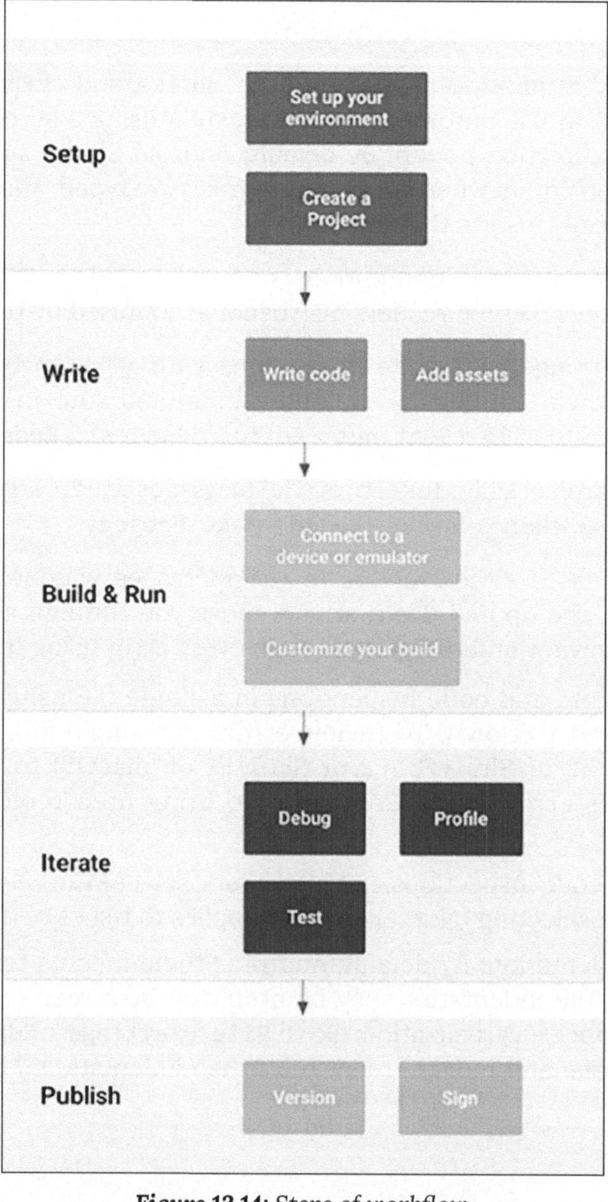

Figure 13.14: *Steps of workflow*

1. The first step in developing an Android app is setting up your workspace.
2. **Create your app:** After organizing your workspace, you can start creating your app. To help you write better code, design a user interface, write resources for various device types, and work more quickly, Android Studio comes with a wide range of tools and intelligence.
3. **Build and run:** In this stage, you create a debuggable APK package for your project, which you can then install and use on an Android-powered device or emulator. During this stage, you can also modify your build. To make your app smaller, you can, for instance, reduce the amount of code and resources it uses and create build variants that generate distinct versions of your app from the same project.
4. **Debug, profile, and test:** During this iterative stage, you keep working on your app while fixing bugs and improving the performance. Use Android Studio to test your app to get assistance with debugging and optimization.
5. **Publish:** To get your app ready for public release, create an Android App Bundle, sign it using a security key, and get set to upload it to the Google Play Store. See the 'Publish your app' page for further details.

Projects Overview [6]

All of the elements that define your Android Studio workspace for an app are contained in a project, including test code, build configurations, source code, and assets. Upon initiating a fresh project, Android Studio generates the essential organization for every file and enables it to be viewed in the Project window. View > Tool Windows > Project is the window that opens.

Modules

An arrangement of source files and build parameters that allow you to divide the functionality of your project into discrete functional units. Your project might have one or more modules, and one module might rely on another. Every module has its own build, test, and debugging processes.

Extra modules come in handy when building code libraries inside your own project or when you want to write distinct code and resource sets for various device kinds, like phones and wearables, but you still want to keep all the files scoped inside the same project and share some code. Then select **`File`** > **`New`** > **`New Module`** to add a new module to your work.

There are several different kinds of modules available in Android Studio: the Android app module, which serves as a container for your app's resource files, build files, and app-level configurations like the Android Manifest and module-level build files. The "**app**" module is the default one that appears when you create a new project. Phone and Tablet Automotive Wear OS Television Baseline Profile Generator Benchmark are among the app module types that Android Studio offers. Each module includes some code templates and necessary files specific to the app or device type that it corresponds to.

Feature Module

Feature module is a modularized feature of your application compatible with Play Feature Delivery. You can offer your users specific app features on demand or as instant experiences via Google Play Instant by utilizing feature modules. The feature modules that Android Studio offers are as follows:

- **Dynamic Feature Module Instant Dynamic Feature Library Module**

  Library module gives you a place to store reusable code that you can import into other projects or use as a dependency in other app modules. Though structurally identical to app modules, library modules cannot be installed on devices because they are built as code archives rather than APKs. The following library module types are available in Android Studio's Create New Module window:

- **Android Library**: This has all file types supported in an Android project, with the exception of native C++ code, such as resources, manifest files, and source code for Kotlin and Java. For your Android app modules, the build output can be added as a dependency in the form of an Android Archive (AAR) file. In analogy to an Android Library, the Android Native Library comprises all file formats that are allowed in an Android project.
- **Native C++ source code**: This, however, can also be found in Android Native Libraries. For your Android app modules, the build output can be added as a dependency in the form of an AAR file.
- **Java or Kotlin Library**: Simply source files for Java or Kotlin are contained here. You can include the Java Archive (JAR) file as a dependency for your Android app modules or other Kotlin or Java projects once the build is complete. Gradle also refers to modules as projects, so sometimes, they are referred to as subprojects. You must declare a library module as follows in order to add it as a dependency to your Android app module: Kotlin dependencies `{ implementation(project(":my-library-module")) }`

Project Files

Android Studio shows your project files in the Android view by default. The actual disk file hierarchy is not reflected in this view. Rather, it is arranged according to modules and file kinds to make it easier to navigate between the important source files for your project, concealing certain files or directories that are not frequently needed.

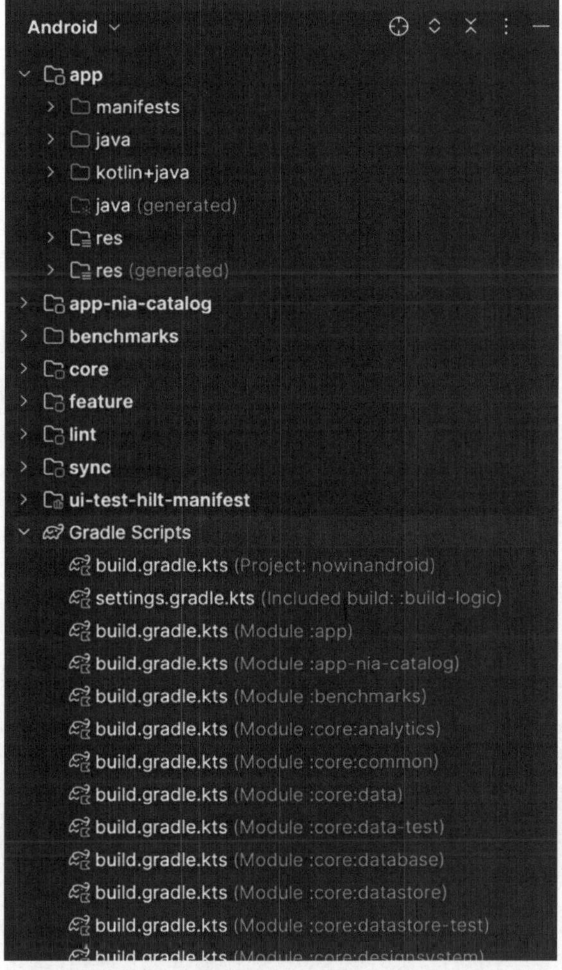

***Figure 13.15**: Project files in the Android view*

- **The Android view** displays all of the project's build-related configuration files in a top-level Gradle Script group, which is one of the structural differences between the Android view and the structure on disk. It displays all of the manifest files for every module in a group at the module level when you have distinct manifest files for various build types and product flavors. Also, it displays every alternative resource file in a single group rather than in a different folder for each resource qualifier.

For instance, you can see side by side all density versions of your launcher icon. Files are displayed in each Android app module under the following groups:

- Manifests: Contains the AndroidManifest, an xml file.

- Java: Includes JUnit test code and contains the source code files for both Kotlin and Java, divided by package names.

  Res: Consists of all non-code resources, separated into their respective subdirectories, including bitmap images and user interface strings.

  Note: *The group structures of various module types vary. A native module, for instance, has a cpp/ folder inside the main group, whereas a Java or Kotlin library is devoid of manifests and res groups.*

  The Project view: To view the project's actual file structure, including all files hidden from the Android view, select `Project` from the Project window's menu.

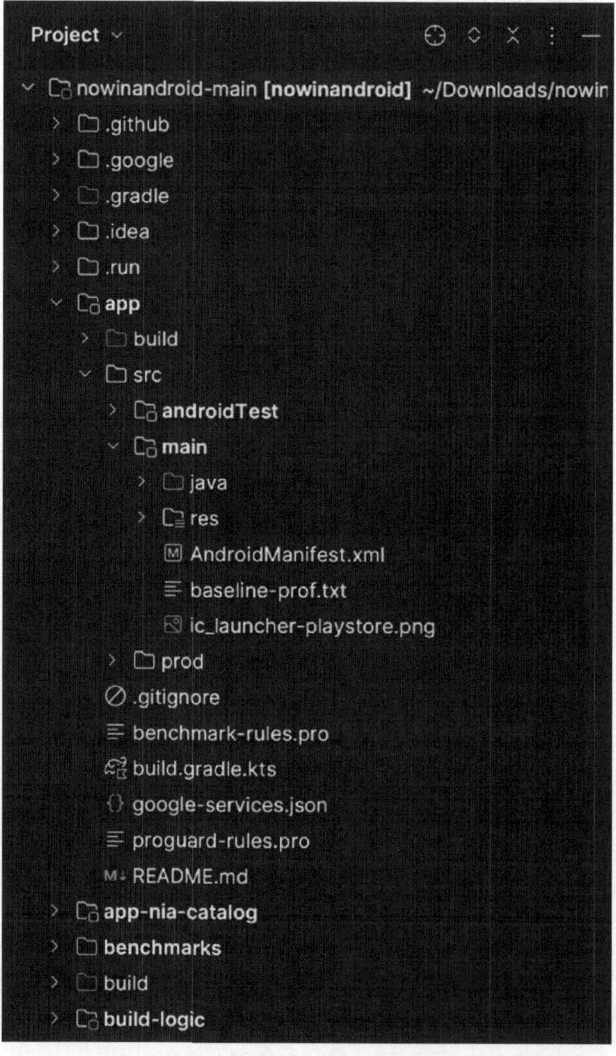

Figure 13.16: *Project view*

Upon choosing the Project view, an abundance of additional files and directories become visible, such as Module-name:

- **build/**: This contains build outputs.
- **libs/**: Includes private libraries in libs/.
- **Src/**: All the module's code and resource files are located in the **src/** subdirectory.
- **androidTest/**: Subdirectory contains the code for instrumentation tests that are executed on an Android device.
- **cpp/**: Contains native code written with the Java Native Interface (JNI) in C or C++. Files for other build variants are located in sibling directories, such as src/debug/ for the debug build type.
- **main/**: Holds the "**main**" source set files:
- **Android Manifest:** The Android code and resources shared by all build variants.
- **xml:** Describes each component of the application and its nature.
- **java/**: Contains source code for either Java or Kotlin, or both,
- **Kotlin/**: if your application has both languages. only includes Kotlin code sources in **kotlin/**.
- **res/**: Holds resources for the application, like UI string files and drawable files.
- **assets/**: Contains files that need to be assembled exactly as is into an APK file. This is a good place, for instance, to store game data and textures.
- **Test/**: This directory can be accessed using URIs just like any other file system, and the **AssetManager** can be used to read files as a stream of bytes. The code for local tests that are executed on your host JVM is located in **test/**.

Project Structure

Click **File** > **Project Structure** to open the **Project Structure** dialog box, where you can modify several project-related settings for your Android Studio project. The following sections are included in it:

- **Project:** This sets the repository location name, Gradle version, and Android Gradle plugin version.
- **SDK Location**: Configures JDK, Android SDK, and Android NDK locations used by your project.
- **Variables:** This feature allows you to modify variables that your build scripts use.
- **Editing module**-specific build configurations, such as the target and minimum SDK, the app signature, and library dependencies, is possible with the module. Each module's settings page is divided into the following tabs:

- **Properties:** Specifies the versions of the SDK and build tools to use to compile the module.
- **Signing**: Specifies the certificate to use to sign your app.
- **Dependencies:** Enumerates the files, libraries, and modules that this module requires. From this pane, you can add, edit, and remove dependencies.
- **Preview:** If a version catalog is being used, note that dependencies added via the Project Structure dialog are added to the **`build.gradle`** file of the module, not the catalog.
- **Build Variants:** Provides you the option to set up various flavors and build kinds for your project.
- **Flavors:** The ability to create different build flavors is provided by flavors, each of which defines a set of configuration parameters, including the target and minimum SDK versions for the module as well as the version code and name. For example, you might define one flavor that has a minimum SDK of 21 and a target SDK of 33.
- **Build Types**: Lets you create and modify build configurations, as described in Configure build variants. By default, every module has debug and release build types, and you can define more as needed.

Create a Project [7]

Android Studio facilitates the creation of Android applications for a range of form factors, including TVs, wear devices, tablets, and phones. The steps for creating a new Android app project and importing an existing project are covered in this section. On the Android Studio Welcome screen, click Start a new Android Studio project to start a new project if you do not already have one open. Choose **`File`** > **`New`** > **`New`** Project from the main menu to start a new project if one is already open.

The Templates Pane

Displays a list of device form factor categories from which you can choose the type of project you want to create in the New Project screen. The project templates for phones and tablets, for instance, are displayed in *Figure* 13.8. Decide on the kind of project you wish to start.

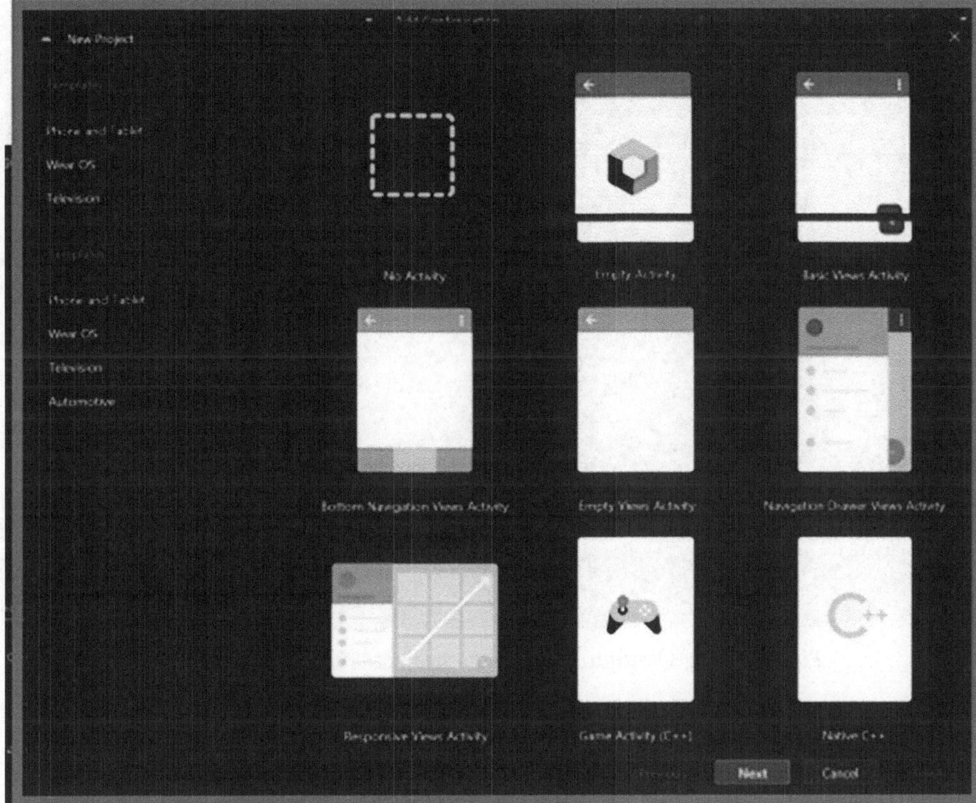

Figure 13.17: *Project Selection Pane*

On the New Project screen, select the kind of project you wish to start.

By choosing your project type, Android Studio can add resources and sample code to your project to assist you in getting started. Click Next after choosing the type of project.

Configure Your Project

The following stage of project creation involves adjusting various parameters, as illustrated in *Figure* 13.9. Set up a few parameters for your new project.

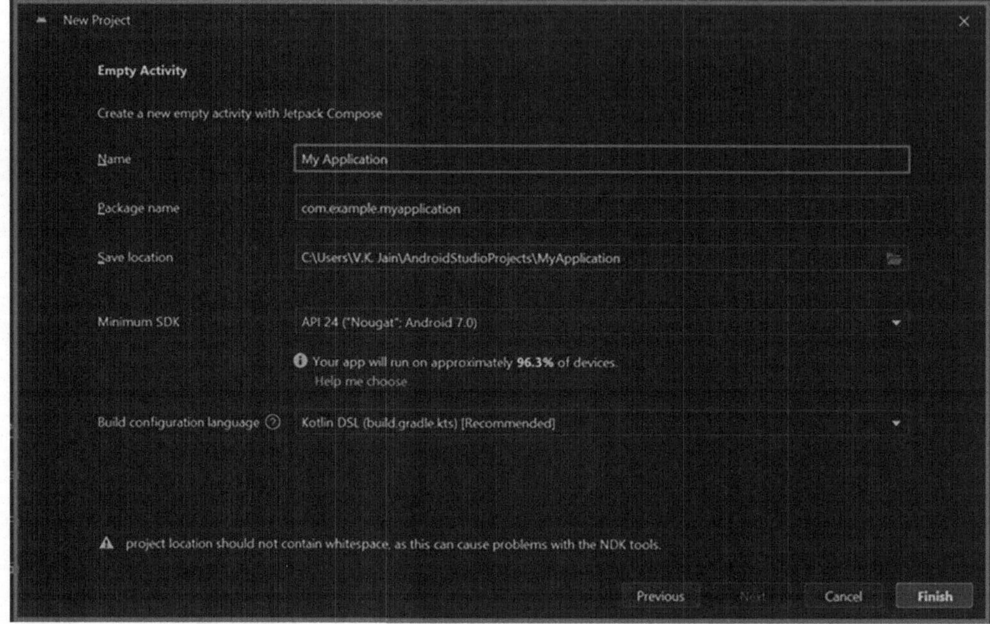

Figure 13.18: *Configure your new project with a few settings*

Specify the Name of Your Project

Give the name of the package. This package name automatically becomes the namespace (which you use to access project resources) and application ID (which you use to publish your project).

Choose the Save location for the local storage of your project. When creating sample code for your new project in Android Studio, choose whether you want it to be in Java or Kotlin. Remember that you are not required to use that language exclusively for the project. Decide which Minimum API level your app should be able to support.

Your app will not be able to use as many contemporary Android APIs if you choose a lower API level. Still, a higher proportion of Android smartphones are capable of using your app. Choosing a higher API level has the opposite effect. Click "`Help me choose`" to view more information that will aid in your decision-making. This opens a dialog where you can see the effect of using different minimum API levels and the cumulative distribution for the selected API level, an aid that displays the various API levels' cumulative distribution.

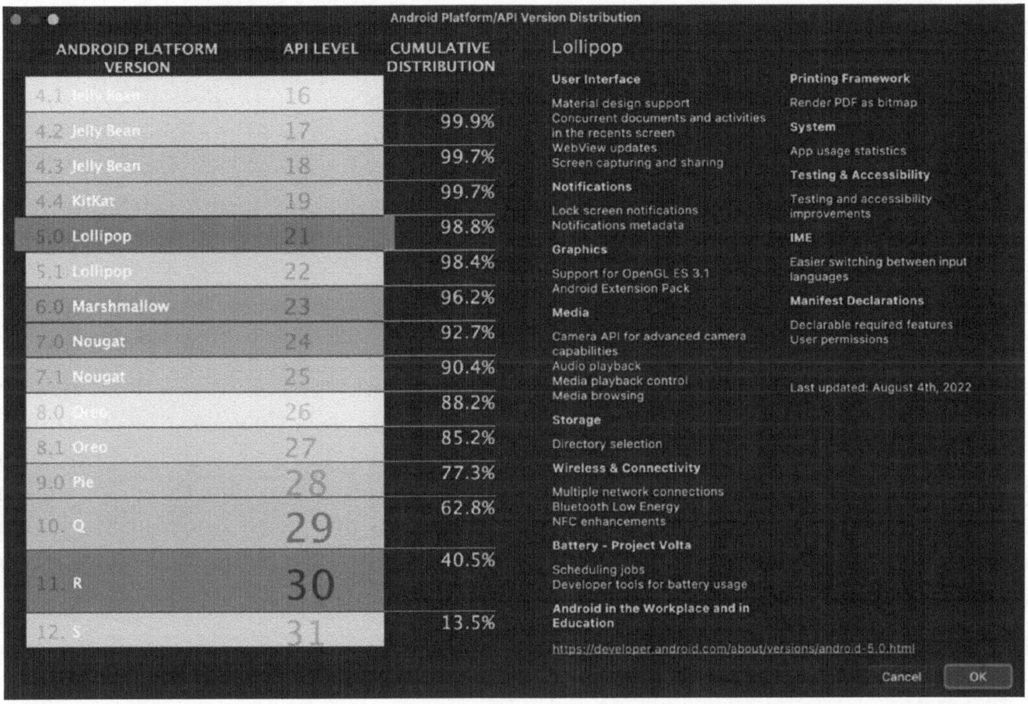

Figure 13.19: *The cumulative distribution of the various API levels is displayed on a help screen*

By default, your project is set up to use Android X libraries instead of Android Support libraries. Choose to use legacy Android support libraries if you would rather use the legacy support libraries. Since the legacy support libraries are no longer supported, doing this is not advised. Click Finish when you're prepared to start working on your project.

To get you started, Android Studio generates a new project for you with some basic code and resources. You can add a module to your project in case you later decide to add support for a different form factor of the device. Additionally, you can create an Android library to share code and resources amongst modules.

Import an Existing Project

To import an existing local project into Android Studio, follow these steps: Click, and then navigate to the project's root directory in the window that appears. Press OK. Android Studio loads the project and indexes its contents in a new IDE window. Choose `File` > `New` > `Project from Version Control` if you are importing a project from version control.

Mobile Linux

Linux for mobile devices, also known as mobile Linux, is used in Linux-based operating systems on portable devices with touchscreens, serving as the primary or only Human Interface Device (HID). It includes tablets and smartphones in the main, as well as some other mobile phones, PDAs (personal digital assistants), and portable media players with separate touchscreens.

Conclusion

In this chapter, first, we have learned the definition and types of mobile devices. Then we discussed the most famous operating system for mobile devices, that is, Android and compared it with Apple-owned iOS. We learned in detail about Android operating system with respect to features and categories of Android applications for making Android-based application. Later, we learned how to deal with Android Studio and Android Studio Integrated Development Environment. At the end of chapter, we learned about Mobile Linux.

In the next chapter, we shall concentrate on operating systems for multiprocessing system.

Questions

1. Enumerate the various categories of Android applications.
2. Describe Android architecture and state its several main components and their sub components.
3. How is a project implemented via Android Studio?

Multiple Choice Questions

1. Android is
    a. an operating system
    b. a web browser
    c. a web server
    d. none of above
2. Under which of the following Android is licensed?
    a. OSS
    b. Sourceforge

   c. Apache/MIT

   d. None of the above

3. The Android is mainly developed for..................

   a. Servers

   b. Desktops

   c. Laptops

   d. Mobile devices

4. Which of the following is the first mobile phone released that ran the Android OS?

   a. HTC Hero

   b. Google gPhone

   c. T - Mobile G1

   d. None of the above

5. Which of the following virtual machines is used by the Android OS?

   a. JVM

   b. Dalvik virtual machine

   c. Simple virtual machine

   d. None of the above

6. Name the language on which Android is based

   a. Java

   b. C++

   c. C

   d. None of the above

7. APK stands for:

   a. Android Phone Kit

   b. Android Page Kit

   c. Android Package Kit

   d. None of the above

8. What does API stand for?
   a. Application Programming Interface
   b. Android Programming Interface
   c. Android Page Interface
   d. Application Page Interface
9. Which of the following converts Java byte code into Dalvik byte code?
   a. Dalvik converter
   b. Dex compiler
   c. Mobile interpretive compiler (MIC)
   d. None of the above
10. How can we stop the services in Android?
    a. By using the `stopSelf()` and `stopService()` method
    b. By using the `finish()` method
    c. By using `system.exit()` method
    d. None of the above
11. What is an activity in Android?
    a. Android class
    b. Android package
    c. A single screen in an application with supporting Java code
    d. None of the above
12. How can we kill an activity in Android?
    a. Using `finish()` method
    b. Using `finishActivity(int requestCode)`
    c. Both (a) and (b)
    d. Neither (a) nor (b)
13. ADB stands for:
    a. Android debug bridge
    b. Android delete bridge

c. Android destroy bridge

d. None of the above

14. On which of the following, developers can test the application, while developing the Android applications?

a. Third-party emulators

b. Emulator included in Android SDK

c. Physical android phone

d. All of the above

15. Which of the following kernels is used in Android?

a. MAC

b. Windows

c. Linux

d. RedHat

16. Which of the following is the first callback method that is invoked by the system during an activity life cycle?

a. `onClick()` method

b. `onCreate()` method

c. `onStart()` method

d. `onRestart()` method

17. Which of the following is not an activity lifecycle callback method?

a. `onClick()` method

b. `onCreate()` method

c. `onStart()` method

d. `onBackPressed()` method

18. We require an AVD to create an emulator. What does AVD stand for?

a. Android Virtual device

b. Android Virtual display

c. Active Virtual display

d. Active Virtual device

19. Does Android support other languages than Java?
    a. Yes
    b. No
    c. Maybe
    d. Cannot say
20. What is the use of a content provider in Android?
    a. For storing the data in the database
    b. For sharing the data between applications
    c. For sending the data from an application to another application
    d. None of the above
21. AAPT stands for
    a. Android Activity Packaging Tool
    b. Android Asset Packaging Tool
    c. Android Action Packaging Tool
    d. None of the above
22. NDK stands for
    a. Native Development Kit
    b. New Development kit
    c. Native Design Kit
    d. None of the above
23. Which of the following methods is used to handle what happens after clicking a button?
    a. onClick
    b. `onCreate`
    c. `onSelect`
    d. None of the above
24. Which of the following Android components displays the part of an activity on screen?
    a. View
    b. Manifest

c. Intent

d. Fragment

25. Which of the following is the parent class of Activity?

 a. context

 b. `object`

 c. `contextThemeWrapper`

 d. None of the above

26. Which of the following is the parent class of service?

 a. context

 b. object

 c. `contextThemeWrapper`

 d. `contextWrapper`

27. OHA in Android stands for

 a. Open Health Academy

 b. Open Handset Alliance

 c. Open Handset Application

 d. Open Handset Association

28. In which of the following tabs is an error shown?

 a. CPU

 b. Memory

 c. ADB Logs

 d. Logcat

29. Which of the following is the topmost layer of Android architecture?

 a. System Libraries and Android Runtime

 b. Linux Kernel

 c. Applications

 d. Applications Framework

30. Which of the layers is below the topmost layer of Android architecture?
    a. System Libraries and Android Runtime
    b. Linux Kernel
    c. Applications
    d. Applications Framework
31. Which of the layers is the lowest layer of Android architecture?
    a. System Libraries and Android Runtime
    b. Linux Kernel
    c. Applications
    d. Applications Framework
32. What is contained in manifest.xml?
    a. Source code
    b. List of strings used in the app
    c. Permission that the application requires
    d. None of the above
33. Which of the following is not a state in the service lifecycle?
    a. Destroyed
    b. Start
    c. Paused
    d. Running
34. Which of the following is a dialog class in Android?
    a. Alert Dialog
    b. `DatePicker Dialog`
    c. `ProgressDialog`
    d. All of the above
35. In which state the activity is, if it is not in focus, but still visible on the screen?
    a. Stopped state
    b. Destroyed state

c. Paused state

d. Running state

36. Which of the following is the built-in database of Android?

a. SQLite

b. MySQL

c. Oracle

d. None of the above

37. Is it true that "`There can be only one running activity at a given time`"?

a. True

b. False

c. Maybe

d. Cannot say

38. Which of the following Android library provides access to the database?

a. `android.content`

b. `android.database`

c. `android.api`

d. None of the above

39. In Android Studio, which of the following callbacks is called when an activity starts interacting with the user?

a. `onDestroy`

b. `onCreate`

c. `onResume`

d. `onStop`

Answers

1.	a	2.	c	3.	d	4.	c	5.	b	6.	a	7.	c
8.	a	9.	b	10.	a	11.	c	12.	c	13.	a	14.	d
15.	c	16.	b	17.	d	18.	a	19.	a	20.	c	21.	b
22.	a	23.	a	24.	d	25.	c	26.	d	27.	b	28.	d
29.	c	30.	d	31.	b	32.	c	33.	c	34.	d	35.	c
36.	a	37.	a	38.	b	39.	c						

References

[1] Android Architecture – Detailed Explanation,https://www.interviewbit.com/blog/android-architecture/

[2] Meet Android Studio, Android Developers,https://developer.android.com/studio/intro

[3] Windows: Download and install Android Studio,https://developer.android.com/codelabs/basic-android-kotlin-compose-install-android-studio#2

[4] Get to know the Android Studio UI, Android Developers,12 Apr 2023, https://developer.android.com › intro › user-interface

[5] Developer Workflow Basics, Android Developers,

[6] Projects overview, Android Developers, Android Studio editor,https://developer.android.com/studio/projects#

[7] Create a project | Android Studio, Android Developers, https://developer.android.com › studio › projects › create...

Chapter 14
Operating Systems for Multiprocessing System

Introduction

Operating system with multiprocessing capabilities: This technology uses several processors in a system to increase efficiency and speed. The multiprocessing operating system allows for the concurrent operation of numerous threads or processes by doing this. A multiprocessing operating system makes use of several processors to function as a single unit. A job can be divided and completed more quickly by connecting multiple CPUs. A final result is produced by compiling the output from each processor once the task is completed. Jobs frequently share other system resources and must share main memory [1].

Structure

In this chapter, we will discuss the following topics:

- Overview of Multiprocessing Operating System
- Working of Multiprocessing Operating System
- Advantages of Multiprocessing Operating System
- Disadvantages of Multiprocessing Operating System
- Types of Multiprocessing Operating Systems
- Disadvantages of Symmetrical Multiprocessing Operating System
- Asymmetrical Multiprocessing Operating System
- Single-processor vs. Multiprocessing operating systems
- Examples of Multiprocessing Operating Systems with Unix

Overview of Multiprocessing Operating System [1]

We have already learned about the scheduling of multiprocessing operating systems in *Chapter* 5, *Scheduling*.

An operating system with multiple processors distributes the workload among its multiple processors or cores. Better performance and quicker execution are made possible by assigning a specific task to each processor. The outcomes from each processor are combined to create a single output once the task is finished. Every processor is given a task that it can effectively complete, thanks to the operating system's management of resource allocation. System performance is maximized, and resources are used more effectively as a result. The organization of a typical multiprocessing operating system is shown in the *Figure* 14.1.

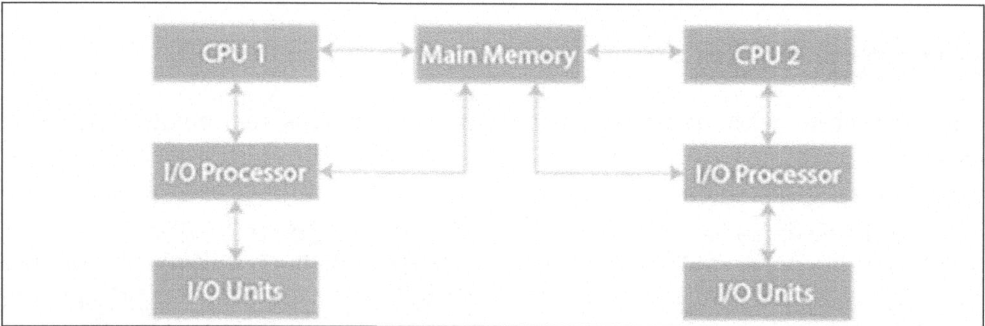

Figure 14.1: *Organization of a typical Multiprocessing Operating System*

Advantages of Multiprocessing Operating System

The following are some advantages multiprocessing operating systems have over other operating systems.

- Multiple processors carry out tasks, which improves system performance and speeds up execution.
- The other processors can carry out the tasks if one stops working. Multiprocessing operating systems therefore guarantee the system's high availability.
- Operating systems with multiple processors are scalable, meaning they can manage growing workloads without compromising system performance.
- Multiprocessing operating systems make effective use of available resources.

Disadvantages of Multiprocessing Operating System

The multiprocessing operating system has the following disadvantages.

- Multiprocessing operating systems are complex and require specialized knowledge.
- The cost of a multiprocessing operating system can be high because of the need for specialized hardware resources.
- They may face compatibility issues with software that is not designed to work with multiprocessing operating systems.
- Achieving synchronization between multiple processors in a multiprocessing operating system is a challenging task.

Types of Multiprocessing Operating Systems

Multiprocessing Operating Systems are of the following types. They are:

- Symmetrical Multiprocessing Operating System
- Asymmetrical Multiprocessing Operating System

Both of these types are discussed in detail in the following section.

Symmetrical Multiprocessing Operating System

Each processor in a symmetric multiprocessing operating system runs the same copy of the operating system, makes independent decisions, and cooperates with other processes to maintain system stability. Simple algorithms are used for CPU scheduling. The least taxed processor can be assigned to each new task that a user assigns. It also results in a system where every processor is constantly 100% occupied. The symmetric multiprocessing operating system is sometimes referred to as a "shared everything" system since the processors share memory and the input-output bus, or data route. There are barely any more than 16 processors in this system. An illustration of a standard symmetrical multiprocessing operating system with shared memory is provided in *Figure* 14.2.

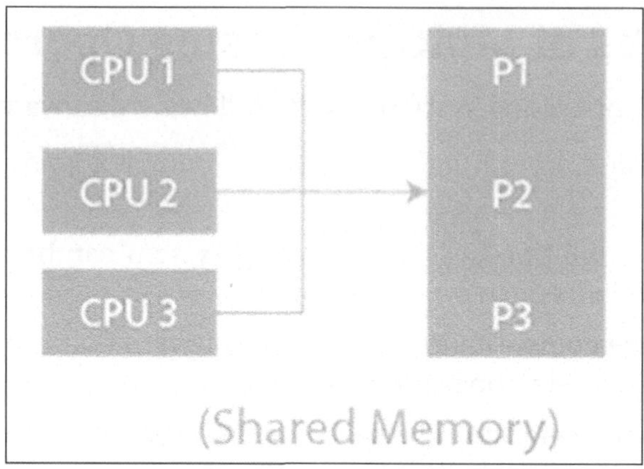

***Figure* 14.2:** *Symmetric Multiprocessing*

Advantages

- Since they are fault-tolerant, the tasks can still be completed by the other processors if one fails
- The asymmetric multiprocessing operating system divides the workload evenly among several processors to use the available resources efficiently

Disadvantages

- They are more complex and require specialized knowledge to manage
- Symmetrical multiprocessing operating systems are much costlier than asymmetric ones
- Synchronization between multiple processors is challenging

Asymmetrical Multiprocessing Operating System

Asymmetrical multiprocessing operating system involves one processor acting as a master and the others as slaves. The master processor assigns ready-to-execute operations to the slave processors. The master processor maintains a ready queue from which slave processors get the processes they need to execute. A scheduler created by the master processor allocates processes to other processors in an asymmetric multiprocessing operating system.

Figure 14.3 depicts a general asymmetrical multiprocessing operating system.

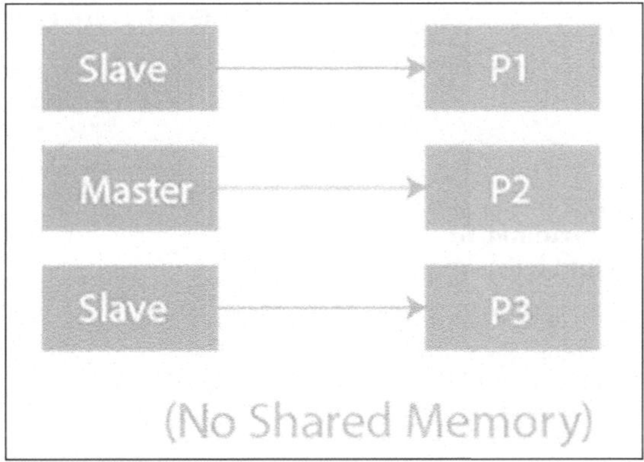

Figure 14.3: *Asymmetrical Multiprocessing Operating System*

Advantages

- Since each CPU can be tailored to a particular task, asymmetric multiprocessing operating systems offer greater scalability.
- Owing to the lack of specialized hardware requirements, asymmetric multiprocessing operating systems are less expensive.
- Designing, handling, and managing them is simpler.

Disadvantages

- Asymmetrical multiprocessing operating system processors can become overloaded in certain cases and remain idle for extended periods in others.
- Since they are made to operate on processors that do not share memory, asymmetric multiprocessing operating systems have limited resource sharing capabilities.

Multiprocessing vs. Single-Processor Operating Systems

Operating systems (OSs) with multiple processors carry out the same tasks as OSs with a single processor. They carry out user-initiated tasks by scheduling and overseeing calculations and operations. The distinction is that multiprocessing OS separate the work into multiple subtasks and then allocate each subtask to a separate central processing unit (CPU). To do this, multiprocessing employs a unique communication architecture. An interprocessor communication system is necessary for an OS with multiple processors so that the processors can schedule and coordinate the completion of tasks. Since multiprocessing OS rely on parallel processing, every processor engaged in a task must be able to communicate with the others regarding its progress. As a result, delays and other inefficiencies can be reduced when performing computations by integrating the work of the processors [2].

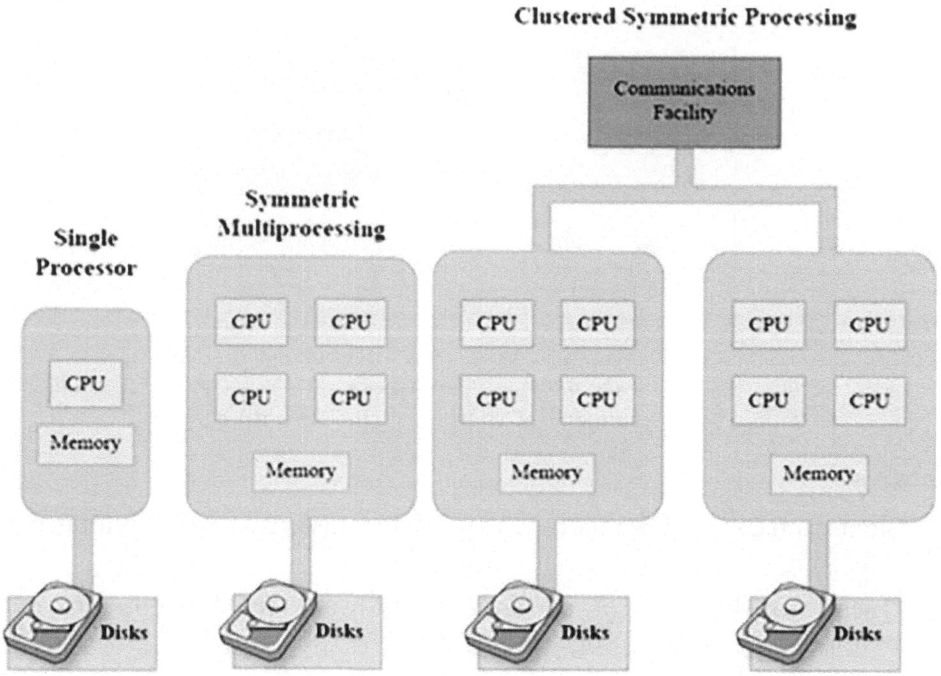

Figure 14.4: Single-Processing vs. Multiprocessing Operating System

Multiprocessing operating systems can handle tasks more quickly and efficiently, as each CPU that becomes available can access the shared memory to complete the task at hand.

Applying Multiprocessing Operating System Effectively

The computer system needs the following to use a multiprocessing operating system effectively:

- **Motherboard Support:** A motherboard has the capacity to support several processors. This entails extra chips for the extra sockets or slots as well as a chipset that can handle the multiprocessing setup.
- **Processor Support**: It refers to processors employed in a system with multiple processors. The operating system assigns distinct tasks to the different processors in the system, managing the entire multiprocessing process. Applications that are divided into smaller, autonomously running routines and intended for use in multiprocessing are referred to as threaded applications. This enables multiprocessing, which enhances performance by allowing the operating system to allow these threads to run concurrently on multiple processors. Processes can operate in parallel on a multiprocessor system. The

capacity of the CPU to handle incoming jobs concurrently is known as parallel processing. In computer systems, this becomes increasingly crucial as the CPU divides and conquers the tasks. In domains such as image processing, weather forecasting, expert systems, artificial intelligence, and others, parallel processing is typically employed. A possible bottleneck in a multiprocessor system could result from the dynamic resource sharing between the different processors.

- **Primary points of contention**: In an operating system designed for multiple processors, there are three primary points of contention:
    - **Locking system**: The locking scheme must safeguard the shared resources among the processors to ensure safe access to them. A locking is used to serialize multiple processors' accesses to the protected resource. The system's performance can be significantly lowered by using locking carelessly. Using locking schemes, avoiding lengthy critical sections, swapping out locks for lock-free algorithms, and, if possible, refraining from sharing can all help to lessen this type of contention.
    - **Data sharing**: The cache coherence protocol serializes the constant accesses to the shared data items by several processors (some of which are capable of writing data). Serialization delays can significantly affect the performance of a system, even one with a moderate size. Moreover, spikes in cache coherence traffic overload the interconnection network or memory bus, slowing down the system as a whole. Replication strategies can be used to lower the frequency of write accesses to the shared data, or if sharing cannot be avoided, to eliminate this type of contention.
    - **False sharing:** This type of contention occurs when disparate data items utilized by various processors are positioned adjacent to one another in memory and consequently share a single cache line. The consequence of false sharing is identical to that of regular sharing, which involves bouncing the cache line among multiple processors; luckily, once it is recognized.

Single-processor OS vs. Multiprocessing Operating Systems - Detailed

As each CPU that becomes available can access the shared memory to complete the task at hand, multiprocessing operating systems can handle tasks more quickly and most efficiently.

For example, if a single-processor OS were running an application requiring it to perform three tasks: one taking five milliseconds, another taking eight milliseconds, and the last taking seven milliseconds, the processor would perform each task in order. The entire application would thus require twenty milliseconds. If a multiprocessing

OS were running the same application, the three tasks would be assigned to separate processors. The first would complete the first task in five milliseconds, the second would do the second task in eight milliseconds, and the third would finish its task in seven milliseconds. Thus, the multiprocessing OS would complete the entire task in eight milliseconds. From this example, it is clear that multiprocessing OSs offer distinct advantages.

- **Coupling:** One type of tightly coupled multiprocessing system has processors sharing memory with each other. This is known as symmetric multiprocessing (SMP). Processor symmetry is present when the multiprocessing OS treats all processors equally, rather than prioritizing a particular one for certain operations. Multiprocessing OSs are designed with special features that support SMP, because the OS must be able to take advantage of the presence of more than one processor. The OS has to "know" that it can divide up certain types of tasks among different processors. It must also be able to track the progress of each task so that the results of each operation can be combined once they conclude. In contrast, asymmetric multiprocessing occurs when a computer assigns system maintenance tasks to some types of processors and application tasks to others. Since the type of task assigned to each processor is not the same, they are out of symmetry. SMP has become more commonplace because it is usually more efficient.
- **Multitasking:** The advent of multiprocessing OSs has had a major influence on how people perform their work. Multiprocessing OSs can execute more than one program at a time. This enables computers to use more user-friendly interfaces based on graphical representations of input and output. It allows users with relatively little training to perform computing tasks that once were highly complex. They can even perform many such tasks at once.

Multiprocessing OSs, though once a major innovation, have become the norm rather than the exception. As each generation of computers must run more and more complex applications, the processing workload becomes greater and greater. Without the advantages offered by multiple processors and OSs tailored to take advantage of them, computers would not be able to keep up.

Examples of Multiprocessing Operating Systems Using Unix

Some common examples of multiprocessing operating systems include Windows Server, Linux, Unix, IBM's z/OS, Solaris, and so on.

Unix Operating System [3]

The UNIX operating system has been implemented on numerous processors, but only recently has it been adapted to multiprocessor (MP) configurations. This expansion increases the range of machines that can run UNIX systems, reinforces the concept of a versatile operating system, and expands the potential applications of UNIX systems.

It also serves as an essential upgrade for projects that initially use UNIX on a mini-computer and subsequently outgrow its capabilities. Currently, UNIX operates in multiprocessing environments on IBM/370 architecture machines, AT&T 3B20A and 3B5 computers, among others.

The following section applies to various machine architectures that support multiprocessor environments. The UNIX systems developed for these multiprocessors offer complete transparency to user programmers, meaning that system calls and commands function identically on multiprocessor systems as they do on single-processor UNIX systems.

Existing C programs can be transferred from single-processor systems to their multiprocessor counterparts without recompilation, except for system-specific code. The terminal interface, file system format, process hierarchy, and all other user-visible aspects of the operating system remain consistent with those on a single-processor UNIX system.

In this context, a multiprocessor hardware configuration refers to a setup with two or more processors sharing a common memory, often referred to as a tightly coupled system. This differs from a loosely coupled system, where each processor has its own private memory, and communication occurs via a networking facility rather than shared memory. Multiprocessor hardware configurations can be further categorized based on their input/output symmetry.

Associated Processor (AP) Configuration

In an Associated Processor (AP) configuration, only one processor is capable of handling I/O operations, while in a true multiprocessor configuration, either processor can do so. Unless specified otherwise, the following discussion pertains to MP and AP configurations. Another multiprocessor UNIX system allows only the master processor to execute the operating system kernel, avoiding the system data corruption issues discussed in *Chapter 3, Concept of a Process and System Calls.* This system has modified the process scheduling algorithm to account for the presence of multiple processors, scheduling only user-level processes to the processor prohibited from executing kernel code, the slave. When a process running on the slave processor makes a system call, the operating system recognizes the origin of the system call on the slave processor, suspends the process, and reschedules it for the master processor.

Challenges with Multiprocessor Capability

Software developers frequently utilize UNIX systems to exchange data and communicate with one another while working on a project. However, several software development projects eventually outgrow their initial processing capacity, meaning that even a single computer can no longer support all users adequately. If a project needs more capacity than a single machine can handle, it can either buy more machines and try to divide the workload among them or upgrade to a bigger machine. However, adding more machines to split the workload presents several challenges:

- There is a significant **networking overhead** when exchanging data between machines.
- Users often need to comprehend the machine/project structure because the network is not always transparent.
- Replicated data may be inconsistent due to concurrent update issues across multiple machines, although data replication is commonly done to minimize network flow.

However, switching to larger machines—sometimes from a different vendor—can be costly in terms of user productivity, data migration, and hardware costs. Projects with a single processor can start small and grow into larger, more powerful systems by adding more processors as needed. This is made possible by a multiprocessor capability. Compared to purchasing a new, larger machine, such growth is typically less costly and disruptive to end users.

A multiprocessor system may also be more reliable, which is another benefit. The system recover even if a hardware malfunction renders one processor unusable. Except for decreased performance, users would not need to take any extra steps and would not notice any differences in system services. Rebooting the systems described here is necessary to restore operation because diagnosing and resolving such issues on a multiprocessor UNIX system while it is in operation is still an open issue. Nevertheless, they function in single-processor mode, allowing the system to be booted and operated on the remaining processors even during a processor failure.

The Problem of Multiprocessors

Because the UNIX system was designed to run on a single processor from the beginning, the code assumes that the kernel is never preempted—that is, except when handling interrupts. Therefore, kernel data structures do not require protection unless they are referred to by an interrupt routine; in that case, interrupt locking can be used to safeguard the data. Raising the processor priority level to a level high enough to stop the type of interrupt from happening is how it is accomplished. Take into consideration, for instance, the snippets of code extracted from figures `getc` and `putc` functions.

Functions are typically utilized for character manipulation and terminal driver queue management. `Clists` are created by chaining together `cblocks`, which are then queued onto them. A character can be removed using the function `getc` from a `clist`, or more accurately, from the first **cblock** of the **clist**. When a **cblock** runs out of characters, it is appended to the start of a free list of **cblocks** and the **clist** is modified appropriately. Specifically, a character is placed onto the final **cblock** of the **clist**, or onto a **clist**, using the put c function. If there is no more room for characters in that **cblock**, a new **cblock** is taken out of the list of available **cblocks**, and the **clist** is changed appropriately. Please refer to the fragments of code in Figure. 14.6.

Pay attention to adding and deleting cblocks from the free list. Let us say a process carries out **getc** statement 1 but is interrupted before **getc** statement 2. The first **cblock** will be removed from the free list if the interrupt handler executes **putc**. Following the interruption, the process resumes control and executes statement 2, resulting in the returned **cblock** being the free list header of **cblocks**. Unfortunately, the **cblock** in **getc** points to the **cblock** and was just removed by **putc**, which severed its previous connection to the free list. The result is that the free list contains only one free **cblock** and one or more busy **cblocks**, and the remaining free **cblocks** are inaccessible.

```
getc(p)
struct clist *p;
{
            struct cblock *cp;
            .
            sp16();
            .
            cp->c_next = cfreelist.c_next;    /* 1 */
            cfreelist.c_next = cp;            /* 2 */
            .
            sp10();
            .
}

putc(c,p)
struct clist *p;
{
            struct cblock *cp;
            .
            sp16();
            .
            cp = cfreelist.c_next;
            cfreelist.c_next = cp->c_next;
            cp->c_next = NULL;
            .
            sp10();
            .
}
```

Figure 14.5: *Raising processor execution level for single processors*

By increasing the processor execution level to avoid interrupts, UNIX systems typically avoid these issues. In Figure. 14.6, the function sp10 lowers the processor execution level to zero, permitting all interrupts, and the function **sp16** raises it to six, meaning that interrupts whose handlers call **putc** are likely to be prevented. Given that there cannot be any interruptions between the calls to **sp16** and **sp10** in *Figure*

14.6. The free list is impervious to corruption. All system data structures are protected when the processor execution level is raised to prevent interrupts because kernel processes cannot be preempted unless they voluntarily give up processor use. Raising the processor execution level, however, does not stop the corruption of system data structures in the multiprocessor systems covered in this paper because kernel code can be executed by each processor concurrently. As an example, one processor could execute **putc** with disastrous consequences, but its **spl** does not guarantee that the other processor will not experience interruptions. As a result, one processor could execute **getc**. Without interruptions, a similar corruption might happen: processors could write to terminals, run putc, and remove the same **cblock** from the free list all at once, with disastrous consequences. To prevent other processors from accessing shared data in multiprocessor systems, kernel code that uses such data must secure it. The method selected for this purpose was based on Dijkstra's. Although semaphores are not new to multiprocessor UNIX systems, their application is more widespread, and the system throughput is significantly higher than previously documented.

Semaphores

Definition: Semaphore is an integer-valued data structure that is used for the limited set of operations listed here.

Init: Initialize the semaphore to an integer value.

psema: Decrement the value of the semaphore. If the resulting value is less than zero, then suspend the executing process and place it on a linked list of processes sleeping on the semaphore. When awakened, the process priority is set to the value supplied as one of the parameters to **psema**. If signals are pending against an awakened process, the value of the priority parameter determines whether they are deferred or caught.

cpsema: If the value of the semaphore is greater than zero, then decrement it and return true. Otherwise, leave the semaphore unmodified and return false.

vsema: Increment the value of the semaphore. If the resulting value is less than or equal to zero, then awaken a process that suspended itself doing a **psema** on the semaphore.

Purpose of Semaphores

First, they are typically initialized to one at system startup; second, they are employed to safeguard particular resources, such as linked lists or tables. A **psema** is applied to the semaphore by a process wishing to use the resource exclusively. This allows the process to proceed while lowering the semaphore value (if any) to zero. At this point, the process uses the resource alone. If another process tries to take control of the resource, its **sema** will drop the value of the semaphore and stop the process from continuing. When a semaphore's absolute value is negative, it indicates how many processes are put on hold while they wait for that resource. A **vsema** is performed on the semaphore by the process responsible for using the resource, which releases it and, if applicable, reawakens any suspended processes. After waking up, a processor can now be scheduled for when it becomes available and does not have any higher-priority tasks executing. When the appointed moment arrives, the awoken process leaves the **psema** call and returns, not realizing that it was briefly suspended. It should execute a **vsema** after utilizing the resource to release the semaphore and awaken any pending processes. When a semaphore is waiting for something to happen, it is initialized to zero. Processes waiting for an event to happen execute a **psema** to suspend themselves, and when they detect it, they execute a **vsema** to wake up inactive processes. A semaphore that counts the resources in the system initializes to the correct value. Since the **vsema** increases when a resource is released and the **psema** decreases when a resource is allocated, semaphore values are always in proportion to the number of resources available. When there are no more resources available, processes will enter sleep mode.

Coding with Semaphores

Process deadlock is a significant issue when using semaphores. A deadlock is demonstrated in *Figure* 14.7 when the code sequences are executed by two processes: A and B. Process B has locked semaphore **sema2**, and process A has locked semaphore **sema1** at time TI.

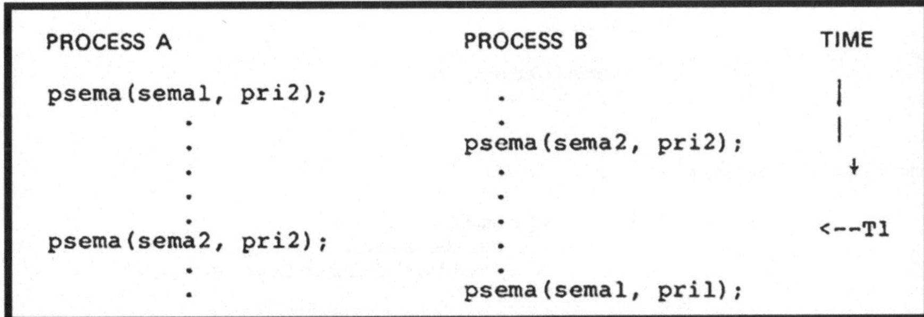

Figure 14.6: *Coding with Semaphores*

Since process B is in control of the semaphore, process A's attempt to lock semaphore sema2 will be suspended. Semaphore sema1 is controlled by process A, so even if process B tries to lock it, it will be suspended. Due to their mutual waiting for a resource, both processes, PROCESS A **psema (semal**, **pri2**); PROCESS B will be suspended indefinitely. The system's different resources are subject to an ordering to prevent deadlocks. To prevent deadlocks, all processes that lock multiple resources at once do so in the specified order. Complex system code and decreased performance would result from more advanced deadlock detection and resolution techniques. Every now and then a process still needs to lock its semaphores in a different order than what is recommended. Since the exec system call accesses the file before deciding whether or not to allocate a text slot, for instance, the system typically locks inodes before text slots. However, the algorithm used to clear the swap space of unused program text first looks through the text table; it only occasionally needs to access the inode, locking it. In these situations, the second semaphore must be locked by the process using a cpsema. To avoid a deadlock, the process must take alternative action if the **cpsema** fails. Typically, this involves releasing the semaphore it is currently holding and waiting for an event before trying to execute the code again. Code that fixes possible deadlock in the *Figure* 14.7 can be found there.

Semaphores in Interrupt Routines

Interrupt handlers usually share kernel data structures with higher-level kernel routines such as the **getc** and **putc** routines for terminal drivers, so semaphore protection is required at the interrupt handler level as well as the rest of the kernel. It is preferable not to sleep in an interrupt routine for two reasons. First, it is desirable to service the interrupt as quickly as possible. Second, the process that would be suspended is often not related to the interrupt being processed. So, interrupt handlers use **cpsemas** instead of **psemas** and take other action if the semaphore is locked elsewhere.

```
PROCESS A                      PROCESS B                              TIME

psema(semal, pril);              .                                      |
    .                          loop:
    .                            .
    .                          psema(sema2, pri2);                      |
    .                            .                                      ↓
    .                            .
    .                            .
psema(sema2, pri2);              .
    .                            .                                    <--Tl
    .                          if (! cpsema(semal)){
    .                                  vsema(sema2);
    .                                  /*other corrective action*/
    .                                  .
    .                                  goto loop;
    .                          }
```

Figure 14.7: *Example of deadlock avoidance*

Semaphores and Performance

To balance the "*granularity*" of semaphore protection–that is, the amount of data protected by a single semaphore–with the frequency of semaphore operations, semaphores must be used carefully. A semaphore may lock up a lot of resources, like the entire buffer pool, or it may be held for a long period. In such cases, many other processes may be suspended while waiting for the semaphore to unlock, which slows down system flow, leading to excessive context switching. Semaphore contention can be quantified by counting the average number of processes that are sleeping on the semaphore and by measuring the degree of contention, or the ratio of the number of times a process was refused access to the semaphore to the number of times it was attempted. The usage of semaphores in the system is out of balance if any of the aforementioned numbers is significantly higher than that of other semaphores.

To lessen semaphore contention, new semaphores should be encoded. Semaphore contention can be minimized by switching out a single semaphore for a group of semaphores. Consider the following scenario: Let us say, there is a linked list of resources that needs to be searched and that needs to have items added or removed. A solitary semaphore may be sufficient to lock the list, but if the list is big and frequently searched, multiple processes may compete for the semaphore, potentially creating a bottleneck in the system. If so, performance can be increased by swapping out the single linked list for a collection of hash buckets, each of which has a linked list with the elements of the original list that hashed to the same value as its heading.

Rather than a single lock spanning the entire list, every hash bucket can have its own lock, distributing the initial load across several semaphores and lowering contention for each one. One semaphore for each buffer, one semaphore for the free list of buffers, and one semaphore for each hashed (by device and block number) buffer queue are all present in the buffer pool, for instance. The system throughput is significantly higher than if there was only one semaphore for the entire buffer pool, even though the free list semaphore has one of the highest contention rates in the system. Regretfully, splitting the free list into distinct lists with independent semaphores without negatively impacting the buffer algorithm's performance is not a feasible solution. Another problem with semaphore performance is deciding whether to lock the semaphore using a **psema** or a **cpsema**. In other words, if the semaphore is locked, should the process sleep until the semaphore becomes free, or should it execute a tight loop, trying to lock the semaphore until it eventually succeeds (see *Figure* 14.8).

```
psema(sema,pri);            while(!cpsema(sema))
                                    ;
```

Figure 14.8: *Sleep and spin lock*

The issue is resolved through a case-by-case analysis of the semaphores by comparing the average amount of time the semaphore is locked to the time it takes to do a context switch. The results depend strongly on CPU performance characteristics.

Semaphore Debugging

Despite their best efforts to follow ordering rules, multiprocessor systems, especially in their early stages of development, are susceptible to deadlocks. Deadlocks can be difficult to diagnose because the underlying cause of the problem has typically long since vanished. A halted system is an indication of a deadlock. Every semaphore operation is logged by the system to make troubleshooting easier. A circular buffer called a log contains entries for each operation done on a semaphore. These entries contain information about the kind of operation carried out, the text address at which it was carried out, the address of the semaphore, the process number, the semaphore value, and other relevant details. The history of processes as they perform kernel operations can be gleaned from the semaphore log. To improve system efficiency, logging can be disabled either during system compilation or, to a lesser extent, during system operation. In addition to the semaphore log, each semaphore has an extra field that contains the process number of the most recent process to take over the semaphore. The process number field in the semaphore structure and the semaphore log can be used to identify bugs in a multiprocessor system that would never occur in a single processor system.

Example

Consider the code in *Figure* 14.9 for the **xumount** function, called when unmounting device **dev**, that frees text slots belonging to the device.

```
xumount(dev)
        register dev_t dev;
{
        register struct inode *ip;
        register struct text *xp;
        register count = 0;

        for (xp = &text[0]; xp < (struct text *)v.ve_text; xp++) {
                if ((ip = xp->x_iptr) == NULL) /* not in use */
                        continue;
                if (dev != NODEV && dev != ip->i_dev) /* on device dev*/
                        continue;
                if (xuntext(xp))
                        count++;
        }
        return(count);
{
```

Figure 14.9: *Single processor code for xumount*

Although unmounting a device and calling xumount is a rare event in xumount (dev) the lifetime of a system, the example illustrates the techniques for converting the code of a single-processor UNZX system to a multiprocessor version. The function checks each text table entry to determine whether the file is present on the device dev and whether it is in use. If so, it makes a call to xuntext to release the text table slot and swap space. *Figure* 14.10 displays the xumount function's multiprocessor version.

```
xumount(dev)
        register dev_t dev;
{
        register struct inode *ip;
        register struct text *xp;
        register count = 0;

        for (xp = &text[0]; xp < (struct text*)v.ve_text;xp++) {
                 if ((ip = xp->x_iptr) == NULL)
                          continue;
                 if (dev != NODEV && dev != ip->i_dev)
                          continue;
                 psema(&ip->i_lock, PSWP);
                 psema(&xp->x_lock, PSWP);
                 if ((ip != xp->x_iptr)
                          |(dev != NODEV && dev != ip->i_dev))
                 {
                          vsema(&xp->x_lock);
                          vsema(&ip->i_lock);
                          continue;
                 }
                 if (xuntext(xp))
                          count++;
                 vsema(&xp->x_lock);
                 vsema(&ip->i_lock);
        }
        return(count);
}
```

Figure 14.10: *Multiprocessor code for xumount, already passed in its search for program text from the device*

The inode and text slot semaphores are locked after the preliminary checks to ensure the text table slot is in use and that its file is on the correct device. The implementation is more effective as demonstrated, but the semaphores could be locked before the checks are completed because **psema** and **vsema** are costly operations and because there is little chance that a text entry will be cleaned up here. However, until the text and inode slots are locked, the text slot's inode pointer or the inode's device number, if either is freed, could be altered by a process running on a different processor. Thus, to call **xuntext** again, the code needs to verify the conditions. If either check is unsuccessful, it needs to release the locked semaphores. As per the protocol set by the exec system call, the inode semaphore is locked before the text semaphore, meaning that the inode is located first and locked before the text slot is assigned. If either **psema** call causes the process to enter sleep mode, it will subsequently be rescheduled to execute at PSWP priority.

Execution of the **xurnount** function does not guarantee that the text table is free of program text from device dev, since a process executing on another processor could allocate a text slot that **xurnount** already passed in its search for program text from the device. The calling code (**sumount**, not shown) prevents the allocation of text slots to make such a guarantee.

Process Execution

In a multiprocessor environment, processes are oblivious to the number of processors they share the system with. The primary engagement between these processes due to the multiprocessor setup revolves around competing for semaphores, although this interaction is subject to certain constraints. Each processor functions independently, managing processes in both kernel and user mode, without adhering to a master/slave structure. Each processor independently chooses processes from a collective pool of available processes using conventional UNIX scheduling techniques. If a process fails to secure selection by one processor, it becomes eligible for selection by other processors. Concurrently, multiple processes can be active in the kernel on different processors, except semaphore interactions. System calls yield consistent results in both single- and multiprocessor systems. The primary states of a process include:

- operational on a processor
- prepared to run and stored in main memory
- prepared to run but not stored in main memory
- resting and stored in main memory
- resting and not stored in main memory
- a zombie (terminated, awaiting its parent's approval)

In the process table of single-processor UNIX systems, no distinguishable flag segregates the first state (currently active on a processor) from the second state (prepared to run and loaded in main memory). Nevertheless, in multiprocessor UNIX systems, a new flag marks that a process is currently active on a processor. Without explicit indication, scheduling a process for simultaneous execution on multiple processors or transferring a currently executing process from one processor to another could occur; both are undesirable situations.

Device Drivers

In terms of conversion for multiprocessor operation, device drivers and other components of the operating system are equivalent, in theory. As previously mentioned, data structures need to be locked, **psema** and **vsema** calls need to be used in place of sleep and wakeup calls, and interrupt routines need to be given extra attention. Device drivers, however, make up more than half of the UNIX operating system at the moment, and they are being added more quickly to support new peripherals and offer improved or new features.

Therefore, in practice, it is challenging to modify drivers for multiprocessor systems and keep them current with changes made for other UNIX systems due to their quantity and volatility; for this reason, it is crucial to maintain the majority of driver code consistency across all implementations. For this to be possible, the system required three modifications. Prior to being called, drivers are locked.

Driver semaphores added to the tables lock and unlock the drivers around driver calls, which are table-driven via the **bdevsw** and **cdevsw** tables. Depending on how the system is configured, different driver protection techniques are encoded.

There are several levels of protection available, ranging from locking per major or minor device type to forcing the process to run on a specific processor (useful in AP configurations where only one processor can perform the I/O). Now, calls to driver lock and driver unlock routines come before and after each call to a driver routine. The second modification involved reimplementing the sleep and wakeup subroutines so that device drivers could call them without altering the original driver code.

The new routines for the UNIX operating system use hash lists of semaphores to suspend the process, whereas the old routines used arbitrary addresses in memory to sleep on. The address being slept on, known as a sleep parameter, is kept in the process table. The wakeup routine only needs to search this list to find all processes that need to be woken up because a semaphore already has a linked list of all processes suspended on the semaphore. While the original process sleeps, the sleep routine unlocks the driver semaphore to allow other processes to access it. When the process wakes up, it relocks the semaphore.

Only drivers are supposed to follow the sleep and wake-up schedules. Still, **psema** and **vsema** are used directly in the main kernel code. Locking must occur before calling driver routines and during interrupt handling, as interrupts can no longer be prevented by increasing the processor execution level (see Section 3.1). The semaphore for the device (if any) is locked using **cpsema** before the device interrupt handler is called. Should the lock fail, the interrupt is queued but not immediately handled; if the lock succeeds, the interrupt is handled when the process is using the **semaphor** at the moment.

AP Systems

AP systems do all I/O from one processor, whereas MP systems can do from all processors. Since the kernel and drivers may have no knowledge of whether they are running on an AP or an MP system, the information is encoded in tables at the lowest software levels that send the direct memory access requests out to the hardware on AP systems. If the process is on the wrong processor, a context switch is done, and a special scheduling parameter forces the process onto the correct processor.

IBM-Specific Issues

The UNIX system for the IBM/370 is a two-level system that runs on IBM hardware indirectly. The resident supervisor of the Time-Sharing System (TSS) is located on the lower level, while the UNIX system code resides on the upper level. Process scheduling, memory management (including paging), hardware error handling, and all machine-dependent I/O operations are managed by the resident supervisor. The file system structure and all UNIX system calls are implemented by the UNIX system layer. The supervisor calls from the UNIX system to the resident supervisor and the pseudo-interrupts that go from the resident supervisor up to the UNIX system make up the interface. This approach has two main benefits: free support for IBM peripherals through the resident supervisor and no need for the UNIX system on the IBM/370 to worry about IBM hardware architecture that might vary from processor to processor. The resident supervisor's system algorithms may not be the best for the UNIX operating system, which is a drawback. Additionally, there is a performance penalty associated with communication between the two layers. For instance, the enqueue-dequeue operations previously present in TSS have been improved with semaphores, which are far more general than what the UNIX system requires.

Computer-Specific Issues

The 3B family of machines is microcoded, so new semaphore instructions were encoded to boost the performance of multiprocessor systems.

The design of the instructions has been optimized for the most frequently occurring cases: when psema usually finds the semaphore unlocked and when vsema usually need not awaken sleeping processes. To this end, the instructions operate on registers containing the semaphore address and, if necessary, the address of a function that puts a process to sleep (for psema) or awakens a process sleeping on the semaphore (for vsema). The use of the new microcoded instructions boosted overall system performance by 30 percent compared to a system that implemented semaphore operations in software.

A 3B hardware feature causes a problem in the implementation of a paging system for a multiprocessor configuration. Paging systems map the virtual address space of a process to physical pages in memory.

The tables that define the mapping reside in memory, but for better performance, they also reside in a special hardware cache called the **Address Translation Buffer** (ATB). Each processor has a private ATB and cannot flush the contents of the other processor's ATB. However, processes executing from shared text or using the shared memory interprocess communication facility can share portions of their virtual address space. So the two processors' views of physical memory can diverge if one processor changes its address mapping, while the other processor continues to use the old mapping still contained in its ATB.

Paging Problem

The paging problem is solved by observing the following protocol:

- A processor flushes the user portion of its ATB during every context switch (this is done in systems without paging anyway since the address mapping of the previously running process is invalid for the currently running process).
- Kernel pages are never swapped from main memory.
- Pages used by a process currently running on another processor cannot be swapped.

Since the paging process cycles through the process table, swapping the oldest pages on a per-process basis, it is easy to satisfy the third rule above, provided the running process uses no shared text or shared data. If the running process does use shared text or shared data, the paging process verifies that the page to be swapped is not shared, or else it does not swap it.

Many UNIX operating system algorithms that use linear searches of system tables did not scale well from single-processor to multiprocessor systems for two reasons. First, multiprocessor systems have greater capacity than their single-processor counterparts, so system tables such as the inode table and the process table have correspondingly more active entries, and consequently, searching for particular entries takes more time. Second, the system tables must be frequently locked so that processes accessing them find a consistent copy until they have finished using them. The two reasons combined imply that the system will spend more time searching the tables, locking them out from other processes, and causing heavy contention for the table semaphores.

Numerous algorithms were redesigned to avoid linear searches of system tables.

Multiprocessor Systems IBM747 is used to prevent such issues. For example, inodes are hashed to a hash chain by device and inode numbers, and search algorithms that used to search the whole inode table for an inode now look for the inode on the hash chain—a far shorter search.

Another instance of how linear searches were dropped to improve performance is the process table. For example, a process that is exiting finds all of its "*children*," reassigns each one's "parent" process identifier to itself, and notifies its parent of the "death of child" signal. The process structure now contains parent, child, and sibling pointers so that the search routines traverse a tree rather than searching the entire process table for parent and child processes.

Approximately 11.7 times faster than a single-processor system, two-processor UNIX systems are demonstrated by benchmarking results, that is,1/7th the number of processes handled in the same amount of time as on single-processor systems.

Although CPU-bound job mixes run slightly faster and I/O-bound job mixes run slightly slower, the figures are based on benchmark programs that run job mixes typical of those found on UNIX systems. Performance improvements are ongoing and should lead to additional gains in these numbers. Less than five percent of `psema` operations on lock semaphores cause the process to go to sleep, indicating that contention for semaphores is minimal. Less than five percent was found to be the overhead of semaphore operations when the multiprocessor system's code was run on a single processor and its performance was compared to a single-processor system running the original UNIX system code. By activating a flag during system compilation, the multiprocessor system can be set up to operate on a single processor. Certain semaphore operations can be disabled by using the macro that the flag controls. Such a system operates at the same level of performance as conventional single-processor systems. One set of source code powers all system configurations, so this has significant implications for system support.

Conclusion

In this chapter, we learned about multiprocessing operating systems, including their working, advantages, and disadvantages. We were introduced to types of multiprocessing operating systems, including symmetrical and asymmetrical multiprocessing operating systems. The comparison between single-processor operating system and multiprocessing operating systems was made. Finally, ample examples of multiprocessing operating systems with Unix were provided, including semaphores, paging, and examples with the IBM 347 computer.

In the next chapter, we will discuss networked operating systems.

References

[1] Multiprocessing Operating System,PrepBytes, https://www.prepbytes.com › Home › Operating system

[2] Multiprocessing Operating Systems (OS), FIELDS OF STUDY,Computer Engineering; Operating Systems,https://science.jrank.org/programming/Multiprocessing_Operating_Syst.html

[3] Multiprocessor UNlX Operating Systems, By M. j. BACH* and S. I. BUROFF* (Manuscript received August 22, 1983)

Chapter 15
Network Operating System

Introduction

Network operating systems (NOS) are specialized software programs created to administer and control network resources. They help all connected devices on the network, including computers, printers, servers, and laptops, communicate and work together. A NOS goes beyond standard operating systems, such as Windows, Linux, or macOS, which manage resources for a single device. Instead, it expands its capabilities to the entire network and all linked devices. By doing this, it gives the entire network operation centralized management, optimization, and improved functionality.

Structure

In this chapter, we are going to learn about the following topics:

- Network Operating Systems
- History
- Need and Functions of Network Operating System
- Types of Network Operating Systems
- Key Role for Network Operations
- Key Features and Capabilities of a Modern
- Proprietary Network Operating Systems
- Components of a Network Operating System
- Client-Server Network Operating System

An Overview of Network Operating System

A network operating system (NOS) is a specialized operating system for a network device, such as a router, switch, or firewall.

Historically, operating systems with networking capabilities were described as network operating systems because they allowed personal computers (PCs) to participate in computer networks and shared file and printer access within a local area network (LAN). This description of operating systems is now largely historical, as common operating systems include a network stack to support a client–server model.

In the end, we shall evaluate the possibility of future development.

History

Early microcomputer operating systems, such as CP/M, MS-DOS and classic Mac OS were designed for one user on one computer. Packet switching networks were developed to share hardware resources, such as a mainframe computer, a printer, or a large and expensive hard disk. As local area network technology became available, two general approaches to handle the sharing of resources on networks arose.

Historically, a network operating system was an operating system for a computer that implemented network capabilities. Operating systems with a network stack allowed personal computers to participate in a client-server architecture in which a server enables multiple clients to share resources, such as printers. Early examples of client-server operating systems that were shipped with fully integrated network capabilities are Novell NetWare, using the Internetwork Packet Exchange (IPX) network protocol, and Banyan VINES, which used a variant of the Xerox Network Systems (XNS) protocols.

These limited client/server networks were gradually replaced by peer-to-peer networks, which used networking capabilities to share resources and files located on a variety of computers of all sizes. A peer-to-peer network sets all connected computers equal; they all share the same abilities to use resources available on the network. The most popular peer-to-peer networks as of 2020 are Ethernet, Wi-Fi, and the Internet protocol suite. Software that allowed users to interact with these networks, despite a lack of networking support in the underlying manufacturer's operating system, was sometimes called a network operating system. Examples of such add-on software include Phil Karn's KA9Q NOS (adding Internet support to CP/M and MS-DOS), PC/TCP Packet Drivers (adding Ethernet and Internet support to MS-DOS), LANtastic (for MS-DOS, Microsoft Windows, and OS/2), and Windows for Workgroups (adding NetBIOS to Windows). Examples of early operating systems with peer-to-peer networking capabilities built in include MacOS (using AppleTalk and LocalTalk), and the Berkeley Software Distribution. [1]

Applications for groupware and distributed computing are commonplace today. A networking stack is a standard component of computer operating systems. The number of networked devices increased quickly during the 1980s, and there was an increasing need to integrate disparate computers with network capabilities. The Internet protocol suite was nearly always used in network architectures, in part because it made multi-vendor interoperability possible and allowed packets to be routed globally as opposed to being limited to a single building. After that, Internet protocols were typically supported by computer operating systems and network device firmware.

Key Role for Network Operations

All connected devices on the network, including PCs, laptops, servers, and printers, can communicate and work together more easily thanks to the management and control provided by a network operating system (NOS), a specialized software program.

A NOS extends its capabilities across the entire network and all connected devices, in contrast to standard operating systems like Windows, Linux, or macOS that manage resources for a single device. In doing so, it offers improved functionality, centralized management, and optimization for the whole network operation.

Types of Network Operating Systems (NOS) [2]

There are two types of network operating systems based on their source:

- **Proprietary NOS**: Hardware or software providers develop these. Hardware manufacturers such as Cisco and Juniper develop NOS tailored for their particular hardware platforms, such as Cisco IOS and Juniper Junos. To meet a wide range of customer needs, software providers such as VMware, Microsoft, and DriveNets create NOS that can operate on a variety of hardware platforms. Microsoft Windows Server and VMware NSX are two examples of proprietary NOS from software providers.
- **Open-source NOS:** Programs such as SONiC and FRRouting (FRR) provide nearly infinite NOS customization to users. Nevertheless, because there is a small developer community, they need a high degree of technical know-how to run, implement, and close any feature gaps.

Need of NOS

In today's digital reality, the demand for reliable and high-performance networks is greater than ever. NOS plays a crucial role in ensuring that all data and services flow smoothly and efficiently across any network, from small local area networks (LANs) to large-scale networks.

Key Features and Capabilities of a Modern NOS

The following are some of the main functions of a network operating system:

- **Resource management**. The NOS effectively distributes resources to linked devices, such as memory, storage capacity, and network bandwidth. Stopping a single device from using up all the resources and slowing down the network guarantees smooth operation.
- **Network security:** The NOS prevents unauthorized access and malicious attacks from entering the network. Features such as firewalls, access control lists (ACLs), user authentication, and more sophisticated routing capabilities are included in this.
- **Service communication and sharing**: Using widely accepted protocols, the NOS enables networked devices to exchange data and services (for example, HTTP, FTP, TCP/IP, and service discovery over a network). Network maintenance is made easier for administrators by the NOS's ability to configure, monitor, and troubleshoot connected devices.

Scaling:

- As more devices are added to a network, a sophisticated NOS can adjust to grow with it.
- Provides the necessary operating system support, including hardware recognition, multiprocessing, and processor and protocol support, among other features.
- Makes it possible to swap printers and software.
- Datasets and file systems can be shared.
- Provides network protection in addition to access control and user authentication.
- Provides online services, internetworking, and a directory. It generates a copy of the data.

Network operating systems can be embedded in a router or hardware firewall that operates the functions in the network layer (layer 3). Notable network operating systems include:

In the last few decades, large-scale networks have undergone tremendous change. In most nations, having access to the internet is a must, and service providers (SPs) have been managing this vital resource while others profit from it. Even with significant changes in the market and changing customer demands, most networks are still built with monolithic chassis and hardware-centric models, just like they were 25 years ago.

This method has produced SP networks that are far too complex. These networks are overburdened with an excessive number of hardware components tailored to individual services, each requiring specialized management skills, rigid software update schedules, and a sizable stock of spare parts.

This strategy limits the innovation potential of service providers while simultaneously increasing operating expenses. High operational overhead as a result overwhelms SPs and hurts their bottom line. Meanwhile, hyperscalers and over-the-top (OTT) media service providers are making the most of these networks by providing cutting-edge services free from similar limitations. Because of this, SPs are looking for different ways to reimagine their networks and are pursuing a model that is more open and software-centric. One of the most important aspects of this change is the way that NOS is evolving. Better flexibility, simplicity, and scalability are required from today's NOS, all while maintaining the performance and dependability that modern carrier-grade networks have come to expect.

Proprietary Network Operating Systems

- Cisco IOS, a family of network operating systems used on Cisco Systems routers and network switches. (Earlier switches ran the Catalyst operating system or CatOS)
- RouterOS by MikroTik ZyNOS, used in network devices made by ZyXEL
- FreeBSD, NetBSD, OpenBSD, and Linux-based operating systems.
- Cisco NX-OS, IOS XE, and IOS XR; families of network operating systems used across various Cisco Systems devices including the Cisco Nexus and Cisco ASR platforms
- Junos OS; a network operating system that runs on Juniper Networks platforms
- Cumulus Linux distribution, which uses the full TCP/IP stack of Linux
- DD-WRT, a Linux kernel-based firmware for wireless routers and access points as well as low-cost networking device platforms such as the Linksys WRT54G
- Dell Networking Operating System; DNOS9 is NetBSD-based, while OS10 uses the Linux kernel
- Extensible Operating System runs on switches from Arista and uses an unmodified Linux kernel
- ExtremeXOS (EXOS), used in network devices made by Extreme Networks
- FTOS (Force10 Operating System), the firmware family used on Force10 Ethernet switches
- ONOS, an open-source SDN operating system (hosted by the Linux Foundation) for communications service providers designed for scalability, high performance, and high availability.
- OpenBSD, an open-source operating system that includes its own implementations of BGP, RPKI, OSPF, MPLS, VXLAN, and other IETF standardized networking protocols, as well as firewall (PF) and load-balancing functionality.

- OpenWrt used to route IP packets on embedded devices
- pfSense, a fork of M0n0wall, which uses PF
- OPNsense, a fork of pfSense
- SONiC, a Linux-based network operating system developed by Microsoft
- VyOS, an open-source fork of the Vyatta routing package

Components of a Network Operating System

The Network Operating System is a fundamental component of the field of interconnected computing, promoting cooperation and resource sharing between a group of connected machines. A network operating system (NOS) is essential for controlling user access, data sharing, and network resources, whether in a local area network (LAN) or a larger global network. The necessity of a reliable and effective network operating system is becoming more apparent as networks change and technology advances. Node.js (NOS) is still an essential part of the orchestration of interconnected computing ecosystems, helping to streamline communication and optimize resource utilization. [3]

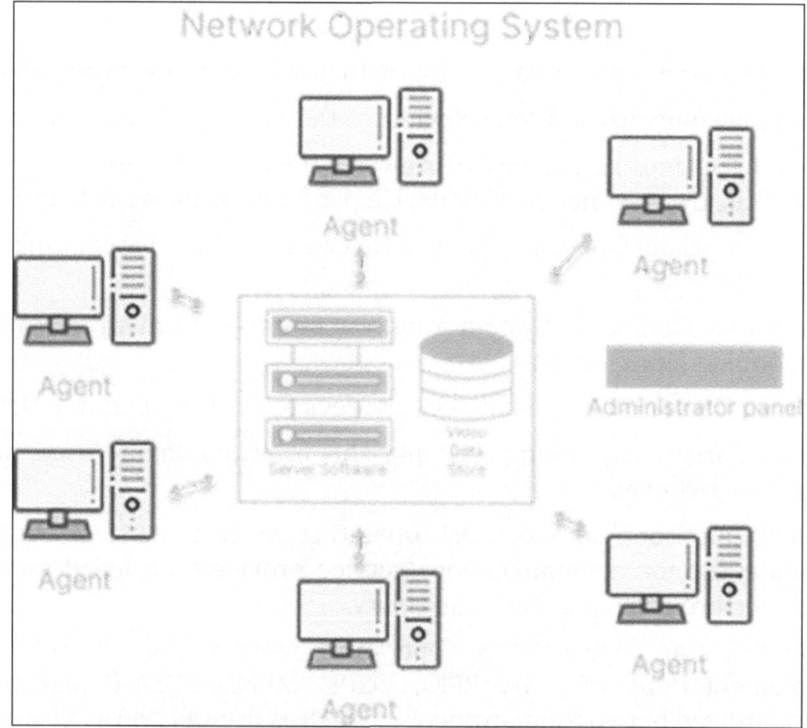

***Figure 15.1**: Components of Network Operating System*

A Network Operating System (NOS) is an operating system specifically designed to manage and facilitate the communication and coordination of activities among a group of interconnected computers or devices within a network. Unlike traditional standalone operating systems that focus on managing a single computer's resources, a network operating system extends its capabilities to address the unique requirements of networked environments. Its primary function is to enable file sharing and provide access to printers on a private network, a local area network, or other networks with many devices. [3]

Functions of Network Operating System

Here are some functions of the network operating system:

- Establishes and maintains user profiles on the network
- Regulates who has access to what network resources
- Controls and configures the network's resources
- Uses protocols over the network to improve the implementation of network functionalities
- Enables a secure connection between two workstations by using access management and user authentication

Types of Network Operating Systems Based on their Configuration

Network operating systems are of two types:

- Peer-to-peer Network Operating System
- Client-Server Network Operating System

Let us talk about each one of them in detail.

Peer-to-Peer Network Operating System

A peer-to-peer network is a group of computers that share equal control and authority over the processing of data. It permits resource sharing across a more manageable and streamlined network. All the devices in the network design are similar to each other in terms of their features, capabilities, and roles. All network's components are connected to all other nodes in the same way.

There is no master-slave relationship between the systems since there is no hierarchy of superiors or inferiors. Several computers can share resources among scanners, printers, and CD-ROMs in smaller settings with no more than 25 workstations using a peer-to-peer network operating system. Peer-to-peer networks are connected by using network adapter cards. Using network cabling and a network hub or switch, we can connect the PCs to one another. Every computer is treated equally, and no one has control over the workgroup. Every device on the network monitors user-profiles and security configurations. There is very little security between the workgroups because there is no centralized login mechanism. Shared resources are accessible to anyone logged into a peer-to-peer network. In the absence of a centralized security system, users can control file and directory sharing, resource sharing, and accessibility through passwords.

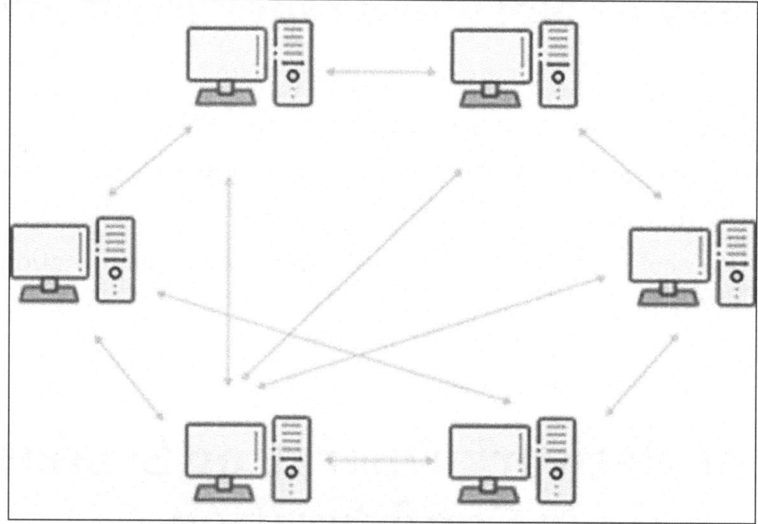

Figure 15.2: *Peer-to-Peer Network Operating System*

Advantages of Peer to Peer Network Operating System

- Lower setup costs and less maintenance due to the lack of a centralized system to manage the network.
- This type of network operating system functions without the use of specific hardware.
- In a peer-to-peer network operating system, setting up network rules does not require a dedicated network administrator.
- Within the network, every user has control over their system by choosing the kinds of files they wish to share.
- In its construction, twisted pair cable is used.

Drawbacks of Peer to Peer Network Operating System:

- One issue that comes up often is security. Share-level protection makes it less secure. When one element of the system network fails, the entire system is affected.

- As the network grows, the system's efficiency decreases. This is the case because each machine on the network has control over it.
- Peer-to-peer operating systems cannot monitor which users are trying to access a given resource.
- There is not a single authority controlling the network. Network administration is not handled by a single individual.
- Rather, all users can access the files and tools on the computer. For control, every shared resource requires a password.
- A network may have a lot of shared resources, making it difficult to remember many passwords.

Client-Server Network Operating System

An operating system for client-server networks has a client in the front and a server in the rear. Additionally, it has a server-based network where users can access tools for processing and storage. Servers and clients split the burden. The main computer offers access.

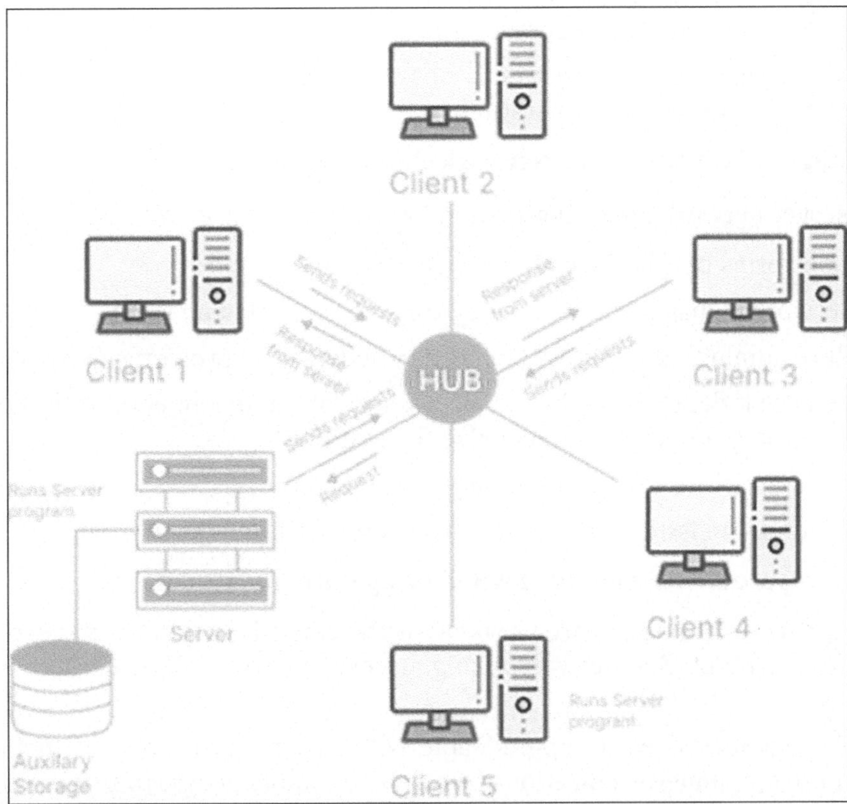

Figure 15.3: *Client-Server Network Operating System*

Customers' requests for printing, digital mail, document storage, and many other services are fulfilled by the server. All group offerings are handled by the server. Within the Client-Server Network Operating System application, a database is viewed by multiple computers connected to the network. The information resides on the server. The consumers send requests to the server, which handles database queries. The clients receive the finished database searches after they are sent over the network. Numerous clients can be served simultaneously by a server.

Advantages of Client-Server Network Operating System

- By dividing up the workload between the clients and the server, network bandwidth is reduced.
- Client-server network operating systems cover far more ground than peer-to-peer network operating systems, which are limited to local areas.
- Peer-to-peer networks are used in environments, such as home networks and small businesses where security is not a concern because users have access to files and resources on the computer.
- Client-server networks are more expansive because additional clients and servers are added as needed to grow the network.
- Remote access to the server is possible from a variety of platforms using a client-server network operating system.

Disadvantages of Client-Server Network Operating Systems

A client-server network operating system has the following drawbacks:

- It performs poorly since all the load is placed on one server.
- Network management is done by trained network managers.
- More administrators must be hired to address the problems more quickly.
- Because it depends on the resources, security, and connections used, a client-server network is more expensive to set up.
- The cost of the server raises the total even more.
- If there is an issue in one area of the network, it fails as a whole.

The following are some benefits of network operating systems:

- High levels of stability are provided by the central computers in these systems. They protect the network using access control and user authentication features.
- The network is easily upgradeable with newer hardware and technologies. There are numerous locations from which remote access to servers is feasible.

- It can be accessed via software, a hardwired network interface, Wi-Fi, or online enrollment.

Cons of Network Operating Systems

The following are the drawbacks of the network operating system:

- Different tasks are completed based on the central location of the server.
- Setting up a network operating system is too expensive because it requires a lot of technical maintenance.
- For it to work correctly, regular updates and maintenance are required.

Conclusion

In this chapter, we have learned about all aspects of designing a network operating systems, including its evolution and history. We have gone through the type, need functions, key features, and key role for network operations. We have also learned about components of a network operating system and various proprietary network operating systems.

The next chapter will be about protection and security of all types of operating systems.

Questions

1. What are the key features and capabilities of modern network operating systems?
2. How many types are there for NOS?
3. What is the key role of network operations and, therefore, network operating systems?
4. Narrate the key features and capabilities of a modern NOS.
5. Write down a brief essay on the history and evolving role of NOS.
6. Discuss proprietary network operating systems.
7. What are the various components of a network operating system?
8. What are the needs and functions of network operating system?
9. Describe the peer-to-peer network operating system with a diagram.
10. What are the various advantages of a peer-to-peer network operating systems?
11. Describe the client-server network operating system with a diagram.

12. What are the various advantages and disadvantages of client-server network operating systems?

13. Discuss various advantages and disadvantages of network operating systems.

Questions with Answers

Q1. Which three network operating systems are there?

Ans. UNIX, Windows, and MS-DOS are the top three operating systems in terms of popularity.

Q2. What distinguishes a network operating system from a standard operating system?

Ans. A network operating system expands its capabilities to supervise and coordinate activities across multiple interconnected computers, whereas a traditional operating system is limited to managing the resources of a single computer. Features such as file sharing, network resource management, and user access control are highlighted.

Q3. What are the network operating system's primary functions?

Ans. One of a network operating system's primary duties is to make file and resource sharing on the network easier. Others are controlling permissions and user access, arranging for device communication to be coordinated, giving network resources centralized control, and putting security measures in place to safeguard networked data.

Q4. Are there any examples of network operating systems available?

Ans. Novell NetWare, Microsoft Windows Server (in its server editions), Linux with networking features, and UNIX versions intended for network environments are a few examples of network operating systems.

Q5. In what ways does a network operating system improve teamwork within a networked environment?

Ans. A network operating system promotes teamwork by offering tools for effective resource allocation, centralized user authentication, and file sharing. As a result, users on the network can cooperate, exchange data without difficulty, and access shared resources with the right authorization.

Q6. What kind of operating system is Windows?

Ans. Under the name Windows, Microsoft developed and distributed several proprietary graphical operating system varieties. Every family caters to a specific market within the computer industry. Among the examples are

Windows NT for end users, Windows Server for servers, and Windows IoT for embedded devices.

Q7. What are the fundamentals of networking?

Ans. Computer networks connect nodes, such as computers, routers, and switches, using wires, fiber optics, or wireless signals. Networked devices can communicate and share resources, thanks to these links. Protocols govern the sending and receiving of messages on networks.

Q8. Is Linux an open-source operating system?

Ans. Linux is an open-source, free operating system distributed by the GNU General Public License (GPL). Anyone may run, examine, alter, distribute, and even sell copies of their modified code as long as they follow the same licence.

References

[1] Network operating system, Wikipedia, the free encyclopedia,https://en.wikipedia.org/wiki/Network_operating_system

[2] What Is a Network Operating System? Key Role for Network Operations,https://drivenets.com/resources/education-center/what-is-a-network-operating-system-nos/

[3] Network Operating System,https://www.prepbytes.com/blog/operating-system/network-operating-system/

CHAPTER 16
Protection and Security

Introduction

Within an operating system (OS), security pertains to the protocols and safeguards put in place to prevent unauthorized access, misuse, modification, or destruction of the system, its resources, and the data it handles. Access control, authorization, encryption, auditing, and intrusion detection/prevention are just a few of the aspects it includes. To ensure that only authorized users can access and manipulate system resources and data, as well as to stop malicious software or unauthorized users from causing harm or taking advantage of vulnerabilities, operating system security serves to protect the confidentiality, integrity, and availability of these elements. File and directory permissions, firewall settings, encryption algorithms, secure boot procedures, antivirus software, and security patches to fix vulnerabilities found over time are examples of security features in an operating system. User authentication mechanisms, such as passwords or biometrics, are the other examples. Securing sensitive data, ensuring system stability, and upholding user confidence in computers depend on strong operating system security.

Structure

In this chapter, we are going to learn about following topics:

- Protection
- Need of Protection in Operating System
- Goals of Protection in Operating System
- Role of Protection in Operating System
- Common Types of Violations
- Program Threats, System, and Network Threats
- Security in Operating Systems
- Security Goals and Policies

- Design Concepts of Protection and Security
- Components of Protection and Security
- Methods to Ensure Protection and Security in Operating System
- Hardware Protection Mechanisms
- Comparison between Protection and Security
- Security Model of UNIX
- Windows XP

Overview: Protection and Security

Protection operation ensures authorized access to system resources, preventing unauthorized users from tampering with or accessing sensitive data. Security operation encompasses measures to safeguard system resources, data, and operations from various threats and vulnerabilities, ensuring system integrity and reliability.

Protection

Protection tackles the system's internal threats. It provides a mechanism for controlling access to processes, programs, and user resources. In simple words, it specifies which files a specific user can access or view and modify to maintain the proper functioning of the system. It allows the safe sharing of common physical address space or common logical address space, which means that multiple users can access the memory due to the physical address space.

What Are We Protecting?

When we state that our operating system should be secure, we are unlikely to achieve effective protection unless we have a fairly comprehensive understanding of what we're trying to protect. Thankfully, an operating system can easily respond to that query, at least in the broadest sense: everything. Although that response may not be very reassuring, it is still advisable to have a realistic grasp of the wider ramifications of operating system security. A standard commodity operating system can do anything the hardware on the computer can do and has total control over all (or nearly all) of its hardware. It can therefore operate the processor, read and write to all registers, access any location in main memory, and carry out any operation that one of its peripherals is capable of. Consequently, the operating system (OS) can do the following:

- Reads, writes, deletes, or corrupts any file on any writeable persistent storage medium, such as hard disks and flash drives
- Changes the scheduling or even stop the execution of any process
- Enables or disables peripheral devices; gives any process access to any other process's resources arbitrarily

- Takes away any resource that a process controls
- Responds to any system call with a maximally harmful lie

In short, processes are at the mercy of the OS. A process can hardly "*protect*" any portion of itself against an evil operating system. Although we usually assume that our operating system is not malicious, it is almost as bad to have a flaw that allows a malicious process to cause the operating system to behave improperly because that process may be able to acquire all of the operating system's capabilities. This should cause you to seriously consider how important it is to create secure operating systems and, more frequently, to update any operating system you use with security patches. Preventing security flaws in your operating system and patching any that are discovered are crucial because they have the potential to completely compromise the machine on which the system is installed. Every computer user needs to safeguard their systems against intentional attacks, both internal and external, from people who want to steal data, corrupt data, or otherwise wreak havoc on their systems on purpose.

Common Types of Violations [1]

Some of the most common types of violations include:

- **Breach of Confidentiality:** Theft of private or confidential information, such as credit card numbers, trade secrets, patents, secret formulas, manufacturing procedures, medical information, financial information, and so on.
- **Breach of Integrity:** Unauthorized modification of data, which may have serious indirect consequences. For example, a popular game or other program's source code could be modified to open up security holes on users systems before being released to the public.
- **Breach of Availability:** Unauthorized destruction of data, often just for the "*fun*" of causing havoc and for bragging rites. Vandalism of websites is a common form of this violation.
- **Theft of Service:** Unauthorized use of resources, such as theft of CPU cycles, installation of daemons running an unauthorized file server, or tapping into the target's telephone or networking services.
- **Denial of Service, DOS:** Preventing legitimate users from using the system, often by overloading and overwhelming the system with an excess of requests for service.
- **Masquerading:** A common attack in which the attacker pretends to be a trusted third party. A variation of this is the man-in-the-middle, in which the attacker masquerades as both ends of the conversation to two targets.
- **Replay Attack:** This involves repeating a valid transmission. Sometimes this can be the entire attack, such as repeating a request for a money transfer, or

other times, the content of the original message is replaced with malicious content.

Let us take an example for a better understanding. Suppose, In a small organization, there are four employees p1, p2, p3, p4, and two data resources, r1 and r2. The various departments frequently exchange information but not sensitive information between all employees. The employees p1 and p2 can only access r1 data resources and employees p3 and p4 can only access r2 resources. If the employee p1 tries to access the data resource r2, then the employee p1 is restricted from accessing that resource. Hence, p1 will not be able to access the r2 resource.

Advantages of Protection

Protection offers many benefits and is essential to preserving the security, integrity, and dependability of an operating system. Here are a few of the main benefits:

- **Data Security:** Security mechanisms protect private information from unwanted access, guaranteeing privacy and averting data breaches or theft.
- **System Integrity**: To maintain the integrity of the operating system and avoid tampering or corruption, protection mechanisms stop unauthorized changes to important files, configurations, and system resources.
- **Elimination of Unauthorized Access:** To stop unauthorized individuals or processes from gaining access to privileged resources or carrying out sensitive tasks, protection mechanisms enforce privilege levels, access control policies, and authentication. Protection mechanisms that log system activities, access attempts, and security events help to promote user accountability. Audit trails provide a record of user activity, which helps with incident response, compliance monitoring, and forensic analysis.
- **Resource Allocation and Fairness:** Protection mechanisms ensure that system resources are distributed among competing processes in a fair and effective manner, preventing resource monopolization and guaranteeing equal access for all users.
- **Protection mechanisms:** This plays a crucial role in maintaining system stability and reliability by safeguarding against potential disruptions, malfunctions, and security incidents. Protection mechanisms support system availability by enforcing security measures and averting service interruptions or downtime.

Need of Protection in Operating System

Various needs for protection in the operating system are as follows:

- There may be security risks, such as unauthorized reading, writing, or modification, or preventing the system from working effectively for authorized users.

- It helps to ensure data security, process security, and program security against
- unauthorized user access or program access.
- It is important to ensure no access rights breaches, no viruses, and no unauthorized access to the existing data.
- Its purpose is to ensure that only the system's policies access programs, resources, and data.

Goals of Protection in Operating System

Various goals of protection in the operating system are as follows:

- The policies define how processes access the computer system's resources, such as the CPU, memory, software, and even the operating system. It is the responsibility of both the operating system designer and the app programmer. These policies are modified at any time.
- Protection is a technique for protecting data and processes from harmful or intentional infiltration. It contains protection policies either established by itself, set by management, or imposed individually by programmers to ensure that their programs are protected to the greatest extent possible.
- It also provides a multiprogramming OS with the security users expect when sharing common space, such as files or directories.

Role of Protection in Operating System

Its primary function is to give computer systems administrators a way to put policies into effect that specify how resources are used. System administrators define certain rules to secure their files and programs, while others are established during the system's design phase. Each program has its own rules about how to use resources, which are subject to change. Consequently, the programmer must also design the protection technique to shield their system from infiltration; system security is not the designer's job.

- **Process-Domain Association**: Processes can move between domains if they possess the required access rights. It could be one of two kinds, as indicated as follows.
- **Static or Fixed**: Processes may be assigned all access rights at the outset in a fixed association. On the other hand, this leads to several access privileges for domain switching. This leads to the discovery of a dynamic method for altering the domain's contents.
- **Adapting or dynamic:** A process can change on the fly, spawning a new domain.

Levels of Protection

A system needs to be secured on four levels:

- **Physical:** Stealing data is simplest when backup tapes are taken. Additionally, special rights are frequently granted to the user who accesses the root console. For example, the user may reboot the system from removable media as root. Although the modern high-speed networking environment presents an increasing number of opportunities for remote attacks, even general access to computer room terminals presents some opportunities for an attacker.
- **Human:** There is a concern that people who are granted access to a system should be reliable and incapable of being forced to violate security. Nonetheless, social engineering–basically, tricking reliable individuals into inadvertently violating security–is becoming an increasingly popular attack method.
    - **Phishing:** Sending a seemingly legitimate email or visiting a website to trick recipients into disclosing personal information is known as phishing. For example, spam emails purporting to be from PayPal, eBay, or any of the many banks or credit-card providers.
    - **Dumpster Diving:** It is the practice of looking through trash or other places for written passwords.
    - **Note:** It is more likely that a user will write down their passwords near their workstation if they are difficult to remember or need to be changed regularly.
    - **Cracking passwords:** This entails figuring out users' passwords by watching them type them in, figuring out personal information about them, such as the names of their pets, or just trying every word in a common dictionary. It should be noted that "good" passwords should have a minimum of characters, contain non-alphabetical characters, not be found in any dictionary (in any language), and be changed regularly. It is also polite to turn away from the keyboard when someone else is typing in their password.
- **Operating System:** The OS needs to defend against security lapses, including programs being launched with unauthorized privileges, memory-access violations, runaway processes (denial of service), and stack overflows, among many other things.
- **Network:** The importance of protecting this part of the system increases with the pervasiveness and importance of network communications in contemporary computing environments. Defending the local system against intrusions via the network as well as defending the network itself against attacks. As wireless communications and portable devices proliferate, this is an increasingly pressing area of concern [2].

Program Threats [3]

Modern systems face numerous common threats. Here we mention a few:

- **Trojan Horse**: A Trojan Horse is a program that, in addition to its apparent actions, secretly carries out some malicious activity. While some Trojan horses are purposefully designed to look like them, others are the product of virus-infected legitimate programs (see the following).

  Long search paths, especially those that include the current directory (), are a risky opening for Trojan horses,, as a segment of the route. An unwary user could unintentionally run the incorrect program if a malicious program with the same name as a legitimate program–or a common misspelling, such as "`sl`" instead of "`ls`"–is placed anywhere on the path.

  An additional traditional Trojan horse is a login emulator, which stores the user's account name and password, notifies them that their password is incorrect, and then terminates their session. After that, the user gives it another go (this time with a legitimate login prompt), logs in successfully, and is unaware that their personal data has been compromised. Two ways to combat Trojan Horses are to make the system print usage statistics when a user logs out and to make logging in require typing non-trappable key combinations such as Control-Alt-Delete. Because regular programs cannot emulate or capture this, modern Windows systems require the Control-Alt-Delete sequence to initiate the login process. The operating system always gains control after pressing that key sequence.

  Spyware is a Trojan Horse variant that is frequently present in "*free*" software downloaded from the Internet. In addition to creating pop-up browser windows, spyware programs can gather user data and send it to a central website. This is an illustration of a covert channel, which is used for covert communications. Spyware also frequently sends out spam emails that are later claimed to be from the afflicted user.

- **Trap Door:** A trap door is created when a programmer, designer, or hacker purposefully introduces a security flaw, so they can access the system later. Once a system has been in an untrustworthy state, it can never be trusted again due to the possibility of trap doors. There could be a copy of a cunningly concealed back door on even the backup tapes. It is possible to embed a clever trapdoor into a compiler, causing any programs compiled with that compiler to have a security flaw. This is particularly risky because there would be no issues found upon inspection of the code being compiled.

- **Logic Bomb**: A Logic Bomb is a code that is meant to wreak havoc only under specific conditions, such as when a specific date or time is reached or when some other notable event takes place. An iconic illustration is the Dead-Man

Switch, which is intended to determine whether a specific individual (for example, the author) is logging in every day, and if they do not log in for a long time (presumably because they have been fired), then the logic bomb goes off and either opens up security holes or causes other problems.

- **Stack and Buffer Overflow:** Using bugs in system code that cause buffers to overflow, this is a classic attack technique. Take a look at the following code, for instance, if **argv**[1] is greater than 256 characters. The **strcpy** command will overwrite nearby memory locations by overflowing the buffer. By limiting the number of characters that can be copied to 255 and leaving space for the null byte, **strncpy** can help prevent this issue.

```
#include
#define BUFFER_SIZE 256

int main( int argc, char * argv[ ] )
{
    char buffer[ BUFFER_SIZE ];

    if( argc < 2 )
        return -1;
    else {
        strcpy( buffer, argv[ 1 ] );
        return 0;
    }
}
```

Figure 16.1: *C program with buffer-overflow condition*

To understand how overflowing the buffer results in a security breach, one must first comprehend how a stack is organized in memory. Specifically, the "*bottom*" of the stack is actually at a high memory address and grows towards lower addresses. On the other hand, higher array elements extend to higher addresses, and an array's address is its lowest address. That is, as an array approaches the bottom of the stack, it "*grows*." Specifically, writing beyond the boundaries of an array–which happens when a buffer fills up too quickly with data–can eventually overwrite the return address, thereby altering the location at which the program ends up jumping when it returns.

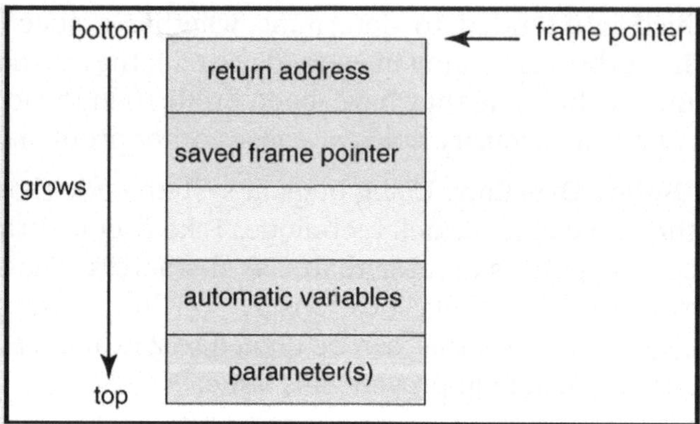

Figure 16.2: *The layout for a typical stack frame*

Having learned how to overwrite the buffer to alter the program's return location, the next step is to insert some malicious code and get the program to jump to it. There is not much room because the input into the buffer is our only way to enter code. Inserting the code for "`exec( /bin/sh )`" is among the easiest and most obvious methods. To accomplish this, a program containing this instruction must first be compiled. Then, the minimal extent that contains the required instructions must be extracted using an assembler or debugger.

The buffer's address is then inserted into the return address location, and the faulty code is padded with as many additional bytes as necessary to fill the buffer to the appropriate amount. Take note that the padding and the faulty code cannot both contain null bytes, as this would cause the **`strcpy`** to end.

The block of data that is produced is given as "*input*," copied into the buffer by the initial program, and then the return statement causes control to jump to the buffer's location and begin running the code to open a shell.

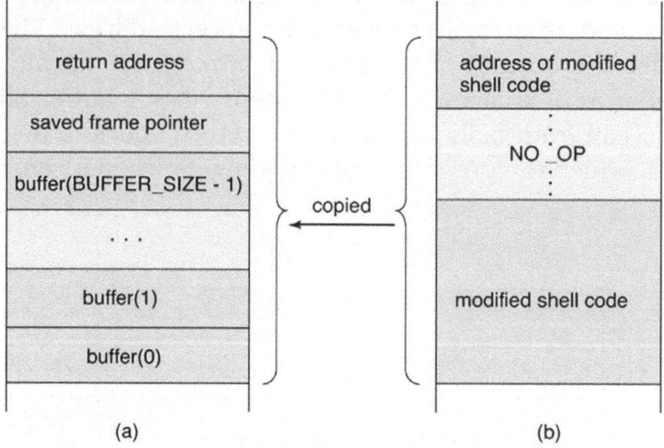

Figure 16.3: *Hypothetical stack frame for Figure 16.1, (a) before and (b) after*

Unfortunately, well-known hacks, like the buffer overflow attack, are widely publicized and understood. It does not take much expertise to follow the directions and begin attacking numerous systems until the law of averages eventually breaks down. Script Kiddies are hackers who can mimic the work of others but only possess very basic hacking abilities. Thankfully, newer hardware now has a feature in the page tables that allows you to mark specific pages as not executable. In this scenario, the buffer overflow attack would function up to a point, but it would crash the program as soon as it attempted to execute statements at that address after "*returning*" to it.

- **Viruses:** A virus is a piece of code inserted into a properly functioning program to spread itself and eventually cause havoc by infecting other programs. PCs are more susceptible to virus infection than UNIX or other multi-user systems because the programs running on those systems have less power to alter other programs or gain access to crucial system components (such as the boot block). Viruses are typically distributed to computers through email or risky downloads, virus droppers, and Trojan Horses. There are numerous types of viruses (see the following). Figure 16.4 shows typical operation of a boot sector virus:

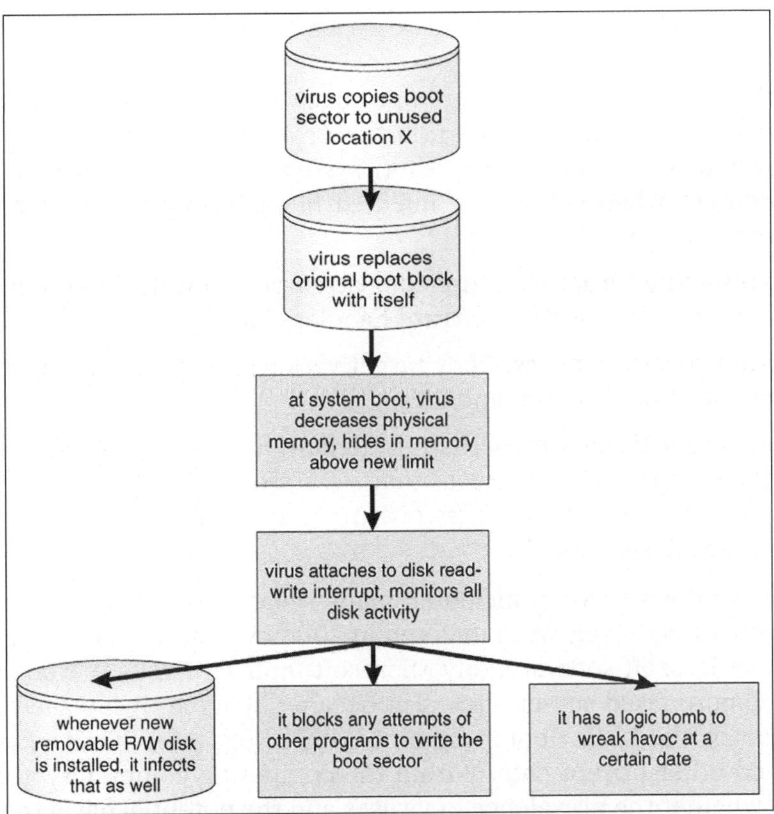

Figure 16.4: *A boot-sector computer virus*

A file virus is one type of virus that attaches itself to an executable file and causes it to launch the virus code first before jumping to the beginning of the original program. These viruses are known as parasitic, because they do not leave any new files on the system and the original program remains fully functional.

- **Boot:** A boot virus runs in the boot sector prior to the OS loading. Because they operate exclusively in memory and do not show up in the file system, these are also referred to as memory viruses.
- **Macros**: These viruses take the form of scripts, or macros, which are launched automatically by some programs that support macros, such as Microsoft Word or Excel. Word processing documents and spreadsheet files may contain these viruses.
- **Source code:** To propagate, source code viruses seek out and infect source code. Every time they proliferate, polymorphic viruses alter only their signature, which serves as a means for virus checkers to identify them rather than their underlying functionality.
- **Encrypted:** To avoid detection, viruses travel in encrypted form. They are actually self-decrypting, which makes it possible for them to spread to other files.
- **Stealth viruses:** They attempt to evade detection by altering system components that may be utilized for detection. One way to change this would be to modify the read() system call to skip over any malicious content when reading an infected file, allowing the reader to view the original, clean file.
- **Tunneling Virus**: Viral tunneling attempts to evade detection by infecting device drivers or the interrupt handler chain.
- **Multipartite Viruses:** They target various system components, including memory, boot sector, and files.
- **Armored Virus:** Anti-virus researchers have a difficult time deciphering and comprehending viruses that are armored. Many files linked to viruses are also concealed, password-protected, or given names that seem innocent, such as ". ".".

Hundreds of Windows servers, including many reliable websites, running Microsoft Internet Information Server, were infected in 2004 by a virus that took advantage of three flaws in Microsoft software. Any Microsoft Internet Explorer web browser that visited any compromised server sites also became infected. It installed a keystroke logger as one of the back door programs, which logs user keystrokes, including passwords and other private data. Within the computing community, there is some debate as to whether the prevalence of viruses and the potential harm they can cause increase in a monoculture, where almost all systems run the same hardware, operating system, and applications.

System and Network Threats [4]

Most of the threats described earlier are termed program threats because they attack specific programs or are carried and distributed in programs. The threats in this section attack the operating system or the network itself or leverage those systems to launch their attacks.

Worms

A worm is a process that replicates itself using the fork/spawn mechanism to inflict damage on a system. As they eat up system resources, worms frequently prevent other, useful processes from operating. Network-propagating worms can be particularly dangerous because they overload network capacity and take down sizable systems.

A Cornell graduate student named Robert Morris launched one of the most well-known worms in November 1988. The worm spread quickly over the Internet, consuming enough resources to bring down numerous systems, and was directed at Sun and VAX computers running BSD UNIX version 4.

The main worm program was transferred onto the target system and launched by the grappling hook program. The worm was composed of two components: a small program known as a grappling hook deposited on the target system through one of three vulnerabilities.

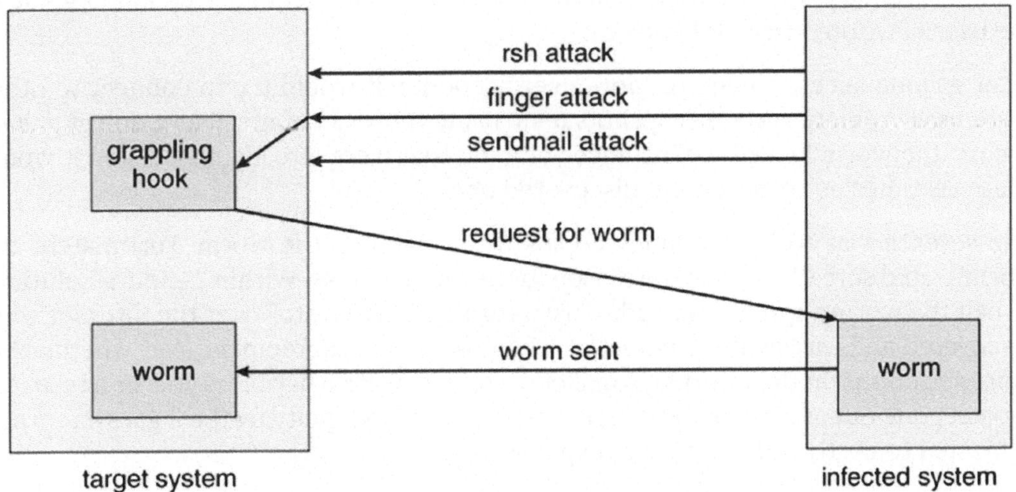

Figure 16.5: *The Morris Internet worm*

The following three vulnerabilities were taken advantage of by the Morris Internet worm:

- **remote shell, or `rsh`**, was a widely used tool at the time for password-free remote system access. It is possible to set up a system so that a user can connect remotely from one computer to another without entering a password if they have accounts on two separate computers with the same name. Numerous systems were set up such that, with the exception of root, any user on system A could log in to system B and access the same account without a password.
- **Finger** is a tool that lets you remotely query a user database to discover more details about a specific account name on a system, including its true name. To retrieve information about **`JoeUser`**, one could send "**`finger joeUser@somemachine.edu`**" to the finger daemon at **`somemachine.edu`**. The worm could fork a shell on the remote system running with root privileges by sending a unique 536-character user name. Regrettably, the finger daemon, which ran with system privileges, had a buffer overflow issue.
- **Sendmail** is a mail sending and forwarding routine with a debugging option to help you check and test the system. Because it was so handy, administrators frequently left the debug feature enabled.

The grappling hook program was copied and run on the remote system by the Morris worm, which took advantage of the debugger. Once installed, the worm launched a series of methodical attacks to find user passwords. Initially, it would look for accounts with the same password as the account name, like "**`guest`**," "**`guest`**." Afterwards, it would attempt to access user accounts by trying every word in the standard UNIX online dictionary. This would be followed by an internal dictionary containing 432 of the user's favorite password choices.

After gaining access to one or more user accounts, it would try to connect to other systems via remote system snapshots (**`rsh`**) using those accounts. Every time it gained access, the worm looked for instances of itself that were already active, and it would cease six times out of seven if it discovered one.

The seventh was to keep phoney copies from stopping the worm. Fortunately, the worm's rapid spread was also the reason for its rapid demise. Within 24 hours, solutions to halt the worm's spread from administrator to administrator over the Internet were discovered and was swiftly eliminated. There is some disagreement over whether Mr. Morris's actions on the Internet, a malicious attack, were a harmless joke or a research project gone out of control. He was, nevertheless, found guilty by the legal system and subjected to costly fines and court expenses.

There have since been many other worm attacks, including the W32.Sobig.F@mm attack, which infected hundreds of thousands of computers and an estimated 1 in 17 e-mails in August 2003. This worm made detection difficult by varying the subject line of the infection-carrying mail message, including "`Thank You!`", "`Your details`", and "`Re: Approved`".

Port Scanning

Port Scanning is technically not an attack but a search for vulnerabilities to attack. The basic idea is to systematically attempt to connect to every known (or common or possible) network port on some remote machine, and to attempt to make contact. Once it is determined that a particular computer is listening to a particular port, then the next step is to determine what daemon is listening and whether or not it is a version containing a known security flaw that can be exploited.

Because port scanning is easily detected and traced, it is usually launched from zombie systems, that is, previously hacked systems that are being used without the knowledge or permission of their rightful owner. For this reason, it is important to protect "*innocuous*" systems and accounts as well as those that contain sensitive information or special privileges.

There are also port scanners available that administrators can use to check their own systems, which report any weaknesses found but do not exploit them or cause any problems. Two such systems are **`nmap`** (http://www.insecure.org/nmap) and **`nessus`** (http://www.nessus.org). The former identifies what OS is found, what firewalls are in place, and what services are listening to what ports. The latter also contains a database of known security holes and identifies any that it finds.

Denial of Service

Denial of Service (DOS) attacks do not attempt to access or damage systems, but merely to clog them up so badly that they cannot be used for any useful work. Tight loops that repeatedly request system services are an obvious form of this attack.

DOS attacks can also involve social engineering, such as the Internet chain letters that say, "**`send this immediately to 10 of your friends, and then go to a certain URL`**", which clogs up not only the Internet mail system but also the webserver to which everyone is directed.

Note: *Sending a "reply all" to such a message notifying everyone that it was just a hoax also clogs up the Internet mail service, just as effectively as if you had forwarded the thing.*

Security systems that lock accounts after a certain number of failed login attempts are subject to DOS attacks, which repeatedly attempt logins to all accounts with invalid passwords strictly to lock up all accounts.

Sometimes, DOS is not the result of deliberate maliciousness. For example:

A website that sees a huge volume of hits due to a successful advertising campaign.

CNN.com occasionally gets overwhelmed on big news days, such as Sept 11, 2001.

CS students given their first programming assignment involving `fork( )` often quickly fill up process tables or otherwise completely consume system resources.

Security in Operating Systems

Security deals with outside threats to the system; the system's resources, including memory, disks, and stored data, are safe and protected from unauthorized access, harmful modifications, and inconsistency by security systems. It offers an analysis of the user prior to granting access to the system mechanism (authentication and encryption).

One meaning of the term "*computer security*" is "*the technology used to implement operating systems with security*.". One effective method of guaranteeing computer security is to use secure operating systems. These are systems for which Unix security describes the security procedures for an operating system that is Unix-like or Unix.

Security Goals and Policies [1]

That is a pretty general statement: "*We want an operating system, or any system, to be secure*." But what exactly does that mean? We essentially mean that we would like a high level of assurance that we get what we want and that there are things in the system that we would like to happen and things that we do not want to happen. We usually have to pay for what we get in life, just like in most other areas. For this reason, it is important to consider exactly what security features and effects we really need and only pay for those, not for extras. It basically comes down to this: we want to identify the objectives we have for the security-relevant behavior of our system and select defense strategies that are likely to help us reach those objectives within a suitable budget. For a long time, security researchers have considered this problem in general terms. They have identified three major security-related objectives at a high conceptual level that are shared by many systems, including operating systems.

- **Confidentiality**: Do not let anyone know about information meant to be kept private. For instance, you would prefer that your credit card number remain private and that no one find out what it is.
- **Integrity:** Prevent an adversary from altering any information or system component intended to be in a specific state. If you ordered a single pepperoni pizza online, for instance, you do not want some nefarious person to alter your order to 1000 anchovy pizzas. Genuineness is a crucial component of integrity.
- A**vailability:** If a service or piece of information is meant to be available for use by you or others, ensure an attacker cannot stop you from using it. It is

frequently crucial to confirm not only that the information has not changed but also that it was created by a specific party and not by an enemy. When your company is having a major sale, for instance, you do not want your rivals to be able to close off the roads surrounding your store and keep customers from getting to you.

An important extra dimension of all three goals is that we want controlled sharing in our systems. We share our secrets with some people and not with others. We allow some people to change our enterprise's databases, but not just anyone. Some systems need to be made available to a particular set of preferred users (such as those who have paid to play your online game) and not to others (who have not). Who is doing the asking matters a lot, in computers as in everyday life.

Another important aspect of security for computer systems is we often want to be sure that when someone told us something, they cannot later deny it. The harder and more expensive it is for someone to repudiate their actions, the easier it is to hold them to account for those actions, and thus the less likely people are to perform malicious actions. After all, they might well get caught and will have trouble denying they did it. Ultimately, of course, the operating system software must do its best to enforce those flexible security goals, which implies we will need to encode those goals in forms that software can understand. We typically must convert our vague understanding of our security goals into highly-specific security policies. For example, in the case of the file described earlier, we might want to specify a policy such as 'users A and B may write to file X, but no other user can write it.' With that degree of specificity, backed by carefully designed and implemented mechanisms, we can hope to achieve our security goals.

Design Concepts

Permissions: A core security feature in these systems is the file system permissions. All files in a typical Unix filesystem have permissions set enabling different access to a file. Unix permissions permit different users access to a file with different privileges (for example,, reading, writing, execution). Like users, different user groups have different permissions on a file.

User groups: Many Unix implementations add an additional layer of security by requiring that a user be a member of the wheel user privileges group to access the **sudo** command [1].

Root access: Sudo command on Ubuntu to temporarily assume root privileges. Most Unix and Unix-like systems have an account or group that enables a user to exert complete control over the system, often known as a root account. If access to this account is gained by an unwanted user, this results in a complete breach of the system. A root account, however, is necessary for administrative purposes, and for the above security reasons, the root account is seldom used for day-to-day purposes (the sudo program is more commonly used), so usage of the root account can be more closely monitored and have achieved certification from an external security-auditing organization, the most popular evaluations are Common Criteria (CC).

User and administrative techniques: Here are the most common user and administrative techniques to effectively manage systems.

- Passwords

  Selecting strong passwords and guarding them properly are important for Unix security.

  On many UNIX systems, user and password information, if stored locally, can be found in the **`/etc/passwd`** and **`/etc/shadow`** file pair.

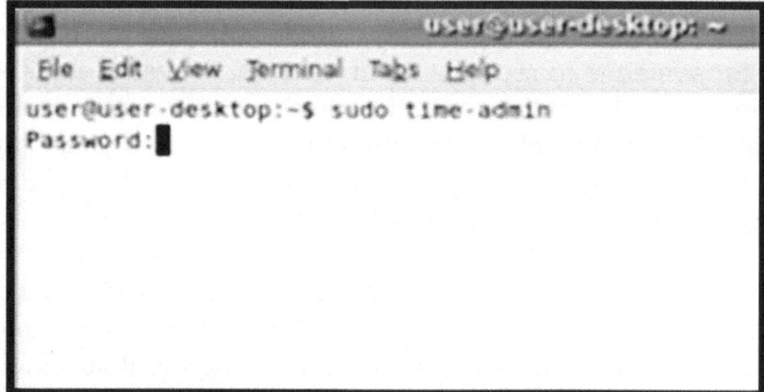

***Figure 16.6:** user and password information*

Software maintenance: Operating systems, like all software, may contain bugs that need fixing or may be enhanced with the addition of new features; many UNIX systems come with a package manager for this. Securely patching the operating system requires that the software come from a trustworthy source and not have been altered since it was packaged. Common methods for verifying that operating system patches have not been altered include using of the digital signature of a cryptographic hash, such as a SHA-256-based checksum or using the read-only media.

Components of Protection and Security

The major components to be dealt with are as follows:

- **Access Control:** The fundamental building block of operating system security are access control mechanisms. They control who has access to what resources and under what circumstances, including privilege management, authorization, and user authentication.
- **Encryption:** Encryption is essential for guaranteeing data confidentiality.

Sensitive information can be intercepted but cannot be read by unauthorized parties because cryptographic algorithms transform plaintext into ciphertext.

- **Firewalls:** Using pre-established security rules to filter incoming and outgoing traffic, firewalls operate as a barrier between trusted internal networks and untrusted external networks. They defend against network-based threats and assist in preventing unwanted access.
- **Antivirus Software:** Malicious software, including Trojan horses, worms, and viruses, is intended to be identified, stopped, and eliminated by antivirus software. To detect questionable activity, it uses heuristic analysis to find known malware signatures in files and processes. Operating systems that resemble Unix are the target of certain worms and viruses. The Morris worm, which was the first computer worm, actually targeted Unix systems.
- **Intrusion Detection and Prevention Systems (IDPS):** IDPS keep an eye on network traffic to look for indications of malicious behavior or infringement of policies. They can stop possible security breaches before they have a negative impact by quickly identifying and addressing threats.
- **Patch management**: It is essential to update and patch operating systems and software regularly to fix known vulnerabilities and reduce the likelihood that attackers will take advantage of them. Systems are kept up to date with the newest security fixes, thanks to patch management procedures.
- **Secure boot:** Only trusted software components are loaded during the system boot process, thanks to a technology known as secure boot. It guards against bootkits and other malware that tries to take over the boot process by preventing the execution of unauthorized code.
- **Auditing and Logging:** These features give administrators access to information about system activity, enabling them to monitor user behavior, spot security events, and carry out forensic analysis in the case of a breach.

Methods to Ensure Protection and Security in Operating System [5]

Preserve a backup copy of your data: Should data become corrupted as a result of security or protection issues, you can always restore it from the backup. Watch out for dubious emails and links: Malicious links can pose a major threat by gaining unauthorized access to our computer systems.

Authentication and Authorization: The operating system should offer secure authentication and authorization to prevent unauthorized access to resources. Users should also take precautions to protect their login credentials.

Use Only Secure WiFi: Occasionally, using free or insecure WIFI might lead to security problems because, in the worst scenario, attackers could record activity or send malicious programs over the network, which could lead to serious issues. Installing anti-virus and malware protection aids in preventing and eliminating malware and viruses from the system.

Handle access sensibly: Since no software can damage our system until it has access, access should only be granted to apps and software after careful examination. As a result, we can ensure that software is accessible to the right people, and we can always monitor the software to see what resources and access it is using. The utilities of firewalls allow us to keep an eye on and filter network traffic.

Use Firewalls: A useful tool for limiting access to and transfer of data to only those who are authorized.

Transferring data content using encryption and decryption: An encryption algorithm that can only be undone with the right decryption key must be used for the data transfer. Your data is shielded by this procedure from unwanted internet access, and in the unlikely event that it is stolen, it will always remain unreadable. Be cautious when disclosing personal information. If you share your credentials and personal information with unreliable sources, attackers may use it against you and jeopardize the security of the system.

Comparison Between Protection and Security

Additionally, available as an alternative to software-only computers, security is hardware-based or assisted computer security. Due to the physical access (or complex backdoor access) needed to be compromised, using tools and techniques, such as dongles, trusted platform modules, intrusion-aware cases, drive locks, blocking USB ports, and mobile-enabled access may be deemed more secure. Each of these is discussed in more detail:

- **USB dongles** can be thought of as a means of preventing unauthorized access to the software on a computer or other device but are also commonly used in software licensing schemes to unlock software capabilities. Between the software program and the key, the dongle, also known as the key, essentially builds a secure encrypted tunnel. The idea behind this is that encrypting the dongle with an Advanced Encryption Standard (AES) scheme makes it more difficult to hack and replicate than it is to just copy and use the native software on a different computer. Virtual Private Networks (VPNs) and other cloud software can be accessed via dongles, another way to use them for security purposes. Furthermore, a USB dongle can lock or unlock a computer.
- **By incorporating cryptographic** capabilities onto access devices via

microprocessors, sometimes known as *"computers-on-a-chip,"* trusted platform modules (TPMs) provide device security. TPMs provide a mechanism to identify and authenticate hardware devices, preventing unwanted network and data access when used in conjunction with server-side software.

- A device that detects when a computer case is opened is known as a computer **case intrusion detection**. Usually, it takes the form of a push-button switch. The BIOS, also known as the firmware, is configured to notify the user the next time the computer boots up.
- **Drive locks** are essentially software tools that encrypt hard drives so that robbers cannot access them. External drive encryption is also possible with dedicated tools.
- One way to protect an otherwise secure computer from unwanted and malicious access is to **disable USB ports**. The most frequent hardware threat to computer networks, according to the magazine Network World, is infected USB dongles connected to a network from a machine inside the firewall.
- **Turning off or disconnecting add-ons,**such as a camera, GPS, portable hard drive, and so on, those are not in operation.
- The widespread use of cell phones has led to an increase in the demand for mobile-enabled access devices. Mobile phones can now connect to access control systems in new and secure ways, thanks to built-in features such as **Bluetooth,** the more recent Bluetooth low energy (LE), near-field communication (NFC) on non-iOS devices, biometric validation through thumbprint readers, and QR code reader software meant for mobile devices. These control systems can be used to manage access to secure buildings in addition to providing computer security.
- **Input Output Memory Management Units** (IOMMUs) allow for hardware-based sandboxing of components in mobile and desktop computers by utilizing direct memory access protections.
- **Physical Unclonable Functions** (PUFs) can be used as a digital fingerprint or a unique identifier for integrated circuits and hardware, providing users with the ability to secure the hardware supply chains going into their systems.

Table 16.1 shows the Comparison between Protection and Security.

Criteria	**Protection**	**Security**
Scope	Focuses specifically on controlling access to system resources and enforcing policies to prevent unauthorized actions within the system	Encompasses a broader range of measures and mechanisms aimed at safeguarding the system, its resources, and data from unauthorized access, misuse, or destruction

Goal	Primarily concerned with preventing unauthorized users or processes from accessing or modifying system resources and enforcing access control policies to maintain system stability and integrity	Aims to ensure the confidentiality, integrity, and availability of system resources and data, protecting them from various threats and vulnerabilities.
Implementation	Implemented through access control mechanisms, such as user permissions, file permissions, and process isolation, to restrict access to system resources based on predefined rules and policies	Implemented through a combination of technical controls (such as encryption, authentication mechanisms, and intrusion detection systems) and procedural measures (such as security policies, user training, and incident response procedures)
Focus	Focuses on enforcing access control policies and mechanisms to ensure that only authorized users or processes can access specific system resources or perform certain actions	Emphasizes proactive measures to identify, mitigate, and prevent security risks and vulnerabilities, often involving continuous monitoring, assessment, and adaptation of security measures
Impact	Primarily affects system performance and usability, as overly restrictive protection mechanisms may hinder legitimate user activities while ensuring system integrity and stability	Has a broader impact on overall system resilience, privacy, and trustworthiness, influencing user confidence and organizational reputation
Location	Protection tackles the system's internal threats	Security tackles the system's external threats

Table 16.1: *Comparison between Protection and Security*

Security Model of UNIX [7]

Hardware-based or assisted computer security is also an option as a substitute for software-only computer security. Using tools and techniques like dongles, trusted platform modules, intrusion-aware cases, drive locks, blocking USB ports, and mobile-enabled access may be considered more secure due to the physical access (or complex backdoor access) that must be compromised.

The following is a more detailed discussion of each of these:

In addition to being used in software licensing schemes to unlock software features,

USB dongles can also be considered a security measure against unauthorized access to the software on a computer or other device. Between the software program and the key, the dongle, also known as the key, essentially builds a secure encrypted tunnel. The idea behind this is that encrypting the dongle with an Advanced Encryption Standard (AES) scheme makes it more difficult to hack and replicate than copying and using the native software on a different computer.

Virtual Private Networks (VPNs) and other cloud software can be accessed via dongles, which is another way to use them for security purposes. Furthermore, a USB dongle can lock or unlock a computer. Using microprocessors, sometimes known as "computers-on-a-chip," trusted platform modules (TPMs) provide device security by incorporating cryptographic capabilities onto access devices. TPMs provide a mechanism to identify and authenticate hardware devices, preventing unwanted network and data access when used in conjunction with server-side software. When a computer case is opened, a device known as a computer case intrusion detection–typically a push-button switch–detects it.

The BIOS, also known as the firmware, is configured to notify the user the next time the computer boots up. Drive locks are essentially software programs that encrypt hard drives, preventing thieves from accessing them. External drive encryption is also possible with dedicated tools. One security measure to stop malicious and unauthorized access to an otherwise secure computer is disabling USB ports.

According to the magazine Network World, infected USB dongles that are connected to a network from a machine inside the firewall pose the most common hardware threat to computer networks. Removing the connection or turning off any peripheral devices (such as a camera, GPS, removable drive, etc. those are not in operation is one way to protect the otherwise secured computer. Because cell phones are so common, mobile-enabled access devices are gaining popularity. Mobile phones can now connect to access control systems in new and secure ways, thanks to built-in features, such as Bluetooth, the more recent Bluetooth low energy (LE), near-field communication (NFC) on non-iOS devices, biometric validation through thumbprint readers, and QR code reader software meant for mobile devices. These control systems can be used to manage access to secure buildings in addition to providing computer security. Hardware-based computer sandboxing is made possible by IOMMUs.

An Example: Windows XP

The general-purpose operating system Windows XP is made to accommodate a large range of security tools and techniques. It is based on user accounts, which are flexible in how they are grouped. A security access token is generated upon login and contains the user's security ID, the security IDs of any groups they are a part of, and a list of any special rights they may have, such as the ability to make backups, restart the computer, and adjust the system clock. A copy of the user's security token, which establishes the privileges of any process operating on the user's behalf, is sent to each process.

Authentication: Passwords are typically used for authentication, but because Windows is modular, other methods, such as fingerprint readers or retinal scans, can also be used. Many common security risks, including successful and unsuccessful logins, logouts, attempts to write to executable files, and access to specific sensitive files, can be tracked, thanks to Windows XP's built-in auditing feature.

Security descriptors define the security attributes of an object. These include the owner's ID, group ownership for POSIX subsystems only, a list of permissible access controls that specify the specific rights that each user or group on the system has with regard to a given object, and auditing control data.

The access control lists contain **`ReadData`**, **`WriteData`**, **`AppendData`**, **`Execute`**, **`ReadAttributes`**, **`WriteAttributes`**, **`ReadExtendedAttribute`**, and **`WriteExtendedAttribute`** for each designated user or group, along with **`AccessAllowed`** or **`AccessDenied`** for the remaining action types.

It makes sense for **container objects**, such as directories, to contain other objects. A new object inherits the permissions of the new container by default when it is created in or copied into one. No additional rights are inherited by **noncontainer objects**. The contained objects' permissions remain unaffected if the container's permissions are subsequently modified.

Even though Windows XP can support a secure system, a good number of security flaws occur on XP systems because many security features are not turned on by default. Whether the system administrator has considered them or not, a sizable number of system daemons and other programs also launch automatically at startup. Currently, 54 processes are active on my system; most of these were not started consciously, and their short, cryptic names make it difficult to figure out exactly what they do or why. When presented with this scenario, most users and administrators tend to ignore things they do not understand.

Conclusion

We have learned there are two different aspects of making a system secure, that is, protection and security. We have seen the need, roles, and goals of protection in operating systems. Before going into details, we are told in this chapter that we should be apprised of common types of violations, program threats, and system and network threats. We have further learned that security in operating systems is dependent on security goals and policies. As such, we discussed the methods to ensure protection and security in the operating systems. We have also learned about hardware protection mechanisms and finally, the security model of UNIX and Windows XP.

Questions

1. What do we mean by the protection of OS, and what are the items the OS designers aim to protect and secure?
2. Write down the names of some of the most common types of violations that are quite often committed in designs of OS.
3. What are the needs and goals of protection in the operating system?
4. What roles are required and provided by protection in the operating system?
5. Discuss the four levels at which a system must be protected.
6. What are the common threats to modern operating systems?
7. Write short notes on any five of the following topics:
   a. Trojan Horse
   b. Worms
   c. Virus
   d. Trap Door
   e. Logic Bomb
   f. Denial of Service
8. What is meant by stack overflow? Describe it with the help of a diagram.
9. At a high conceptual level, what are the three big security-related goals that are common?
10. What are the various components of protection and security?
11. Write down the various methods to ensure protection and security in the operating system.
12. List down the hardware protection mechanisms of various hardware components.
13. Describe the security model of UNIX.
14. Describe the various features of Windows XP as a general-purpose OS.

Questions with Answers

Q1. What is an operating system's main purpose for security and protection?

Ans. The main objective is to protect system resources–data, memory, and CPU time–from malicious activity and unauthorized access while maintaining availability, confidentiality, and integrity.

Q2. What is the difference between security and protection in an operating system?

Ans. While security covers a wider range of activities, such as protection mechanisms, authentication, encryption, audit trails, and policies to guard against threats and vulnerabilities, protection primarily focuses on limiting access to system resources.

Q3. What constitutes an operating system's security model's core constituents?

Ans. Authentication methods, audit trails, intrusion detection systems (IDS), encryption techniques, access control lists (ACLs), and security policies are usually the main components.

Q4. What part does access control play in an operating system's resource protection?

Ans. Who has access to what resources and what actions they can take with those resources are controlled by access control. To enforce security policies, it utilizes strategies, such as access control lists, user authentication, and permissions.

Q5. What are a few popular operating system authentication techniques?

Ans. Passwords, biometric authentication (fingerprint, iris scan), multi-factor authentication (password plus token), and public key infrastructure (PKI) certificates are examples of common authentication techniques.

References

[1] Introduction to Operating System Security Chapter by Peter Reiher (UCLA),https://pages.cs.wisc.edu/~remzi/OSTEP/security-intro.pdf

[2] Operating Systems: Security, University of Illinois Chicago, https://www.cs.uic.edu › Operating Systems › 15_Security

[3] Protecting Systems from Deliberate Attacks: A Security Overview,Course Hero,https://www.coursehero.com ›

[4] Operating Systems: Security, University of Illinois Chicago, https://www.cs.uic.edu › OperatingSystems ›

[5] Protection and Security in Operating System,Scaler,https://www.scaler.com › topics › protection-and-security..., 25 Jun 2024

[6] Hardware protection mechanisms, LinkedIn · Faisal Paray

[7] Computer security, Wikipedia, https://en.wikipedia.org › wiki › Computer_security

Index

D

E

P

T